ASCENT®
CENTER FOR TECHNICAL KNOWLEDGE

Autodesk® Revit® 2027 Fundamentals for Architecture

Learning Guide

Imperial Units - Edition 1.0

ASCENT - Center for Technical Knowledge®
Autodesk® Revit® 2027
Fundamentals for Architecture
Imperial Units - Edition 1.0

Prepared and produced by:

ASCENT Center for Technical Knowledge
11201 Dolfield Blvd, Suite 112
Owings Mills, MD 21117

866-527-2368
www.ASCENTed.com

Lead Contributor: Cherisse Biddulph

ASCENT - Center for Technical Knowledge (a division of Rand Worldwide Inc.) is a leading developer of professional learning materials and knowledge products for engineering software applications. ASCENT specializes in designing targeted content that facilitates application-based learning with hands-on software experience. For over 25 years, ASCENT has helped users become more productive through tailored custom learning solutions.

We welcome any comments you may have regarding this guide, or any of our products. To contact us please email: feedback@ASCENTed.com.

AS-RAR2701-FND1IM-SG // IS-RAR2701-FND1IM-SG

Contents

Design Development

Chapter 12: Modeling Roofs 12-1

Chapter 13: Modeling Stairs, Railings, and Ramps 13-1

Construction Documentation

Preface

The Autodesk® Revit® software is a powerful Building Information Modeling (BIM) program that works the way architects think. The program streamlines the design process through the use of a central 3D model, where changes made in one view update across all views and on the printable sheets.

The objective of the *Autodesk® Revit® 2027: Fundamentals for Architecture* guide is to enable you to create a full 3D architectural project model, including walls, doors, windows, components, floors, ceilings, roofs, and stairs, using the basic tools that the majority of architectural users need. This includes how to navigate the user interface and use the basic drawing, editing, and viewing tools.The final part of the guide focuses on creating construction documents.

Topics Covered

- Understanding the purpose of BIM and how it is applied in the Autodesk Revit software.
- Navigating the Revit workspace and interface.
- Selecting a template and linking CAD and Revit files as the basis of a project.
- Creating levels and grids as datum elements for the model.
- Understanding the Project Browser and working with views.
- Understanding Revit families and components.
- Working with the basic sketching and modifying tools.
- Creating a 3D building model with columns, walls, curtain walls, windows, and doors.
- Adding floors, ceilings, and roofs to the building model.
- Modeling stairs, railings, and ramps.
- Setting up sheets for plotting with text, dimensions, details, tags, and schedules.
- Creating details.

Prerequisites

- Access to the 2027.0 version of the software, to ensure compatibility with this learning content. Future software updates that are released by Autodesk may include changes that are not reflected in this content. The practices and files included are not compatible with prior versions of the software (e.g., 2026).
- An understanding of architectural terminology is an asset.

Note on Software Setup

This content assumes a standard installation of the software using default preferences. This includes the Revit templates and Revit Content (families) that can be found on the Autodesk website at https://knowledge.autodesk.com/ by searching "*How to download Revit Content*".

Note on Learning Guide Content

ASCENT's learning guides are intended to teach the technical aspects of using the software and do not focus on professional design principles and standards. The practices aim to demonstrate the capabilities and flexibility of the software rather than following specific design codes or standards.

Lead Contributor: Cherisse Biddulph

Cherisse is an Autodesk Certified Professional for Revit as well as an Autodesk Certified Instructor. She brings over 20 years of industry, teaching, and technical support experience to her role as a Learning Content Developer with ASCENT. With a passion for design and architecture, she has worked in the industry assisting firms with their Building Information Modeling (BIM) management and software implementation needs as they modernize to a BIM design environment. Although her main devotion is the Revit design product, she is also proficient in AutoCAD, Autodesk Forma, and Autodesk Navisworks. Today, Cherisse continues to expand her knowledge in the ever-evolving AEC industry and the software used to support it.

Cherisse Biddulph has been the Lead Contributor for *Autodesk Revit: Fundamentals for Architecture* since 2020.

In This Guide

The following highlights the key features of this guide.

Feature	Description
Practice Files	The Practice Files page includes a link to the practice files and instructions on how to download and install them. The practice files are required to complete the practices in this guide.
Chapters	A chapter consists of the following: Learning Objectives, Instructional Content, Practices, Chapter Review Questions, and Command Summary. • **Learning Objectives** define the skills you can acquire by learning the content provided in the chapter. • **Instructional Content**, which begins right after Learning Objectives, refers to the descriptive and procedural information related to various topics. Each main topic introduces a product feature, discusses various aspects of that feature, and provides step-by-step procedures on how to use that feature. Where relevant, examples, figures, helpful hints, and notes are provided. • **Practice** for a topic follows the instructional content. Practices enable you to use the software to perform a hands-on review of a topic. It is required that you download the practice files (using the link found on the Practice Files page) prior to starting the first practice. • **Chapter Review Questions**, located close to the end of a chapter, enable you to test your knowledge of the key concepts discussed in the chapter. • **Command Summary** concludes a chapter. It contains a list of the software commands that are used throughout the chapter and provides information on where the command can be found in the software.

Practice Files

To download the practice files for this guide, use the following steps:

1. Type the URL *exactly as shown below* into the address bar of your Internet browser to access the Course File Download page.

   Note: If you are using the ebook, you do not have to type the URL. Instead, you can access the page simply by clicking the URL below.

   https://www.ascented.com/getfile/id/viscidulaPF

2. On the Course File Download page, click the **DOWNLOAD NOW** button, as shown below, to download the .ZIP file that contains the practice files.

3. Once the download is complete, unzip the file and extract its contents.

   The recommended practice files folder location is:
   C:\Revit 2027 Fundamentals for Architecture Practice Files

   Note: It is recommended that you do not change the location of the practice files folder. Doing so may cause errors when completing the practices.

Introduction to Autodesk Revit and Project Setup

This guide is divided into three sections: Introduction to Autodesk Revit and Project Setup, Design Development, and Construction Documentation.

The first section provides an introduction to the Autodesk® Revit® software, including working with the software interface, setting up a drawing, incorporating datum elements, adding families, and using the basic sketch and modify tools.

This section includes the following chapters:

- Chapter 1: Introduction to Revit
- Chapter 2: Starting a Revit Project
- Chapter 3: Working with Views
- Chapter 4: Revit Families
- Chapter 5: Basic Sketching and Modify Tools

Chapter 1

Introduction to Revit

Building Information Modeling (BIM) and Revit® work hand in hand to help you create smart, 3D models that are useful at all stages in the building process. Understanding the software interface and terminology enhances your ability to create and navigate around in the various views of the model.

Learning Objectives

- Describe the concept of Building Information Modeling in conjunction with applying Revit.
- Navigate the graphic user interface, including the ribbon (where most of the tools are found), Properties (where you make modifications to element information), and the Project Browser (where you can open various views of the model).
- Open existing projects and save projects.
- Use viewing commands to navigate around the model in 2D and 3D views.

1.1 BIM and Revit

Building Information Modeling (BIM) is an approach to the entire building life cycle, including design, construction, and facilities management. The BIM process supports the ability to coordinate, update, and share design data with team members across disciplines.

Revit is a model authoring software. It enables you to create complete 3D building models (as shown on the left in Figure 1–1) that provide considerable information reported through construction documents, and enables you to share these models with other programs for more extensive analysis.

> ***Note:*** *The software includes tools for architectural, mechanical, electrical, plumbing, and structural design.*

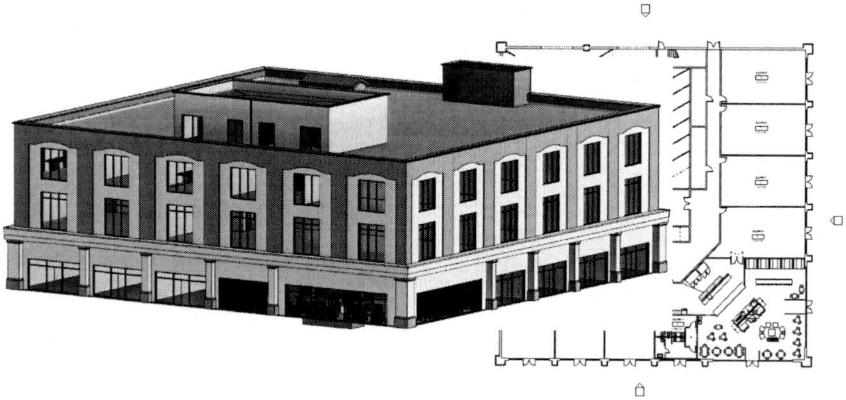

Figure 1–1

Revit is a Parametric Building Modeler software:

- *Parametric:* A relationship is established between building elements: when one element changes, all other related elements and/or geometry is modified as well. For example, when you place a door in a wall, the door removes part of the wall and stays inside that wall if it moves.
- *Building:* The software is designed for working with buildings and the surrounding landscape, as opposed to gears or highways.
- *Modeler:* A project is built in a single file based on the 3D building model, as shown on the left in Figure 1–1. All views, such as plans (as shown on the right in Figure 1–1), elevations, sections, details, construction documents, and reports are generated based on the model. When working in a project, you are almost always working in 3D no matter what type of view you are in.
- It is important that everyone who is collaborating on a project works in the same version and build of the software.

BIM Workflow

BIM has changed the process of how a building is planned, budgeted, designed, constructed, and (in some cases) operated and maintained.

When using 2D drafting software, construction documents, such as floor plans, sections, elevations, and detail drawings, are created separately. These programs typically work on a geometric level, so if you add or move an element (like a wall, fixture, or column) in one view, the change is not automatically made in the other views. The designer has to go through and update each affected drawing and schedule manually to keep everything consistent. Sometimes, a separate 3D model is also created for visualization, but it is usually not connected to the 2D drawings. This adds more work and increases the chance of errors.

In BIM, the design process revolves around the model, as shown in Figure 1–2. Plans, elevations, and sections are simply 2D versions of the 3D model, while schedules are a report of the information stored in the model. Changes made in one view automatically update in all views and related schedules. Even construction documents update automatically with callout tags in sync with the sheet numbers. This is called *bidirectional associativity*.

By creating complete models and associated views of those models, Revit takes much of the tediousness out of producing a building design.

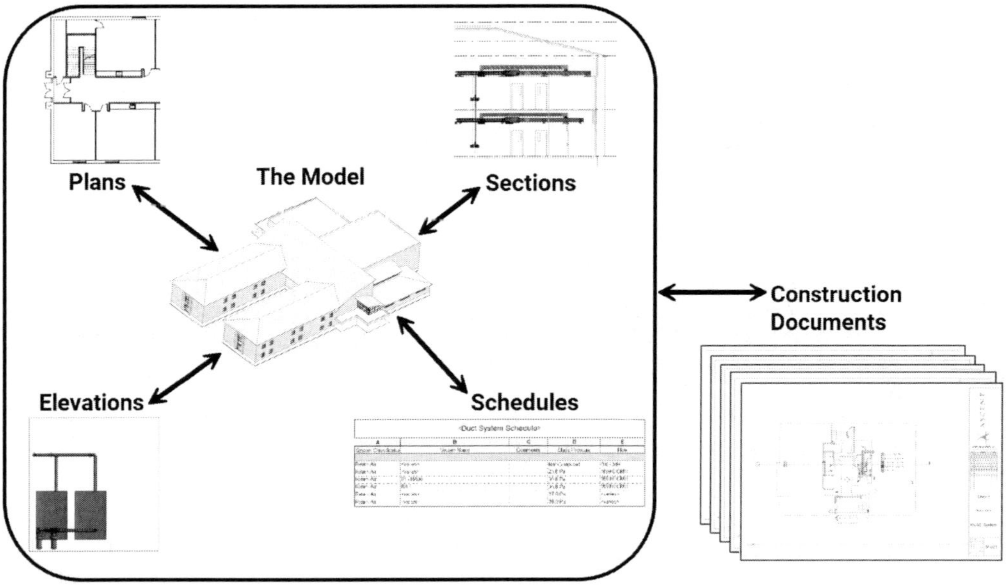

Figure 1–2

Revit Terms

When working in Revit, it is important to know the typical terms used to describe items. Views and reports display information about the elements that form a project. There are three main types of elements: model, datum, and view-specific, as shown in Figure 1–3 and described below.

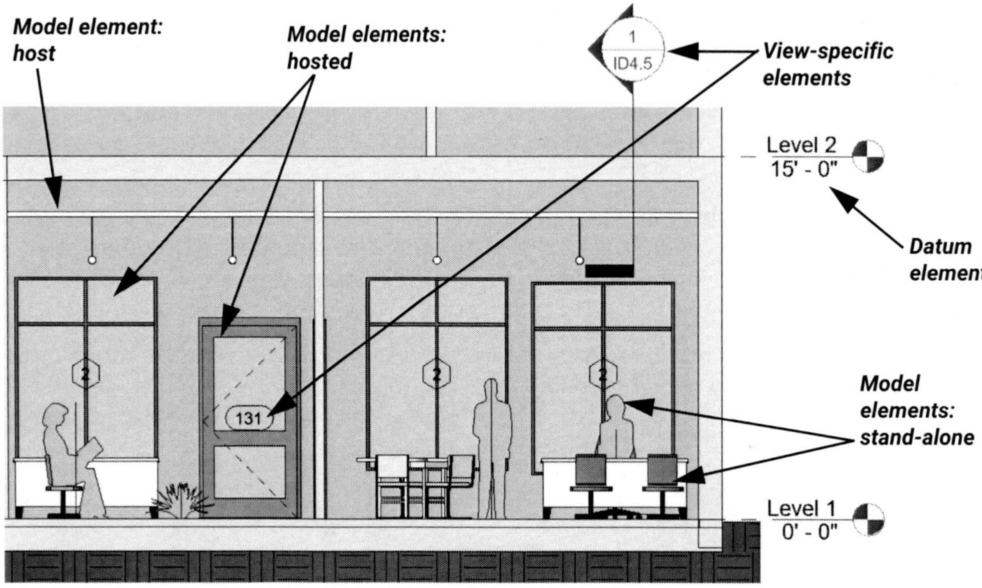

Figure 1–3

Views	Views enable you to display and manipulate the model. For example, you can view and work in floor plans, ceiling plans, elevations, sections, schedules, and 3D views. You can change a design from any view. All views are stored in the project.
Reports	Reports, including schedules, gather information from the building model element that can be presented in the construction documents or used for analysis.
Model Elements	Model elements include all parts of a building, such as walls, floors, ceilings, and roofs, and appear in all relevant views.
Component Elements	Component elements are placed from inserted families, such as plumbing fixtures, lighting fixtures, mechanical equipment, columns, beams, furniture, and plants. • Host elements, such as walls, support other categories of components like doors, windows, and casework. • Hosted elements must be attached to a host element, such as doors must be placed on a (host) wall. • Stand-alone elements do not require hosts.

Datum Elements	Datum elements define the project context, such as the levels for the floors, grids, and reference planes.
View-specific Elements	View-specific elements only display in the view in which they are placed. The view scale controls their size. These include annotation elements such as dimensions, text, tags, and symbols as well as detail elements such as detail lines, filled regions, and 2D detail components.

- Revit elements are "smart": the software recognizes them as walls, columns, plants, ducts, lighting fixtures, etc. This means that the information stored in their properties automatically updates in schedules, which ensures that views and reports are coordinated across an entire project, and are generated from a single model.

Revit and Construction Documents

In the traditional workflow, the most time-consuming part of the project is the construction documents. With BIM, the base views of those documents (i.e., plans, elevations, sections, and schedules) are produced automatically and update as the model is updated, saving hours of work. The views are then placed on sheets that form the construction document set.

For example, a floor plan is duplicated. Then, in the new view, all but the required categories of elements are hidden or set to halftone and annotations are added. The plan is then placed on a sheet, as shown in Figure 1–4.

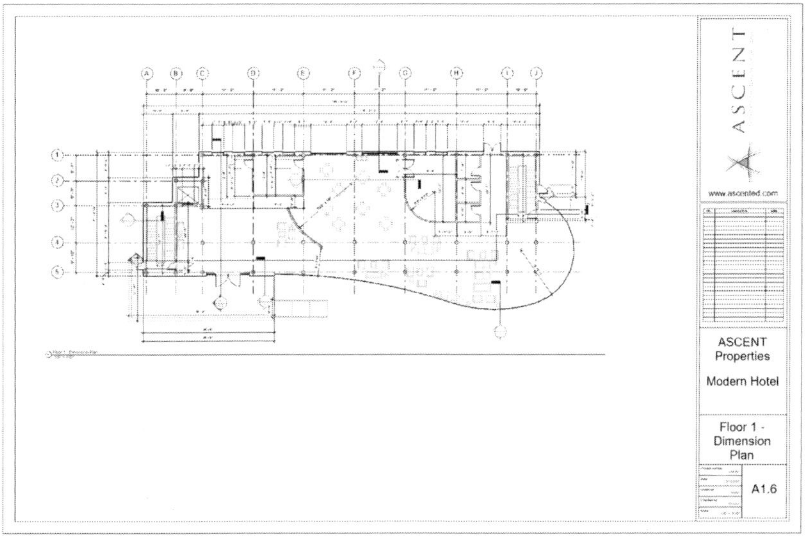

Figure 1–4

- Work can continue on a view and is automatically updated on the sheet.
- Annotating views in the preliminary design phase is often not required. You might be able to wait until you are further along in the project.

1.2 Overview of the Interface

The Revit interface is designed for intuitive and efficient access to commands and views. It includes the ribbon, Quick Access Toolbar, Navigation Bar, and Status Bar, which are common to most of the Autodesk software. It also includes tools that are specific to Revit, including Properties, the Project Browser, and the View Control Bar. Revit includes access to tools for architectural, mechanical, electrical, plumbing, and structural design but can be altered by setting up a customized workspace that is more tailored to your specific discipline. A breakdown of the Revit interface is shown in Figure 1–5.

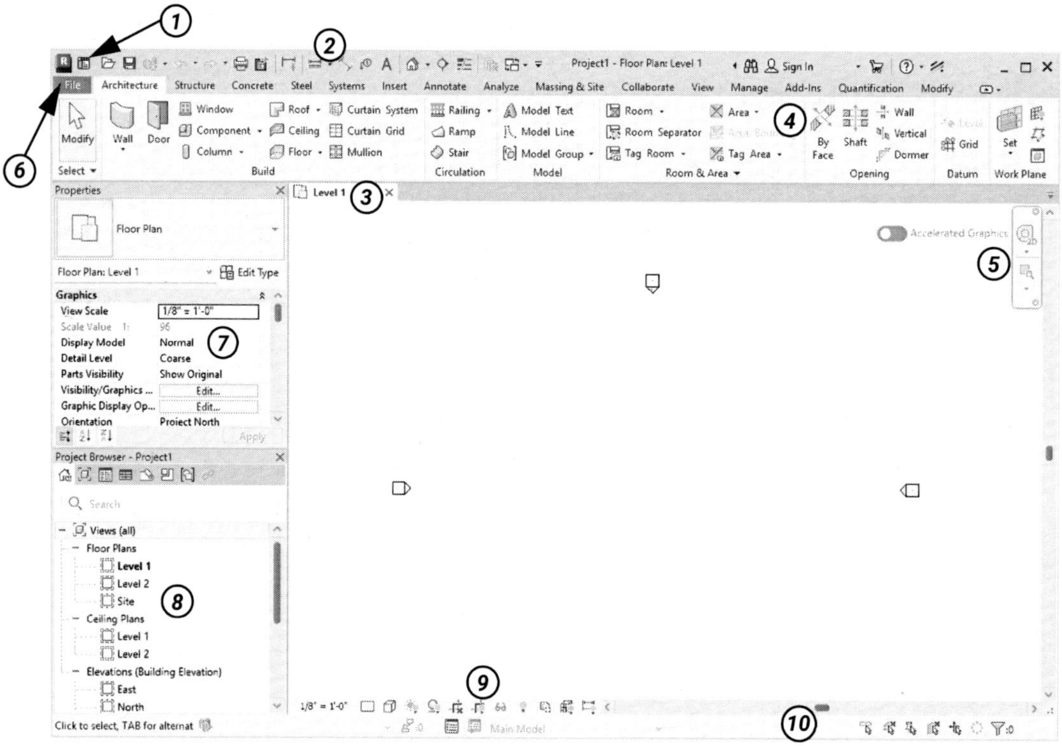

Figure 1–5

1. Home Screen
2. Quick Access Toolbar
3. View Tabs
4. Ribbon
5. Navigation Bar
6. File Tab
7. Properties
8. Project Browser
9. View Control Bar
10. Status Bar

> ***Note:*** *The Accelerated Graphics toggle, shown near the Navigation Bar in Figure 1–5, is a new feature as of Revit 2026. Most of the images in this guide were created with Accelerated Graphics disabled for both the toolbar and right-click menu and will not show it. For more information, refer to* ***Accelerated Graphics*** *on page* ***1-13****.*

1. The Home Screen

When you first open Revit, the Home screen displays with recently used projects and families, as shown in Figure 1–6. Click an option along the left side of the interface to open or start a new model or family. There are other feature options you can access, like **Autodesk Projects** and **My Insights**, as well as a toggle to turn off and on the **New Revit Home**, which shows all recent files for both models and families. There are also links to **What's new**, **Online help**, **Community forum**, and **Customer support**.

In the upper-right corner is the (Autodesk Assistant), which is an AI-powered tool that allows you to ask questions about how to use a feature, ask for assistance in designing or creating documents, and troubleshoot issues within Revit. You can also click (Explore new features and tips) to see a list of feature recommendations.

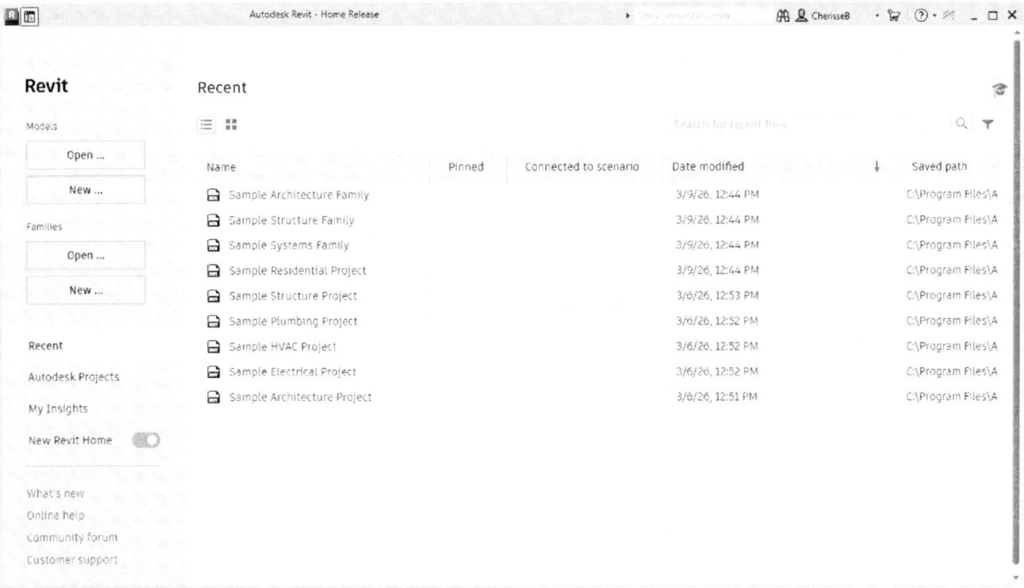

Figure 1–6

- You can open files directly from the **Recent** page (shown above in Figure 1–6). (List View) displays the file names in a list format and (Grid View) displays the files as thumbnail images.
- In the Quick Access Toolbar, click (Home) to switch between the active project model and the Home screen.
- To access Autodesk Forma models, click **Autodesk Projects**.
- To view personalized insights based on your usage data, click **My Insights**. The Insights cards will display topics such as Revit usage details, new commands, and feature recommendations.

2. Quick Access Toolbar

The Quick Access Toolbar (shown in Figure 1–7) includes commonly used commands, such as **Home, Open**, **Save**, **Undo**, **Redo, Print**, and **PDF**. It also includes **Activate Controls and Dimensions** to reduce clutter when selecting multiple elements in a view, and frequently used annotation tools, including measuring tools, **Aligned Dimension**, **Tag by Category**, and **Text**. Viewing tools, including several different 3D views and sections, are also easily accessed here.

Figure 1–7

The top toolbar also hosts the InfoCenter (shown in Figure 1–8), which includes a search field to find help topics on the web, access to Autodesk Account and the Autodesk App Store, help options, and the Autodesk Assistant.

Figure 1–8

Autodesk Assistant is an AI-powered tool integrated into the software. It provides conversational support, self-service features, and personalized assistance within Revit. You can ask questions in the chat box to get responses in the form of context-specific answers, helpful resources, or command suggestions.

How To: Use Autodesk Assistant

1. With a project open, in the InfoCenter, click  (Autodesk Assistant) to open the *Autodesk Assistant* panel, as shown in Figure 1–9.

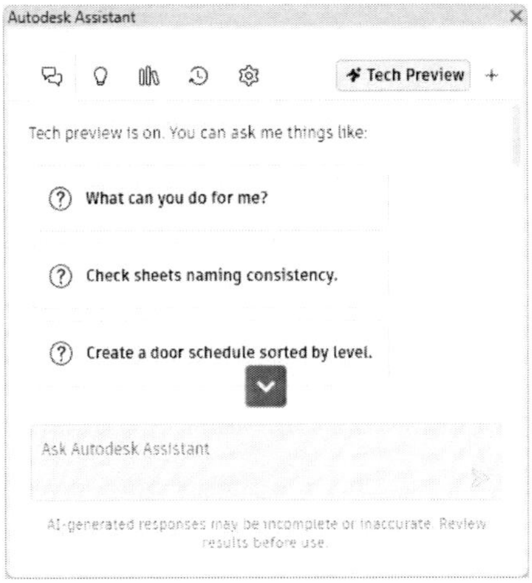

Figure 1–9

*Note: **Autodesk Assistant** was introduced in Autodesk Revit 2027, and its capabilities are expected to evolve in future releases. By default, **Tech Preview** mode is activated, but you can disable it by clicking (Settings) in the Autodesk Assistant panel and toggling off the option. Disabling the **Tech Preview** mode does not disable all Autodesk Assistant features; rather, it limits the Assistant to offering guidance only based on existing Autodesk resources.*

2. Enter your question in the chat box, as shown on the left in Figure 1–10. Autodesk Assistant responds with AI-generated answers, as shown on the right in Figure 1–10.

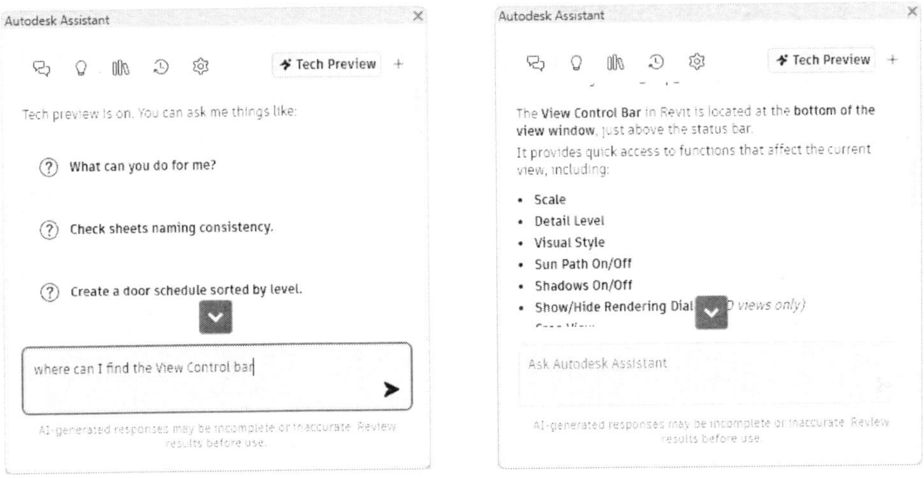

Figure 1–10

3. You can continue the conversation with Autodesk Assistant by entering additional prompts in the panel, or start a new chat by clicking +, then clicking **Got it**.

Note: Chats are saved on the (Chat History) tab until you explicitly delete them. To delete a chat, hover over it in the list and click . The chat history also persists between Revit sessions.

To use prompts more efficiently, consider the following:

- You can save existing prompts by hovering over them in the panel and clicking (Save prompt). All saved prompts are stored in the (Prompt Library) tab for reuse.
- You can copy an existing prompt from your conversation by hovering over it in the panel and clicking (Copy prompt).

As Autodesk Assistant evolves and matures, it is anticipated that it will be able to handle more complex questions about the model, automate repetitive tasks, and even validate the model. Continue to review this tool to learn more about how you can leverage AI to access information from Autodesk's resources and review your model.

3. View Tabs

Each view of a project opens in its own tab and can be pulled out of the application window and moved to another monitor. Each view displays a Navigation Bar (for quick access to viewing tools), the View Control Bar, and elevation markers, as shown in Figure 1–11.

> **Note:** *In 3D views, you can also use the ViewCube to orbit the view.*

- To close a tab, click the **X** that displays when you hover over the tab or the name in the list, as shown in Figure 1–11.

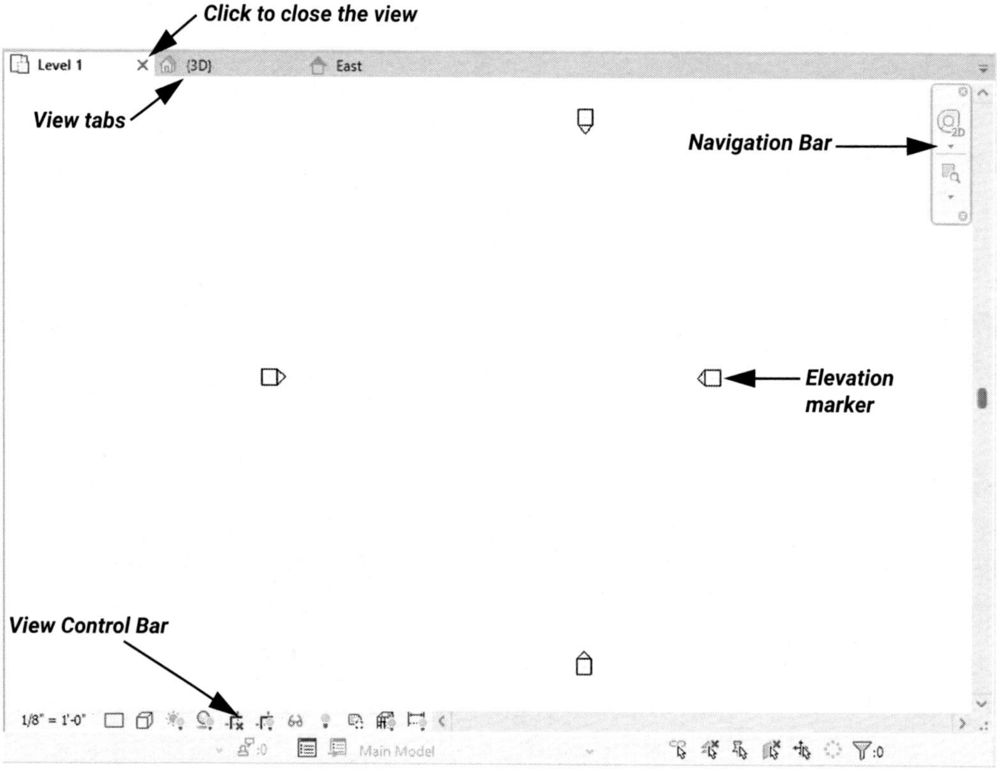

Figure 1–11

Hint: Elevation Markers

You can hover your cursor over an elevation marker's arrowhead to see what the view name is, as shown in Figure 1–12. You can also double-click on the arrowhead to open the view.

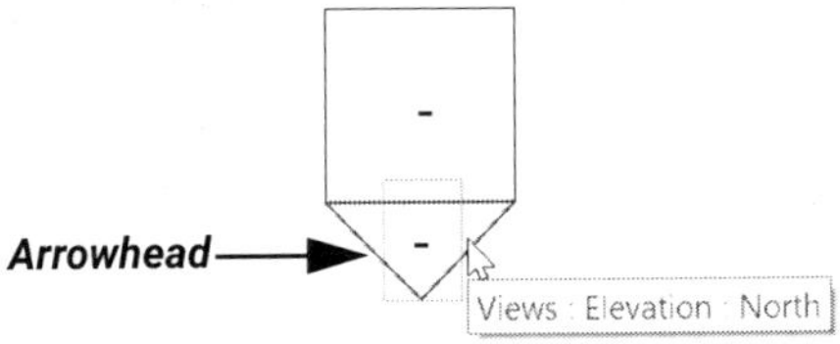

Figure 1–12

Hint: Using Thin Lines

The software automatically applies line weights to views, as shown for a section on the left in Figure 1–13. If a line weight seems heavy or obscures your work on the elements, toggle off the line weights. In the Quick Access Toolbar or in the *View* tab>*Graphics* panel, click (Thin Lines), or type **TL**. The lines display with the same weight, as shown on the right in Figure 1–13.

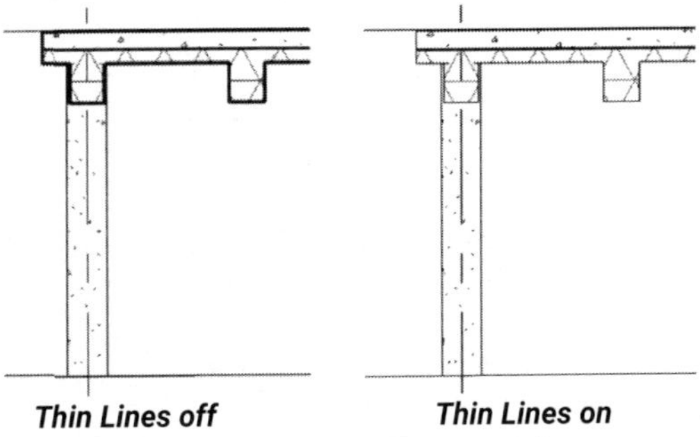

Figure 1–13

The **Thin Line** setting is remembered until you change it, even if you shut down and restart the software.

- Click on the tab along the top of the drawing area to switch between views. You can also:
  - Press <Ctrl>+<Tab>.
  - Select the view in the Project Browser.
  - In the Quick Access Toolbar (shown on the left in Figure 1–14) or *View* tab>*Windows* panel (shown on the right in Figure 1–14), expand (Switch Windows) and select the view from the list.

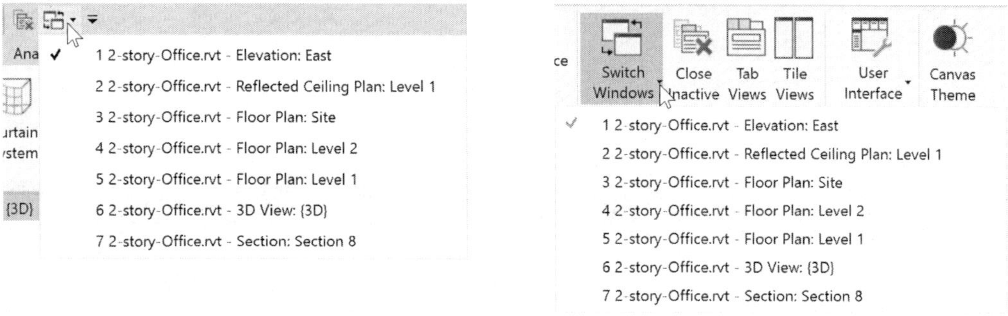

Figure 1–14

  - Expand the drop-down list at the far end of the tabs, as shown in Figure 1–15 to select a view from the list.

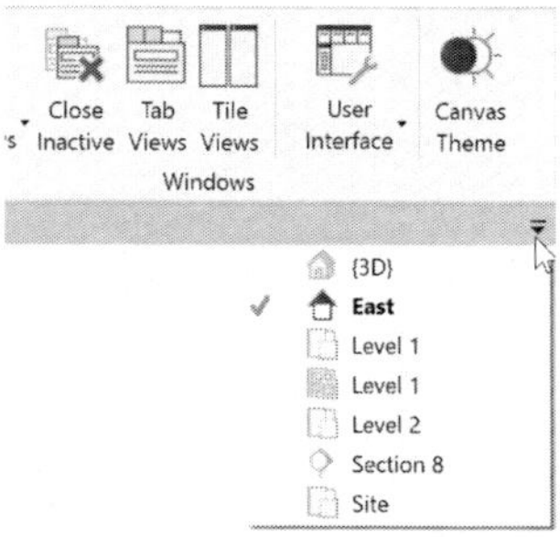

Figure 1–15

- To close all open views except the current view, in the Quick Access Toolbar or *View* tab> *Windows* panel, click (Close Inactive Views). If you have multiple projects open, one view of each project remains open. If you have dragged a view to another monitor, that view will need to be manually closed by clicking the **X** in the upper-right corner.

- You can switch between tabbed and tiled views from the *View* tab>*Windows* panel or by typing shortcuts. For tabbed views (as shown on the left in Figure 1–16), click  (Tab Views) or type **TW**. For tiled views (as shown on the right in Figure 1–16), click  (Tile Views) or type **WT**.

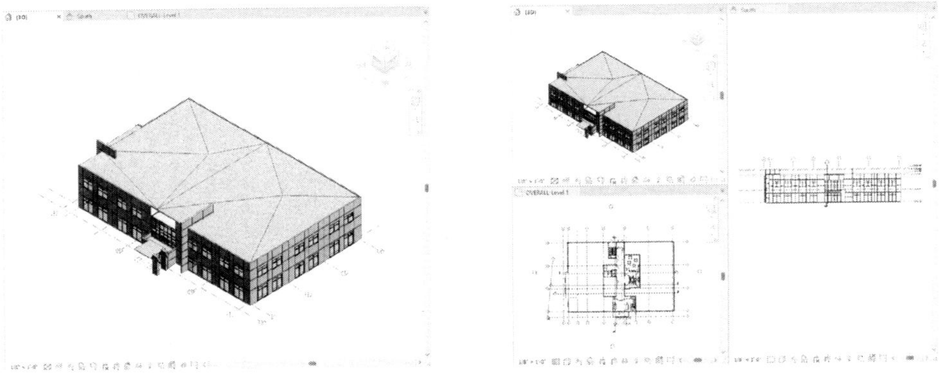

Figure 1–16

- When you are working with tiled views, you can type **ZA** (Zoom All to Fit) to zoom to fit the full model in each of the different views.
- Drag the edge of tiled views to resize them as needed.

Accelerated Graphics

The **Accelerated Graphics** toggle lets you use a new, faster graphics system in Revit. When you turn it on for a view, Revit uses your computer's graphics card more efficiently to make moving around your model feel quicker and smoother. It does not change your model or settings – it just improves how the view runs while it is open. Once you close the view or the model, the faster graphics mode turns off automatically.

- Click the toggle next to **Accelerated Graphics** to turn it on. A blue border around the view displays with *Accelerated Graphics* in the upper-left corner, as shown in Figure 1–17. To turn it off, click the toggle again, and the blue border no longer displays.

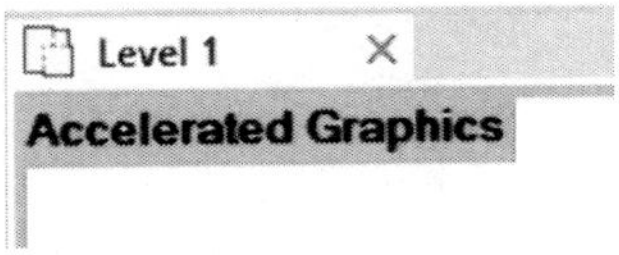

Figure 1–17

- To move the toolbar in the view area, hover over the *Accelerated Graphics* toolbar (shown on the left in Figure 1–18) and click the arrow to expand the menu. From the list of options, choose the one you prefer. If you select **Close this toolbar**, the toolbar will be turned off in all views and will remain off in all future projects.

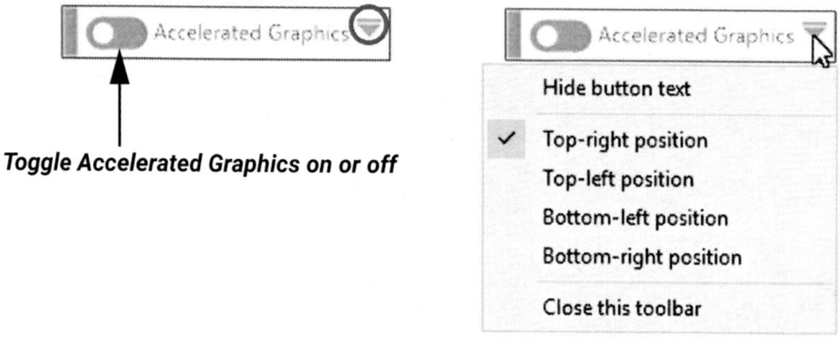

Figure 1–18

- If you closed the toolbar and want to enable the *Accelerated Graphics* mode for a specific view, right-click in the view and select **Accelerated Graphics**, as shown in Figure 1–19. To turn off this mode, right-click in the view and select **Accelerated Graphics** again.

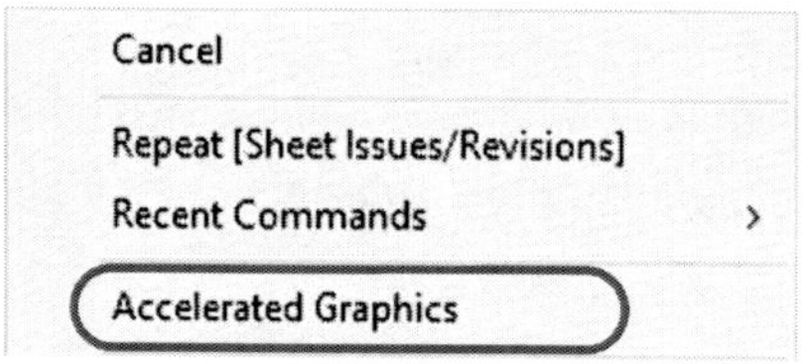

Figure 1–19

How To: Enable Accelerated Graphics

1. In the *File* tab, click **Options**.
2. In the *Options* dialog box>*Graphics* tab, in the *Accelerated Graphics* section, ensure the **Enable Accelerated Graphics** option is checked.
3. Select **Show onscreen toolbar and toggle with right click menu** or **Toggle with right click menu only**, as shown in Figure 1–20, and click **OK**.

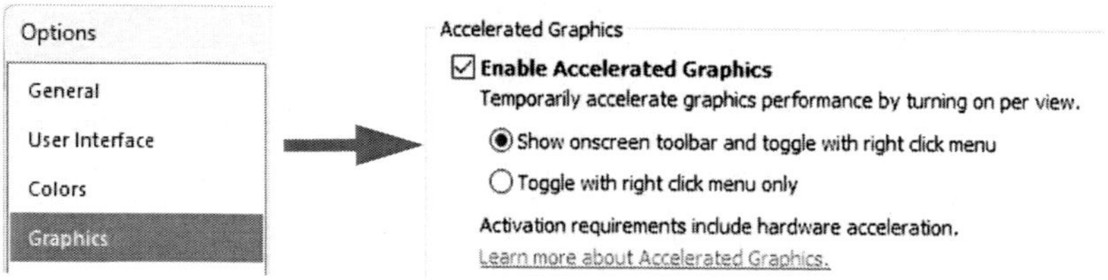

Figure 1–20

- To disable both the toolbar and the right-click menu option, uncheck **Enable Accelerated Graphics**.

4. Ribbon

The ribbon contains tools in a series of tabs and panels. Selecting a tab displays a group of related panels. The panels contain a variety of tools, grouped by task. Depending on which tool is started or which element is selected in the drawing view, a contextual tab will display with additional tools for sketching, modifying, hosting, or placement options. You will learn more about sketching and modifying tools in ***Chapter 5 Basic Sketching and Modify Tools***.

When you start a command to create new elements, the ribbon displays the *Modify* contextual tab for that tool. For example, when starting the **Column** command, the contextual tab gives you additional tools specific to the command, as shown on the left in Figure 1–21; when starting the **Lighting Fixture** command, you get a different set of *Placement* tools than for columns, as shown on the right in Figure 1–21.

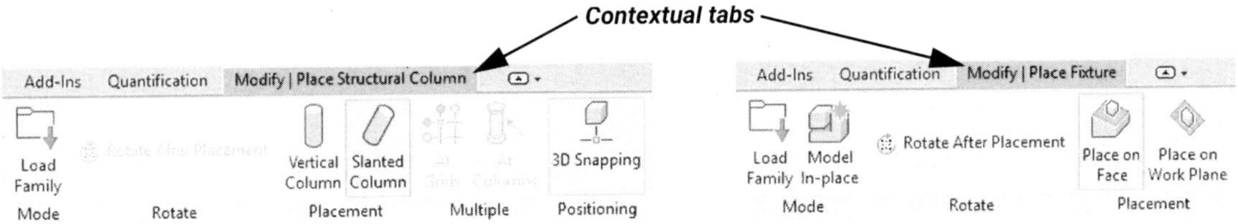

Figure 1–21

When a tool requires you to draw the element rather than placing it, like for a door, air terminal, or plumbing fixture, you will see a group of sketching aids in the *Draw* panel, as shown in Figure 1–22. For example, you can draw a wall by using one of the sketch tools to select the starting point and the end point.

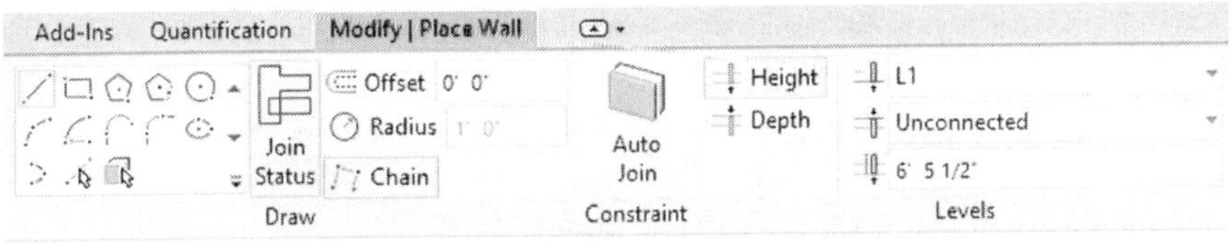

Figure 1–22

Some tools, like the **Stairs**, **Roof**, **Sketch Ceiling**, and **Floor** commands, will display finish and cancel buttons among the *Modify* options, as shown in Figure 1–23. To complete the command, you will need to click (Finish Edit Mode) or (Cancel Edit Mode).

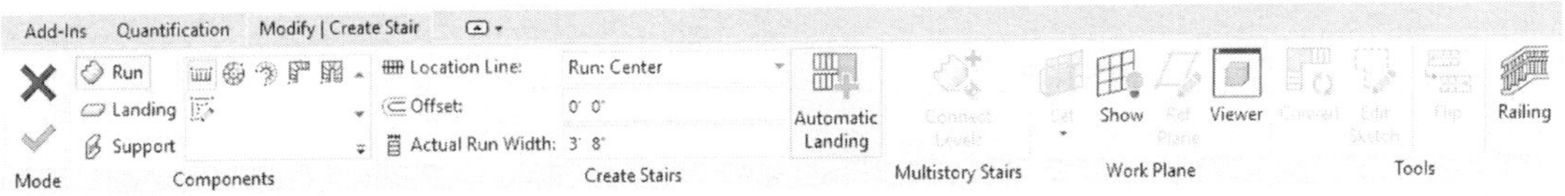

Figure 1–23

When you select an element in the drawing view to be edited, the ribbon displays the *Modify* contextual tab, which contains general editing commands and command-specific tools. For example, when selecting a wall in a view, the contextual tab shows the *Mode*, *Modify Wall*, and *Manage Host* tools, as shown in Figure 1–24.

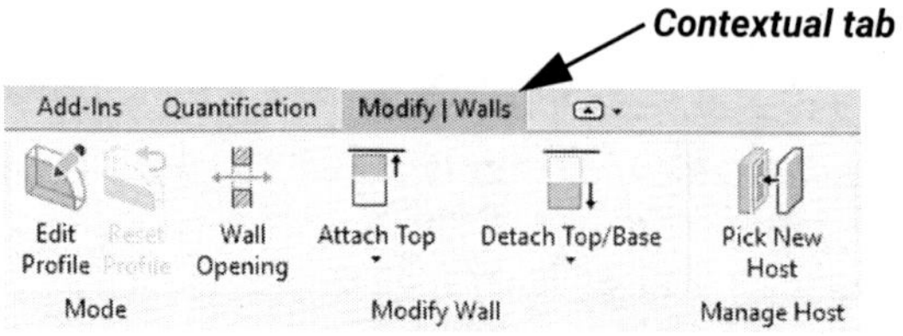

Figure 1–24

- When a command is one that you can toggle on and off, the icon will be highlighted in blue if the command is toggled on. When it is toggled off, the icon is gray (not highlighted), as shown in Figure 1–25.

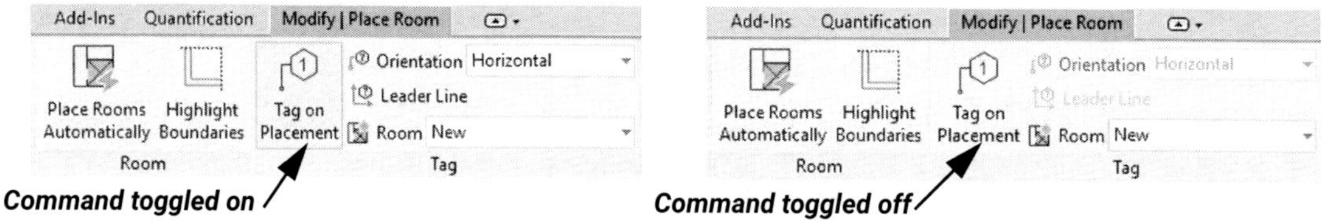

Figure 1–25

- When you hover over a tool on the ribbon, tooltips display the tool's name and a short description. If you continue hovering over the tool, a graphic displays (and sometimes a video), as shown in Figure 1–26.

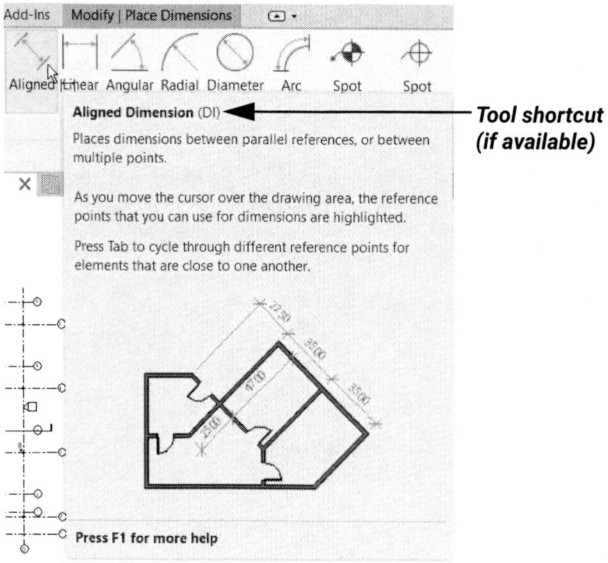

Figure 1–26

- Many commands have shortcut keys. For example, type **AL** for **Align** or **MV** for **Move**. They are listed next to the name of the command in the tooltips. Do not press <Enter> when typing shortcuts. A list of shortcuts can be found in the Autodesk Revit Help, which can be accessed by clicking ⓘ (Help) in the upper-right corner of the interface or pressing <F1>.
  - For convenience, both the **RVTKeyboardShortcuts.xlsx** and **RVTKeyboardShortcuts.pdf** files have been downloaded for you and can be found in the practice files *Reference* folder.
- To arrange the order in which the ribbon tabs are displayed, select the tab, hold <Ctrl>, and drag it to a new location. The location is remembered when you restart the software.
- Any panel can be dragged by its title into the view window to become a floating panel. Click the **Return Panels to Ribbon** button (as shown in Figure 1–27) to reposition the panel in the ribbon.

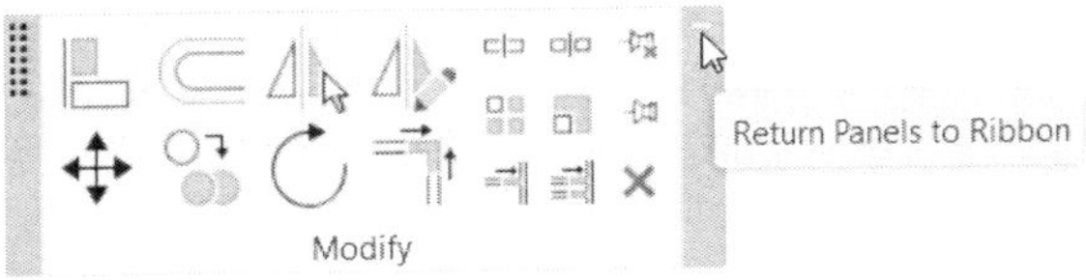

Figure 1–27

Hint: Ending a Command

When you are finished working with a tool, you typically default back to the **Modify** command. To end a command, use one of the following methods:

- In any tab on the ribbon, click (Modify).
- Type the shortcut **MD**.
- Press <Esc> once or twice to revert to **Modify**.
- Right-click and select **Cancel**, then repeat again to cancel the command.
- Start another command.

5. Navigation Bar

The Navigation Bar enables you to access the 2D (when in plan views) and Full Navigation (when in 3D views) SteeringWheels to navigate the view, as well as the Zoom commands, as shown in Figure 1–28. In a 3D perspective view (camera), you can use the **Fly** command to look around in the view.

> ***Note:*** *The Zoom or SteeringWheel command last used in the Navigation Bar will be the default command until it is manually changed. Using the zoom shortcut commands will not affect the Zoom command that displays in the Navigation Bar.*

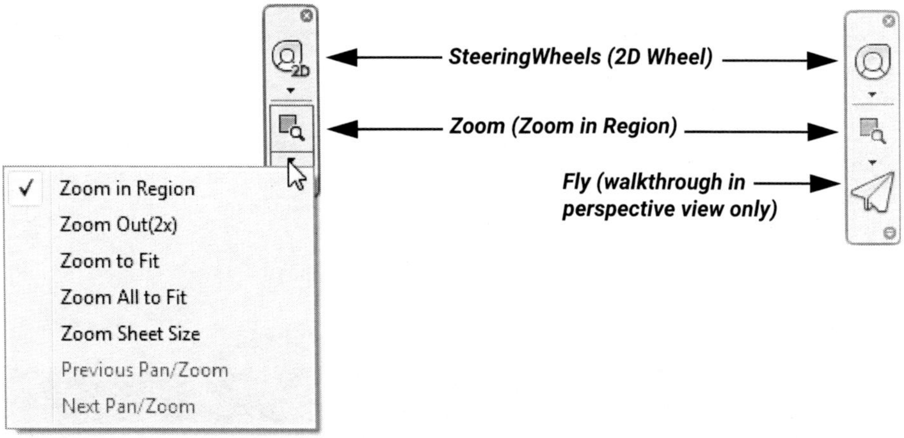

Figure 1–28

6. File Tab

When clicking on the *File* tab in the ribbon (also known as the *File* menu), a menu expands providing access to file commands, like **New**, **Open**, **Save**, **Save As**, **Export**, and **Print**, as well as the **Options** settings, as shown in Figure 1–29. Hover the cursor over a command to display a list of additional tools.

> ***Note:*** *If you click the primary icon (e.g.,* ***New*** *or* ***Open****) rather than the arrow, it starts the default command (except for* ***Save As*** *and* ***Export****, which require an option to be selected).*

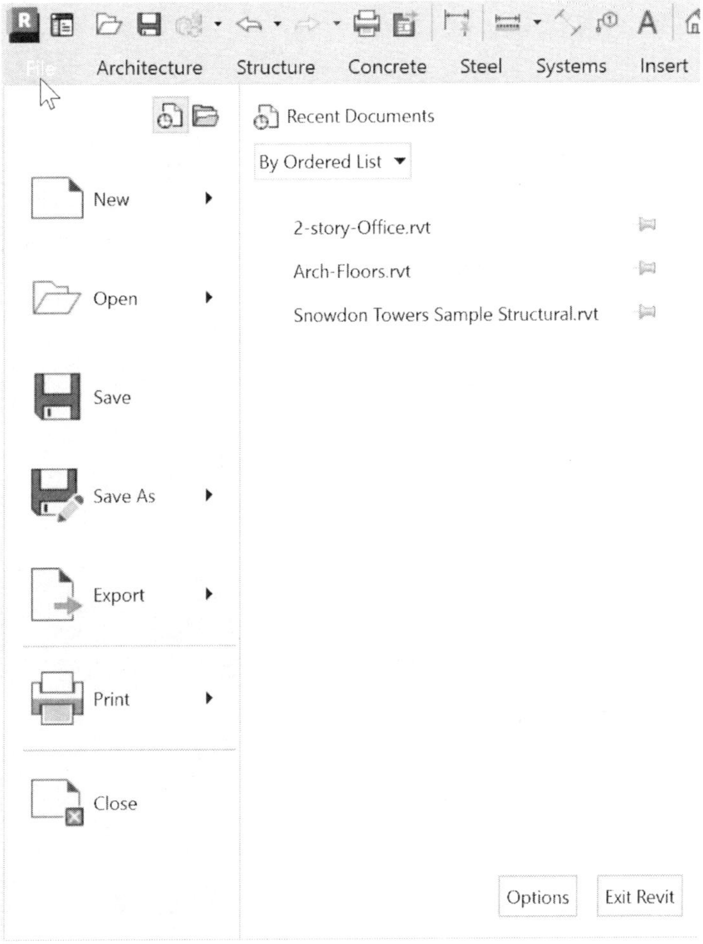

Figure 1–29

- To display a list of recently used documents, click (Recent Documents). The documents can be reordered as shown in Figure 1–30. You can click (Pin) next to a document name to keep it available.

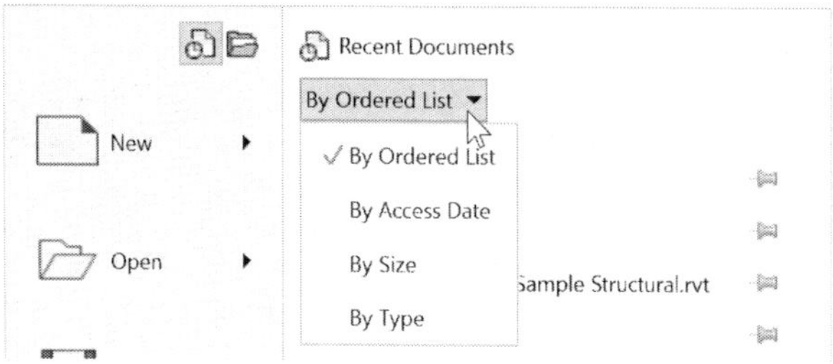

Figure 1–30

- To display a list of open documents and views, click (Open Documents). The list displays the documents and views that are open, as shown in Figure 1–31. You can use the *Open Documents* list to change between views.

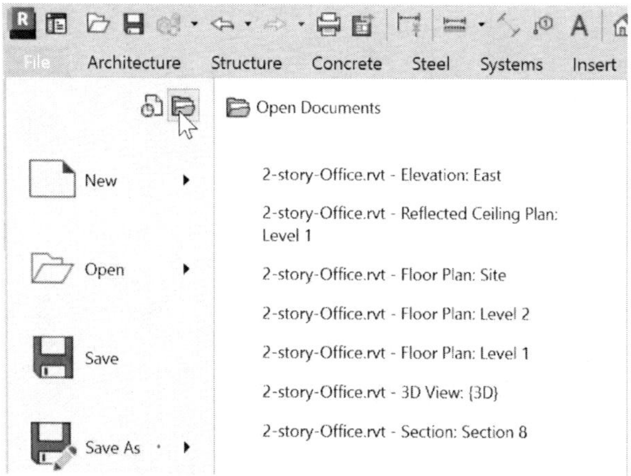

Figure 1–31

- Click (Close) to close the current project.
- At the bottom of the menu, click **Options** to open the *Options* dialog box or click **Exit Revit** to exit the software.

7. Properties

Properties (also known as the Properties palette) contains several parts, as shown in Figure 1–32. The Type Selector can be found at the top, which enables you to choose the size or style of the element you are adding or modifying. The options available in Properties enable you to make changes to information (parameters). There are two types of properties:

- **Instance properties** are set for the individual element(s) you are creating or modifying.
- **Type properties** control options for all elements of the same type. If you modify these parameter values, all elements of the selected type change.

Properties is usually kept open while working on a project to easily permit changes at any time.

If it does not display, in the *Modify* tab>*Properties* panel, click (Properties), or type **PP**. Alternatively, you can right-click in the view and select **Properties**. At the bottom of the Properties palette, you have buttons for sorting the properties and type properties parameters in the default order or in ascending or descending alphanumeric order. This only sorts the parameters within each of the sections and not the section titles.

> ***Note:*** *Some parameters are only available when you are editing an element. They are grayed out when unavailable.*

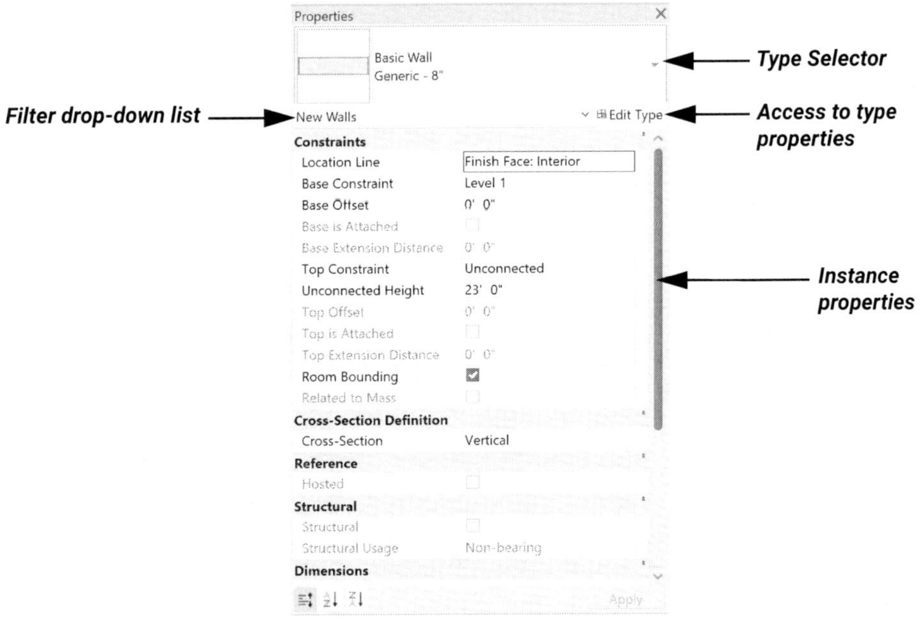

Figure 1–32

- Options for the current view display if the **Modify** command is active, but you have not selected an element.
- If a command or element is selected, the options for the associated element display.

- You can save the changes either by moving the cursor off of Properties, by pressing <Enter>, or by clicking **Apply**.
- When you start a command or select an element, you can set the element type in the Type Selector, as shown in Figure 1–33.

Note: *You can limit what shows in the drop-down list by typing in the search box.*

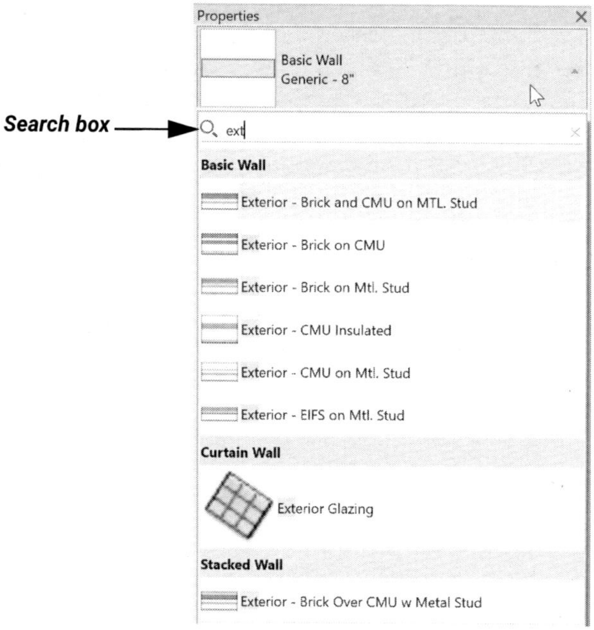

Figure 1–33

- When multiple elements are selected, you can filter the type of elements that display using the drop-down list, as shown in Figure 1–34.

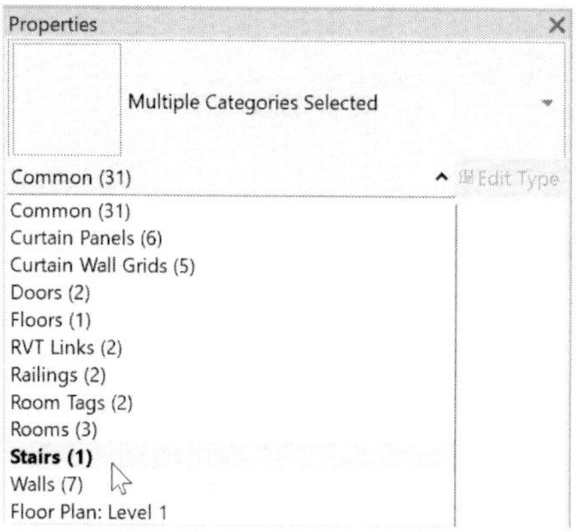

Figure 1–34

- Properties can be placed on a second monitor, or floated, resized, and docked on top of the Project Browser, as shown in Figure 1–35. Click a tab to display its associated information.

Figure 1–35

8. Project Browser

The Project Browser (shown in Figure 1–36) lists all the views of the model in which you can work and any additional views that you create, such as floor plans, ceiling plans, 3D views, elevations, sections, etc. It also includes schedules, legends, sheets (for plotting), lists of families by category, groups, and Revit links. The name of the active view is bold, and views that are placed on sheets will have a status icon next to the level's name.

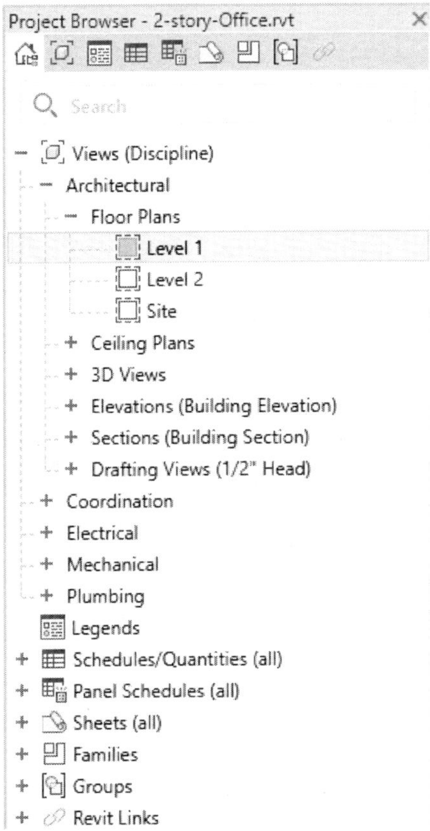

Figure 1–36

- To display the views associated with a view type (e.g., floor plans, ceiling plans, etc.), click (Expand) next to the section name. To hide the views in the section, click (Collapse). You can also expand and collapse sets using the shortcut menu, as shown in Figure 1–37.

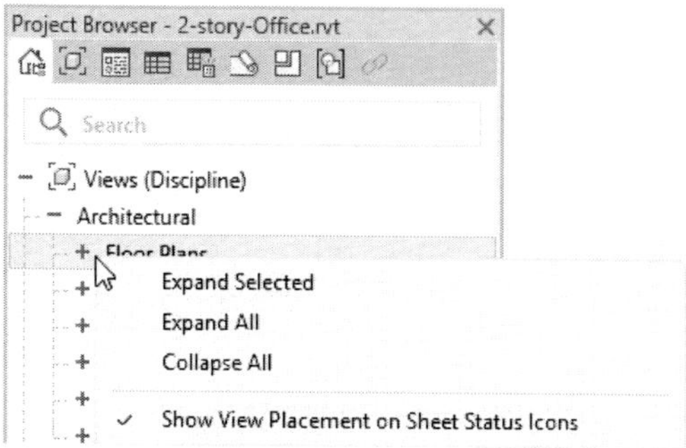

Figure 1–37

- To open a view, double-click on the view name or right-click and select **Open**.
- To open a sheet, right-click on the view in the Project Browser and select **Open Sheet**, as shown in Figure 1–38.
- To rename a view, slowly click twice on the view name and the text will highlight so it can be changed. You can also right-click on a view name and select **Rename...**, as shown in Figure 1–38, or press <F2>.

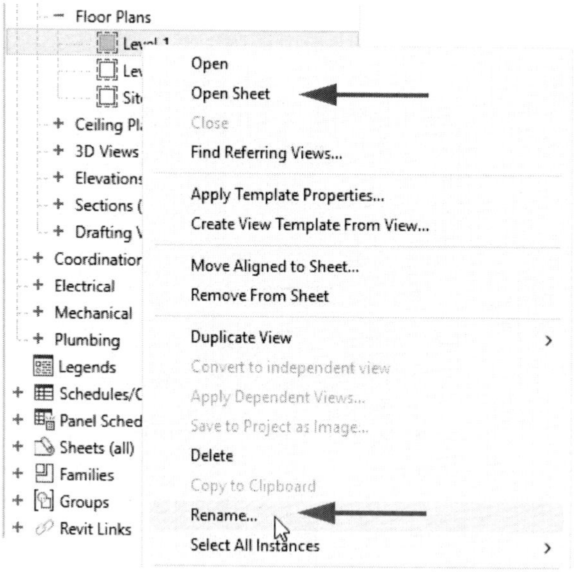

Figure 1–38

- You can zoom the Project Browser content to make the text larger and easier to see. Hover the cursor over the Project Browser, then press and hold <Ctrl> and use your mouse wheel to zoom or press the arrow keys on your keyboard up or down to zoom in and out.

Setting the Discipline of a View

You can utilize discipline in a view to display discipline-specific elements and to organize the Project Browser. When you duplicate or create a view, if it is not in the expected grouping in the Project Browser, you would need to set the *Discipline* in Properties. The view properties of the *Discipline* parameter (shown on the left in Figure 1–39) control the visibility of some elements and applies grouping in the Project Browser. For example, you can separate the coordination plans from the architectural plans, as shown on the right.

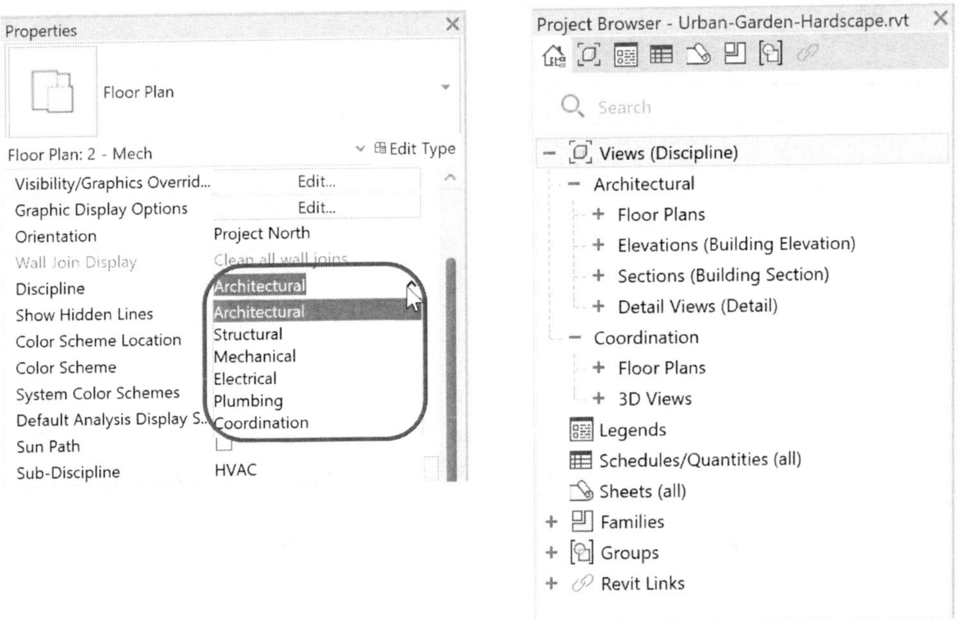

Figure 1–39

9. View Control Bar

The View Control Bar (shown in Figure 1–40) displays at the bottom of each view window. It controls aspects of that view, such as the scale and detail level. It also includes tools that display parts of the view and hide or isolate elements in the view.

Figure 1–40

- The number of options in the View Control Bar change when you are in a 3D view, as shown in Figure 1–41.

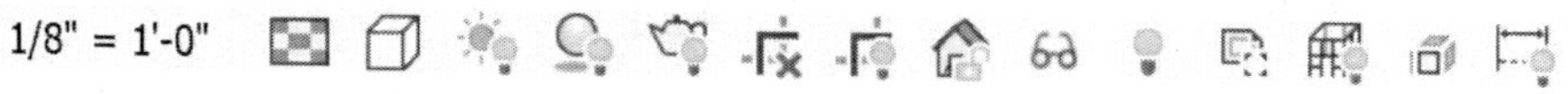

Figure 1–41

Tool	Tooltip	Description
1/8" = 1'-0"	**View Scale**	Set the scale of individual views.
	Detail Level	Set the detail level of a view.
	Visual Style	Various graphic style representations.
	Sun Path On/Off	Controls the visibility of the sun's path.
	Shadows On/Off	Controls elements' shadow visibility in a view.
	Show/Hide Rendering Dialog	Available in 3D only. Shows or hides the rendering dialog box.
	Crop View	Define the crop boundaries for a view.
	Show/Hide Crop Region	Display the crop region in a view.
	Unlocked/Locked 3D Views	Lock a 3D view's orientation.
	Temporary Hide/Isolate	Temporarily isolate/hide by category or element (view specific).
	Reveal Hidden Elements	View hidden elements or unhide them in the active view.
	Worksharing Display	Available when worksharing is enabled. Controls display settings.
	Temporary View Properties	Enable, apply or restore view properties and display recent templates and apply them.
	Show or Hide the Analytical Model	Only used for Structural and MEP to display the analytical information.
	Highlight Displacement Sets	Also known as exploded views.
	Reveal Constraints	Temporarily view the dimension and alignment constraints in the active view.

10. Status Bar

The left-hand side of the Status Bar provides information about the current process, such as the next step for a command, as shown in Figure 1–42.

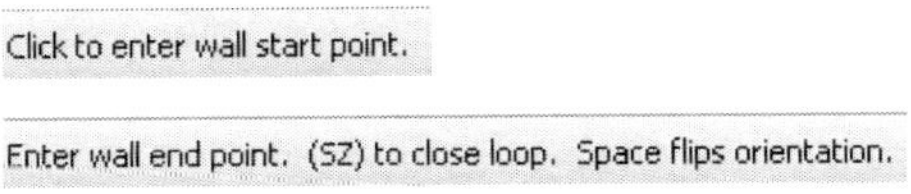

Figure 1–42

The right-hand side of the Status Bar provides selection options that enable you to control how the software selects specific elements in a project by toggling selection options on and off. When a selection option is toggled off, the icon will have a red X on it, as shown in Figure 1–43.

Figure 1–43

- (Select links): When this option is toggled on, you can select linked CAD drawings or Revit models. When it is toggled off, you cannot select them when using **Modify** or **Move**.
- (Select underlay elements): When this option is toggled on, you can select underlay elements. When it is toggled off, you cannot select them when using **Modify** or **Move**.
- (Select pinned elements): When this option is toggled on, you can select pinned elements. When it is toggled off, you cannot select them when using **Modify** or **Move**.
- (Select elements by face): When this option is toggled on, you can select elements (such as the floors or walls in an elevation) by selecting the interior face or selecting an edge. When it is toggled off, you can only select elements by selecting an edge.
- (Drag elements on selection): When this option is toggled on, you can hover over an element, select it, and drag it to a new location. When it is toggled off, the Crossing or Box select mode starts when you press and drag, even if you are on top of an element. Once elements have been selected, they can still be dragged to a new location.

You can also set the selection option from the ribbon. Expand the *Select* panel's title and select the option(s), as shown in Figure 1–44.

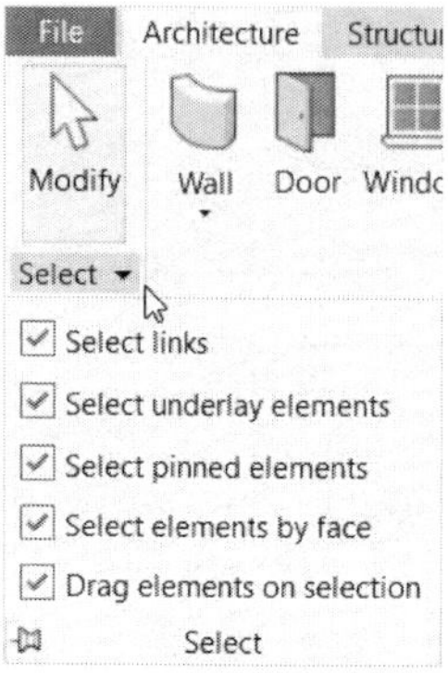

Figure 1–44

Other options in the Status Bar are related to worksets and design options (advanced tools).

Hint: Shortcut Menus

Shortcut menus help you to work smoothly and efficiently by enabling you to quickly access required commands. These menus provide access to basic viewing commands, recently used commands, and the available browsers, as shown in Figure 1–45. Additional options vary depending on the element or command that you are using.

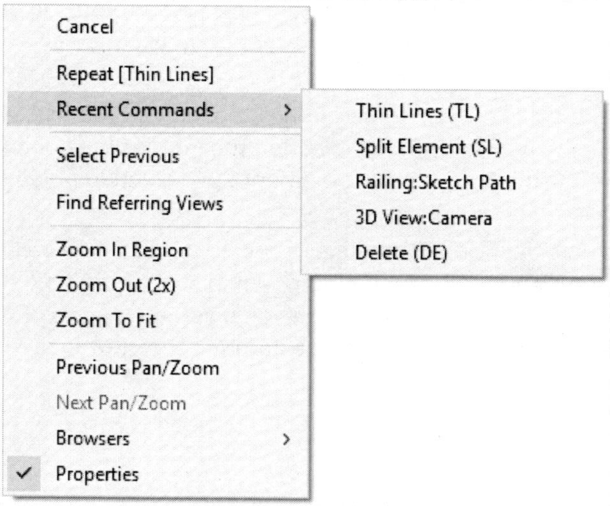

Figure 1–45

Change Interface to Dark Mode

You can change Revit's entire interface to a dark mode or you can change just the drawing area to dark mode. You can also set the interface to dark mode, then click (Canvas Theme) to change the drawing area back to white.

How To: Change the Entire Interface to Dark Mode

1. In the *File* tab, click **Options**.
2. In the *Options* dialog box, select the *Colors* tab.
3. Expand the *UI active theme* drop-down list and select **Dark**, as shown in Figure 1–46.

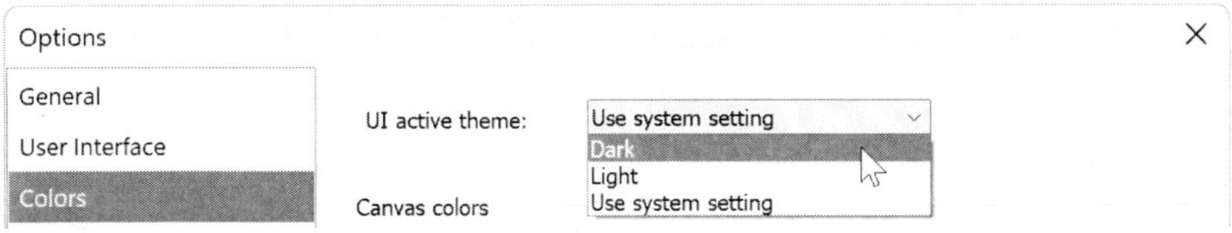

Figure 1–46

4. The entire interface is now in dark mode.

- To return to the interface to the default setting, in the *Options* dialog box>*Colors* tab, expand the *UI active theme* drop-down list and select **Use system setting**.

How To: Change the Drawing Area to Dark Mode

1. In the *View* tab>*Windows* panel, click (Canvas Theme).
2. Just the drawing area will change to dark mode.
   - If the interface is set to dark mode, you can use this to set the drawing area to display a light background.

1.3 Opening and Saving Projects

File operations to open existing files, create new files from a template, and save files in Revit are found on the Home screen or in the *File* tab, as shown in Figure 1–47.

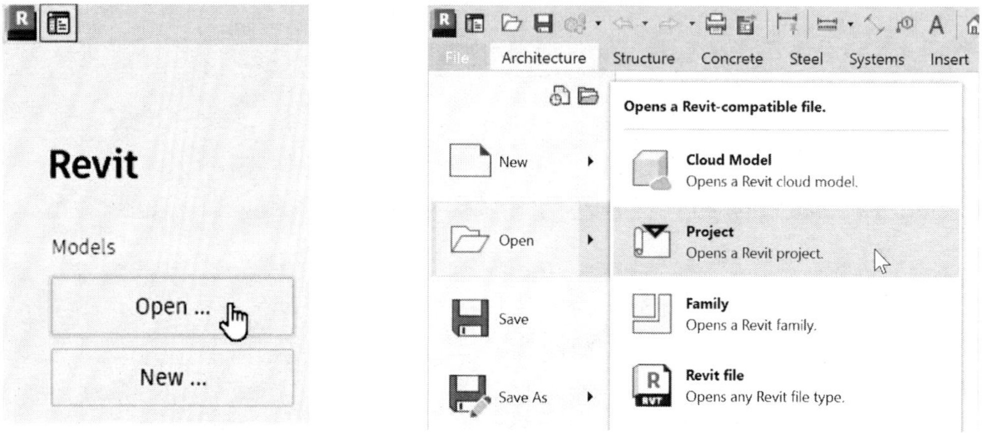

Home screen ***File tab***

Figure 1–47

There are three main file formats:

- **Project files (.rvt):** These are where you do the majority of your work in the building model by adding elements, creating views, annotating views, and setting up printable sheets. They are initially based on template files.
- **Family files (.rfa):** These are separate components that can be inserted in a project. They include elements that can stand alone (e.g., a table or piece of mechanical equipment) or are items that are hosted in other elements (e.g., a door in a wall or a lighting fixture in a ceiling). Title block and annotation symbol files are special types of family files.
- **Template files (.rte and .rft):** These are the base files for any new project or family. Project templates (**.rte**) hold standard information and settings for creating new project files. The software includes several templates for various types of projects. You can also create custom templates. Family templates (**.rft**) include base information for creating families. Template files are usually saved as a new file.

Opening Projects

To open an existing project, click **Open** from the Home screen, or in the Quick Access Toolbar or *File* tab, click (Open). You can also press <Ctrl>+<O>. The *Open* dialog box opens, and you can navigate to the required folder and select a project file. An example of the *Open* dialog box is shown in Figure 1–48.

Figure 1–48

- The software release version of the currently selected project displays below the preview. Do not open a drawing that should remain in an earlier version, as you cannot save back to previous versions.

  Note: It is important that everyone working on a project uses the same software version (e.g., 2027) and is on the same updated version (e.g., 2027.1). While your software may be able to open files created in its earlier versions, it will not be able to open files created in versions newer than the one you are using currently as Revit is not backwards compatible. For example, if you are working in Revit 2026, you cannot open a model created in Revit 2027.

- When you open a file created in an earlier version, the *Model Upgrade* dialog box indicates the release of a file and the release to which it will be upgraded. If needed, you can cancel the upgrade before it completes.
- When you encounter an *Unresolved References* dialog box upon opening a project, you have two options. You can either click **Ignore and Continue opening the project** to proceed with opening the project, or click **Open Manage Links to correct the problem** to resolve the issue. The details of the *Manage Links* dialog box will be explained in the next chapter.

Saving Projects

It is important to save your projects frequently. In the Quick Access Toolbar or *File* tab, click (Save), or press <Ctrl>+<S> to save your project. If the project has not yet been saved, the *Save As* dialog box opens, where you can specify a file location and name.

- To save an existing project with a new name, in the *File* tab, expand (Save As) and click (Project).
- If you have not saved in a certain amount of time, the software will notify you with the Project Not Saved Recently alert box, as shown in Figure 1–49. Select **Save the project**. If you want to set reminder intervals or not save at this time, select one of the other two options shown in Figure 1–49.

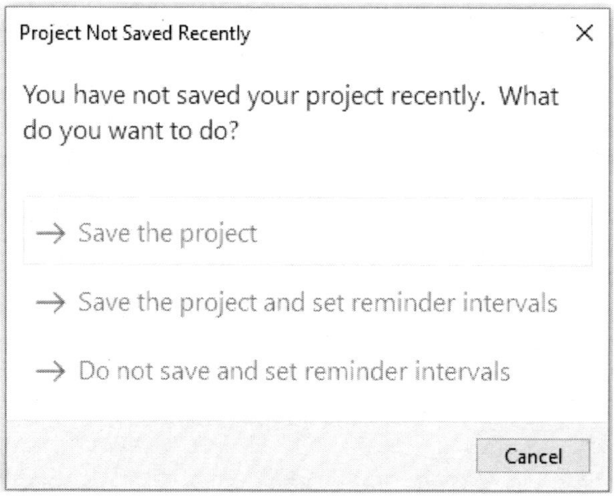

Figure 1–49

- You can set the *Save reminder interval* to **15** or **30 minutes**, **One**, **Two**, or **Four hours**, or to have **No reminders** display. In the *File* tab, click **Options** to open the *Options* dialog box. Select **General** and set the interval, as shown in Figure 1–50.

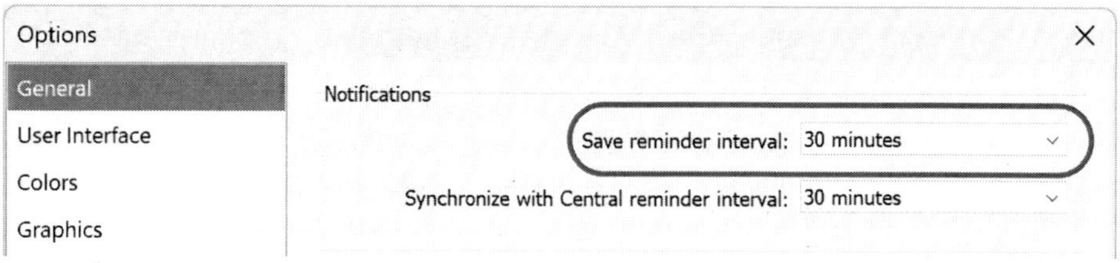

Figure 1–50

Saving Backup Copies

By default, the software saves a backup copy of a project file when you save the project. Backup copies are numbered incrementally (e.g., **My Project.0001.rvt**, **My Project.0002.rvt**, etc.) and are saved in the same folder as the original file. In the *Save As* dialog box, click **Options...** to control how many backup copies are saved. The default number is three backups. If you exceed this number, the software deletes the oldest backup file.

Hint: Setting a Starting View

To save time when opening a complex model with worksharing activated, you can specify a *starting view*. This could be a cover sheet or a drafting view with information about the project. The idea is that the contents of the starting view are simple elements rather than model elements.

- To set the starting view, in the *Manage* tab>*Manage Project* panel, click (Starting View). In the *Starting View* dialog box, select the view name, as shown in Figure 1–51.

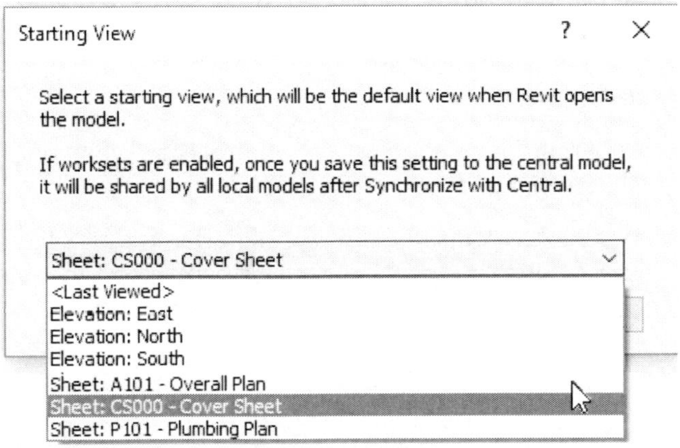

Figure 1–51

1.4 Viewing Commands

Viewing commands are crucial to working efficiently in most drawing and modeling programs and Revit is no exception. Once in a view, you can use the Zoom controls to navigate in it. You can zoom in and out and pan in any view. There are also special tools for viewing in 3D.

Zooming and Panning

Use the mouse wheel as the main method of zooming and panning around the models.

- Scroll the wheel on the mouse up to zoom in and down to zoom out.
- Hold the wheel and move the mouse to pan.
- Double-click on the wheel to zoom to the extents of the view.
- In a 3D view, hold <Shift> and the mouse wheel and move the mouse to orbit around the model.

When you save a model and exit the software, the pan and zoom location of each view is remembered. This is especially important for complex models.

Additional Zoom Controls

A number of additional zoom methods enable you to control the screen display. **Zoom** and **Pan** can be performed at any time while using other commands.

- You can access the **Zoom** commands in the Navigation Bar in the upper right corner of the view (as shown in Figure 1–52). You can also access them from most shortcut menus and by typing the shortcut commands.

Note:  *(2D Wheel) provides cursor-specific access to **Zoom** and **Pan**.*

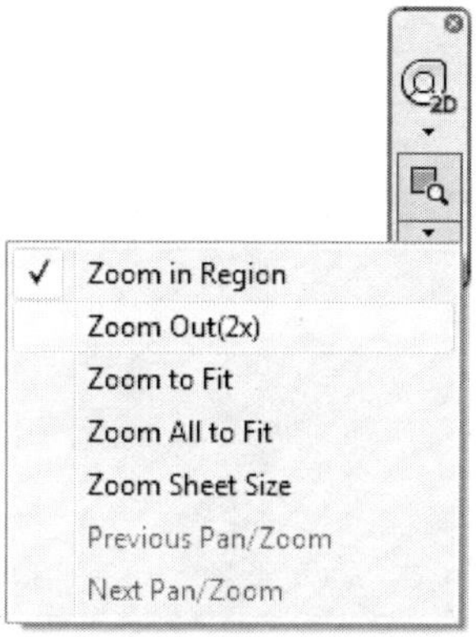

Figure 1–52

Zoom Commands

	Zoom In Region (ZR)	Zooms in to a region that you define. Drag the cursor or select two points to define the rectangular area you want to zoom in to. This is the default command.
	Zoom Out(2x) (ZO)	Zooms out to half the current magnification around the center of the elements.
	Zoom to Fit (ZF or ZE)	Zooms out so that the entire contents of the project only display on the screen in the current view.
	Zoom All to Fit (ZA)	Zooms out so that the entire contents of the project display on the screen in all open views.
	Zoom Sheet Size (ZS)	Zooms in or out in relation to the sheet size.
N/A	**Previous Pan/Zoom (ZP)**	Steps back one **Zoom** command.
N/A	**Next Pan/Zoom**	Steps forward one **Zoom** command if you have done a **Previous Pan/Zoom**.

Viewing in 3D

Even if you started a project entirely in plan views, you can quickly create 3D views of the model, as shown in Figure 1–53. There are two types of 3D views: orthographic views created by the **Default 3D View** command and perspective views created by the **Camera** command.

Figure 1–53

Working in 3D views helps you visualize the project and position some of the elements correctly. You can create and modify elements in both orthographic and perspective 3D views, just as you can in plan views.

- Once you have created a 3D view, you can save it and easily return to it.
- Perspective 3D views are visual representations of what the model would look like if you were standing in the model.

- Orthographic 3D views can have a scale applied to them so that the entire model's components are at the same size no matter where the camera is positioned or its distance from the model.
- You can add, delete, modify, and move elements in 3D perspective views.
- Perspective views can be placed on sheets.

How To: Create and Save a 3D View

1. In the Quick Access Toolbar or *View* tab>*Create* panel, click (Default 3D View). The default 3D southeast view opens, as shown in Figure 1–54.

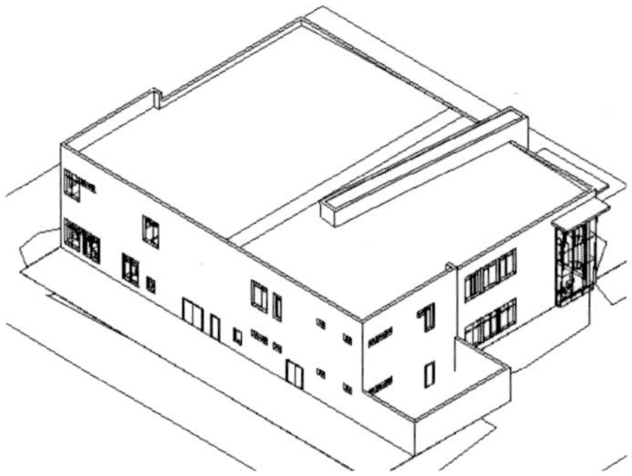

Figure 1–54

Note: *You can spin the view to a different angle using the mouse wheel or the middle button of a three-button mouse. Hold <Shift> as you press the wheel or middle button and drag the cursor.*

2. Modify the view to display the building from other directions.
3. In the Project Browser, slowly click twice on the {3D} view or right-click on the {3D} view and select **Rename...**. The name is placed in a text box with the original name highlighted, as shown in Figure 1–55.

Figure 1–55

4. Type a new name in the text box, as shown in Figure 1–56.

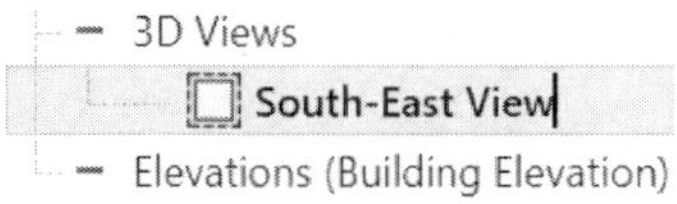

Figure 1–56

Note: *All types of views can be renamed.*

- When you modified the default 3D view but did not save it to a new name, the **Default 3D View** command opens the view in the last orientation you specified.

How To: Create a Camera 3D View

1. Switch to a floor plan view.
2. In the Quick Access Toolbar or *View* tab>*Create* panel, expand (Default 3D View) and click (Camera).
3. In Properties, verify **Perspective** is set for *Projection Mode*. In the *Modify | Camera* tab> *Camera* panel, set the *Offset* and the *From* setting for which level the camera will be placed on, as shown in Figure 1–57.

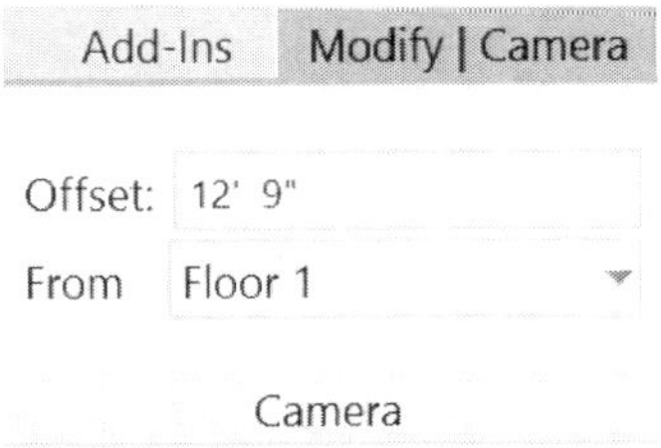

Figure 1–57

4. Place the camera on the view.
5. Point the camera in the direction in which you want it to shoot by placing the target on the view, as shown in Figure 1–58.

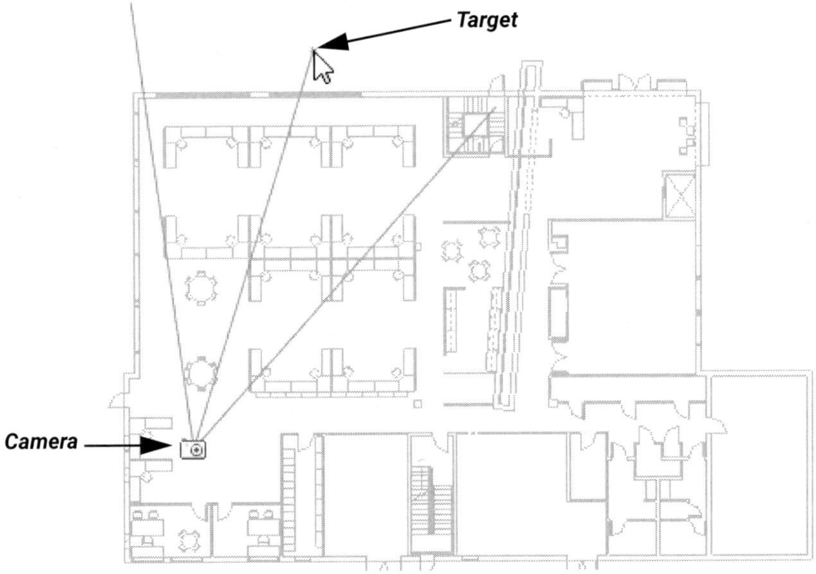

Figure 1–58

A new view is displayed, as shown in Figure 1–59.

Figure 1–59

- You can use the round controls to modify the display size of the view and press <Shift> + the mouse wheel to change the view.

- To perform a walkthrough in a perspective view, in the Navigation Bar, click (Fly).
  - Use the arrow keys on the keyboard to move around the model.
  - Hold down <Shift> and scroll your mouse wheel up or down to adjust the speed of movements while doing a walkthrough. Watch the Status Bar to see the **Fly and walk speed factor** change, and stop scrolling when the desired speed displays.
  - To adjust the eye elevation, press <E> to move up or <Q> to move down. You can also adjust the *Eye Elevation* and *Target Elevation* parameters in Properties.
  - If you would like to select on an element while performing a walkthrough, click (Modify) and select the element. To continue the walkthrough, click **Fly** in the Navigation Bar to proceed.
  - To get out of the **Fly** command, press <Esc> or select a new command.

How To: Create an Orthographic 3D View

1. Switch to a floor plan view.
2. In the Quick Access Toolbar or *View* tab>*Create* panel, expand (Default 3D View) and click (Camera).
3. In Properties, expand *Projection Mode* and select **Orthographic**. In the *Modify | Camera* tab>*Camera* panel, set the *Offset* and the *From* setting for which level the camera will be placed on.

4. Place the camera on the view.
5. Point the camera in the direction in which you want it to shoot by placing the target on the view, as shown in Figure 1–60.

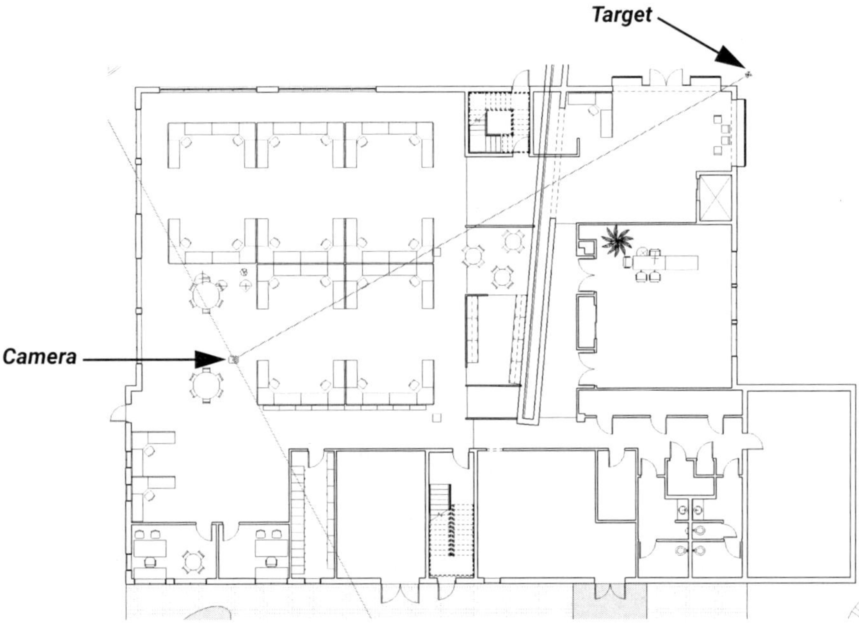

Figure 1–60

- A new view is displayed, as shown in Figure 1–61. If needed, the *Eye Elevation* and *Target Elevation* can be adjusted in Properties.

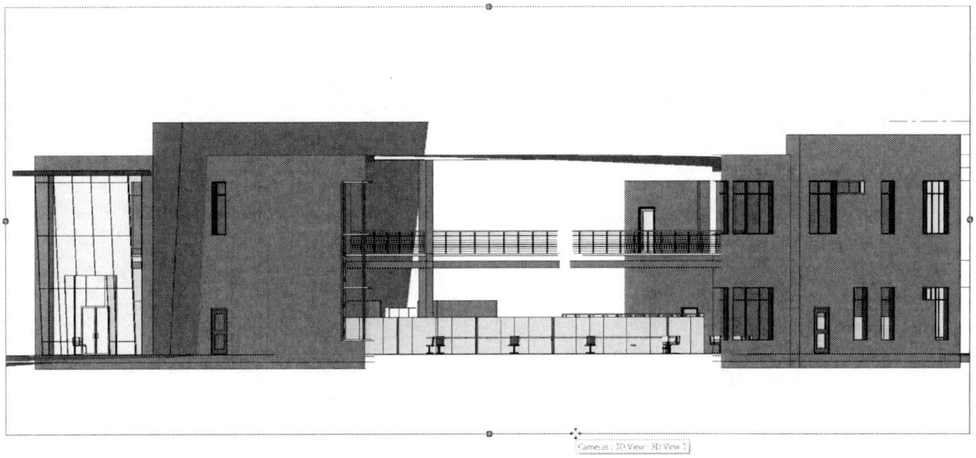

Figure 1–61

6. In Properties, scroll down and adjust the *Eye Elevation* and *Target Elevation* as needed.

How To: Modify Camera 3D Views

1. In a plan view, select the camera or target icon and drag it within the view to reposition the placement.
2. In Properties, scroll down and adjust the *Eye Elevation* and *Target Elevation* as needed.

- To display the camera and camera controls in a plan view, select the camera's crop boundary in the perspective view, then switch back to the plan view.
  - Alternatively, while in a plan view, you can right-click on the perspective 3D view in the Project Browser and select **Show Camera**, as shown in Figure 1–62. The camera and camera crop boundaries will display.

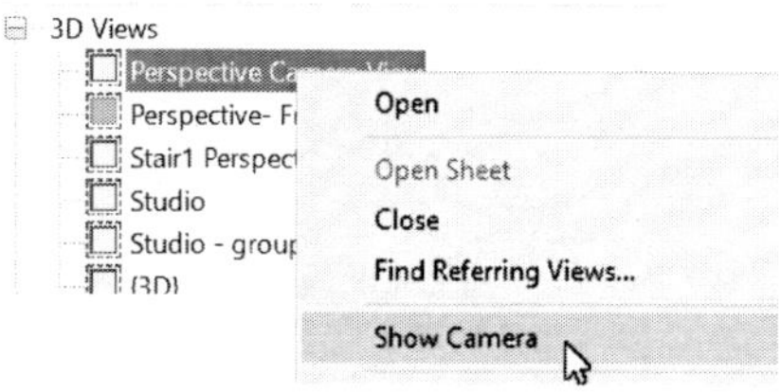

Figure 1–62

- For perspective 3D views, if the view becomes distorted, reset the target so that it is centered in the boundary of the view (called the crop region). In the *Modify | Cameras* tab> *Camera* panel, click (Reset Target).

ViewCube

The ViewCube provides visual clues as to where you are in a 3D view. It helps you move around the model with quick access to specific views (such as top, front, and right), as well as corner and directional views, as shown in Figure 1–63.

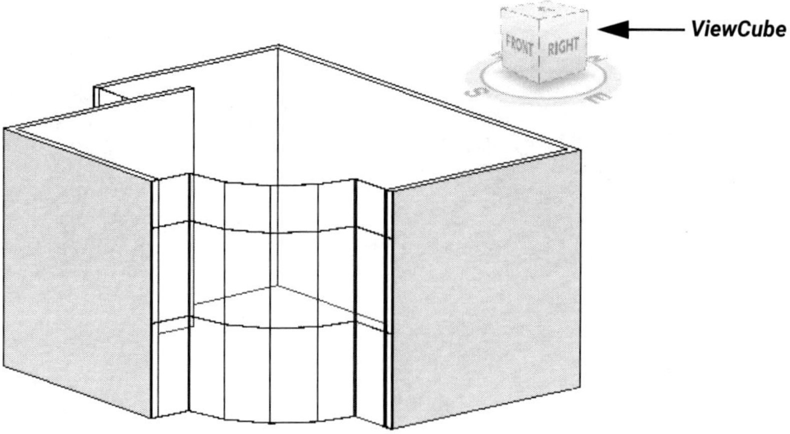

Figure 1–63

Move the cursor over any face of the ViewCube to highlight it. Once a face is highlighted, you can select it to reorient the model. You can also click and drag on the ViewCube to orbit the box, which rotates the model.

- (Home) displays when you roll the cursor over the ViewCube. Click it to return to the view defined as **Home**. To change the Home view, set the view as you want it, right-click on the ViewCube, and select **Set Current View as Home**.
- The ViewCube is available in orthographic and perspective views.

You can switch between Perspective and Orthographic mode by right-clicking on the ViewCube (as shown on the left in Figure 1–64) or clicking on (ViewCube contextual menu) to the lower right of the ViewCube (as shown on the right in Figure 1–64) and selecting **Perspective** or **Orthographic**.

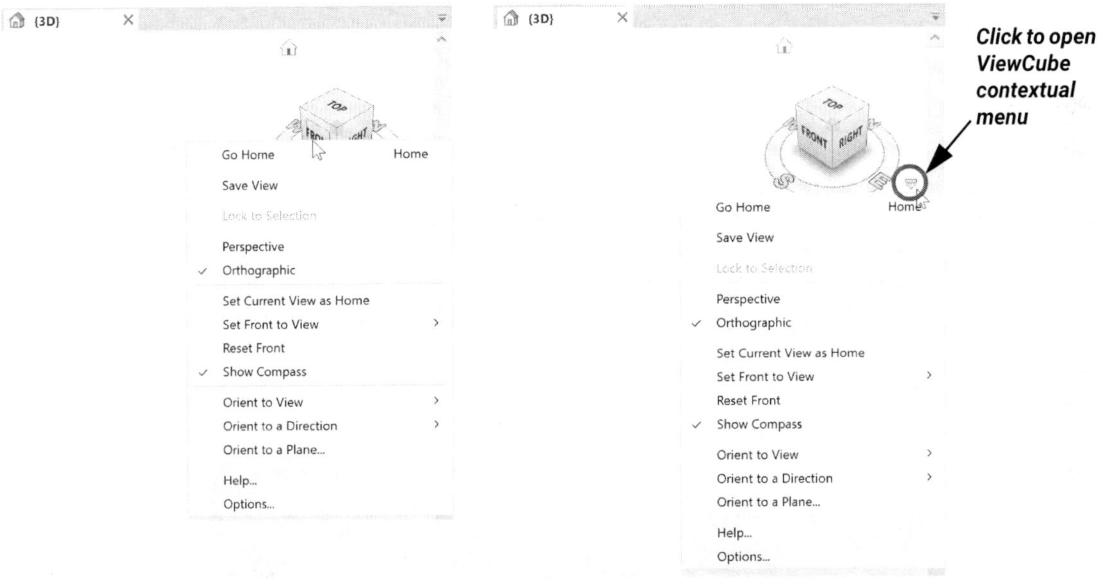

Right-click on ViewCube ***ViewCube contextual menu***

Figure 1–64

You can create 3D views that are oriented to a specific view. For more information, refer to ***Chapter 3 Working with Views***.

Visual Styles

Any view can have a visual style applied. The **Visual Style** options found in the View Control Bar (shown in Figure 1–65) specify the shading of the building model. These options apply to plan, elevation, section, and 3D views.

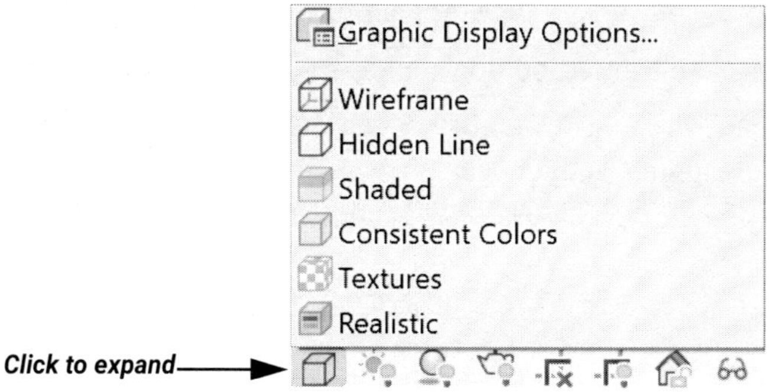

Figure 1–65

- (Wireframe) displays the lines and edges that make up elements, but hides the surfaces. This can be useful when you are dealing with complex intersections.
- (Hidden Line) displays the lines, edges, and surfaces of the elements, but it does not display any colors. This is the most common visual style to use while working on a design.
- (Shaded) displays the view with colors and shadows to show the affect of indirect light, as shown in Figure 1–66.

Figure 1–66

- (Consistent Colors) give you a sense of the material's color, regardless of the angle of the view, including transparent glass. An example showing an exterior view using Consistent Colors is shown in Figure 1–67. Landscape components will display as gray outlines of the objects until the Realistic visual style is used.

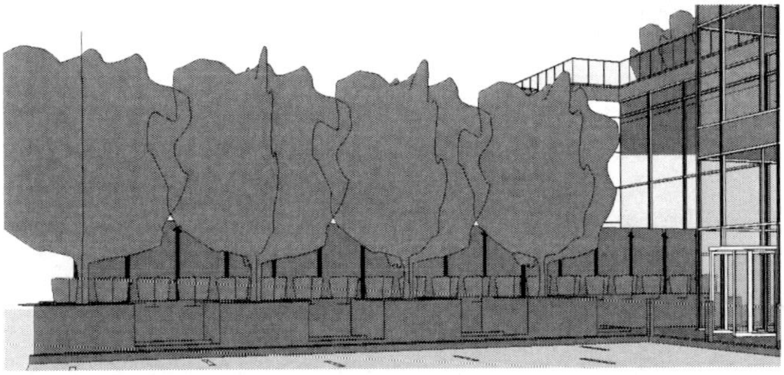

Figure 1–67

- (Textures) displays the view using Consistent Colors, but if a component has a material applied to it, the Textures visual style displays the material's texture as well. For example, Figure 1–68 appears as if it is using Consistent Colors but it is also showing the texture of the brick material on the planters.

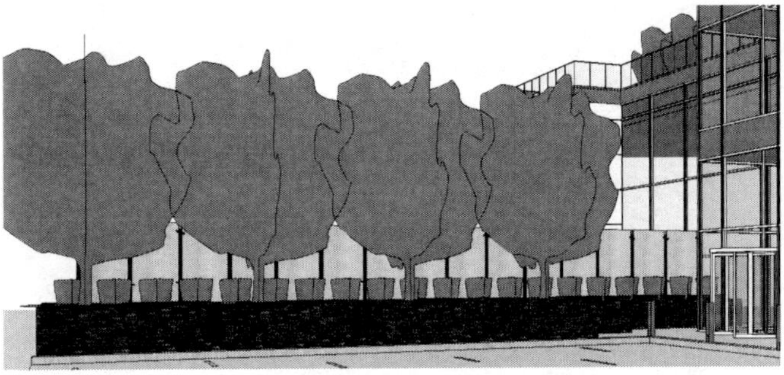

Figure 1–68

- (Realistic) displays artificial lights in addition to the material's appearance (if material has been applied to a component), as shown in Figure 1–69. It takes a lot of computer power to execute this visual style, so it is better to use the other visual styles most of the time as you are working.

Figure 1–69

Select and Identify Elements in a Project

When selecting an element in the drawing area, the element highlights (as shown on the left in Figure 1–70) and information about the element displays in Properties, helping you further identify the element. When you position the cursor over or near an element in the drawing area (as shown on the right in Figure 1–70), the outline of the element is highlighted with a thicker line weight and a tooltip appears. Additionally, the Status Bar at the bottom of the Revit window displays a description of the element.

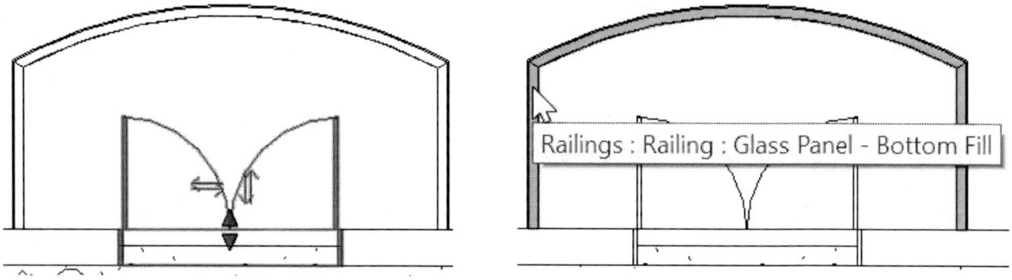

Figure 1–70

To deselect an element, you can do one of the following:

- In any tab on the ribbon, click  (Modify).
- Type the shortcut **MD**.
- Click in an empty area in the drawing area to clear the selection.
- Press <Esc> once to revert to **Modify**.
- Right-click and select **Cancel...** once or twice.
- Select another element.

Practice 1a
Open and Review a Project

Practice Objectives

- Navigate the graphic user interface.
- Manipulate 2D and 3D views by zooming and panning.
- Create 3D orthographic and perspective views.
- Set the visual style of a view.

In this practice, you will open a project file and view each of the various areas in the interface. You will investigate elements, commands, and their options. You will also open views through the Project Browser and view the model in 3D, as shown in Figure 1–71.

Figure 1–71

- This is a version of the main project you will work on throughout this guide.

Task 1: Explore the interface and model.

1. On the Home screen, in the *Models* section, click **Open...**, as shown on the left in Figure 1–72. Alternatively, if you have a project open, on the *File* tab, expand (Open) and click (Project), as shown on the right.

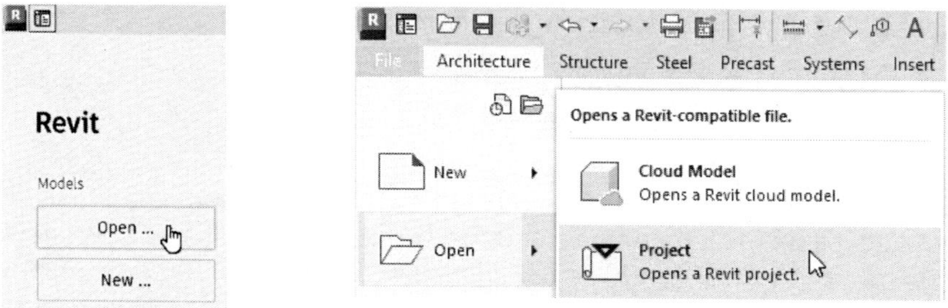

Home screen ***File tab***

Figure 1–72

2. In the *Open* dialog box, navigate to the *Revit 2027 Fundamentals for Architecture Practice Files* folder and select **Arch-Final.rvt**.
3. Click **Open**. The 3D view of the hotel opens in the view window.
4. In the Project Browser, expand the *Floor Plans* section. Double-click on **Floor 1** to open it. This view is referred to as **Floor Plans: Floor 1**.
5. Take time to review the floor plan to get acquainted with it.
6. Review the various parts of the screen and the different rooms in the hotel as they will be referenced throughout the practices.
7. In the view, hover the cursor over one of the doors. A tooltip displays describing the element, as shown in Figure 1–73. Information about the element also displays in the Status Bar, but not in Properties.

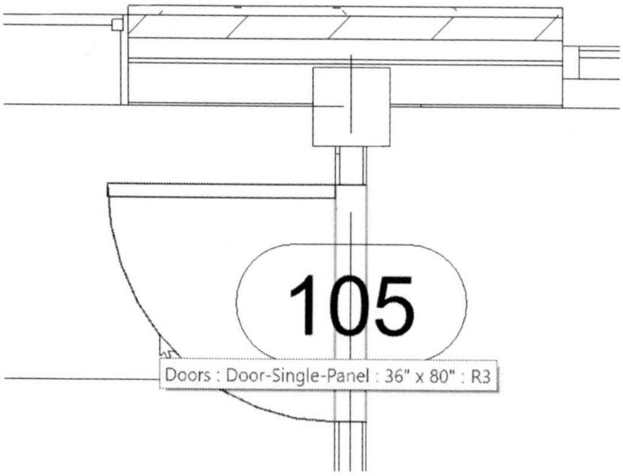

Figure 1–73

8. Hover the cursor over another element to display its description.
9. Select a door. The ribbon changes to the *Modify | Doors* tab and Properties displays the door type and parameter information about the door family.
10. Click in an empty space in the view, outside of the building, to release the selection.
11. Hold <Ctrl> and select several elements and datums of different types. The ribbon changes to the *Modify | Multi-Select* tab and Properties displays **Multiple Categories Selected**.
12. In the ribbon, in the *Select* panel, click (Modify) to clear the selection.
13. In the *Architecture* tab>*Build* panel, click (Wall), or type the shortcut **WA**. The *Modify | Place Wall* tab displays at the end of the ribbon, containing the tools and options that enable you to draw walls, like the sketch tools, *Chain*, *Offset*, *Radius*, *Constraint*, and *Level*. Properties shows the wall type and wall parameters.
14. Click (Modify) to end the command. Note that the contextual tab on the ribbon no longer displays.
15. In the *Architecture* tab>*Build* panel, click (Door), or type the shortcut **DR**. The ribbon changes to the *Modify* | *Place Door* tab and displays the options and tools you can use to place doors. Properties displays the door type and the door parameters.
16. Click (Modify) to return to the main ribbon.
17. In the Quick Access Toolbar, click (Save) to save the project.

Task 2: Use the Project Browser to open views.

1. In the Project Browser, note that some views have a blue icon next to them, which indicates that they have been placed on a sheet.
   - You might need to widen the Project Browser to display the full names of the views.
2. Right-click on **Floor 1** and select **Open Sheet**, as shown in Figure 1–74. The **A1.1 - Ground Floor Plan** sheet opens.

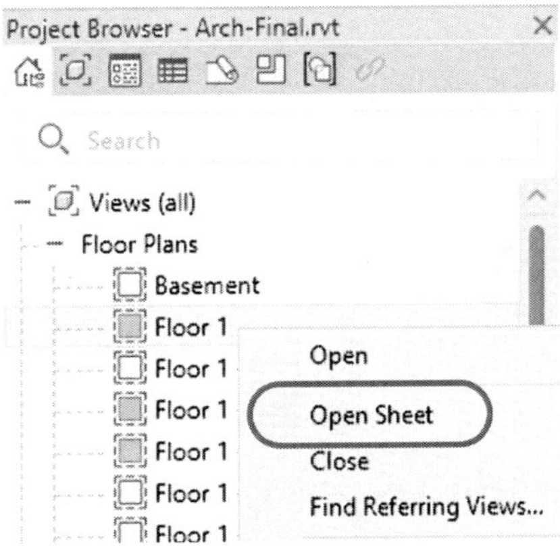

Figure 1–74

3. On the *A1.1 - Ground Floor Plan* tab, click on the X to close the view, as shown in Figure 1–75.

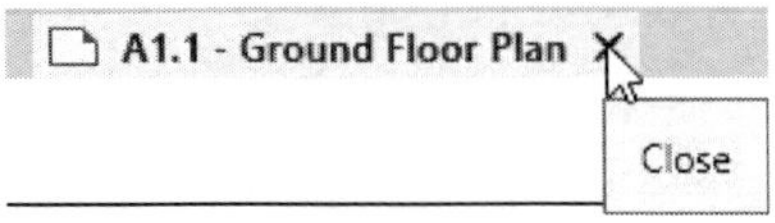

Figure 1–75

4. In the Project Browser, double-click on the **Floor 1 - Furniture Plan** view.
5. This floor plan displays with the furniture, but without the annotations that were displayed in the **Floor 1** view.
6. Open the **Floor 1 - Life Safety Plan** view by double-clicking on it. The walls and furniture display, but the furniture is grayed out and red lines describing important life safety information display.
7. At the top of the views, click each tab to switch between the open views. End back on the **Floor 1 - Life Safety Plan** view.
8. In the *View* tab>*Windows* panel, click (Tile Views), or type **WT**. All of the open views are tiled. Type **ZA** to zoom out to the extents of all the opened views, as shown in Figure 1–76.
   - Depending on which view was the active view when you tiled the views, the order they tiled in may differ from what is shown in the image.

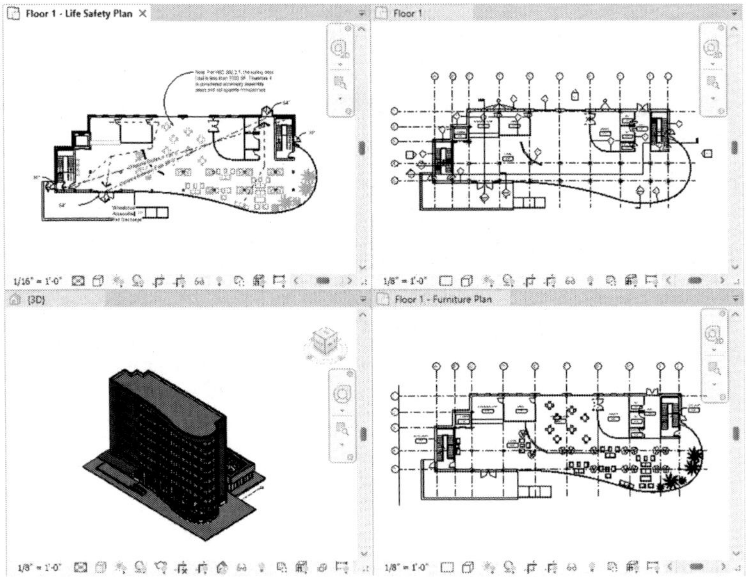

Figure 1–76

9. Click inside the **Floor 1** view to make it active.

10. In the *View* tab>*Windows* panel, click (Tab Views), or type **TW**. The views return to the tabs and the Floor 1 view is first in the group of view tabs.
11. Type **ZF** to zoom all in the view.
12. Using your mouse wheel, zoom in to the right side of the view so that you can clearly see the east elevation marker, as shown in Figure 1–77.

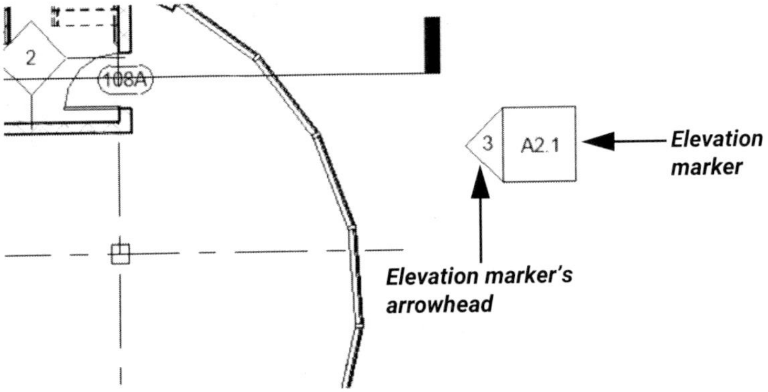

Figure 1–77

13. Double-click on the elevation marker's arrowhead to open the view. The **East** elevation view opens.
14. In the *View* tab>*Windows* panel, expand (Switch Windows) and select **Arch-Final.rvt - Floor Plan: Floor 1**, then type **ZF** to zoom all.
15. Using your mouse wheel, zoom in to the west side of the building at the west stairs and double-click on the **1/A2.2** section marker's arrowhead, as shown in Figure 1–78.

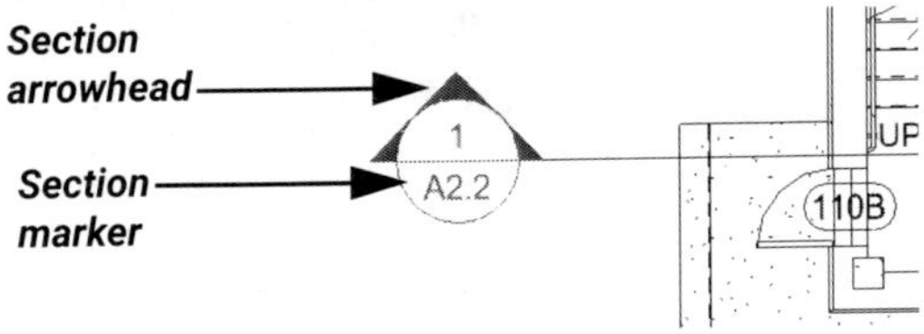

Figure 1–78

16. The **E/W Building Section** view opens.
17. In the Project Browser, expand the *Sections (Building Section)* section and note that the **E/W Building Section** view is bold, meaning it is the active view.
18. At the bottom of the view window, in the View Control Bar, click **Visual Style** and select (Shaded). The elements in the view are now easier to read.
19. In the Project Browser, scroll down and expand the *Sheets (all)* section.

20. Double-click on several of the sheets to open and view them. Some have views already applied (e.g., **A1.5 - Floor 2 - Floor Plan View**, as shown in Figure 1–79).

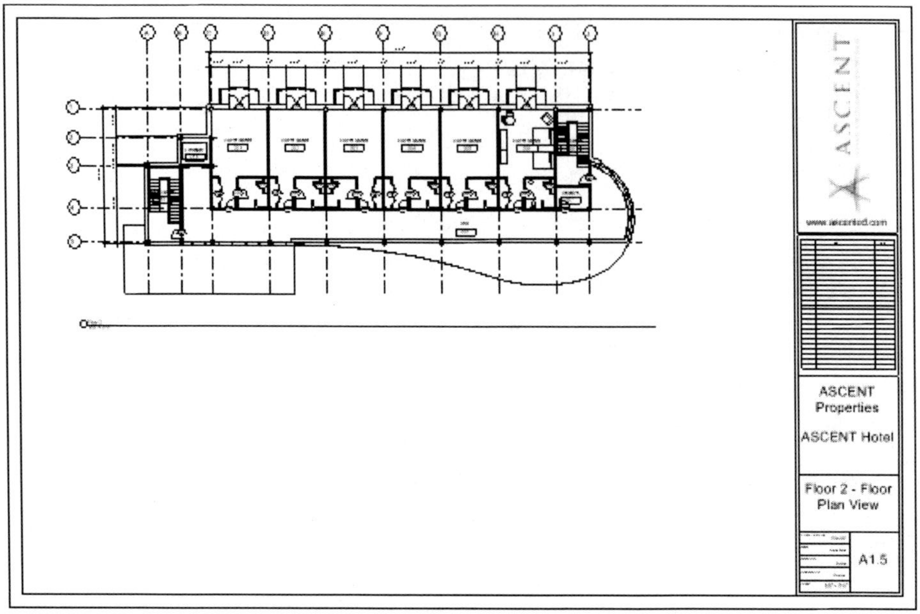

Figure 1–79

21. Save the project.

Task 3: Practice viewing tools.

1. At the far right of the view tabs, expand **Switch Windows** and select **Floor 1**, as shown in Figure 1–80. Type **ZF** to zoom all in the view.

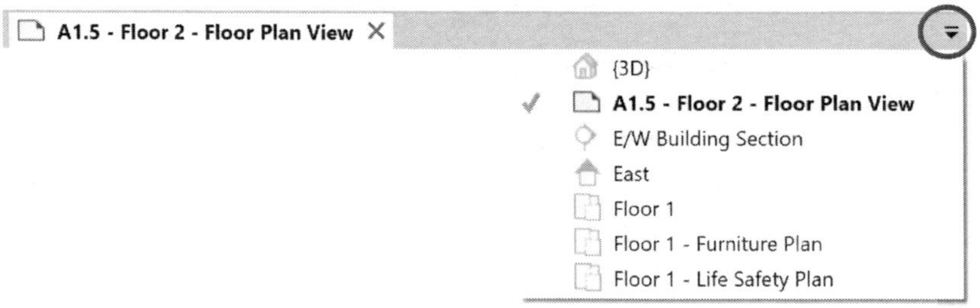

Figure 1–80

2. In the Navigation Bar, expand **Zoom** and select (Zoom In Region), or type **ZR**. Zoom in on one of the stairs.

*Note: The Navigation Bar displays the last-used Zoom command, so if the one you need to use is displayed, you can click it without expanding **Zoom**.*

3. Pan to another part of the building by holding down the middle mouse button or wheel and dragging the mouse. Alternatively, you can use the (2D Wheel) SteeringWheel in the Navigation Bar. To end the SteeringWheel, click the tool in the Navigation Bar.
4. Double-click on the mouse wheel to zoom out to fit the extents of the view.
5. In the Quick Access Toolbar, click (Default 3D View) to open the default 3D view, as shown in Figure 1–81.

Figure 1–81

6. Hold down <Shift> + the middle mouse button or wheel and move your mouse around to orbit the model in the 3D view.
7. In the View Control Bar, change the *Visual Style* to (Shaded), then try the other visual styles.
8. In the upper-right corner of the view area, click on the corners of the ViewCube to switch to a different angle other than the southeast one you started out in.
9. In the Project Browser, expand *3D Views*, right-click on the **{3D}** view and select **Rename...**. Alternatively, you can slowly click twice on the view name. Type in **3D Model** for the new name and press <Enter>.
10. Review the other 3D views that have already been created.

Task 4: Create a camera view.

1. In the Quick Access Toolbar, click (Default 3D View). Note that a new **{3D}** view is created and appears in the Project Browser within the *3D Views* section.
2. Press <Ctrl>+<Tab> to cycle through the open views.
3. In the Quick Access Toolbar, expand (Switch Windows) and select the **Arch-Final.rvt - Floor Plan: Floor 1** view.

4. In the Quick Access Toolbar, click (Close Inactive Views). This closes all the views except the one you are working in.
5. In the Quick Access Toolbar, expand (Default 3D View) and select (Camera), as shown in Figure 1–82.

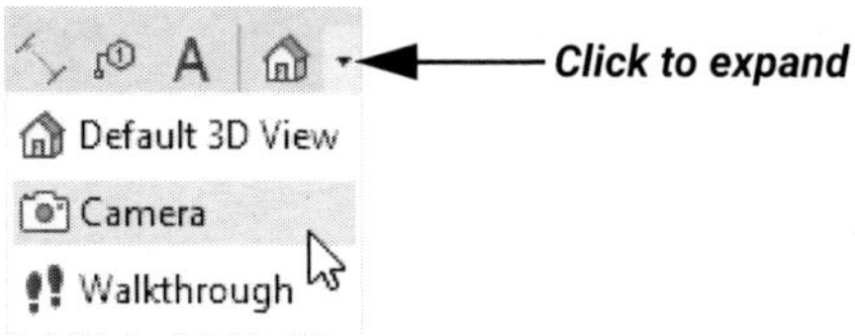

Figure 1–82

6. Click the first point near the Kitchen room area and click the second point (target) outside the building, as shown in Figure 1–83.

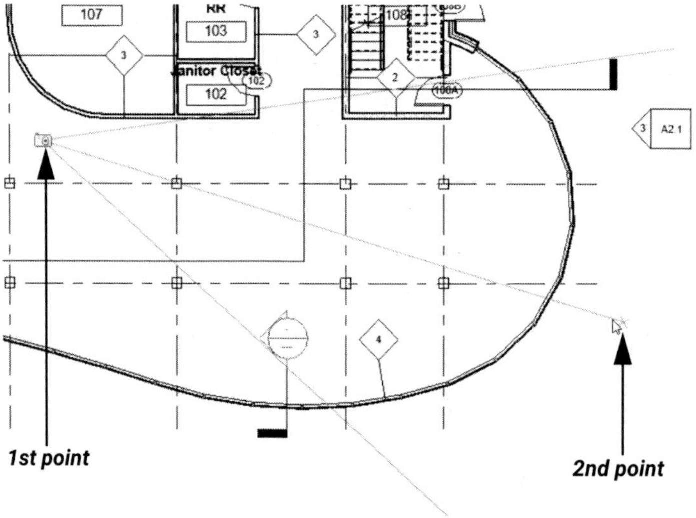

Figure 1–83

7. A new 3D view opens and displays the camera view. The furniture and planters display even though they did not display in the floor plan view.
8. In the Navigation Bar, click (Fly), then click and hold down the left mouse button to move around the view.
9. In the View Control Bar, set the *Visual Style* to (Realistic).
10. In the Project Browser, in the *3D Views* section, note the new camera view called **3D View 1**.
11. In the Quick Access Toolbar, click (Save) to save the project.
12. In the *File* tab, click (Close). This closes the entire project.

End of practice

Chapter Review Questions

1. When working in a project in Revit, do you work in 3D or 2D?
    a. You work in 2D in plan views and in 3D in non-plan views.
    b. You work in 3D almost all of the time, even when you are working in what looks like a flat view.
    c. You work in 2D or 3D depending on how you toggle the 2D/3D control.
    d. You work in 2D in plan and section views and in 3D views.

2. What is the purpose of the Project Browser?
    a. It lets you browse through the building project, similar to a walk through.
    b. It is used to adjust the properties and settings of individual elements.
    c. It manages multiple Revit projects as an alternative to using File Explorer.
    d. It is used to access and manage the views of the project.

3. Where do you change the visual style?
    a. Ribbon
    b. View Control Bar
    c. Project Browser
    d. Properties

4. What is the difference between Type Properties and Properties?
    a. Properties stores parameters that apply to the selected individual element. Type Properties stores parameters that impact every element of the same type in the project.
    b. Properties stores the location parameters of an element. Type Properties stores the size and identity parameters of an element.
    c. Properties only stores parameters of the view. Type Properties stores parameters of model components.

5. When you start a new project, how do you make sure the base information (units, views, and settings) will be in the new file?

a. Transfer the base information from an existing project.

b. Select the right template for the task.

c. Revit automatically extracts the base information from imported or linked file(s).

6. What is the main difference between a view made using (Default 3D View) and a view made using (Camera)?

a. Use **Default 3D View** for exterior views and **Camera** for interiors.

b. **Default 3D View** creates a static image and a **Camera** view is live and always updated.

c. **Default 3D View** is orthographic and a **Camera** view is perspective.

d. **Default 3D View** is used for the overall building and a **Camera** view is used for looking in tight spaces.

Command Summary

Button	Command	Location
General Tools		
	**Home**	• **Quick Access Toolbar** • **Shortcut:** <Ctrl>+<D>
	**Modify**	• **Ribbon:** All tabs>*Select* panel • **Shortcut:** MD
	**New**	• ***File* tab** • **Shortcut:** <Ctrl>+<N>
	**Open**	• **Quick Access Toolbar** • ***File*** tab • **Shortcut:** <Ctrl>+<O>
	**Open Documents**	• ***File*** tab
	**Properties**	• **Ribbon:** *Modify* tab>*Properties* panel • **Shortcut:** PP
	**Recent Documents**	• ***File* tab**
	**Save**	• **Quick Access Toolbar** • ***File* tab** • **Shortcut:** <Ctrl>+<S>
	**Type Properties**	• **Ribbon:** *Modify* tab>*Properties* panel • **Properties**>Edit Type
Select Tools		
	**Drag elements on selection**	• **Ribbon:** All tabs>expanded *Select* panel • **Status Bar**
	**Filter**	• **Ribbon:** *Modify | Multi-Select* tab>*Filter* panel • **Status Bar**
	**Select Elements By Face**	• **Ribbon:** All tabs>expanded *Select* panel • **Status Bar**
	**Select Links**	• **Ribbon:** All tabs>expanded *Select* panel • **Status Bar**
	**Select Pinned Elements**	• **Ribbon:** All tabs>expanded *Select* panel • **Status Bar**
	**Select Underlay Elements**	• **Ribbon:** All tabs>expanded *Select* panel • **Status Bar**

Button	Command	Location
Viewing Tools		
	**Camera**	• **Quick Access Toolbar**, expand Default 3D View • **Ribbon:** *View* tab>*Create* panel, expand Default 3D View
	**Close Inactive Views**	• **Quick Access Toolbar** • **Ribbon:** *View* tab>*Windows* panel
	**Default 3D View**	• **Quick Access Toolbar** • **Ribbon:** *View* tab>*Create* panel
N/A	**Next Pan/Zoom**	• **Navigation Bar** • **Shortcut Menu**
N/A	**Previous Pan/Zoom**	• **Navigation Bar** • **Shortcut Menu** • **Shortcut:** ZP
	**Shadows On/Off**	• **View Control Bar**
	**Show Rendering Dialog/ Render**	• **View Control Bar** • **Ribbon:** *View* tab>*Graphics* panel • **Shortcut:** RR
	**Switch Windows**	• **Quick Access Toolbar** • **Ribbon:** *View* tab>*Windows* panel
	**Tab Views**	• **Ribbon:** *View* tab>*Windows* panel • Shortcut: TW
	**Tile Views**	• **Ribbon:** *View* tab>*Windows* panel • Shortcut: WT
	**ViewCube Home**	• **ViewCube**
	**Zoom All to Fit**	• **Navigation Bar** • **Shortcut:** ZA
	**Zoom in Region**	• **Navigation Bar** • **Shortcut Menu** • **Shortcut:** ZR
	**Zoom Out (2x)**	• **Navigation Bar** • **Shortcut Menu** • **Shortcut:** ZO

Button	Command	Location
	**Zoom Sheet Size**	• **Navigation Bar** • **Shortcut:** ZS
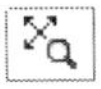	**Zoom to Fit**	• **Navigation Bar** • **Shortcut Menu** • **Shortcut:** ZF, ZE
Visual Styles		
	**Consistent Colors**	• **View Control Bar**
	**Hidden Line**	• **View Control Bar** • **Shortcut:** HL
	**Realistic**	• **View Control Bar**
	**Shaded**	• **View Control Bar** • **Shortcut:** SD
	**Textures**	• **View Control Bar**
	**Wireframe**	• **View Control Bar** • **Shortcut:** WF

Chapter 2

Starting a Revit Project

Starting a Revit project begins by using a template. You can then link in a CAD file or an existing Revit model, if these are available. From there, you can add the framework for a design, including levels to define vertical heights and grids to help define the Revit elements' layout.

Learning Objectives

- Select and open a project template.
- Link and import CAD files to be used as a basis for developing a design.
- Link existing Revit models to develop and coordinate with other disciplines.
- Add and modify levels to define floor-to-floor heights and other vertical references.
- Add and modify grids to provide locations for model elements.

2.1 Selecting a Project Template

New projects are based on a project template file. The template file includes preset levels, views, and some families, such as wall styles and text styles. When using templates, most of the views are set to display only the elements specific to the template, so it is best practice to select a template that reflects your company's discipline.

Check with your BIM manager about which template you need to use for your projects. Your company might have more than one based on the type of project you are designing. Ideally, you should not start your work inside of another discipline or model. Instead, you should start from one of the default Revit templates or your company's custom template and link the architectural model into your project. If you link a Revit model into your project, you can use the monitoring and coordinating features to copy/monitor necessary items, such as walls, floors, and grids, from the architect. To learn more about copying/monitoring, see ASCENT's *Autodesk Revit: Collaboration Tools* guide.

How To: Start a New Project

1. On the Home screen under *Models*, click **New**. Alternatively, in the *File* tab, expand  (New) and click  (Project), as shown in Figure 2–1, or press <Ctrl>+<N>.

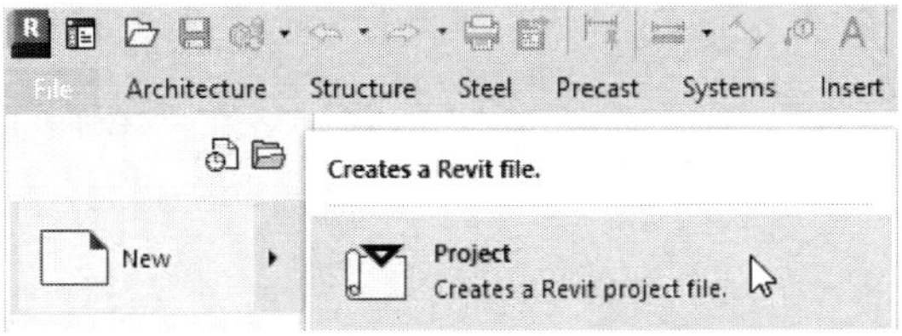

Figure 2–1

2. In the *New Project* dialog box (shown in Figure 2–2), select the template that you want to use and click **OK**.

   Note: *The list of template files is set in the Options dialog box in the File Locations tab. It might vary depending on the installed product and company standards.*

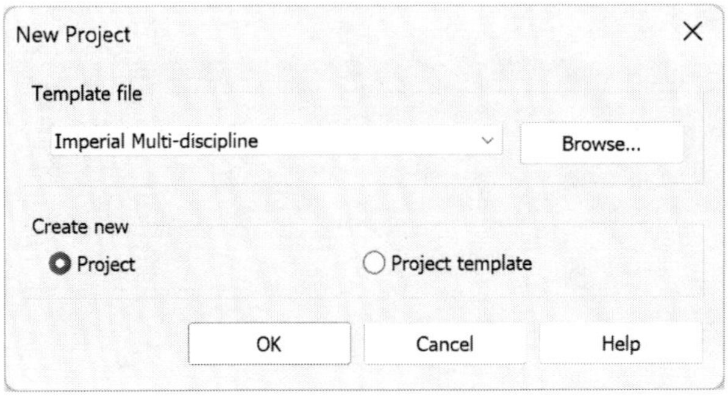

Figure 2–2

Hint: Revit Worksharing

If established by your company that worksharing is needed, you would typically want to start a worksharing project on your local network once a project has been created.

- For more information about establishing and using worksets, refer to ASCENT's *Autodesk Revit: Collaboration Tools* guide.

Recommended Project Setup

A multidiscipline approach to design and data sharing is the recommended best practice for all Revit projects. It allows multiple teams to create and work on their own trade-specific designs and then easily share the models with other teams so they can consolidate all design data into one host model by linking in other disciplines, as illustrated in Figure 2–3.

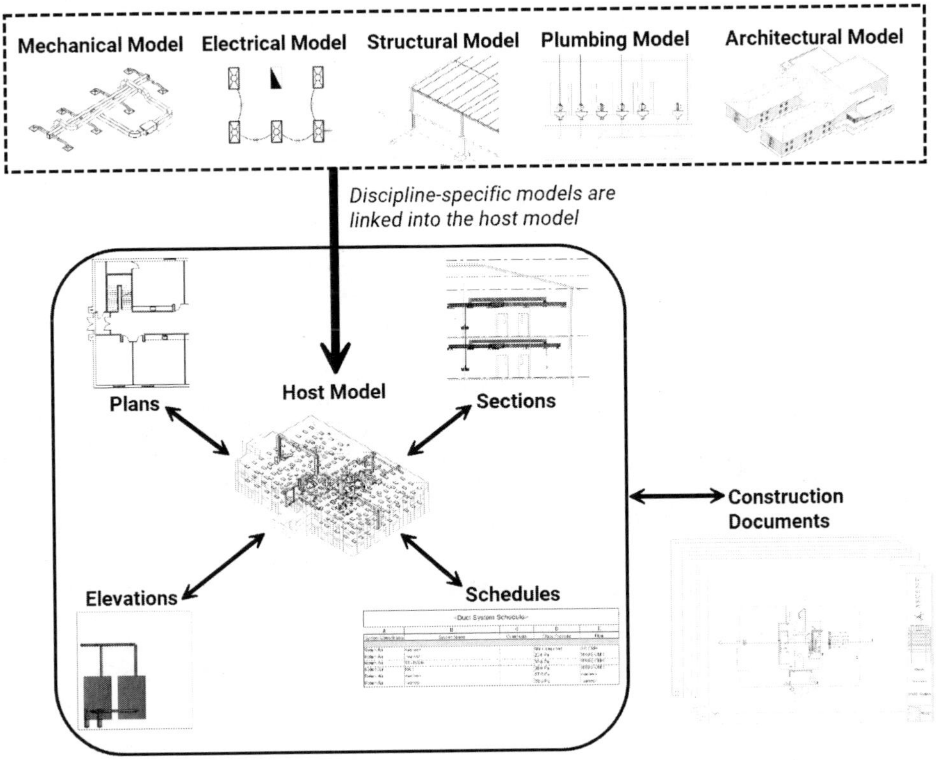

Figure 2–3

In Revit, models from different disciplines (such as architectural, mechanical, electrical, plumbing, and structural) can be linked together into one project. For example, mechanical and structural models can be linked into an architectural model, allowing teams to coordinate designs while maintaining separate project files.

Once saved, the links are part of the current project, and if any of the linked files are modified, the updated projects can be reloaded. Alternatively, each time a project is opened, it automatically loads the latest version of the linked projects. All links can be managed using the *Manage Links* dialog box, as shown in Figure 2–4. To open it, click (Manage Links) in the *Insert* tab>*Link* panel or in the *Manage* tab>*Manage Projects* panel.

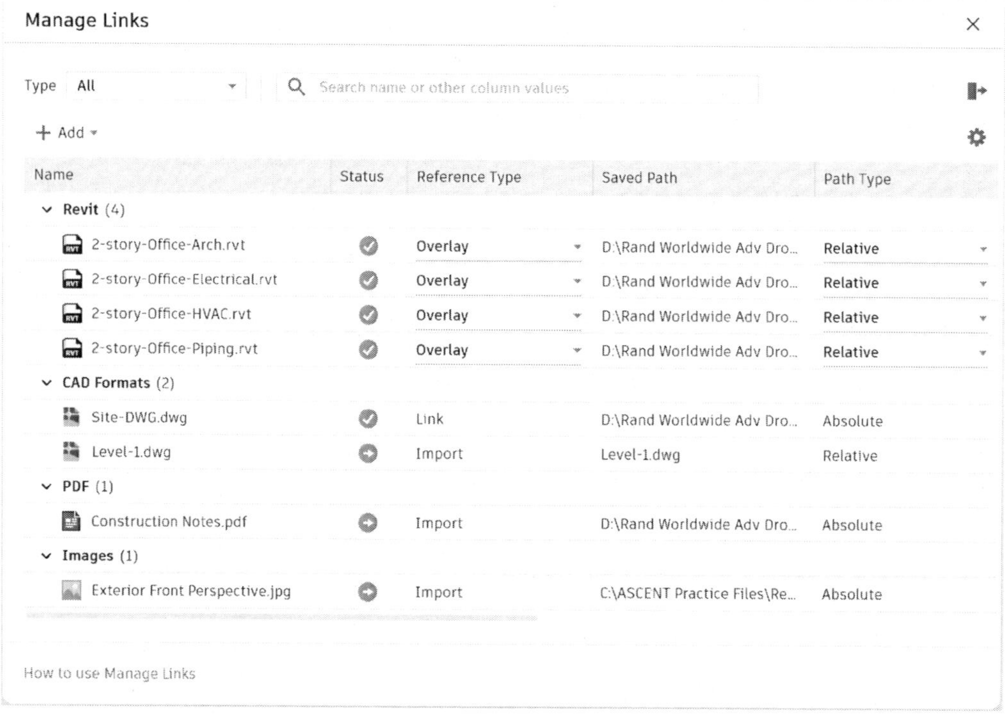

Figure 2–4

2.2 Linking and Importing CAD Files

CAD files can be imported or linked into a Revit project. As an example, a designer might lay out a floor plan using the standard 2D AutoCAD software, and you then need to incorporate that information into your structural model. In addition, many renovation projects start with existing 2D drawings. Instead of redrawing from scratch, link or import the CAD file (as shown in Figure 2–5) and trace over it in Revit. You can also print a hybrid drawing that is part Revit project and part imported/linked drawing.

> **Note:** *When you hover over an imported or linked CAD file, you can see in the tooltip that it is called an Import Symbol.*

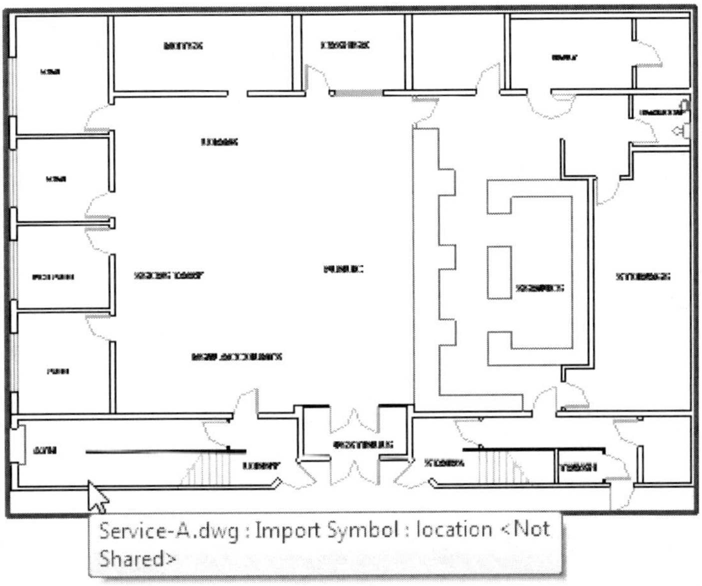

Figure 2–5

- CAD file formats that can be imported or linked include AutoCAD® (DWG and DXF), FormIt (AXM), 3D ACIS modeling kernel (SAT), MicroStation (DGN), 3D Shape (OBJ, STL, STEP, STP, and STPZ), Rhino (3dm), and Trimble SketchUp (SKP).
- When linking or importing a CAD file, you can specify a level or a named horizontal reference plane in the project to position the CAD file at.

> **Note:** *The reference plane needs to be at or below the level where you are trying to insert a CAD file.*

- You can specify the linking or import units (e.g., feet, meter, or US survey feet).

Linking vs. Importing

- **Link:** A connection is maintained with the original file and the link updates if the original file is updated. Within the *Manage Links* dialog box (as shown in Figure 2–6), you can manually **Reload** the linked CAD file if updates occur. There are also options to **Unload, Remove**, or **Import**.

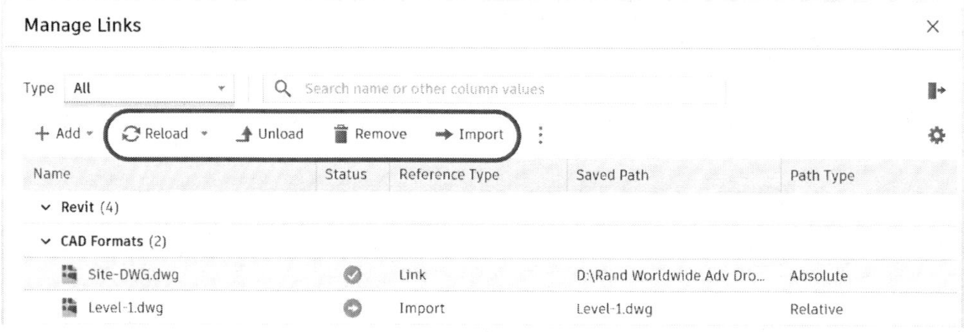

Figure 2–6

- **Import:** No connection is maintained with the original file. It becomes a separate element in the Revit model. Within the *Manage Links* dialog box, you only have the option to **Remove** the imported CAD file, as shown in Figure 2–7.

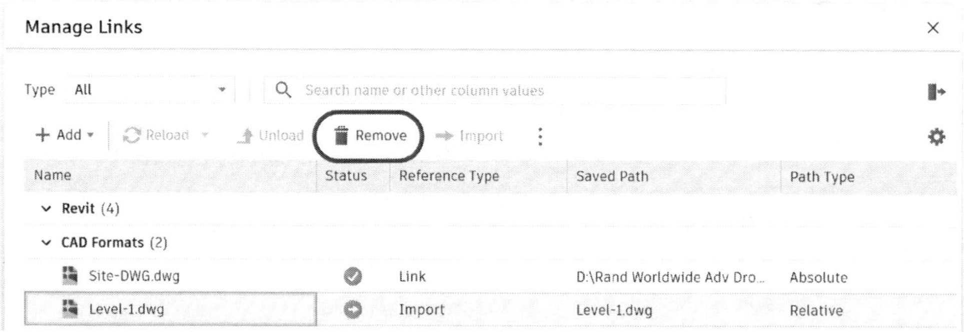

Figure 2–7

How To: Link or Import a CAD File

1. Open the view into which you want to link or import the file.
   - For a 2D file, this should be a 2D view. For a 3D file, open a 3D view.
2. In the *Insert* tab>*Link* panel, click (Link CAD), or in the *Insert* tab>*Import* panel, click (Import CAD).

3. In the *Link CAD Formats* (shown in Figure 2–8) or *Import CAD Formats* dialog box, select the file that you want to link or import.
    - Select a file format in the *Files of type* drop-down list to limit the files that are displayed.

Note: *The dialog box settings for Link CAD Formats and Import CAD Formats are the same.*

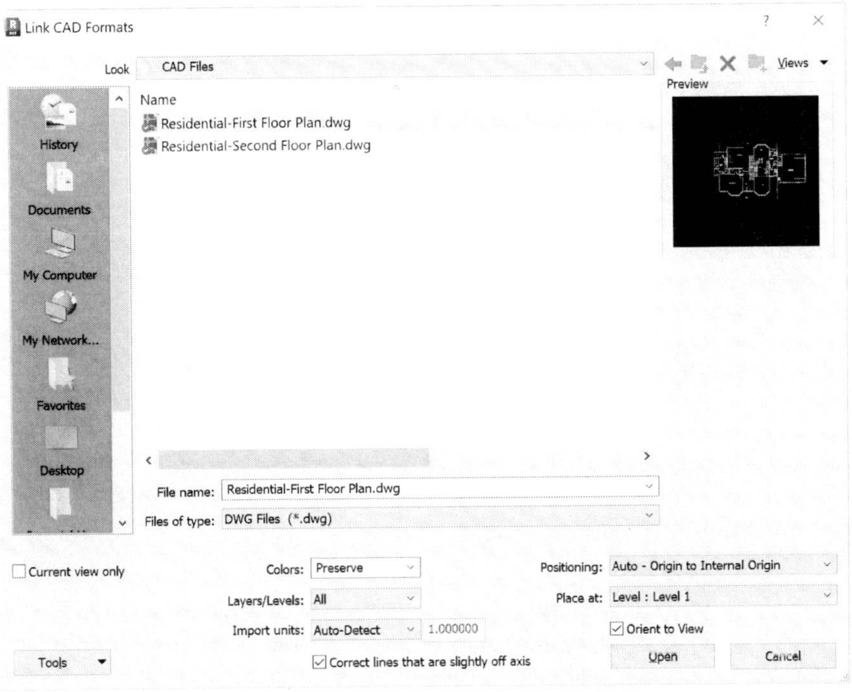

Figure 2–8

4. If **Current view only** is selected, as shown in Figure 2–9, you can set all options except the *Place at* and the *Orient to View* options. The view will only display in the current view.

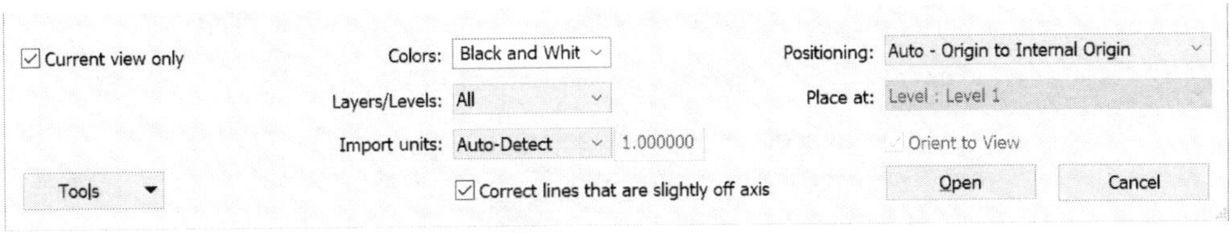

Figure 2–9

5. If you would like to place the CAD file at a level or reference plane, verify **Current view only** is unchecked and set the *Place at* option, as shown in Figure 2–10. Click **Open**.

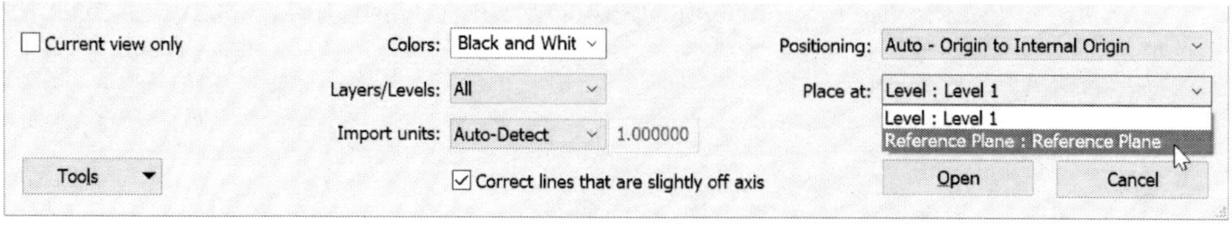

Figure 2–10

Link and Import Options

Current view only	Determine whether the CAD file is placed in every view, or only in the current view. This is especially useful if you are working with a 2D floor plan that you only need to have in one view.
Colors	Specify the color settings. Typical Revit projects are mainly black and white. However, other software frequently uses color. You can **Invert** the original colors, **Preserve** them, or change everything to **Black and White**.
Layers/Levels	Indicates which CAD layers are going to be brought into the model. Select how you want layers to be imported: **All**, **Visible**, or **Specify...**.
Import units	Select the units of the original file, as required. **Auto-Detect** works in most cases.
Correct lines...	If lines in a CAD file are off axis by less than 0.1 degree, selecting this option straightens them. It is selected by default.
Positioning	Specify how you want the imported file to be positioned in the current project: 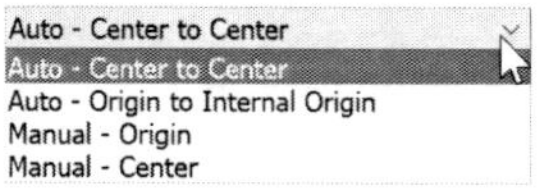 ***Import options*** 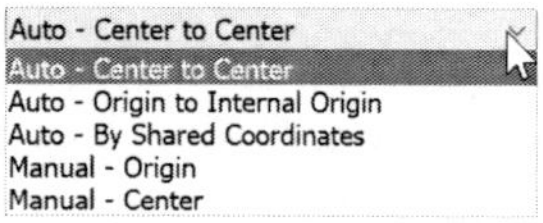 ***Linking options*** The last option used will be the default position.
Place at	Select a level or named reference plane at which to place the imported file. If you selected **Current view only**, this option is grayed out.
Orient to View	Used to orient the CAD file on import/link.

- When a file is positioned **Auto - Origin to Internal Origin**, it is pinned in place and cannot be moved. To move the file, click on the pin to unpin it, as shown in Figure 2–11.

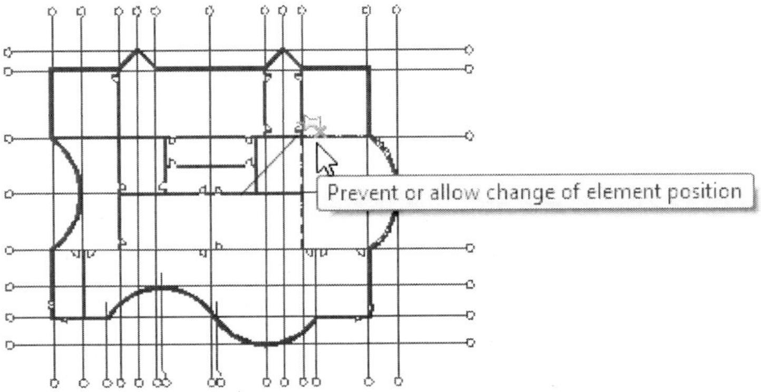

Figure 2–11

2.3 Modifying Imported/Linked CAD Files

An imported/linked CAD file is called an *import symbol* once it is inserted into a project, as shown in Figure 2–12. When you select an imported/linked file, you can modify it by arranging the *Foreground/Background* status, modifying its type properties, querying information about elements in the file, and deleting layers. You can also modify the visibility/graphic overrides of each imported/linked file instance.

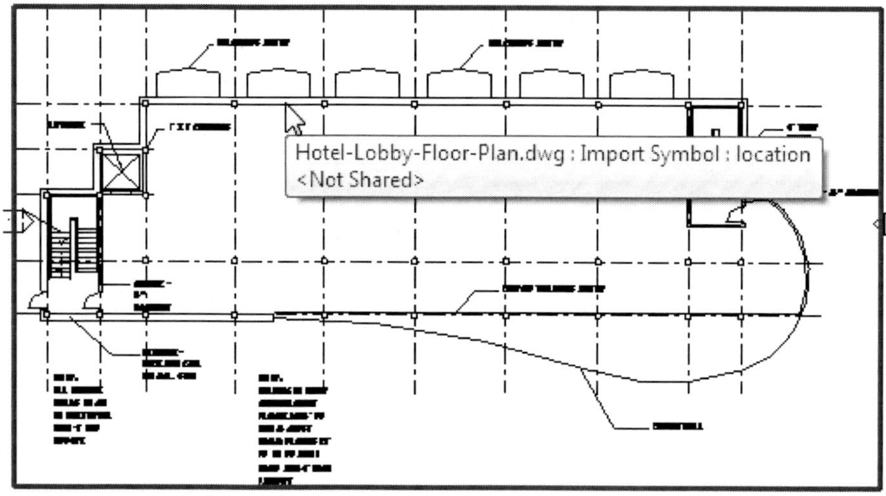

Figure 2–12

Arrange Linked/Imported CAD Files

CAD files that are linked or imported using the **Current view only** setting have the option to set the file to display in the foreground or background.

- Select the CAD file in the view and in Properties, expand *Draw Layer (*as shown on the left in Figure 2–13) and select either **Foreground** or **Background**.
- In the contextual tab>*Arrange* panel (shown on the right in Figure 2–13), select either **Bring to Front** or **Send to Back** or expand them to see more options to move linked files to the front or back of the host elements.

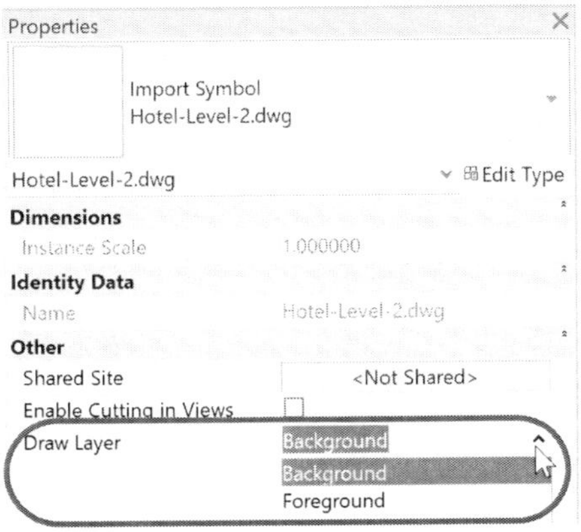

Properties

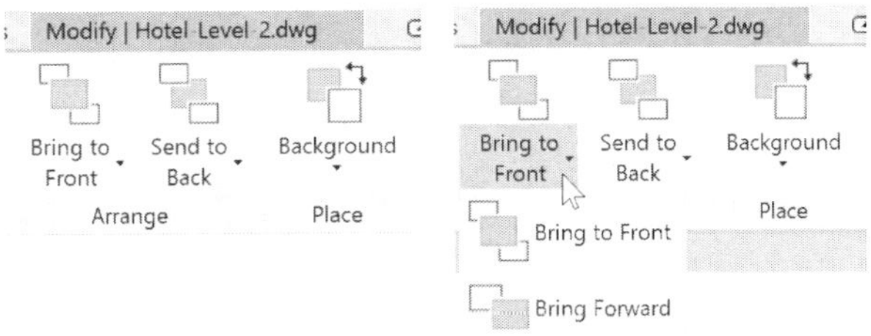

Contextual ribbon

Figure 2–13

Visibility/Graphic Overrides – Imported Categories

Imported or linked CAD files have their own visibility settings in the *Visibility/Graphic Overrides* dialog box on the *Imported Categories* tab. You can control the display of individual layers within the CAD file by turning them on or off in the *Visibility* column (as shown in Figure 2–14) and changing their colors, line weights, and line patterns. This helps ensure that the CAD file appears clean and consistent with your Revit project's graphic standards. This is also where you can set your imported or linked CAD file to display in the view in halftone or turn it off completely.

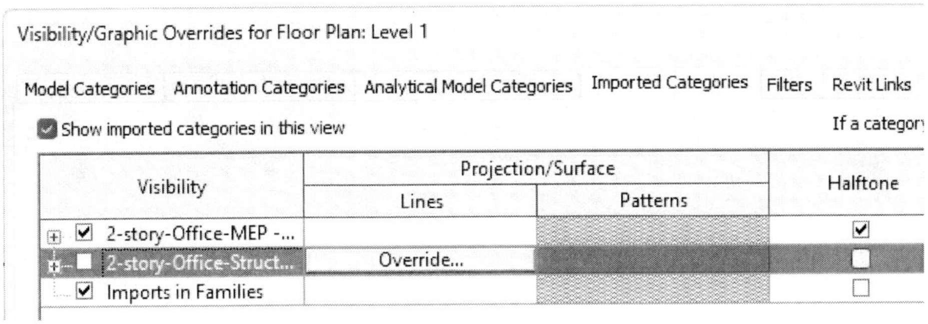

Figure 2–14

How To: Hide Individual CAD File Layers

1. In the *View* tab>*Graphics* panel, click (Visibility/Graphics), or type **VG** or **VV** to open the *Visibility/Graphic Overrides* dialog box.
2. Select the *Imported Categories* tab. It displays a list of each imported instance and its layers/levels, as shown in Figure 2–15.
3. To have the linked/imported file display in halftone, check the box in the *Halftone* column.
4. Click the plus sign beside the file name to expand the list of the layers in that file.
5. Clear the checkmark from the individual layers that you do not want to display.
    - Typically, these layers contain similar information, such as all windows or all notes in a drawing. However, it is not as definite as using Revit elements. An item might have been misplaced on a different layer and, if so, it does not toggle off.

- To toggle off the entire file, clear the checkmark next to the file name in the *Visibility* column.

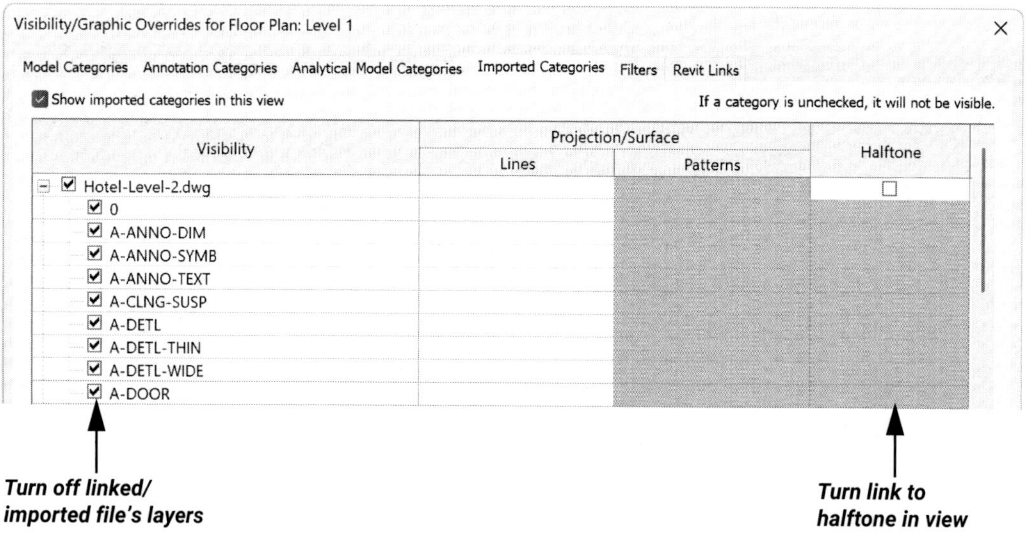

Figure 2–15

6. Close the dialog box.

Setting an Imported or Linked CAD File to Halftone in View

To see the difference between the host model elements and the linked or imported CAD file, you can set the linked/imported file to halftone, as shown in Figure 2–16.

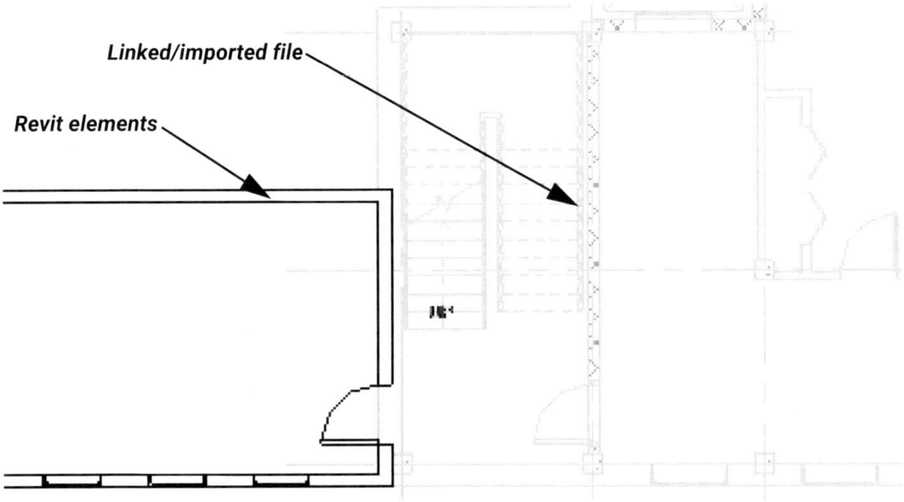

Figure 2–16

How To: Set a CAD File to Halftone in a View

1. Select the imported/linked CAD file.
2. Right-click and select **Override Graphics in View>By Element...** or **By Category...**, as shown in Figure 2–17.

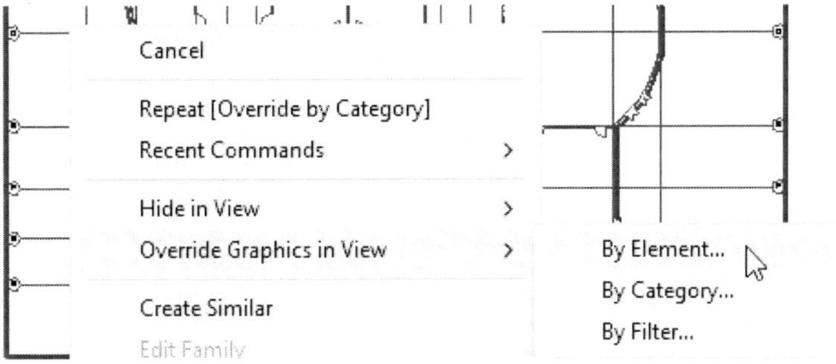

Figure 2–17

3. In the *View Specific Element* (or *Category*) *Graphics* dialog box, select **Halftone**, as shown in Figure 2–18.
    - If halftone is set using **By Element**, the setting will not show up in the *Visibility/Graphic Override* dialog box. You will need to select the CAD file, right-click, and select **Override Graphics in View>By Element** to turn it off in the *View Specific Element Graphics* dialog box.
    - If halftone is set using **By Category**, you can turn it off in the *View Specific Category Graphics* dialog box or using the *Visibility/Graphic Overrides* dialog box.

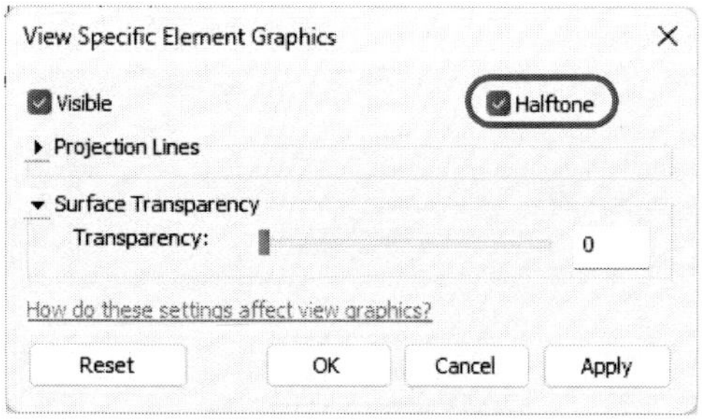

Override by Element

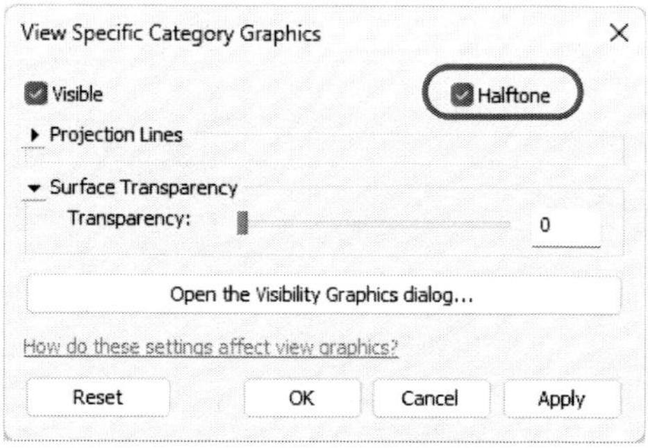

Override by Category

Figure 2–18

4. Click **OK**.

2.4 Linking in Revit Models

You can link Revit models directly into a project. These models can be an existing building that you are creating an addition to, as shown in Figure 2–19, or engineering models that you are checking to ensure that they line up with your model. This can also be used for campus-like projects where the same building is repeated multiple times. The Revit models that are linked are full 3D models.

> ***Note:*** *A linked model automatically updates when the original file is changed.*

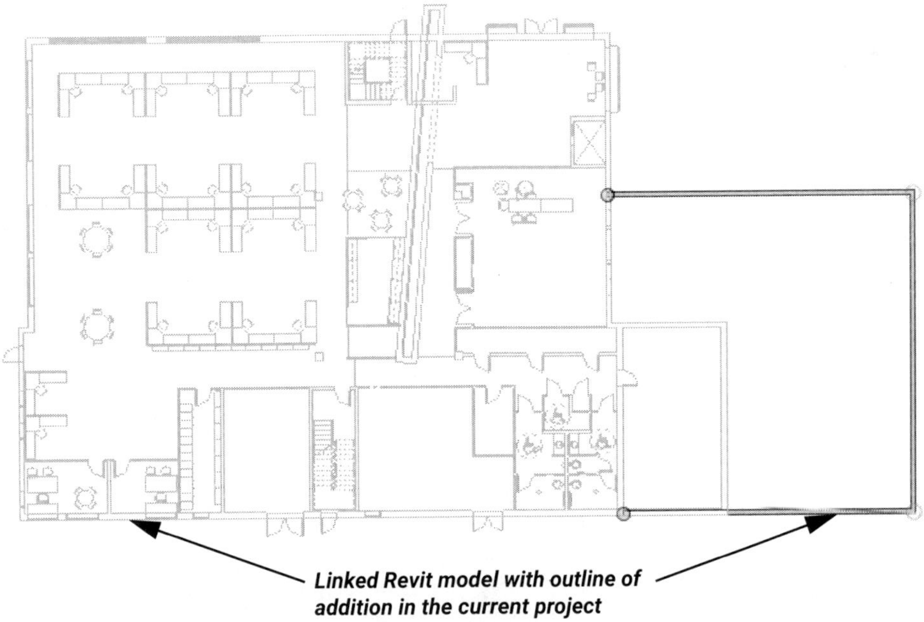

Figure 2–19

- Architectural, structural, and MEP models created in Revit can be linked into each other. It is best practice to always link Revit models that are from the same release cycle.
- When you link Revit models, clashes between disciplines can be detected and information can be passed between disciplines.
- Revit models are always linked. They cannot be imported.

How To: Add a Linked Model to a Host Project

1. In the *Insert* tab>*Link* panel, click (Link Revit).
2. In the *Import/Link RVT* dialog box, select the file that you want to link. Before opening the file, set the *Positioning*, as shown in Figure 2–20.

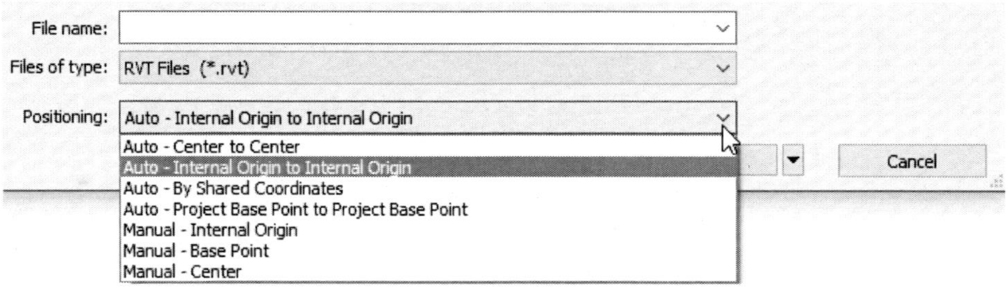

Figure 2–20

3. Click **Open**.

- Depending on how you decide to position the file, it is automatically placed in the project or you can manually place it with the cursor. The more links present in a project, the longer it takes to load.

2.5 Modifying Linked Revit Models

A Revit linked model is a separate Revit file that you bring into your current project to use as a reference. It is often used when different teams are working on different parts of a building, like architecture, structure, or MEP. Linking the model lets you see and coordinate with other disciplines' work without editing their files directly. You can control how the linked model looks and behaves in your views, but the original file stays unchanged.

It is best practice to adjust a linked Revit model's visibility using the *Revit Links* tab in the *Visibility/Graphic Overrides* dialog box.

Visibility/Graphic Overrides – Revit Links

The *Revit Links* tab in the *Visibility/Graphic Overrides* dialog box (shown in Figure 2–21) allows you to control how linked Revit models appear in your views. In the *Visibility* column, you can turn on or off each link to show or hide it in the current view. The *Halftone* column lets you set the link to a gray tone, making it easier to distinguish from the main model. Checking the box in the *Underlay* column shows the linked model as a background reference. In the *Display Settings* column, **By Host View** means the linked model will follow the visibility settings of the current view in the host project for all view settings and visibility/graphic overrides settings for the model, annotation, analytical model, and imported categories.

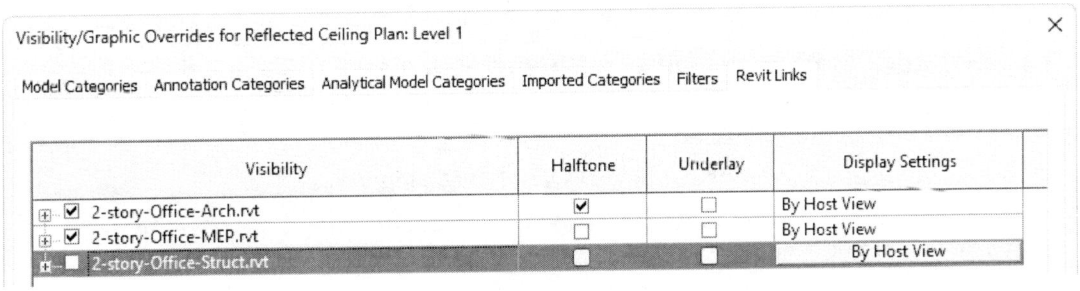

Figure 2–21

How To: Use Visibility/Graphic Overrides to Set the Revit Model to Halftone

1. In the *View* tab>*Graphics* panel, click (Visibility/Graphics), or type **VG** or **VV** to open the *Visibility/Graphic Overrides* dialog box.

2. In the *Visibility/Graphic Overrides* dialog box, on the *Revit Links* tab, check the checkbox for a specific Revit linked model in the *Halftone* column, as shown in Figure 2–22.

- If you want to turn off the Revit model in the view, uncheck the checkbox next to the model's name in the *Visibility* column.

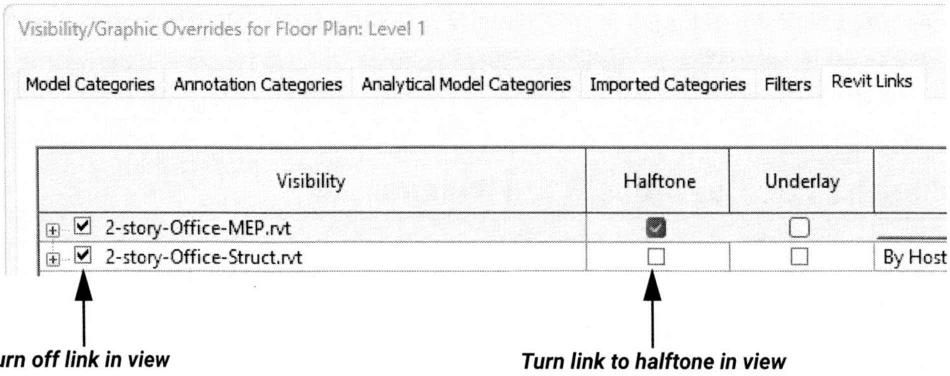

Figure 2–22

- If you select a Revit linked model and type **VH**, it will hide all Revit links in the model. To unhide the links, you will need to use **Reveal Hidden Elements** in the View Control Bar.

How To: Set Revit Models to Halftone Directly in a View

1. In the view, select a Revit model.
2. Right-click and select **Override Graphics in View>By Category...**.
3. In the *View Specific Category Graphics* dialog box, select the checkbox for **Halftone**, as shown in Figure 2–23, and click **OK**. All linked Revit models in the view are set to halftone.

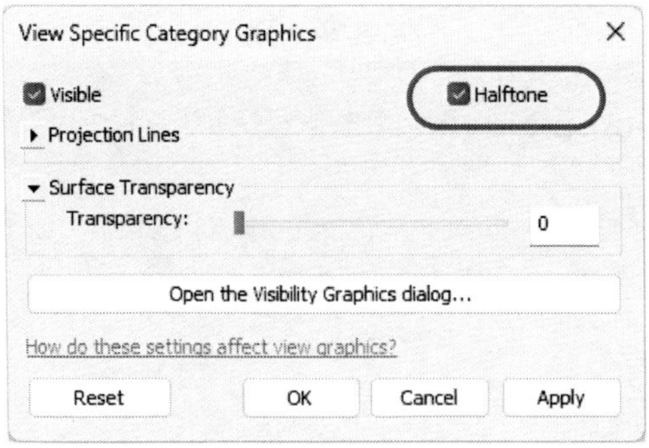

Figure 2–23

- You will need to remember that you set the linked Revit models to halftone using this dialog box, as the setting will not be reflected in the *Visibility/Graphic Overrides* dialog box as it is with CAD files.

2.6 Temporary Hide/Isolate

You might want to temporarily remove linked or imported CAD files and models from a view, modify the project, and then restore the elements. Instead of completely toggling the elements off, you can temporarily hide them.

Select the elements you want to hide (make invisible) or isolate (keep displayed while all other elements are hidden) and click (Temporary Hide/Isolate). Select the method you want to use, as shown in Figure 2–24.

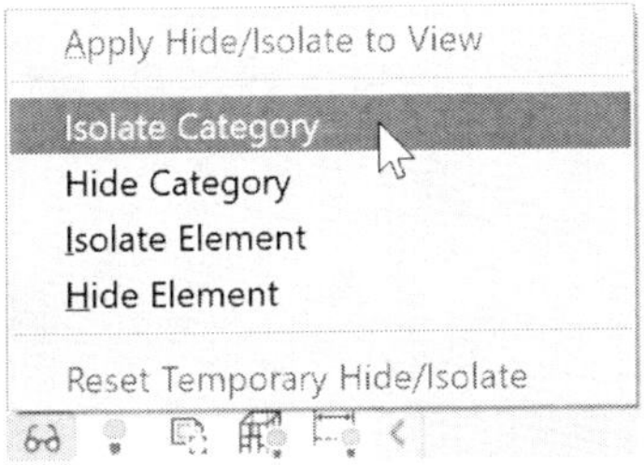

Figure 2–24

- The category or elements are hidden or isolated. A cyan border displays around the view with a note in the upper-left corner, as shown in Figure 2–25. It indicates that the view contains temporarily hidden or isolated elements.

Figure 2–25

- Click (Temporary Hide/Isolate) again and select **Reset Temporary Hide/Isolate** to restore the elements to the view.
- If you want to permanently hide the elements in the view, select **Apply Hide/Isolate to View**.
- Elements that are temporarily hidden in a view are not hidden when the view is printed.

2.7 Managing Links

The *Manage Links* dialog box (shown in Figure 2–26) enables you to reload, unload, add, and remove links. You can also convert a linked CAD file to an imported file. If you accidentally click **Import**, you can close the *Manage Links* dialog box and click **Undo** in the Quick Access Toolbar.

There are three ways to open the *Manage Links* dialog box:

- In the *Insert* tab>*Manage* panel, click (Manage Links).
- In the *Manage* tab>*Manage Project* panel, click (Manage Links).
- Select the Revit link and click (Manage Links) in the *Modify | RVT Links* tab>*Link* panel.

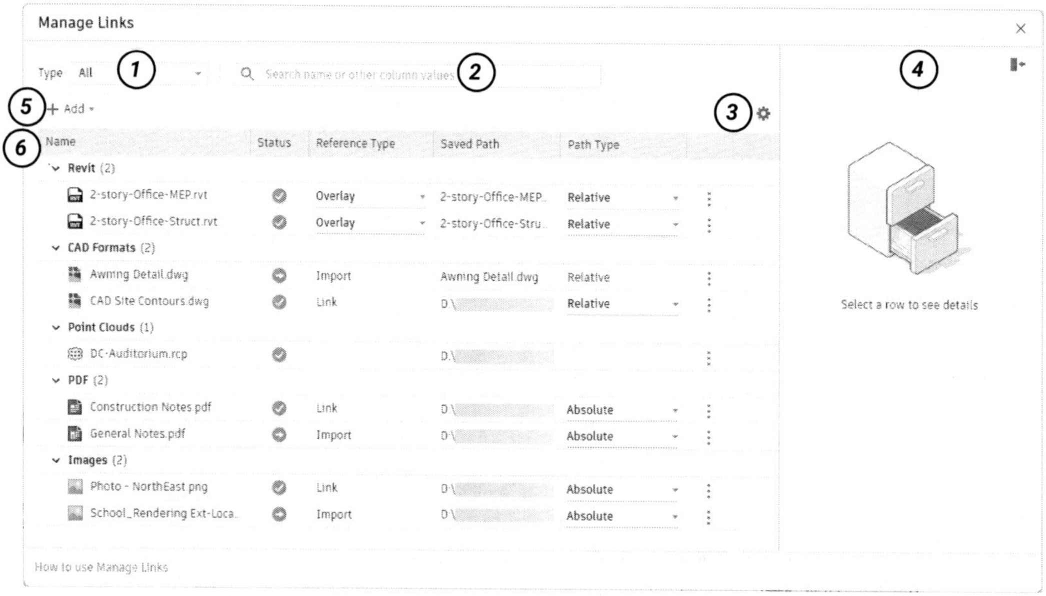

Figure 2–26

1. *Type* Drop-Down List
2. Search Bar
3. *Show Columns* List
4. File Detail Panel
5. **Add** Menu
6. File List

1. Type Drop-Down List

By default, the *Manage Links* dialog box is set to show all file types. You can adjust this by expanding the *Type* drop-down list and changing it from **All** to a specific type, as shown in Figure 2–27. The *Manage Links* dialog box shows both linked and imported CAD files.

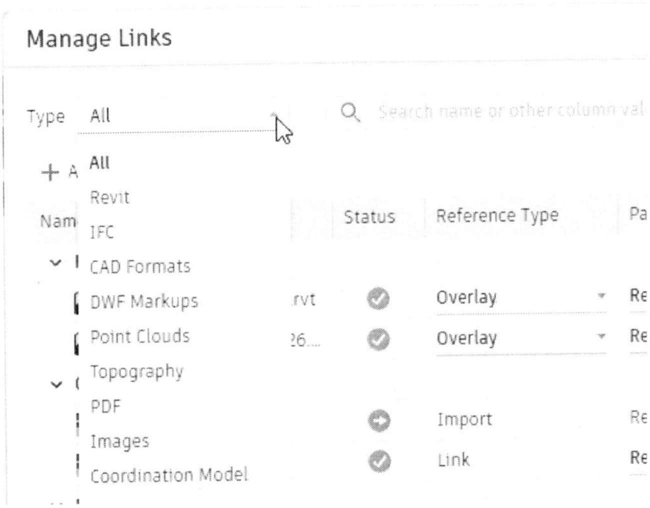

Figure 2–27

2. Search Bar

At the top of the *Manage Links* dialog box is a search bar to narrow down the list of linked and imported files that display. As soon as you start typing in the search bar, the list of files below will automatically update. It will only show the files that match the letters or words you are typing. Click the X in the search bar (shown in Figure 2–28) to clear the search and return to the full list.

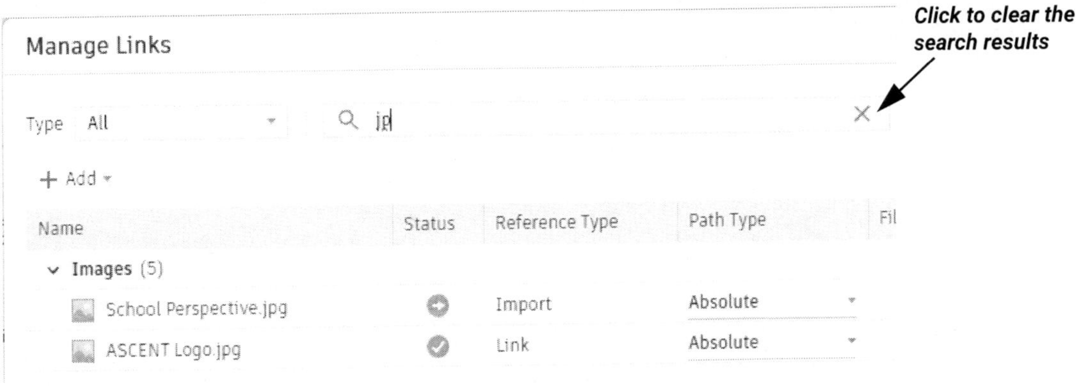

Figure 2–28

3. Show Columns List

To choose which columns you want to see in the *Manage Links* dialog box, click the gear icon to expand a list of all available columns, as shown in Figure 2–29. You can check the boxes for the columns you want to show, and uncheck the ones you do not need. When you are done, click the gear icon again to close the list.

Figure 2–29

4. File Detail Panel

When you select a file in the file list, the file detail panel displays information about the file. This panel can be expanded and collapsed by clicking the icon in the upper-right corner. Depending on the file that is selected, you can modify things like *Path type* and *Reference type*, as shown in Figure 2–30.

- You can also select multiple files in the file list and change the *Reference type* and/or *Path type* in the file detail panel.

Figure 2–30

5. Add Menu

At the top of the *Manage Links* dialog box is the **Add** menu. When you click to expand it, as shown in Figure 2–31, a list displays of file types that you can add, including **Revit**, **CAD Formats**, **PDF**, and **Images**. When you select a type, it will open the respective import or link dialog box, where you can navigate to the file to bring it into the model. For file types that allow you to position the file manually, the manual options will not be available in the link or import dialog box. For example, if you select **Revit**, the *Link Revit* dialog box's *Positioning* options will not include any manual options.

Figure 2–31

6. File List

By default, imported and linked file types display in the *Manage Links* dialog box within a tree structure that organizes the file types into their respective categories. When you select a file, operation tools display along the top of the dialog box, depending on which file type was selected. The tools are also available by right-clicking on a file or expanding the more menu at the end of the file. Figure 2–32 shows the operation tools that display when a Revit file is selected.

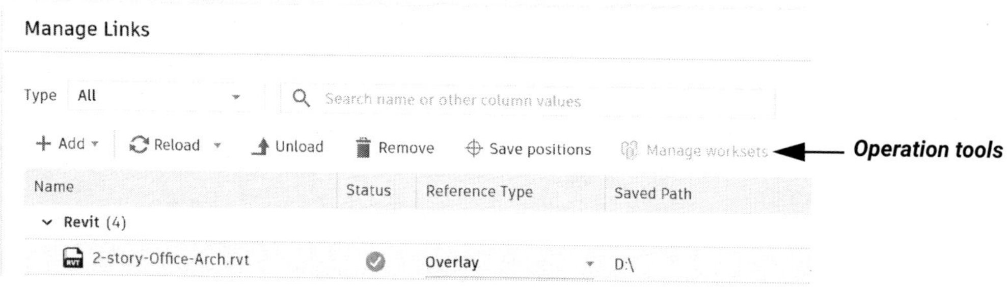

Figure 2–32

The *Saved Path* column shows the location where the file is stored on your computer or network. To copy the saved path for a file, hover your cursor over the file's saved path, as shown in Figure 2–33, triple-click on the path name to select the full path, and press <Ctrl>+<C> to copy the information.

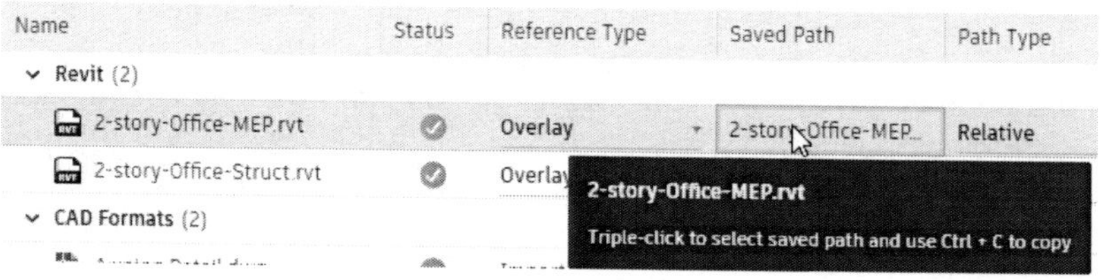

Figure 2–33

The following options are available:

- **Reload:** Reloads the file without additional prompts.
- **Reload From:** Opens the *Add Link* dialog box, which enables you to select the file you want to reload. Use this if the linked file location or name has changed. This is accessed by expanding **Reload**.
- **Unload:** Unloads the file so that the link is kept, but the file is not displayed or calculated in the project. Use **Reload** to restore it.

  Note: *For Revit links, some of these options are also available in the Project Browser. Expand the Revit Links section, then right-click on the Revit link and select* ***Reload, Unload,*** *or* ***Reload From...***.

- **Remove:** Deletes the link or imported file from the host model.

- **Import:** Converts the linked file to an imported file.

Links can be nested into one another. How a link responds when the host project is linked into another project depends on the option in the *Reference Type* column.

- **Overlay:** The nested linked model is not referenced in the new host project.
- **Attach:** The nested linked model displays in the new host project.

The option in the *Path Type* column controls how the location of the link is remembered.

- **Relative**
    - Searches the root folder of the current project.
    - If the file is moved, the software still searches for it.
- **Absolute**
    - Searches the entire file path where the file was originally saved.
    - If the original file is moved, the software is not able to find it.
- Other options control how the linked file interfaces with worksets and shared positioning.

Unresolved Reference

When opening a project with linked files that have been moved or deleted, an *Unresolved References* dialog box will appear after the project opens in Revit, as shown in Figure 2–34. This message will only display for files that have been linked into the project and not for imported files. At the bottom of the dialog box, click **Show details** to view a list of the files that have unresolved issues.

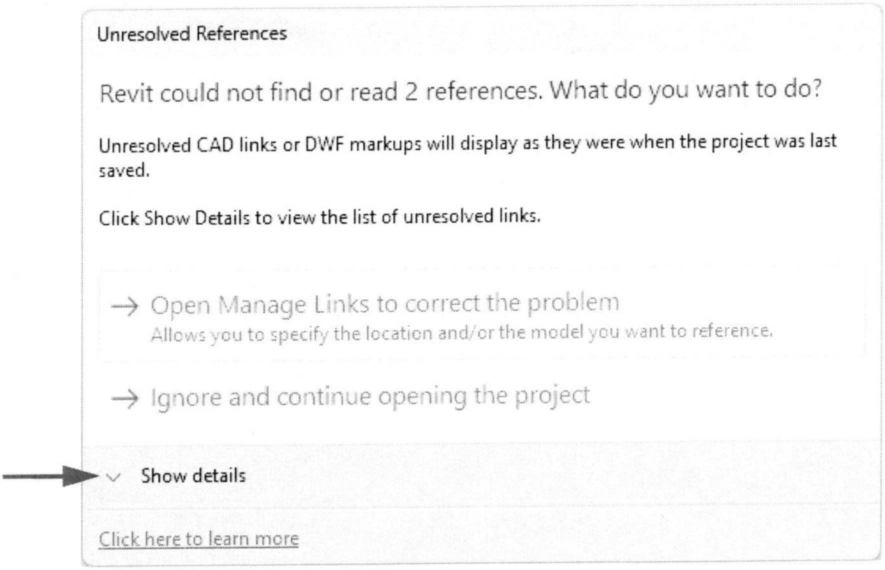

Figure 2–34

How To: Fix Unresolved References

1. After you open a Revit project that contains linked files, the *Unresolved References* dialog box displays.
2. In the *Unresolved References* dialog box, click **Open Manage Links to correct the problem**.
   - Alternatively, if you click **Ignore and continue opening the project**, you can open the *Manage Links* dialog box and resolve the issues at a later time. Note that if any elements in the project are hosted to a surface or element in a linked Revit model, the hosted elements will be orphaned or disassociated, potentially causing further issues.
3. In the *Manage Links* dialog box, any file that is missing will have a warning symbol in the *Status* column, as shown in Figure 2–35.

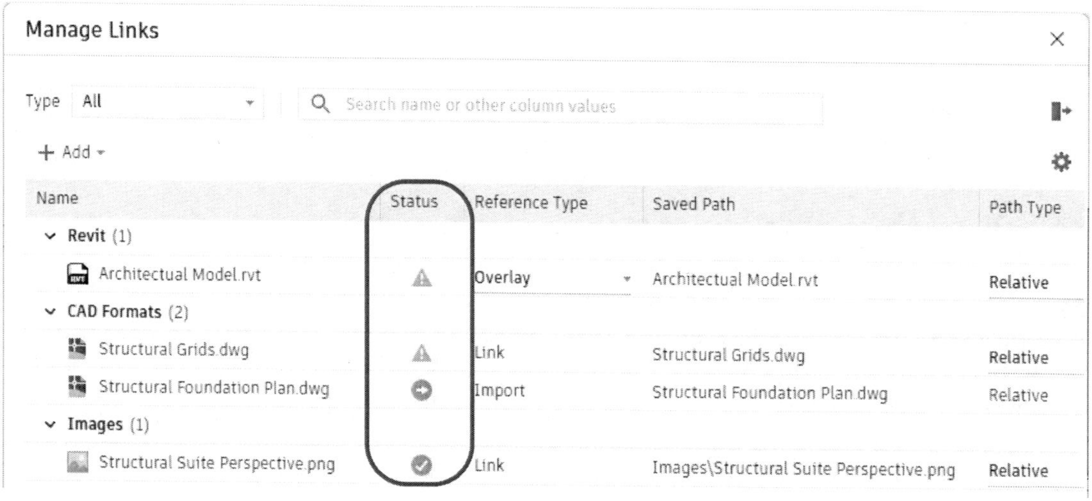

Figure 2–35

4. Click on the file in the *Name* column. The operation tools display at the top of the columns, as shown in Figure 2–36. Expand **Reload** and select **Reload from...**.

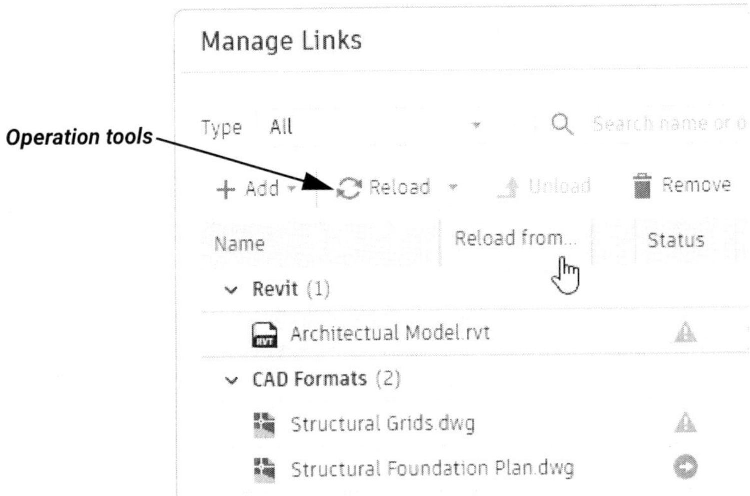

Figure 2–36

5. In the file browser dialog box, navigate to the file and click **Open**.

Practice 2a
Start a Project and Link Files

Practice Objectives

- Start a Revit project.
- Link a CAD file.
- Link a Revit file.
- Modify the linked files in a view.

In this practice, you will start a Revit project, then import floor plans created in AutoCAD and use them as a base layout for the first floor lobby and for a typical guest floor. You will then link in a Revit model that includes a standard poolhouse and platform for the building. Figure 2–37 shows the completed practice.

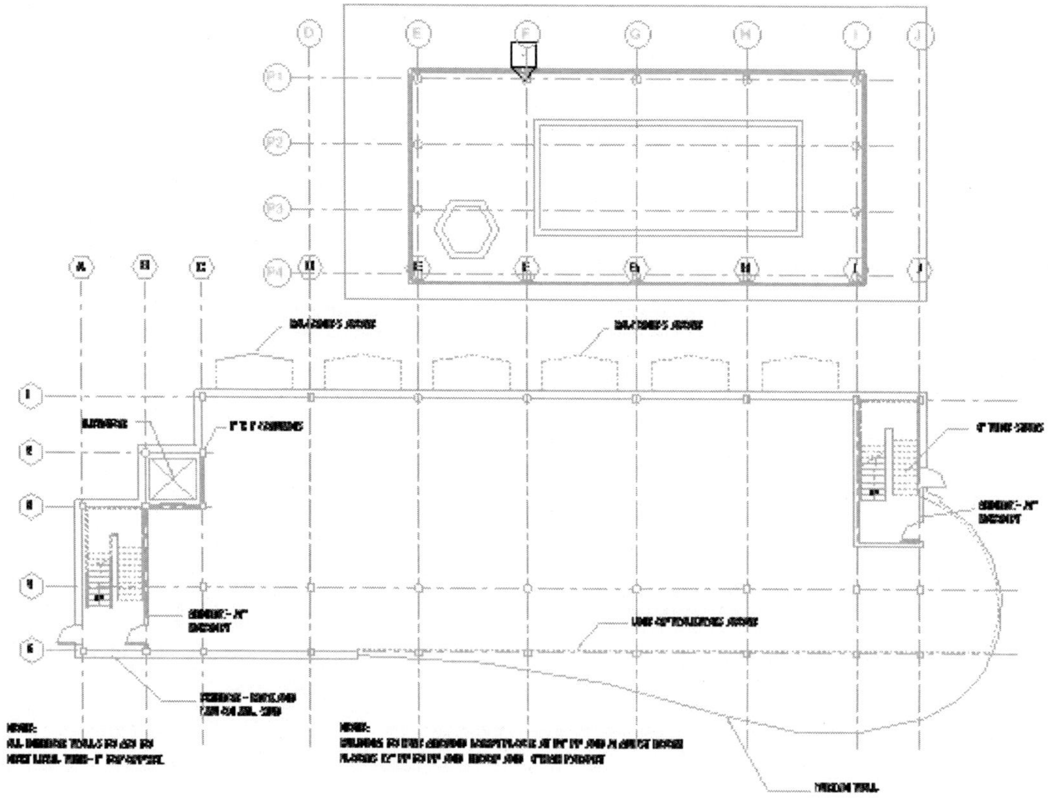

Figure 2–37

Task 1: Start a project.

1. On the Home screen, in the *Models* section, click **New**. Alternatively, in the *File* tab, expand (New) and click (Project).
2. In the *New Project* dialog box, click **Browse...**.
3. In the *Choose Template* dialog box, navigate to the practice files *Templates* folder, select **Imperial-Arch Template**, and click **Open**.
4. In the *New Project* dialog box, click **OK**. (There are no elements in this file, only datums and basic views.)
5. In the *File* tab, expand (Save As) and select (Project). In the *Save As* dialog box, navigate to the practice files folder and name the project as **Hotel-Start.rvt**. Click **Save**.
6. Review the Project Browser and note that the project has default floor plan, ceiling plan, and elevation views. By default, the **Floor Plans: Level 1** view is open and displays in bold in the Project Browser, as shown in Figure 2–38.

Figure 2–38

Task 2: Link a CAD file.

1. Verify you are in the **Floor Plans: Level 1** view. In the *Insert* tab>*Link* panel, click (Link CAD).
2. In the *Link CAD Formats* dialog box, navigate to the practice files *CAD Files* folder and select the file **Hotel-Level-1.dwg**, then set the following options, as shown in Figure 2–39:
    - Check the checkbox next to **Current view only**
    - *Colors:* **Black and White**
    - *Layers/Levels:* **All**
    - *Import Units:* **Auto-Detect**
    - *Positioning:* **Auto - Origin to Internal Origin**

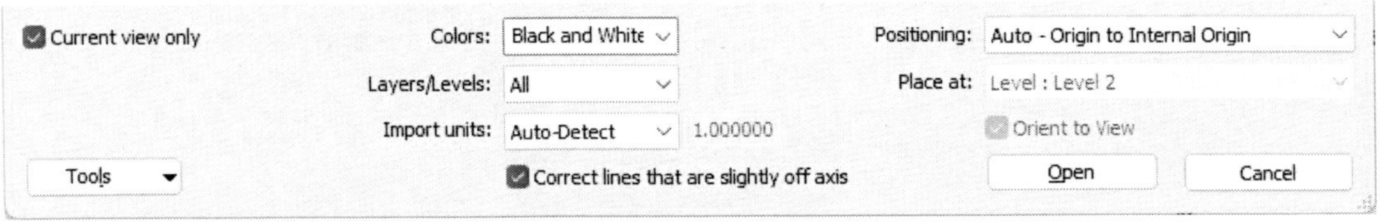

Figure 2–39

3. Click **Open**. The linked CAD file is placed in the project on the **Floor Plans: Level 1** view.
4. Select the linked CAD file. In Properties, note that it displays as **Import Symbol** and is pinned in place because it was imported origin to internal origin.
5. With the linked CAD file still selected, in Properties, in the *Other* section, change the *Draw Layer* to **Foreground**. Alternatively, this can be set in the *Modify | Hotel-Level-1.dwg* tab> *Arrange* panel.

    Note: *As you are drawing walls, floors, ceilings, and roofs within your project, you will want to change how the DWG is displaying in your view from Foreground to Background, depending on what you need to see.*

6. With the CAD file still selected, right-click in the draw area and select **Override Graphics in View>By Category...**.
7. In the *View Specific Category Graphics* dialog box, select **Halftone** and click **OK**.

8. Click in an empty space in the view to release the selection. The linked file displays in halftone, as shown in Figure 2–40.

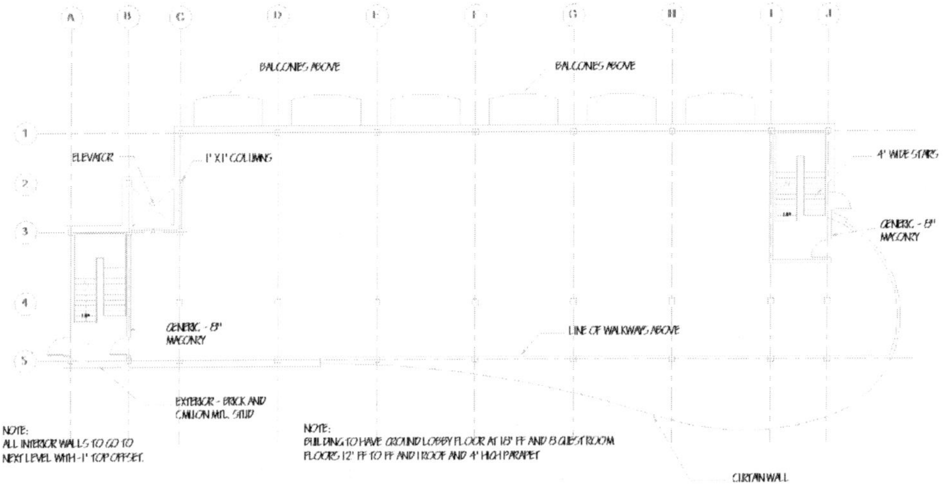

Figure 2–40

9. From the Project Browser, open the **Floor Plans: Level 2** view. The CAD file linked in Level 1 does not display because you specified to link the CAD file with **Current view only** selected.
10. Link the CAD file **Hotel-Level-2.dwg** using the options that were used for Level 1. Set the *Draw Layer* to **Foreground**.
11. Override the graphics and set the linked file to **Halftone**.
12. Save the project.

Task 3: Link in a Revit model.

1. In the Quick Access Toolbar, click (Default 3D View). Neither of the linked CAD files display in this view.
2. In the *Insert* tab>*Link* panel, click (Link Revit).
3. In the *Import/Link RVT* dialog box, navigate to the practice files *Revit Link Files* folder and select **Hotel-Pool.rvt**. Verify that the *Positioning* is set to **Auto - Internal Origin to Internal Origin** and click **Open**.
4. In the View Control Bar, change the *Visual Style* to (Shaded).
5. In the *View* tab>*Graphics* panel, click (Visibility/Graphics), or type **VG** or **VV** to open the *Visibility/Graphic Overrides* dialog box.

6. Select the *Annotation Categories* tab, then scroll down to **Levels** and uncheck it, as shown in Figure 2–41. Click **OK**.

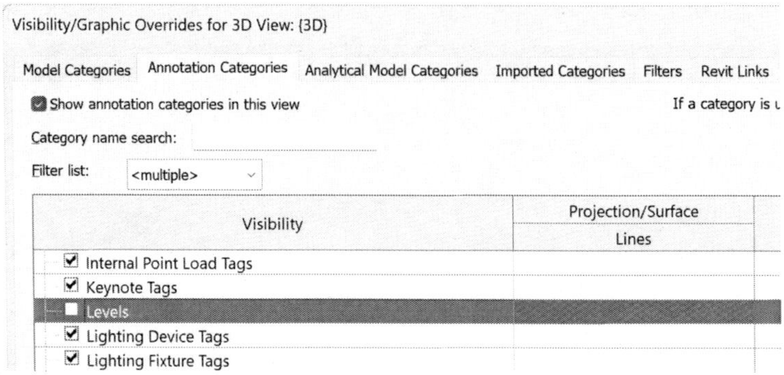

Figure 2–41

7. Type **ZF** to zoom to fit all visible objects.
8. Along the top of the view window, select the *Level 1* view tab to switch back to this view. Both the linked CAD file and linked Revit model display in this view. If needed, type **ZF**.
9. Type **VG** or **VV** to open the *Visibility/Graphic Overrides* dialog box.
10. Select the *Revit Links* tab. Next to **Hotel Pool.rvt**, check the checkbox for **Halftone**, as shown in Figure 2–42.

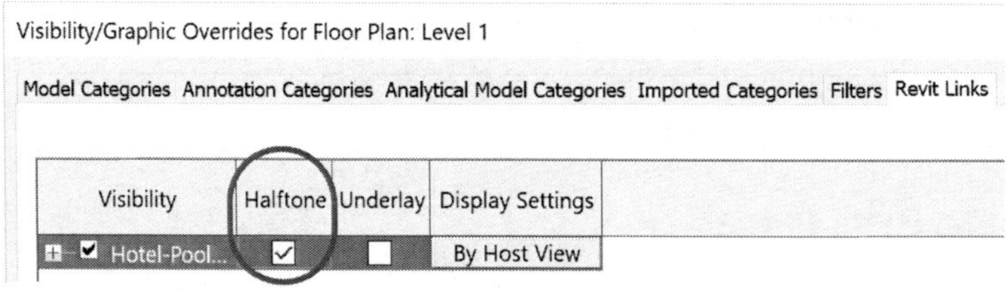

Figure 2–42

11. Select the *Imported Categories* tab and note that the linked **Hotel-Level-1.dwg** is set to *Halftone*. This is because you used **Override Graphics in View>By Category...** to set the file to halftone and did not use **By Element**.

    Note: *If you set the DWG to halftone using **By Element**, you would need to select the DWG, right-click, and select **Override Graphics in View>By Element**, then uncheck **Halftone** to turn it off.*

12. Click **OK**.
13. Select the *Level 2* view tab and note that the linked Revit model displays, but is not halftone in this view. This is because the *Visibility/Graphic Overrides* dialog box modifies per view.
14. Save and close the project.

End of practice

2.8 Setting Up Levels

Levels define floors and vertical heights in a project, like the first and second floor. The default template starts with two levels, but you can add as many as needed, including negative heights for things like basements or footings, as shown in Figure 2–43. Levels must be created in an elevation or section view, and once an element is attached to a level, it will move with that level if it changes. Levels can be shown or hidden in the default 3D view, where they can be modified and copied, but not created.

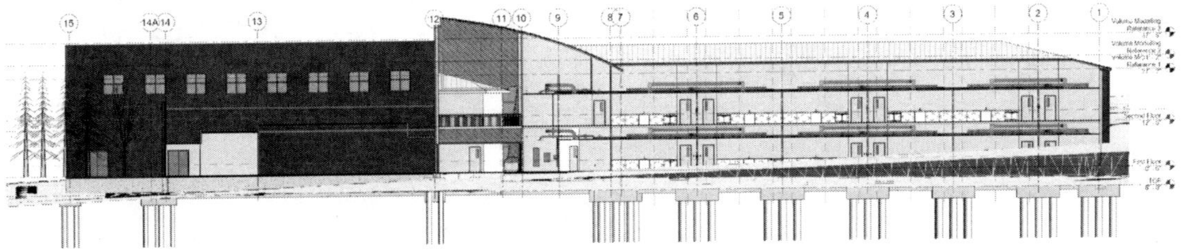

Figure 2–43

There are tools that you can utilize while drawing levels, such as modify tools, sketch tools, and drawing aids like temporary dimensions, preview lines, and alignment lines. You will learn more about these tools in ***Chapter 5 Basic Sketching and Modify Tools***.

How To: Create Levels

1. Open an elevation or section view.
2. In the *Architecture* or *Structure* tab>*Datum* panel, click (Level), or type **LL**.
3. In the Type Selector, set the level head type, if needed.
4. In the *Modify | Place Level* tab>*Plan Views* panel, check **Create Plan View**, as shown in Figure 2–44. If left unchecked, no plan view will be created when a level line is added to the project.

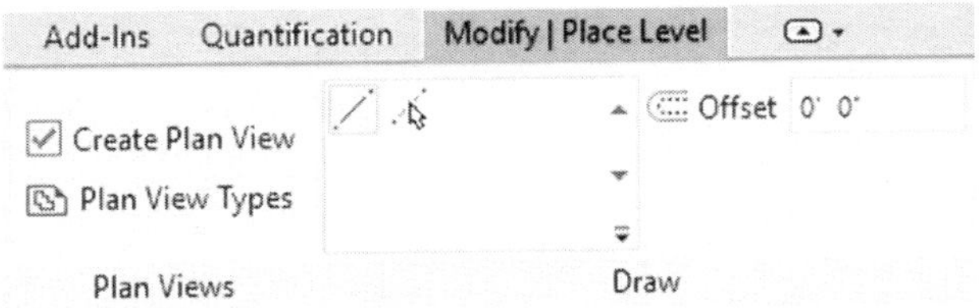

Figure 2–44

5. Click **Plan View Types** to open the *Plan View Types* dialog box (shown in Figure 2–45) to select or unselect the types of views to create when you place the level. When finished, click **OK**.

   Note: *If you have* ***Structure tab and tools*** *turned off in the Options dialog box>User Interface tab, you will not see* ***Structural Plan*** *in the Plan View Types dialog box.*

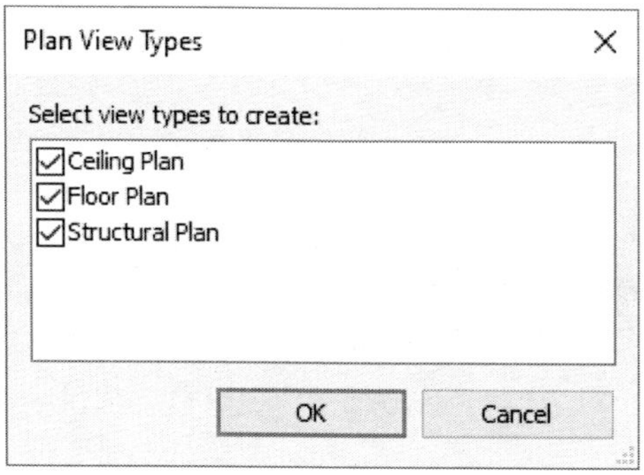

Figure 2–45

6. In the *Modify | Place Level* tab>*Draw* panel, click either (Pick Lines) to select an element or (Line) to sketch a level.

Pick Lines Option

A fast way to create multiple levels is to use the **Pick Lines** option.

1. In the *Modify | Place Level* tab>*Draw* panel, click (Pick Lines).
2. Set the (Offset) and press <Enter>. This ensures you do not place the new level on top of an existing one.
3. Hover over an existing level and verify the offset preview line is in the right location, as shown in Figure 2–46, then click to place the new level.

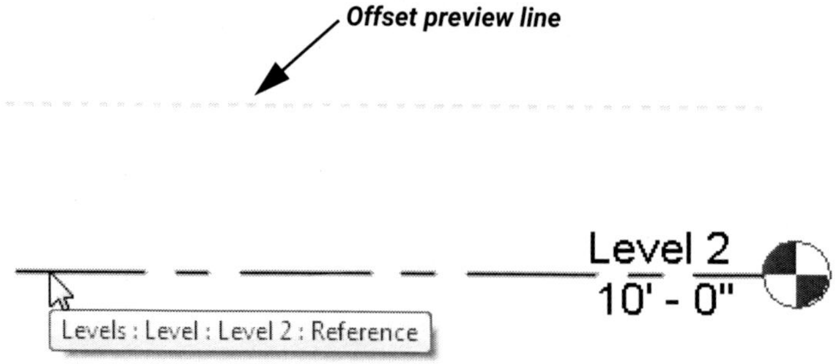

Figure 2–46

Line Option

1. In the *Modify | Place Level* tab>*Draw* panel, click (Line).
2. Sketch the level lines in a consistent direction, either from left to right or right to left. Alignment lines and temporary dimensions can help you place the level line correctly, as shown in Figure 2–47.

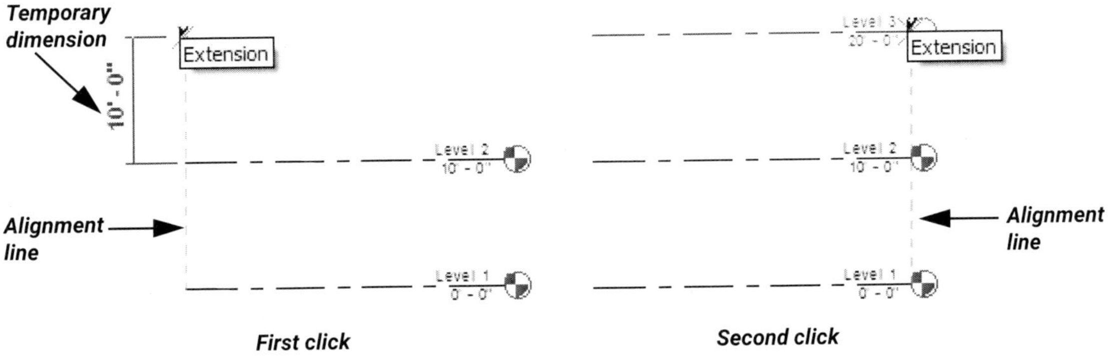

Figure 2–47

- When using the **Line** option, you can set the (Offset) and pick a point along an existing level as the start point. A grayscale preview level line displays to show where the new level will be in reference to the existing level, as shown in Figure 2–48. Click a second point along the existing level to finish the command. The level line becomes permanent.

Note: *Before clicking the second point, if the preview of the level is not in the correct position (i.e., above or below the existing level), press <Spacebar> to toggle the offset of the new level.*

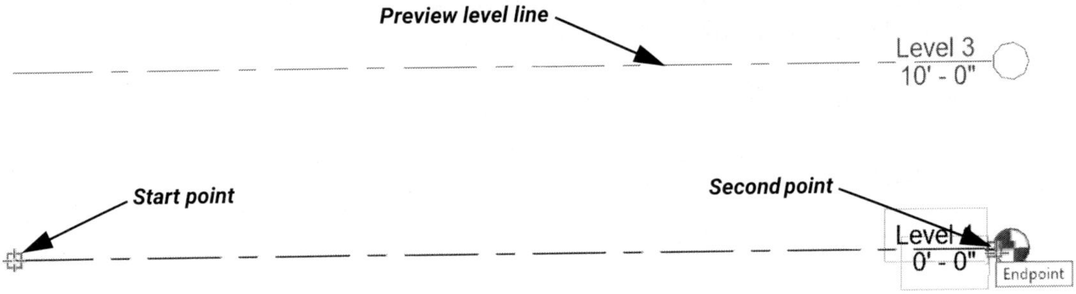

Figure 2–48

- Use tools in the *Modify* panel like (Copy) to duplicate level lines. The level names are incremented but plan views are not created. These are called **reference levels**.
- Level names are automatically incremented as you place them. This automatic numbering is most effective when you use names such as Floor 1, Floor 2, etc. (as opposed to First Floor, Second Floor, etc.). In addition, this makes it easier to find the view in the Project Browser.

Modifying Levels

You can change levels using standard controls and temporary dimensions, as shown in Figure 2–49 to the levels' appearance. You can also make changes to the name and height of the level by selecting on the individual items in the view as well as change these in Properties. You can change just the name of the level in the Project Browser but not the height.

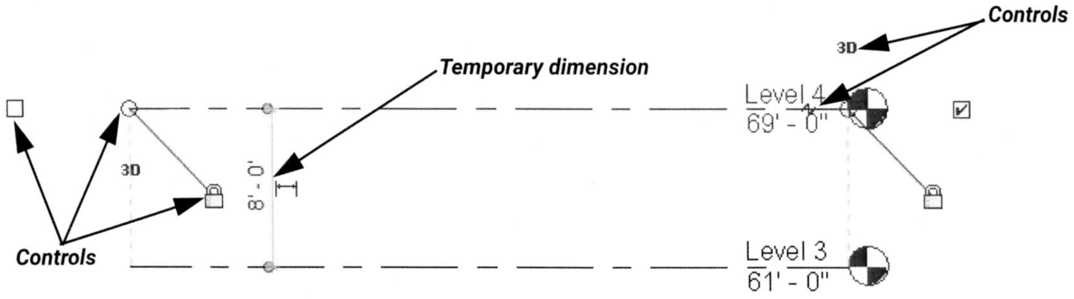

Figure 2–49

- (Hide/Show Bubble) displays on either end of the level line and toggles the level head symbol and level information on or off.
- 2D 3D (Switch to 3d/2d extents) controls whether any movement or adjustment to the level line is reflected in other views (3D) or only affects the current view (2D).
- (Modify the level by dragging its model end) at each end of the line enables you to drag the level head to a new location.
- (Create or remove a length or alignment constraint) controls whether the level is locked in alignment with the other levels. If it is locked and the level line is stretched, all of the other level lines stretch as well. If it is unlocked, the level line stretches independent of the other levels.
- Temporary dimensions let you change the height of level lines.
- Click (Add Elbow) to add a jog to the level line, as shown in Figure 2–50. Drag the shape handles to new locations as needed. This is a view-specific change.

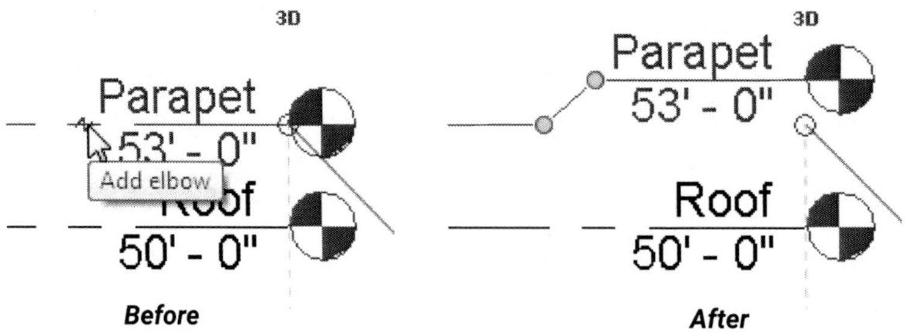

Figure 2–50

How To: Modify a Level's Name and Elevation

1. To change the level name or elevation, double-click on the information next to the level head, or select the level and modify the *Name* or *Elevation* fields in Properties, as shown in Figure 2–51.

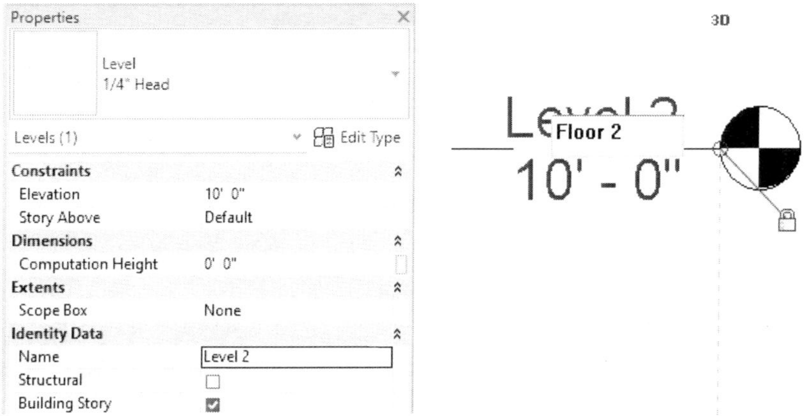

Figure 2–51

2. A *Confirm Level Rename* dialog box displays, prompting you to rename the corresponding views, as shown in Figure 2–52. Click **Yes** if you want to rename the view in the Project Browser.

   - If you change the name in the Project Browser, a *Confirm Plan View Rename* dialog box displays and you are asked if you would like to rename the corresponding level and views.

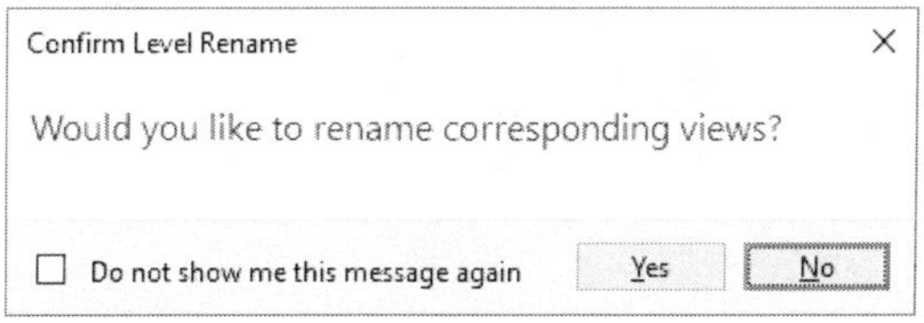

Figure 2–52

Hint: Modifying Measurements

For imperial measurements (feet and inches), the software uses a default of feet. For example, when you type **4** and press <Enter>, it assumes **4'-0"**. For a distance such as 4'-6", you can type any of the following: **4'-6"**, **4'6**, **4-6**, or **4 6** (the numbers separated by a space). To indicate distances less than one foot, type the inch mark (") after the distance, or enter **0**, a space, and then the distance.

- If you delete a level, the views related to that level are also deleted. A warning displays, as shown in Figure 2–53.

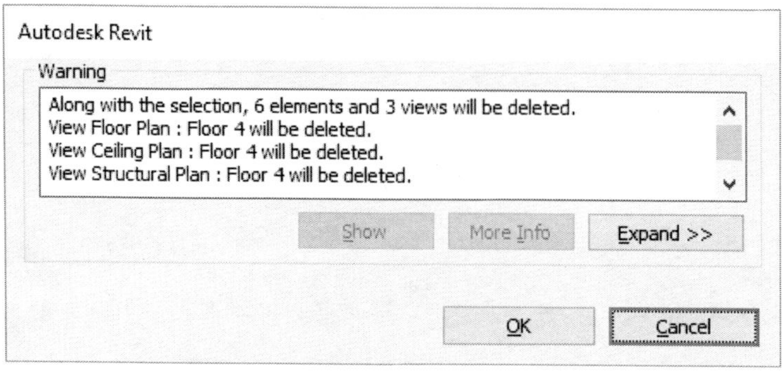

Figure 2–53

> **Hint: Copying Levels and Grids from Other Projects**
>
> Levels and grid lines can be added by drawing over existing levels or grids in an imported or linked file. They can also be copied and monitored from a linked Revit file. Some projects might require both methods.

Creating Plan Views

When you place a level, verify in the contextual tab that **Create Plan View** is selected. There may be instances where you do not need to create plan views for levels that only mark data points, such as the top of a storefront window or the top of a parapet. In these cases, either ensure the **Create Plan View** option is unchecked or copy the level. If needed, you can create a plan view manually. Level heads with views appear in blue, while those without views are black, as shown in Figure 2–54.

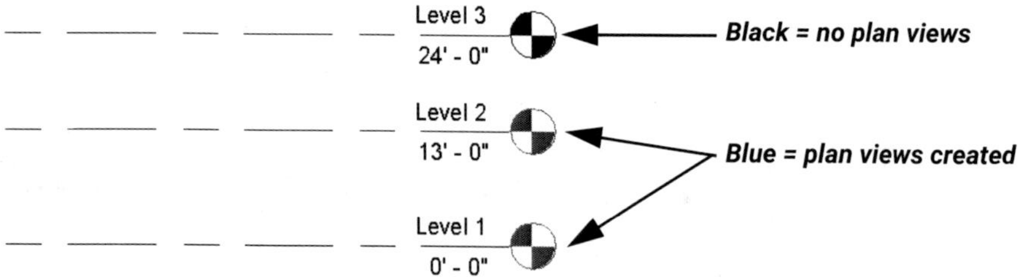

Figure 2–54

How To: Create Plan Views

1. In the *View* tab>*Create* panel, expand (Plan Views) and select the type of plan view you want to create, as shown in Figure 2–55.

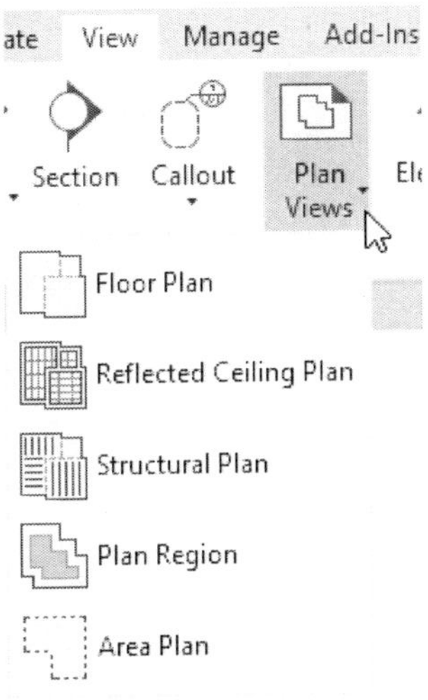

Figure 2–55

2. In the *New Plan* dialog box (shown in Figure 2–56 for a floor plan), select the levels for which you want to create plan views. Hold <Ctrl> to select more than one level.
   - Clear **Do not duplicate existing views** to create a copy of an existing view.

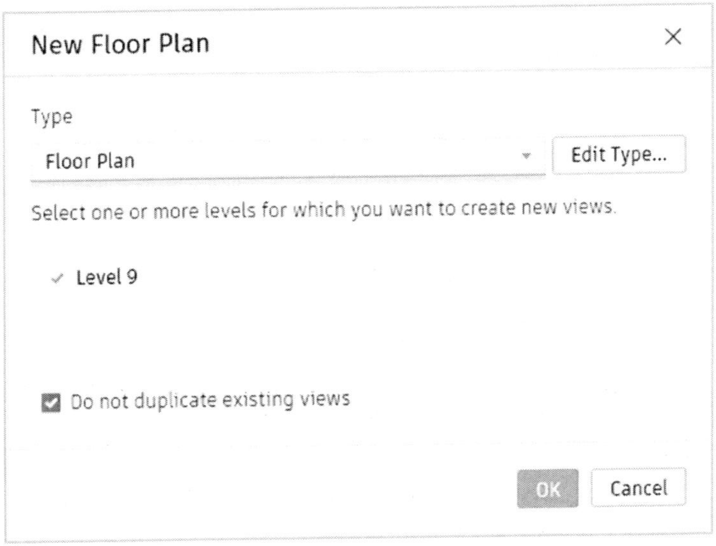

Figure 2–56

3. Click **OK**.

- Once a plan view is made from a level, you can double-click on the level head to open the related floor plan view. You create other plan views similar to creating a floor plan. Ceiling plans are typically created by default when you add a level with a view and have not specified which views to create in the *Plan View Types* dialog box. If you do not want a level to have a ceiling plan, you can right-click on its name in the Project Browser and select **Delete**, as shown in Figure 2–57.

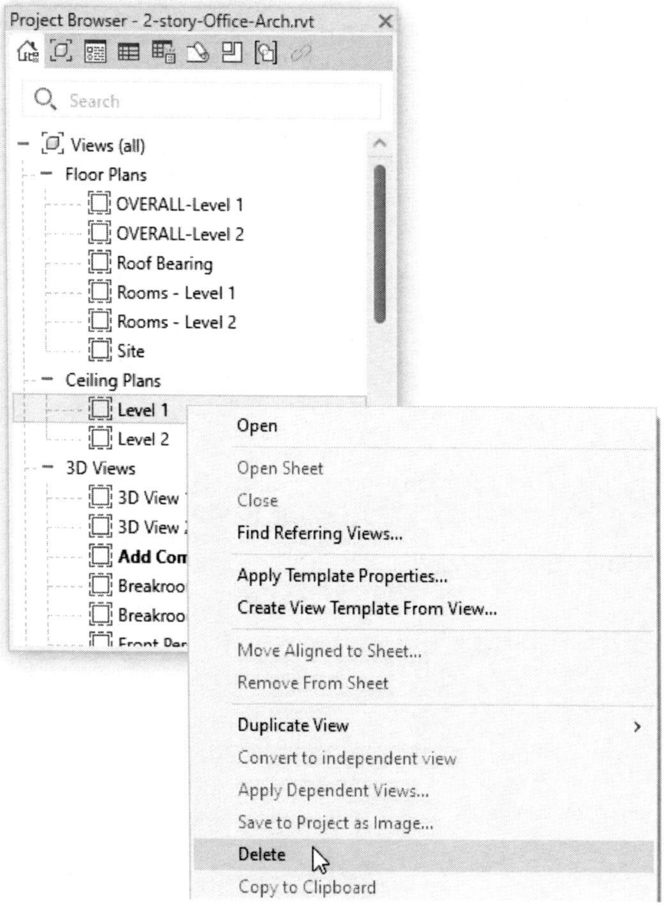

Figure 2–57

Practice 2b
Set Up Levels

Practice Objectives

- Add and modify levels
- Create a plan view.

In this practice, you will set up the levels required in the hotel project, including the floors, top of the footing, basement, and parapet levels. Figure 2–58 shows the completed practice.

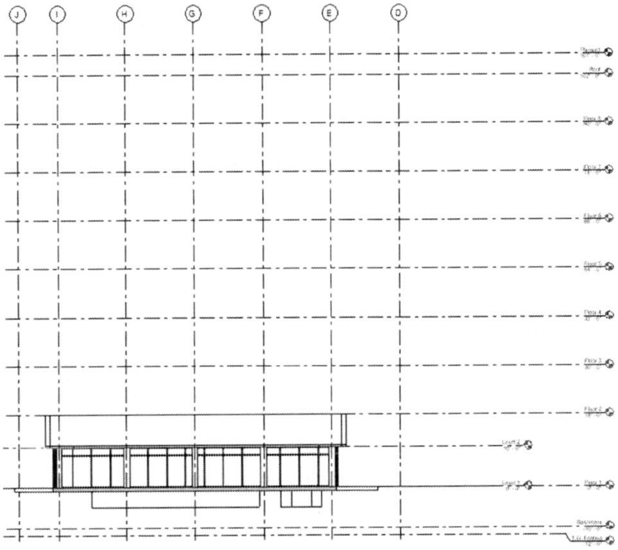

Figure 2–58

1. Open the project **Arch-Levels.rvt** from the practice files folder.
2. In the Project Browser, open the **Elevations (Building Elevation): North** view. You will see your project's **Level 1** and **Level 2** levels, as well as the Level 1 and Level 2 levels and grid lines that are part of the linked Revit file.
3. Select the linked Revit file.
4. In the View Control Bar, expand (Temporary Hide/Isolate) and select **Hide Element**. This toggles off the linked Revit file in the current view.
5. Zoom in on the level heads and names.

6. Slowly click twice on the name *Level 1* and rename it to **Floor 1,** as shown in Figure 2–59. Press <Enter>.

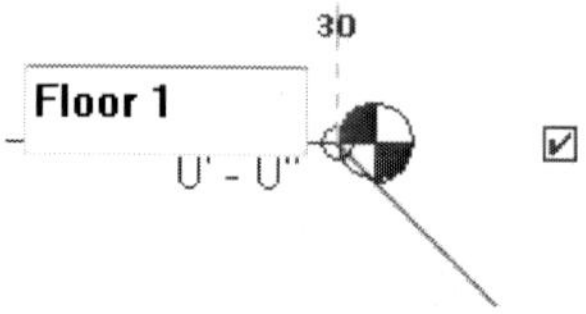

Figure 2–59

7. In the *Confirm Level Rename* dialog box, click **Yes** or press <Y> when prompted to rename the corresponding views and note that in the Project Browser, in the *Floor Plans* section, the view name has changed as well.
8. Repeat the process and rename *Level 2* as **Floor 2**. Press <Enter>. In the *Confirm Level Rename* dialog box, click **Yes** to rename the corresponding views.
9. Click on the height of Floor 2. Change it from **10'-0"** to **18'-0"** and press <Enter>.

   Note: *Instead of typing the hyphen, press <Spacebar> between the feet and inches. When doing this, you do not need to add the symbols for feet or inches as well.*

10. Click (Modify).
11. In the *Architecture* tab>*Datum* panel, click (Level).
12. In the *Modify | Place Level* tab>*Plan Views* panel, check **Create Plan View**, then click **Plan View Types**.
13. In the *Plan View Types* dialog box, uncheck **Structural Plan** to deselect it (so that only **Ceiling Plan** and **Floor Plan** are selected), as shown in Figure 2–60. Click **OK**.

    Note: *If you have **Structural tabs and tools** turned off in the Options dialog box>User Interface tab, you will not see **Structural Plan** in the Plan View Types dialog box.*

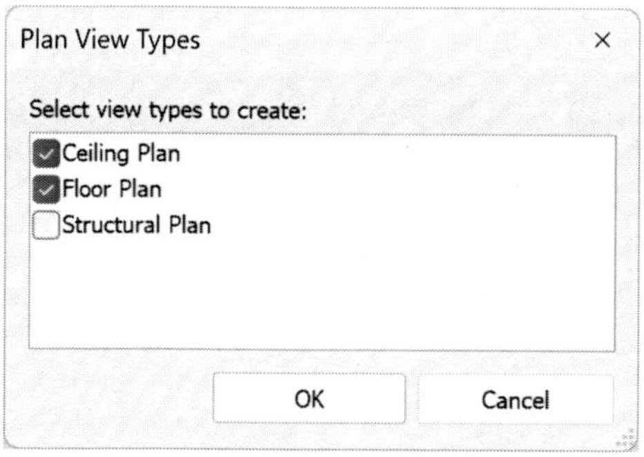

Figure 2–60

14. In the *Modify | Place Level* tab>*Draw* panel, click (Pick Lines). In the *Modify | Place Level* tab>*Draw* panel, set the (Offset) to **12'-0"** and press <Enter>.

15. Hover the cursor over the level line of **Floor 2** and move the cursor slightly upward until you see the dashed preview line display above the **Floor 2** level, as shown in Figure 2–61. Click to create the new level **Floor 3**.

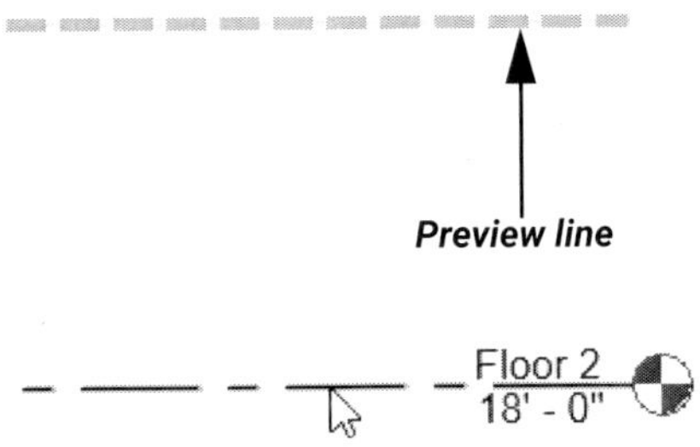

Figure 2–61

16. Create additional levels until there are a total of nine levels, all with the *Offset* of **12'-0"**.

    Note: *While in the **Level** command, you can press and hold your mouse wheel down and move the mouse to pan in the view.*

17. Click (Modify), then zoom to the **Floor 9** level so that you can see the entire level line and select it.
18. Rename *Floor 9* as **Roof** and press <Enter>. (Rename the corresponding views.)
19. Click (Modify).
20. Start the **Level** command again.
21. In the *Modify | Place Level* tab>*Draw* panel, click (Line).
22. In the *Plan Views* panel, uncheck the **Create Plan View** option. (This level does not need a plan view.)
23. In the *Draw* panel, set the (Offset) to **5'-0"** and press <Enter>.
24. Create one additional level above the **Roof** level by clicking the far-left end of the Roof level line as the start point, then clicking the right-hand endpoint of the Roof level head as the second point, as shown in Figure 2–62.

    Note: *You will see a grayed-out preview of Floor 10. Once the second point is selected, Floor 10 becomes a level.*

Figure 2–62

25. Click (Modify).

26. Rename the top level as **Parapet**.

    Note: *You do not get the request to rename corresponding views because you unchecked* ***Create Plan View****, so no view was created when the level was placed in the view. The Parapet level head is black, as shown in Figure 2–63, as opposed to blue like the rest of the levels. A black level head means that there are no views created for this level.*

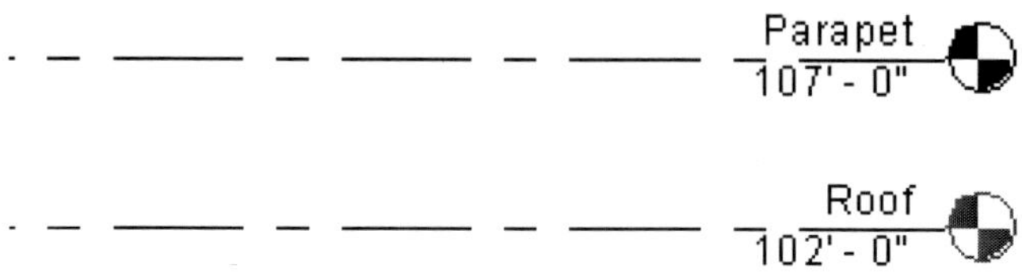

Figure 2–63

27. Click (Modify).
28. Zoom and pan to the Floor 1 level.
29. Select the Floor 1 level line. In the *Modify | Levels* tab>*Modify* panel, click (Copy).
30. In the *Modify | Copy* tab>*Copy* panel, verify **Multiple** is selected, as shown in Figure 2–64.

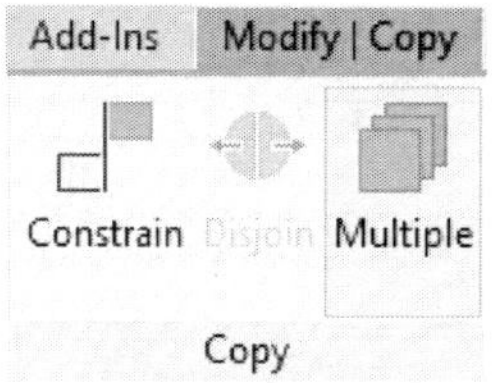

Figure 2–64

31. In the view, click Floor 1's level line for the copy start point. For the second point, click below Floor 1 (the distance does not matter right now as you will set this in the next few steps).
32. Click again below the level you just placed to make another new level. There should now be two new levels below Floor 1.
33. Click (Modify).

34. Select the new level below Floor 1. In Properties, in the *Identity Data* section, type **Basement** next to *Name*. In the *Constraints* section, set the *Elevation* to (negative) **-10'-0"**, as shown in Figure 2–65.

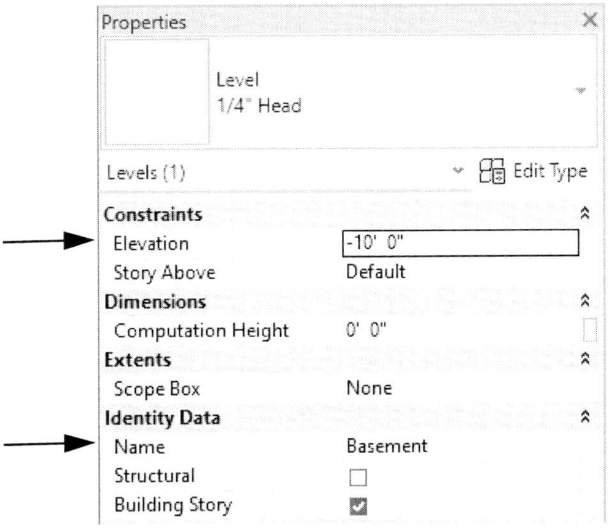

Figure 2–65

35. In Properties, click **Apply**, or move your cursor into the drawing area to apply the changes.
36. Rename the level below Basement to **T.O. Footing** and set the *Elevation* to (negative) **-12'-0"**, as shown in Figure 2–66.
37. Click (Modify).

38. The **Basement** and **T.O. Footing** level names are overlapping in the view. Select the **T.O. Footing** level and click the (Add elbow) control between the level name and height. Use the **Drag** circle grips (shown in Figure 2–66) to adjust the level line so it does not run through the text.

Note: Zoom in if you cannot see the ***Add elbow*** *control on the level line.*

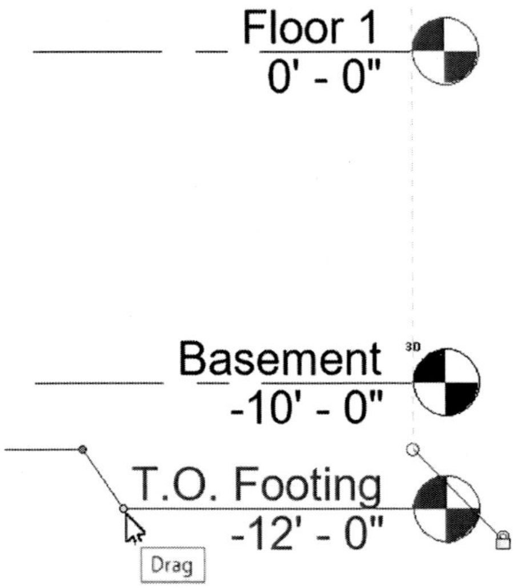

Figure 2–66

39. In the View Control Bar, select (Temporary Hide/Isolate) and select **Reset Temporary Hide/Isolate**.

40. Select the Floor 1 level line, then select the (Drag the extents of the level in the model) control and drag the level over until it is far enough away from the linked model levels. The other levels will follow because of the alignment constraint. If some levels do not follow, drag them to meet up with the others.

41. Zoom out to display the entire project.

Note: Because the Basement and T.O. Footing were copies of Floor 1, you need to create floor plan views. Note that these two views' level heads are black as opposed to the rest of the levels that have views created that have blue level heads.

42. In the *View* tab>*Create* panel, expand (Plan Views) and select (Floor Plan).

43. In the *New Floor Plan* dialog box, select **Basement** and **T.O. Footing**, as shown in Figure 2–67. (Hint: Use <Ctrl> to select the two levels.)

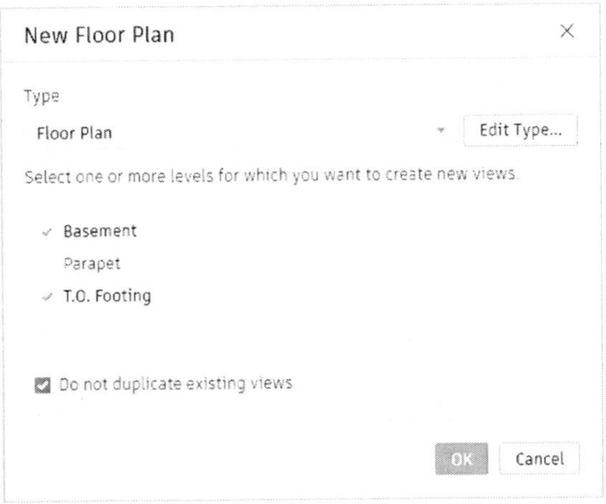

Figure 2–67

44. Click **OK**. The floor plan views now show in the Project Browser and the T.O. Footing view (or the last view to be created) becomes the active view.
45. Switch back to the **North** elevation view and note that the **Basement** and **T.O. Footing** level heads are now blue.
46. To create a new ceiling plan view, in the *View* tab>*Create* panel, expand (Plan Views) and select (Reflected Ceiling Plan).
47. In the *New RCP* dialog box, select **Basement** and click **OK**.
48. Select the *Floor 1* view tab to make it the active view.
49. Close any open views by clicking (Close Inactive Views) in the Quick Access Toolbar.
50. Open the **Default 3D** view.
51. Because you hid the levels when linking in the models, you need to unhide them. In the View Control Bar, click (Reveal Hidden Elements).
52. Using your mouse wheel, zoom out so you can see the level lines.
53. Select one level and in the *Modify | Levels* tab>*Reveal Hidden Elements* panel, click (Unhide Category).
54. In the View Control Bar, click (Close Reveal Hidden Elements).
55. In the Project Browser, select the **Roof** view in the *Ceiling Plans* section. Right-click and select **Delete** to delete the view.
56. Save and close the project.

End of practice

2.9 Creating Grids

Grids are annotation elements that display in most views, including plan, ceiling, section, elevation, and 3D views. They help organize your design when developing a layout and describe the pattern and location for columns, as shown in Figure 2–68. Grids can be multi-segmented, arcs, or straight lines, and they can be hidden in the view if needed. Each line or arc in a grid is a separate entity and can be placed, moved, and modified individually. Grids cannot be drawn in a 3D view but grids can be displayed in a 3D view, perspective view, or in a 3D view with a selection box, and when you click on a grid, the surface contour displays.

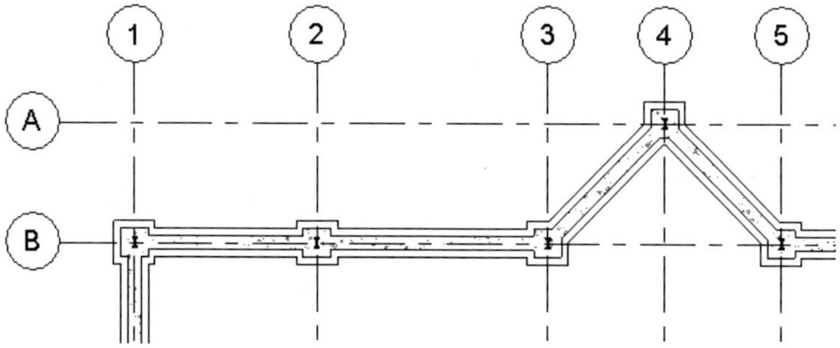

Figure 2–68

How To: Create a Grid

1. In the *Architecture* or *Structure* tab>*Datum* panel, click (Grid), or type **GR**.
2. In the Properties, in the Type Selector, select the grid type, which will control the size of the bubble and the linestyle.
3. In the *Modify | Place Grid* tab>*Draw* panel (shown in Figure 2–69), select the sketch tool you want to use.
4. Depending on the tool selected, you can enter a value for (Offset), or to set the radius, click (Radius) and enter the radius value. To toggle radius off, click (Radius) again.

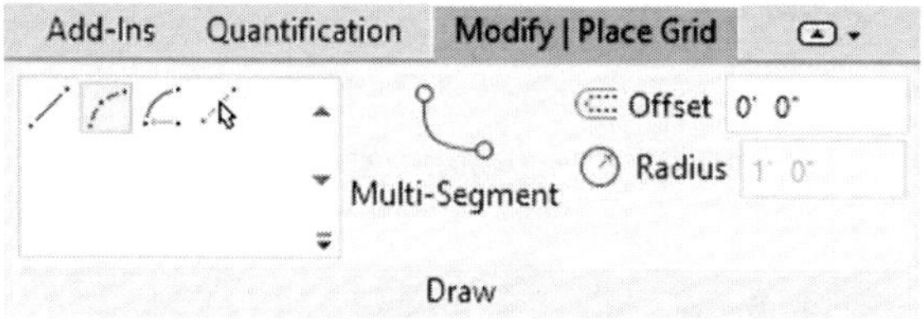

Figure 2–69

5. Start drawing grid lines. Grids can be sketched at any angle, but you should ensure that all parallel grids are sketched in the same direction (e.g., from left to right or from bottom to top).

How To: Create a Multi-Segment Grid

1. In the *Architecture* or *Structure* tab>*Datum* panel, click (Grid), or type **GR**.
2. In the *Modify | Place Grid* tab>*Draw* panel, toggle on (Multi-Segment). You are put into Edit Sketch mode.
3. In the *Modify | Edit Sketch* tab>*Draw* panel, select a sketch tool, as shown in Figure 2–70.
   - Depending on the tool selected, you can set a value for an (Offset), or to set the radius, click (Radius) and enter the radius value.
   - You can toggle (Chain) on or off, as shown in Figure 2–70 toggled on with the **Line** tool selected.

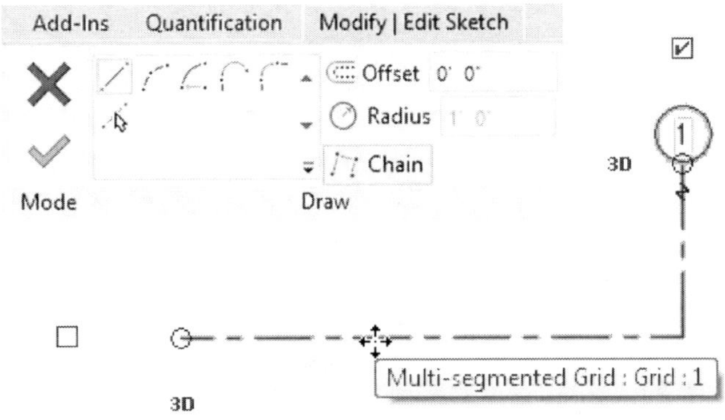

Figure 2–70

4. When finished, click (Finish Edit Mode) in the *Mode* panel to complete the command. Alternatively, if you need to cancel the Edit Sketch mode, click (Cancel Edit Mode). In the *Sketch Discarded* dialog box, read the message and click **Yes**.

How To: Turn On or Off Grids in 3D

1. Open a 3D or perspective view and click (Modify) to verify nothing is selected.
2. In Properties, click **Edit...** next to *Show Grids*, as shown in Figure 2–71.

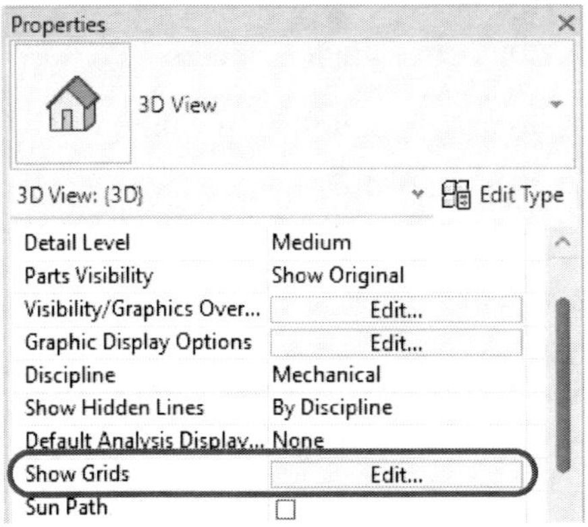

Figure 2–71

3. In the *Show Grids* dialog box, select the level(s) that you want the grids to display at in the 3D view, as shown in Figure 2–72.

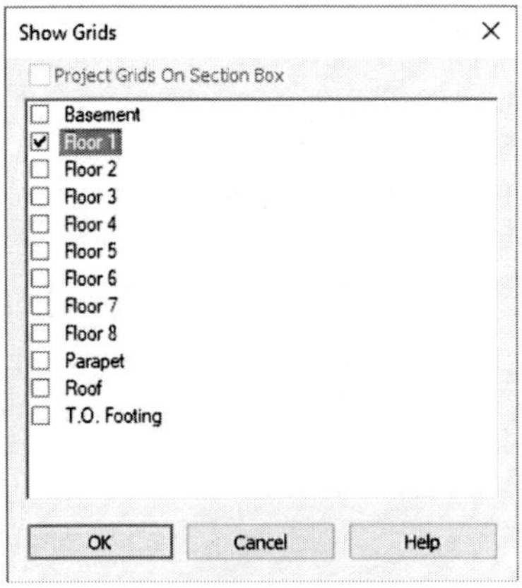

Figure 2–72

4. Click **OK**.

How To: Display Grids on Section Box

1. To display the grids on the bottom of a section box, in Properties, verify that **Section Box** is selected and click **Edit...** next to *Show Grids*.

2. In the *Show Grids* dialog box, select only the **Project Grids On Section Box** option, as shown in Figure 2–73, and click **OK**. Note that you can display the grids at a specific level as well as project the grids on the section box by also selecting a level in the *Show Grids* dialog box.

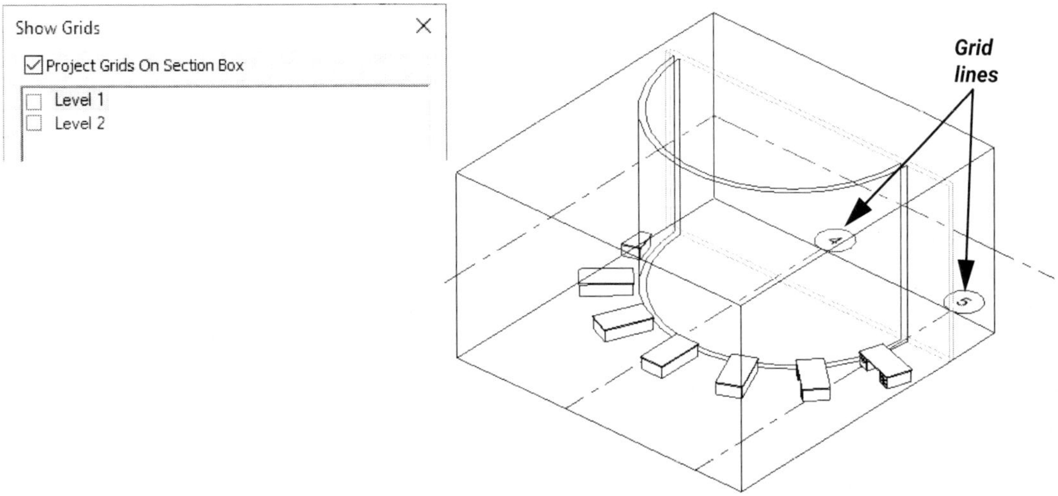

Figure 2–73

Modifying Grid Lines

Grid lines, like levels, are datum elements that you can adjust using controls, alignments, and temporary dimensions in the view, as shown in Figure 2–74. You can change the type using the Type Selector, and grid numbers can be letters, numbers, or a mix of both. To modify a grid number, double-click the bubble and type the new value, or change the *Name* in Properties. In MEP disciplines, grids serve as a reference guide to help align MEP elements with the architectural and structural models.

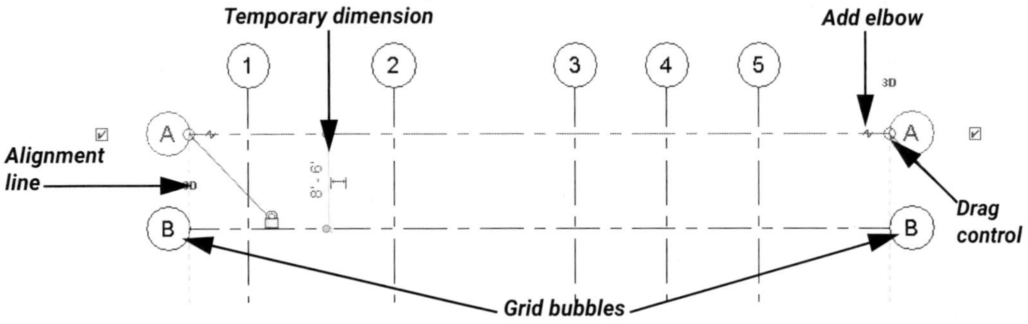

Figure 2–74

To modify the length of the grid line, select the grid line and click and drag the ⊕ (Modify the grid by dragging its model end) control to the new location, as shown in Figure 2–75.

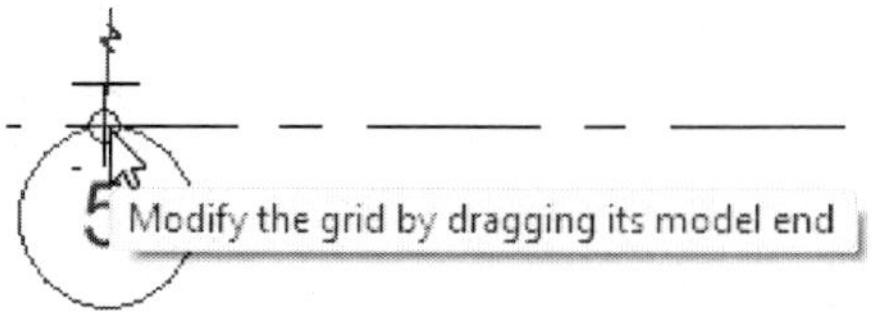

Figure 2–75

In 3D views, grid lines can be edited just like in plan views – you can rename them, adjust their length using the drag control, and change the spacing by modifying temporary dimensions. To change how the grid symbols appear at each end of the grid line, use the *Type Properties* dialog box, where the first pick point is *End 1* and the second is *End 2*, as shown in Figure 2–76.

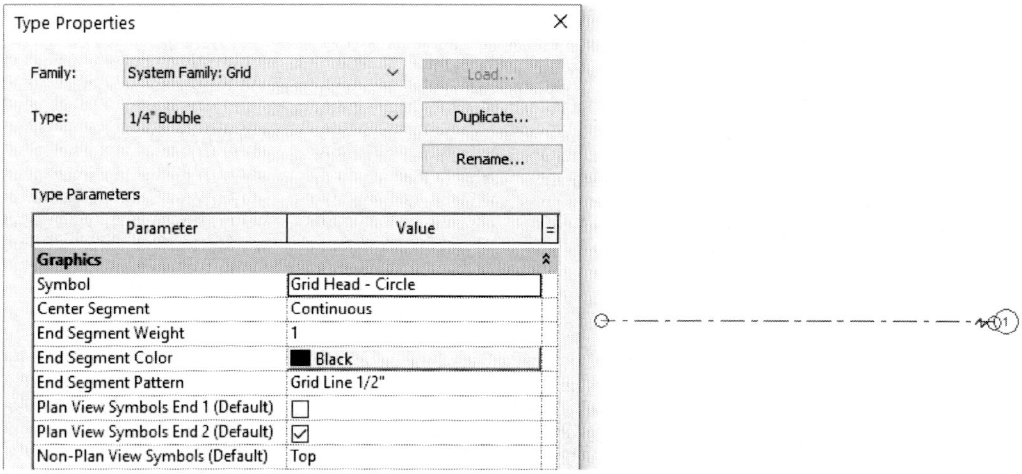

Figure 2–76

Hint: Propagating Datum Extents

If column grids do not display in a view, this might be due to adding a level after the grid lines were added. To display the grid lines in plan views, select the grid lines in a view in which they are displayed. In the *Modify | Grids* tab>*Datum* panel, click (Propagate Extents). In the *Propagate datum extents* dialog box (shown in Figure 2–77), select the views to project the grid lines to.

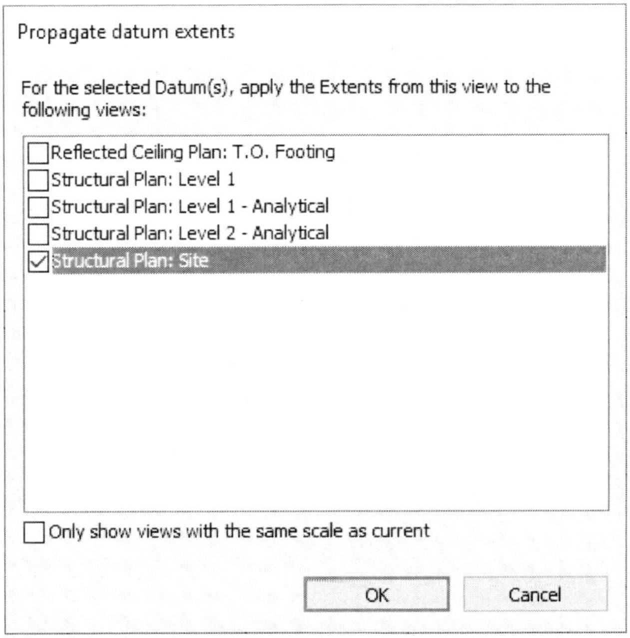

Figure 2–77

- This also works for levels.
- (Propagate Extents) is particularly useful to make grid lines display the same in all views.

Practice 2c
Add Grids

Practice Objectives

- Add and modify grid lines.
- Modify grid properties in a 3D view.

In this practice, you will place grid lines using the linked CAD model as a guide. You will then turn grid lines on in a 3D view.

1. Open the project **Arch-Grids.rvt** from the practice files folder.
2. From the Project Browser, open the **Floor Plans: Floor 1** view.
3. Select the linked Revit file with the pool (**Hotel-Pool.rvt**). In the View Control Bar, expand (Temporary Hide/Isolate) and select **Hide Element**.
4. In the *Architecture* tab>*Datum* panel, click (Grid).
5. In the *Modify | Place Grid* tab>*Draw* panel, click (Pick Lines).
6. Select grid line **A** from the linked DWG file to create a grid line in the Revit model.
7. Click (Modify) to end the command.
8. Zoom in to the new grid line bubble and click inside of it. Type **A** and press <Enter>.

   Note: *If you zoom in to the bubble and click on the number or letter, you can change the value without exiting the command.*

9. Start the **Grid** command again and use **Pick Lines** to continue selecting the vertical grid lines displayed in the imported file. The letters automatically increment.
10. Click to place the first horizontal grid line, then click (Modify). Change the letter in the bubble to **1** and press <Enter>.
11. Start the **Grid** command again and use **Pick Lines** to continue selecting the horizontal grid lines. The numbers automatically increment.
12. Click (Modify) to end the command.
13. Select the CAD file (**Hotel-Level-1.dwg**). In the View Control Bar, expand (Temporary Hide/Isolate) and select **Hide Element**.

14. Only the grids display, as shown in Figure 2–78.

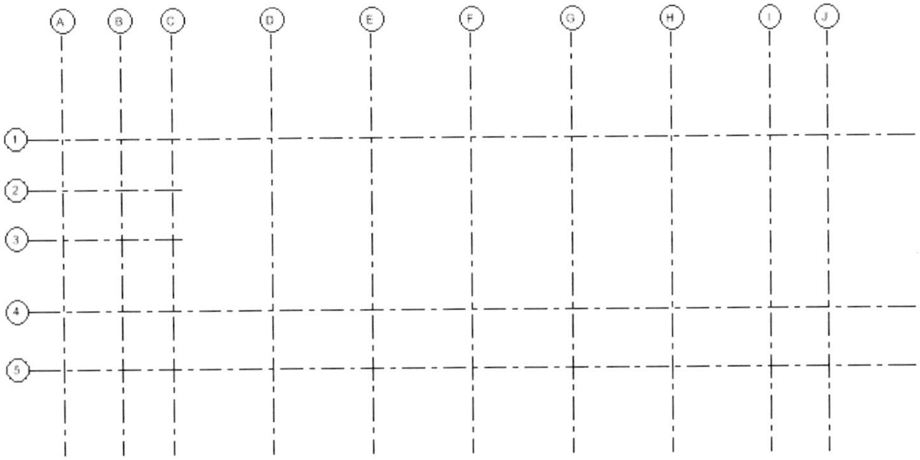

Figure 2–78

15. In the View Control Bar, select (Temporary Hide/Isolate) and select **Reset Temporary Hide/Isolate**. The imported DWG and linked RVT now display.

16. Open the default 3D view by selecting the view tab at the top of the view. Note that you do not see the grids.

17. Click (Modify) to verify nothing is selected in the view.

18. In Properties, in the *Graphics* section, click **Edit...** next to *Show Grids*.

19. In the *Show Grids* dialog box, select **Floor 1** and click **OK**.

20. The grids now display. Select the linked Revit file with the pool (**Hotel-Pool.rvt**).

21. In the View Control Bar, expand (Temporary Hide/Isolate) and select **Hide Element** to see the grids unobstructed as shown in Figure 2–79.

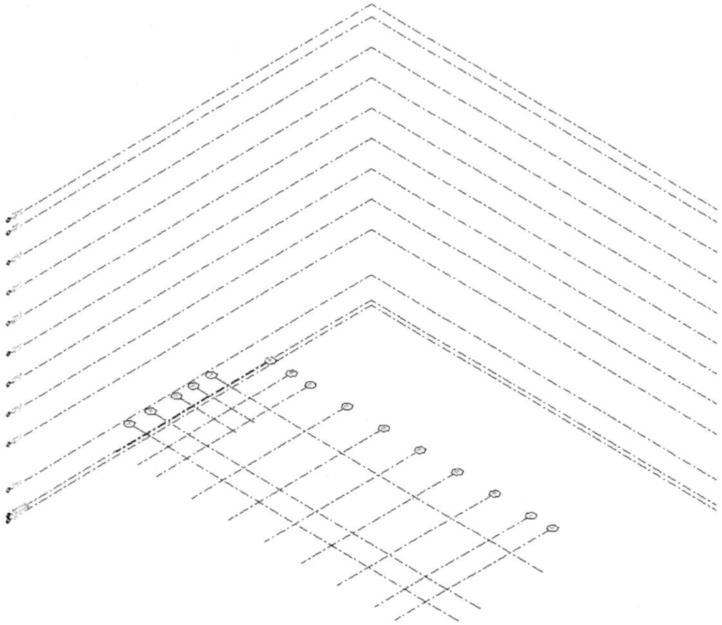

Figure 2–79

22. Select one of the grid lines. In Properties, click **Edit Type**.
23. In the *Type Properties* dialog box, in the *Graphics* section, check the checkbox next to **Plan View Symbols End 1 (Default)**.
24. Click **OK**. There are now grid bubbles on both ends of the grid line.
25. Click (Modify) to deselect the grid line.

26. Zoom in to grid lines 2 and 3. Select grid line **2** and uncheck the checkbox to turn off the grid bubble that is inside the building area, as shown in Figure 2–80.

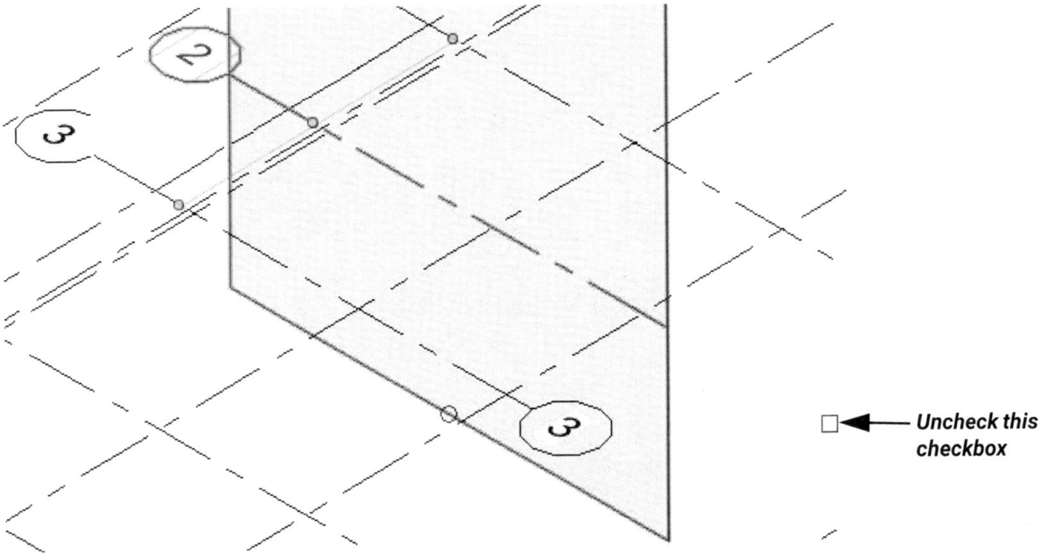

Figure 2–80

27. In the View Control Bar, select (Temporary Hide/Isolate) and select **Reset Temporary Hide/Isolate**.

28. Save and close the project.

End of practice

Chapter Review Questions

1. What type of view do you need to be in to add a level to your project?

a. Any 3D view.

b. As this is done using a dialog box, the view does not matter.

c. Any plan view.

d. Any section or elevation view.

2. How do you line up grid lines that might be different lengths, as shown in Figure 2–81?

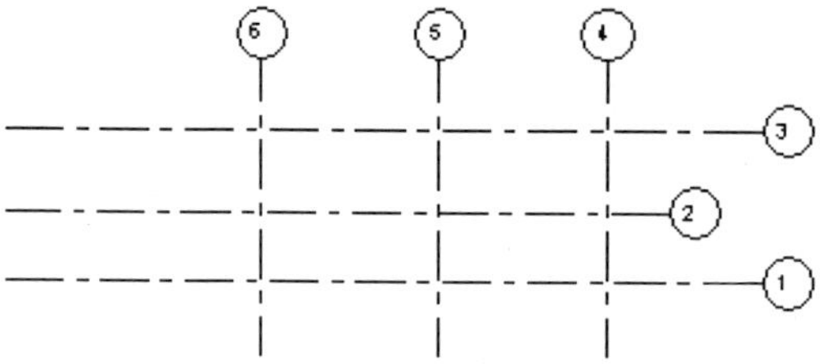

Figure 2–81

a. Delete and redraw the grid lines.

b. Select the grid line and use the drag control to line up with the other grid lines.

c. Select the grid line, right-click, and select **Auto-Align**.

d. In Properties, change the *Length* to get them into position.

3. Grids can be displayed in a 3D view.

a. True

b. False

4. Which of the following types of CAD formats can you import into Revit? (Select all that apply.)

a. .DWG

b. .XLS

c. .SAT

d. .DGN

5. To modify linked CAD files, you need to open what dialog box?

a. Type Properties

b. Link CAD

c. Manage Links

d. Insert from File

6. When linking a Revit model, what should be done to keep the linked model from moving?

a. Lock the model.

b. Pin the model.

c. Center the model.

d. Coordinate the model.

7. When creating a new level, you have to change all corresponding views.

a. True

b. False

8. Where can you change a level's name?

a. In the View Control Bar.

b. In a plan view by clicking on the level.

c. In the Project Browser, in Properties, or in an elevation view by clicking on the level's name.

d. You cannot change the name after the level has been placed in the view.

9. If imported with the **Current view only** option selected, you can set the imported DWG to be in the foreground or background throughout the project's life cycle.

a. True

b. False

Command Summary

Button	Command	Location
	**Grid**	• **Ribbon:** *Architecture* tab>*Datum* panel • **Shortcut:** GR
	**Import CAD**	• **Ribbon:** *Insert* tab>*Import* panel
	**Import PDF**	• **Ribbon:** *Insert* tab>*Import* panel
	**Level**	• **Ribbon:** *Architecture* tab>*Datum* panel • **Shortcut:** LL
	**Link CAD**	• **Ribbon:** *Insert* tab>*Link* panel
	**Link PDF**	• **Ribbon:** *Insert* tab>*Link* panel
	**Link Revit**	• **Ribbon:** *Insert* tab>*Link* panel
	**Manage Links**	• **Ribbon:** *Insert* tab>*Manage* panel or *Manage* tab>*Manage Project* panel • **Ribbon:** (with link selected) *Modify | RVT Links* tab>*Link* panel
	**Multi-Segment (Grid)**	• **Ribbon:** *Modify | Place Grid* tab>*Draw* panel
	**Offset**	• **Ribbon:** *Modify | Place Level* or *Modify | Place Grid* tab>*Draw* panel • **Ribbon:** *(Multi-Segment) Modify | Edit Sketch* tab>*Draw* panel
	**Propagate Extents**	• **Ribbon:** *Modify | Grids* or *Modify | Levels* tab>*Datum* panel
	**Radius**	• **Ribbon:** *Modify | Place Grid* tab>*Draw* panel
	**Temporary Hide/Isolate**	• **View Control Bar**

Chapter 3

Working with Views

Views are the cornerstone of working with Revit® models as they enable you to see the model in both 2D and 3D. As you are progressing through your project, you can duplicate and change views to display different information based on the same view of the model. Callouts, elevations, and sections are especially important views for construction documents.

Learning Objectives

- Understand the Project Browser.
- Duplicate views so that you can modify the display as you are creating the model and for construction documents.
- Change the way elements display in different views to show required information and set views for construction documents.
- Create callout views of parts of plans, sections, or elevations for detailing.
- Add building and interior elevations that can be used to demonstrate how a building will be built.
- Create wall sections to help you create the model and to include in construction documents.
- Create 3D section views using selection boxes and Orient to View.

3.1 Understanding the Project Browser

When starting a project using the supplied Revit templates, the Project Browser displays the default organization for the view tabs as **all** (as shown in Figure 3–1). There is also a status icon next to the view that indicates if the view has been added to a sheet: a white box indicates the view is not on a sheet while a colored box indicates the view is on a sheet.

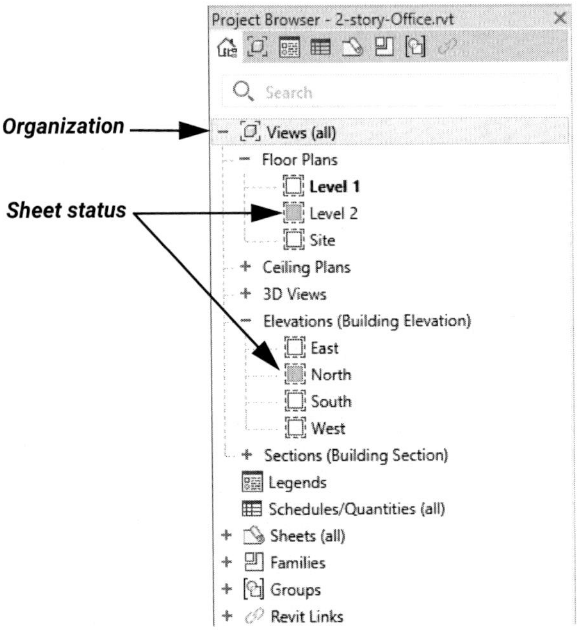

Figure 3–1

If you no longer require a view, you can delete it. Right-click on its name in the Project Browser and select **Delete**.

> ***Note:*** *The Project Browser can be floated, resized, or docked on top of Properties. It can also be customized by changing the Browser Organization or its location within the application.*

How To: Open Multiple Views

1. To open multiple views, press and hold either <Shift> or <Ctrl> and select the views, right-click, and select **Open**, as shown in Figure 3–2.

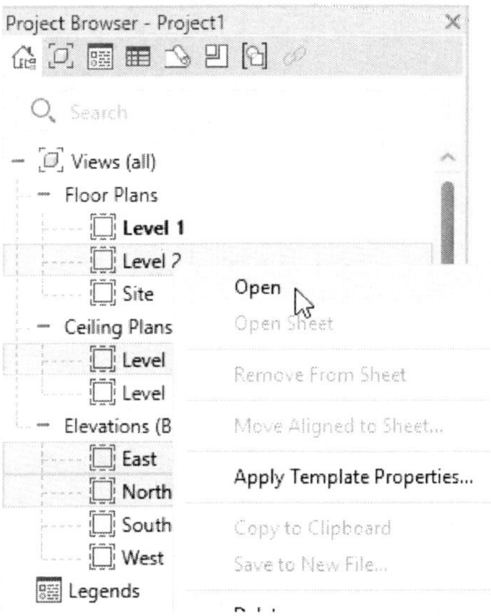

Figure 3–2

2. In the *Open View* dialog box (shown in Figure 3–3), click **OK**.

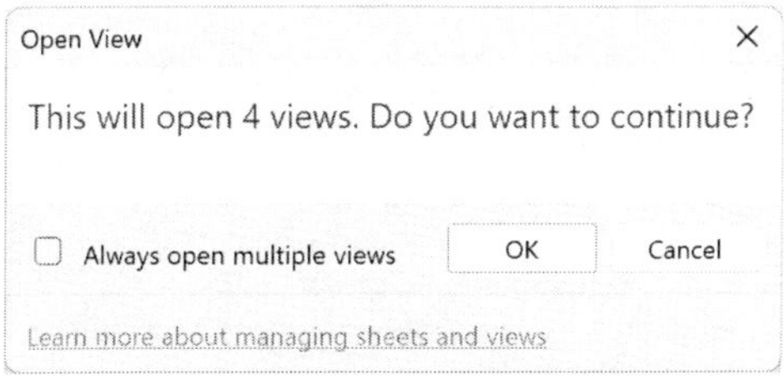

Figure 3–3

- To bypass the *Open View* dialog box in future, check the **Always open multiple views** checkbox.

Filter the Project Browser

The tabs at the top of the Project Browser can be selected to filter what is being displayed. By default, the persistent tabs will always display: (All), (Views), (Legends), (Schedules), (Sheets), (Families), (Groups), and (Links). As you create more specific views, new tabs will appear in the Project Browser, such as (Panel Schedules), (Reports), or (Assemblies). These are called dynamic tabs. These tabs reduce the amount of information you need to sort through when looking for a specific type of view in your project.

View Placement on Sheet Status Icon

The box to the left of the view name indicates if the view has been placed on a sheet.

- A box that's filled in indicates the view is on a sheet.
- A white (empty) box indicates the view is not on a sheet.
- A half-filled box indicates the view is partially placed on a sheet (e.g., in the case where a schedule has multiple views because of the schedule's length).

How To: Turn Off the Sheet Status Icon

1. In the Project Browser, right-click on any of the view names or on the **Views (all)** node at the top.
2. Select **Show View Placement on Sheet Status Icons**, as shown in Figure 3–4.

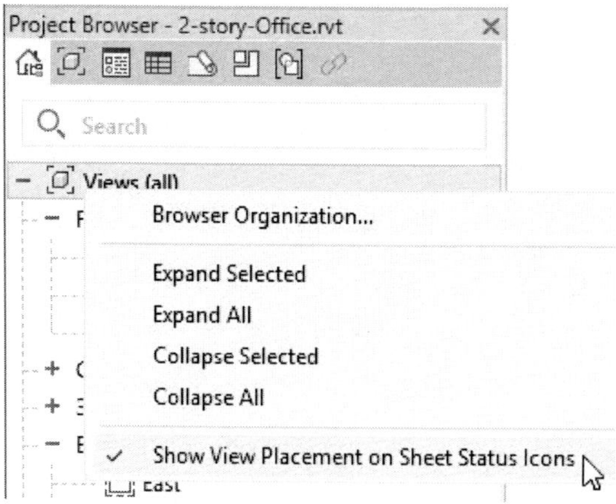

Figure 3–4

Search in Project Browser

At the top of the Project Browser is a search bar so you can quickly find within each parent or child node anything that has the search word in it, as shown in Figure 3–5. When working in a view, you can locate its location in the Project Browser by right-clicking in an empty area in the view (with nothing selected) and selecting **Find in Project Browser**. The view will highlight in the Project Browser. You can also locate an element in the Project Browser by selecting the element in a view, right-clicking, and selecting **Find in Project Browser**.

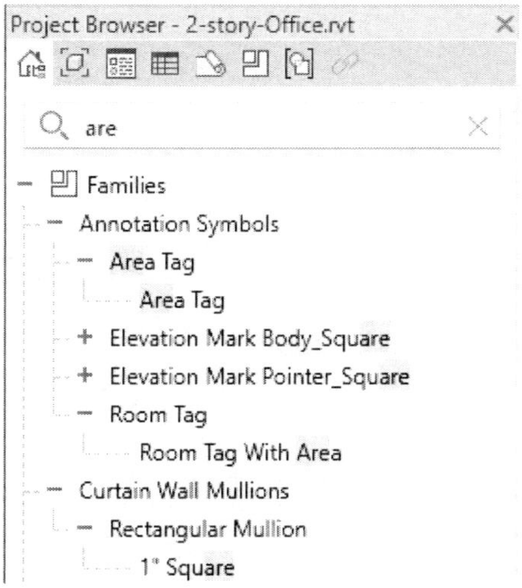

Figure 3–5

3.2 Duplicating Views

Once you have created a model, you do not have to recreate the elements at different scales or copy them so that they can be used on more than one sheet. Instead, you can duplicate the required views and modify the view to suit your needs.

Duplication Types

Duplicate creates a copy of the view that only includes the building elements and view properties, as shown in Figure 3–6. Annotation and detailing are not copied into the new view. Building model elements automatically change in all views, but view-specific changes made to the new view are not reflected in the original view.

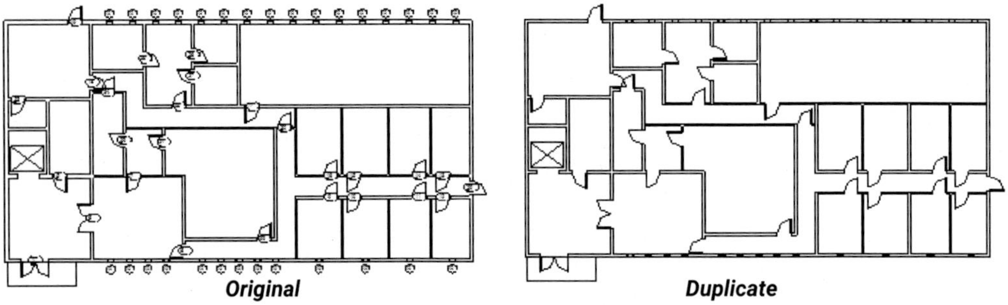

Figure 3–6

Duplicate with Detailing creates a copy of the view and includes all annotation and detail elements (such as tags), as shown in Figure 3–7. Any annotation or view-specific elements created in the new view are not reflected in the original view.

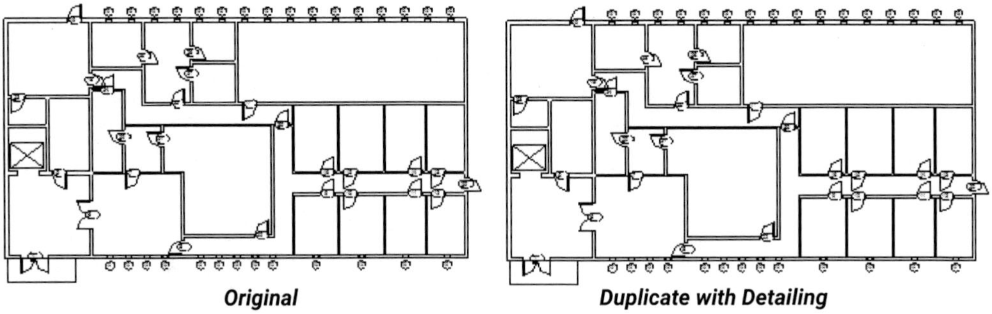

Figure 3–7

Duplicate as Dependent creates a copy of the view and links it to the original (parent) view, as shown in the Project Browser in Figure 3–8. View-specific changes made to the overall view, such as changing the *Scale*, are also reflected in the dependent (child) views and vice-versa.

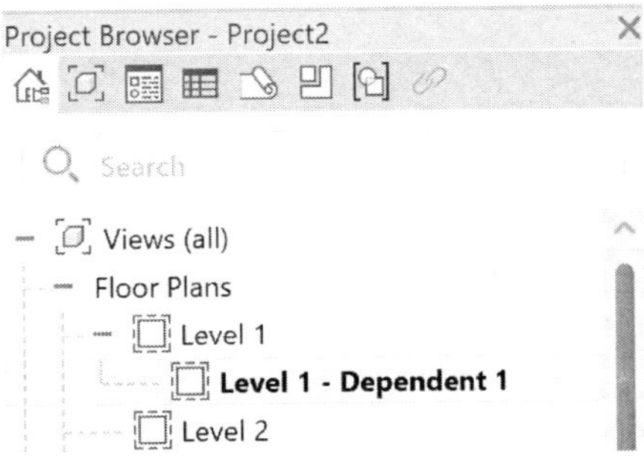

Figure 3–8

- Use dependent views when the building model is so large that you need to split the building onto separate sheets, while ensuring that the views are all at the same scale.
- If you want to separate a dependent view from the original view, right-click on the dependent view and select **Convert to independent view**.

How To: Create Duplicate Views

1. Open the view you want to duplicate.
2. In the *View* tab>*Create* panel, expand **Duplicate View** and select the type of duplicate view you want to create, as shown in Figure 3–9. Most types of views can be duplicated.

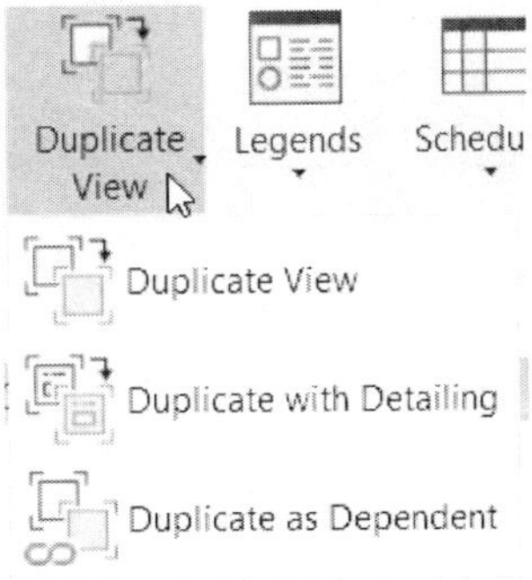

Figure 3–9

- Alternatively, you can right-click on a view in the Project Browser and select the duplicate type you want to use, as shown in Figure 3–10.

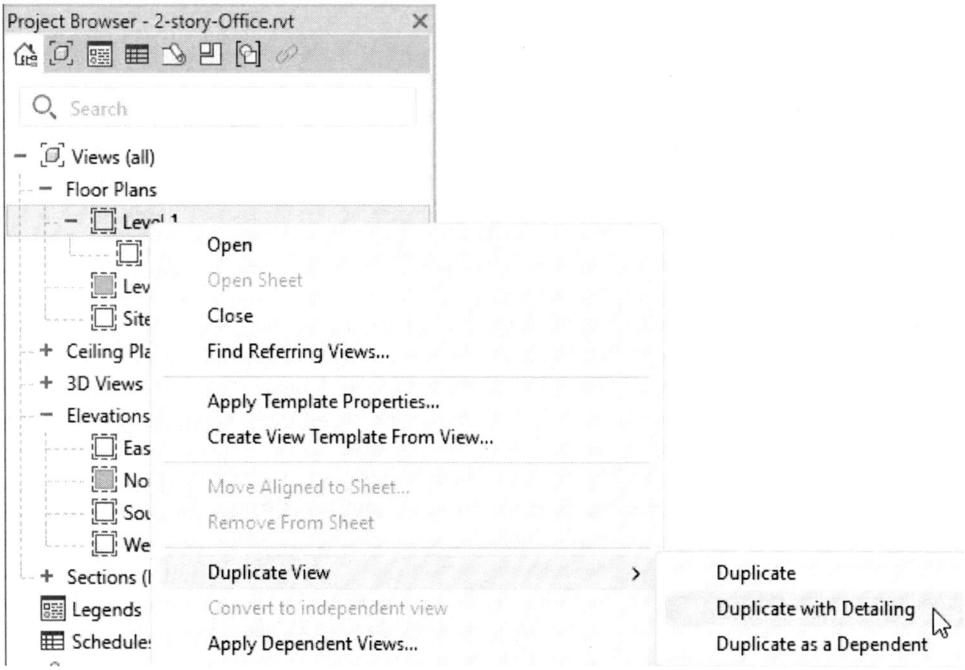

Figure 3–10

- To rename a view, slowly click twice on the view name so the text highlights, as shown in Figure 3–11. You can also right-click on a view name and select **Rename...**, or press <F2>.

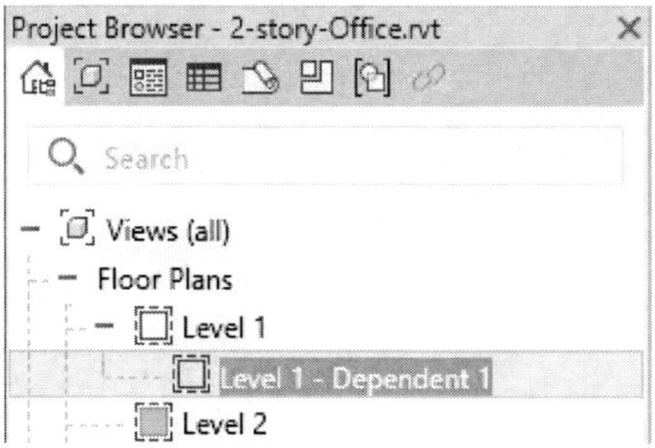

Figure 3–11

- Ceiling plans are typically created by default when you add a level with a view. If you do not want a level to have a ceiling plan, you can right-click on its name in the Project Browser and select **Delete**, as shown in Figure 3–12.

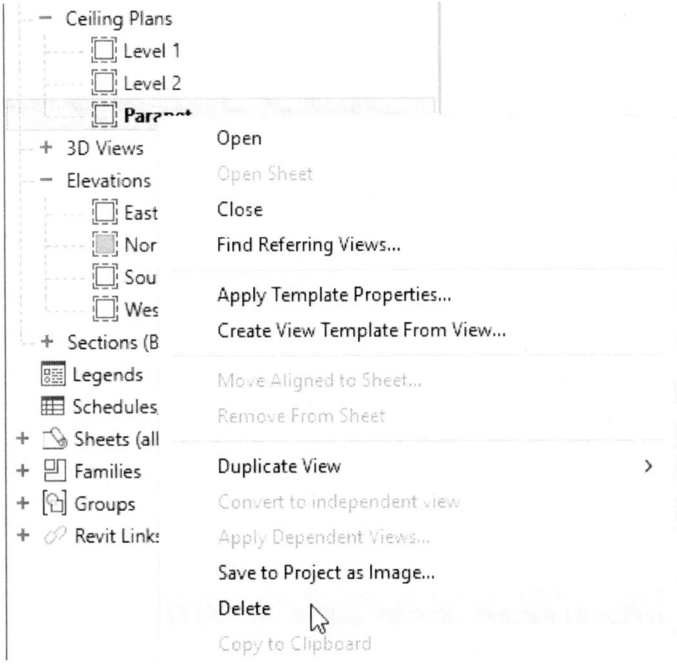

Figure 3–12

3.3 Modifying How the View Displays

Views are powerful tools that enable you to create multiple versions of a model without having to recreate building elements. For example, you can have views that are specifically used for working on the model, while other views are annotated and used for construction documents, as shown in Figure 3–13. Different disciplines can have different views that show only the features they require, as shown in Figure 3–13. Properties of one view can be independent of the properties in other views. Once you have modified how a view needs to display, you can create a view template and apply that template to other views.

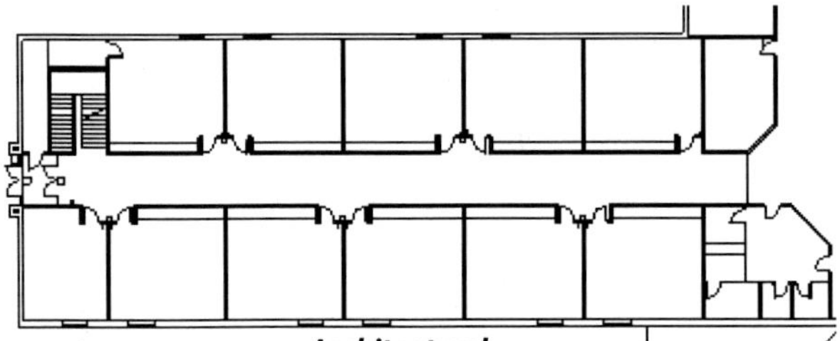

Architectural

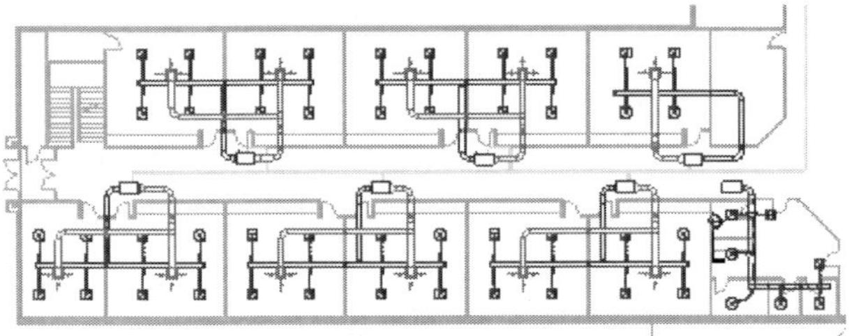

Mechanical

Figure 3–13

The view display can be modified in the following locations:

- View Control Bar
- Properties
- Shortcut menu
- *Visibility/Graphic Overrides* dialog box

View Control Bar

The most basic properties of a view are accessed using the View Control Bar (shown in Figure 3–14). These include the *Scale*, *Detail Level*, and *Visual Style* options. Additional options include temporary overrides and other advanced settings.

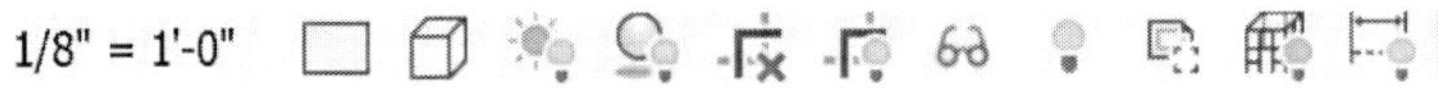

Figure 3–14

- The **Detail Level** controls whether you see compound structure of elements (**Coarse**) or full scale elements (**Medium** or **Fine**), as shown in Figure 3–15.

Medium/Fine ***Coarse***

Figure 3–15

View Properties

You can modify how a view displays by modifying the view's properties, as shown in Figure 3–16. These properties include *Underlays* and *View Range*, as well as many others. The *Discipline* of a view can also be set here.

- The options in Properties vary according to the type of view. A plan view has different properties than a 3D view.

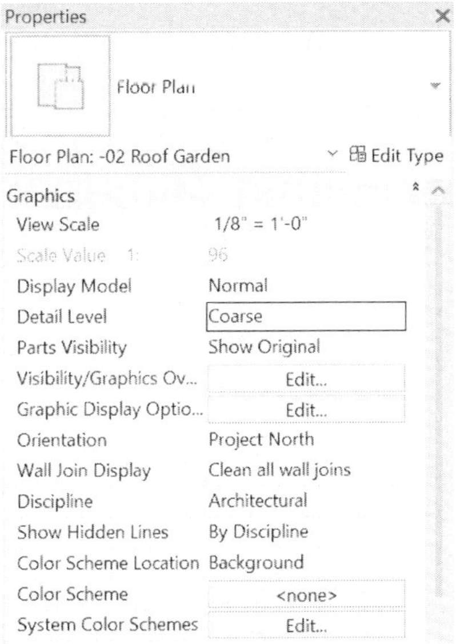

Figure 3–16

Setting an Underlay

Setting an *Underlay* is helpful if you need to display elements on a different level, such as the second floor plan shown with an underlay of the first floor plan in Figure 3–17. You can then use the elements to trace over or even copy to the current level of the view.

> ***Note:*** *Underlays are only available in Floor Plan and Ceiling Plan views.*

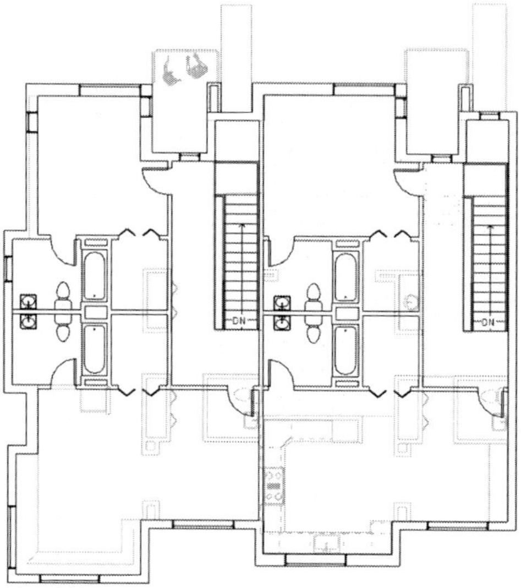

Figure 3–17

In Properties, in the *Underlay* section, specify the *Range: Base Level* and the *Range: Top Level*. You can also specify the *Underlay Orientation* to **Look down** or **Look up**, as shown in Figure 3–18.

Underlay	
Range: Base Level	Floor 2
Range: Top Level	Floor 3
Underlay Orientation	Look down

Figure 3–18

- To prevent moving elements in the underlay by mistake, turn off **Select Underlay Elements** by either expanding the *Select* panel title (shown in Figure 3–19) and clearing the checkbox or clicking (Select Underlay Elements) in the Status Bar to toggle it off ( ).

Figure 3–19

Setting the View Range

The *View Range* controls the cut planes that control the visibility of plan views, as shown in the *Sample View Range* key in Figure 3–20. Elements outside the cut planes do not display unless you include an underlay.

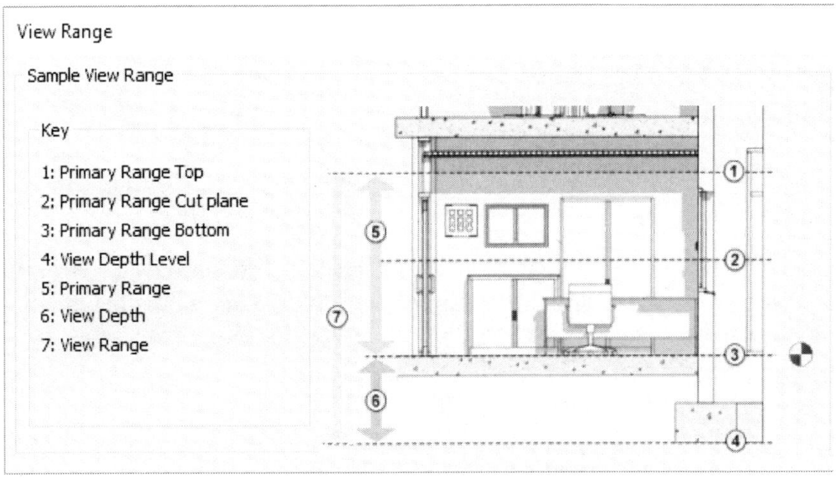

Figure 3–20

How To: Set the View Range

1. In Properties, in the *Extents* section beside *View Range*, select **Edit...**, or type **VR**.
2. In the *View Range* dialog box, as shown in Figure 3–21, modify the levels and offsets for the *Primary Range* and *View Depth*.
    - Click **<<Show** to display the *Sample View Range* key.
3. Click **OK**.

Figure 3–21

- If the settings used cannot be represented graphically, a warning displays, stating the inconsistency.
- A reflected ceiling plan (RCP) is created, as if the ceiling is reflected by a mirror on the floor, so that the ceiling is the same orientation as the floor plan. The cutline is placed just below the ceiling to ensure that any windows and doors below do not display.

Visibility/Graphic Overrides – Elements

The options in the *Visibility/Graphic Overrides* dialog box (shown in Figure 3–22) control how every category and sub-category of elements is displayed per view. You can toggle categories on and off, override the *Projection/Surface* and *Cut* information, set categories to *Halftone*, and change the *Detail Level*. To reduce the time it takes to find a category, you can use the *Category name search* to narrow down your search.

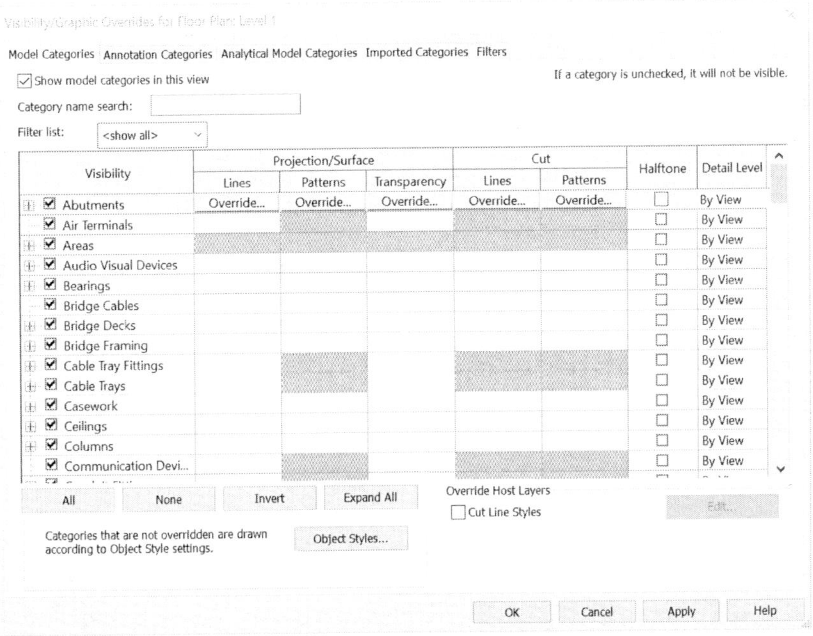

Figure 3–22

In the *View* tab>*Graphics* panel, click (Visibility/Graphics). To quickly open the *Visibility/ Graphic Overrides* dialog box, type **VV** or **VG**. It is also available in Properties: in the *Graphics* section, beside *Visibility/Graphic Overrides*, click **Edit...**.

- The visibility/graphic overrides are divided into the *Model*, *Annotation*, *Analytical Model*, *Imported*, and *Filters* categories.
- Other categories might be available if specific data has been included in the project, including *Design Options*, *Linked Files*, and *Worksets*.

- To limit the number of categories showing in the dialog box, you can select a discipline from the *Filter list* drop-down list, as shown in Figure 3–23.

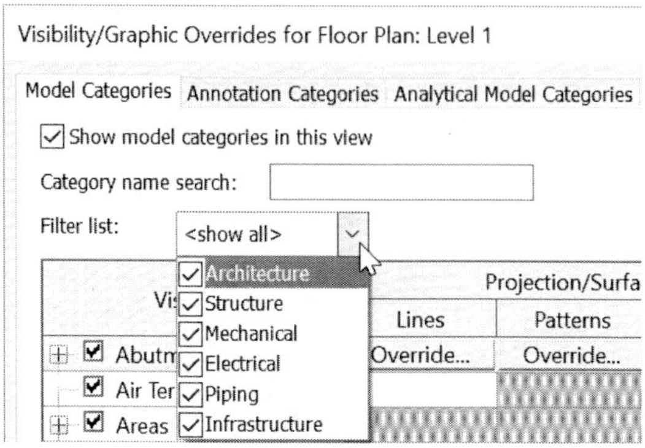

Figure 3–23

- To help you select categories, at the bottom of the *Visibility/Graphic Overrides* dialog box, use the **All**, **None**, and **Invert** buttons. The **Expand All** button displays all of the sub-categories.

Hiding and Overriding Graphics

There are additional ways to customize a view by hiding individual elements or a category in a view and by modifying how elements display graphically in a view by element or category (e.g., altering lineweight, color, or pattern).

An element is an individual object such as one wall or a piece of furniture in a view, while a category includes all instances of a selected element, such as all the walls or furniture in a view.

In the example shown in Figure 3–24, a furniture plan has been created by toggling off the structural grids category and then graying out all of the walls and columns.

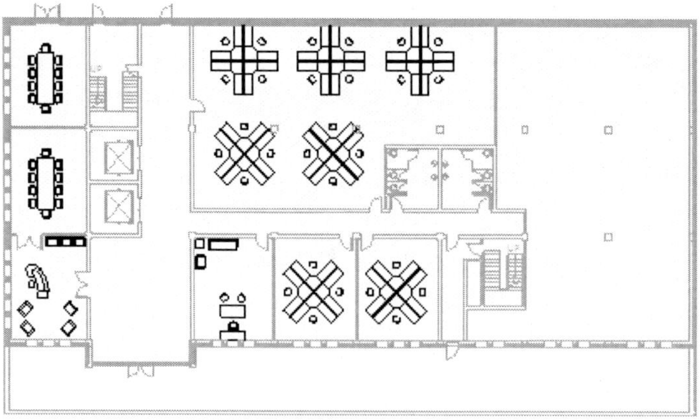

Figure 3–24

How To: Hide Elements or Categories in a View

1. Select the elements or categories you want to hide.
2. Right-click and select **Hide in View>Elements** or **Hide in View>Category**, as shown in Figure 3–25.
   - A quick way to hide entire categories is to select an element(s) and type **VH**.

   Note: *The elements or categories are hidden in the current view only.*

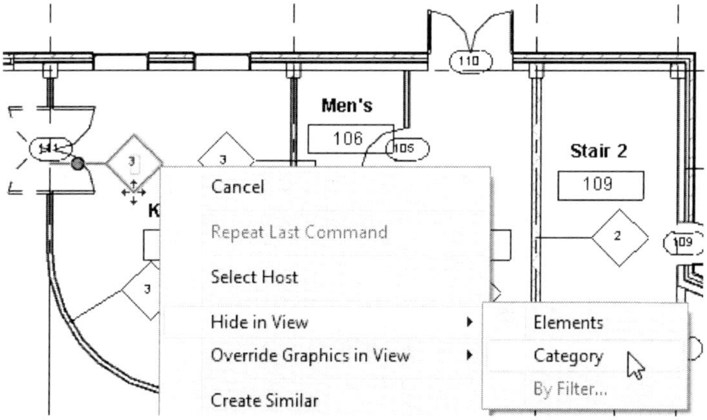

Figure 3–25

- If you select **Elements**, these overrides cannot be overwritten by view templates or within the *Visibility/Graphic Overrides* dialog box. The only way to display these hidden elements is to use **Reveal Hidden Elements** from the View Control Bar (see ***Reveal Hidden Elements*** on page *19*).
- If you select **Category**, these overrides can be removed by going into the *Visibility/Graphic Overrides* dialog box.

How To: Override Graphics of Elements or Categories in a View

1. Select the element(s) you want to modify.
2. Right-click and select **Override Graphics in View>By Element** or **By Category**.
   - If you select **By Element**, these overrides cannot be overwritten by view templates or within the *Visibility/Graphic Overrides* dialog box. You need to remember that you have overridden those element graphics in the view, then select those elements, right-click, and select **Override Graphics in View>By Element**, and reset or change the overrides to remove them.
   - If you select **By Category**, these overrides can be removed by going into the *Visibility/Graphic Overrides* dialog box.

3. The *View Specific Element* (or *Category*) *Graphics* dialog box opens, as shown in Figure 3–26. The exact options in the dialog box vary depending on the type of elements selected.

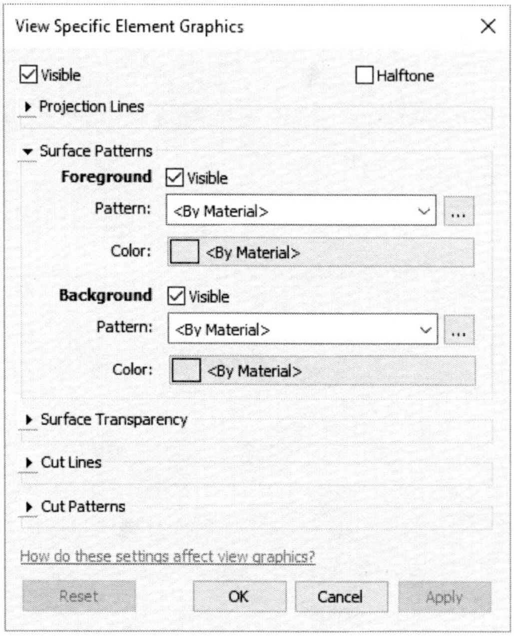

Figure 3–26

4. Select the changes you want to make and click **OK**.

View-Specific Options

- Clearing the **Visible** option is the same as hiding the elements or categories.
- Selecting the **Halftone** option grays out the elements or categories.
- The options for *Projection Lines* and *Cut Lines* include **Weight**, **Color**, and **Pattern**. The options for *Surface Patterns* and *Cut Patterns* include **Visibility**, **Pattern**, and **Color** for the *Foreground* and *Background*, as shown above in Figure 3–26.
- **Surface Transparency** can be set by moving the *Transparency* slider bar, as shown in Figure 3–27.

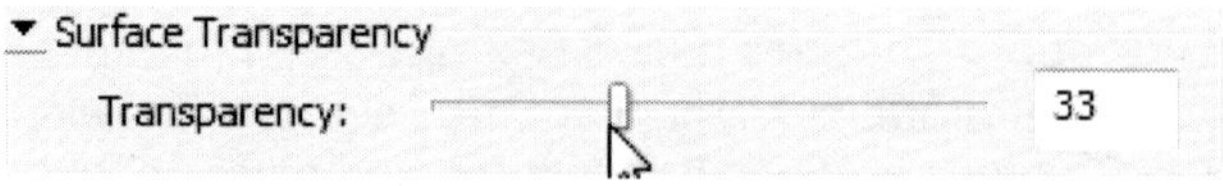

Figure 3–27

- The *View Specific Category Graphics* dialog box includes **Open the Visibility Graphics dialog...**, which opens the full dialog box of options.

Reveal Hidden Elements

If you have hidden links/imports or elements in a view by selecting them in the view and typing **VH**, by right-clicking and selecting **Hide in View**, or by turning them off inside the *Visibility/Graphic Overrides* dialog box, you can restore their visibility by selecting **Reveal Hidden Elements** in the View Control Bar.

1. In the View Control Bar, click (Reveal Hidden Elements). The border and all hidden elements are displayed in magenta, while visible elements in the view are grayed out, as shown in Figure 3–28.

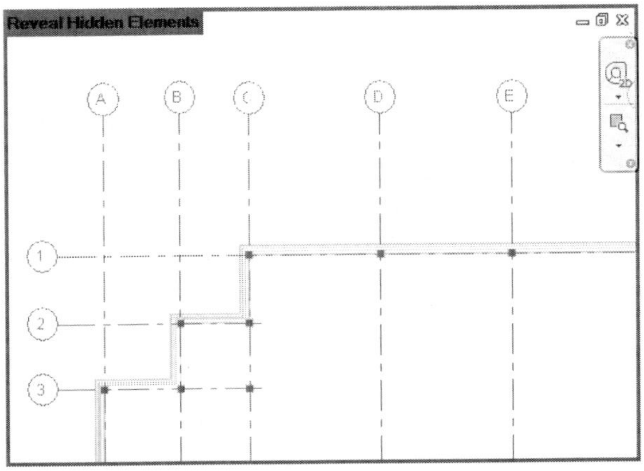

Figure 3–28

2. Select the hidden elements you want to restore, right-click, and select **Unhide in View>Elements** or **Unhide in View>Category**. Alternatively, in the *Modify* contextual tab>*Reveal Hidden Elements* panel, click (Unhide Element) or (Unhide Category).

- When you are finished, in the View Control Bar, click (Close Reveal Hidden Elements) or, in the *Modify* contextual tab>*Reveal Hidden Elements* panel, click (Toggle Reveal Hidden Elements Mode).

Working with Crop Regions

Plans, sections, elevations, and 3D views can all be modified by changing how much of the model is displayed in a view. One way to do this is to set the model crop region. If there are dimensions, tags, or text near the crop region, you can also use the annotation crop region to include these, as shown in Figure 3–29.

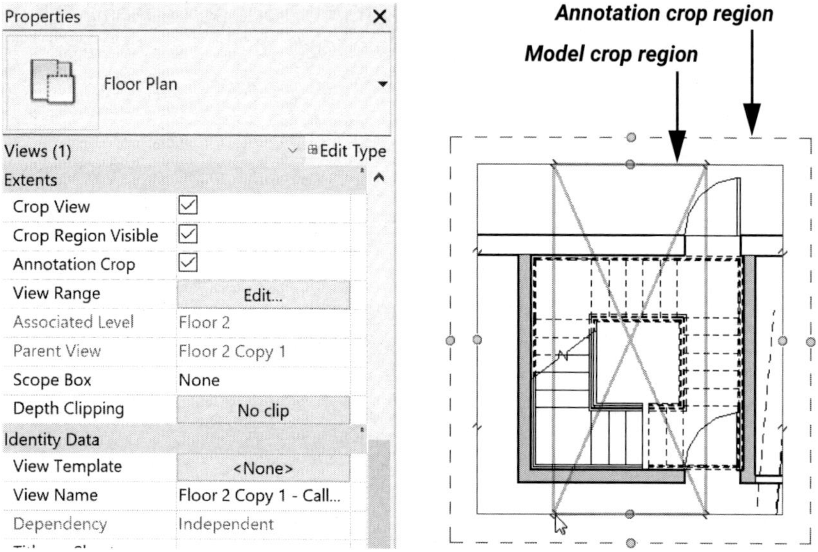

Figure 3–29

- To display the crop region, in the View Control Bar, click (Show Crop Region). Alternatively, in Properties, in the *Extents* section, select the checkbox next to *Crop Region Visible*. *Annotation Crop* is also available in this area.

  Note: *Zoom out if you do not see the crop region when you set it to be displayed.*

- It is best practice to hide a crop region before placing a view on a sheet. In the View Control Bar, click (Hide Crop Region).
- Resize the crop region using the control on each side of the region.
- Click (Break Line) control to split the view into two regions, horizontally or vertically. Each part of the view can then be modified in size to display what is needed and be moved independently.

  Note: *Breaking the crop region is typically used with sections or details.*

- The annotation crop region crops any annotation outside of the crop region and any annotations that it touches. If the model crop region crops an element that is tagged, the tag or annotation will automatically be cropped as well. You can turn on **Annotation Crop** and resize the crop region closer to the model crop region using the segment handles or by using the *Crop Region Size* dialog box, as shown in Figure 3–30. In the *Modify* contextual tab>*Crop* panel, click  (Size Crop) to open the dialog box.

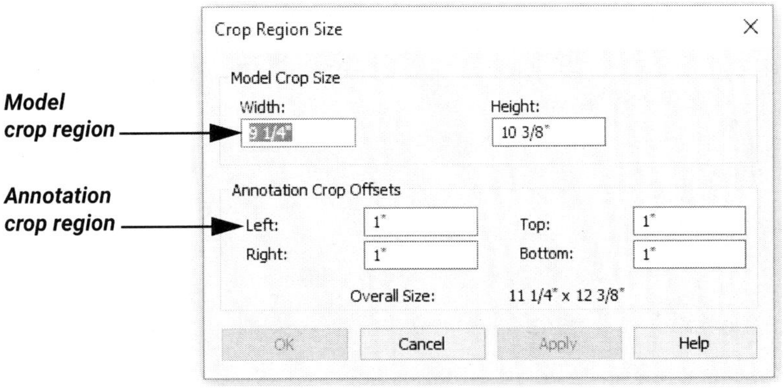

Figure 3–30

Plan Regions

When you have a plan view with multiple levels of floors or ceilings, you can create plan regions that enable you to set a different view range for part of a view (as shown in Figure 3–31 for a set of clerestory windows).

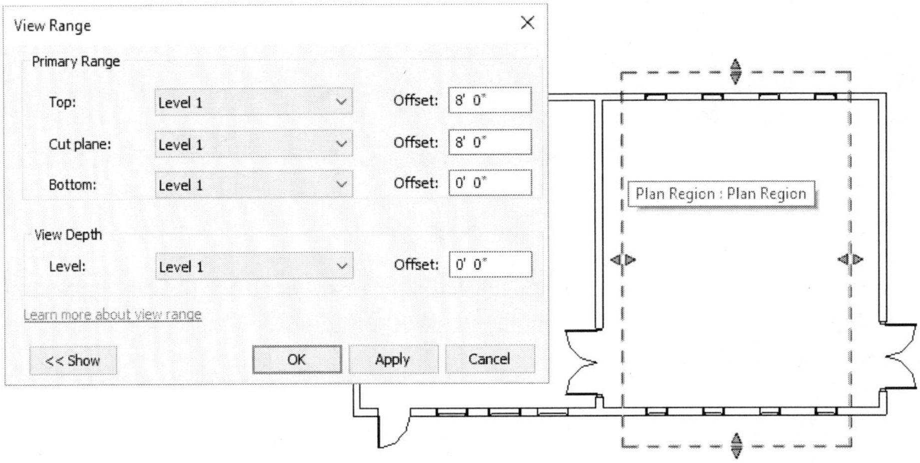

Figure 3–31

How To: Create Plan Regions

1. In a plan view, in the *View* tab>*Create* panel, expand (Plan Views) and select (Plan Region).
2. In the *Modify | Create Plan Region Boundary* tab>*Draw* panel, select a sketch tool and create the boundary for the plan region.
   - The boundary must be closed and cannot overlap other plan region boundaries, but the boundaries can be side by side.
3. In Properties, click **Edit...** next to *View Range*.
4. In the *View Range* dialog box, specify the offsets for the plan region and click **OK**. The plan region is applied to the selected area.
5. Click (Finish Edit Mode).

- Plan regions can be copied to the clipboard and then pasted into other plan views.
- You can use shape handles to resize plan region boundaries without having to edit the boundary.
- If a plan region is above a door, the door swing displays, but the door opening does not display, as shown in Figure 3–32.

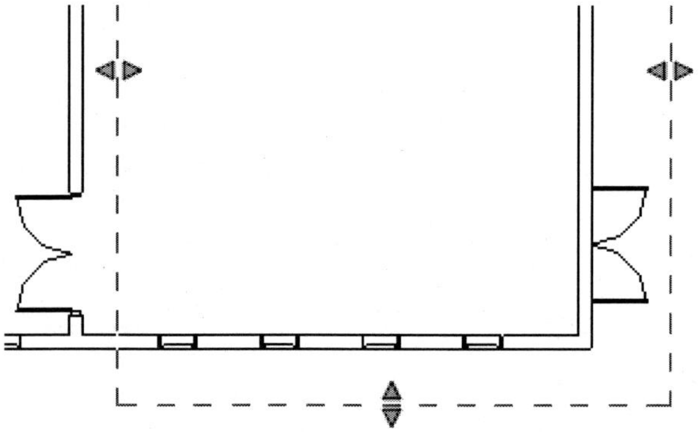

Figure 3–32

- Plan regions can be toggled on and off in the *Visibility/Graphic Overrides* dialog box on the *Annotation Categories* tab. If they are displayed, the plan regions are not included when printing and exporting.

Hint: Depth Clipping and Far Clipping

Depth Clipping (shown on the left in Figure 3–33) is a viewing option that sets how sloped walls are displayed if the *View Range* of a plan is set to a limited view. **Far Clipping** (shown on the right) is available for section and elevation views.

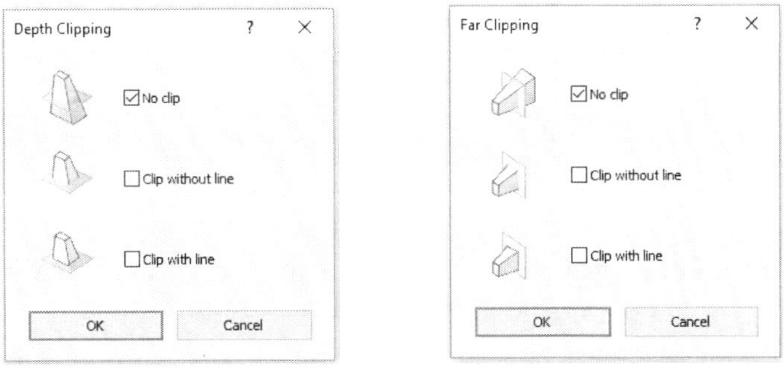

Figure 3–33

- An additional graphic display option enables you to specify *Depth Cueing*, so that items that are in the distance will be made lighter.

View Templates

A powerful way to use views effectively is to set up a view and then save it as a view template. You can apply view templates to views individually or through Properties. Setting the view template using Properties helps to ensure that you do not accidentally modify the view while interacting with it.

How To: Create a View Template from a View

1. Set up a view, as needed.
2. In the Project Browser, right-click on the view and select **Create View Template from View**. Alternatively, in the *View* tab>*Graphics* panel, expand **View Templates** and select **Create Template from Current View**.
3. In the *New View Template* dialog box, type in a name and click **OK**.
4. The new view template is listed in the *View Templates* dialog box. Make any modifications needed in the *View properties* section.
5. Click **OK**.

How To: Specify a View Template for a View

From Properties:

1. In the Project Browser, select the view or views to which you want to apply a view template.
2. In Properties, scroll down to the *Identity Data* section and click the button beside *View Template*.
3. In the *Assign View Template* dialog box, select a view template from the list and click **OK**.

From the Project Browser:

1. In the Project Browser, select one or more similar views (e.g., plan views), right-click, and select **Apply Template Properties...**. Alternatively, in the *View* tab>*Graphic* panel, expand **View Templates** and select **Apply Template Properties to Current View**.
2. In the *Apply View Template* dialog box, select the view template from the list, as shown in Figure 3–34, and click **OK**.

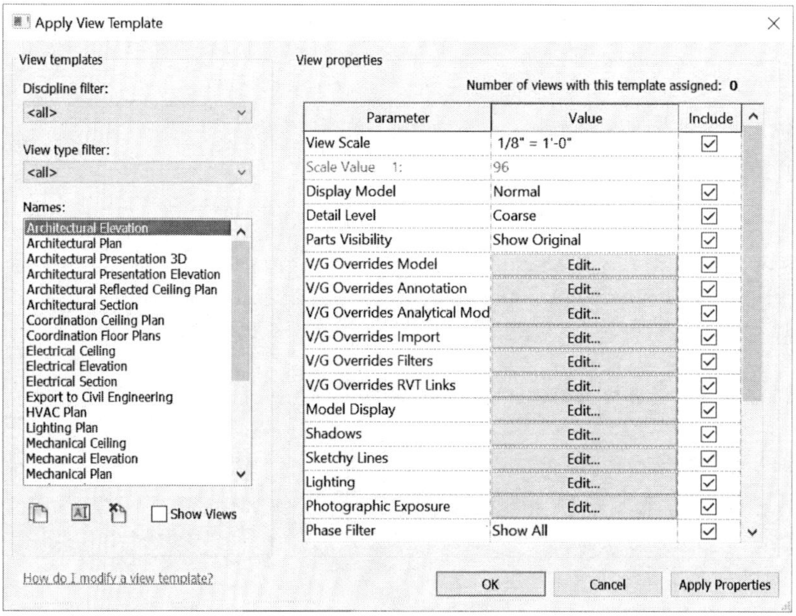

Figure 3–34

From the View Control Bar:

1. In the View Control Bar, click (Temporary View Properties).
2. If you select **Enable Temporary View Properties**, you can modify the view's instance properties.
3. If you select **Temporarily Apply Template Properties...**, in the *Temporarily Apply Template Properties* dialog box, select a view template and click **OK** to temporarily apply a view template to a view.

   Note: *If any view templates have been applied previously, there will be a Recent Templates section displaying the recently used view templates, as shown in Figure 3–35.*

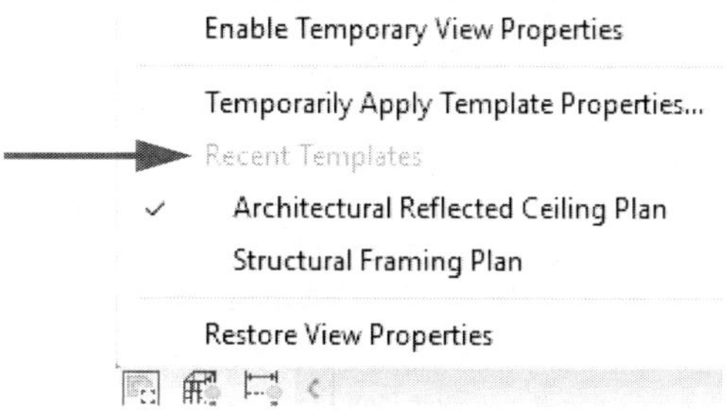

Figure 3–35

- A colored border will display with *Temporary View Properties* in the upper-left corner of the view.
- To disable temporary view properties mode, click (Temporary View Properties) and select **Restore View Properties**.

Practice 3a
Duplicate Views and Set the View Display

Practice Objectives

- Duplicate and rename views.
- Hide elements in views.
- Modify the graphic display of elements in views.

In this practice, you will duplicate views and then modify them by changing the scale, hiding elements, and changing other elements to halftone to prepare them to be used in construction documents. The finished views of the second floor are shown in Figure 3–36.

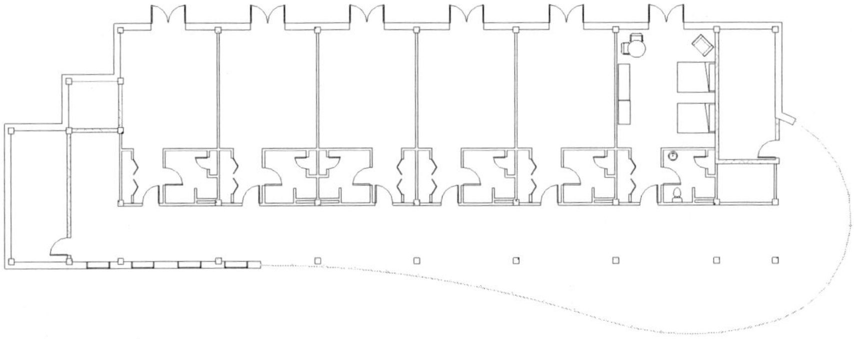

Figure 3–36

- Elements have been added to this model to demonstrate what happens when working with views.

Task 1: Duplicate and modify the Floor 1 floor plan view.

1. Open the project **Arch-Display.rvt** from the practice files folder.
2. Close any other projects you may have open.
3. Open the **Floor Plans: Floor 1** view. This view shows the room and door tags.
4. In the Project Browser, right-click on the **Floor Plans: Floor 1** view and select **Duplicate View>Duplicate with Detailing**. This creates a view with all the tags, grids, and elevation markers.
5. In the Project Browser, slowly click twice on the duplicated view name. Rename it **Floor 1 - Reference Plan** and press <Enter> or click in an empty area in the view to apply the change. You will use this view later to place callouts and sections.

6. In the Project Browser, right-click on the **Floor Plans: Floor 1** view and select **Duplicate View>Duplicate**. This creates a view without all of the tags, but includes the grids and elevation markers.
7. Rename it to **Floor 1 - Overall Plan**.
8. With the **Floor 1 - Overall Plan** view active, in the View Control Bar, change the *Scale* to **1/16"=1'-0"** by clicking on the current viewport scale and selecting the new scale from the list.
   - All of the annotations become larger, as they need to plot correctly at this scale.
9. Activate the 3D view by clicking its tab along the top of the view.
10. Type **WT** to tile the four open windows and then type **ZA** to zoom out to fit all the view in their new windows. Compare the various floor plans.
11. Save the project.

Task 2: Duplicate and modify the Floor 2 floor plan view.

1. With the 3D view still active, type **TW** to return to the tab views and type **ZA** to zoom to fit the view.
2. Click the X, as shown in Figure 3–37, to close the **Floor 1 - Overall Plan** and **Floor 1 - Reference Plan** views. (Your views may differ from what is in the image below.)

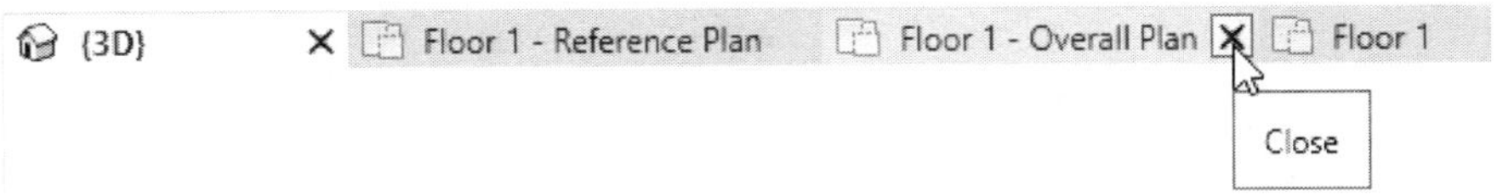

Figure 3–37

3. Open the **Floor Plans: Floor 2** view. Note that the view displays door and room tags, as well as the CAD and Revit linked files.
4. In the Project Browser, right-click on the **Floor 2** view and select **Duplicate View>Duplicate**. This creates a new view without any annotations or the CAD file.
5. Rename this view to **Typical Guest Room Plan** and press <Enter>.
6. Type **VV** to open the *Visibility/Graphic Overrides* dialog box. On the *Revit Links* tab, clear the checkbox in the *Visibility* column for the **Hotel-Pool.rvt** option.
7. Select the *Annotation Categories* tab, scroll down in the *Visibility* column list, and clear the checkbox for the **Grids** option.
8. Click **OK**.
9. Select everything in the view with a crossing window. In the *Modify | Multi-Select* tab> *Selection* panel, click  (Filter).
10. In the *Filter* dialog box, click **Check None**, then only check the check boxes for **Curtain Panels, Curtain Wall Grids**, and **Curtain Wall Mullions**.

11. Click **OK**.
12. With all the curtain walls selected, right-click and select **Override Graphics in View>By Category...**.
13. In the *View Specific Category Graphics* dialog box, select **Halftone** and click **OK**. The curtain walls are now halftone.
14. Click in an empty space in the view to release the selection.
15. Save and close the project.

End of practice

3.4 Adding Callout Views

Callouts are details of plan, elevation, or section views. When you place a callout in a view, as shown on the left in Figure 3–38, it automatically creates a new view clipped to the boundary of the callout, as shown on the right. You can create rectangular or sketched callout boundaries or reference an existing view.

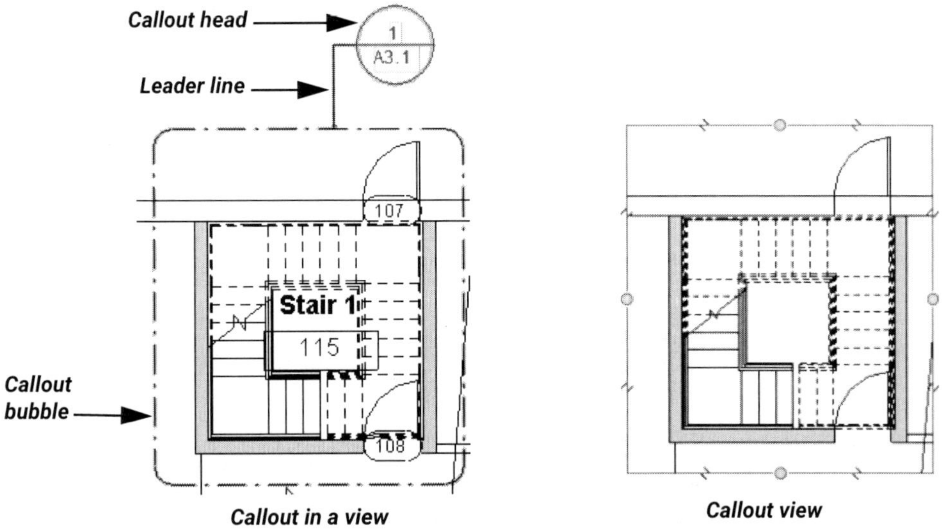

Figure 3–38

- When using the option to reference an existing view, Revit will not create a new callout view in the project as it is simply referencing a view to help further show design intent.
- Callout views are saved in the same section in the Project Browser as the original view. For example, the callout view of a floor plan is placed within the *Floor Plans* section.
- To open the callout view, double-click on its name in the Project Browser or on the callout head (verify that the callout bubble is not selected before you double-click on it).

How To: Create a Rectangular Callout

1. In the *View* tab>*Create* panel, click (Callout).
2. Select points for two opposite corners to define the callout bubble around the area you want to detail.
3. Select the callout bubble and use the shape handles to modify the location of the bubble and any other edges that might need changing.
4. In the Project Browser, rename the callout view, if needed.

How To: Create a Sketched Callout

1. In the *View* tab>*Create* panel, expand (Callout) and click (Sketch).
2. Sketch the shape of the callout bubble using the tools in the *Modify | Edit Profile* tab>*Draw* panel, as shown in Figure 3–39.

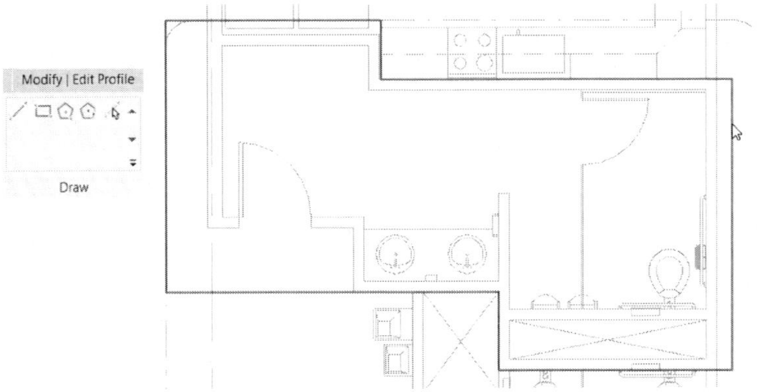

Figure 3–39

3. Click (Finish) to complete the boundary.
4. Select the callout bubble and use the shape handles to modify the location of the bubble and any other edges that might need to be changed.
5. In the Project Browser, rename the callout view, if needed.

Modifying Callouts

Callouts are cropped versions of the original view. When you modify them, you are changing the crop region of the view.

- You can select the callout bubble then the **Drag Head** grip of the callout marker (as shown in Figure 3–40) to move the callout head to a different location. You can modify the leader landing by dragging the grip at the landing.

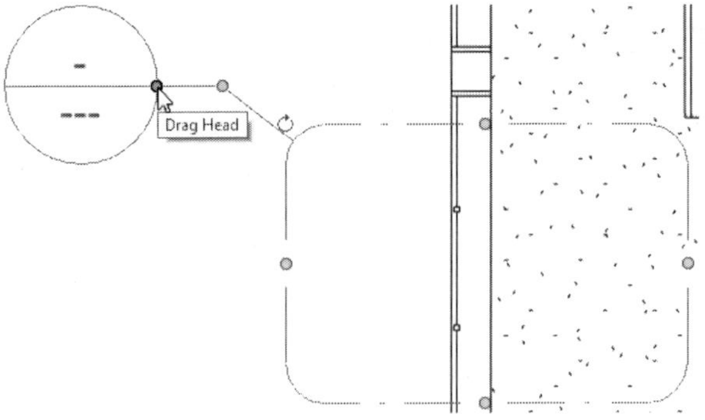

Figure 3–40

In the callout view, you can modify the crop region with shape handles and view breaks, as shown in Figure 3–41. If you change the size of the callout bubble in the original view, it automatically updates the callout view and vice-versa.

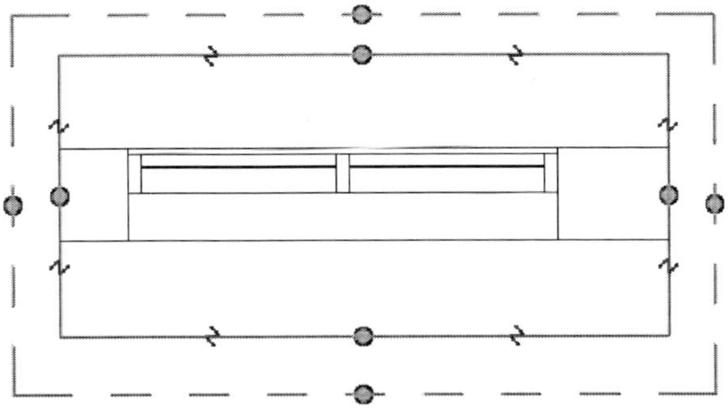

Figure 3–41

How To: Edit the Callout's Crop Region

1. Select the crop region.
2. In the *Modify | Views* tab>*Mode* panel, click (Edit Crop). Reshape the crop region boundary, as needed.
3. Click (Finish) to complete the boundary.

- If you want to return a modified crop region to the original rectangular configuration, click (Reset Crop).

Callout View Associations

In a callout view, you can specify in Properties where the callout will show, in either **Intersecting Views** or just the **Parent View Only**, as shown in Figure 3–42.

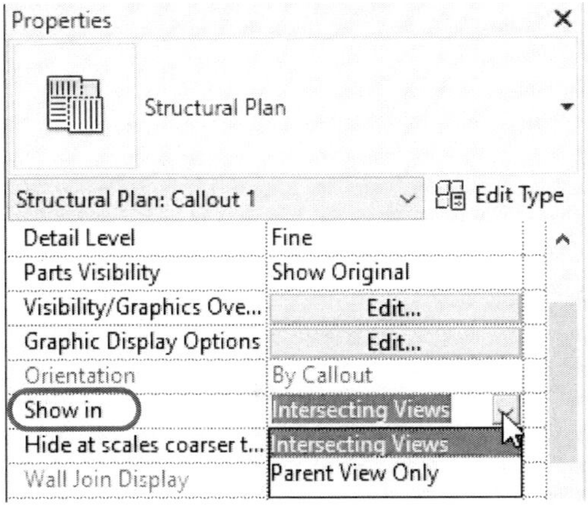

Figure 3–42

Callout views can be preserved if the parent view is deleted. Open the callout view and, in Properties, set the *Parent View* to **<none>**, as shown in Figure 3–43.

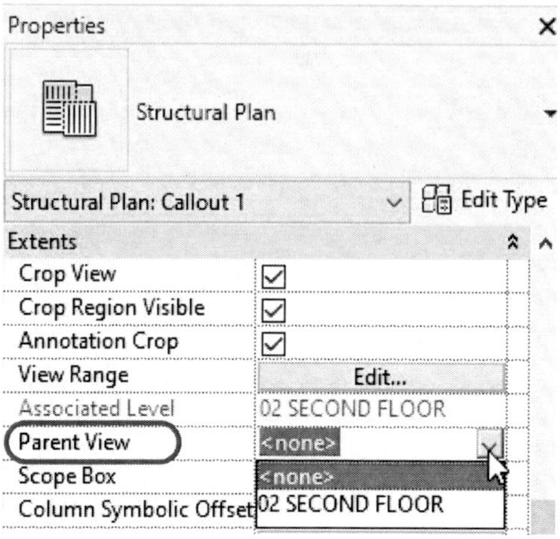

Figure 3–43

If a parent view is deleted, a *Dependent Callouts* dialog box will appear, as shown in Figure 3–44, asking if you want to make the callout view that is associated with the deleted parent view an independent view or delete it.

Note: *Click* ***Show details*** *to get more information about the associated callout view(s).*

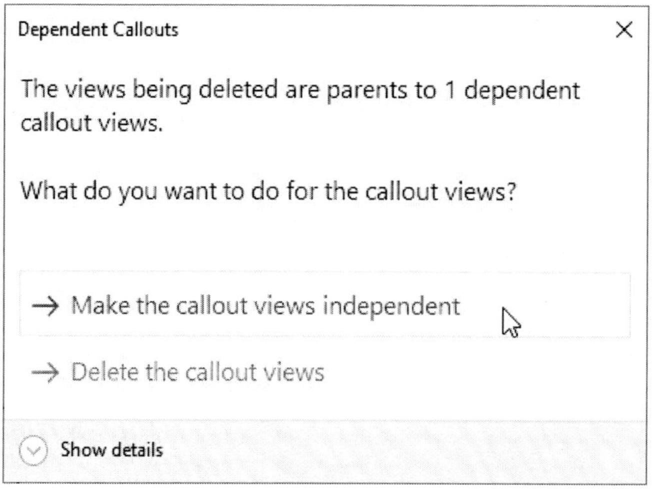

Figure 3–44

If a parent view is deleted, the callout view's *Show in* property defaults to **Intersecting Views** and is grayed out.

Practice 3b
Add Callout Views

Practice Objectives

- Modify crop regions.
- Create callouts.
- Override visibility and graphic styles in views.
- Create view templates.

In this practice, you will create callout views of a guest room and make modifications to the visibility graphics so that one displays the furniture and the other does not. Figure 3–45 shows Floor 1 with callouts completed. Then, you will create view templates from the view to use in other practices. You will also add callout views for other areas that need enlarged plans.

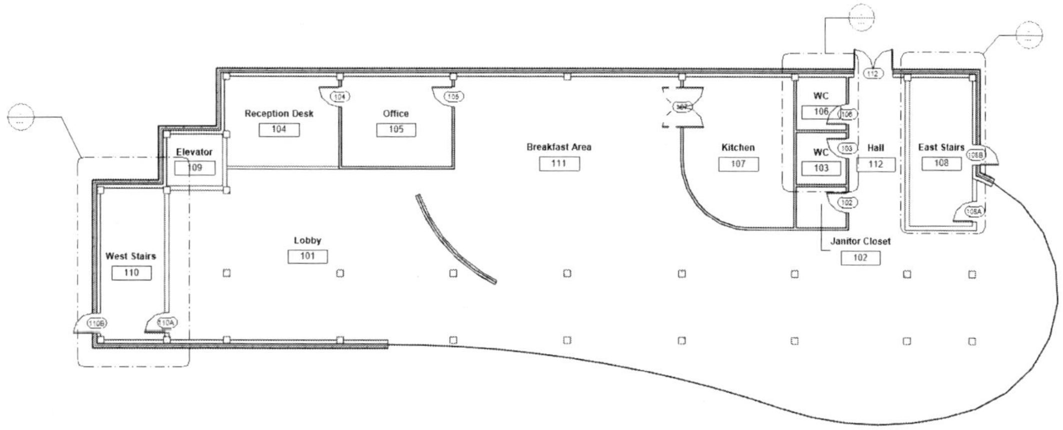

Figure 3–45

- Furniture and dimensions have been added to this model to demonstrate what happens when working with views.

Task 1: Add callout views.

1. Open the project **Arch-Callouts.rvt** from the practice files folder.
2. Open the **Floor Plans: Typical Guest Room Plan** view. (Dimensions, furniture, and plumbing fixtures have been added to one of the guest rooms.)
   - Note that the *Scale* is set to **1/8"=1'-0"**.

3. In the *View* tab>*Create* panel, expand (Callout) and select (Rectangle).
4. In the Type Selector, verify that **Floor Plan** is selected.
5. Place a callout around the guest room with furniture, as shown in Figure 3–46, by clicking the upper-left corner of the room as the first pick and the lower-right corner of the room (including the bathroom) as the second pick.
6. Select the callout to display the grips. Hold and drag the grips to adjust the callout bubble, callout head, and leader line, as needed.

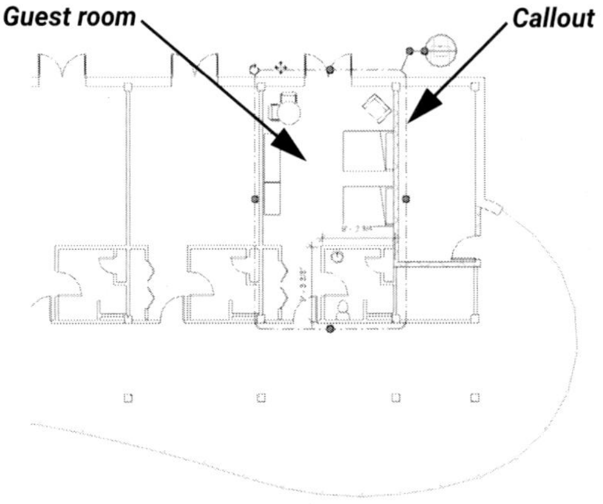

Figure 3–46

7. Click in an empty space in the view to release the selection.
8. Double-click on the callout head to display the view. Note that the *Scale* is automatically set to **1/4"=1'-0"**, as it is a partial plan view.
9. In the Project Browser within the *Floor Plans* section, rename the Typical Guest Room Plan - Callout 1 view to **Typical Guest Room - Furniture Plan**. Note that the dimensions do not display because callouts will not copy them from the original view.
10. Save the project.

Task 2: Override graphics in views.

1. Click the *Typical Guest Room Plan* view tab to make it the active view.
2. Open the *Visibility/Graphic Overrides* dialog box by typing **VV**.

3. In the dialog box, on the *Model Categories* tab, set the *Filter list* to **Architecture** (by clearing the checkmarks for the other options). In the *Visibility* column, clear **Casework** (as shown in Figure 3–47), **Furniture**, **Furniture Systems**, and **Plumbing Fixtures** (not shown).

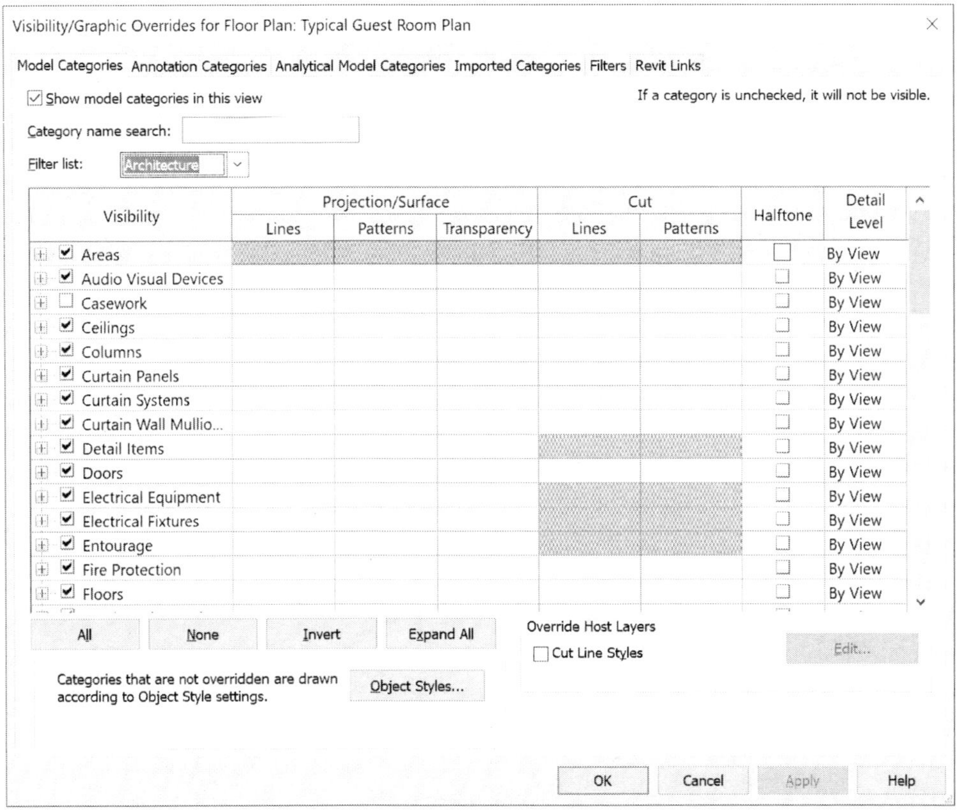

Figure 3–47

4. Click **OK**. The furniture and plumbing fixtures are removed from the view, but the dimensions still display.

5. Click the *Typical Guest Room - Furniture Plan* view tab to make it the active view. Note that the furniture and plumbing fixtures still show in this view.

6. Open the *Visibility/Graphic Overrides* dialog box. On the *Model Categories* tab, at the bottom of the table, click **All** and place a checkmark in one of the *Halftone* columns. Click **Apply**. All of the elements are set to halftone.

7. Click **None** to clear all categories that are selected.

8. In the *Halftone* column, clear the checkboxes for the **Casework**, **Furniture**, **Furniture Systems**, and **Plumbing Fixtures** categories.

9. Click **Apply** to set the changes without exiting the dialog box.

10. In the *Annotation Categories* tab, clear the checkbox for **Show annotation categories in this view**, as shown in Figure 3–48. No annotation elements will display in this view even if they are added in other views of this part of the model.

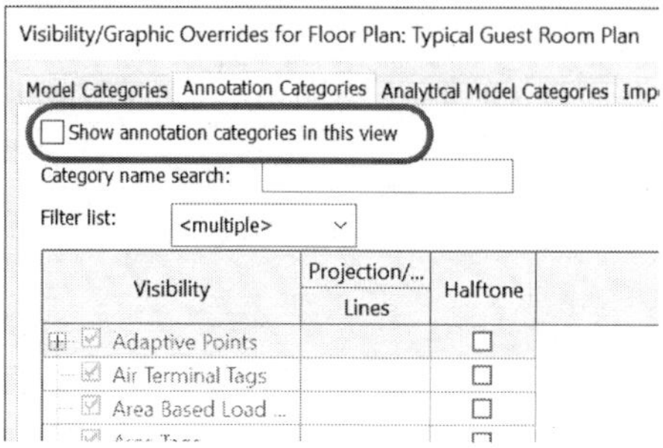

Figure 3–48

11. Click **OK** to close the dialog box. The view should display as shown in Figure 3–49.

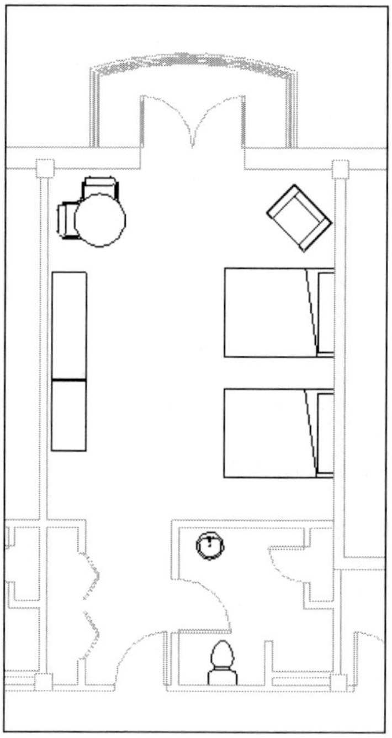

Figure 3–49

12. Save the project.

Task 3: Create a view template.

1. In the Project Browser, right-click on the **Typical Guest Room Plan** view and select **Create View Template From View...**.
2. In the *New View Template* dialog box, type **Dimension Plan** and click **OK**.
3. In the *View Templates* dialog box, click **OK**.
4. Repeat creating a view template but using the **Typical Guest Room - Furniture Plan** view. Name the new view template **Furniture Plan**.
    - Creating a view template from a view can be used on other plan views as needed.
5. Save the project.

Task 4: Create additional callouts.

1. Open the **Floor Plans: Floor 1 - Reference Plan** view.
2. In the *View* tab>*Create* panel, click (Callout) and add floor plan callouts to the stairs and restrooms areas, as shown in Figure 3–50.
3. In the Project Browser, rename the created callout views as shown in Figure 3–50 (grids have been hidden in the figure for clarity).

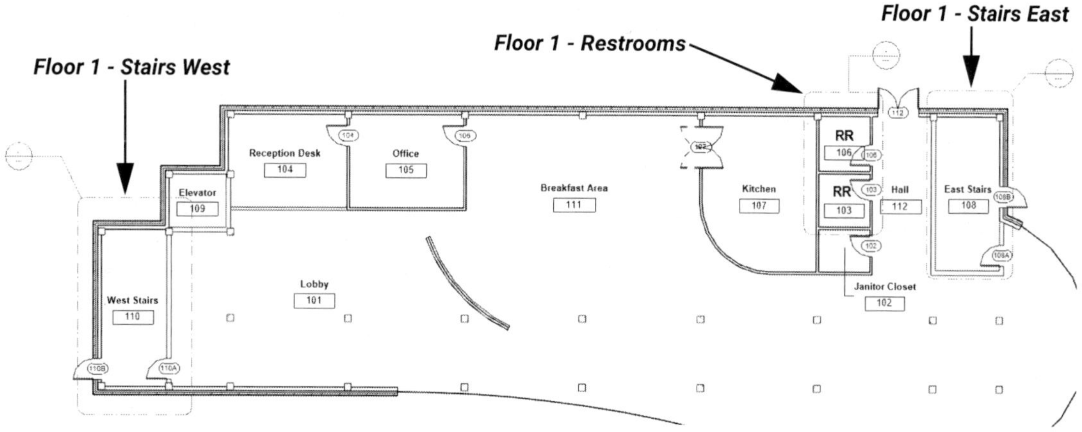

Figure 3–50

4. Save and close the project.

End of practice

3.5 Creating Elevations and Sections

Elevations and sections are critical elements of construction documents and can assist you as you are working on a model. Any changes made in one of these views (such as the section in Figure 3–51) changes the entire model, and any changes made to the project model are also displayed in the elevations and sections.

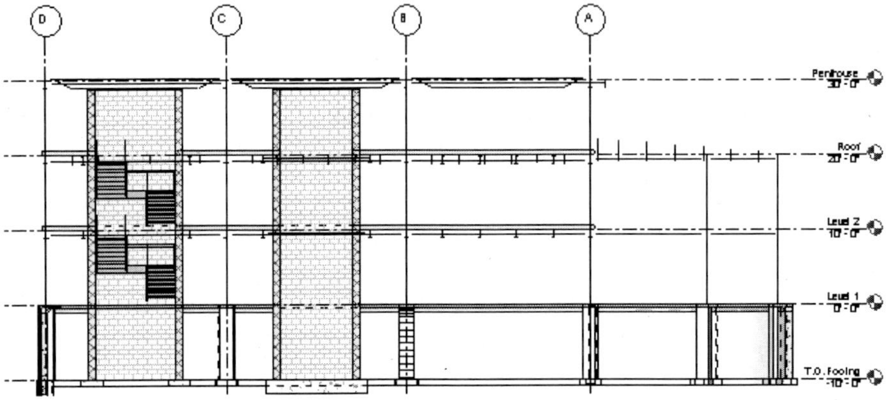

Figure 3–51

In the Project Browser, elevations are separated by elevation type and sections are separated by section type, as shown in Figure 3–52. To open an elevation or section view, double-click on the marker's arrowhead or on its name in the Project Browser.

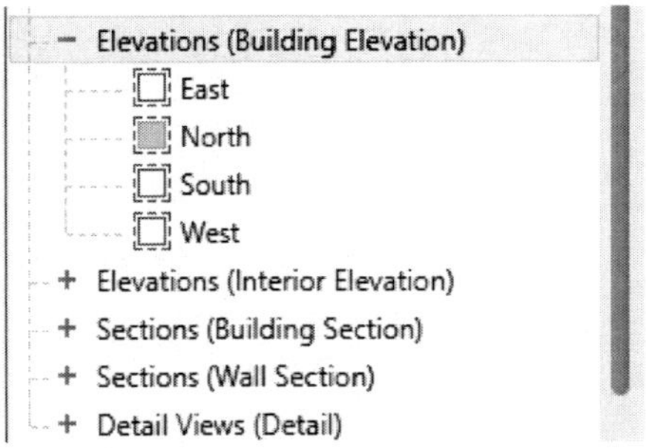

Figure 3–52

Elevations

Elevations are *face-on* views of the interiors or exteriors of a building. Four exterior building elevation views are defined in the default template: **North**, **South**, **East**, and **West**. You can create additional building elevation views at other angles or interior elevation views. When you place an elevation marker, a new elevation view is created. When selecting an elevation marker's arrowhead in the view, you will see the elevation line, handles, shape controls, and elevation view region, as shown in Figure 3–53. Double-click on the arrowhead to open the view. You can also choose to reference an existing view instead of creating a new one. In this case, double-clicking on the elevation marker's arrowhead will open the referenced view, but you will not see the elevation view region or its controls.

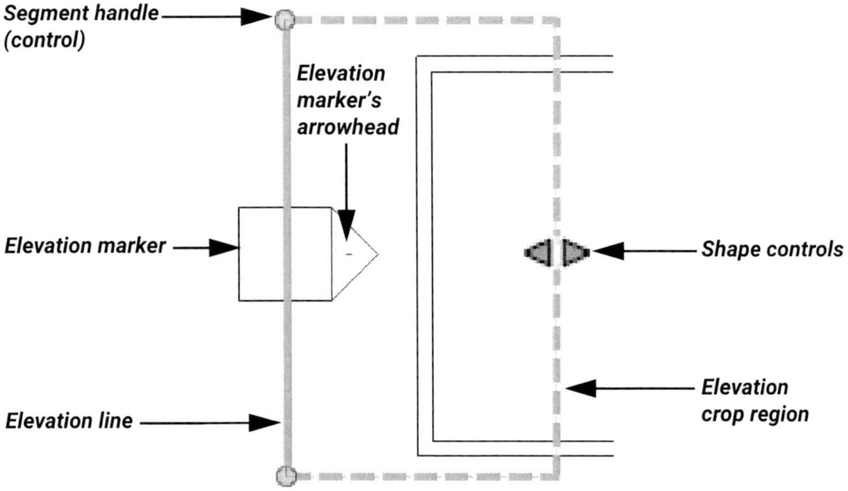

Figure 3–53

There are two types of elevations that you can create from the **Elevation** command: **Building Elevation** is typically used on the exterior of a building and **Interior Elevation** is typically used on the interior of a building. Elevation markers must be placed in plan views. When you add an elevation view to a sheet, the detail and sheet number are automatically added to the view title and elevation marker. When you rename the elevation in the Project Browser, the name changes on the elevation marker's arrowhead.

How To: Create an Elevation

1. In the *View* tab>*Create* panel, expand (Elevation) and click (Elevation).

   Note: *The software remembers the last elevation type used, so you can click the top button if you want to use the same elevation command.*

2. In the Type Selector, select the elevation type: **Building Elevation** or **Interior Elevation**.
3. Move the cursor near one of the walls that defines the elevation. The marker follows the angle of the wall.

4. Click to place the marker. To give the elevation a new name, in the Project Browser either slowly click twice on the name or right-click on it and select **Rename...**, or in Properties, change the *View Name* in the *Identity Data* section.

- The length, width, and height of an elevation are defined by the walls and ceiling/floor at which the elevation marker is pointing.
- When creating interior elevations, ensure that the floor or ceiling above is in place before creating the elevation or you will need to modify the elevation crop region so that the elevation markers do not show on all floors.

How To: Create an Elevation That References an Existing View

1. Start the **Elevation** command.
2. In the *Modify | Elevation* tab>*Reference* panel, check the **Reference Other View** checkbox, expand the drop-down list, and select a view, as shown in Figure 3–54. If the list of views is too long, use the search to narrow down the list of views.
    - Note that if you do not select a view and just keep **<New Drafting View>** selected, you will create a new drafting view. The elevation will reference the new drafting view in the *Drafting Views* section of the Project Browser. Refer to ***Chapter 17 Creating Details*** for more information on drafting views.

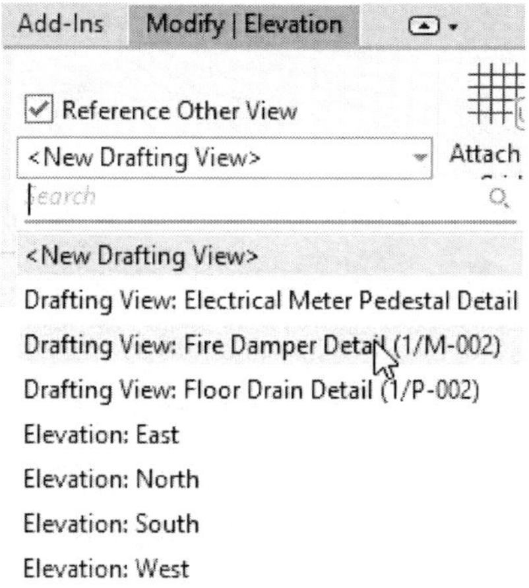

Figure 3–54

3. Place the elevation in the view.

Sections

Sections are slices through a model, and can be created through an entire building, through a wall, or to create a detail. Each section type has its own graphic display and appears in a different section of the Project Browser. They can be created in plan, elevation, and other section views. Figure 3–55 shows all the components of a section. Double-clicking on the arrowhead will open the section view. You can flip, resize, or split a section using the controls, and you can rename the section view that is shown in the Project Browser in the same ways you can rename an elevation view.

- When placing a section, you can reference an existing view. In this case, double-clicking on the section marker's arrowhead will open the referenced view, and you will not get the shape controls to adjust the view depth of the section.

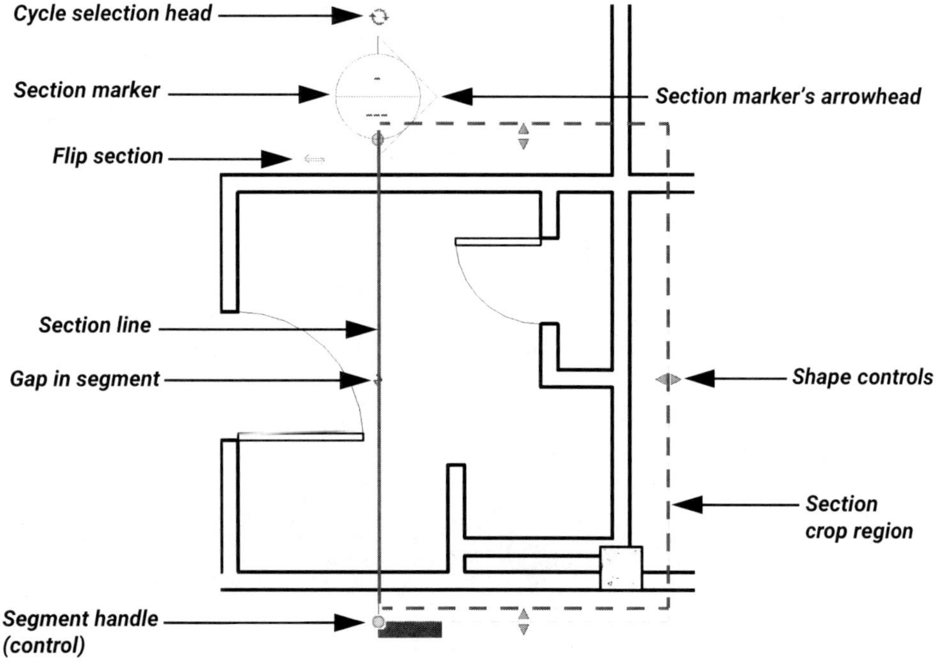

Figure 3–55

How To: Create a Section

1. In the *View* tab>*Create* panel or in the Quick Access Toolbar, click (Section).
2. In the Type Selector, select **Section: Building Section** or **Section: Wall Section**. If you want a section in a drafting view, select **Detail View: Detail.**
3. In the view, select a point where you want to locate the crop region and section marker.
4. Select the second or end point that defines the section.

5. The shape controls display. You can flip the arrow and change the size of the cutting plane, as well as the location of the bubble and flag.

- When placing a section you can snap to other elements in the model as the start and end points of the section line. You can also use the modify tools, such as the **Align** command, to reorient a section line to an element such as an angled wall.
- Section lines can also be used as an alignment object and can be snapped to when placing other geometry.

How To: Create a Section That References an Existing View

1. Start the **Section** command.
2. In the *Modify | Section* tab>*Reference* panel, check the **Reference Other View** checkbox, expand the drop-down list, and select a view, as shown in Figure 3–56. If the list of views is too long, you can use the search to narrow it down.
    - Note that if you do not select a view and just keep **<New Drafting View>** selected, you will create a new drafting view. The section will reference the new drafting view in the *Drafting Views* section of the Project Browser. Refer to ***Chapter 17 Creating Details*** for more information on drafting views.

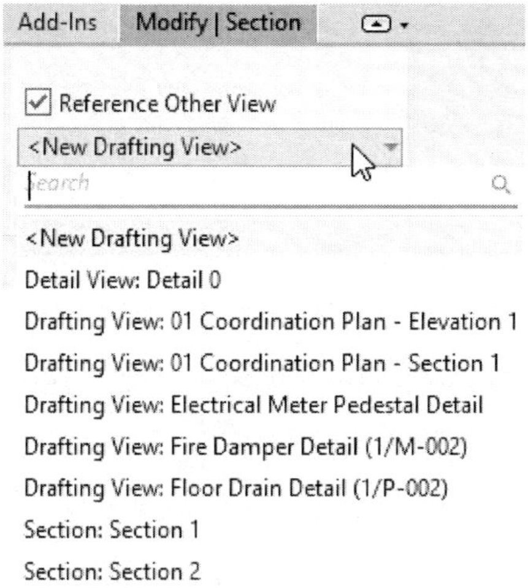

Figure 3–56

3. Place the section in the view.

Modifying Elevations and Sections

There are two parts to modifying elevations and sections:

- To modify the markers (as shown in Figure 3–57), in the plan view, select the arrowhead (triangle) part of the section marker and use the segment handles to change the length and depth of elevations and sections. You can also modify the crop region, split the crop region segment, and split the crop region with a gap.

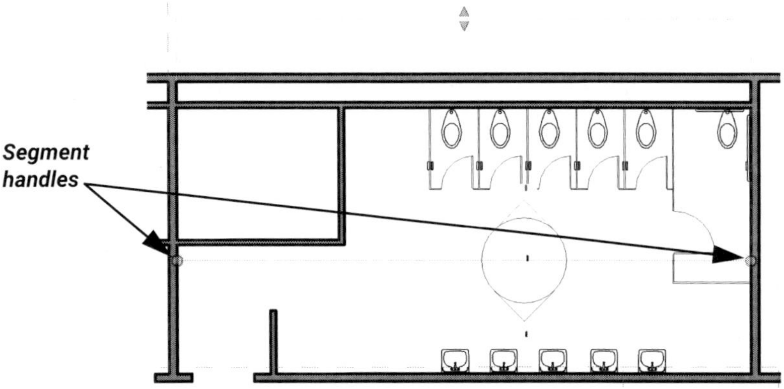

Figure 3–57

- To modify the view (as shown in Figure 3–58), select the crop region and use the segment handles to modify the size or create view breaks.

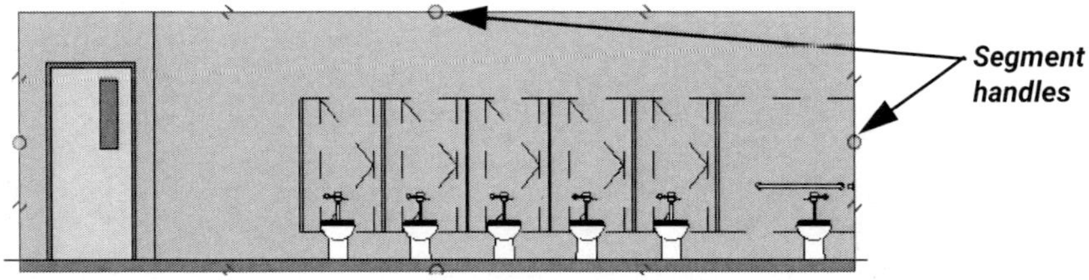

Figure 3–58

Modifying Elevation Markers

When you modify elevation markers, you can specify the length and depth of the clip plane, as shown in Figure 3–59.

- Select the arrowhead of either the interior or building elevation marker (not the circle or square portion) to display the clip plane.
- Drag the round shape handles to lengthen or shorten the elevation.
- Adjust the (Drag) shape controls to modify the depth of the elevation.

To display additional elevations from one marker, select the circle or square portion (not the arrowhead) and place a checkmark in the **Show Arrow** box in the directions that you want to display, as shown in Figure 3–59.

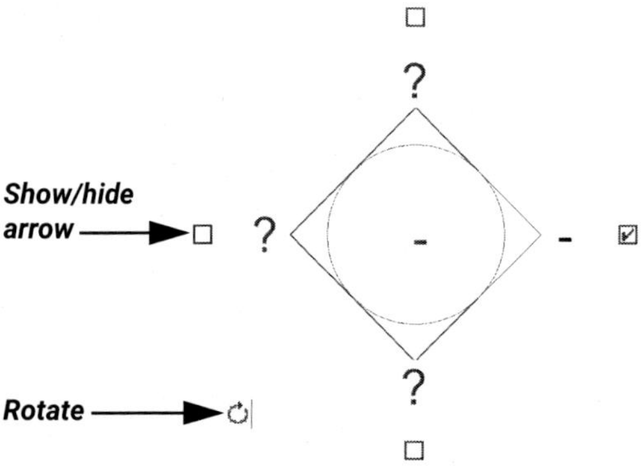

Figure 3–59

- Use the (Rotate) control to angle the marker (e.g., for a room with angled walls).

Modifying Section Markers

When you modify section markers, various shape handles and controls enable you to modify a section, as shown in Figure 3–60.

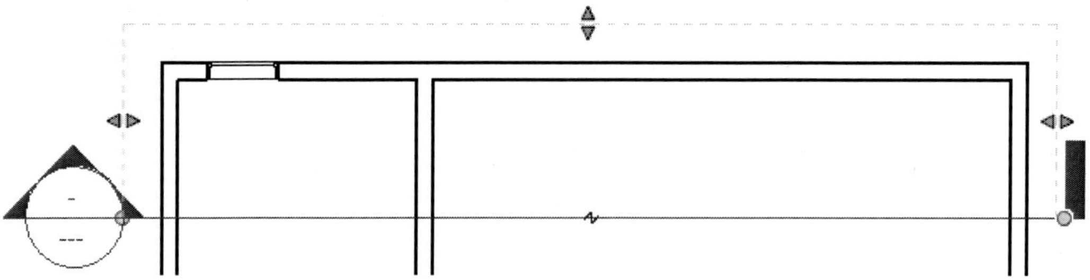

Figure 3–60

- Adjust the (Drag) shape controls to change the length and depth of the cut plane.
- Drag the segment handle controls at either end of the section line to change the location of the arrow or flag without changing the cut boundary.
- Click (Flip Section) to change the direction of the arrowhead, which also flips the entire section.
- Click (Cycle Section Head/Tail) to switch between an arrowhead, flag, or nothing on each end of the section.
- Click (Gaps in Segments) to create an opening in section lines, as shown in Figure 3–61. Select it again to restore the full section cut.

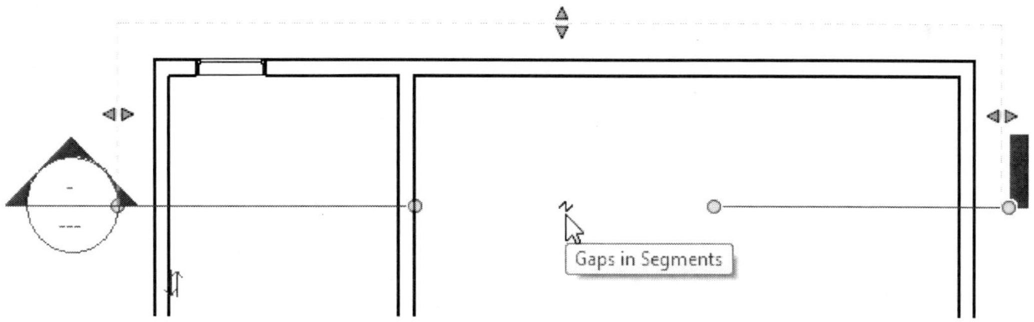

Figure 3–61

How To: Add a Jog to a Section or Elevation Line

1. Select the elevation or section line you want to modify.
2. In the *Modify | Views* tab>*Section* panel, click (Split Segment).
3. Select the point along the section line where you want to create the split, as shown in Figure 3–62.

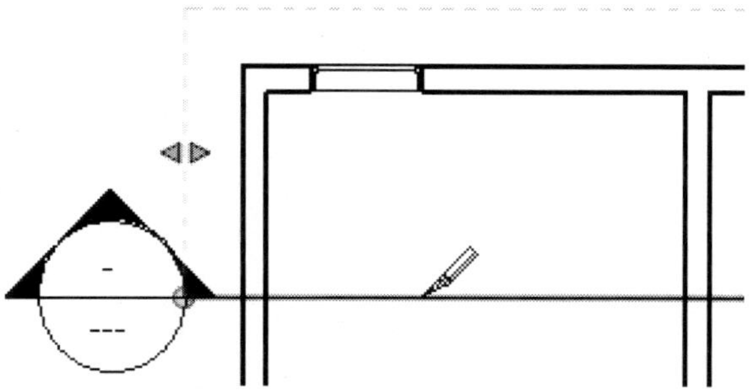

Figure 3–62

4. Specify the location of the split line, as shown in Figure 3–63.

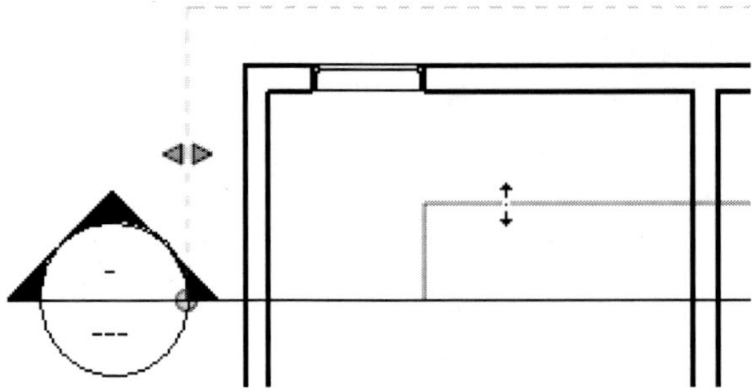

Figure 3–63

- If you need to adjust the location of any segment on the section line, modify it and drag the shape handles along each segment of the line, as shown in Figure 3–64.

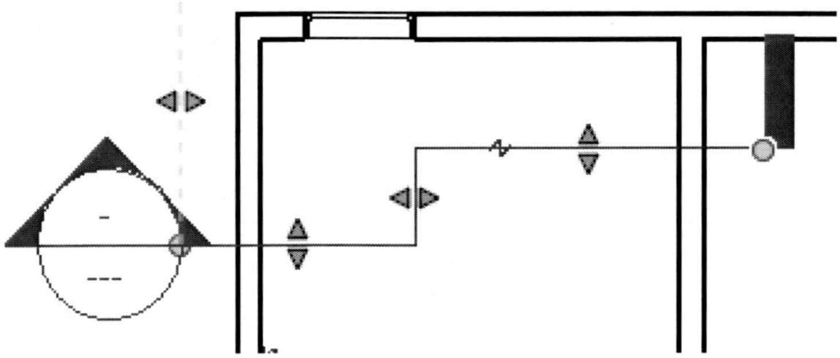

Figure 3–64

- To bring a split section line back into place, use the shape handle to drag the jogged line until it is at the same level with the rest of the line.

3D Section Views

There are three ways you can create section views of your 3D model: by selecting elements in a view and starting the **Selection Box** command, turning on **Section Box** in a 3D view (as shown in Figure 3–65), and orienting a 3D view to a specific view. These are all very helpful as you are working and also can be used in construction documents and presentations.

- This allows you to rotate and view the elements unobstructed. You can adjust the sizing of the selection section box by dragging the handles as needed.

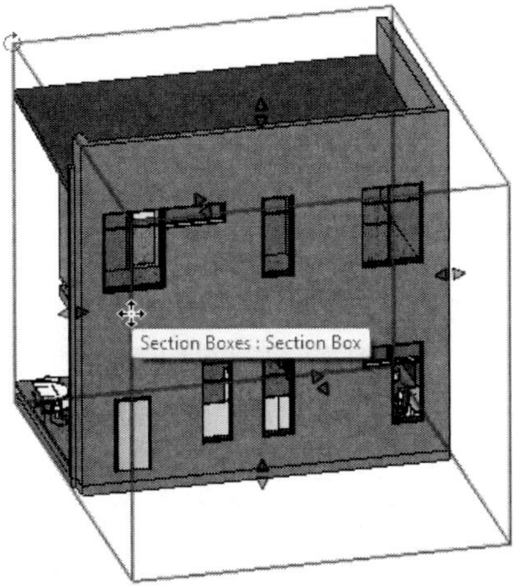

Figure 3–65

How To: Create a Selection Box by Selecting Elements in a View

1. In a view, select the elements you want to isolate. In the example shown above in Figure 3–65, the front wall was selected.
2. In the *Modify* tab>*View* panel, click  (Selection Box), or type **BX**.
3. The default 3D view opens displaying a section box around the selected item(s).
4. Use the controls of the section box to modify the size of the box to show exactly what you want.

- To toggle off a section box and restore the full model, in the view's Properties, in the *Extents* section, clear the checkmark from *Section Box*.

How To: Turn on Section Box in a 3D View

1. Open a 3D view.
2. With nothing selected, in Properties, in the *Extents* section, click the box next to *Section Box*.
3. A section box appears around the entire 3D model. Use the grips to adjust what you want to display.

How To: Orient a 3D View to a View

1. Open a 3D view.
2. Right-click on the ViewCube and select **Orient to View>Floor Plans**, **Elevations**, **Sections**, or **3D Views**, as shown in Figure 3–66, then select the view from the list.

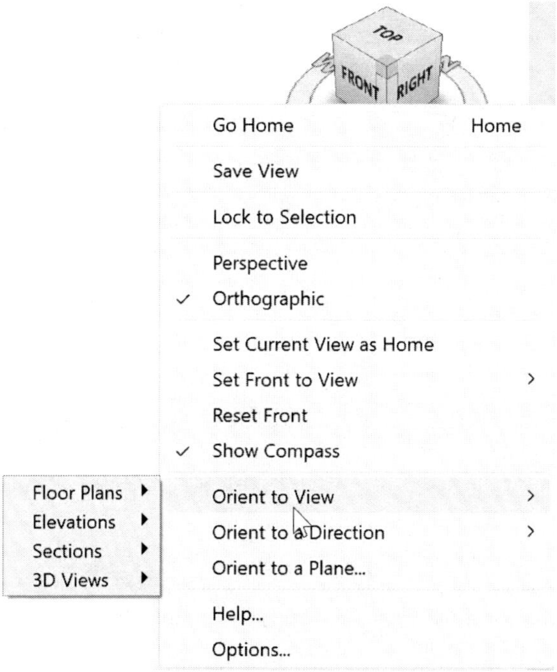

Figure 3–66

3. The view displays, as shown in the partial floor plan view of a stair on the left in Figure 3–67. Use the 3D view rotation tools to navigate around the 3D model, as shown on the right.

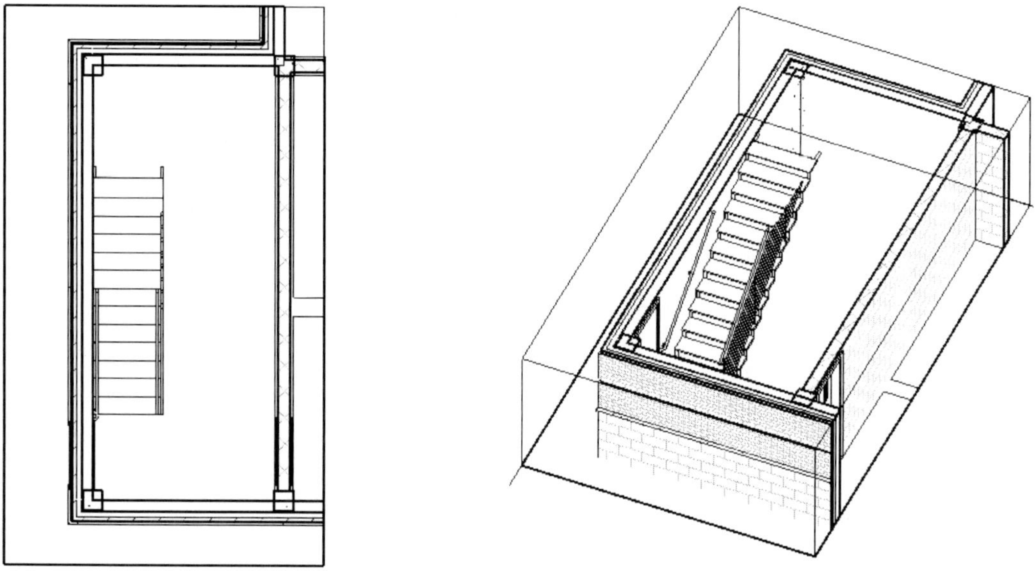

Figure 3–67

- **Orient to a Direction** enables you to position the view in a specific direction, as shown in Figure 3–68. This is similar to using the orientation planes of the ViewCube.

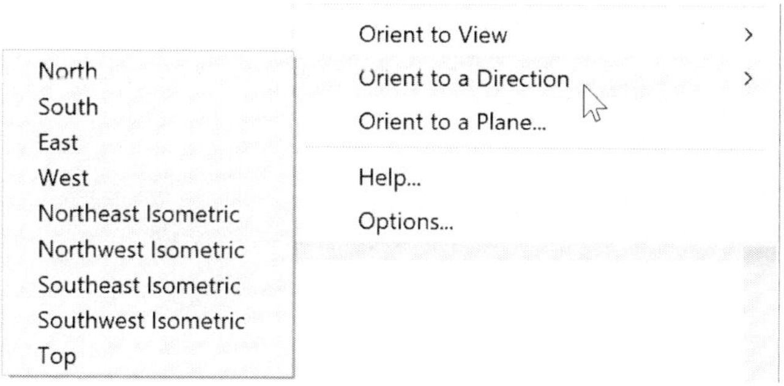

Figure 3–68

- **Orient to a Plane** opens the *Select Orientation Plane* dialog box and enables you to specify a level, grid, or named reference plane, or pick a plane or a line, as shown in Figure 3–69. The view is not cut at the plane but oriented in that direction.

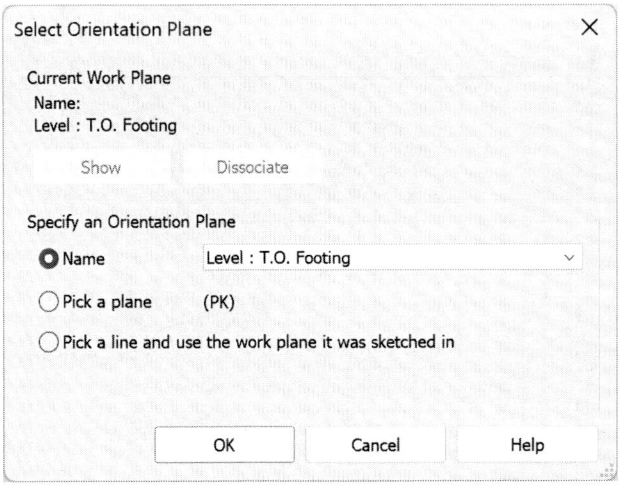

Figure 3–69

Practice 3c
Create Elevations and Sections

Practice Objectives

- Create exterior and interior elevations.
- Add building sections and wall sections.

In this practice, you will create exterior elevations of the poolhouse and interior elevations of the restrooms. You will also add building sections and several wall sections to the project. Figure 3–70 shows the created building section in a shaded visual style.

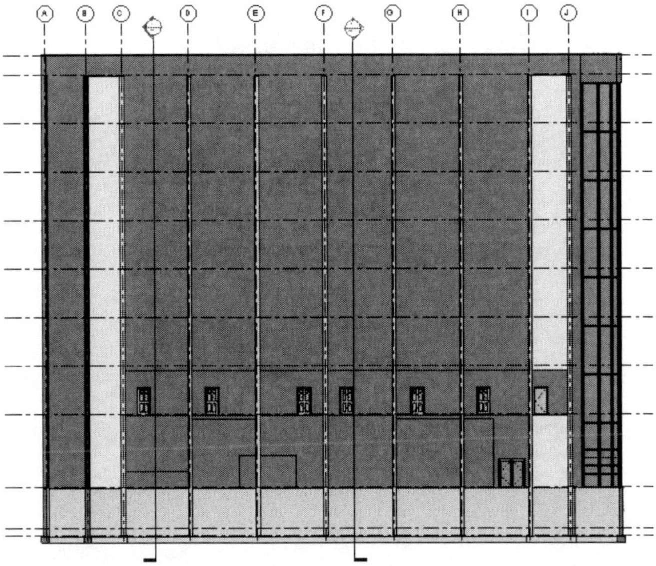

Figure 3–70

Task 1: Add exterior elevations.

1. Open the project **Arch-Elevations.rvt** from the practice files folder.
2. Verify you are in the **Floor Plans - Floor 1** view. Find and note the two restrooms in the hotel labeled **RR-106** and **RR-103**.
3. Open the **Floor Plans: Floor 1 - Reference Plan** view. In the view, double-click the mouse wheel to zoom extents.
4. In the Status Bar, toggle off (Select Links).
    - When off, the icon will display a red X ( ). This allows you to select items that are on top of linked files without selecting the linked file.

5. Click on the square portion of the **North** elevation marker and drag it between grid lines C and D, as shown in Figure 3–71.

   Note: *In this project, north is considered the top of the project.*

6. In the View Control Bar, click (Show Crop Region).
7. Ensure that there is enough space above the poolhouse to add an elevation mark at this scale. If not, move the crop region up.
8. In the *View* tab>*Create* panel, expand (Elevation) and click (Elevation). In the Type Selector, select **Elevation: Building Elevation**, if not already selected.
9. Place an elevation marker outside of the poolhouse building between grid lines F and G, as shown in Figure 3–71. Note that the marker displays pointing towards the wrong direction, which will be corrected in an upcoming step.

   Note: *Because the poolhouse is a linked file, the elevation marker does not know in which direction to point the elevation's arrowhead.*

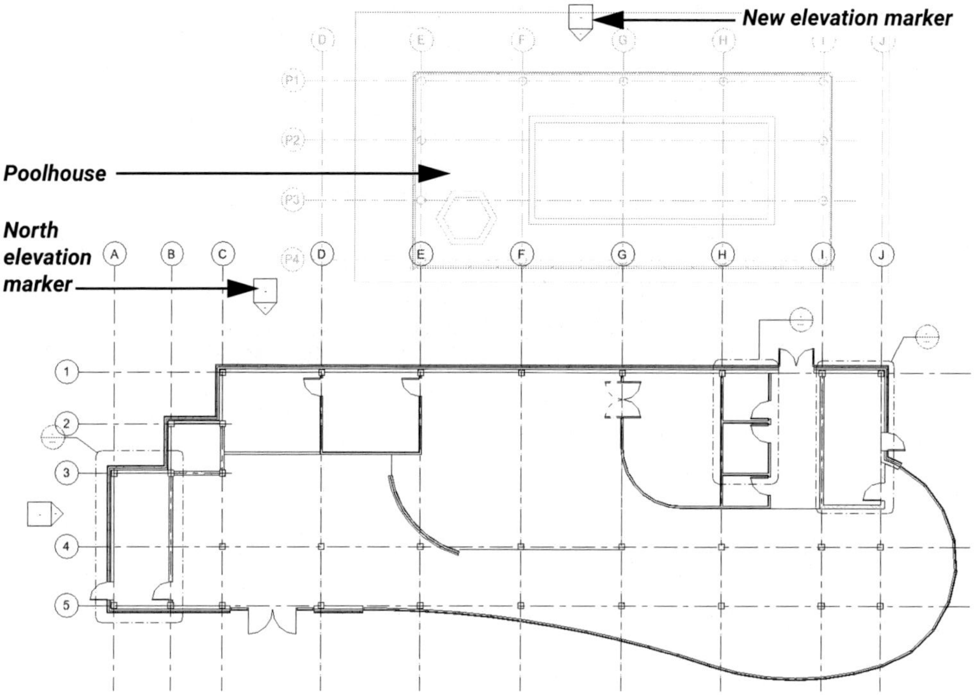

Figure 3–71

10. Click (Modify).

11. Select the square portion of the elevation marker and clear the checkbox for the incorrect direction. When prompted that a view elevation will be deleted, click **OK**.
12. Check the checkbox for the correct direction (pointing downwards), as shown in Figure 3–72.

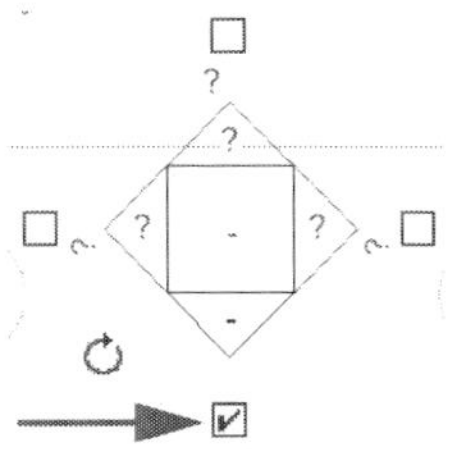

Figure 3–72

13. Click (Modify), then select the arrowhead on the new elevation marker to display the elevation crop region.
14. Using the segment handles and shape controls, change the length and depth of the elevation crop region to just be around the poolhouse, as shown in Figure 3–73. (The elevation crop region in the image is enhanced for clarity.)

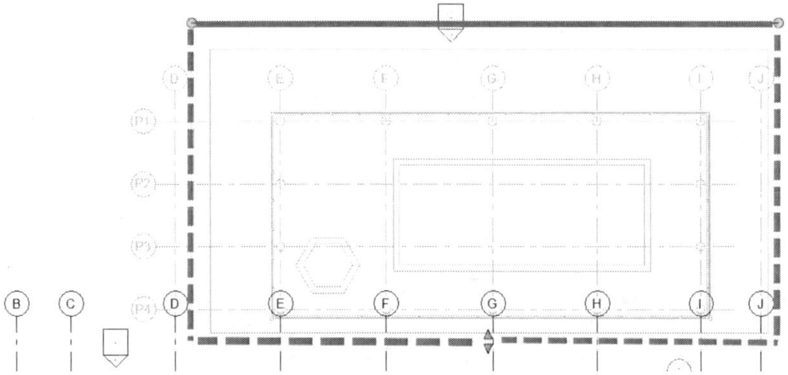

Figure 3–73

15. Double-click on the arrowhead of the elevation marker to open the elevation view.

16. In the elevation view, select the crop region and use the crop region segment handles to change the crop region so that the height is up to **Floor 3** and the bottom is just below the floor line. Bring the sides in close to the pool building, as shown in Figure 3–74.

17. Type **VV**. In the *Visibility/Graphic Overrides* dialog box, on the *Annotation Categories* tab, turn off the *Visibility* for the **Grids** and **Levels** so that the elevation is similar to that shown in Figure 3–74.

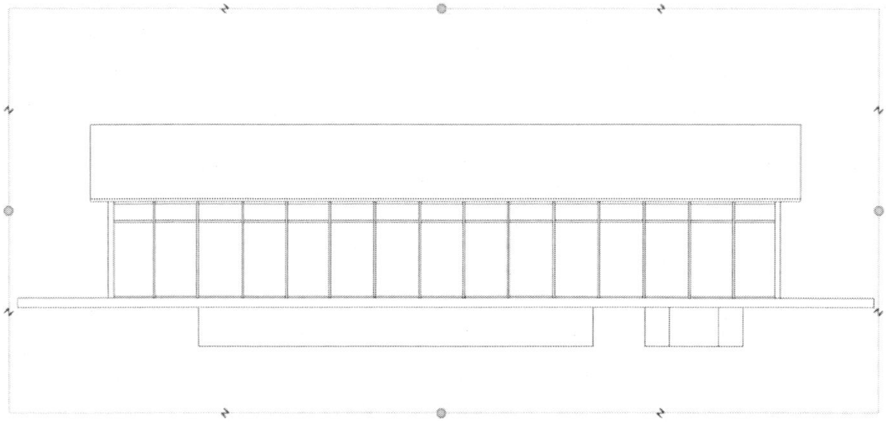

Figure 3–74

18. In the View Control Bar, click  (Hide Crop Region).

19. In the Project Browser, in the *Elevations (Building Elevation)* section, the new elevation view will display as bold because it is the active view.

20. Right-click on the new elevation view and select **Rename...**. Rename it **Pool-North** and press <Enter>.

21. Return to the **Floor 1 - Reference Plan** view.

22. Add elevation markers to the other three sides of the poolhouse, as shown in Figure 3–75.

23. Open the new elevations. Resize, hide grids and levels, and rename the elevations accordingly. If needed, hover over the elevation marker and the tooltip will display the name of the view (as shown in Figure 3–75).

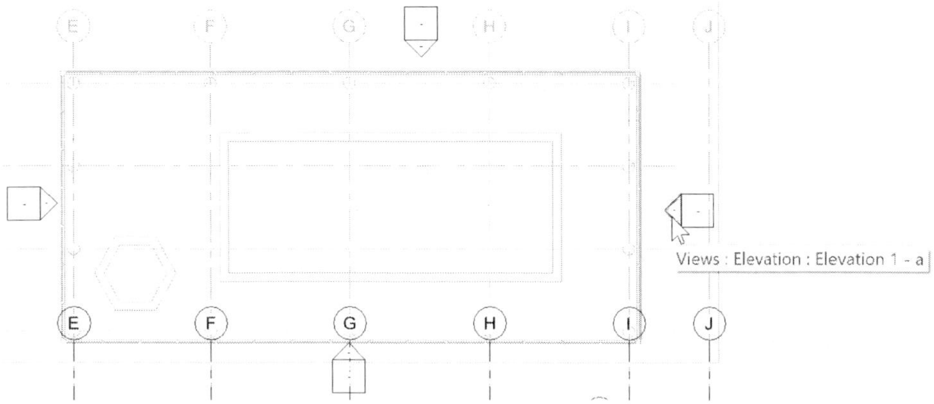

Figure 3–75

24. Save the project.

Task 2: Add interior elevations.

1. Open the **Floor Plans: Floor 1 - Restrooms** view.
2. In the *View* tab>*Create* panel, click (Elevation).
3. In the Type Selector, select **Elevation: Interior Elevation**.
4. Place an elevation in the top restroom with the elevation arrowhead pointing to the west wall (west direction). Note that the elevation arrowhead changes directions as you are placing it, depending on the closest wall.
5. Click (Modify).
6. Select the circle part of the interior elevation marker and check the box opposite the current checkbox, as shown in Figure 3–76. This places an elevation arrowhead in each direction.

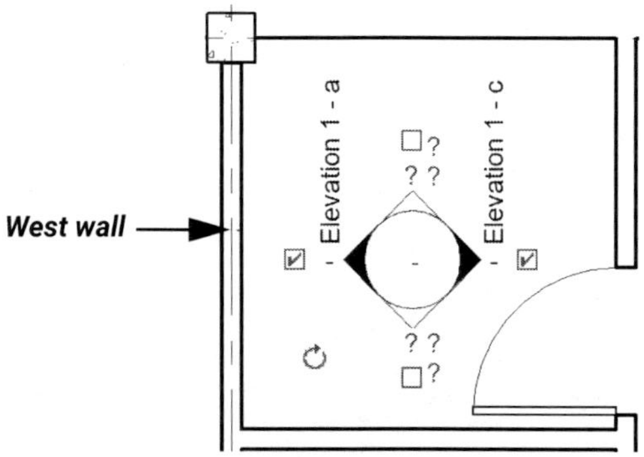

Figure 3–76

7. Repeat the process to add an interior elevation marker to the other restroom and verify the checkboxes are selected for both the west and east directions.
8. In the topmost restroom, select the elevation marker arrow that is pointing west. In Properties (shown in Figure 3–77), change the view's name in the *Identity Data* section according to the room number and which direction the arrow is facing (so this elevation marker arrowhead will be named **RR106-West**).

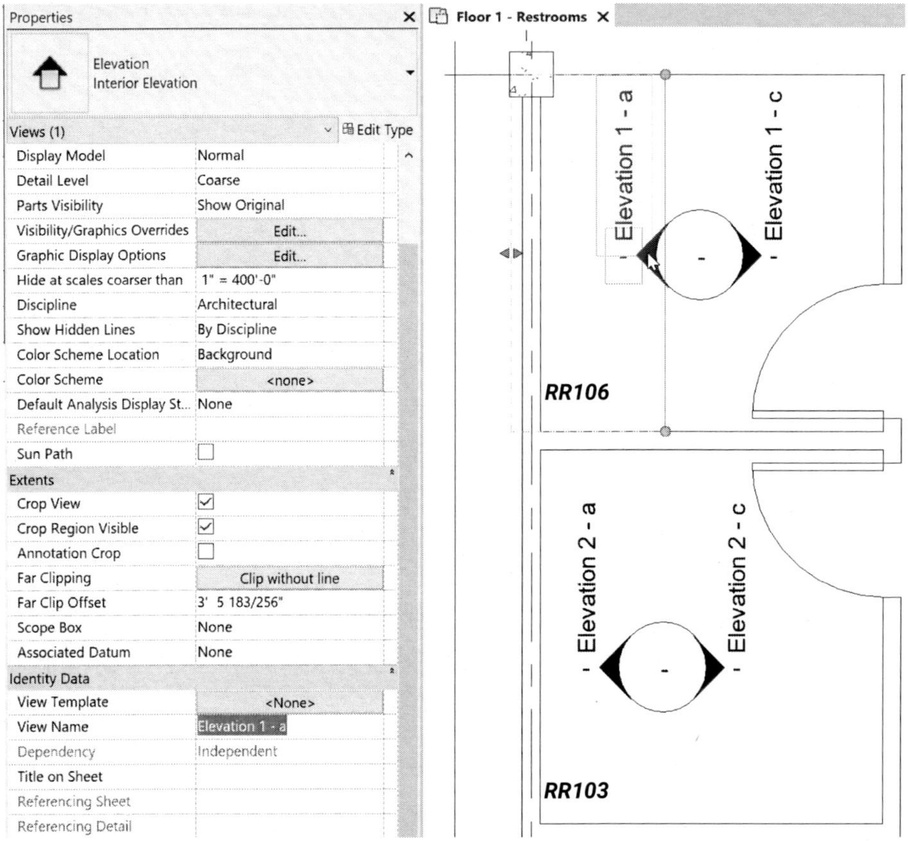

Figure 3–77

9. Repeat to rename the rest of the elevation markers' views. The topmost restroom's east elevation arrowhead will be named **RR106-East**, and the arrowheads for the restroom below that will be renamed to **RR103-West** and **RR103-East** respectively.

10. Press and hold <Ctrl> (to select more than one element) and select all of the elevation marker arrowheads (not the squares). In Properties, in the *Graphics* section, set the *Hide at scales coarser than* to **1/4"=1'-0"**, as shown in Figure 3–78.

Note: *Doing this keeps these markers from showing up in other plans at larger scales.*

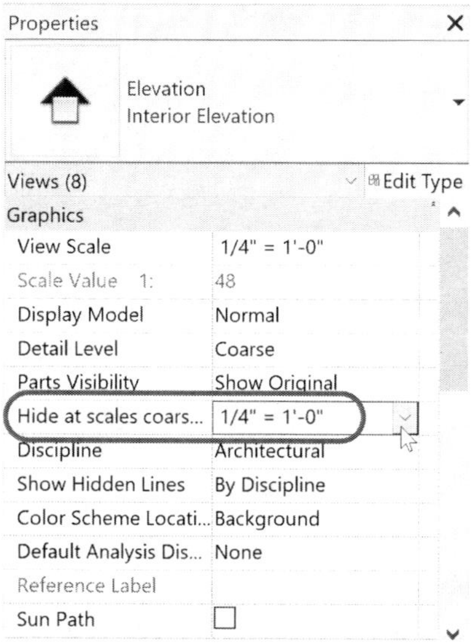

Figure 3–78

11. Open the elevation **RR103-East**. The interior elevation should automatically stop at the boundaries of the walls and ceiling.

12. Save the project.

Task 3: Clean up a view and add building sections.

1. Open the **Floor Plans: Floor 1 - Reference Plan** view. Note that the restroom interior elevation markers do not display in this view. This is because of the *Hide at scales coarser than* value you just set.
2. Type **ZF** (Zoom to Fit) to zoom out to the extents of the view.
3. In the *View* tab>*Create* panel, click (Section).
4. In the Type Selector, select **Section: Building Section**, if not already selected.

5. Draw a horizontal section and a vertical section through the building, as shown in Figure 3–79. (Elevation markers are turned off in the image for clarity.)

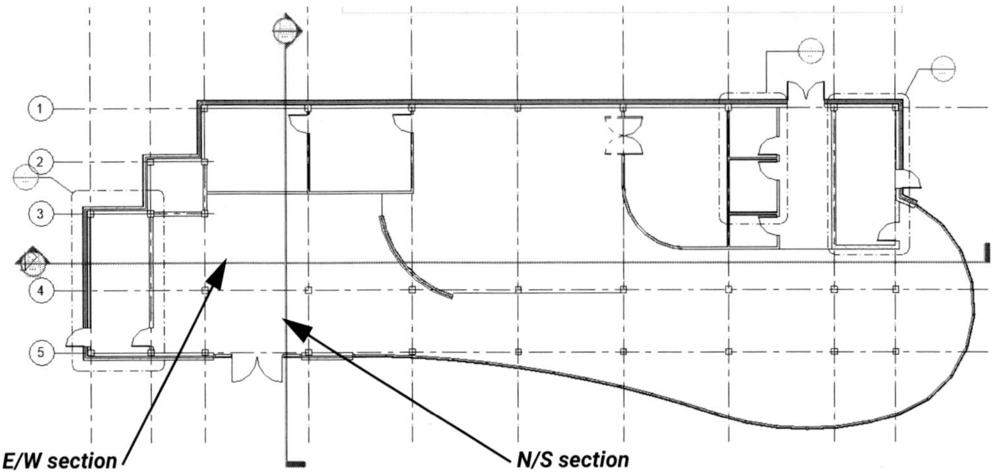

Figure 3–79

6. In the Project Browser, under *Sections (Building Section)*, rename the new sections to **E/W Building Section** and **N/S Building Section**.
7. Select the **E/W Building Section** line and drag the section down so it goes through the stairwell doors and above grid line 5, as shown in Figure 3–80.

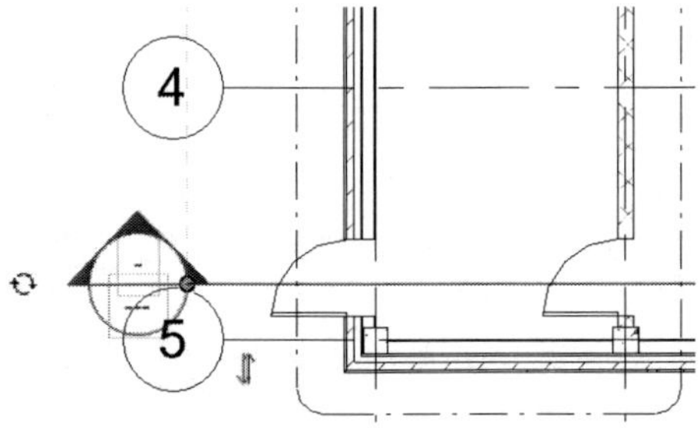

Figure 3–80

8. View each of the building sections.
9. Save the project.

Task 4: Add wall sections.

In this task, you will be using the **Floor 2** view to place the wall sections as you want to ensure that they go through certain features, such as doors and windows.

1. Open the **Floor Plans: Floor 2** view.
2. In the *View* tab>*Create* panel, click (Section). In the Type Selector, select **Section: Wall Section**.
3. Draw four wall sections, as shown in Figure 3–81. To draw the individual sections, you must start the **Section** command each time. To quickly do so, click (Section) in the Quick Access Toolbar. Ensure that the front wall section passes through a window and the back wall section passes through a door.

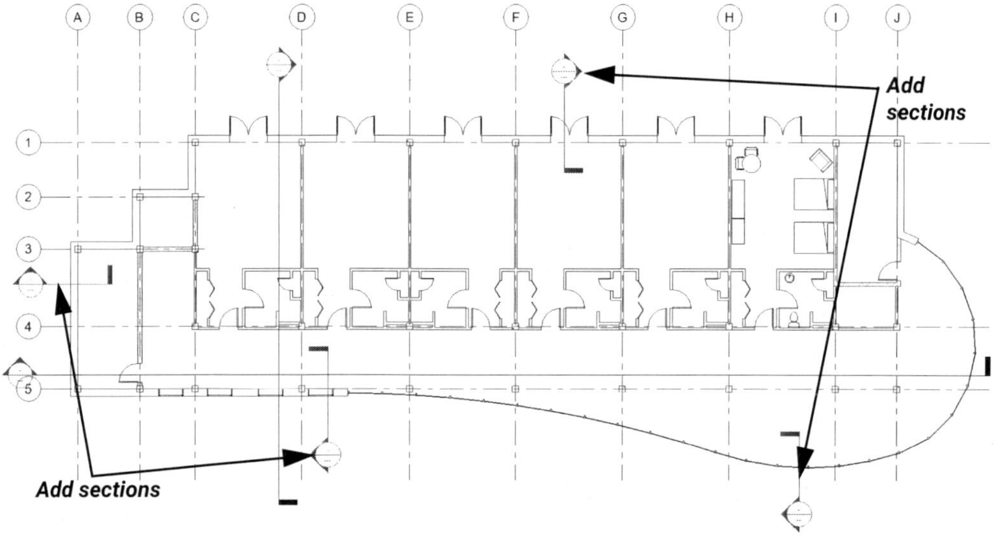

Figure 3–81

4. View each of the wall sections.
5. In the Status Bar, toggle on (Select Links) so that it displays without the red X above it ( ).
6. Save and close the project.

End of practice

Chapter Review Questions

1. Which of the following commands creates a view that results in an independent view displaying the same model geometry and containing a copy of the annotation?
    a. Duplicate
    b. Duplicate with Detailing
    c. Duplicate as a Dependent

2. What is the primary purpose of the *Visibility/Graphic Overrides* dialog box?
    a. To manage the visibility and appearance of categories and subcategories in the current view.
    b. To control the rendering quality of 3D views.
    c. To override the global project units for specific families.
    d. To change the color of individual elements in the entire model.

3. If you want to hide just one of the elevation markers in a view, what do you have to do?
    a. Select the elevation marker, then right-click and select **Hide in View>By Filter**.
    b. Select the elevation marker, then right-click and select **Hide in View>Category**.
    c. Select the elevation marker, then right-click and select **Hide in View>Elements**.
    d. In the *Visibility/Graphic Overrides* dialog box, uncheck **Elevations**.

4. What is the purpose of creating a callout?
    a. To create a boundary around part of the model that needs revising, similar to a revision cloud.
    b. To create a view of part of the model to export to the AutoCAD software for further detailing.
    c. To create a view of part of the model that is linked to the main view from which it is taken.
    d. To create a 2D view of part of the model.

5. What is the function of the annotation crop region in a Revit view?
   a. It limits the printing area for a sheet.
   b. It hides model elements that are outside the crop region.
   c. It controls the visibility of annotation elements like text, tags, and dimensions within a defined boundary.
   d. It scales annotation elements to a different view scale.

6. How do you create multiple interior elevations in one room?
   a. Start the **Interior Elevation** command and place the elevation marker.
   b. Start the **Elevation** command and select **Interior Elevation** in the Type Selector, then place the first marker, select it, and select the appropriate Show Arrow boxes.
   c. Start the **Interior Elevation** command and place an elevation marker for each wall of the room you want to display.
   d. Start the **Elevation** command, select **Multiple Elevation** in the Type Selector, and place the elevation marker.

7. How do you create a jog in a building section, such as that shown in Figure 3–82?

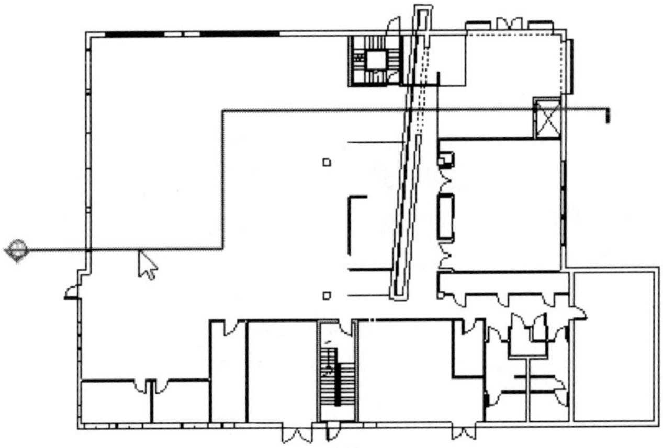

Figure 3–82

   a. Use the **Split Element** tool in the *Modify* tab>*Modify* panel.
   b. Select the building section and then click **Split Segment** in the contextual tab.
   c. Select the building section and click the blue control in the middle of the section line.
   d. Draw two separate sections and use the **Section Jog** tool to combine them into a jogged section.

Command Summary

Button	Command	Location
Views		
	**Callout: Rectangle**	• **Ribbon:** *View* tab>*Create* panel, expand Callout
	**Callout: Sketch**	• **Ribbon:** *View* tab>*Create* panel, expand Callout
	**Duplicate**	• **Ribbon:** *View* tab>*Create* panel, expand Duplicate View • **Right-click:** (*on a view in the Project Browser*) expand Duplicate View
	**Duplicate as Dependent**	• **Ribbon:** *View* tab>*Create* panel, expand Duplicate View • **Right-click:** (*on a view in the Project Browser*) expand Duplicate View
	**Duplicate with Detailing**	• **Ribbon:** *View* tab>*Create* panel, expand Duplicate View • **Right-click:** (*on a view in the Project Browser*) Duplicate View
	**Elevation**	• **Ribbon:** *View* tab>*Create* panel, expand Elevation
	**Plan Region**	• **Ribbon:** *View* tab>*Create* panel, expand Plan Views
	**Section**	• **Ribbon:** *View* tab>*Create* panel • **Quick Access Toolbar**
	**Split Segment**	• **Ribbon:** (*when the elevation or section marker is selected*) *Modify | Views* tab>*Section* panel
Crop Views		
	**Crop View**	• **View Control Bar** • **View Properties:** Crop View (*check*)
	**Do Not Crop View**	• **View Control Bar** • **View Properties:** Crop View (*clear*)
	**Edit Crop**	• **Ribbon:** (*when the crop region of a callout, elevation, or section view is selected*) *Modify | Views* tab>*Mode* panel
	**Hide Crop Region**	• **View Control Bar** • **View Properties:** Crop Region Visible (*clear*)

Button	Command	Location
	**Reset Crop**	• **Ribbon:** *(when the crop region of a callout, elevation or section view is selected) Modify | Views* tab>*Mode* panel
	**Show Crop Region**	• **View Control Bar** • **View Properties:** Crop Region Visible (*check*)
	**Size Crop**	• **Ribbon:** (*when the crop region of a callout, elevation or section view is selected*) *Modify | Views* tab>*Mode* panel
View Display		
	**Hide in View**	• **Ribbon:** *Modify* tab>*View Graphics* panel>Hide> Elements *or* By Category • **Right-click:** *(when an element is selected)* Hide in View>Elements *or* Category
	**Override Graphics in View**	• **Ribbon:** *Modify* tab>*View Graphics* panel>Hide> Elements *or* By Category • **Right-click:** *(when an element is selected)* Override Graphics in View>By Element *or* By Category • **Shortcut:** *(category only)* VV or VG
	**Reveal Hidden Elements**	• **View Control Bar**
	**Selection Box**	• **Ribbon:** *Modify* tab>*View* panel • **Shortcut:** BX
	**Temporary Hide/Isolate**	• **View Control Bar**
	**Temporary View Properties**	• **View Control Bar**

Chapter 4

Revit Families

To develop your 3D model, you will need to add various Revit® family elements, such as furniture, lighting fixtures, mechanical equipment, and structural framing elements. These components can be loaded from your company's template, the Revit Library, or a custom library. If the family elements are parametric, you can modify the components to have different sizes to control the visibility of items as needed to relay design intent for various aspects of the project.

Learning Objectives

- Place components in a project to further develop the design.
- Load components from the Revit Library.
- Change component types and locations.
- Create additional family types.

4.1 About Revit Families

All elements added to your projects are created with families. A family contains different elements, materials, and properties (called parameters). Within the family, you can have multiple family types with different parameters. For example, you can have a column family that contains various family types for different sizes of it.

Components are elements that can be loaded externally. These can include freestanding components, such as the VAV terminal unit, base cabinets, tables, and chairs shown in Figure 4–1. They can also include wall-, ceiling-, floor-, roof-, face-, and line-hosted components. These hosted components must be placed on the referenced element, such as the wall-based upper cabinets and ceiling-based air terminal shown in Figure 4–1.

Note: *Family creation is covered in the ASCENT's Autodesk Revit BIM Management: Template and Family Creation guide.*

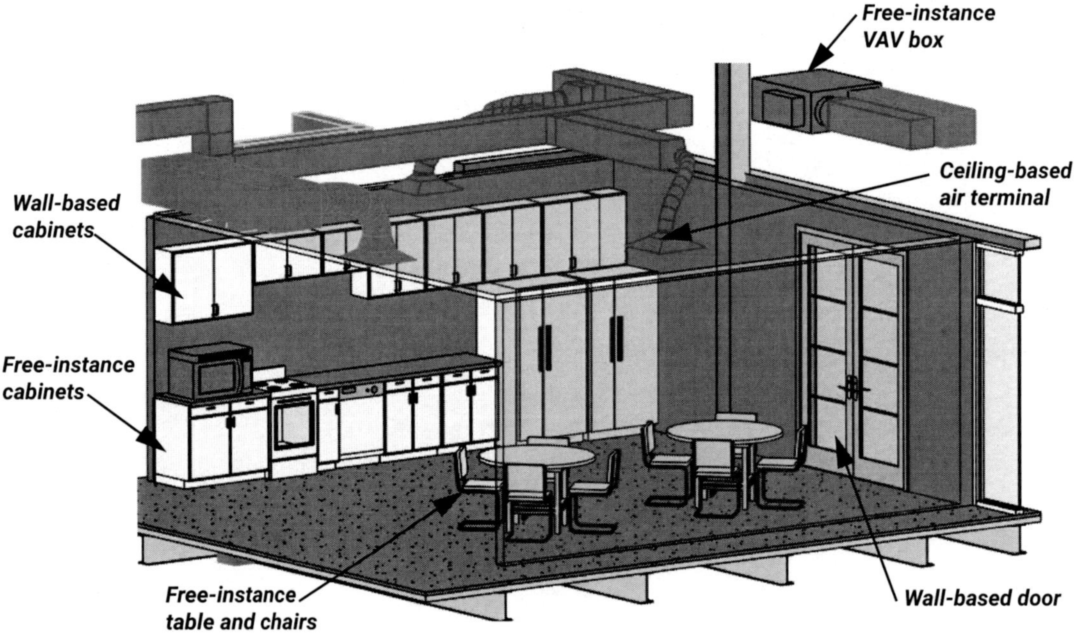

Figure 4–1

Host-based vs. Free-instance Families

- *Host-based* families are dependent on a host. Examples include a pendant lighting fixture (which requires a ceiling) and a clock or mirror (which requires a wall), as shown in Figure 4–2.
- *Free-instance* families do not need a host. Examples include the sideboard and candle holder shown in Figure 4–2.

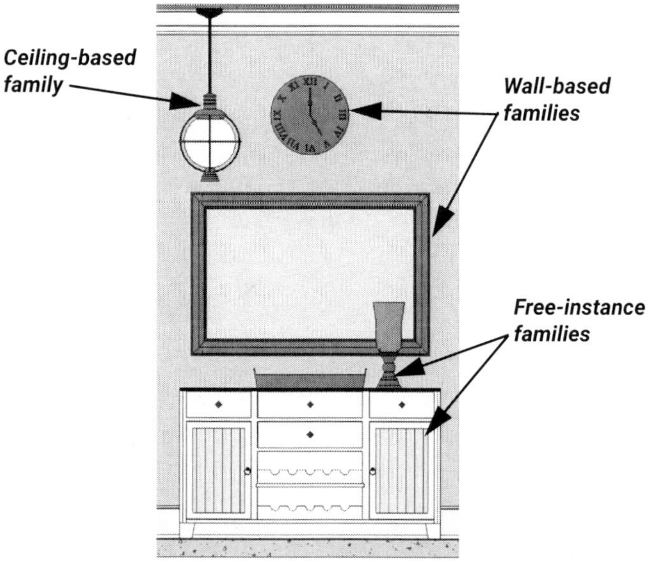

Figure 4–2

The Different Kinds of Families

There are three kinds of families: system families, loadable families, and in-place families. Loadable and system families are what are typically used in a project, whereas in-place families are reserved for custom objects that are unique to the project.

System Families

System families are families that are predefined in Revit projects and templates. System families include walls, wall foundations, floors, structural slabs, ceilings, stairs, railings, and roofs, as shown in Figure 4–3. They also include duct, pipe, cable tray, and conduit types, as well as some annotation types, such as text and dimensions.

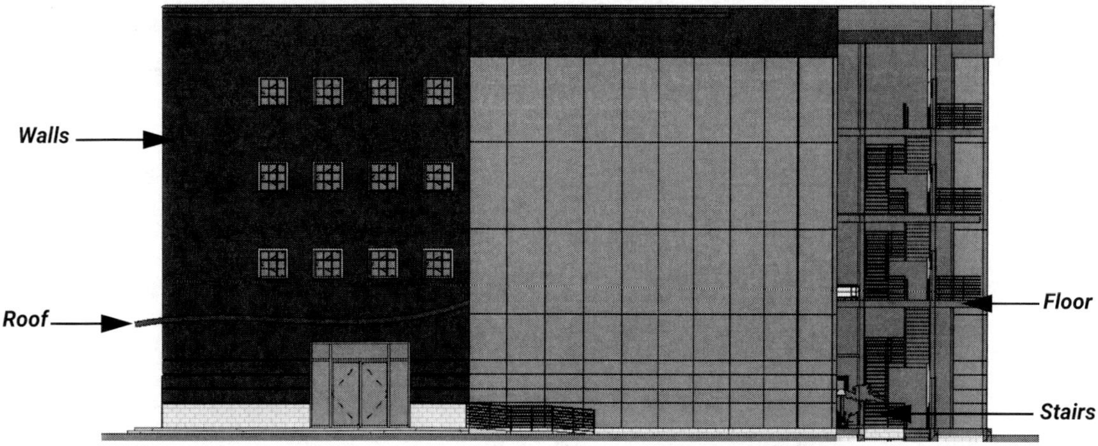

Figure 4–3

- System families are added to the model by starting a specific command from the appropriate tab in the ribbon. These will be further discussed in the *Design Development* section.
- System families cannot be saved out of a project or loaded from a library, but they can be customized by duplicating an existing type and modifying the *Type Parameters*, as shown in Figure 4–4. This can only be done within a project and helps to establish the company standards for the families set up in a template file. System families can be shared by using the **Transfer Project Standards** tool.

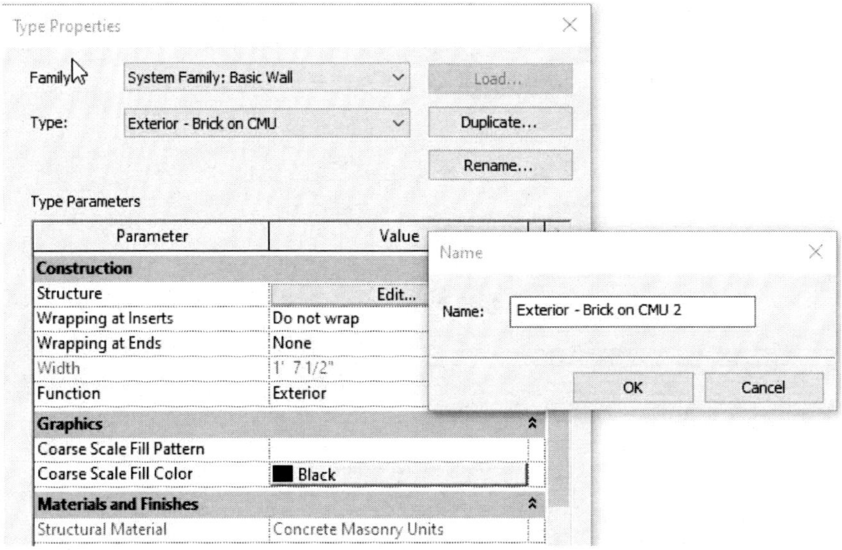

Figure 4–4

Loadable Families

Loadable families are external component families that are created outside of the project, such as furniture, plants, windows, doors, and casework, as shown in Figure 4–5. Frequently used components can be saved to a custom library for future use.

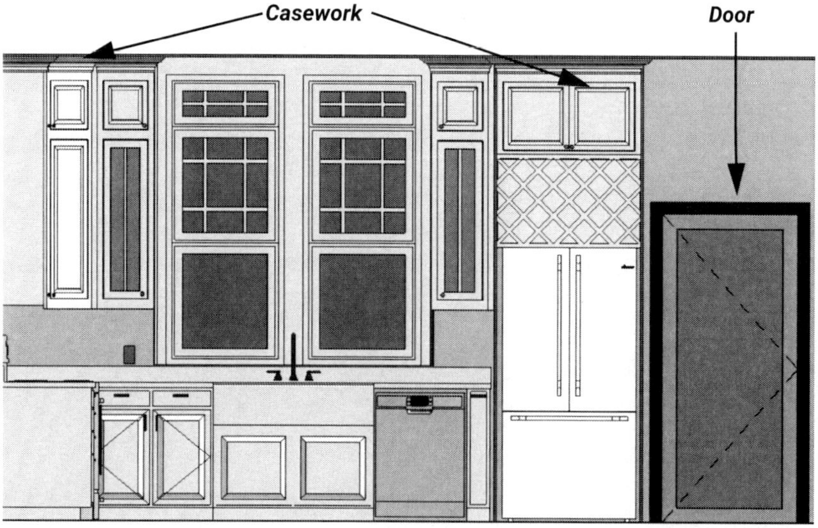

Figure 4–5

- Annotation components are tags (shown in Figure 4–6), symbols, and title blocks. (They will be discussed further in ***Chapter 16 Adding Tags and Schedules***.)

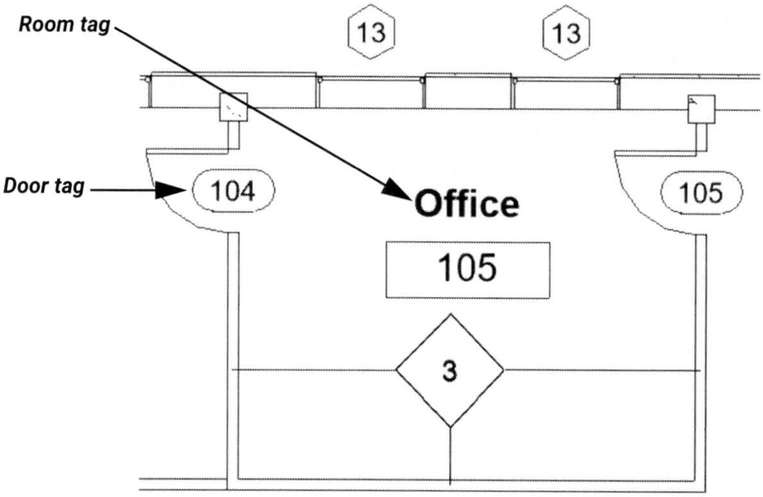

Figure 4–6

In-Place Families

In-place families are families that are created within a project that are unique to the project and will most likely not be used in another, for example a custom built-in shelf system (as shown in Figure 4–7) that needs to be built to suit.

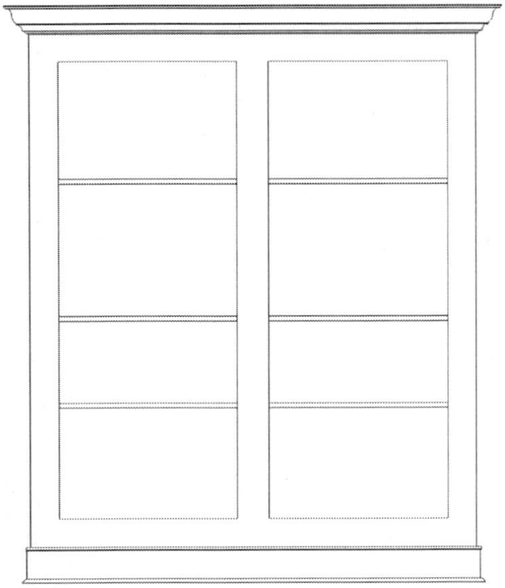

Figure 4–7

Working with Component Families

To optimize project size and improve performance, by default the Revit project templates are not fully loaded with all available Revit families. However, you can load more families with multi-options from the Revit Library or the Autodesk website. You can also load your company's custom component family or families from other manufacturers that you may have available on your local machine. Some Revit component families have a type catalog associated with them that enables you to select specific types of that family to load. This helps with keeping the file size down.

- You can also check which custom component families your company has and find vendor-specific components. More BIM objects can be found at bimobject.com.
- You can copy a component family to the clipboard in one project and paste it into a different project that is open in the same session of Revit.
- You can load as many components into a project as needed or create your own.
- Components are family files with the extension .RFA. For example, a component family named Desk.rfa can contain several types and sizes.

4.2 Loading Components

You can load components from the Revit Library or from a custom library before starting the component command, or you can load after starting the command. Components (also known as families) are full 3D elements that can be placed at appropriate locations and heights, and which interact with the building elements around them. For example, a lighting fixture can be designed to be hosted by a face (such as a wall or ceiling), or to stand alone by itself.

How To: Use Load Family

1. In the *Insert* tab>*Load from Library* panel, click (Load Family).

   Note: *To use the Load Family method, you must install the **Autodesk Revit 2027 Content** in your desired language.*

2. In the *Load Family* dialog box, locate the folder that contains the family or families you want to load and select them, as shown in Figure 4–8. To load more than one family at a time, hold <Ctrl> while selecting.

   - If the *Load Family* dialog box does not default to the Revit Library folder, click on **Imperial Library** in the *Places* panel.

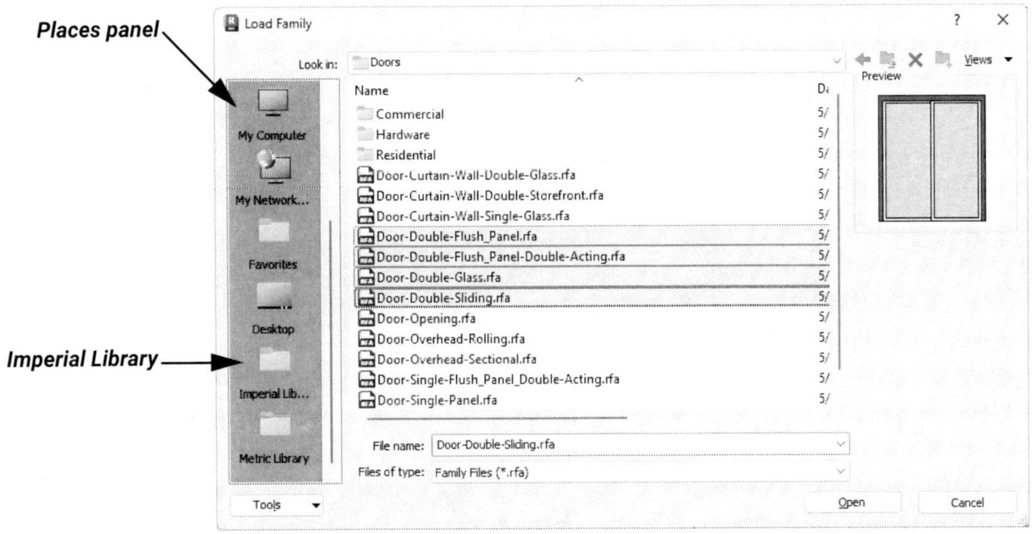

Figure 4–8

   - The program remembers the last-used folder.

3. Click **Open**.

4. For some families, the *Specify Types* dialog box displays, as shown for a door in Figure 4–9. Select the types you want to include in your project and click **OK**.
   - To select more than one type, hold <Ctrl> as you select.
   - You can use the drop-down lists under the columns to filter the sizes.
   - When loading several families with extra types, you can choose the element from the *Family* list on the right side and then pick the *Types* on the left side. Repeat for each of the elements listed. Once you are finished, click **OK**.

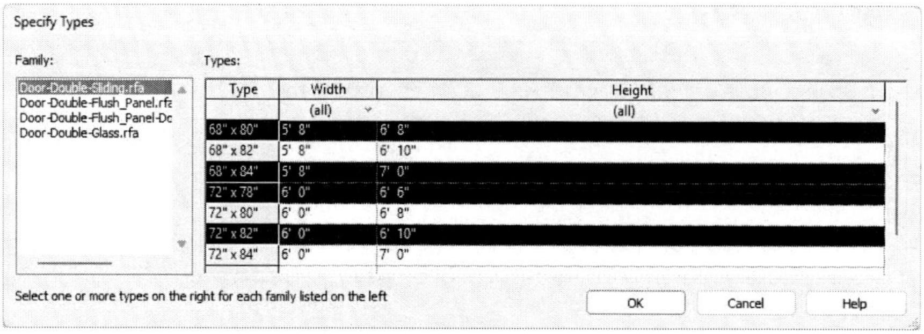

Figure 4–9

5. Once the family (or families) is loaded, in the Type Selector, select the type you want to use, as shown in Figure 4–10 .

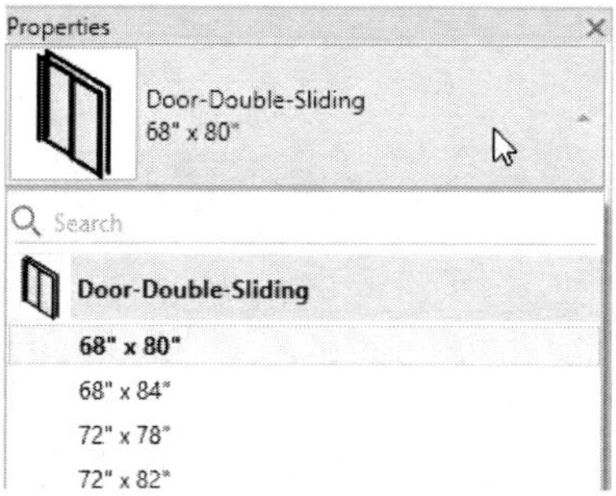

Figure 4–10

Hint: Using Families with This Learning Content

For the practices in this learning content, all families that are used have been provided with the practice files. This was done to ensure that all users can easily locate and use the required files to successfully complete all practices. In general, it is recommended that you use families from the provided Autodesk Revit Content via downloaded content or the cloud, or from your own custom company library.

How To: Use Load Autodesk Family

1. In the *Insert* tab>*Load from Library* panel, click (Load Autodesk Family).
2. In the *Load Autodesk Family* dialog box, filter your search by typing in what kind of family you are looking for and pressing <Enter> or clicking (Search), or click on a category in the *Browse* section, as shown in Figure 4–11.

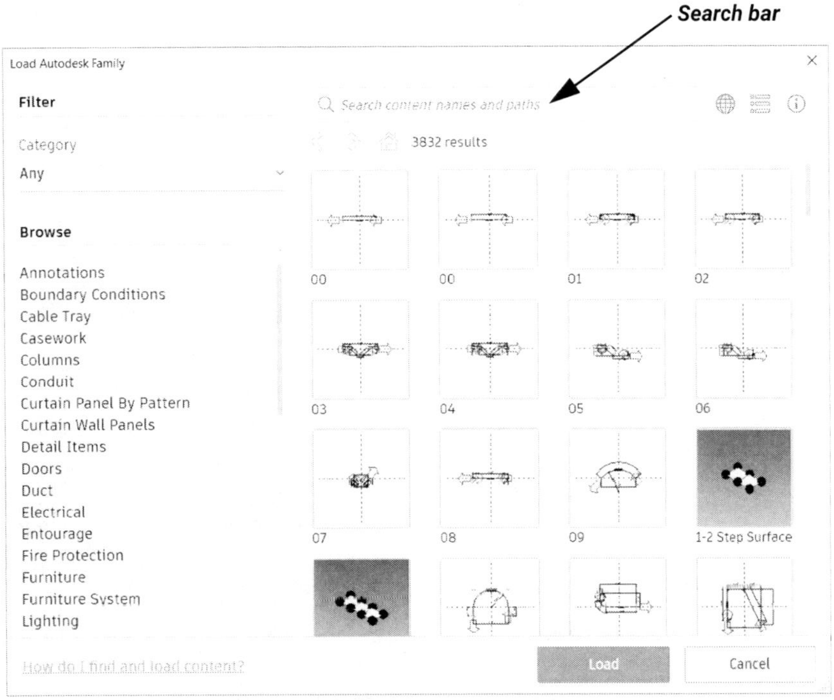

Figure 4–11

3. You can select as many families as needed, then click **Load** to load them into your project.

Placing Components

When placing components, you have several options available to you, including specifying a placement, utilizing snaps, and using snap overrides.

How To: Place a Component

1. In the *Architecture* tab>*Build* panel, click (Place a Component), or type **CM**.
   - If you have not yet loaded your component, in the *Modify | Place Component* tab>*Mode* panel, click (Load Family) and load your component.
2. In the Type Selector, select the component you want to add to the project.
3. To place the component in the model, proceed as follows, based on the type of component used:

If the component is...	Then...
Not hosted	The element's host is the level it is placed in. Set the *Level* and *Offset* in Properties, as shown in Figure 4–12.
Wall hosted	Place the element on the required surface. If applicable, set the *Elevation from Level* in Properties, as shown in Figure 4–13.
Face hosted	When placing an element that requires a host, you can override the host on which the element will be placed by selecting one of the following options found in the contextual tab>*Placement* panel (as shown in Figure 4–14): • **Place on Vertical Face:** Vertical faces include walls and columns. • **Place on Face:** Faces include ceilings, beams, and roofs. • **Place on Work Plane:** Work planes can be set to levels, faces, and named reference planes. If the element does not require a host, these options are not available.

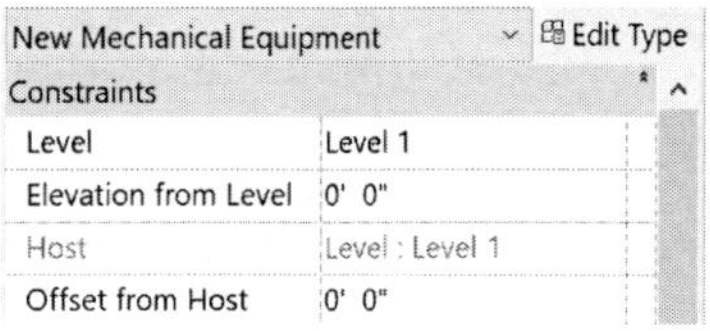

Figure 4–12

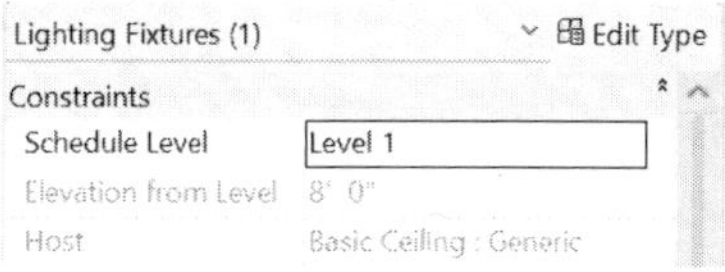

Figure 4–13

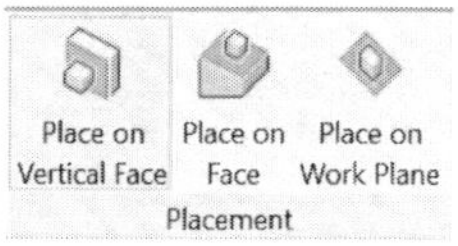

Figure 4–14

- Work plane-based families will default to the last work plane option used.
- Many components can be rotated by pressing <Spacebar> when placing them. This will rotate them in 90° increments, unless your cursor is over an angled wall, reference plane, or grid line.

- In the contextual tab>*Rotate* panel, some components will have an option to (Rotate After Placement), as shown in Figure 4–15. This enables you to rotate the element by any degree immediately after placing the family.

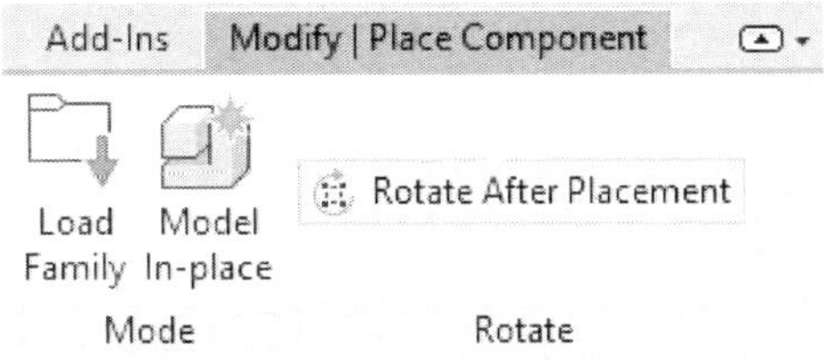

Figure 4–15

A fast way to add components that match those already in your project is to select one, right-click on it, and select **Create Similar**, as shown in Figure 4–16. This starts the appropriate command with the same type selected. **Create Similar** works with all elements.

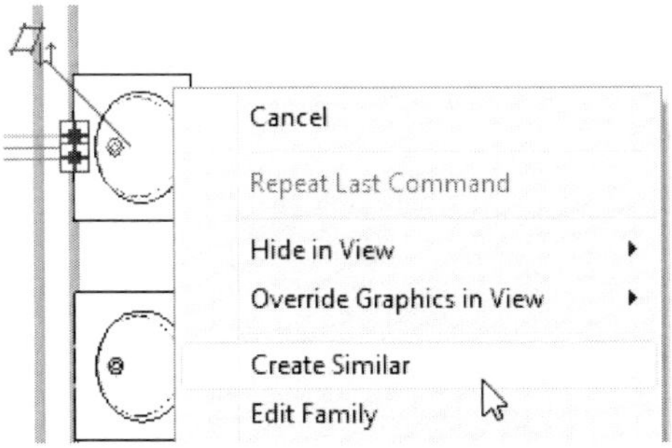

Figure 4–16

Using Snaps

When you move the cursor over an element, the snap symbol displays. Each snap location type displays with a different symbol. Snaps are key points that help you reference existing elements to exact points when modeling, as shown in Figure 4–17.

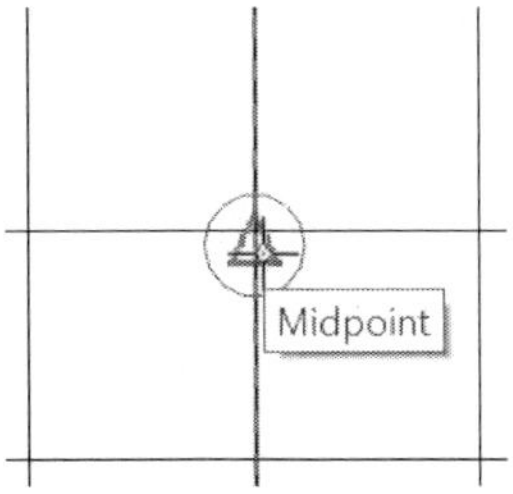

Figure 4–17

Snap Overrides

When placing a component, you can use the **Snap Mid Between 2 Points** temporary snap override by selecting it from the right-click menu (as shown in Figure 4–18) or typing **S2**, then selecting two points in the view.

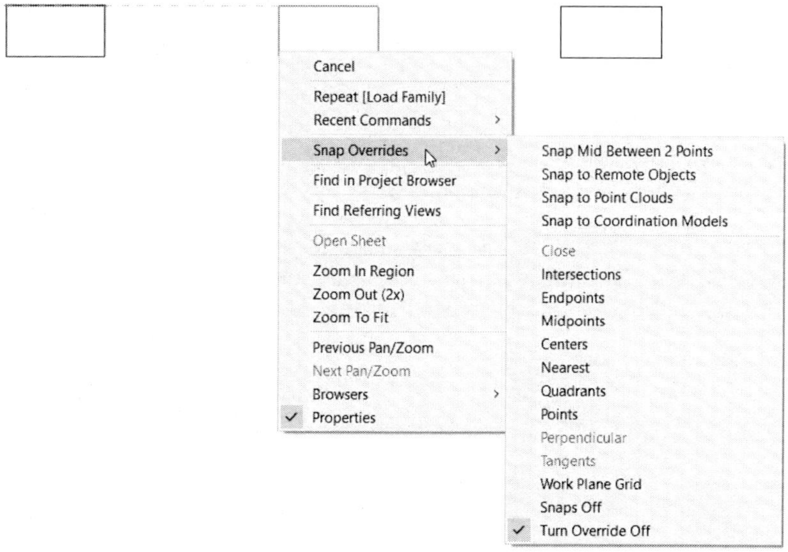

Figure 4–18

- Keyboard shortcuts for each snap can be used to override the automatic snapping. Temporary overrides only affect a single pick, but can be very helpful when there are snaps nearby other than the one you want to use.
- An example of using snap overrides: if you want to place a non-hosted element between two elements, you can type **S2** for *Snap Mid Between 2 Points* then select two points in the view. The new element is placed at the middle of the two selected points, as shown in Figure 4–19.

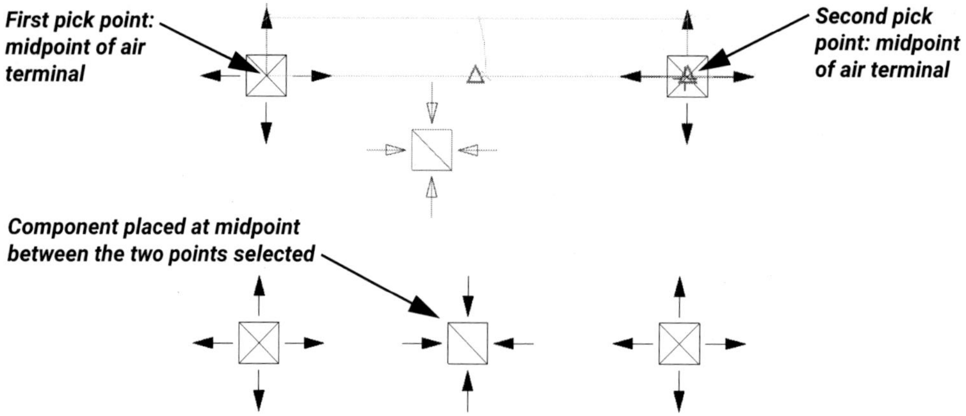

Figure 4–19

Snaps Settings

In the *Manage* tab>*Settings* panel, click (Snaps) to open the *Snaps* dialog box (shown in Figure 4–20). The *Snaps* dialog box enables you to set which snap points are active and set the dimension increments displayed for temporary dimensions (both linear and angular).

- The *Snaps* dialog box shows the keyboard shortcuts for both *Object Snaps* and *Temporary Overrides*.

Figure 4–20

4.3 Modifying Components

Components can be modified when they are selected by changing the type in the Type Selector. For example, you might have placed a floor drain in a project (as shown in Figure 4–21), but now you need to change it to a different type or size. With some types, you can use controls to modify the component. You can also select a new host for a component and move components with nearby elements.

Figure 4–21

How To: Swap Out a Component

1. Select an element in the model.
2. In the Type Selector, select the family type that you want to change it to.
   - If needed, modify the component's instance or type properties.

Modify Host Elements

If you need to move a component from the level on which it was inserted, you can change its host using  (Pick New Host). For example, the floor drain in Figure 4–22 is floating above the floor. It was placed on Level 1 when it was inserted, but it needs to be located on the floor that is below the level.

Figure 4–22

- You can select a floor, surface, or level to be the new host for the components depending on the requirements of the component.

Moving with Nearby Host Elements

Components have the capacity to move with nearby host elements (such as walls) when they are moved. Select the component and in Properties, select the checkbox next to *Moves With Nearby Elements*. The component is automatically assigned to the closest host elements.

For example, a desk near the corner of two walls is linked to those two walls. If you move either wall, the desk moves as well. However, you can still move the desk independently of the walls.

- You cannot specify which elements the component should be linked to; the software determines this automatically. This option only works with host elements (such as walls), not with other components.

Hint: Copying Elements to Levels

The standard Windows commands (Cut to Clipboard or <Ctrl>+<X>), (Copy to Clipboard or <Ctrl>+<C>), and (Paste from Clipboard or <Ctrl>+<V>) work in Revit just as they do in other Windows-compatible software. They are available in the *Modify* tab>*Clipboard* panel, but not in the shortcut menu.

In the software, you can also paste elements aligned to various views or levels, as shown in Figure 4–23.

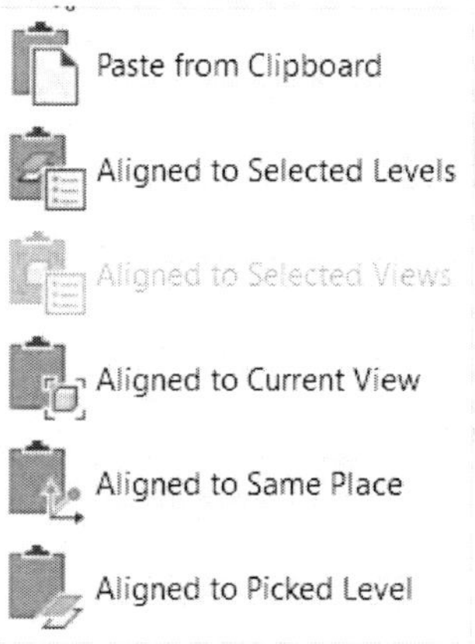

Figure 4–23

- **Aligned to Selected Levels:** Opens a dialog box where you can select the level to which you want to copy. This enables you to copy items on one level and paste them to the same location on another level (e.g., windows in a high-rise building).
- **Aligned to Selected Views:** Copies view-specific elements (such as text or dimensions) into a view that you select in a dialog box. Only the floor plan or reflected ceiling plan views are available.
- **Aligned to Current View:** Pastes elements copied in one view to the same location in another view.
- **Aligned to Same Place:** Pastes elements to the same location in the same view.
- **Aligned to Picked Level:** Pastes elements to the level you select in an elevation or section view.

4.4 Creating Additional Family Types in a Project

As you work within your project, you may find that you need different sizes of families than what is provided. For example, a sink family only has one size, but you need several different sizes, as shown on the left in Figure 4–24. You can also duplicate a family type and have the same family but with different structural layers and materials. Both loadable and system families can be duplicated to modify the parameters within the instance and type properties. Once you duplicate the existing family type, you can choose it in the Type Selector, as shown on the right in Figure 4–24.

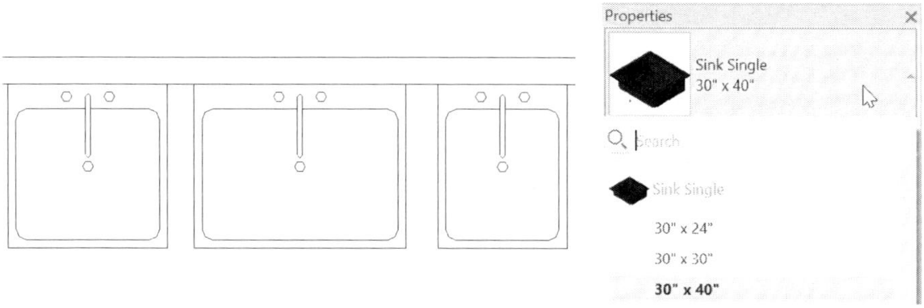

Figure 4–24

- A new family type that is created in a project will only exist in that project.

How To: Create Additional Family Types

1. Start the **Component** command.
2. In the Type Selector, select the type you want to modify. In Properties, click (Edit Type) or in the *Modify* tab>*Properties* panel, click (Type Properties).
3. In the *Type Properties* dialog box, click **Duplicate**.
4. Type a new name for the element and click **OK**.
5. In the *Type Properties* dialog box, change the various parameters to the desired values.

6. If duplicating a wall or floor system family type, you can edit the structure and materials, if required.
    a. In the *Type Properties* dialog box, click **Edit...** next to the *Structure* parameter, as shown in Figure 4–25, to open the *Edit Assembly* dialog box.

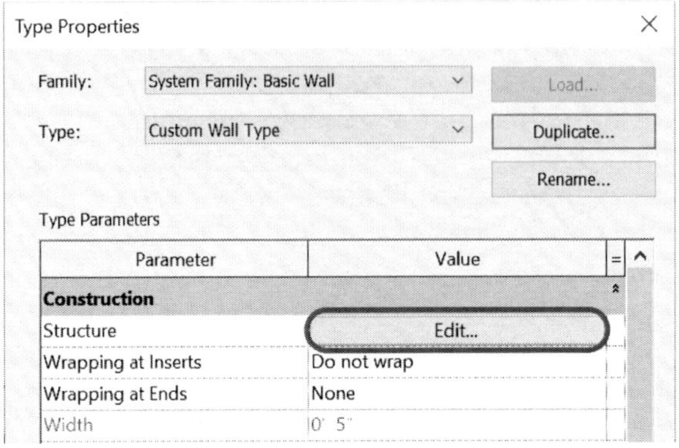

Figure 4–25

    b. In the *Edit Assembly* dialog box, you can edit the structure by inserting, deleting, editing, or reordering layers, as well as changing the thickness.

    c. To change a layer's material, select the cell in the *Material* column and click ⋯ (Browse) (as shown on the left in Figure 4–26) to open the *Material Browser* dialog box (as shown on the right). Make the required edits and click **OK** to return to the *Edit Assembly* dialog box.

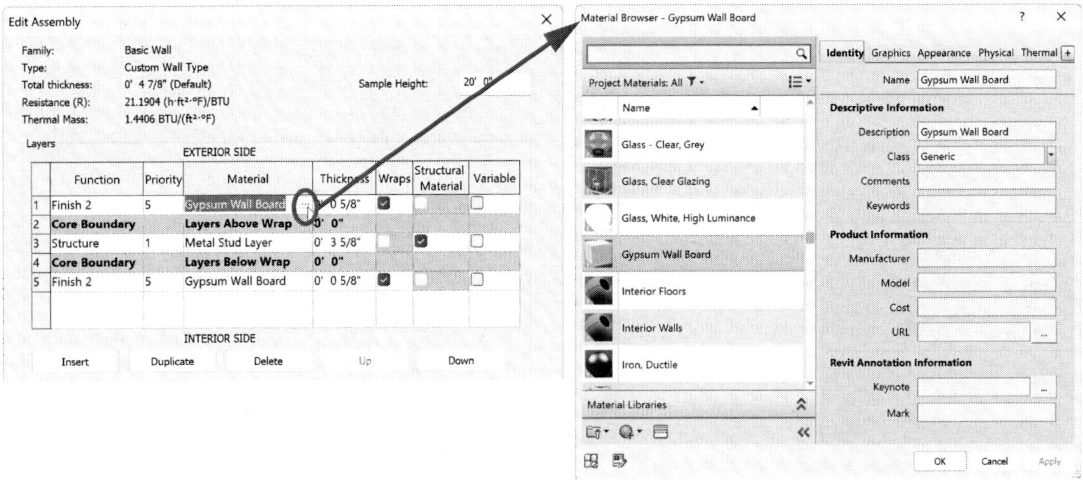

Figure 4–26

    d. When finished editing the assembly, click **OK** to close the *Edit Assembly* dialog box.

7. Click **OK** to close the *Type Properties* dialog box. The new type is now available for use.

Families with Connectors

Revit's default library comes with loadable mechanical, plumbing, and electrical fixtures, as well as equipment that has connectors.

Fixtures are families that are placed using the (Component) command or from the *System* tab using the respective command. For example, the emergency recessed lighting fixture shown in Figure 4–27 can be placed using (Lighting Fixture) in the *Systems* tab>*Electrical* panel. Many of the fixture families included with Revit have multiple sizes. The recessed light shown in Figure 4–27 has different sizes and voltages.

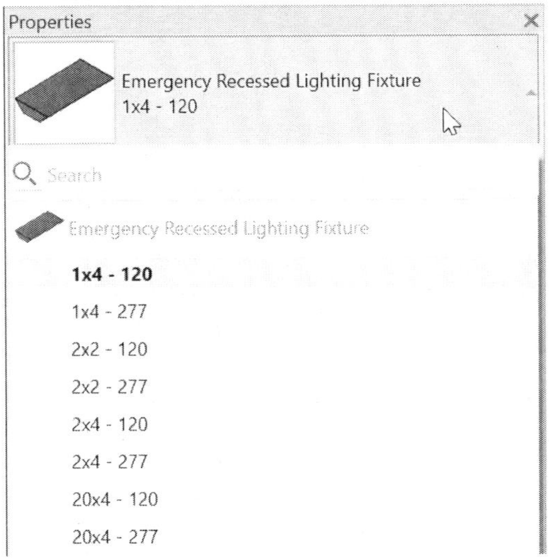

Figure 4–27

- Lighting, plumbing, mechanical, and electrical fixtures and equipment have folders for both architectural and MEP. The fixtures that are in the *Architectural* folder are families that do not have connectors, whereas the fixtures in the *MEP* folder contain connectors. For example, the MEP furnace shown in Figure 4–28 contains connectors that are used to connect ducts and pipes to create systems as well as to calculate loads within a project.

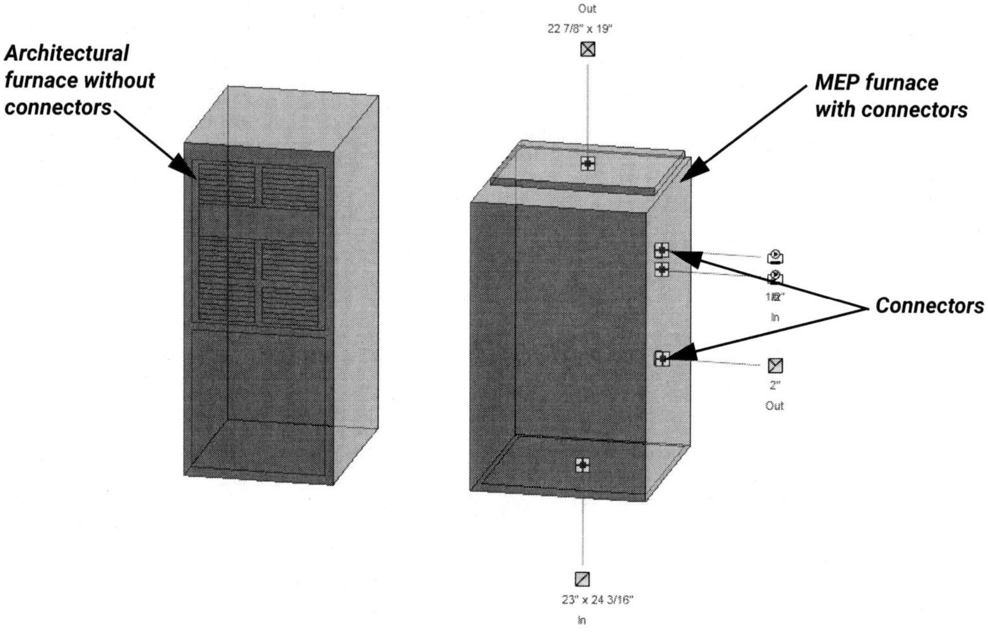

Figure 4–28

Practice 4a
Load Components

Practice Objective

- Load and add components.

In this practice, you will add furniture to the lobby of the hotel. Figure 4–29 shows a sample furniture arrangement. You will load a component from a custom library and use controls to modify the placement. Finally, you will create new loadable and system family types.

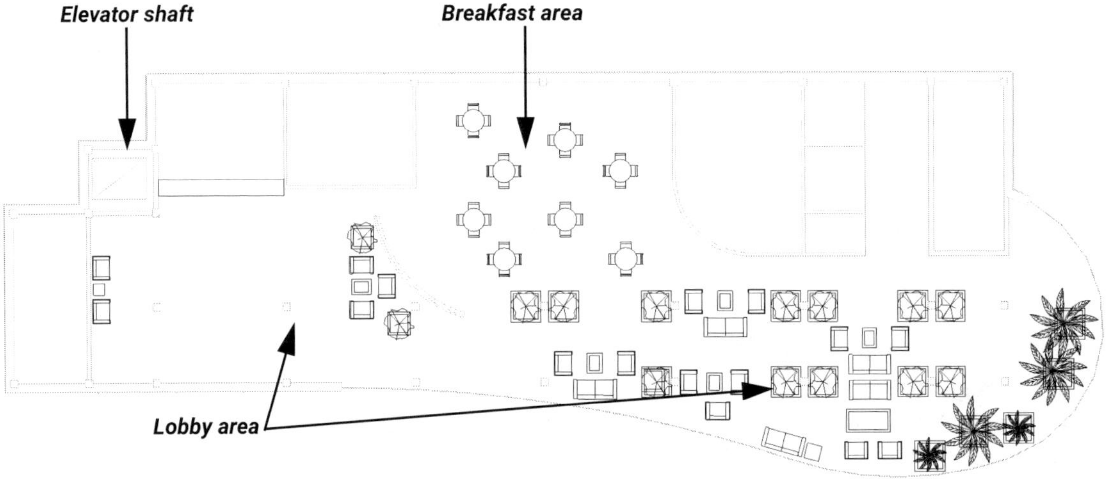

Figure 4–29

Task 1: Duplicate a view and apply a view template.

1. Open the project **Arch-Components.rvt** from the practice files folder.
2. In the Project Browser, duplicate the **Floor 1** view.
3. Rename it to **Floor 1 - Furniture Plan**. The view is now the active view.
4. In the Project Browser, right-click on **Floor 1 - Furniture Plan** and select **Apply Template Properties...**.

5. In the *Apply View Template* dialog box, in the *Name* section, select **Furniture Plan** (as shown in Figure 4–30) and click **OK**.

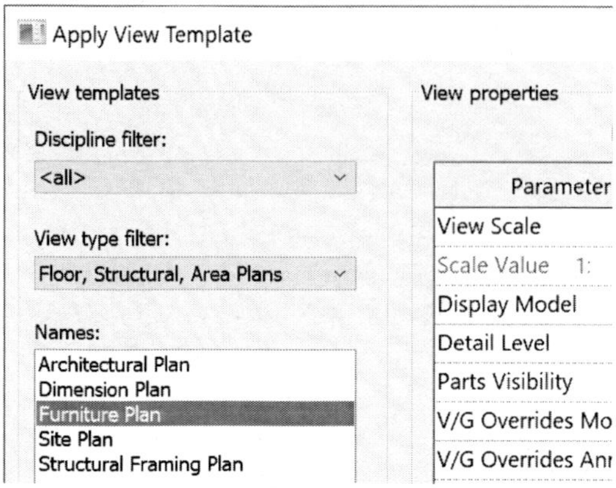

Figure 4–30

6. Type **VV** to open the *Visibility/Graphic Overrides* dialog box. Click on the *Revit Links* tab and clear the checkbox in the *Visibility* column for **Hotel-Pool.rvt**.
7. Click **OK**.
8. Test the view to check the applied view template. In the *Architecture* tab>*Build* panel, expand (Component) and click (Place a Component).
9. In the Type Selector, review the various furniture components that are available for the project. Select **Chair-Corbu** and place it in the lobby area near the curved curtain walls in the lower-right corner of the building.
   - Use <Spacebar> to rotate the component, as needed. If you want the component to follow the curve of a wall, hover over the wall and press <Spacebar> and the component will rotate about the curve or angle. Once it is in the direction you want, you can move your cursor to the location you want to place it and click to place.
10. Click (Modify).
11. Open the **Floor Plans: Floor 1** view. The chair does not display in this view because the Furniture category (and several others) has been toggled off.
12. Return to the **Floor Plans: Floor 1 - Furniture Plan**.
13. Save the project.

Task 2: Load families.

1. In the *Insert* tab>*Load from Library* panel, click (Load Family).

2. In the *Load Family* dialog box, navigate to the practice files *Families* folder. Load the following components:

   - *Doors* folder: **Elevator-Door-Center.rfa**
   - *Furniture* folder: **Countertop-Lobby.rfa**
   - *Planting* folder: **RPC Plant-Tropical.rfa** and **RPC Tree-Tropical.rfa**
   - *Site* folder: **Planter.rfa**
   - *Specialty Equip* folder: **Elevator-Electric.rfa**

   Note: *You will need to click* ***Open*** *after selecting families within a folder, then click* ***Load Family*** *again to select families from a different folder. You can press <Enter> to repeat the last command, which will open the Load Family dialog box.*

3. Save the project.

Task 3: Load families from Load Autodesk Family.

1. In the *Insert* tab>*Load from Library* panel, click  (Load Autodesk Family).

   Note: *You must have an Internet connection and be signed in to the software to use the Load Autodesk Family method. These families are also provided in the practice files Families>Tables and Families>Details folders.*

2. In the *Load Autodesk Family* dialog box, type **table dining round w chairs** in the search field and press <Enter>. Select the image of the **Table-Dining Round w Chairs** (as shown in Figure 4–31) and click **Load**.

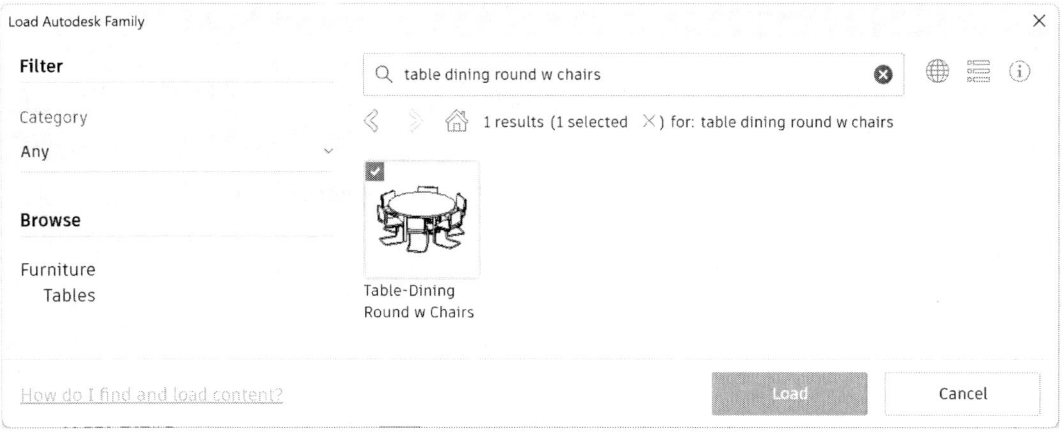

Figure 4–31

3. Start the **Load Autodesk Family** command again.

4. In the *Load Autodesk Family* dialog box, type **Break line** in the search field and press <Enter>.

5. Select the image of the **Break Line** and click **Load**.
6. Save the project.

Task 4: Place components.

In this task, you are simply learning how to place components. Do not be too concerned with the exact placement as you will learn how to use modifying tools in the next chapter.

1. Start the **Component** command.
2. Place and arrange the components, placing the dining tables in the breakfast area and other elements in the lounge, as shown in Figure 4–32. Place at least one plant in a planter. You can follow the suggested layout or create your own design.
    - To arrange components once placed, select the placed element, then click and hold the left mouse button to drag the element to the desired location. You can also use the up, down, left, and right arrows on your keyboard.

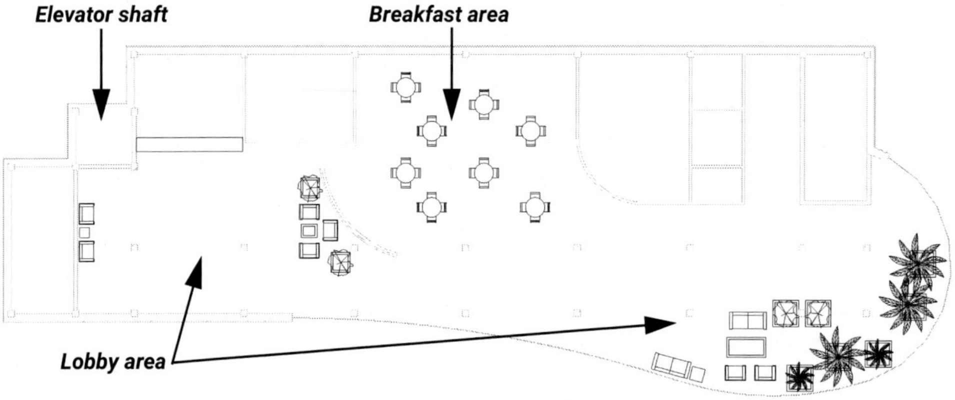

Figure 4–32

3. Click (Modify).
4. Start the **Component** command again. In the Type Selector, select **Elevator-Electric 2500 lbs** and place it inside the elevator shaft.

5. In the Type Selector, select the **Elevator Door - Center 42" x 84"** and place it in the wall, as shown in Figure 4–33.

   Note: *The image shows the elevator shaft cropped for better viewing.*

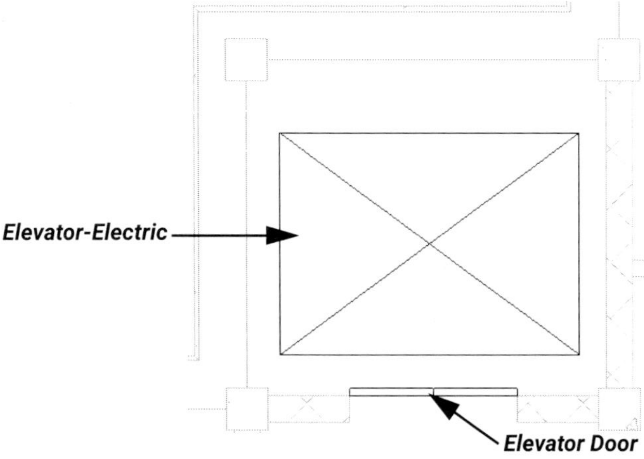

Figure 4–33

6. Select the elevator door component and make sure the flip grips are on the outside of the wall.
7. In the *Modify | Specialty Equipment* tab>*Clipboard* panel, click (Copy to the Clipboard).
8. In the *Clipboard* panel, expand (Paste) and click (Aligned to Selected Levels).
9. In the *Select Levels* dialog box, select **Basement** and **Floor 2** through **Floor 8**, as shown in Figure 4–34. (Select more than one level by holding down <Ctrl> while selecting them.) Click **OK**. This copies the door to the rest of the levels.

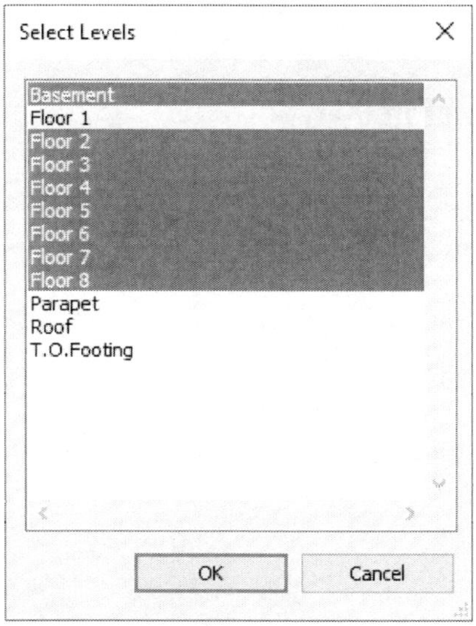

Figure 4–34

10. Open the Floor 2 view and other floor plan views to see the elevator door.
11. Save the project.

Task 5: Create a new loadable family size.

1. In the *Architecture* tab>*Build* panel, click (Structural Column).
2. In the Type Selector, select one of the **Concrete-Rectangular-Column** types.
3. In Properties, click (Edit Type).
4. In the *Type Properties* dialog box, click **Duplicate**.
5. Rename the column to **24 x 24**. Click **OK**.
6. In the *Type Properties* dialog box, change the dimensions for both *b* (base) and *h* (height) to **2'-0"**, as shown in Figure 4–35.

Type Parameters

Parameter	Value
Structural	
Section Shape	Not Defined
Dimensions	
b	2' 0"
h	2' 0"

Figure 4–35

7. Click **OK**.
8. Click (Modify).
9. Save the project.

Task 6: Create a new system family type.

1. In the *Structure* tab>*Foundation* panel, click (Structural Foundation: Wall), or type **FT**.
2. In the Type Selector, select the **Wall Foundation: Bearing Footing - 36" x 12"**, if not already selected.
3. In Properties, click (Edit Type).
4. In the *Type Properties* dialog box, click **Duplicate...**.
5. In the *Name* dialog box, type **Bearing Footing - 24" x 12"** and click **OK**.

6. In the *Type Properties* dialog box, under *Dimensions*, set the *Width* to **2'-0"**, as shown in Figure 4–36.

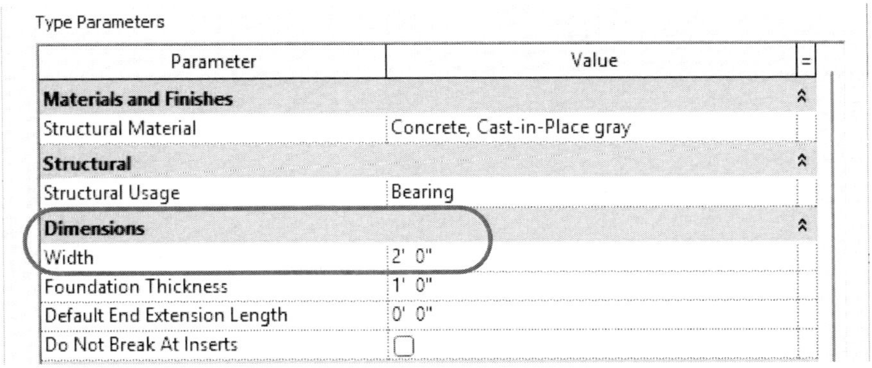
Type Parameters

Parameter	Value
Materials and Finishes	
Structural Material	Concrete, Cast-in-Place gray
Structural	
Structural Usage	Bearing
Dimensions	
Width	2' 0"
Foundation Thickness	1' 0"
Default End Extension Length	0' 0"
Do Not Break At Inserts	☐

Figure 4–36

7. Click **OK**.
8. Click (Modify).
9. Save and close the project.

End of practice

Chapter Review Questions

1. How do you change the family type when inserting a component?
    a. Quick Access Toolbar
    b. Type Selector
    c. Contextual tab
    d. Properties

2. If the component you want to use is not available in the current project, where do you go to get the component? (Select all that apply.)
    a. In another project, copy the component to the clipboard and paste it into the current project.
    b. In the current project, use  (Insert from File) and select the family from the list in the dialog box.
    c. In the current project, use  (Load Family) and select the family from the list in the dialog box.
    d. Search a manufacturer's site for a component and download it.

3. When you use the **Moves with Nearby Elements** option, can you control which elements a component moves with?
    a. Yes, select the element with which you want it to move.
    b. No, it moves with the closest host element.

4. Which of the following commands would you use if you want to move a furniture component to a floor that is lower than the level where it was original placed, as shown in Figure 4–37?

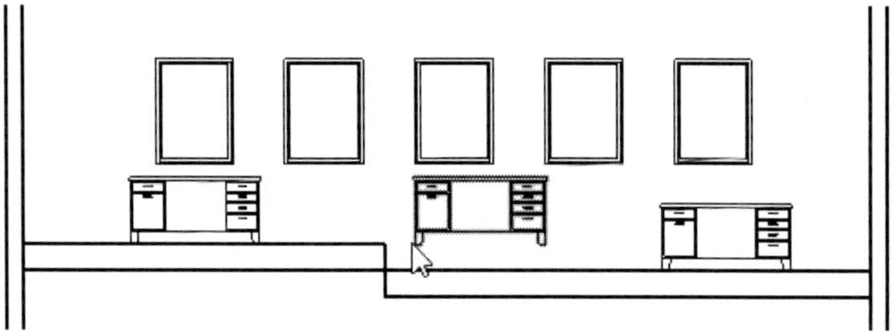

Figure 4–37

a. Use (Level) and add a level at the height of the lower floor.

b. Use (Ref Plane) and draw a plane aligned with the lower floor.

c. Use (Pick New Host) and select the lower floor.

d. Use (Edit Family) and change the work plane in the family so that it matches the height of the lower floor.

5. To use **Load Autodesk Family** to load a new family into your project, you must install the Autodesk Revit Content in your desired language from the Autodesk website.

a. True

b. False

Command Summary

Button	Command	Location
	**Copy to Clipboard**	• **Ribbon:** *Modify* tab>*Clipboard* panel • **Shortcut:** <Ctrl>+<C>
	**Cut to the Clipboard**	• **Ribbon:** *Modify* tab>*Clipboard* panel • **Shortcut:** <Ctrl>+<X>
	**Paste - Aligned to Current View**	• **Ribbon:** *Modify* tab>*Clipboard* panel, expand Paste
	**Paste - Aligned to Same Place**	• **Ribbon:** *Modify* tab>*Clipboard* panel, expand Paste
	**Paste - Aligned to Selected Levels**	• **Ribbon:** *Modify* tab>*Clipboard* panel, expand Paste
	**Paste - Aligned to Selected Views**	• **Ribbon:** *Modify* tab>*Clipboard* panel, expand Paste
	**Paste - Aligned to Picked Level**	• **Ribbon:** *Modify* tab>*Clipboard* panel, expand Paste
	**Paste from Clipboard**	• **Ribbon:** *Modify* tab>*Clipboard* panel • **Shortcut:** <Ctrl>+<V>
	**Load Autodesk Family**	• **Ribbon:** *Modify | Place Component* tab>*Load* panel or *Insert* tab>*Load from Library* panel
	**Load Family**	• **Ribbon:** *Modify | Place Component* tab>*Load* panel or *Insert* tab>*Load from Library* panel
	**Pick New Host**	• **Ribbon:** *Modify | Multi-Select* or *component type* contextual tab>*Host* panel
	**Place Component**	• **Ribbon:** *Architecture* tab>*Build* panel, expand Component • **Shortcut:** CM

Chapter 5

Basic Sketching and Modify Tools

When you start adding general building elements (e.g., walls, floors, and ceilings) to a project, you will use basic sketching, selecting, and modifying tools. Using these tools with drawing aids helps you to place and modify elements to create accurate building models.

Learning Objectives

- Sketch linear elements such as walls.
- Add components.
- Ease the placement of elements by incorporating drawing aids such as alignment and preview lines, preview images, temporary dimensions, and snaps.
- Place reference planes as temporary guide lines.
- Use techniques to select and filter groups of elements.
- Modify elements using a contextual tab, Properties, temporary dimensions, and controls.
- Move, copy, rotate, and mirror elements and create array copies in linear and radial patterns.
- Align, trim, and extend elements with the edges of other elements.
- Split linear elements anywhere along their length.
- Offset elements to create duplicates a specific distance away from the original.

5.1 Adding General Building Elements

General building element commands are found on the *Architecture* tab (shown in Figure 5–1) and are how you place elements such as walls, doors, roofs, etc. into your project. You can change the type of these elements using the Type Selector in Properties.

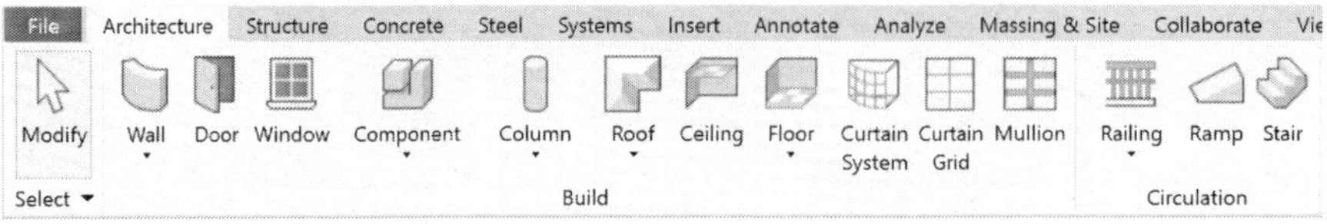

Figure 5–1

When you start a general building element command from the *Architecture* tab, the contextual tab and Properties (shown in Figure 5–2) enable you to modify element-specific features for the new element you are placing in the project. As you are working, several features called *drawing aids* display, as shown in Figure 5–2. They help you to create designs quickly and accurately. There will be different drawing aid and contextual tab options depending on which building element command is started.

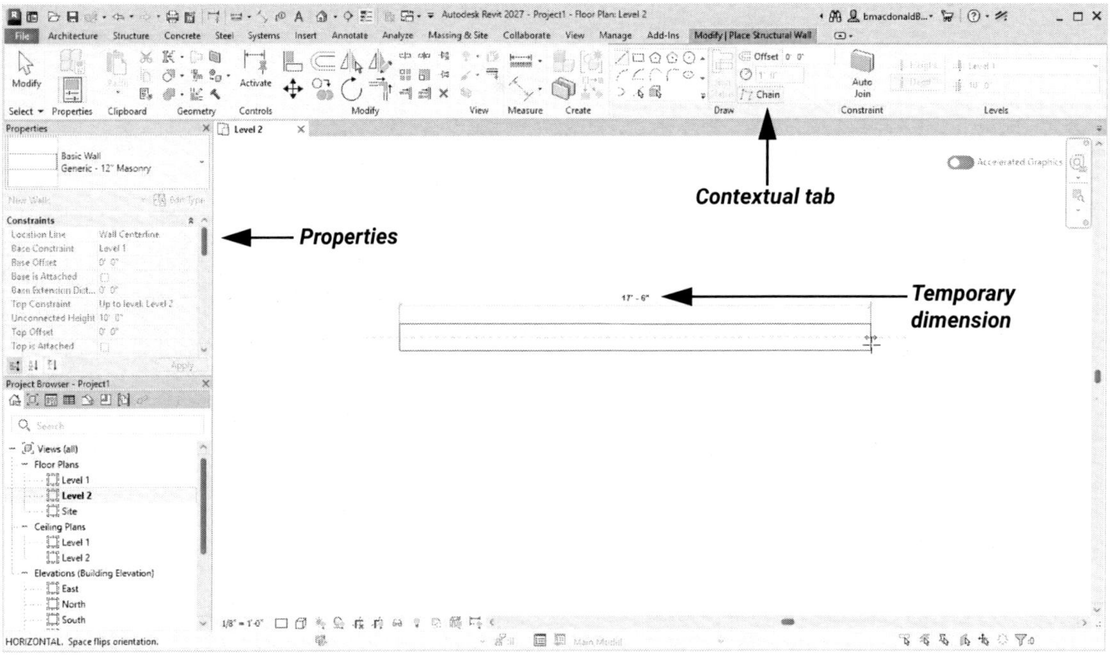

Figure 5–2

- In Revit, you are most frequently creating 3D model elements rather than 2D sketches. These tools work with both 3D and 2D elements in the software.

How To: Add Walls

In this How To, a wall has been used as an example, but these steps apply to any general building element command in the ribbon.

1. In the *Architecture* tab>*Build* panel or *Structure* tab>*Structure* panel, expand (Wall) and select (Wall: Structural) or (Wall: Architectural).
2. In Properties, verify or change the wall type (for example, **Basic Wall: Generic - 8"**) in the Type Selector and set any parameters like *Base Constraint*, *Base Offset*, and *Top Constraint*.
3. Place the wall in the model using the sketch tools.

How To: Add a Door

1. In the *Architecture* tab>*Build* panel, click (Door), or type **DR**.
2. In the Type Selector, select the type of door.
3. Hover over the wall that you want to place the door on. Use the temporary dimensions and/or other drawing aids to properly locate where you want the door.
   - Press <Spacebar> to change the swing of the door before placing it.
4. Select the wall once you are in the correct location to place the door.
5. Continue adding other doors as needed.

- While placing or modifying doors or windows, you can adjust the element using temporary dimensions and the **Flip the instance facing** and **Flip the instance hand** controls to change the swing and hinge locations, as shown in Figure 5–3. With windows, you can flip the interior and exterior using the same technique.

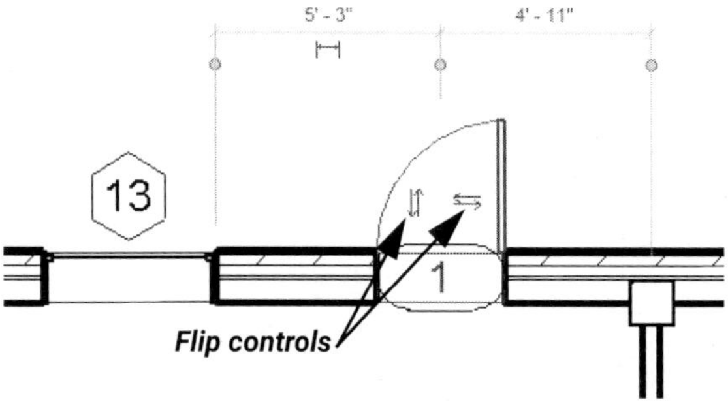

Figure 5–3

Draw Panel

Many elements (such as walls, beams, and braces) are modeled using the sketch tools in the contextual tab's *Draw* panel. Other elements (such as floors, ceilings, roofs, beam systems, and slabs) have boundaries that are sketched using many of the same tools. Sketch tools are also used when you create details or schematic drawings. Once you select a tool, additional settings will display in the contextual tab, such as (Offset) and (Radius).

> **Note:** *The exact tools and options vary according to the element being modeled.*

- When you use the **Create Similar** command on a element that was added using a sketch tool, like **Start-End-Radius Arc** or **Circle**, Revit will remember the tool that was used to create the element and use it again.

The following methods are available with most commands:

- *Draw* the element using a sketch tool.
- *Pick* an existing element (such as a line, face, or wall) as the basis for the new sketch.

How To: Use Sketch Tools

1. Start the command you want to use.
2. In the contextual tab>*Draw* panel (shown for the **Wall** command in Figure 5–4), select a sketch tool.

   Note: *You can change from one sketch tool to another in the middle of a command.*

3. Set the other options available in the contextual tab, as shown for the **Wall** command in Figure 5–4.

   Note: *Different options display according to the type of element that is selected or the command that is active.*

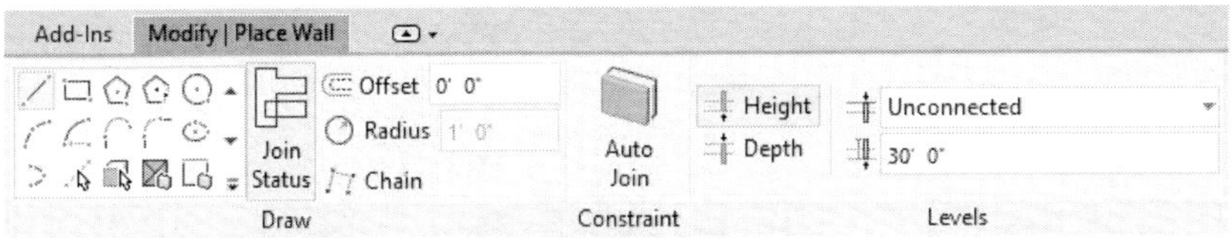

Figure 5–4

4. Depending on the sketch tool selected, select points to sketch the elements or watch the Status Bar, in the lower-left corner, for hints on what to do.

Sketch Tools and Options

The following are some of the sketch tools and options available in the *Draw* panel:

Draw Tools		
	Line	Draws a straight line defined by the first and last points. If **Chain** is enabled, you can continue selecting end points for multiple segments.
	Rectangle	Draws a rectangle defined by two opposing corner points. You can adjust the dimensions after selecting both points.
	Inscribed Polygon	Draws a polygon inscribed in a hypothetical circle with the number of sides specified in the contextual tab>*Draw* panel.
	Circumscribed Polygon	Draws a polygon circumscribed around a hypothetical circle with the number of sides specified in the contextual tab>*Draw* panel.
	Circle	Draws a circle defined by a center point and radius.
	Start-End-Radius Arc	Draws a curve defined by a start, end, and radius of the arc. The outside dimension shown is the included angle of the arc. The inside dimension is the radius.
	Center-ends Arc	Draws a curve defined by a center, radius, and included angle. The selected point of the radius also defines the start point of the arc.
	Tangent End Arc	Draws a curve tangent to another element. Select an end point for the first point, but do not select the intersection of two or more elements. Then, select a second point based on the included angle of the arc.
	Fillet Arc	Draws a curve defined by two other elements and a radius. Because it is difficult to select the correct radius by clicking, this command automatically moves to edit mode. Select the dimension and then modify the radius of the fillet.
	Spline	Draws a spline curve based on selected points. The curve does not actually touch the points (sketches, model lines, and detail lines only).
	Ellipse	Draws an ellipse from a primary and secondary axis (walls, sketches, model lines, and detail lines only).
	Partial Ellipse	Draws only one side of the ellipse, like an arc. A partial ellipse also has a primary and secondary axis (sketches, model lines, and detail lines only).
Pick Tools		
	Pick Lines	Use this option to select existing linear elements in the project. This is useful when you start the project from an imported 2D drawing.
	Pick Face	Use this option to select the face of a 3D massing element (walls and 3D views only).
	Pick Walls	Use this option to select an existing wall in the project to be the basis for a new sketch line (floors, ceilings, etc.).

Draw Panel Options		
	Join Status	Allows automatic wall joins.
	Offset	Enables you to enter values so you can create linear elements at a specified distance from the selected points or element.
	Radius	Enables you to enter values when using a radial tool or to add a radius to the corners of linear elements as you sketch them.
	Chain	Controls how many segments are created in one process. If this option is not selected, the **Line** and **Arc** tools only create one segment at a time. If it is selected, you can continue adding segments until you press <Esc> or select the command again.

Drawing Aids

As soon as you start sketching, placing, or modifying elements, drawing aids display, as shown in Figure 5–5, depending on which tool you are using. The drawing aids include:

- Alignment lines
- Preview lines
- Preview images
- Temporary dimensions
- Snaps

These aids are available with most modeling and many modification commands.

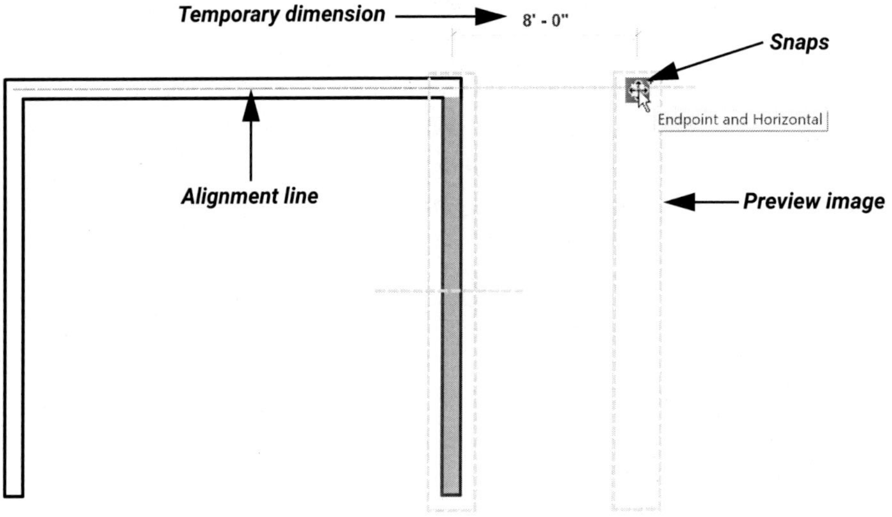

Figure 5–5

An **alignment line** displays as soon as you are in alignment horizontally, vertically, or at an angle with another object, such as the wall shown in Figure 5–6. They also line up with the implied intersections of walls and other elements.

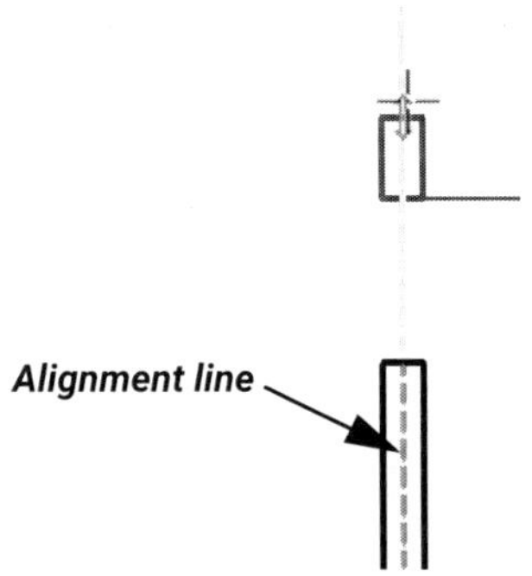

Figure 5–6

- Hold <Shift> to force the alignments to be orthogonal (90° angles only).

Preview lines display to help you visualize the outcome when using tools like **Offset** (shown in Figure 5–7) or while in a command like **Wall** that has the option to enter a numerical value for the offset. It also displays where the results will be permanently, depending on which side of the element you are hovering over.

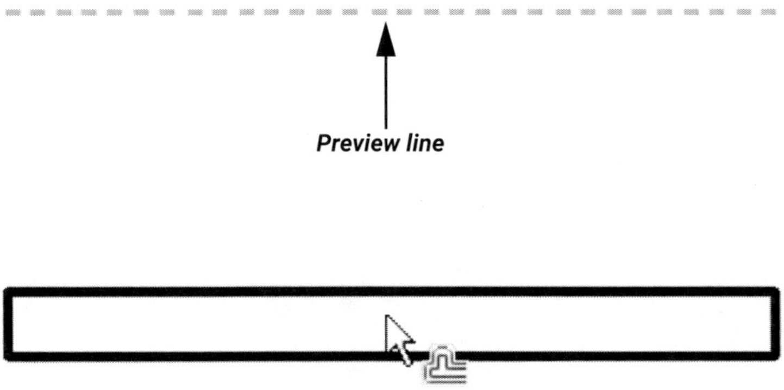

Figure 5–7

When using modify tools like **Copy** or **Move**, a **preview image** displays with dashed lines showing the approximate size and position of the element you are copying or moving (as shown in Figure 5–8). It helps you visualize placement and includes an alignment line to indicate when the element is horizontally or vertically aligned with nearby elements.

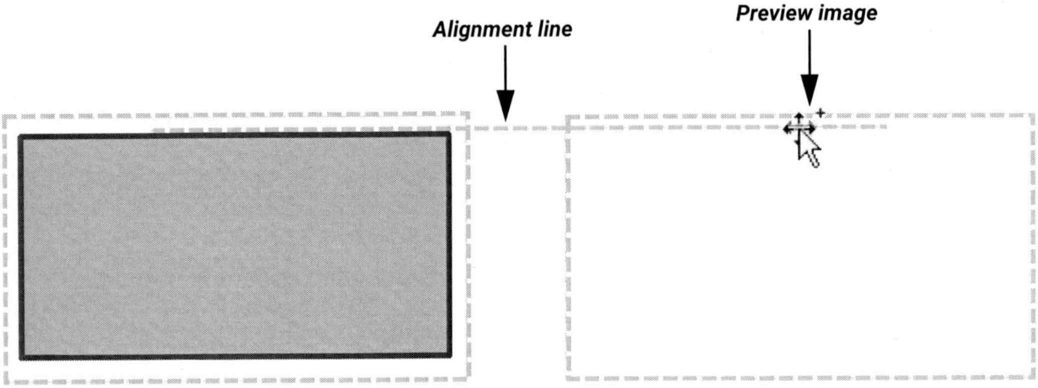

Figure 5–8

Temporary dimensions display when selecting elements in a view to help place elements at the correct length, angle, and location. As soon as you deselect an element, temporary dimensions no longer display in the view.

- To use temporary dimensions while placing an element, you can type in a value or move the cursor until you see the dimension you want, or you can place the element and then modify the value as needed.
- If you want to make temporary dimensions permanent, click the (Make this temporary dimension permanent) dimension symbol located under the dimension value, as shown in Figure 5–9.

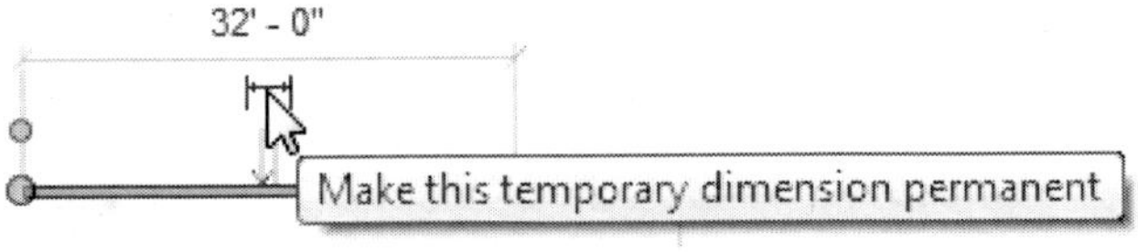

Figure 5–9

Snaps are key points that help you reference existing elements to exact points when modeling, as shown in Figure 5–10.

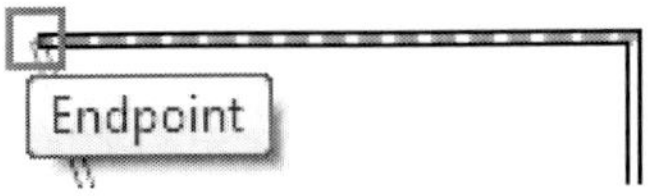

Figure 5–10

- When you move the cursor over an element, the snap symbol displays. Each snap location type displays with a different symbol.

Reference Planes

As you develop designs in Revit, there are times when you need lines to help you define certain locations. You can sketch *reference planes* (displayed as dashed green lines) and snap to them whenever you need to line up elements. For the example shown in Figure 5–11, the lighting fixtures in the reflected ceiling plan are placed using reference planes.

- To insert a reference plane, in the *Architecture, Structure*, or *Systems* tab>*Work Plane* panel, click  (Ref Plane), or type **RP**.

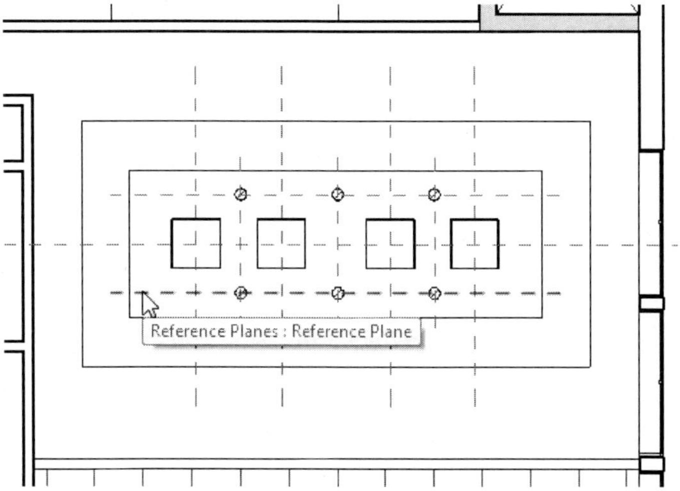

Figure 5–11

- Reference planes display in associated views because they are infinite planes and not just lines.

  Note: *Reference planes do not display in 3D views.*

- You can name reference planes by clicking **<Click to name>** and typing in the text box, as shown in Figure 5–12.

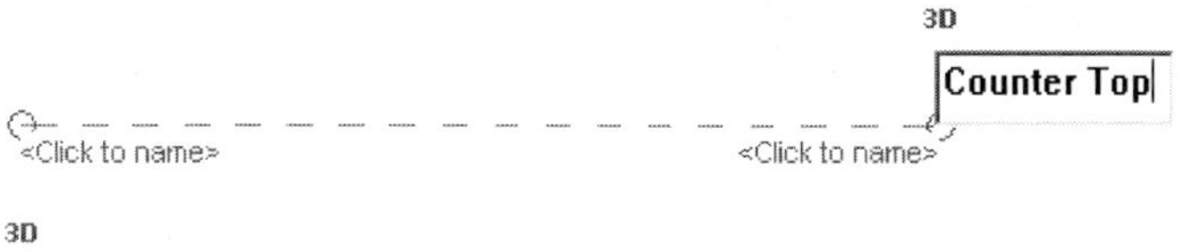

Figure 5–12

- If you sketch a reference plane in sketch mode (used with floors and similar elements), it does not display once the sketch is finished.
- Reference planes can have different line styles if they have been defined in the project. In Properties, select a style from the *Subcategory* list.

- It is possible to generate additional subcategories for reference planes using different line styles, lineweights, and colors, which can help you distinguish reference planes used for different functions. Moreover, you can manage the visibility of reference plane subcategories separately.

Hint: Model Line vs. Detail Line

While most of the elements that you create are representations of actual building elements, there are times you may need to add lines to clarify the design intent. These can be either detail lines, as shown in Figure 5–13, or model lines. Detail lines are also useful as references because they are only reflected in the view in which you sketch them.

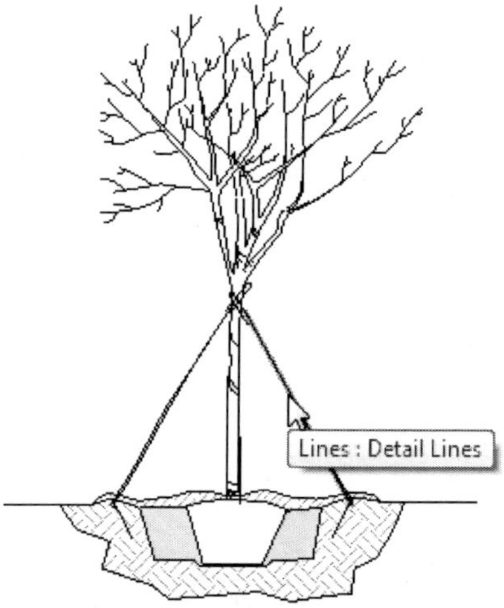

Figure 5–13

- A model line (*Architecture* or *Structure* tab>*Model* panel> (Model Line)) functions as a 3D element and displays in all views.
- A detail line (*Annotate* tab>*Detail* panel> (Detail Line)) is strictly a 2D element that only displays in the view in which it is drawn.
- In the *Modify* contextual tab, select a *Line Style* and then the sketch tool that you want to use to draw the model or detail line.

Editing Building Elements

Projects typically involve extensive changes to the model, and Revit was designed to make changes quickly and efficiently. You can change an element using the following methods, as shown in Figure 5–14:

- The Type Selector enables you to specify a different type. This is frequently used to change the size and/or style of the elements.
- Properties enables you to modify the information (parameters) associated just with the selected elements. These are referred to as **instance properties**.
- **Type properties** are accessed through Properties by clicking **Edit Type**. They enable you to modify parameters for all of the same element type in the model.
- The contextual tab in the ribbon contains the *Modify* commands and element-specific tools.
- Temporary dimensions enable you to change the element's dimensions or position.
- Controls enable you to drag, flip, lock, and rotate the element.
- Shape handles enable you to drag elements to modify their height or length.

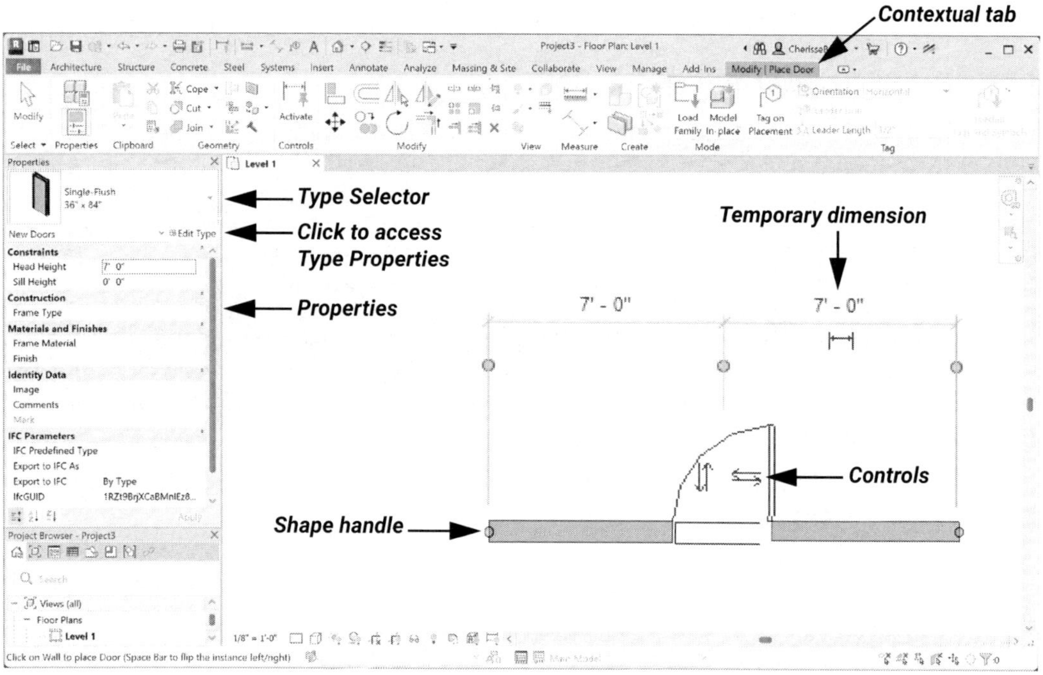

Figure 5–14

- To delete an element, select it and press <Delete>, right-click and select **Delete**, or in the *Modify* panel, click (Delete).

Working with Controls and Shape Handles

When you select an element, various controls and shape handles display depending on the element and view. For example, in plan view you can use controls to drag the ends of a wall and change its orientation. You can also use the controls to drag the wall ends in a 3D view and use the arrow shape handles to change the height of the wall, as shown in Figure 5–15.

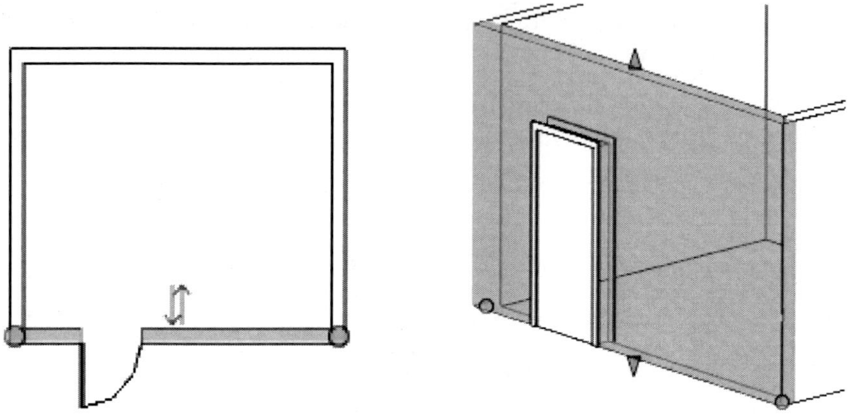

Figure 5–15

- If you hover the cursor over the control or shape handle, a tooltip displays showing its function.

Editing Temporary Dimensions

Temporary dimensions automatically snap to the closest elements that are perpendicular to each other. To change where the dimension has snapped to, drag the Move Witness Line control, as shown in Figure 5–16, to connect to a new reference. Note that temporary dimensions work with actual elements in the view and not with linked elements. You can also right-click on the Move Witness Line control and select **Move Witness Line**; the witness line attaches to your cursor and you can click a new location on an element to place the witness line.

- For walls, you can click on the Move Witness Line control to cycle through the different layers in the wall, or while dragging the Move Witness Line control, you can hover over a wall, press <Tab> to cycle through the different layers of the wall, and click to place the witness line once the layer you want highlights.
- You can change the font size of temporary dimensions as well as set the preference for how temporary dimensions display.

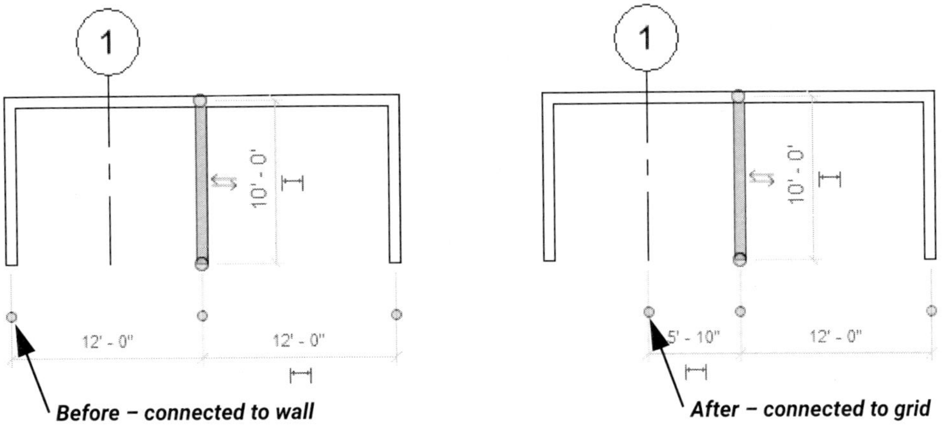

Figure 5–16

- The new location of a temporary dimension for an element is remembered as long as you are in the same session of the software.
- You can control the size of the temporary dimension text in the *Options* dialog box on the *Graphics* tab. In the *Temporary dimension text appearance* area, change the *Size* to a larger or smaller scale.

How To: Change the Size of Temporary Dimensions

1. In the *File* tab, click **Options**.
2. In the *Options* dialog box, select the *Graphics* tab.
3. In the *Temporary dimension text appearance* section, expand the *Size* drop-down list and select a different size, as shown in Figure 5–17. Click **OK**.

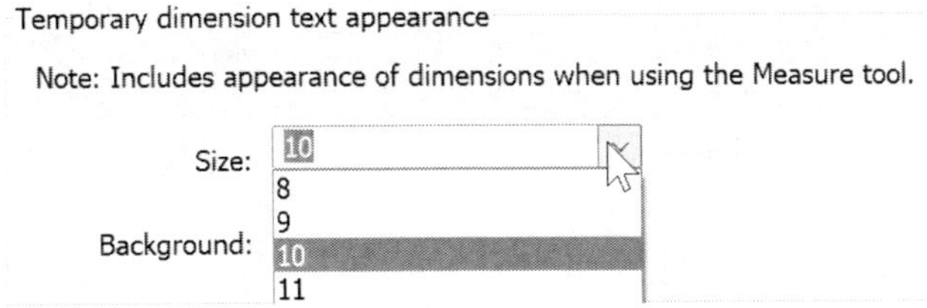

Figure 5–17

How To: Set the Temporary Dimension Properties

1. In the *Manage* tab>*Settings* panel, expand (Additional Settings), hover over (Annotations) and select (Temporary Dimensions).
2. In the *Temporary Dimensions Properties* dialog box (shown in Figure 5–18), select the desired options and click **OK**.

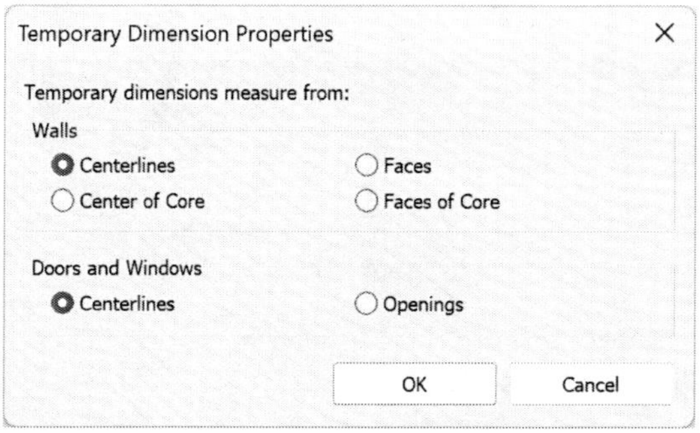

Figure 5–18

Selecting Multiple Elements

You can select more than one element at a time using the various methods described below, as well as remove elements from a group of selected elements by filtering out specific categories. When selecting more than one element in a model, you may also see controls like temporary dimensions and pin controls, as shown in Figure 5–19. You have the ability to hide these controls and temporary dimensions if they make viewing the selected elements difficult using the **Activate Controls and Dimensions** option.

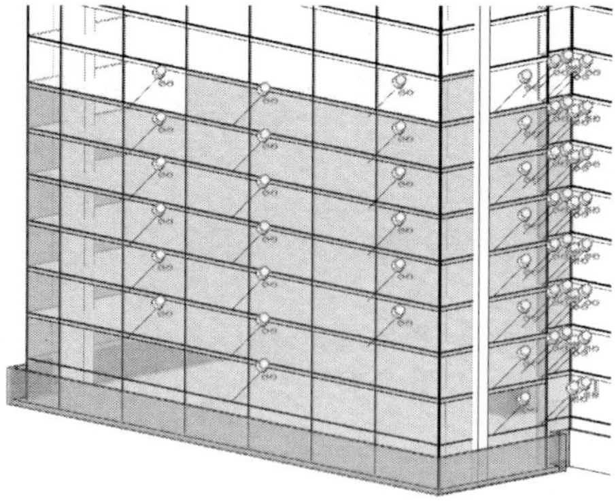

Figure 5–19

Note: *You can save selections and use them again*

How To: Manually Select Multiple Elements

1. Once you have selected at least one element, hold <Ctrl> and select another item to add it to your selection.
2. To remove an element from a group of selected elements, hold <Shift> and select the element you want removed.
    - If several elements are on or near each other, hover your cursor over an edge and press <Tab> to cycle through them before you click.
    - If there are elements that might be linked to each other, such as walls that are connected, pressing <Tab> selects the chain of elements.

How To: Select Multiple Elements with a Window Selection

1. Click and drag the cursor to *window* around elements using one of two selection options:
    - **Selection window (or containing window):** Click and drag your cursor from left to right (as shown in Figure 5–20). With this option, you only select the elements completely inside the window.
    - **Crossing window:** Click and drag your cursor from right to left (as shown in Figure 5–20). With this option, you select elements that are both inside and crossing the window.

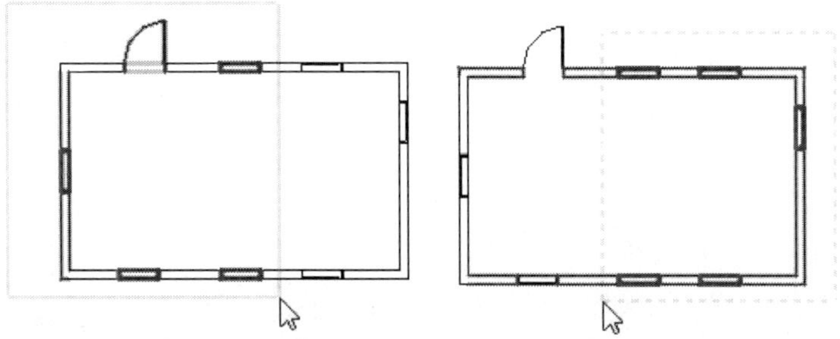

Selection window: left to right ***Crossing window: right to left***

Figure 5–20

- If you are accidentally clicking on elements and dragging them out of place when trying to window around elements, you can toggle off (Drag Elements on Selection) in the lower-right corner of the Status Bar. When off, the icon will display with a red X ( ).

How To: Quickly Select a Previous Group of Selected Elements

1. Press <Ctrl>+<Left Arrow> to reselect the previous group of element selection.
    - Alternatively, right-click in the view window with nothing selected and select **Select Previous**.

How To: Quickly Select All of the Same Element

1. To select all elements of a specific type, right-click on an element.
2. In the menu, select **Select All Instances>Visible in View, In Entire Project**, or **In Entire Project Including Legends**, as shown in Figure 5–21. For example, if you select a column of a specific size and use this command, only the columns of the same size are selected.

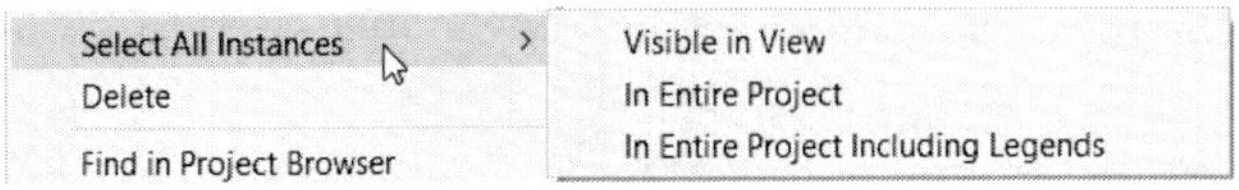

Figure 5–21

- Alternatively, select the element in the view and type **SA**. This selects all elements of the same type in the view.

How To: Use Activate Controls and Dimensions

1. With multiple elements selected in the model, in the *Modify* contextual tab>*Controls* panel, click (Activate Controls and Dimensions) to toggle it on (the icon will be highlighted in blue if the command is toggled on).
   - Alternatively, in the Quick Access Toolbar, click (Activate Controls and Dimensions), or type **AC**.
2. When this option is toggled on, the controls and temporary dimensions are shown in the view, as shown on the left in Figure 5–22. Toggle (Activate Controls and Dimensions) off to hide the controls and dimensions again, as shown on the right.

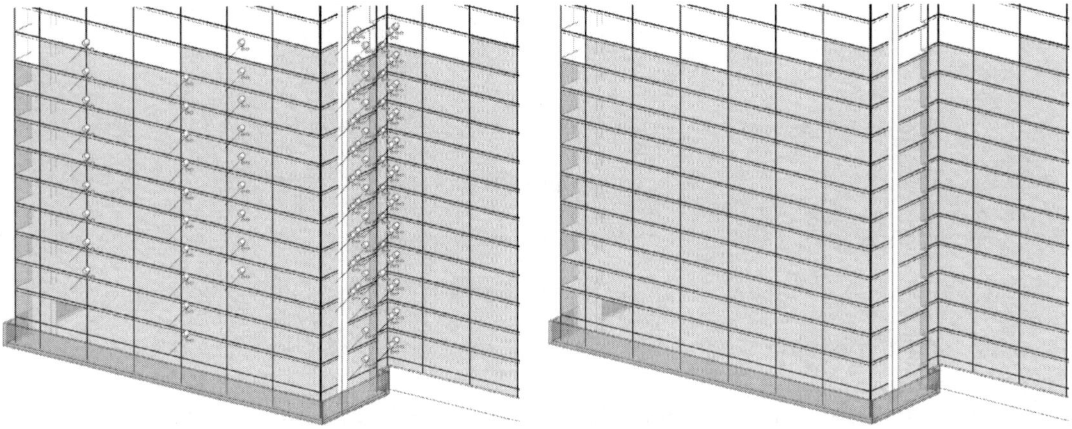

Activate Controls and Dimensions toggled on ***Activate Controls and Dimensions toggled off***

Figure 5–22

Measuring Tool

When modifying a model, it is useful to know the distance between elements. This can be done with temporary dimensions or, more frequently, by using the measuring tools found in the Quick Access Toolbar or in the *Modify* tab>*Measure* panel, as shown in Figure 5–23.

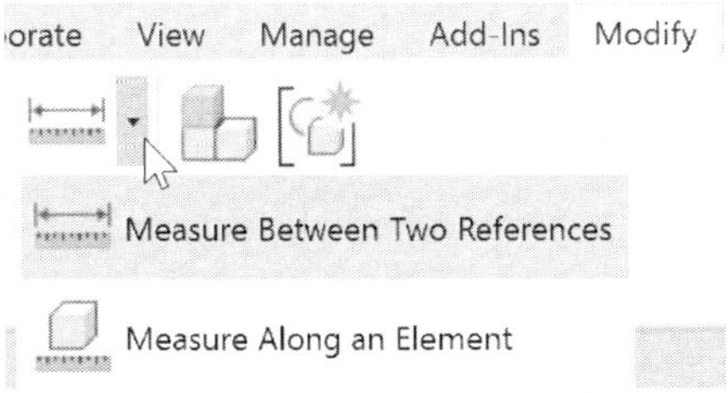

Figure 5–23

-  (Measure Between Two References): Select two elements and the measurement displays. This can be done in both 2D and 3D views.
  - If you select **Chain** in the *Modify | Measure* tab>*Measurement* panel (as shown in Figure 5–24), you can get the total length of multiple measurements.

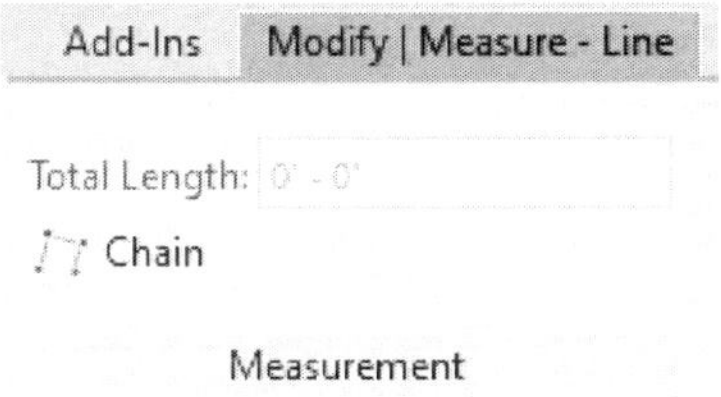

Figure 5–24

-  (Measure Along An Element): Select the edge of a linear element and the total length displays. Use <Tab> to highlight other elements and then click to measure along all of them, as shown in Figure 5–25. This can be done in 2D views only.

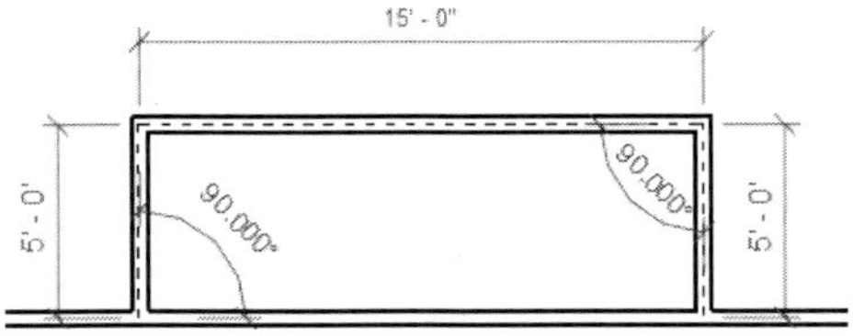

Figure 5–25

- References include any snap point, wall lines, or other parts of elements (such as door center lines).

Filtering Selection of Multiple Elements

When multiple element categories are selected, the *Multi-Select* contextual tab opens in the ribbon. This gives you access to all of the modify tools and the **Filter** command. The **Filter** command enables you to specify the types of elements to select. For example, you might only want to select columns, as shown in Figure 5–26.

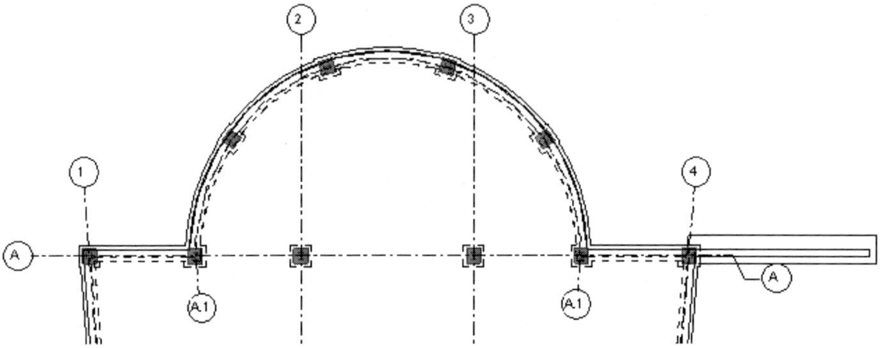

Figure 5–26

How To: Filter a Selection of Multiple Elements

1. Select everything in the area using either a crossing window or window selection that includes the elements you want to work with.
2. In the *Modify | Multi-Select* tab>*Selection* panel or in the Status Bar, click (Filter). The *Filter* dialog box opens, as shown in Figure 5–27.

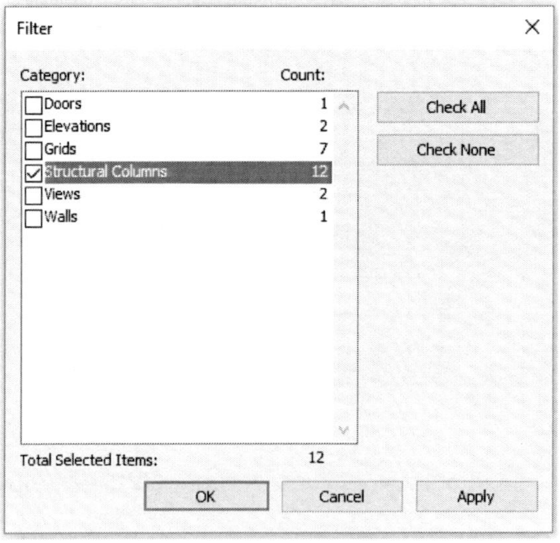

Figure 5–27

3. The *Filter* dialog box displays all types of elements in the original selection. Click **Check None** to clear all of the options or **Check All** to select all of the options. You can also select or clear individual categories as needed.
4. Click **OK**. The selection is now limited to the elements you specified.

- The number of elements selected displays on the right end of the Status Bar and in Properties.

Practice 5a
Sketch and Edit Elements

Practice Objective

- Use sketch tools and drawing aids.

In this practice, you will use the **Wall** command along with sketching tools and drawing aids, such as temporary dimensions and snaps. You will use the **Modify** command and modify the walls using grips, temporary dimensions, the Type Selector, and Properties. You will add a door and modify it using temporary dimensions and controls.

A simple model is used for this exercise so you can practice using the tools before working on the main building model. The completed model is shown in Figure 5–28.

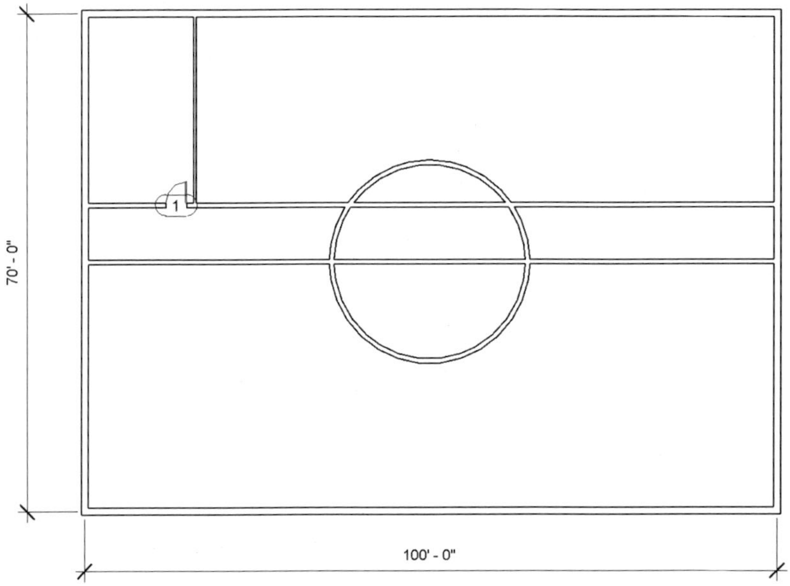

Figure 5–28

Task 1: Use sketching tools and temporary dimensions to model and modify walls.

1. On the Home screen, in the *Models* section, click **New...**. Alternatively, if you are in a project, in the *File* tab, click (New)> (Project).
2. In the *New Project* dialog box, click **Browse...**.
3. In the *Choose Template* dialog box, navigate to the practice files *Templates* folder, select **Imperial-Arch Template**, and click **Open**.

4. In the *New Project* dialog box, click **OK**.
5. In the Quick Access Toolbar, click (Save). When prompted, name the project **Starting Project.rvt** and save it in the practice files folder.
6. In the *Manage* tab>*Settings* panel, expand (Additional Settings), hover over (Annotations), and select (Temporary Dimensions).
7. In the *Temporary Dimensions Properties* dialog box, in both the *Walls* and *Doors and Windows* sections, select **Centerlines** (if not already selected), as shown in Figure 5–29, and click **OK**.

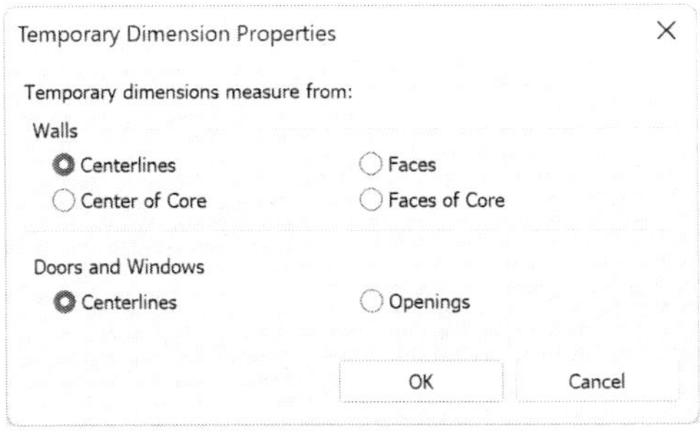

Figure 5–29

8. In the *Architecture* tab>*Build* panel, click (Wall), or type **WA**.
9. In Properties, verify the wall type is set to **Basic Wall Generic - 8"**.
10. In the *Modify | Place Wall* tab>*Draw* panel, click (Rectangle) and verify that (Join Status) is toggled on.
11. In the *Constraint* panel, verify that (Auto Join) is toggled off (not highlighted).
12. In the *Levels* panel, leave the **Height** and **Depth** as is.

    Note: *You want to draw your walls within the four elevation markers (these can be moved at anytime during a project if needed). Keep an eye on the Status Bar in the lower-left corner for command prompts.*

13. Click a starting point for the rectangle to the left (near the North and West elevation markers), then drag your mouse in a diagonal direction to the right until the rectangle is approximately **90' x 60'**, and click to finish. You do not have to be precise because you can change the dimensions later. Note that temporary dimensions display while you are drawing the rectangle and after.
14. Click (Modify). Note that temporary dimensions no longer display after you click **Modify**.
15. Select an elevation marker and type **VH** to hide them in view.

16. Zoom in to the walls and select the bottom horizontally drawn wall. The first vertical wall's temporary dimension becomes active (changes to blue). Click on it and type **70**, as shown in Figure 5–30, then press <Enter>.

Note: *Because the project's units are set to feet and fractional inches, you can type the numbers separated by a space without entering the units (for example,* ***4 6*** *for 4'-6"), then press <Enter> and the software knows how to convert it to the proper units.*

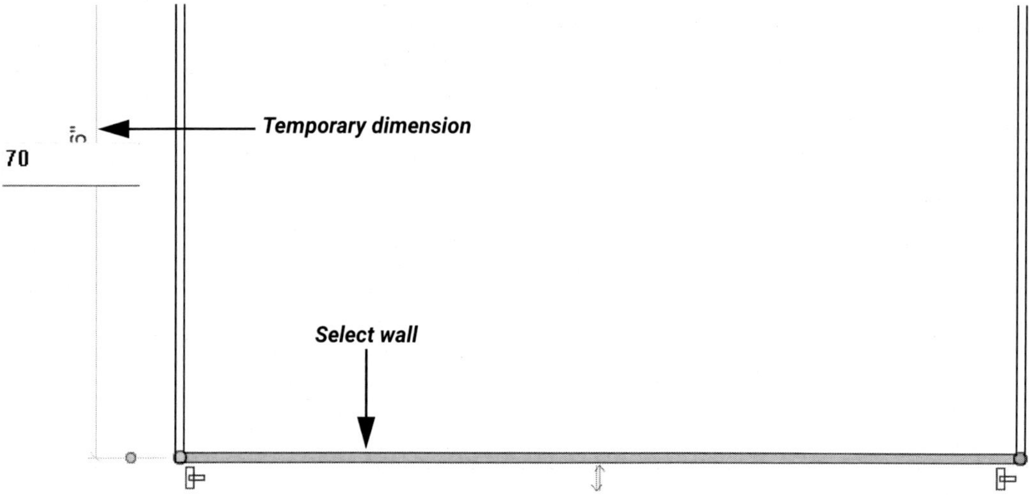

Figure 5–30

17. The dimension still displays as temporary. Click the dimension control of the dimension to make it permanent, as shown in Figure 5–31.

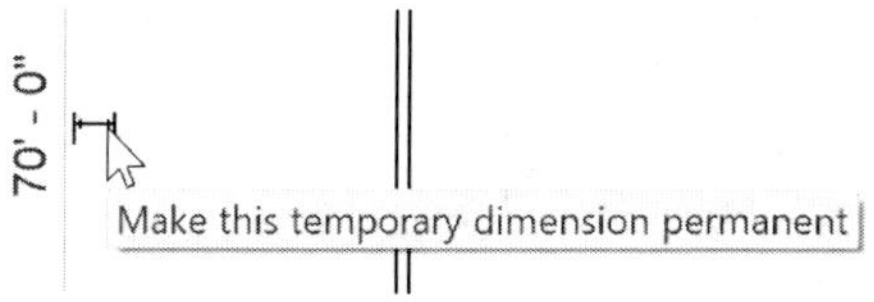

Figure 5–31

18. Click (Modify).

19. Select the right vertically drawn wall, as shown in Figure 5–32. The bottom horizontal dimension becomes active. Click the dimension text, type **100** (as shown in Figure 5–32), and press <Enter>. Make the dimension permanent.

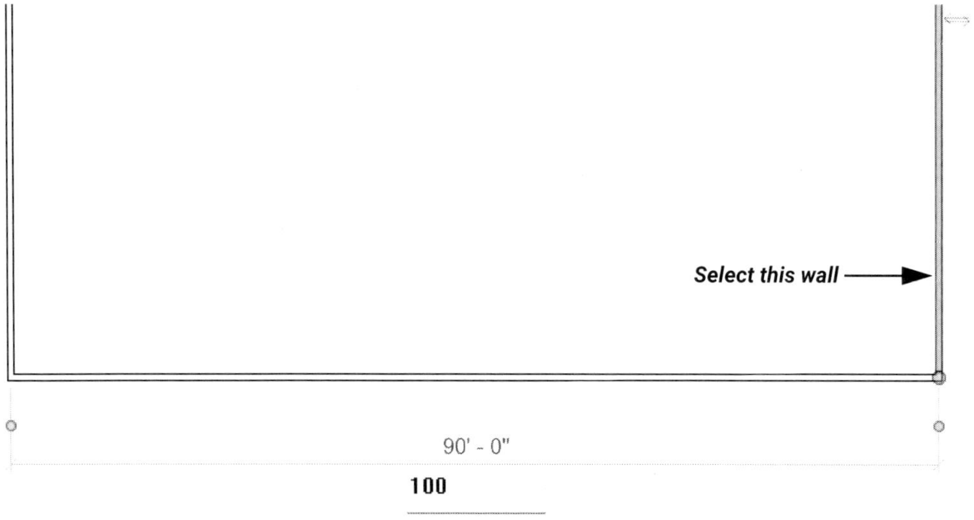

Figure 5–32

20. Click (Modify) or click in an empty space in the view to end the selection.

21. Start the **Wall** command and use the same wall type.

22. In the *Draw* panel, verify that (Line) is selected and toggle off (Chain). Sketch a wall going left to right horizontally from midpoint to midpoint of the vertical walls. Hint: The midpoint snap icon is a triangle. Move your cursor along the vertical wall until the triangle displays, then click to select it.

23. To draw another horizontal wall, move your cursor along the leftmost vertical wall above the middle horizontal wall until the temporary dimension displays as **8'-0"**, as shown in Figure 5–33. Click to place the wall start point, then click the rightmost vertical wall for the second point.

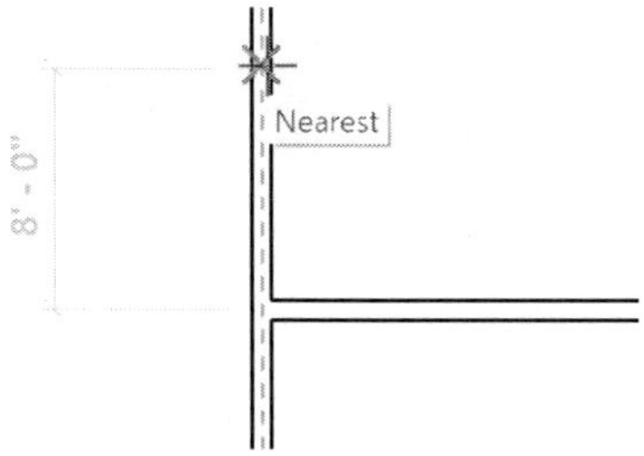

Figure 5–33

24. Click (Modify).

Note: *If needed, you can adjust the distance between the two horizontal walls by selecting the wall you just drew and using the temporary dimension to adjust the wall's distance. Note that if you were to select the bottom vertical wall and change the temporary dimension, that wall would be the wall that moves.*

25. Start the **Wall** command. From the horizontal wall you just drew, draw a wall in the vertical direction **16'-0"** away from the outermost wall, as shown in Figure 5–34, to created an enclosed room.

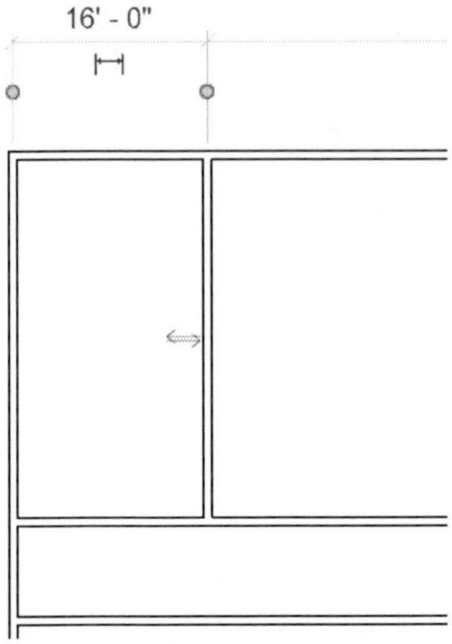

Figure 5–34

26. Stay in the **Wall** command. In the *Draw* panel, click (Circle) and sketch a **14'-0"** radius circular wall at the midpoint of the lower interior horizontally drawn wall, as shown in Figure 5–35. Hint: After you click your first pick point, you can type your measurement and press <Enter> to create the circle.

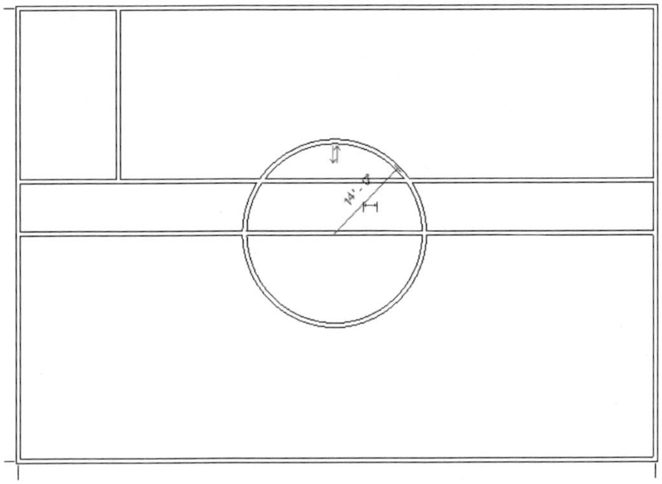

Figure 5–35

27. Click (Modify).

28. Hover the cursor over one of the outside walls, press <Tab> to highlight the chain of outside walls, and click to select the walls.
29. In the Type Selector, select **Basic Wall: Generic - 12"**, as shown in Figure 5–36. The thickness of the outside walls change.

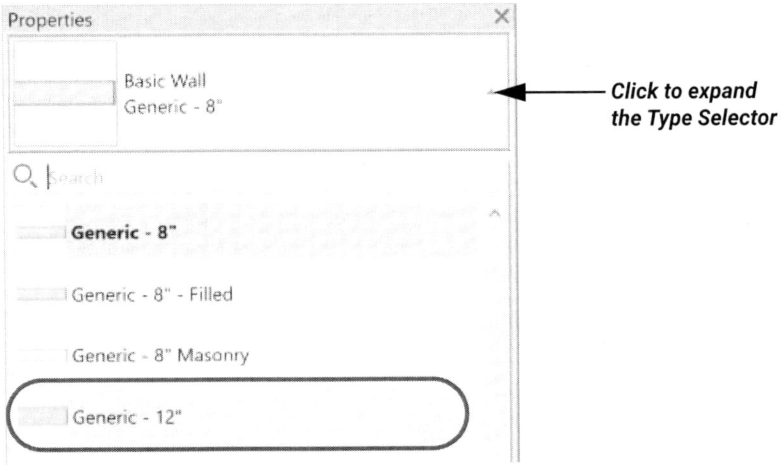

Figure 5–36

30. Click in an empty space in the view to release the selection.
31. Select the vertically drawn wall in the upper-left room. In the Type Selector, change the wall to one of the interior partition wall types. Note that the dimension does not change from **16'-0"**
32. Click in an empty space in the view to release the selection.
33. Save the project.

Task 2: Add and modify a door.

1. Zoom in on the room in the upper-left corner.
2. In the *Architecture* tab>*Build* panel, click (Door), or type **DR**.
3. In the *Modify | Place Door* tab>*Tag* panel, click (Tag on Placement) and verify the *Orientation* is set to **Horizontal**.

4. Place a door in the hallway in the upper-left room, as shown in Figure 5–37.
5. Click (Modify).
6. Select the door. Use temporary dimensions to move it so it is **2'-6"** from the right interior vertical wall. If needed, use controls to flip the door so it swings into the room, as shown in Figure 5–37.

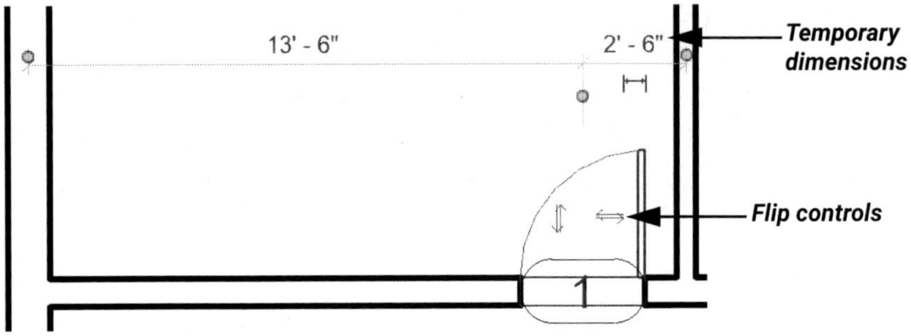

Figure 5–37

7. Type **ZE** to zoom out to the full view.
8. Save and close the project.

End of practice

5.2 Working with Basic Modify Tools

The basic modifying tools, **Move**, **Copy**, **Rotate**, **Mirror**, **Align**, and **Array**, can be used with individual elements or any selection of elements. They are found in the *Modify* panel (shown in Figure 5–38), in the *Modify* tab, and in contextual tabs.

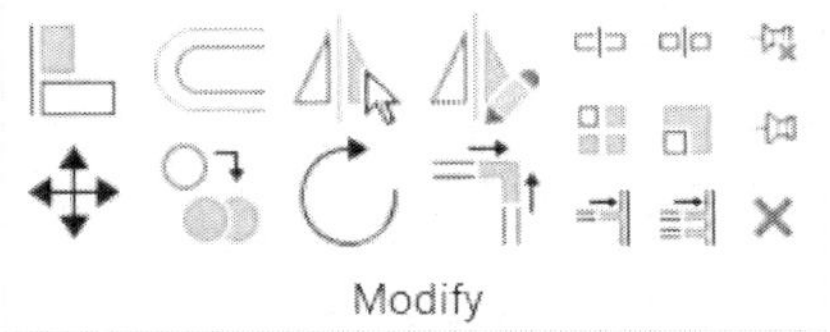

Figure 5–38

- For these modify commands, you can either select the elements and start the command, or start the command, select the elements, and press <Enter> to finish the selection and move to the next step in the command.

  Note: *Watch the Status Bar in the lower-left corner of the interface for the command prompts.*

Moving and Copying Elements

The **Move** and **Copy** commands enable you to select the element(s) and move or copy them from one place to another. You can use drawing aids to help place a second element, as shown in Figure 5–39.

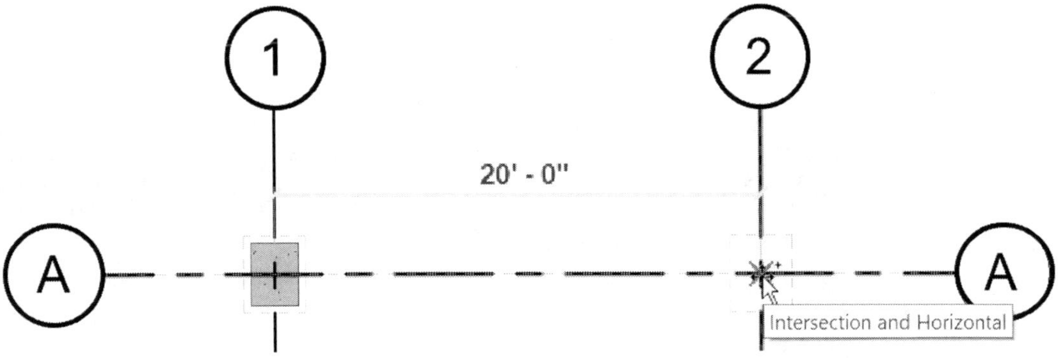

Figure 5–39

How To: Move or Copy Elements

1. Select the elements you want to move or copy.
2. In the *Modify* panel, click (Move) or (Copy). Alternatively, you can type **MV** for **Move** and **CO** for **Copy**. A boundary box displays around the selected elements.
3. Select a start point on or near the element.
4. Select a second point.
5. When you are finished, you can start another *Modify* command using the elements that remain selected, or click (Modify) to end the command.

- You can drag elements to new locations without starting the **Move** command by selecting an element, holding down the left mouse button, and dragging your cursor to move the element.
- Select an element, press and hold <Ctrl>, and drag your cursor away from the element to create a copy of it. This is quick but not very precise.

Move/Copy Elements Options

The **Move** and **Copy** commands have several options that display in the ribbon's contextual tab, as shown in Figure 5–40.

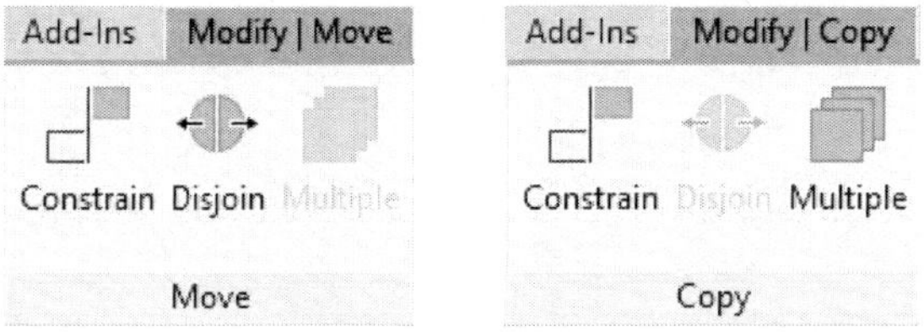

Figure 5–40

Constrain	Restricts the movement of the cursor to horizontal or vertical, or along the axis of an item that is at an angle. This keeps you from selecting a point at an angle by mistake. **Constrain** is off by default.
Disjoin (Move only)	Breaks any connections between the elements being moved and other elements. If **Disjoin** is on, the elements move separately. If it is off, the connected elements also move or stretch. **Disjoin** is off by default.
Multiple (Copy only)	Enables you to make multiple copies of one selection.

- These commands only work in the current view, not between views or projects. To copy between views or projects, in the *Modify* tab>*Clipboard* panel, use (Copy to Clipboard), (Cut to the Clipboard), and (Paste from Clipboard).

Hint: Pinning Elements

If you do not want elements to be moved, you can pin them in place, as shown in Figure 5–41. Select the elements and in the *Modify* tab>*Modify* panel, click (Pin), or type **PN**. Pinned elements can be copied, but not moved. If you try to delete a pinned element, a warning dialog box displays reminding you that you must unpin the element before the command can be started.

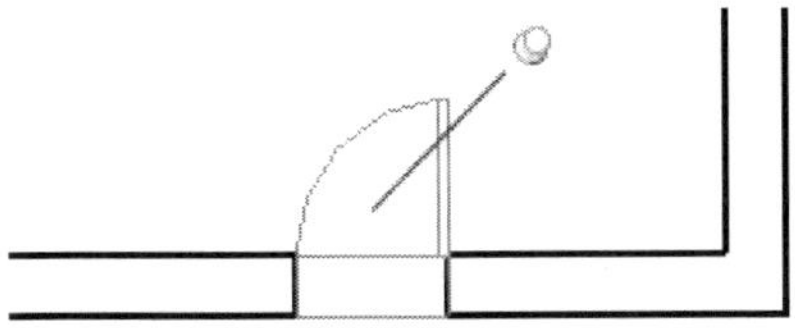

Figure 5–41

Select the element and click (Unpin) or type **UP** to unpin the element.

Rotating Elements

The **Rotate** command enables you to rotate selected elements around a center point or origin, as shown in Figure 5–42. You can use preview images, temporary dimensions, and snaps to help specify the center of rotation and the angle. You can also create copies of the element as it is being rotated.

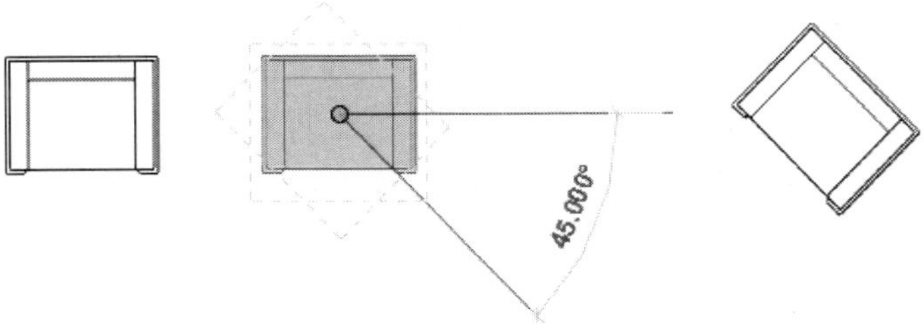

Figure 5–42

How To: Rotate Elements

1. Select the element(s) you want to rotate.
2. In the *Modify* panel, click (Rotate), or type **RO**.

3. In the *Modify | Rotate* tab>*Rotate* panel, select either (Place), as shown on the left in Figure 5–43, to manually place the center of rotation on the element or (Center), as shown on the right in Figure 5–43, to automatically set to the center of the element or group of elements.

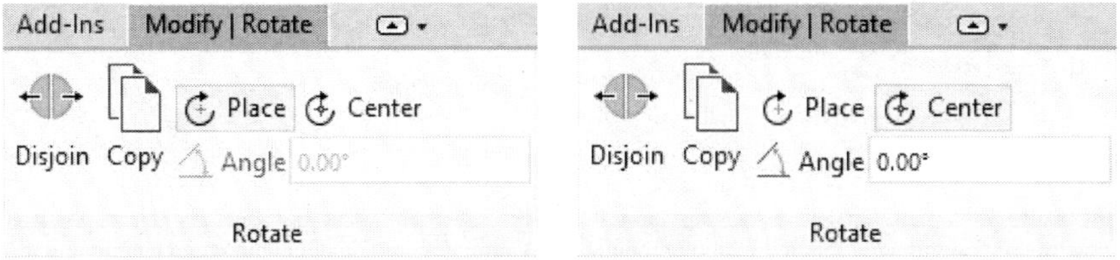

Figure 5–43

4. To change the center of rotation (as shown in Figure 5–44) when using the **Place** option, use one of the following:
   - Drag the center of rotation grip control to a new point.
   - Click the center of rotation then select a different location on the element.
   - Press <Spacebar> to select the center of rotation and remove it from its current location, then click a new location to move it to.

   ***Note:** To start the **Rotate** command with the ability to select the center of rotation, select the elements first and type **R3**.*

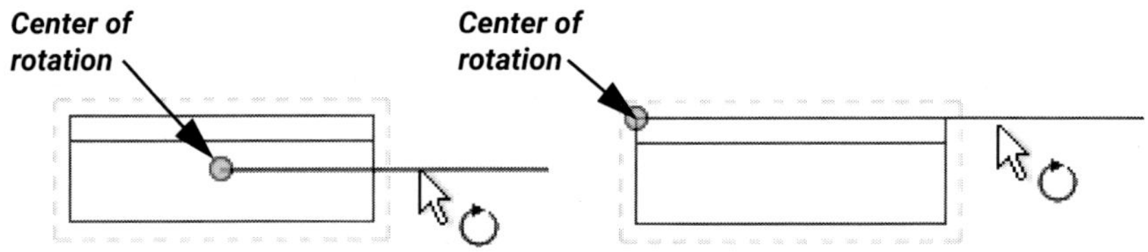

Figure 5–44

5. Once the center of rotation is established, in the *Modify | Rotate* tab>*Rotate* panel, specify if you want to make a copy by selecting (Copy), type an angle in the (Angle) field, and press <Enter>. You can also specify the angle on screen using temporary dimensions after the first selection point.
6. To rotate an element that has a connection between other elements, such as a wall or a single duct or pipe in a run, select the element and in the *Modify | Rotate* tab>*Rotate* panel, select (Disjoin). This will allow you to only rotate the selected element without getting an error message. This does not work if an element has been hosted to an element such as toilet or sink that is hosted to a wall.
7. The rotated element(s) remain highlighted, enabling you to start another command using the same selection, or click (Modify) to finish.

Mirroring Elements

The **Mirror** command enables you to mirror elements about an axis defined by a selected element, as shown in Figure 5–45, or by selected points. It is important to understand that if you mirror components with multiple connectors, it will flip the connectors. For example, when you mirror a sink, the hot and cold connectors on the copied or flipped element will be on the opposite sides. Always verify the elements that you mirror.

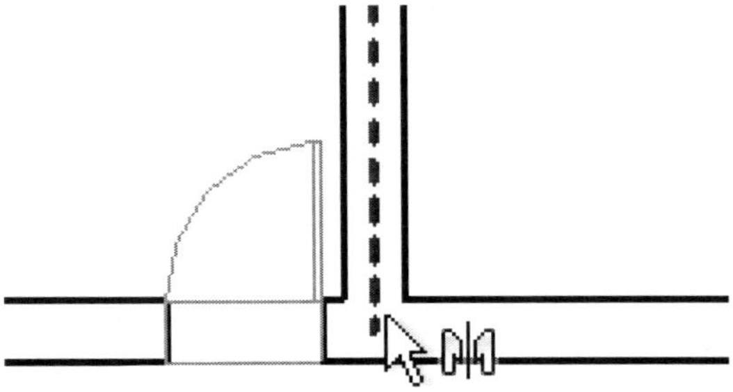

Figure 5–45

How To: Mirror Elements

1. Select the element(s) to mirror.
2. In the *Modify* panel, select the method you want to use:
   - Click (Mirror - Pick Axis) or type **MM**. This prompts you to select an element as the **Axis of Reflection** (mirror line).
   - Click (Mirror - Draw Axis) or type **DM**. This prompts you to select two points to define the axis about which the elements mirror.
3. In the *Modify | Mirror* tab>*Mirror* panel, select or deselect (Copy).
4. The new mirrored element(s) remain highlighted, enabling you to start another command, or return to **Modify** to finish.

Hint: Scale

Revit is designed with full-size elements. Therefore, not much should be scaled. For example, scaling a wall increases its length but does not impact the width, which is set by the wall type. However, you can use (Scale) in reference planes, images, and imported files from other programs.

Creating Linear and Radial Arrays

The **Array** command creates multiple copies of selected elements in a linear or radial pattern, as shown in Figure 5–46. For example, you can array a row of columns to create a row of evenly spaced columns on a grid, or array a row of parking spaces. The arrayed elements can be grouped or placed as separate elements.

> ***Note:*** *A linear array creates a straight line pattern of elements, while a radial array creates a circular pattern around a center point.*

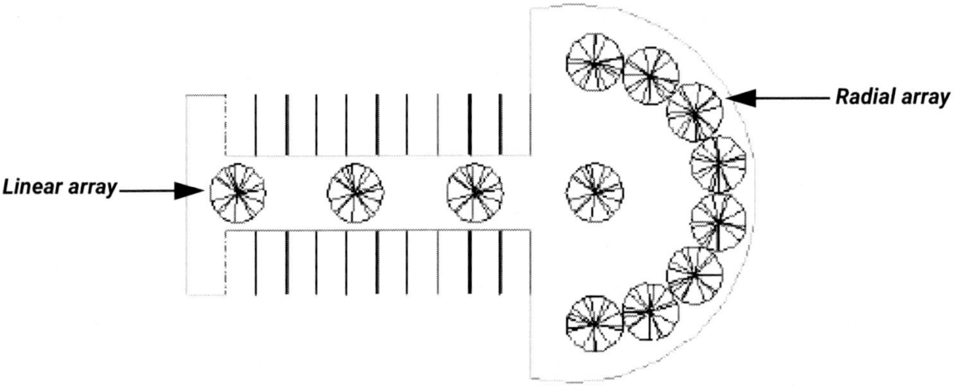

Figure 5–46

Array Options

In the *Modify | Array* contextual tab, set up the options in the *Array* panel for a **Linear** array (as shown on the top of Figure 5–47) or **Radial** array (as shown on the bottom).

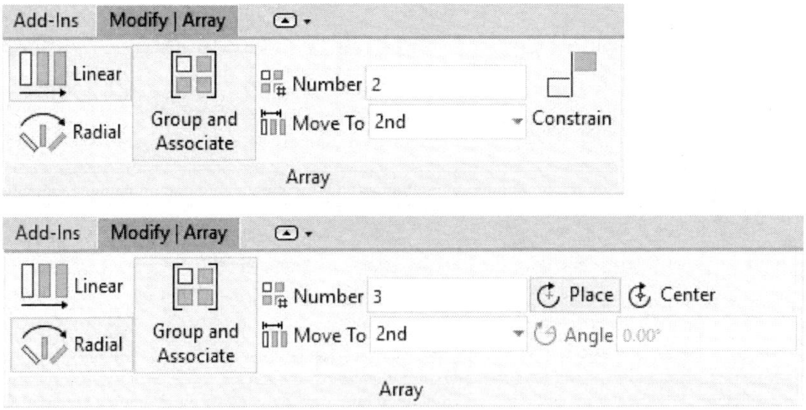

Figure 5–47

Group and Associate	Creates an array group element out of all arrayed elements. Groups can be selected by selecting any elements in the group.
Number	Specifies how many instances you want in the array.
Move To	**2nd** specifies the distance or angle between the center points of the two elements. **Last** specifies the overall distance or angle of the entire array.
Constrain	Restricts the direction of the array to only vertical or horizontal (Linear only).
Angle	Specifies the angle (Radial only).
Place or Center	Specifies a location for the origin about which the elements rotate (Radial only). Select **Place** to manually place the center of rotation on the element or select **Center** to automatically set it to the center of the element or group of elements

How To: Create a Linear Array

1. Select the element(s) to array.
2. In the *Modify* panel, click (Array), or type **AR**.
3. In the *Modify | Array* tab>*Array* panel, click (Linear).
4. Specify the (Number) and the (Move To) option.
5. Select a start point and an end point to set the spacing and direction of the array. The array is displayed.
6. If (Group and Associate) is selected, you are prompted again for the number of items, as shown in Figure 5–48. Type a new number or click on the screen to finish the command.

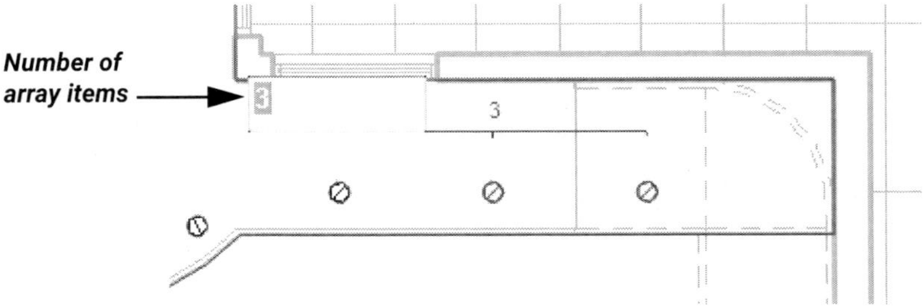

Figure 5–48

- To make a linear array in two directions, you need to array one direction first, select the arrayed elements, and then array them again in the other direction.

How To: Create a Radial Array

1. Select the element(s) to array.
2. In the *Modify* panel, click (Array).

3. In the *Modify | Array* tab>*Array* panel, click (Radial).
4. Specify the (Number) and the (Move To) option.
5. Similar to the **Rotate** command, select either (Place) to the move the center of rotation to the appropriate location, as shown in Figure 5–49, or (Center) to automatically position the center of rotation at the center of the element.
6. When the center of rotation is set, you can specify an (Angle) and press <Enter> or specify the rotation angle by selecting points on the screen.

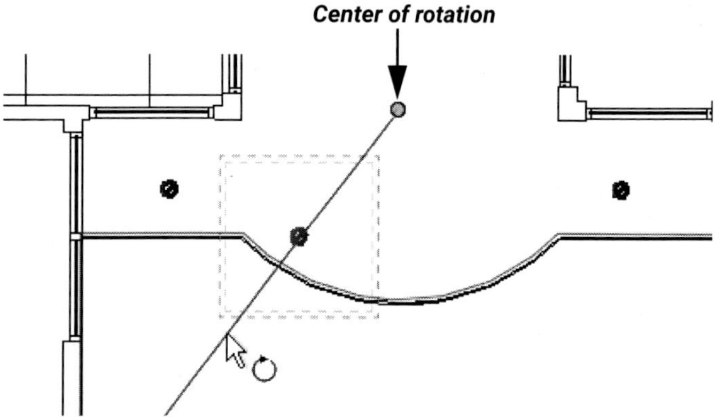

Figure 5–49

7. If (Group and Associate) is selected, you are prompted again for the number of items. Type a new number or click on the screen to finish the command.

Modifying Array Groups

When you select an element in an array that has been grouped, you can change the number of instances in the array, as shown in Figure 5–50. For radial arrays, you can also modify the distance to the center.

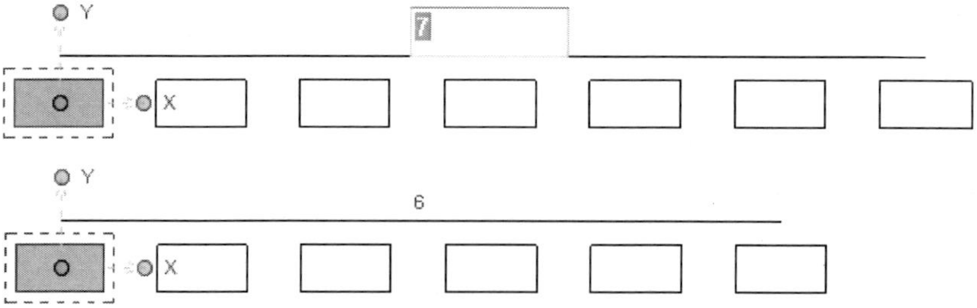

Figure 5–50

- Dashed lines surround the element(s) in a group, and the XY control lets you move the origin point of the group.

If you move one of the elements in the array group, the other elements move in response based on the distance and/or angle, as shown in Figure 5–51.

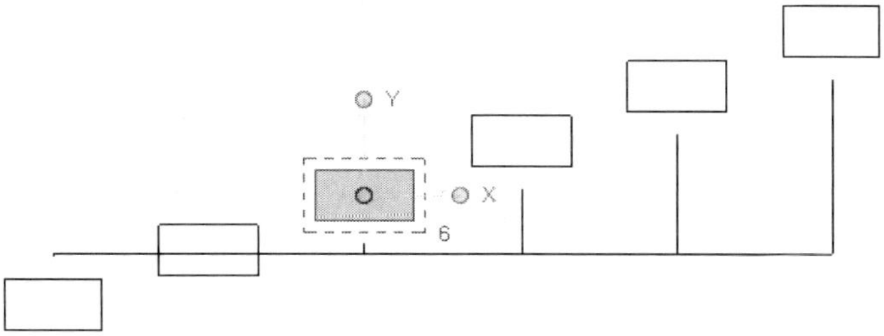

Figure 5–51

- To remove the array constraint on the group, select all of the elements in the array group and, in the *Modify* contextual tab>*Group* panel, click (Ungroup).
- If you select an individual element in an array and click (Ungroup), the element you selected is removed from the array, while the rest of the elements remain in the array group.
- You can use (Filter) to ensure that you are selecting only **Model Groups**.

Aligning Elements

The **Align** command enables you to line up one element with another, as shown in Figure 5–52. Most Revit elements can be aligned. For example, you can line up the tops of windows with the top of a door, or line up furniture with a wall.

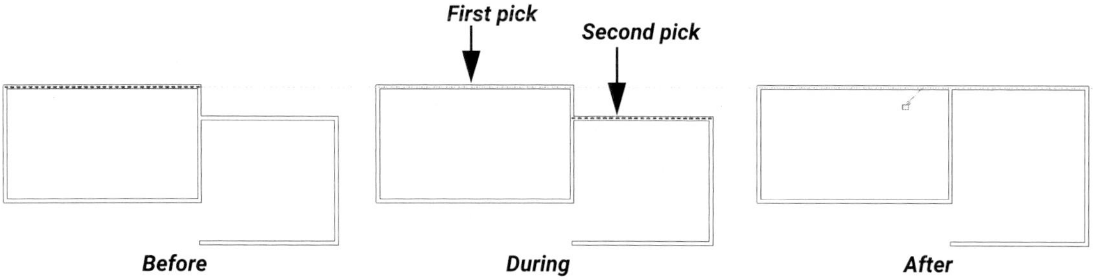

Figure 5–52

- The **Align** command works in all model views, including parallel and perspective 3D views.

How To: Align Elements

1. In the *Modify* tab>*Modify* panel, click (Align), or type **AL**.
2. Select a line or point on the element that is going to remain stationary.

   Note: *For elements that are close together, press <Tab> to select the correct element.*

3. Select a line or point on the element to be aligned. The second element moves into alignment with the first one.

- You can manually lock alignments so that the elements move together if either one is moved.
- Once you have created the alignment, a padlock is displayed. Click on the padlock to lock it, as shown in Figure 5–53.

Note: *Locking elements enlarges the size of the project file, so use this option carefully.*

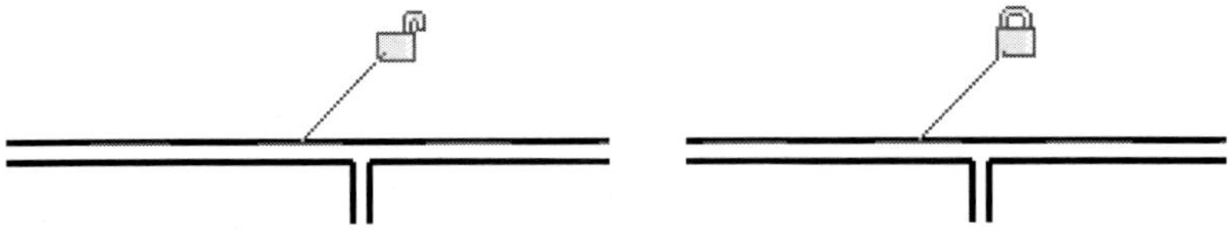

Figure 5–53

Align Contextual Tab Options

- If you need to align multiple elements, in the *Modify | Align* tab>*Align* panel (shown in Figure 5–54), select **Multiple Alignment** to select multiple elements to align with the first element. You can also hold <Ctrl> to select multiple elements to align.
- If you want to lock your alignments as you go, in the *Modify | Align* tab>*Align* panel, you can check the checkbox for **Lock** to lock any alignments made so you do not need to go back and lock them manually.
- For walls, you can set (Prefer) to specify if you want the command to prefer **Wall centerlines**, **Wall faces**, **Center of core**, or **Faces of core**. The core refers to the structural members of a wall as opposed to facing materials, such as sheet rock.
- For (Pattern), you can choose how surface patterns are aligned by selecting either the **Entire Surface** or **Selected Face** option. If you select **Entire Surface**, the pattern will be aligned across the entire surface, creating a seamless and consistent appearance. On the other hand, if you choose **Selected Face**, each face of the element can have its own pattern alignment, allowing for greater flexibility and customization. Ultimately, the choice between these options depends on your specific design needs and preferences.

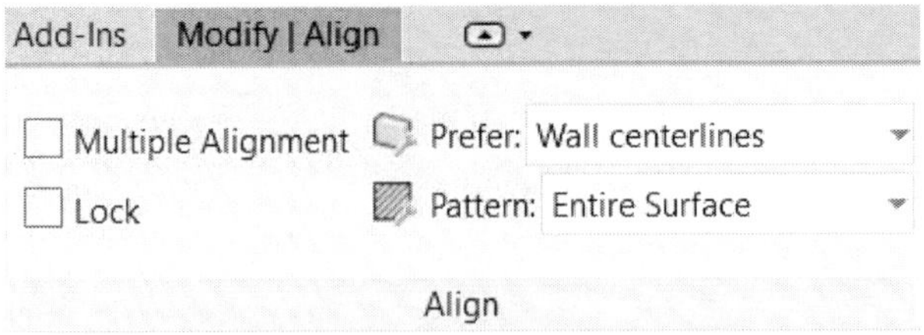

Figure 5–54

Practice 5b
Work with Basic Modify Tools

Practice Objective

- Use basic modify tools such as Move, Copy, Rotate, and Array.

In this practice, you will create a series of offices using the **Copy** and **Mirror** commands. You will then array desks around a circular wall, then rotate and array a pair of columns across the front of a simple building. Figure 5–55 shows the completed practice.

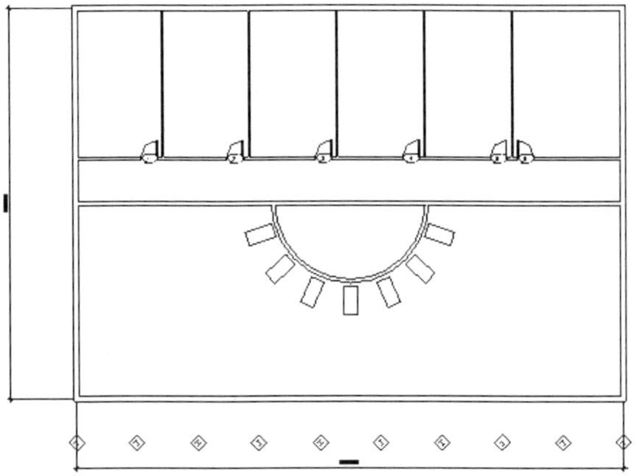

Figure 5–55

- A simple model is used for this exercise so you can practice using the tools before working on the main building model.

Task 1: Modify walls and doors.

1. Open the project **Simple Building-1.rvt** from the practice files folder.
2. Select the top arc of the circular wall.
3. In the *Modify* panel, click (Delete), or type **DE**. The walls that the circular wall crossed are automatically cleaned up.
   - You can also press <Delete> or right-click and select **Delete**.
4. Zoom in to the upper-left corner and select the vertical interior wall, door, and door tag.

   Note: *Hold <Ctrl> to select more than one element, or use a selection window. If you select something other than the above items, hold <Shift> and select the element to remove it from the selection.*

5. In the *Modify | Multi-Select* tab>*Modify* panel, click (Copy), or type **CO**.

6. In the *Modify | Copy* tab>*Copy* panel, select (Constrain) and (Multiple), if required (the tool showing as highlighted means it is turned on). The **Constrain** option forces the cursor to move only horizontally or vertically.
7. Select the top inside of the vertical wall as the start point and, using the temporary dimensions, pick the end point **16'-0"** away from the start point, as shown in Figure 5–56. The wall, door, and door tag are copied to the right and the door tag displays *2*.

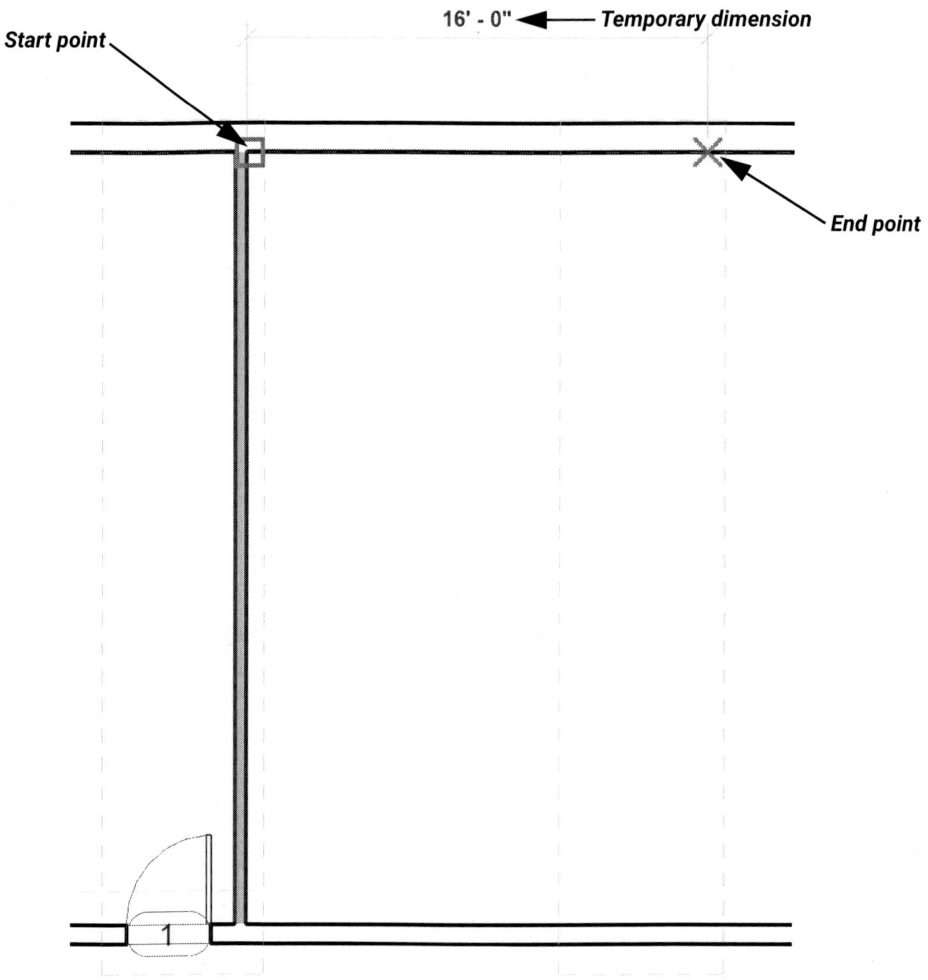

Figure 5–56

8. The new elements are still selected. Continue to copy the elements across the building by moving your cursor away from the newly placed elements. Type **16** (16'-0") and press <Enter> to set the distance between each copy. The final layout is shown in Figure 5–57 (the tags in the image have been enlarged for clarity).

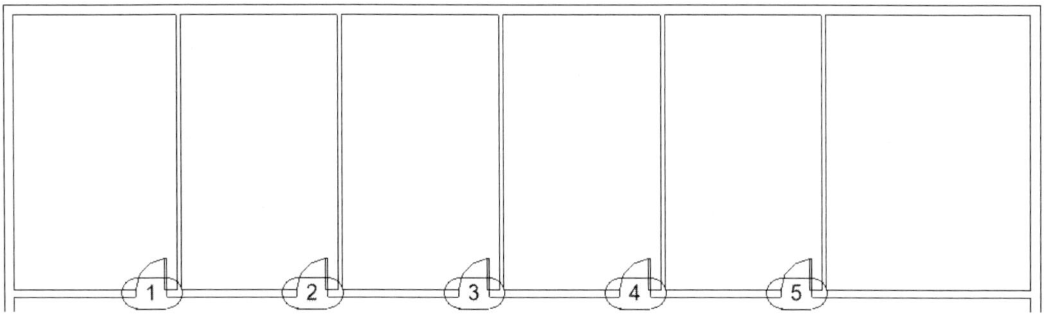

Figure 5–57

9. Click (Modify).
10. Zoom in and pan to the room to the far right.
11. Select door #5 and the associated door tag.
12. In the *Modify* panel, click (Mirror - Pick Axis), or type **MM**. In the *Modify | Mirror* tab> *Mirror* panel, ensure that (Copy) is selected.
13. Hover your cursor over the vertical wall that is located to the right of door 5. When the mirror axis line displays along the center of the wall, as shown on the left in Figure 5–58, click to select it. The door is copied, as shown on the right in Figure 5–58.

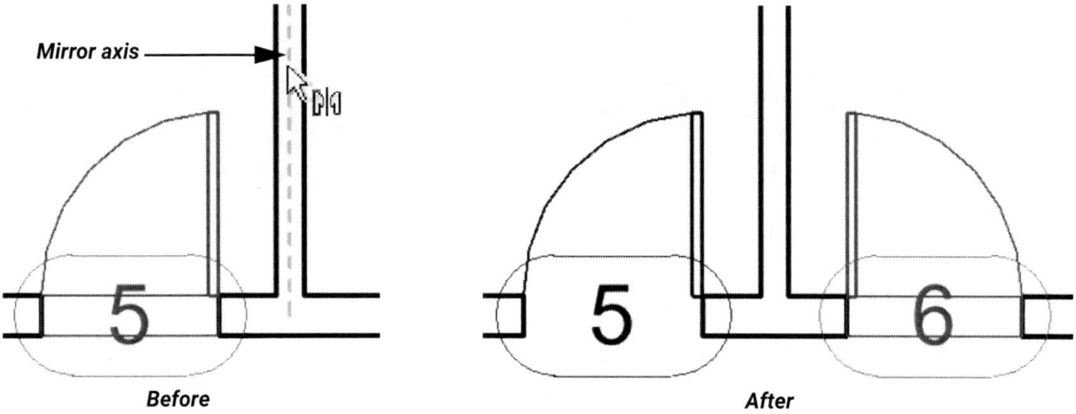

Figure 5–58

14. Click in an empty space in the view to release the selection.
15. Type **ZE** to zoom out to the full view.
16. Save the project.

Task 2: Add reference planes and use them to place a component.

1. In the *Architecture* tab>*Work Plane* panel, click (Ref Plane).
2. In the *Modify | Place Reference Plane* tab>*Draw* panel, select (Line). Click the midpoint of the wall or center of the half circle wall as the start point. Draw down past the arch wall and click to select the second point of the reference plane, as shown in Figure 5–59.
3. In the *Draw* panel, select (Pick Lines), then for (Offset), type **20'-0"** and press <Enter>. In the view, hover your cursor over the top of the horizontal wall with the half circle wall until the blue preview line displays, as shown in Figure 5–59, then click to place a horizontal reference plane. Use the end grips to shorten the horizontal reference plane.

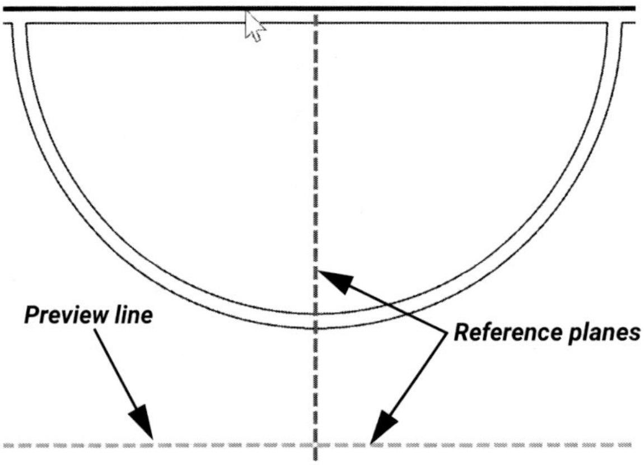

Figure 5–59

4. Click (Modify).

Task 3: Place and modify components.

1. In the *Architecture* tab>*Build* panel, click (Component), or type **CM**.

2. In the Properties, in the Type Selector, verify that **Desk: 60" x 30"** is selected, as shown in Figure 5–60.

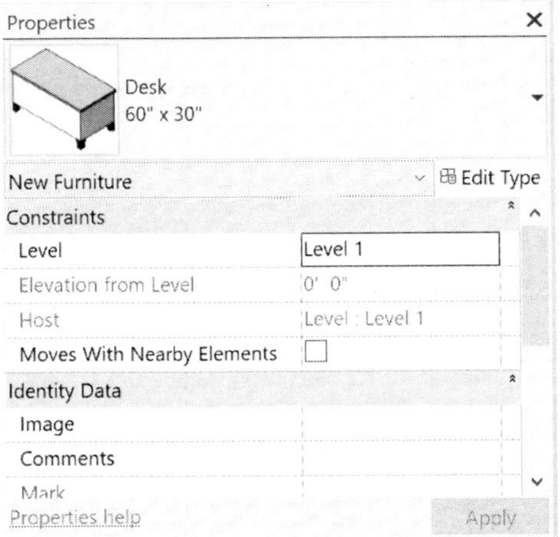

Figure 5–60

3. As you move the cursor, you can see that the desk is horizontal. Press <Spacebar> to rotate the desk 90°.
4. Place the desk at the intersection of the two reference planes, as shown in Figure 5–61. Zoom in as needed to ensure that you are connected to the reference.

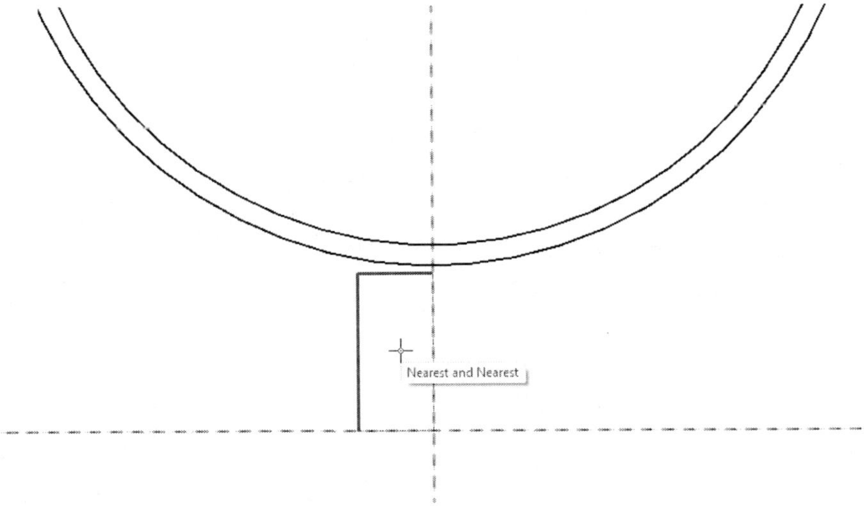

Figure 5–61

5. Click (Modify) and select the desk you just placed.

6. In the *Modify* panel, click (Move). In the *Modify | Move* tab>*Move* panel, select (Constrain).
7. Select the top midpoint of the desk as the start point of the move and select the intersection of the desk and the reference plane as the end point, as shown in Figure 5–62.
   - You can type **SM** to snap to midpoint and **SI** to snap to intersection.

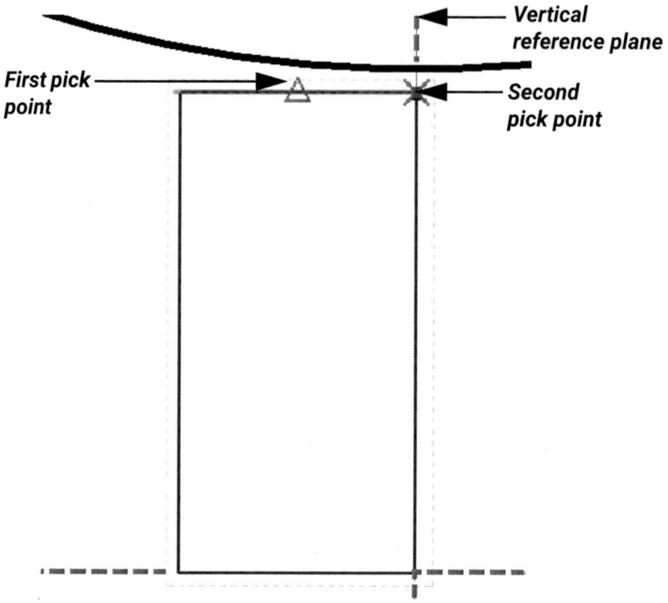

Figure 5–62

8. Click in an empty space in the view to clear the selection.
9. Save the project.

Task 4: Create a radial array.

1. Select the desk.
2. In the *Modify* panel, click (Array), or type **AR**.
3. In the *Modify | Array* tab>*Array* panel, click (Radial). Toggle off (Group and Associate), set (Number) to **15** and (Move To) to **2nd**, and select (Place).

4. Select the midpoint of the wall, as shown in Figure 5–63.

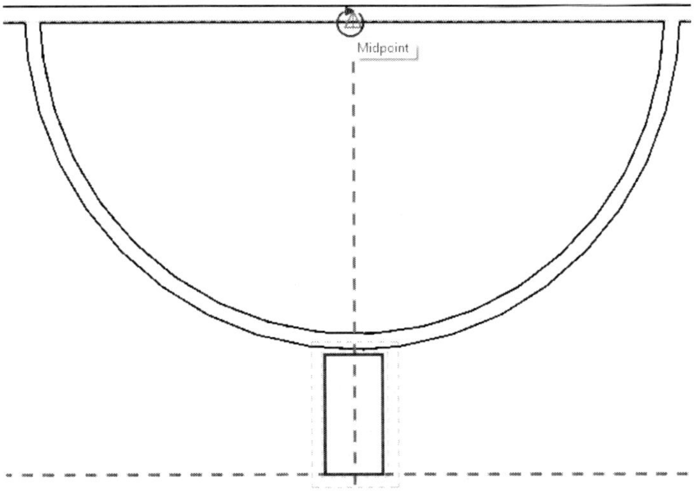

Figure 5–63

5. Return to the *Array* panel and set (Angle) to **360**. Press <Enter>. The array displays as shown in Figure 5–64.

   Note: *Sometimes it is easier to create more elements then you need, and then delete the ones that are not required, as is done in this example.*

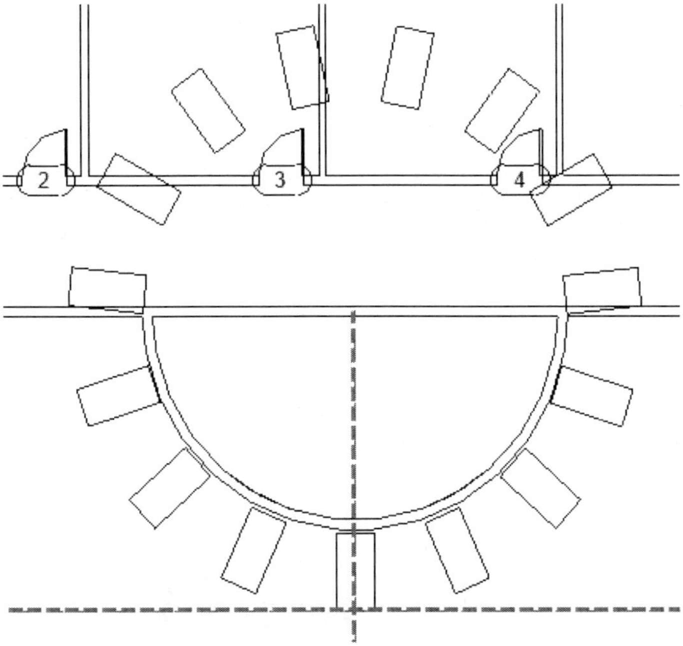

Figure 5–64

6. Delete all the desks that are outside of the room; keep the ones that are around the half circular wall.
7. Zoom out to display the entire view.
8. Save the project.

Task 5: Modify columns.

1. Pan and zoom to the lower-left side of the model. Two columns (one architectural and one structural) have been added to the project.
2. Select the square architectural column and click and hold the left mouse button to drag it over so that the column lines up with the centerline of the wall, as shown in Figure 5–65. Use the temporary dimension to set the distance off the wall to **8'-0"**.

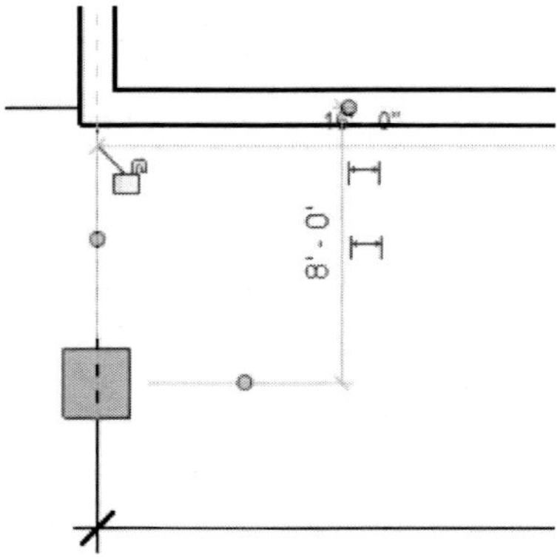

Figure 5–65

3. Select the structural column. Drag the column to the center of the architectural column, as shown in Figure 5–66. You can also use the **Move** command, verify **Constrain** is toggled off, and use the **Midpoint** snap of the structural column and architectural column.

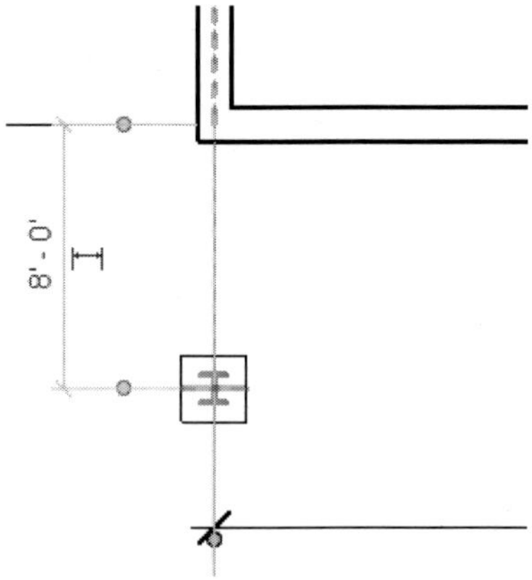

Figure 5–66

4. Save the project.

Task 6: Rotate and array the columns.

1. Click (Modify) and select the two columns.
2. In the *Modify | Multi-Select* tab>*Modify* panel, click (Rotate), or type **RO**. In the *Rotate* panel, toggle off (Copy) and select (Center).
3. For the start ray, click horizontally to the right of the column, as shown in Figure 5–67.

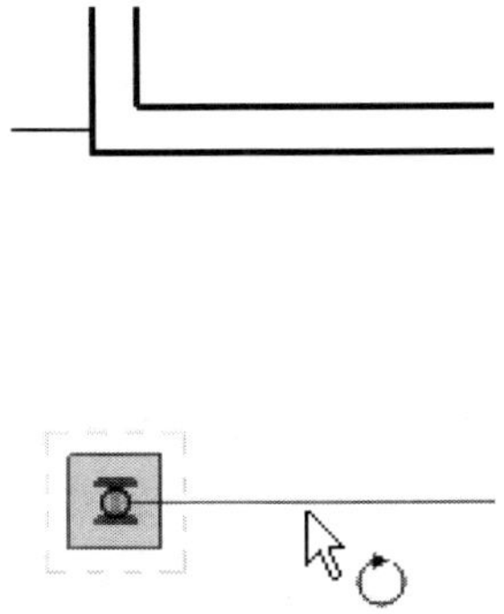

Figure 5–67

4. Move the ray line up until you see the temporary dimension display **45.00°**, as shown in Figure 5–68, and click to rotate the columns.

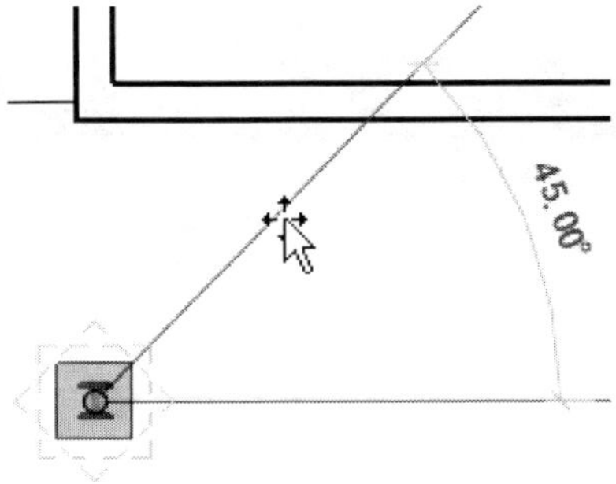

Figure 5–68

5. With the two columns still selected, in the *Modify | Multi-Select* tab>*Modify* panel, click (Array), or type **AR**.

6. In the *Array* panel, click (Linear), verify (Group and Associate) is toggled off, set (Number) to **10** and (Move To) to **Last**, and toggle on (Constrain).

   Note: *Remember after starting a command, review the Status Bar (lower-left corner of the interface) for command prompts.*

7. For the start point, click the midpoint of the columns. For the endpoint of the array, select the **Horizontal and Extension** of the centerline of the far right wall as shown in Figure 5–69.

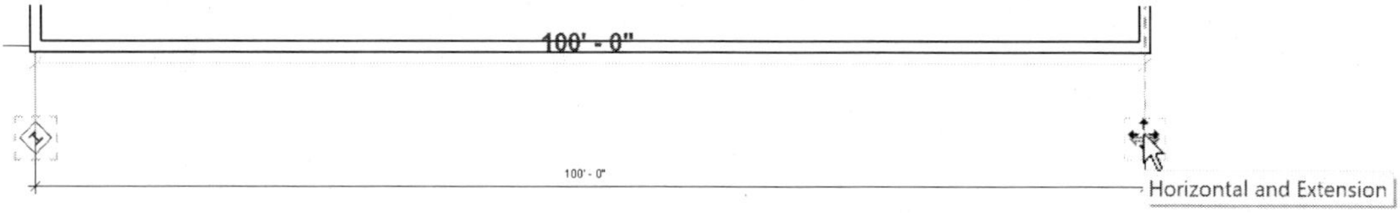

Figure 5–69

8. Zoom out to display the entire building.
9. The columns are arrayed evenly across the front of the building as shown in Figure 5–70.

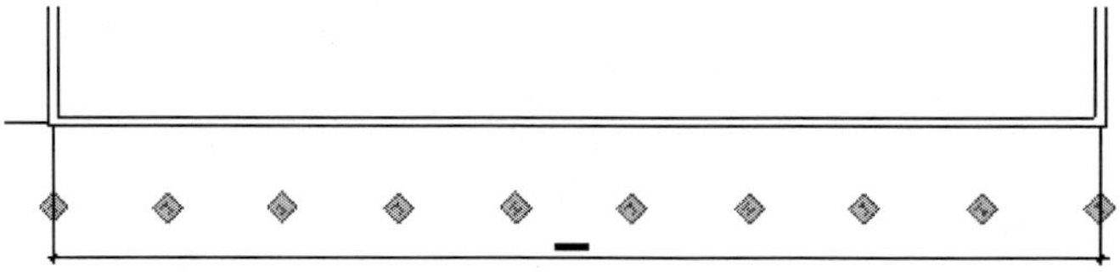

Figure 5–70

10. Save and close the project.

End of practice

5.3 Working with Additional Modify Tools

As you work on a project, some additional tools found on the *Modify* tab>*Modify* panel (shown in Figure 5–71) can help you with placing, modifying, and constraining elements. **Align** can be used with a variety of elements, while **Split Element**, **Trim/Extend**, and **Offset** can only be used with linear elements.

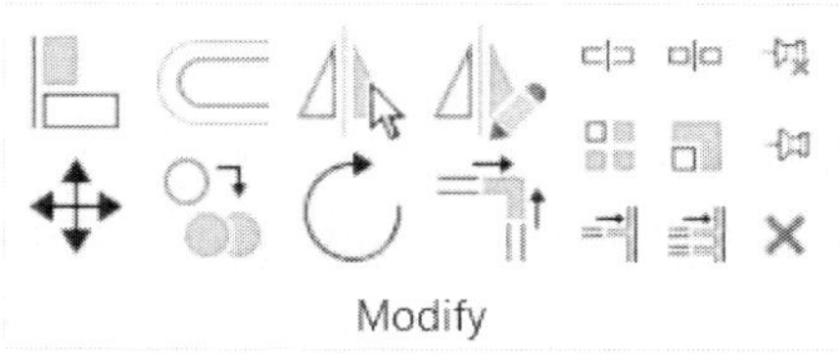

Figure 5–71

Splitting Linear Elements

The **Split Element** command enables you to break a linear element at a specific point. You can use drawing aids to help place the split point. After you have split the linear element, you can use other editing commands to modify the two parts, or change the type of one part, as shown with walls in Figure 5–72. You can split walls in plan, elevation, or 3D views.

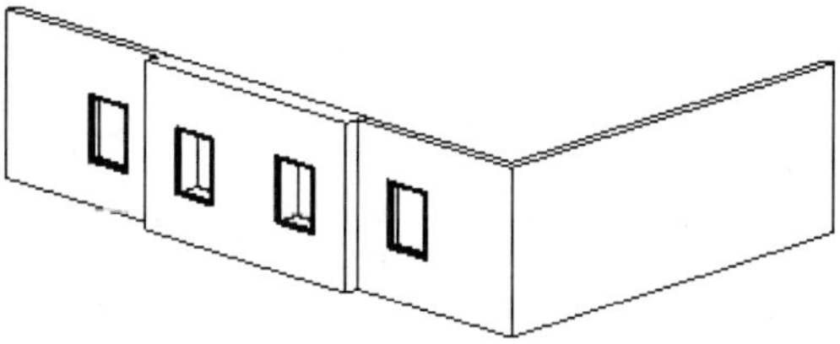

Figure 5–72

How To: Split Linear Elements

1. In the *Modify* tab>*Modify* panel, click (Split Element), or type **SL**.
2. In the *Modify | Split* tab>*Adjustments* panel, select or clear the **Delete Inner Segment** option.
3. Move the cursor to the point you want to split and select the point.
4. Repeat for any additional split locations.
5. Modify the elements that were split, as needed.

- The **Delete Inner Segment** option is used when you select two split points along a linear element. When the option is selected, the segment between the two split points is automatically removed.

- In the *Modify* tab>*Modify* panel, click (Split with Gap) to split the linear element at the point you select, as shown in Figure 5–73, but also create a *Joint Gap* specified in the *Modify | Split Elements With Gap* tab>*Constraints* panel.

Note: *This command is typically used with structural precast walls.*

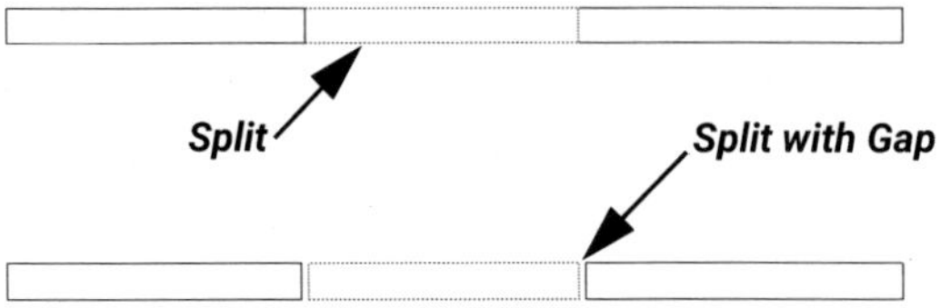

Figure 5–73

Trimming and Extending

There are three trim/extend methods that you can use with linear elements: **Trim/Extend to Corner**, **Trim/Extend Single Element**, and **Trim/Extend Multiple Elements**.

- When selecting elements to trim, click the part of the element that you want to keep. The opposite part of the line is then trimmed.

How To: Trim/Extend to Corner

1. In the *Modify* tab>*Modify* panel, click (Trim/Extend to Corner), or type **TR**.
2. Select the first linear element on the side you want to keep.
3. Select the second linear element on the side you want to keep, as shown in Figure 5–74.

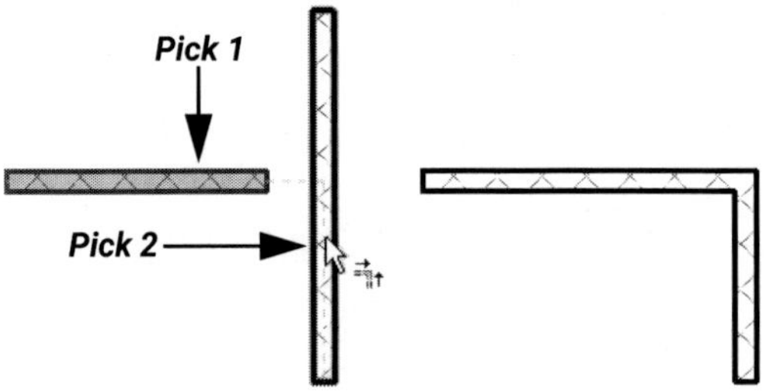

Figure 5–74

How To: Trim/Extend a Single Element

1. In the *Modify* tab>*Modify* panel, click (Trim/Extend Single Element).
2. Select the cutting or boundary edge.
3. Select the linear element to be trimmed or extended, as shown in Figure 5–75.

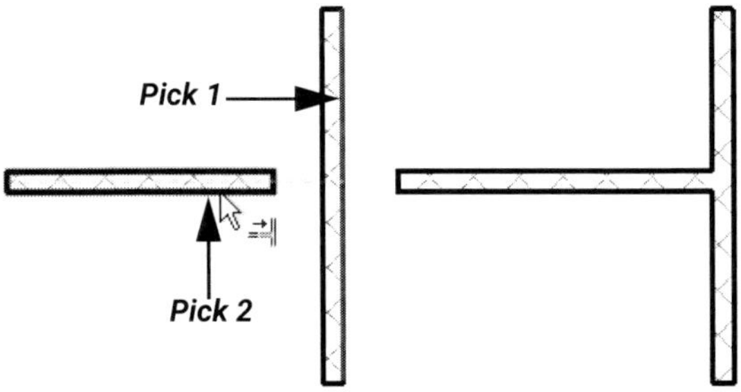

Figure 5–75

How To: Trim/Extend Multiple Elements

1. In the *Modify* tab>*Modify* panel, click (Trim/Extend Multiple Elements).
2. Select the cutting or boundary edge.
3. Select the linear elements that you want to trim or extend by selecting one at a time, or by using a crossing window, as shown in Figure 5–76. For trimming, select the side you want to keep.

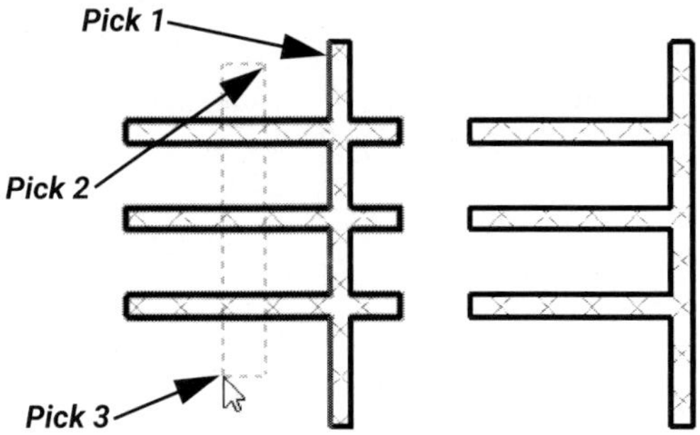

Figure 5–76

- You can click in an empty space in the view to clear the selection and select another cutting edge or boundary.

Offsetting Elements

The **Offset** command is an easy way of creating parallel copies of linear elements at a specified distance, with a dashed preview line indicating the preset distance location of where the copied element will be placed, as shown in Figure 5–77. Walls, beams, braces, and lines are among the elements that can be offset.

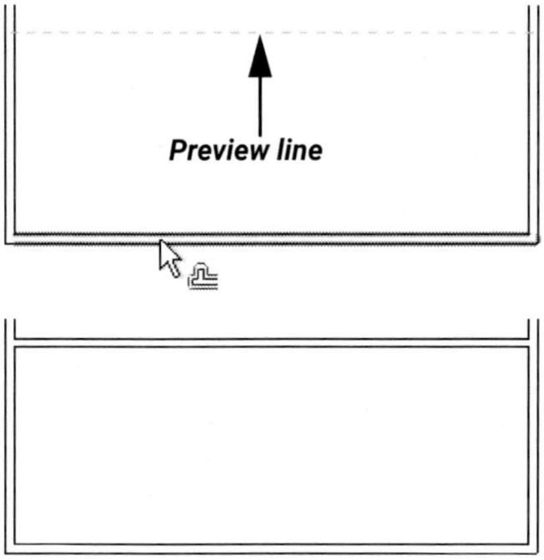

Figure 5–77

- If you offset a wall that has a door or window embedded in it, the elements are copied with the offset wall.
- You can specify the offset distance by selecting (Numerical) and typing an offset distance in the (Offset) field, as shown in Figure 5–78.
- You can also choose to manually select the offset distance by selecting (Graphical) and selecting two points in the drawing area.

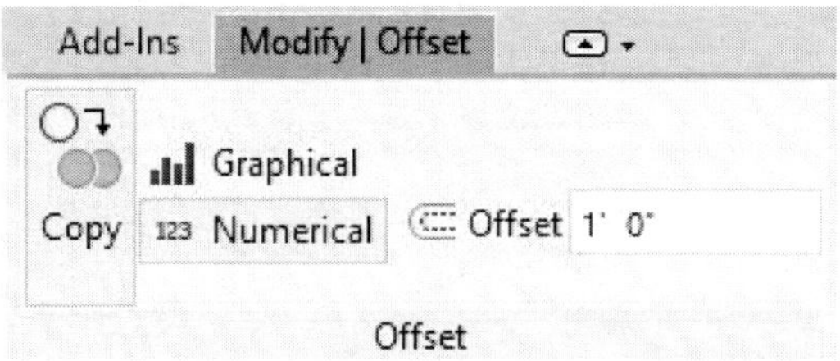

Figure 5–78

How To: Offset Using the Numerical Method

1. In the *Modify* tab>*Modify* panel, click (Offset), or type **OF**.
2. In the *Modify | Offset* tab>*Offset* panel, select (Numerical), then type the required distance in the (Offset) field and press <Enter>.
   - In the *Offset* panel, the (Copy) option (which is on by default) makes a copy of the element being offset. If this option is not selected, the **Offset** command moves the element the set offset distance.
3. Move the cursor over the element you want to offset. A dashed line previews the offset location. Move the cursor to flip the sides, as needed.
4. Click to create the offset.
5. Repeat Steps 4 and 5 to offset other elements by the same distance, or to change the distance for another offset.

- With the **Numerical** option, you can select multiple connected elements for offsetting. Hover the cursor over an element and press <Tab> until the other connected elements are highlighted, as shown in Figure 5–79. Click to select the element to offset all of the elements at the same time.

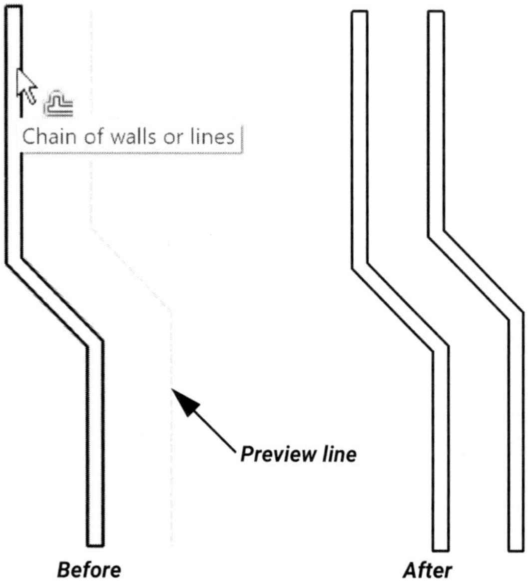

Figure 5–79

How To: Offset Using the Graphical Method

1. In the *Modify* tab>*Modify* panel, click (Offset), or type **OF**.
2. In the *Modify | Offset* tab>*Offset* panel, select (Graphical) .
3. Select the linear element to offset. You cannot select more than one element at a time.
4. Select two points that define the distance of the offset and which side to apply it. You can type an override in the temporary dimension for the second point.

- Most linear elements connected at a corner automatically trim or extend to meet at the offset distance, as shown in Figure 5–80.

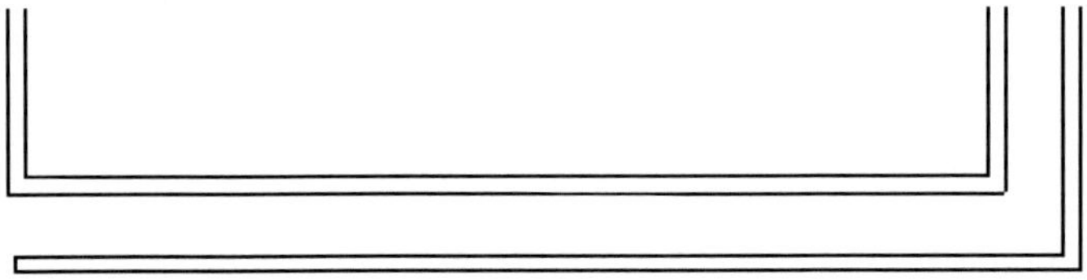

Figure 5–80

Practice 5c
Work with Additional Modify Tools

Practice Objective

- Align, Split, Trim/Extend, and Offset elements.

In this practice, you will split a wall into three parts and delete the middle portion. You will offset walls and then trim or extend them to form new rooms. You will then align the new walls to match existing walls. Figure 5–81 shows the completed practice.

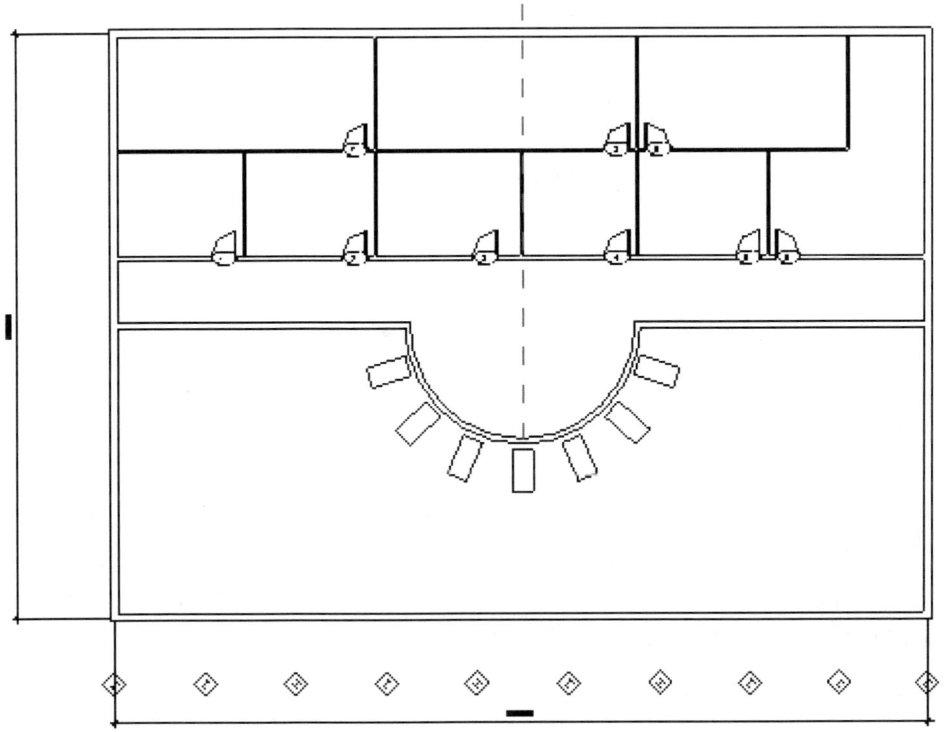

Figure 5–81

- A simple model is used for this exercise so you can practice using the tools before working on the main building model.

Task 1: Split and remove walls.

1. Open the project **Simple Building-2.rvt** from the practice files folder.
2. In the *Modify* tab>*Modify* panel, click (Split Element), or type **SL**.
3. In the *Modify | Split* tab>*Adjustments* panel, select **Delete Inner Segment**.
4. Click on the horizontally drawn wall where it intersects with the curved wall at both ends. The wall segment between these points is removed, as shown in Figure 5–82. (The desks have been hidden in the image for clarity.)

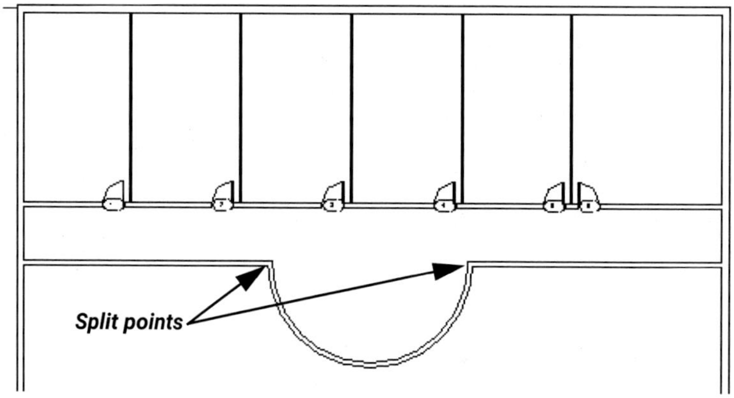

Figure 5–82

5. Click (Modify) to finish.
6. Save the project.

Task 2: Offset and trim walls.

1. In the *Modify* tab>*Modify* panel, click (Offset), or type **OF**.
2. In the *Modify | Offset* tab>*Offset* panel, verify (Numerical) is selected. Set the (Offset) to **14'-0"** and press <Enter>, then ensure that (Copy) is turned on.

3. Select the top horizontally drawn wall while ensuring that the dashed preview line displays inside the building, as shown in Figure 5–83.

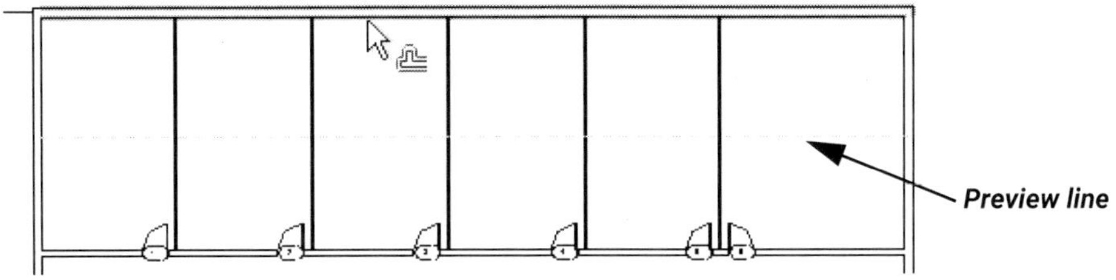

Figure 5–83

4. With the **Offset** command still active, change the (Offset) value to **10'-0"** and press <Enter>, then offset the last vertically drawn interior wall to the right, as shown in Figure 5–84.

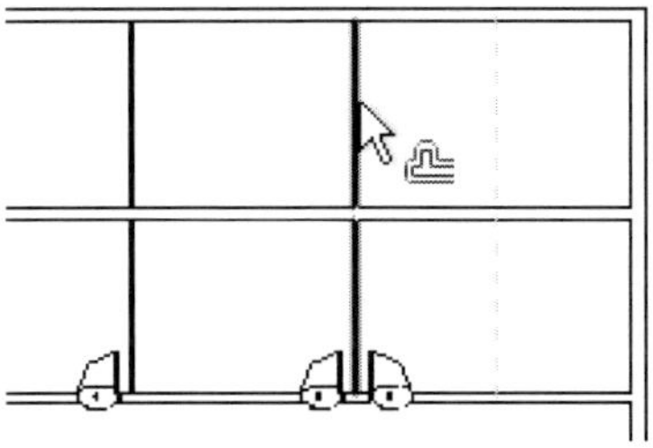

Figure 5–84

5. Click (Modify) and select the new horizontally drawn wall that was created from the exterior wall. Change the wall to **Basic Wall: Interior - 3 1/8" Partition (1-hr)**. The layout of the new walls should display as shown in Figure 5–85.

   Note: *The vertically drawn wall does not need to be changed because it was offset from an interior wall.*

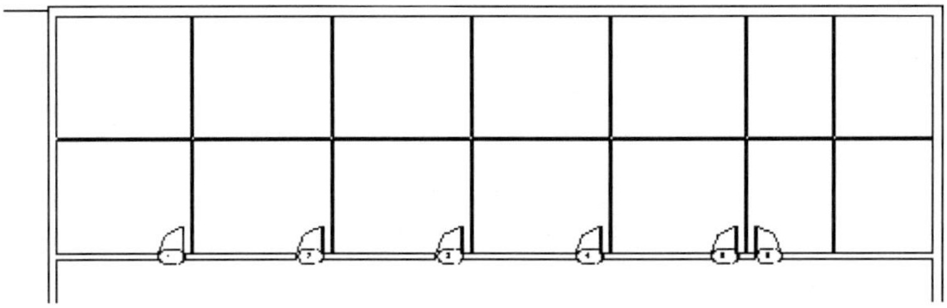

Figure 5–85

6. In the *Modify* tab>*Modify* panel, click (Trim/Extend Multiple Elements).
7. Select the new horizontally drawn wall as the element to trim against.

8. Select every other wall *below* the new wall. (Remember, you select the elements that you want to keep.) The walls should display as shown in Figure 5–86.

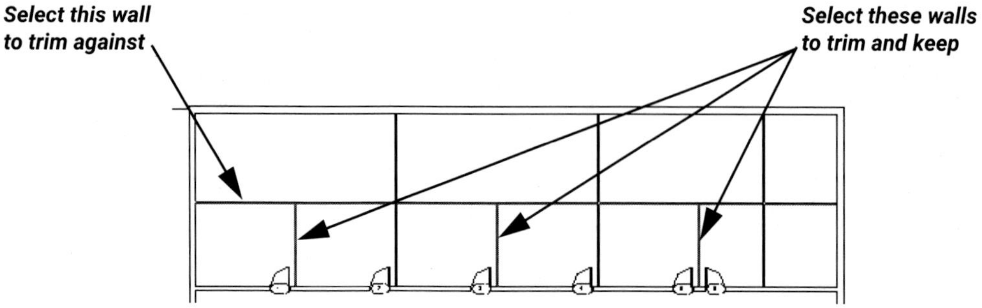

Figure 5–86

9. In the *Modify* tab>*Modify* panel, click (Trim/Extend to Corner), or type **TR**. Select the two walls to trim, as shown in Figure 5–87.

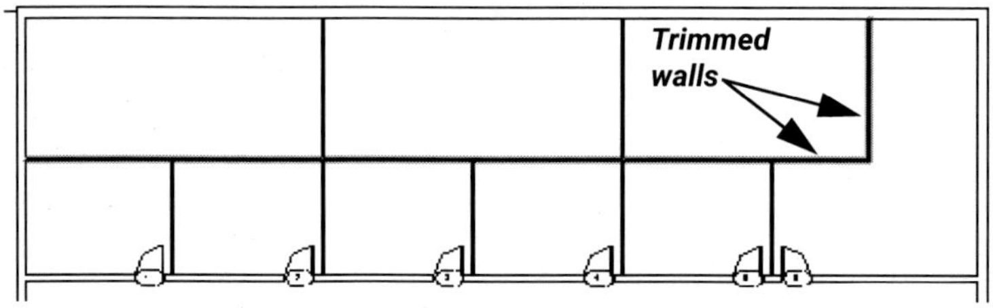

Figure 5–87

10. Click (Modify).
11. In the *Architecture* tab>*Build* panel, select (Door) and add doors into the three new rooms, as shown in Figure 5–88.
12. Click (Modify)
13. Save the project.

Task 3: Align walls.

1. Select and extend the vertical reference plane. Use the control to drag the top end so it extends beyond the outer wall, as shown in Figure 5–88.

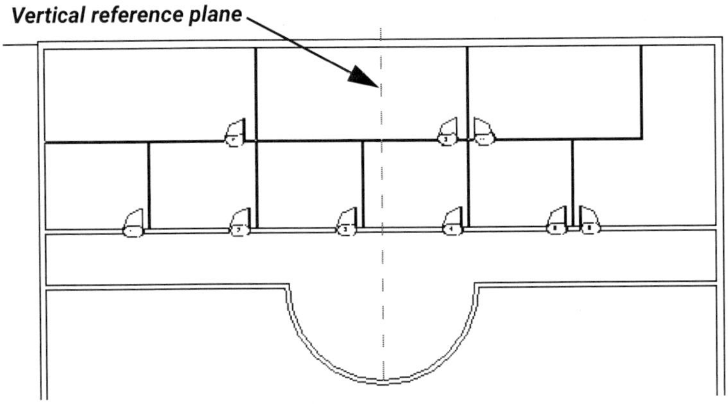

Figure 5–88

2. In the *Modify* tab>*Modify* panel, click (Align), or type **AL**.
3. Select the reference plane, and then the wall to the left. The wall should line up with the reference plane.

   Note: *If you want to align the wall precisely, press <Tab> while hovering over the wall to highlight either the edge of the wall or the centerline of the wall.*

4. Save and close the project.

End of practice

Chapter Review Questions

1. What is the purpose of an alignment line?
   a. Displays when the new element you are placing or modeling is aligned with the grid system.
   b. Indicates that the new element you are placing or modeling is aligned with an existing element.
   c. Displays when the new element you are placing or modeling is aligned with a selected tracking point.
   d. Indicates that the new element is aligned with true north rather than project north.

2. Temporary dimensions snap to the nearest perpendicular element.
   a. True
   b. False

3. When you are modeling (not editing) a linear element, how do you edit the temporary dimension?
   a. Select the temporary dimension and change the dimension value in Properties.
   b. Type a new value and press <Enter>.
   c. Type a new value in the *Distance/Length* field in the contextual tab and press <Enter>.

4. How do you select all elements of a specific type in a view?
   a. Select the element category in the Project Browser.
   b. Select one element, right-click, and select **Select All Instances>Visible in View**.
   c. Select all of the elements in the view and use  (Filter) to clear the other categories and only select the needed category.
   d. Select one element and click  (Select Multiple) in the ribbon.

5. When starting commands such as **Move**, **Copy**, **Rotate**, **Mirror**, and **Array**, you must select the element before starting the command.

a. True

b. False

6. How do you change the element type for a selected element?

a. Change the type properties.

b. In the contextual tab, click **Change Element Type**.

c. Select the dynamic control next to the selected element and select a new type in the drop-down list.

d. In Properties, select a new type in the Type Selector.

7. Both **Rotate** and **Radial Array** have a center of rotation that defaults to the center of the element or group of elements you have selected. How do you move the center of rotation to another point? (Select all that apply.)

a. In the contextual tab, click (Center) to display the center of rotation grip control on the element and drag it to a new location.

b. Right-click and select **Place** and select the new point.

c. In the contextual tab, click (Place) and select the new point.

d. Right-click and select **Snap Overrides>Centers** and select the new point.

8. Which command would you use to remove a part or a segment of a wall?

a. (Split Element)

b. (Wall Joins)

c. (Cut Geometry)

d. (Demolish)

9. Which of the following are ways in which you can create additional parallel walls? (Select all that apply.)

a. Use the **Trim/Extend Multiple Elements** tool.

b. Use the **Offset** tool in the *Modify* tab.

c. Select an existing wall, hold <Ctrl>, and drag the wall away to create an additional wall.

d. Use the **Align** command with an offset.

10. Which command do you use if you want two walls that are not touching to come together and clean up, as shown in Figure 5–89?

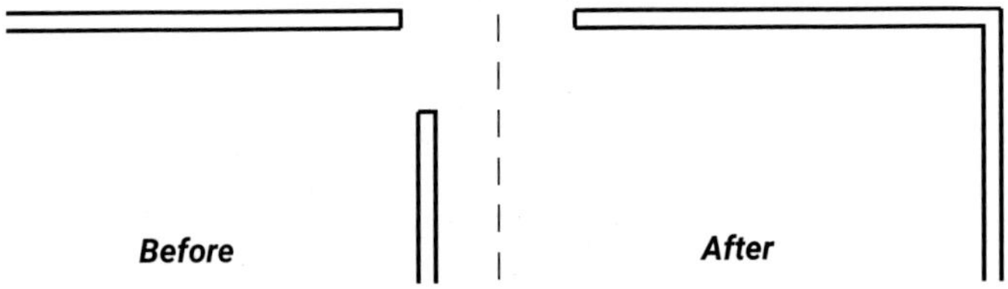

Figure 5–89

a.  (Edit Wall Joins)

b.  (Trim/Extend to Corner)

c.  (Join Geometry)

d.  (Edit Profile)

Command Summary

Button	Command	Location
Sketch Tools		
	**Center-ends Arc**	• **Ribbon:** *Modify | (various linear elements)* tab>*Draw* panel
	**Circle**	• **Ribbon:** *Modify | (various linear elements)* tab>*Draw* panel
	**Circumscribed Polygon**	• **Ribbon:** *Modify | (various linear elements)* tab>*Draw* panel
	**Ellipse**	• **Ribbon:** *Modify | (various linear elements)* tab>*Draw* panel
	**Ellipse Arc**	• **Ribbon:** *Modify | (various linear elements)* tab>*Draw* panel
	**Fillet Arc**	• **Ribbon:** *Modify | (various linear elements)* tab>*Draw* panel
	**Inscribed Polygon**	• **Ribbon:** *Modify | (various linear elements)* tab>*Draw* panel
	**Line**	• **Ribbon:** *Modify | (various linear elements)* tab>*Draw* panel
	**Pick Faces**	• **Ribbon:** *Modify | Place Wall*>*Draw* panel
	**Pick Lines**	• **Ribbon:** *Modify | (various linear elements)* tab>*Draw* panel
	**Pick Walls**	• **Ribbon:** *Modify | (various boundary sketches)*>*Draw* panel
	**Rectangle**	• **Ribbon:** *Modify | (various linear elements)* tab>*Draw* panel
	**Spline**	• **Ribbon:** *Modify | Place Lines, Place Detail Lines, and various boundary sketches*>*Draw* panel
	**Start-End-Radius Arc**	• **Ribbon:** *Modify | (various linear elements)* tab>*Draw* panel
	**Tangent End Arc**	• **Ribbon:** *Modify | (various linear elements)* tab>*Draw* panel

Button	Command	Location
Modify Tools		
	**Align**	• **Ribbon:** *Modify* tab>*Modify* panel • **Shortcut:** AL
	**Array**	• **Ribbon:** *Modify* tab>*Modify* panel • **Shortcut:** AR
	**Copy**	• **Ribbon:** *Modify* tab>*Modify* panel • **Shortcut:** CO
	**Copy to Clipboard**	• **Ribbon:** *Modify* tab>*Clipboard* panel • **Shortcut:** <Ctrl>+<C>
	**Delete**	• **Ribbon:** *Modify* tab>*Modify* panel • **Shortcut:** DE
	**Mirror - Draw Axis**	• **Ribbon:** *Modify* tab>*Modify* panel • **Shortcut:** DM
	**Mirror - Pick Axis**	• **Ribbon:** *Modify* tab>*Modify* panel • **Shortcut:** MM
	**Move**	• **Ribbon:** *Modify* tab>*Modify* panel • **Shortcut:** MV
	**Offset**	• **Ribbon:** *Modify* tab>*Modify* panel • **Shortcut:** OF
	**Paste**	• **Ribbon:** *Modify* tab>*Clipboard* panel • **Shortcut:** <Ctrl>+<V>
	**Pin**	• **Ribbon:** *Modify* tab>*Modify* panel • **Shortcut:** PN
	**Rotate**	• **Ribbon:** *Modify* tab>*Modify* panel • **Shortcut:** RO, R3
	**Scale**	• **Ribbon:** *Modify* tab>*Modify* panel • **Shortcut:** RE
	**Split Element**	• **Ribbon:** *Modify* tab>*Modify* panel • **Shortcut:** SL
	**Split with Gap**	• **Ribbon:** *Modify* tab>*Modify* panel
	**Trim/Extend Multiple Elements**	• **Ribbon:** *Modify* tab>*Modify* panel
	**Trim/Extend Single Element**	• **Ribbon:** *Modify* tab>*Modify* panel

Button	Command	Location
	**Trim/Extend to Corner**	• **Ribbon:** *Modify* tab>*Modify* panel • **Shortcut:** TR
	**Unpin**	• **Ribbon:** *Modify* tab>*Modify* panel • **Shortcut:** UP
Additional Tools		
	**Aligned Dimension**	• **Ribbon:** *Modify* tab>*Measure* panel • **Quick Access Toolbar**
	**Component**	• **Ribbon:** *Architecture/Structure/Systems* tab • Shortcut: CM
	**Detail Line**	• **Ribbon:** *Annotate* tab>*Detail* panel • **Shortcut:** DL
	**Filter**	• **Ribbon:** *Modify | Multi-Select* tab>*Filter* panel • **Status Bar**
	**Model Line**	• **Ribbon:** *Architecture* tab>*Model* panel • **Shortcut:** LI
	**Reference Plane**	• **Ribbon:** *Architecture/Structure/Systems* tab>*Work Plane* panel

Design Development

The second section of this guide focuses on teaching you how to use the tools available in Revit® to create the building model.

This section includes the following chapters:

- Chapter 6: Adding Columns
- Chapter 7: Modeling Walls
- Chapter 8: Working with Doors and Windows
- Chapter 9: Working with Curtain Walls
- Chapter 10: Modeling Floors
- Chapter 11: Modeling Ceilings
- Chapter 12: Modeling Roofs
- Chapter 13: Modeling Stairs, Railings, and Ramps

Chapter 6

Adding Columns

Revit includes two types of columns: architectural and structural. Architectural columns are placeholders or decorative elements, while structural columns include more precise information relative to strength and load-bearing parameters.

Learning Objectives

- Learn the differences between architectural and structural columns in Revit.
- Add structural columns to the project as the first design consideration.
- Place structural footings at the center of the columns.

6.1 Adding Columns

Architectural columns (displayed on the left in Figure 6–1) are usually situated vertically from the current level up to a specified height. Their placement is limited to vertical positioning, and settings can be adjusted in the contextual tab and Properties. Architectural columns cannot be placed automatically at grid lines or in a slanted orientation.

On the other hand, structural columns (depicted on the right in Figure 6–1) are typically positioned from the current level down to a specific depth. They offer more flexibility, allowing vertical or slanted placement at grids or columns, and can be tagged during placement. Structural column settings can also be modified in the contextual tab and Properties.

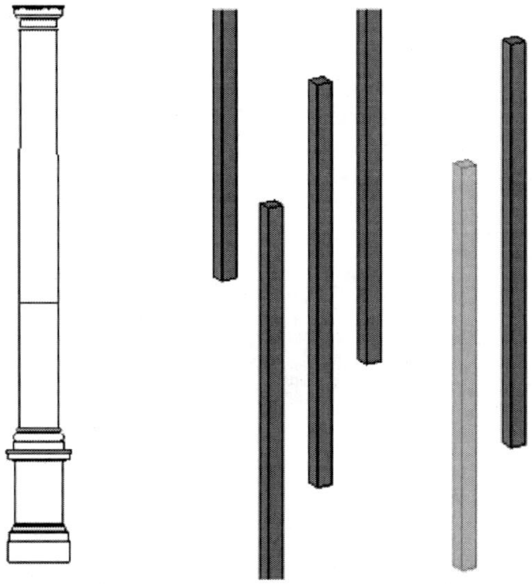

Architectural column ***Structural columns***

Figure 6–1

How To: Add Vertical Columns

1. In the *Architecture* tab>*Build* panel, expand (Column) and click either (Column: Architectural) or (Structural Column). Note that (Structural Column) is always the default.
2. In the Type Selector, select the column you want to use.
3. If placing a structural column, in the *Modify | Place Structural Column* tab>*Placement* panel, select (Vertical).

   Note: *When placing an architectural column, the ribbon will only display the Rotate and Levels panels. The Placement panel is not available for architectural columns as they can only be vertical.*

4. In the *Levels* panel (shown in Figure 6–2 for a structural column), select one of the following options:
    - (Height): Set (Top) to either a level or **Unconnected**. If **Unconnected** is selected, specify the (Unconnected Height) value that is measured from the level.
    - (Depth): Set the (Bottom) to either a level or **Unconnected**. If **Unconnected** is selected, specify the (Depth) value.

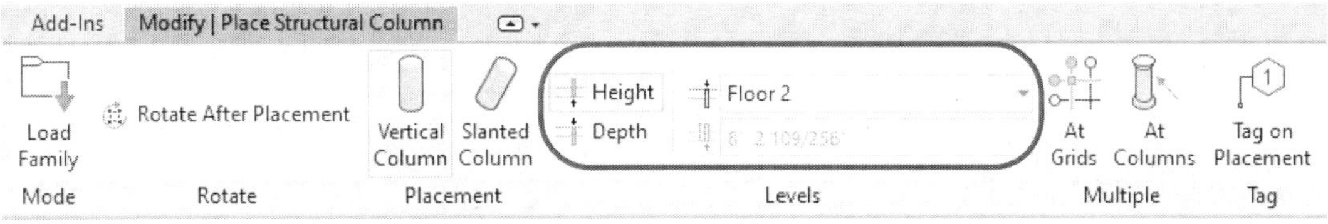

Figure 6–2

5. When placing columns, they will snap to grid lines and walls, but can also be placed as free instances unconnected to any grid lines or walls.
    - If you have (Rotate After Placement) selected in the *Rotate* panel, you will be prompted for a rotation angle after you select the insertion point for the column.

- If you are working with structural columns, you will have two additional options for placing columns in the *Modify | Place Structural Column* tab>*Multiple* panel:
    - To place structural columns at the intersection of grid lines, click (At Grids) and select the grid lines. Columns will only be placed at the intersections of the selected grid lines.
    - To place structural columns wherever you have an architectural column, in the *Modify | Place Structural Column* tab>*Multiple* panel, click (At Columns) and select the architectural columns. The structural columns are placed at the center of the architectural columns, as shown in Figure 6–3.

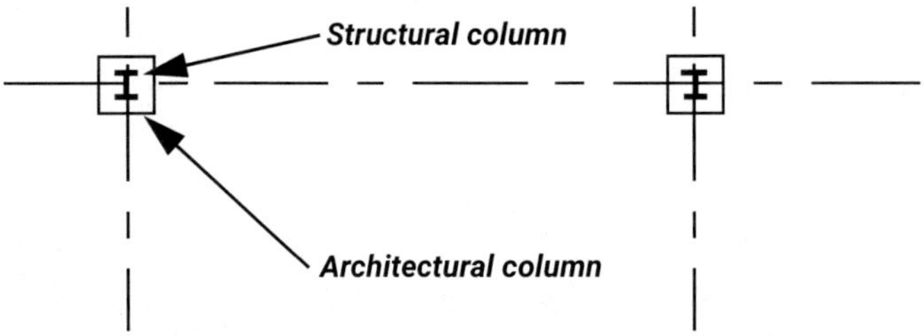

Figure 6–3

- An architectural column placed in a wall is automatically cleaned up if the material of the column and wall match. Structural columns remain separate even if they are the same material as the surrounding walls, as shown in Figure 6–4.

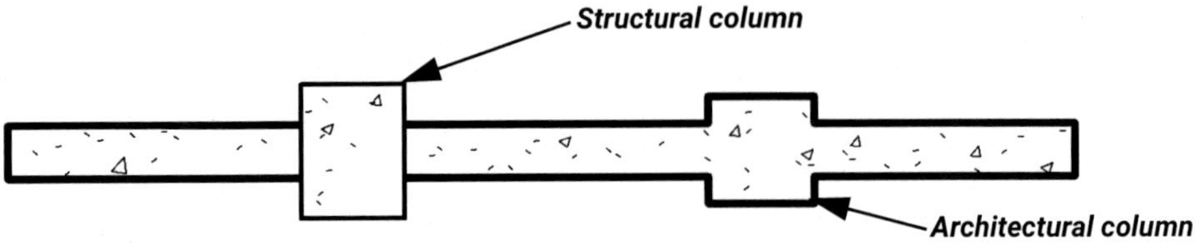

Figure 6–4

- You can select additional column types from the *Columns* (for architectural) or *Structural Columns* folders in the Revit Library, as shown in Figure 6–5. (Note that the Revit content libraries are a separate installation.)

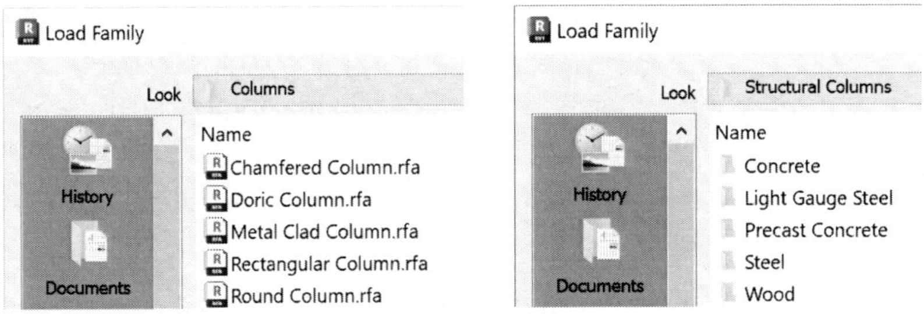

Figure 6–5

- When loading some structural column families, you will be prompted to choose from a list of types, as shown in Figure 6–6. Hold <Ctrl> or <Shift> to select more than one and click **OK** to load them.

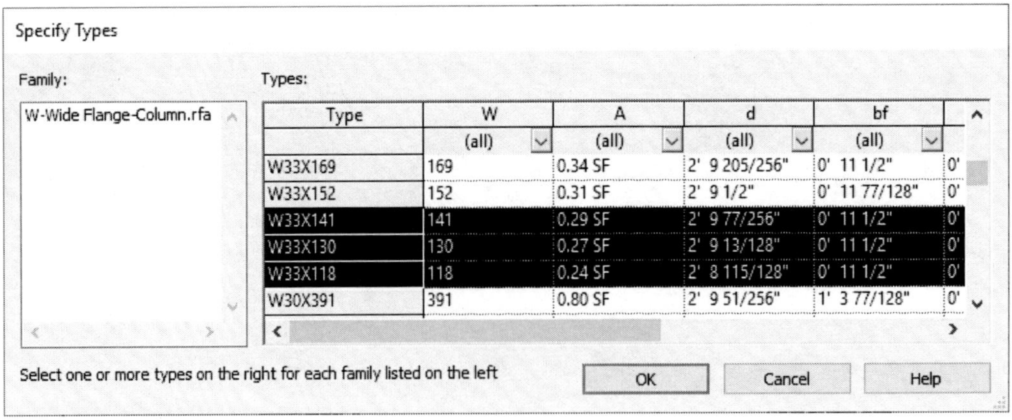

Figure 6–6

Modifying Columns

When selecting a column, you can modify the constraints within Properties and change the *Base Level* and *Top Level*, as well as the offsets from these levels and several other options, as shown in Figure 6–7. You can also attach columns to other elements so that they move with those elements.

Note: *Structural columns have additional parameters.*

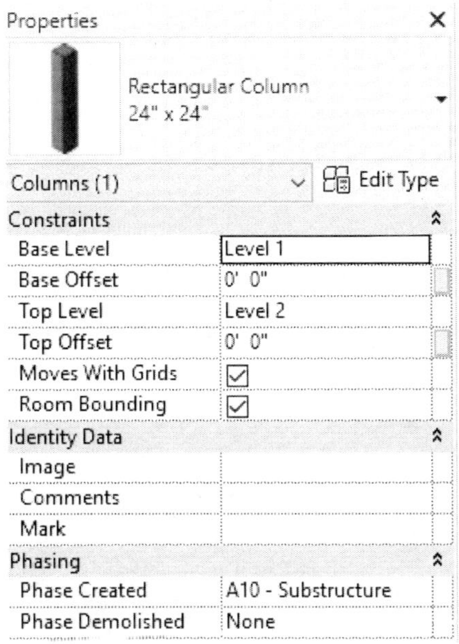

Figure 6–7

- When changing the top and base levels and offsets, you should make these changes in a logical order, as having a zero or negative height column results in an error message.
- Deleting a grid line or wall does not delete the columns placed on them.
- By default, columns placed at grid intersections will move with the grids, although you can still move the columns independently of the grid. Select the column(s) and, in Properties, select or clear **Move With Grids** to change the method. This toggle is normally on by default, but it is good practice to check its status.

- In the *Modify | Columns* tab>*Modify Column* panel (shown in Figure 6–8), you can attach or detach a column's top and base to floors, ceilings, roofs, reference planes, and structural framing.

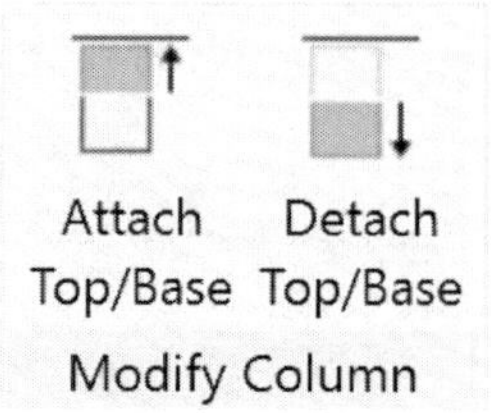

Figure 6–8

How To: Attach Columns to Other Elements

1. Select a column or group of columns.
2. In the *Modify | [Structural] Columns* tab>*Modify Column* panel, click (Attach Top/Base).
3. In the *Attach Top/Base* panel that appears (as shown in Figure 6–9), select **Top** or **Base** and set the *Attachment Style* , *Attachment Justification*, and *Offset From Attachment*.

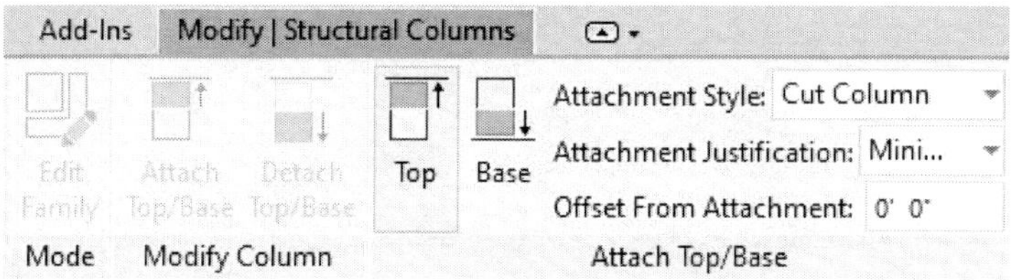

Figure 6–9

4. Select the floor, roof, footing, beam, reference plane, or level to which you want the column(s) attached.

- Attaching columns to other objects associates or constrains certain parameters, such as the height.
- If you want to detach a column that has been attached, select the column and click (Detach Top/Base).
- You can use the **Attach Top/Base** command to attach structural columns to isolated foundations and footings. If the foundation height changes, the length of the column changes with it.

6.2 Adding Isolated Footings

Footings for columns (shown in Figure 6–10) are placed using the **Structural Foundation: Isolated** command. When you select a column, the footing automatically attaches to the bottom of the column. This is true even when the bottom of the column is on a lower level than the view you are working in.

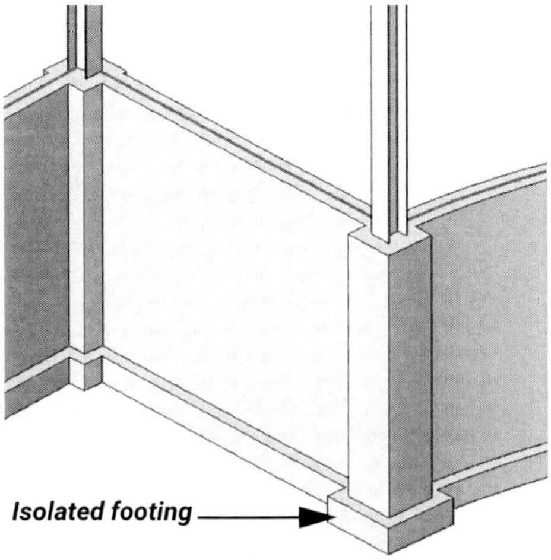

Figure 6–10

- Isolated footings can be placed in a plan or 3D view.

How To: Place an Isolated Footing

1. In the *Structure* tab>*Foundation* panel, click (Isolated) to start the **Structural Foundation: Isolated** command.
2. In the Type Selector, select a footing type.
3. In the view, click to place the individual footing, as shown in Figure 6–11.
    - If needed, press <Spacebar> to rotate the isolated footings after they are placed.

*Note: When hovering your cursor over a column, type **SM** to snap to the midpoint.*

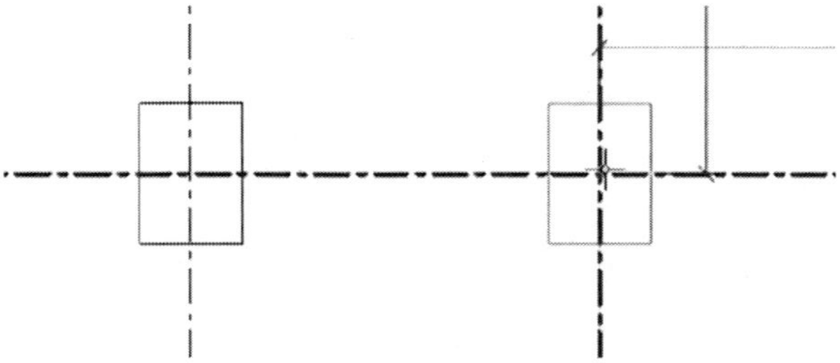

Figure 6–11

- Once you have placed at least one footing, you can use the **Copy** command to add others. Ensure that you are copying from the column midpoint. (Figure 6–12 shows copying more than one footing at a time.)

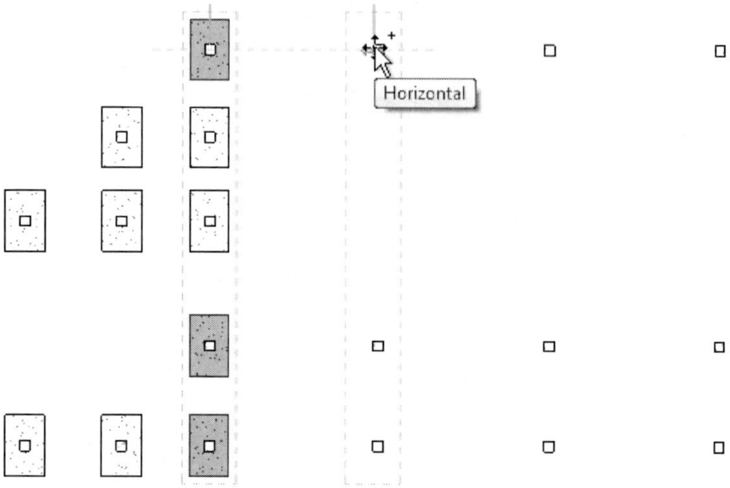

Figure 6–12

- To save time when placing footings, in the *Modify | Place Isolated Foundation* tab>*Multiple* panel, click either (At Grids) and select all of the grids or (At Columns) and select all of the columns in the view. When you are finished, click (Finish).
  - If needed, press <Spacebar> to rotate the isolated footings after they are placed.
- If the material of the wall footing and the material of the isolated footing are the same, they automatically join, as shown in Figure 6–13.

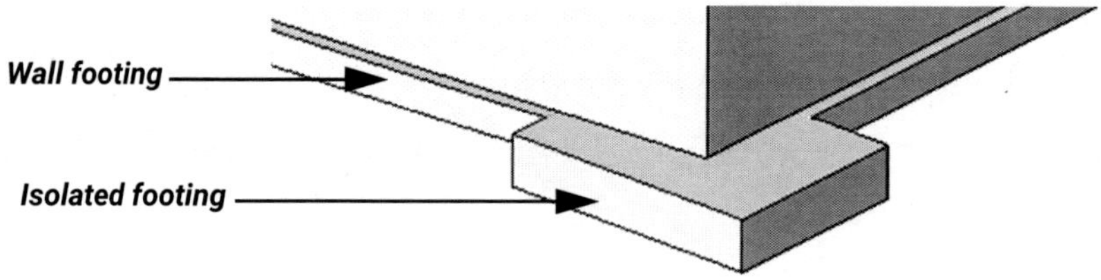

Figure 6–13

Hint: Foundation Element Properties

Some of the element properties are automatically generated from the location and size of the element in the model and are grayed out, for example *Host*, *Elevation at Top*, and *Elevation at Bottom*, as shown in Figure 6–14. These can be used in tags and schedules.

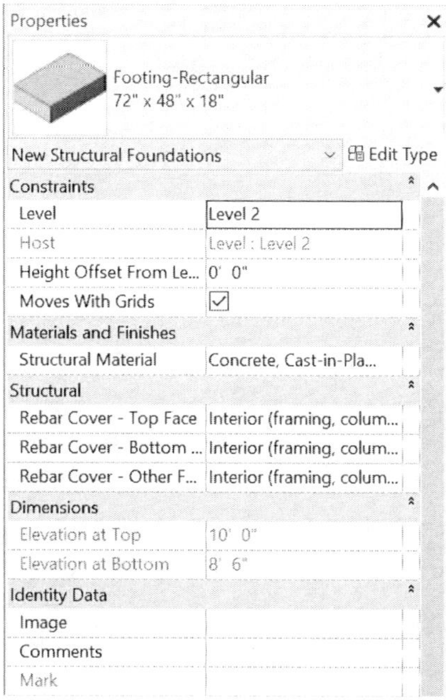

Figure 6–14

Practice 6a
Add Columns

Practice Objectives

- Add structural columns.
- Add footings by using copying, at grids, and manually placing them.

In this practice, you will add structural columns to grids and modify the height of the columns. Figure 6–15 shows the completed practice.

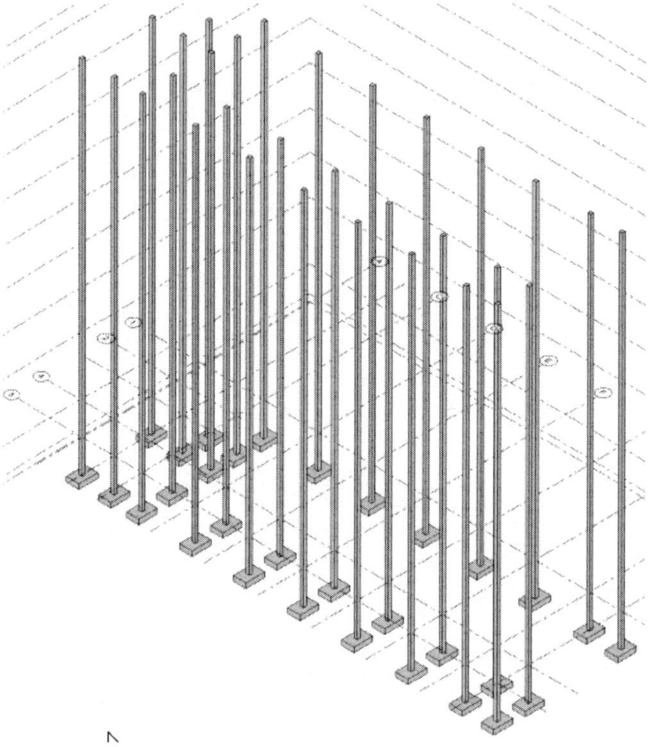

Figure 6–15

- Now that you have practiced the basics in previous exercises using a simple model, you will return to the main building model project to add the columns.

Task 1: Add columns.

1. Open the project **Arch-Columns.rvt** from the practice files folder.
2. Verify you are in the **Floor Plans: Floor 1** view.

3. Open the Visibility/Graphic Overrides by typing **VV**.
4. In the *Visibility/Graphic Overrides* dialog box, select the *Imported Categories* tab.
5. In the *Visibility* column, click on the node next to **Hotel-Level-1.dwg** to expand it and see all the layers, as shown in Figure 6–16.
6. Uncheck **A-ANNO-DIM**, **A-ANNO-SYMB**, and **A-ANNO-TEXT** (as shown in Figure 6–16) and click **OK**. Note that the DWG's annotations are no longer displaying in the view.

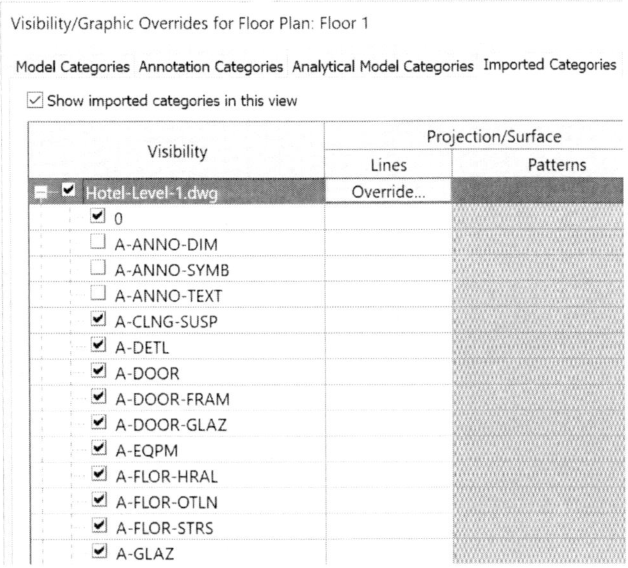

Figure 6–16

7. In the *Architecture* tab>*Build* panel, click (Structural Column).
8. In the Type Selector, select **Precast-Square Column: 12" x 12"**, if not already selected.
9. In the *Modify | Place Structural Column* tab>*Placement* panel, verify that (Vertical Column) is selected.
10. In the *Rotate* panel, verify that (Rotate After Placement) is not selected. In the *Levels* panel, verify that (Height) is selected, then for (Top), select **Floor 2** from the drop-down list, if not already selected.
11. In Properties, verify that the checkbox next to *Room Bounding* is checked.
12. In the *Modify | Place Structural Column* tab>*Multiple* panel, click (At Grids).
13. Select all of the horizontal and vertical grid lines in the project using a crossing window (right to left).
14. In the *Modify | Place Structural Column > At Grid Intersection* tab>*Multiple* panel, click (Finish).

15. Click (Modify).
16. Delete the columns at locations **A1**, **A2**, **A4**, **B1**, and **B4**, as shown in Figure 6–17.

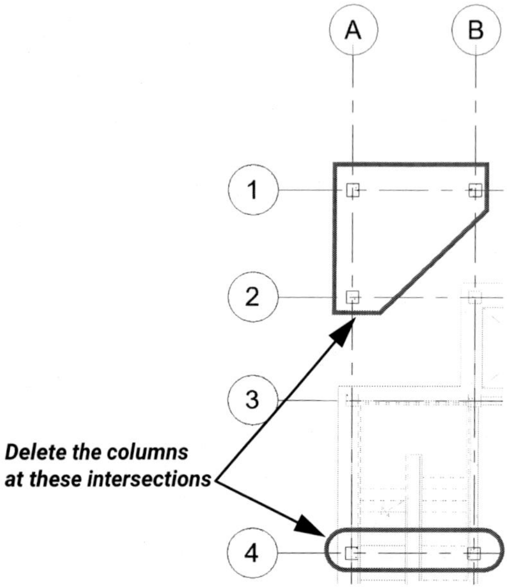

Figure 6–17

17. Save the project.

Task 2: Modify the columns.

1. In the Quick Access Toolbar, click (Default 3D View).
2. Select the poolhouse and type **VH** to hide it in the view.

3. Note that the columns are only set to a base level of Floor 1 and a top level of Floor 2, as shown in Figure 6–18.

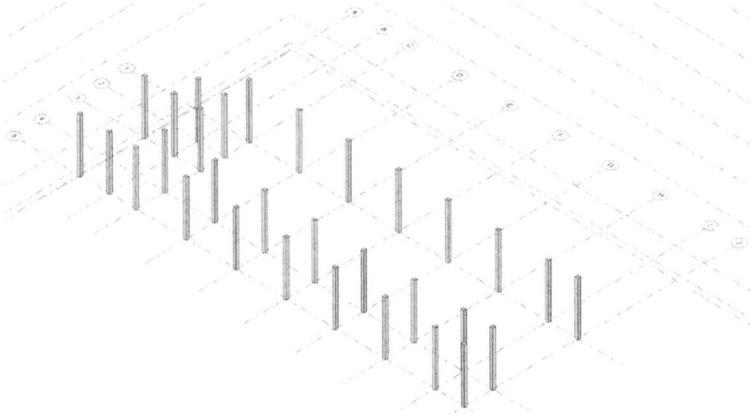

Figure 6–18

4. Select all of the columns. You can select one column, then right-click and select **Select All Instances>Visible in View**.
5. In Properties, in the *Constraints* section, change the following:
   - *Base Level* to **T.O. Footing**
   - *Top Level* to **Roof**
6. Click **Apply** or move the cursor into the view window. The columns now extend from the top of the footing to the roof level.
7. In the 3D view, select the **T.O. Footing** level line. This highlights the entire level surface in the view to help with visualization, as shown in Figure 6–19.

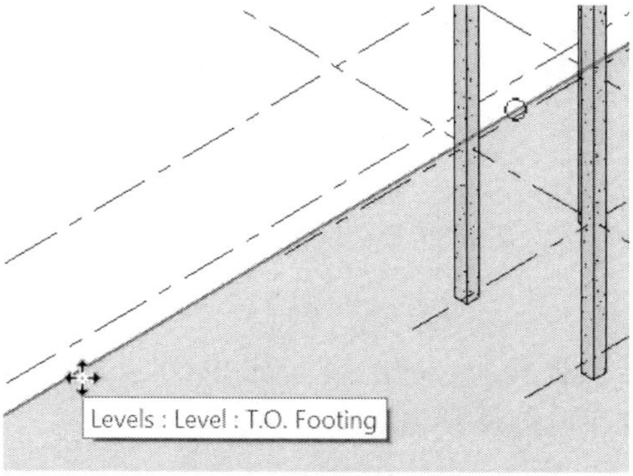

Figure 6–19

8. Save the project.

Task 3: Add column footings.

1. Open the **Floor Plans: T.O. Footing** view and select everything in the view.
2. In the Status Bar or in the *Modify | Multi-select* tab>*Selection* panel, click (Filter).
3. In the *Filter* dialog box, clear **Structural Columns** and click **OK**.
4. In the View Control Bar, click (Temporary Hide/Isolate) and select **Hide Element**.
   - Everything except the columns should be hidden, as shown in Figure 6–20. It is now easier to identify the locations of the footings.

Figure 6–20

5. In the *Structure* tab>*Foundation* panel, click (Isolated).
6. A dialog box displays that there is no structural foundations family loaded, as shown in Figure 6–21. Click **Yes** to load a foundations family.

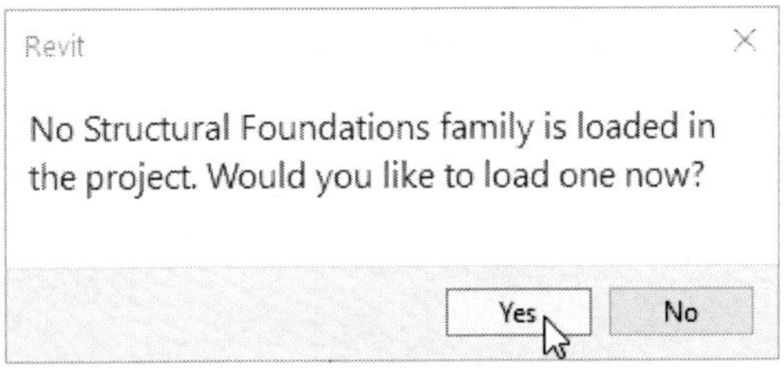

Figure 6–21

7. In the *Load Family* dialog box, navigate to the practice files *Families>Structural* folder, select **Footing-Rectangular.rfa**, and click **Open**.
8. In Properties, verify that **Footing-Rectangular: 72" x 48" x 18"** is selected in the Type Selector and that the *Level* is set to **T.O. Footing**.

9. Place a footing at each column's midpoint, as shown in Figure 6–22. (Hint: When hovering your cursor over a column, type **SM** to snap to the midpoint.)

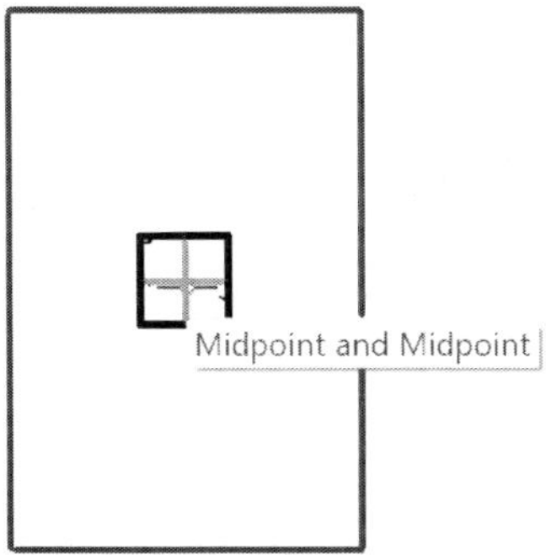

Figure 6–22

10. Click (Modify).
11. In the View Control Bar, click (Temporary Hide/Isolate) and select **Reset Temporary Hide/Isolate**.
12. Save and close the project.

End of practice

Chapter Review Questions

1. Where can columns be placed?
   a. Columns can only be placed on grids.
   b. Architectural columns can be placed anywhere, but structural columns can only be placed on grids.
   c. Both architectural and structural columns can be placed wherever you want.
   d. Grid-based column types must be placed on the grid, but free-standing column types can be placed anywhere.

2. In order for architectural columns to move with grids, what needs to be selected when placing the column?
   a. In the contextual tab, select **At Grids**.
   b. Set the *Top Constraint* to grids.
   c. Columns always move with grids no matter what type.
   d. In Properties, select **Moves With Grids**.

3. To draw a slanted column, you need to start the **Structural Column** command.
   a. True
   b. False

Command Summary

Button	Command	Location
	**At Architectural Columns**	• **Ribbon:** *Modify | Place Structural Column* tab>*Multiple* panel
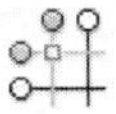	**At Grids**	• **Ribbon:** *Modify | Place Structural Column* tab>*Multiple* panel
	**At Structural Columns**	• **Ribbon:** *Modify | Place Isolated Foundation* tab>*Multiple* panel
	**Column**	• **Ribbon:** *Architecture* tab>*Build* panel
	**Column: Architectural**	• **Ribbon:** *Architecture* tab>*Build* panel, expand Column
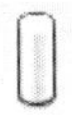	**Structural Column**	• **Ribbon:** *Architecture* tab>*Build* panel, expand Column

Chapter 7

Modeling Walls

Walls are the primary elements that define rooms in buildings for both 2D and 3D representation. They are important for communicating the project to both customer and contractor. Walls can demonstrate the relationship between materials, lighting, texture, and the overall visual effect in a particular space. You can draw walls in Revit by tracing an imported file, taking measurements from blueprints, or using physical measurements. Revit contains a variety of wall types that are available in different widths and materials. You can change the height, length, type, and layers of walls as needed.

Learning Objectives

- Model walls using specific wall types.
- Modify walls by changing the wall type, height, length, and profile.
- Define how walls join at intersections.
- Add wall openings that are not cased or filled with a door or window.
- Add room elements and tags that display the room name and room number.

7.1 Modeling Walls

Walls in Revit are more than just two lines on a plan. They are full 3D elements that store detailed information, including height, thickness, and materials. This means they are useful in 2D and 3D views, and also impact material takeoff schedules, as shown in Figure 7–1.

- Walls are a system family that is predefined in the Revit template file and cannot be loaded in from an external location or saved out to a external location.
- Walls can be customized to suit your company needs, if necessary.
- To ensure that your walls are oriented correctly, it is best practice to draw your walls in a clockwise manner.

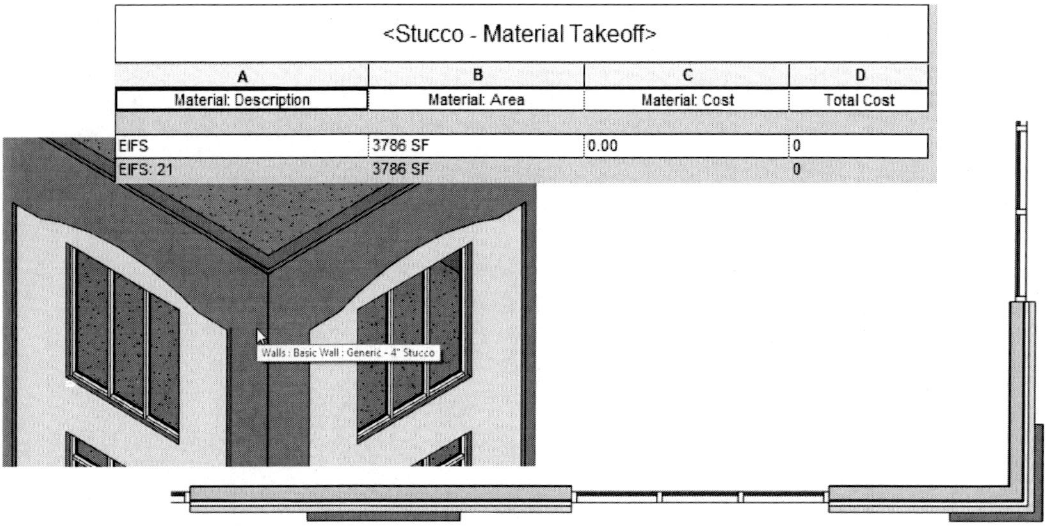

Figure 7–1

In a building, different types of walls serve different purposes. Structural walls are load-bearing, carrying the weight of the roof and floors and helping to support the building. Non-load-bearing walls do not support any weight and are mainly used to divide spaces inside. A face wall is the outer wall of a building, which closes off the space and may also be decorative. A finish wall is the layer added to the surface of a wall, like paint, tiles, wallpaper, or paneling, best used for presentations.

In Revit, there are three broad categories of walls:

- **Basic walls:** Compound walls that contain one or more layers (e.g., blocks, air space, bricks, etc.).
- **Curtain walls:** Walls that are divided horizontally and vertically into a grid system.
- **Stacked walls:** Consist of two or more basic walls stacked vertically, such as a brick wall over a concrete wall.

Wall Cross-Section

The *Cross-Section* for the basic wall category can be modified to be **Vertical**, **Slanted**, or **Tapered**, as shown in Figure 7–2.

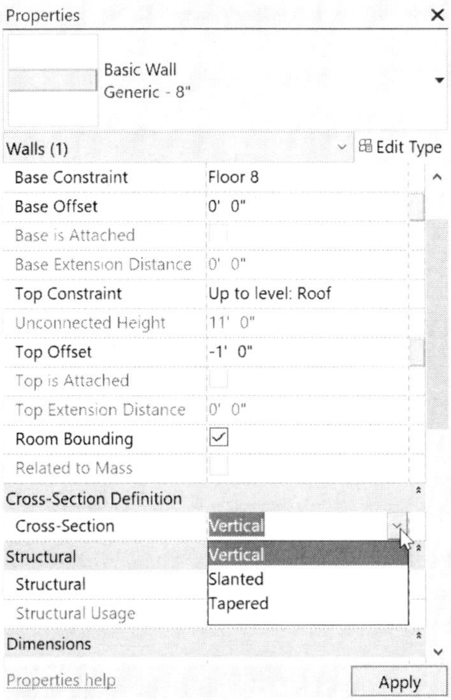

Figure 7–2

Vertical Wall

All walls are drawn by default as a vertical wall and are at a 0° vertical when comparing it to a slanted wall type.

> ***Note:*** *If you change a wall's cross-section to* ***Tapered*** *and adjust the settings for the tapered wall, then you will see only the Tapered wall types displayed in the Type Selector. If you need to draw a vertical or slanted wall after the tapered wall is drawn, you will need to set the cross-section back to* ***Vertical*** *or* ***Slanted*** *so that you can see all the wall types in the Type Selector.*

Slanted Wall

You can draw a slanted wall type and specify the **Angle From Vertical** degree value in Properties. The slant degree needs to be within -90° to 90°. You can also change a vertically drawn wall to a slanted wall type. If there are any doors, door openings or window added to the wall, you will need to select those objects and, in Properties, specify their *Orientation*. The direction to which the wall has been drawn (right to left or left to right) will determine the direction the angle will go. Figure 7–3 shows that when drawing from left to right the wall slant will go in the negative direction, and drawing from right to left the slant wall goes in the positive direction.

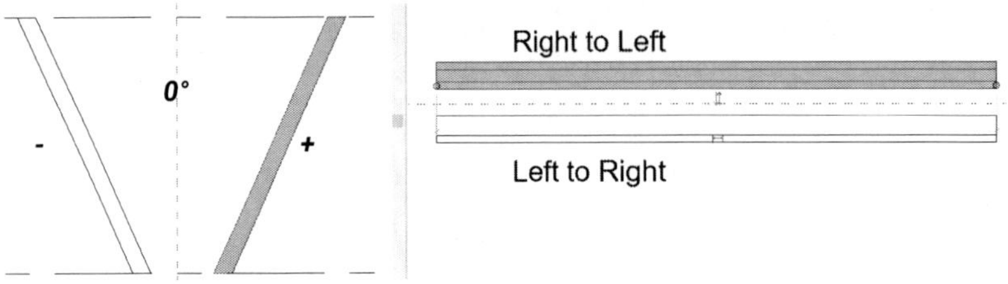

Figure 7–3

- Slanted walls can be modified in a plan, 3D, section, and perspective views.
- You can create a slanted wall with curved, circle, arc, polygon, or elliptical paths.
- If the angle is not going in the correct direction, + or -, you can add a (negative) - symbol in front of the degree value in Properties.

Tapered Wall

You can create a tapered wall from any wall type except walls with sweeps and reveals. You must first edit the structure of the wall to set the variable thickness for the available wall layers. If not, you are prompted to set this before drawing the wall, as shown in Figure 7–4.

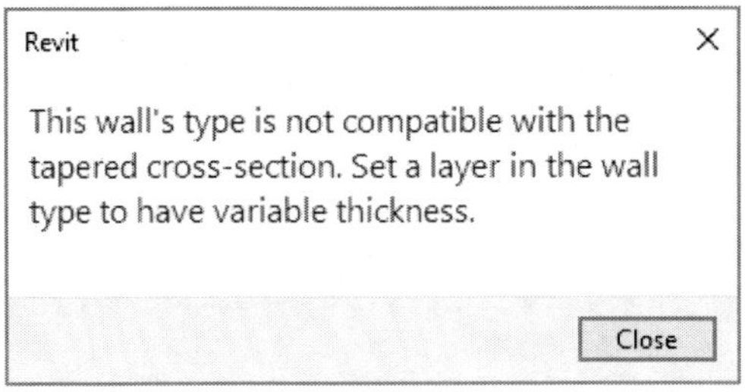

Figure 7–4

- To set the default angles of the tapered wall, you can set the *Default Exterior* and *Interior Angle* in the *Type Properties* dialog box.

- If you have multiple instances of the same tapered wall type, you can select a tapered wall, and in Properties, override the angles by checking the checkbox next to *Enable Angle Overrides* and setting the *Exterior Angle* and *Interior Angle*, as shown in Figure 7–5.

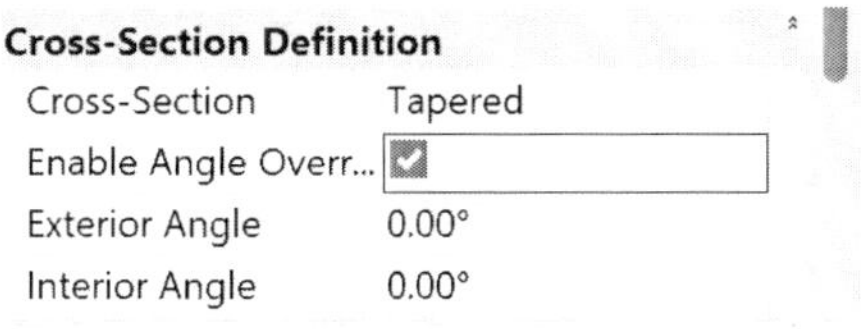

Figure 7–5

- Curtain walls and stacked wall types cannot be tapered.
- If doors, door openings, or windows are placed in a tapered wall, you can specify the orientation of the door and wall. See *"Modifying Door and Window Properties"* on page *8-4*.

Wall Display per View

You can alter the way a wall is displayed in the active view by setting the *Detail Level*, as shown in Figure 7–6. You can also override the visibility settings of all walls in a view by opening the *Visibility/Graphic Overrides* dialog box and modifying the **Wall** category. To change the way selected walls display in the active view, you would override the setting for graphics in view by element. To display the hatching in all walls in the active view where a wall is being cut through, in the View Control Bar, set the *Detail Level* to **Medium** or **Fine**, as shown in Figure 7–6.

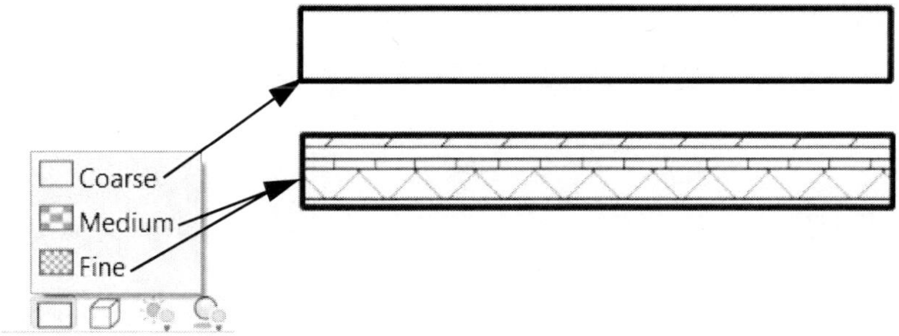

Figure 7–6

- To access the *Visibility/Graphic Overrides* dialog box to change all walls in a view, go to the *View* tab>*Graphics* panel and click (Visibility/Graphics), or type **VG** or **VV**. You can uncheck **Non-Core Layers** (as shown in Figure 7–7) to only view the core layer in the view. This overrides all walls in the view.

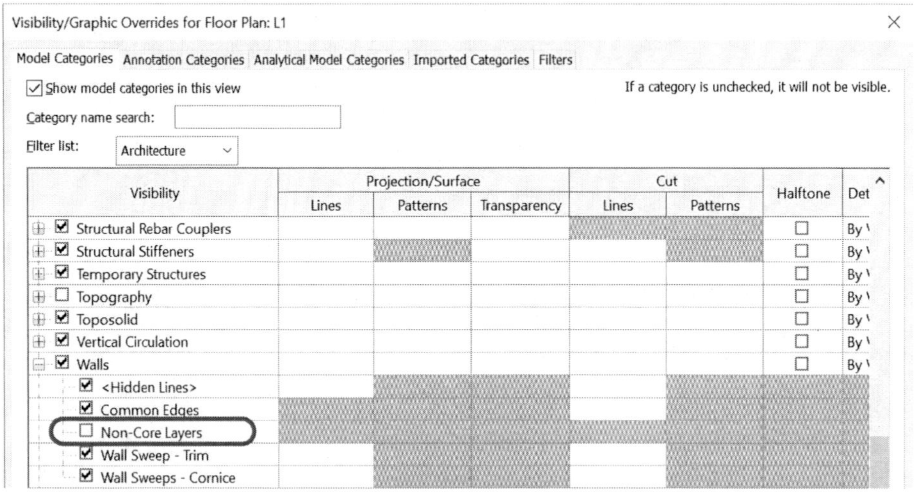

Figure 7–7

- To modify a single or a select few walls in the view, select the walls, right-click, and select **Override Graphics in View>By Element**, as shown in Figure 7–8.

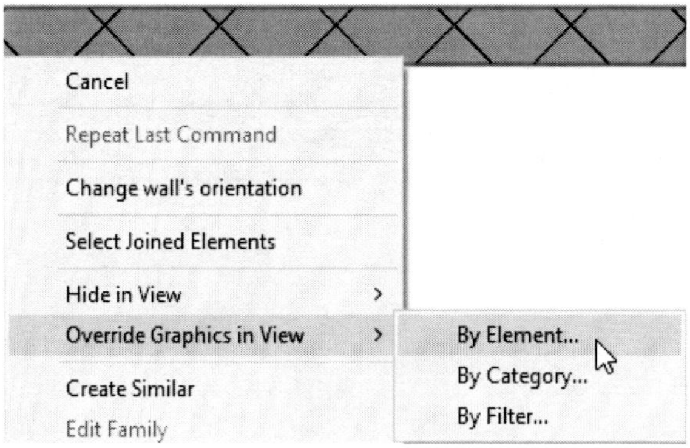

Figure 7–8

How To: Model a Wall

1. In the *Architecture* tab>*Build* panel, click (Wall), or type **WA**.
2. In the Type Selector, select a wall type, as shown in Figure 7–9. You can use the search box to quickly find specific types of walls.

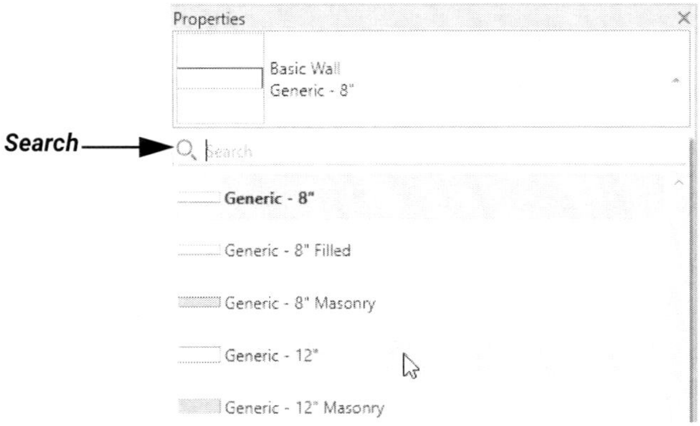

Figure 7–9

3. In Properties, set the *Cross-Section* to **Vertical**, **Slanted**, or **Tapered**, depending on the wall you need to create, as shown in Figure 7–10. Specify the properties and type properties as needed. If this is not set at the beginning of drawing a wall, the last cross-section used will be the default.
   - If you set the *Cross-Section* to **Slanted**, you are able to set the *Angle From Vertical* degree, as shown in Figure 7–10.

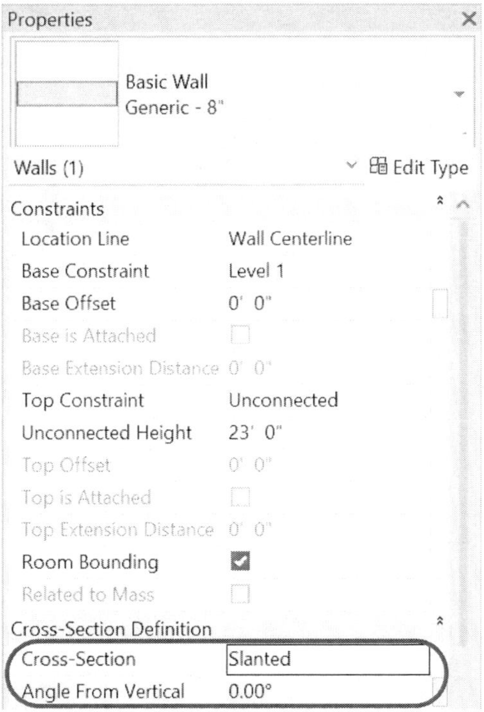

Figure 7–10

- If you set the *Cross-Section* to **Tapered**, you will get a warning about the wall type. You must first edit the structure of the wall before setting the *Cross-Section* to **Tapered**.
    - **a.** With the wall type selected, click **Edit Type** in Properties.
    - **b.** Click **Edit...** next to *Structure*.
    - **c.** In the *Edit Assembly* dialog box, check the checkbox in the *Variable* column (as shown in Figure 7–11) for the layer that you want tapered.

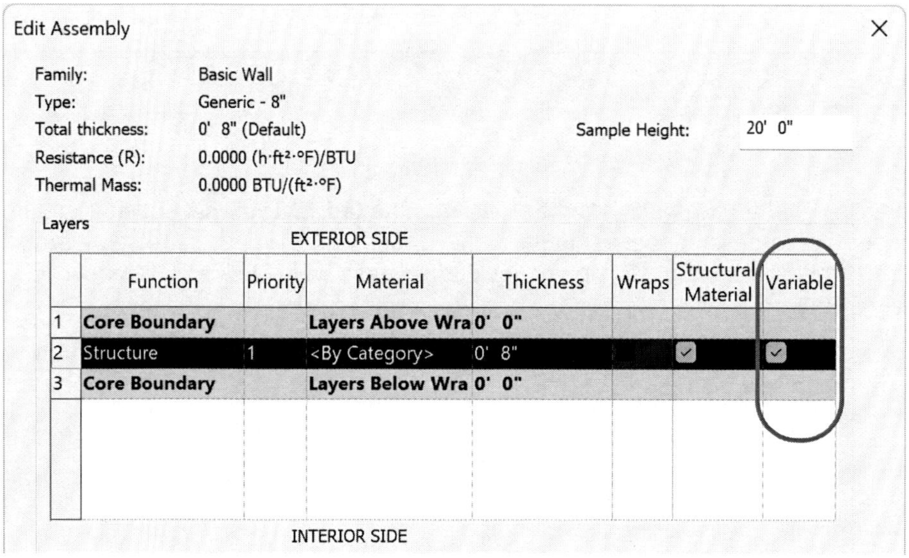

Figure 7–11

- **d.** Click **OK**.

e. In the *Type Properties* dialog box, you will now have the ability to set the *Cross Section Definition*, as shown in Figure 7–12.

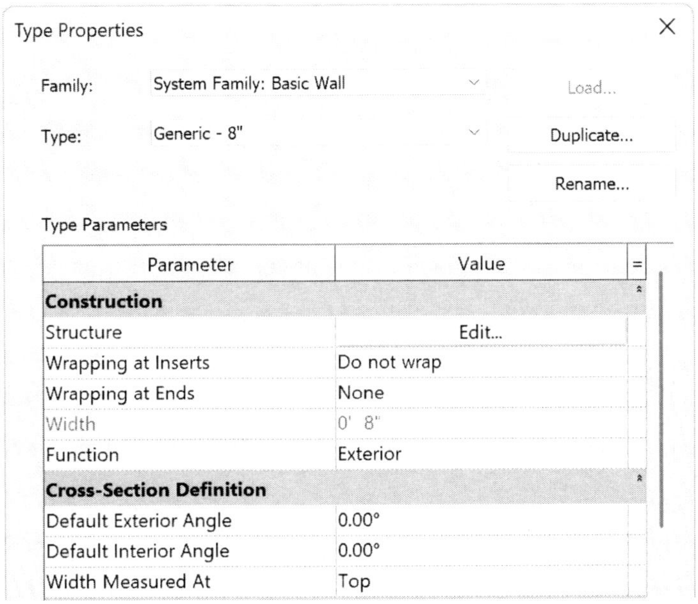

Figure 7–12

4. In the *Modify | Place Wall* tab (shown in Figure 7–13), select one of the sketch tools from the *Draw* panel, then specify any of the options in the *Draw*, *Constraint*, and *Levels* panels before you start modeling.

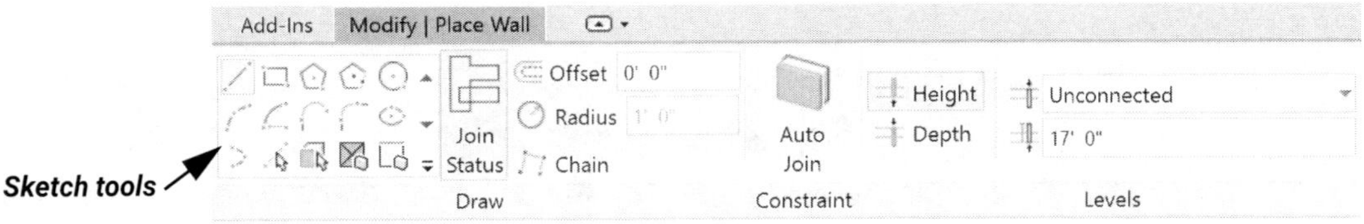

Figure 7–13

Draw Panel Options

- (Join Status): Allows automatic wall joins.
- (Offset): Enables you to enter the distance at which a new wall is created from an existing element.

Note: *(Offset) in the Modify | Place Wall contextual tab offsets the wall from where you are drawing it and not from a level perspective, like Base and Top Offset do in Properties.*

- (Radius): Adds a curve of a specified radius to connected walls as you model.
- (Chain): Enables you to model multiple connected walls.

Constraint Panel Options

- (Auto Join): Similarly to **Join Geometry**, allows the wall to be joined with any walls that touch it.

Levels Panel Options

- (Height): Set (Top) to either a level or **Unconnected**. If **Unconnected** is selected, specify the (Unconnected Height) value that is measured from the level.
- (Depth): Set the (Bottom) to either a level or **Unconnected**. If **Unconnected** is selected, specify the (Depth) value.

5. Draw the wall.

- Use drawing aids to help you while sketching walls.
- As you are sketching, you can press <Spacebar> to flip the orientation of walls.
- When using the **Chain** option, press <Esc> once to finish the string of walls and remain in the **Wall** command or press <Esc> twice to get out of the Wall command completely. Hint: <Esc> works similarly on other commands.

Hosted Walls

During the design process, instead of duplicating or modifying an existing wall type to change the finish of a wall, you can add a hosted wall (also called a finish wall) to the exterior or interior side of an existing architectural wall (the host wall). Use **Place By Room** or **Place By Segment** and select either **Exterior Side** or **Interior Side**. Adding a hosted wall allows you to visually see different finishes.

To avoid drawing hosted walls over doors or windows when using these tools, use **Auto Join**. Figure 7–14 shows a wall with doors and windows and a hosted wall applied both with and without **Auto Join** turned on.

- The **Place By Room** and **Place By Segment** tools are not available for structural wall types.

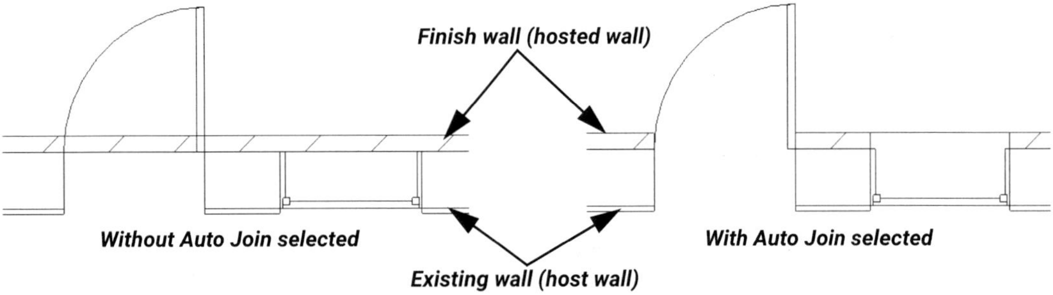

Figure 7–14

Hosted Wall Sketch Tools

- (Place By Room): Allows you to place hosted walls on all the walls in a room. Hover your cursor over a room until the walls are outlined in red, as shown in Figure 7–15, then click to place the hosted wall.

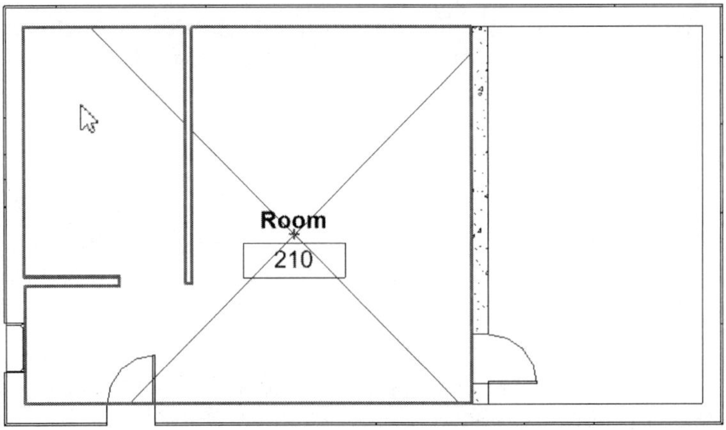

Figure 7–15

- (Place By Segment): Allows you to place a hosted wall on a single segment of a wall. Hover your cursor over a wall until the wall segment is outlined in red, as shown in Figure 7–16. You can move your cursor to the inside or outside of the wall, depending on which side you want the hosted wall to be on, and click to place it.

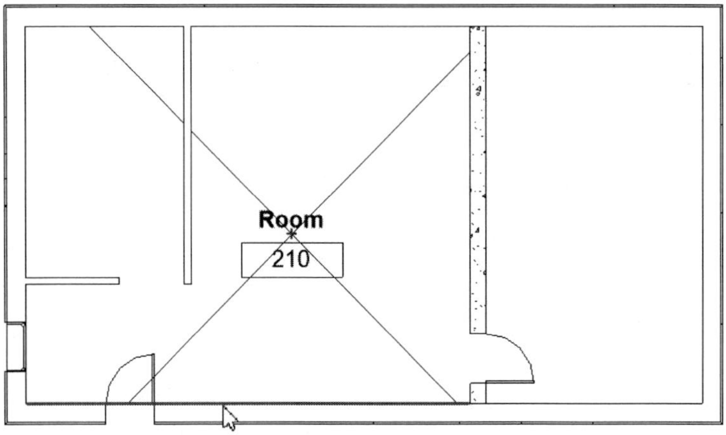

Figure 7–16

- You can manually draw a hosted wall using the **Wall** command as long as you do not have **Place By Room** or **Place By Segment** selected. Toggle on **Auto Join** so if the host wall is moved or modified, a warning will display.

Hosted Wall Placement Options

- (Interior Side): Places the hosted wall's interior side against the selected host.
- (Exterior Side): Places the hosted wall's exterior side against the selected host.

- Instead of selecting one of the wall placement options, you can press <Spacebar> to flip between the two options quickly while sketching the hosted wall.

Hosted Wall Constraint Options

- (Hosted Wall): Displays when either **Place By Room** or **Place By Segment** is selected in the *Draw* panel. You can create a hosted wall on a host wall (existing wall) and remain connected to the host wall if it is moved. Once a hosted wall is placed, you can specify an offset between the host and the hosted wall by selecting the hosted wall and entering a value for *Offset from Host* in Properties.
  - If a host wall's length changes, the hosted wall does not change in length and would need to be modified independently. Also, if a door or window is placed, it will not cut through both the host and hosted wall; to achieve that, you will need to toggle on **Auto Join**.

- (Auto Join): When placing a hosted wall with **Auto Join** selected, the hosted wall will join to the host wall. If the host wall is moved or deleted, the hosted wall will remain in place and you will receive a warning, as shown in Figure 7–17, prompting if you would like to unjoin the wall elements from each other. Using **Auto Join** allows for some doors and windows to cut through both the host and hosted walls.

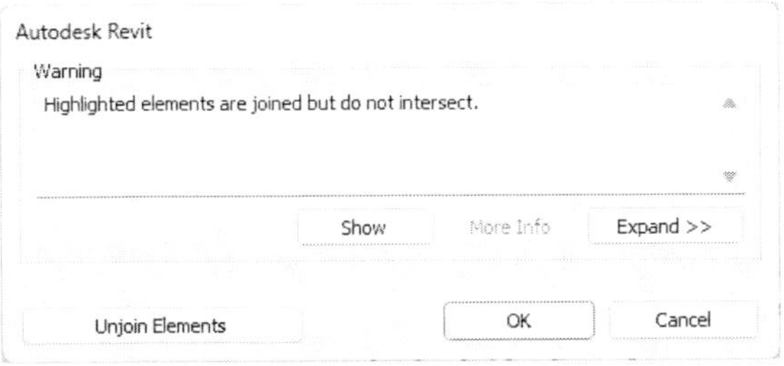

Figure 7–17

How To: Place a Hosted Wall

1. In the *Architecture* tab>*Build* panel, click (Wall: Architectural), or type **WA**.
2. In Properties, select the wall type in the Type Selector and verify the *Location Line* is set correctly.

   Note: *To avoid overlapping, it is best to work with walls that have their Location Line set to* ***Finish Face: Exterior*** *or* ***Interior*** *or* ***Core Face: Exterior*** *or* ***Interior****.*

3. In the *Modify | Place Wall* tab>*Draw* panel, select either (Place By Room) or (Place By Segment). Toggle (Join Status) on or off, as needed.
4. In the *Modify | Place Wall* tab>*Placement* panel, select either (Exterior Side) or (Interior Side).
5. In the *Modify | Place Wall* tab>*Constraint* panel, toggle on (Hosted Wall) to constrain the new wall to the existing wall and/or (Auto Join) if you know geometry needs to cut through the host and hosted walls.

   Note: *If you start the Wall command using* ***Wall: Structural****, the placement and join tools will not display on the ribbon.*

6. Click to place the wall, as shown in Figure 7–18.

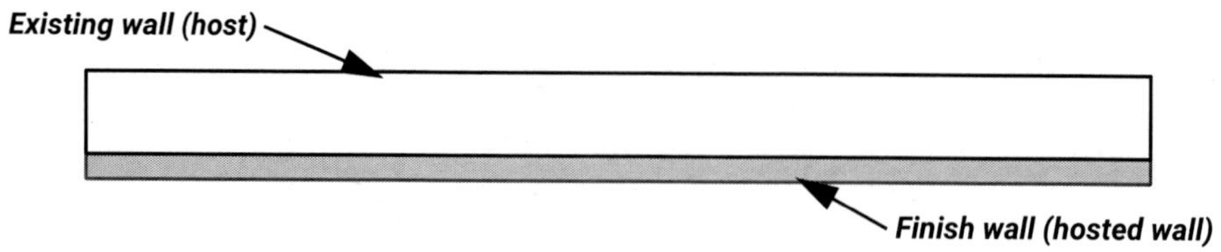

Figure 7–18

Modifying Hosted Walls with Hosts

You can modify a hosted wall using the options in the *Modify | Walls* tab>*Manage Host* panel, as follows:

- (Select Main Host): If you need to find the host wall, select the hosted wall and select **Select Main Host**. The host wall highlights in the view.
- (Remove Hosted Relationship): If a hosted wall was placed with (Hosted Wall) toggled on, select the hosted wall and click **Remove Hosted Relationship** to remove the relationship between the host and the hosted wall.
- (Pick New Host): If you need to select a new host for the hosted wall, select the hosted wall and click **Pick New Host**, then select a wall that is parallel to the hosted wall.
  - If you receive a warning that the highlighted elements are joined but do not intersect, click **Unjoin Elements** to continue. You do not need to remove the hosted relationship before you pick a new host.

7.2 Modifying Walls

There are several methods of modifying walls. You can change the type of wall using the Type Selector, modify the Properties, use controls and shape handles to modify the length and wall orientation, and use temporary and permanent dimensions to change the location or length of a wall in 2D and 3D views, as shown in Figure 7–19. Additional tools enable you to modify wall joins, edit the profile of a wall, and add wall openings.

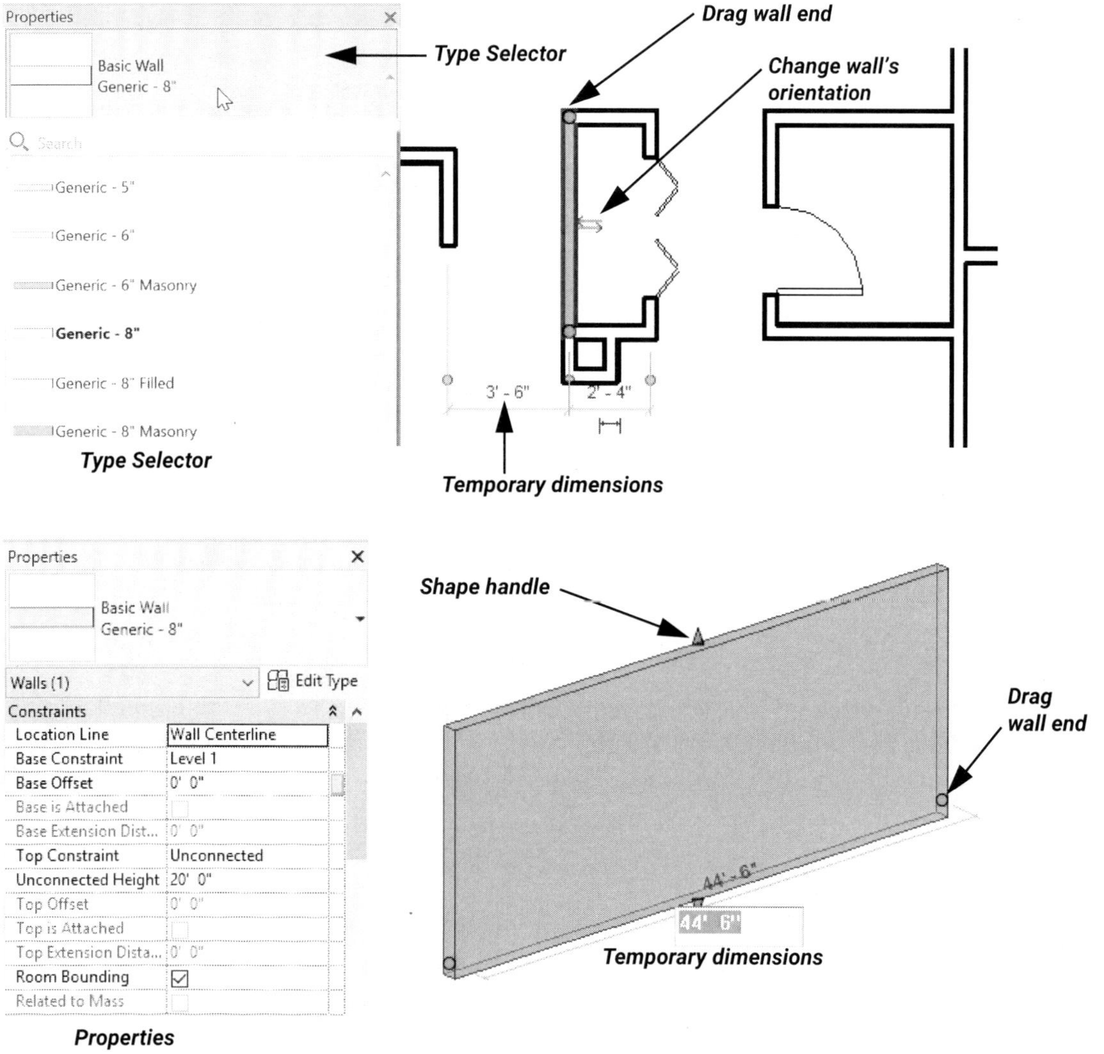

Figure 7–19

Modifying Slanted and Tapered Walls

Modifying a slanted or tapered wall is similar to modifying a vertical wall type with the exception of modifying the angle.

- When modifying a slanted wall type, you have the ability to modify the Drag Wall Slant grip or modify the temporary dimension in a 3D, section, elevation, or isometric view, as shown in Figure 7–20.

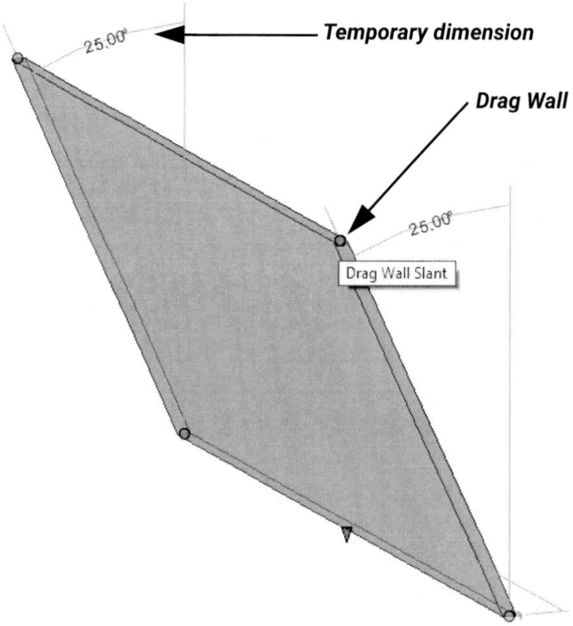

Figure 7–20

- When modifying a tapered wall, you have the ability to modify the **Drag Wall Exterior Face Slant** and **Drag Wall Interior Face Slant** grips or modify the temporary dimension in a 3D, section, elevation, or isometric view, as shown in Figure 7–21.

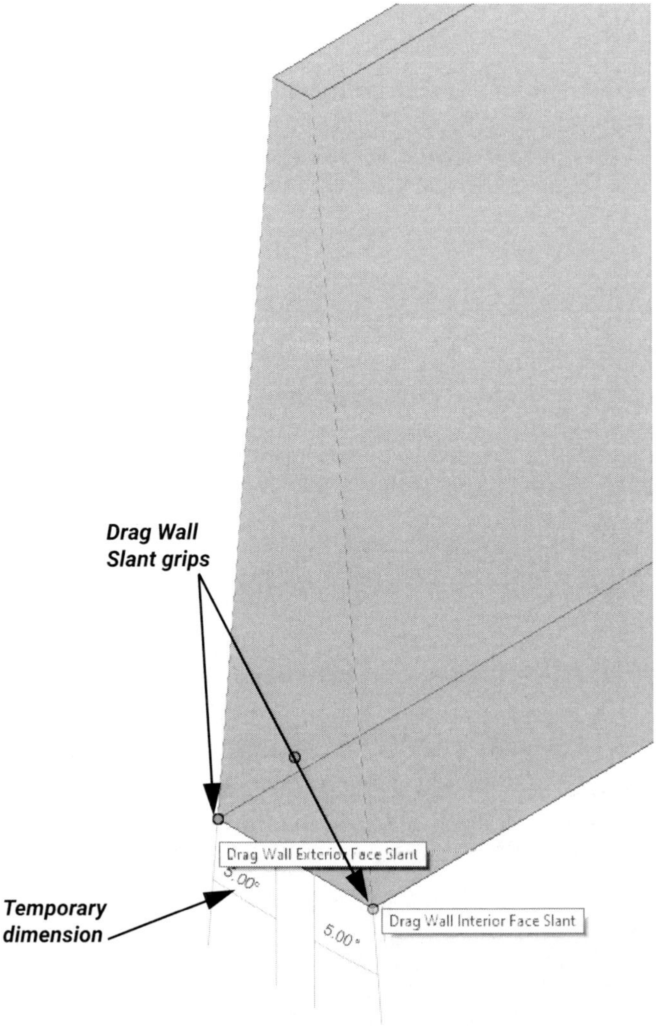

Figure 7–21

- You can set the wall's structural properties as **Non-bearing**, **Bearing**, **Shear**, or **Structural combined**, as shown in Figure 7–22.

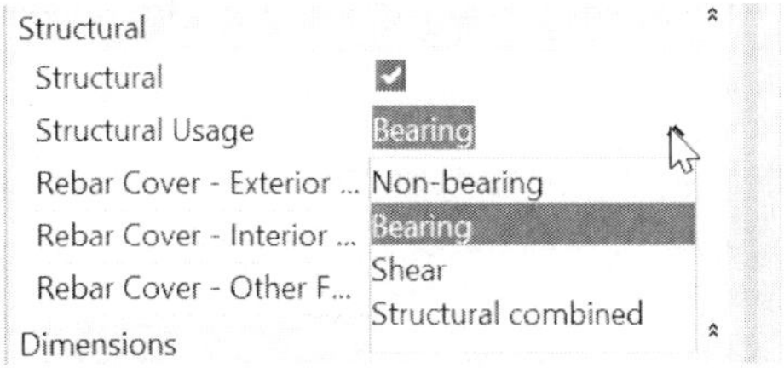

Figure 7–22

Wall Joins

The software automatically joins walls with common materials when they come together at an intersection, as shown on the left in Figure 7–23. However, there are times when you do not want the walls to clean up, such as when one fire-rated wall butts into another, or when a wall touches a column surround, as shown on the right in Figure 7–23.

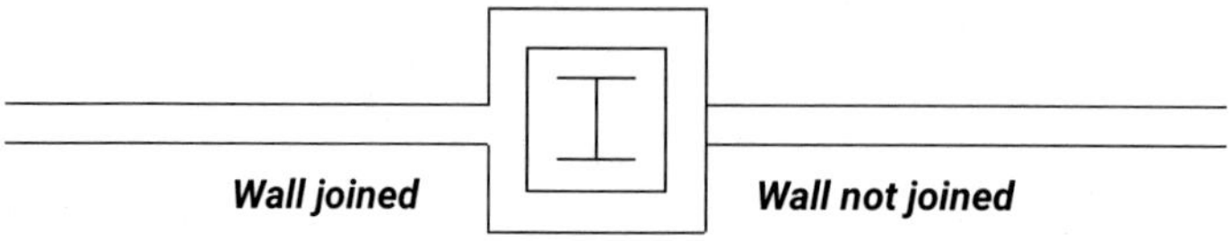

Figure 7–23

- While you are creating walls, you can toggle **Join Status** on or off in the *Modify | Place Wall* tab>*Draw* panel, as shown in Figure 7–24.

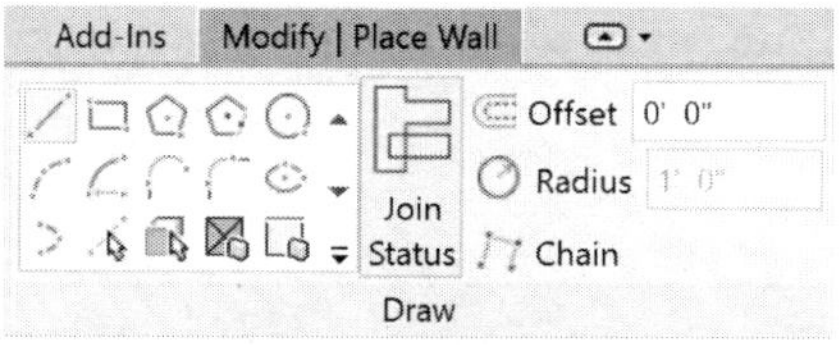

Figure 7–24

- If a wall is already placed, select the wall, right-click on the **Drag Wall End** control at the end of the wall, and select **Disallow Join**, as shown on the left in Figure 7–25. Once the end is not joined, you can drag it to the appropriate location, as shown on the right in Figure 7–25.

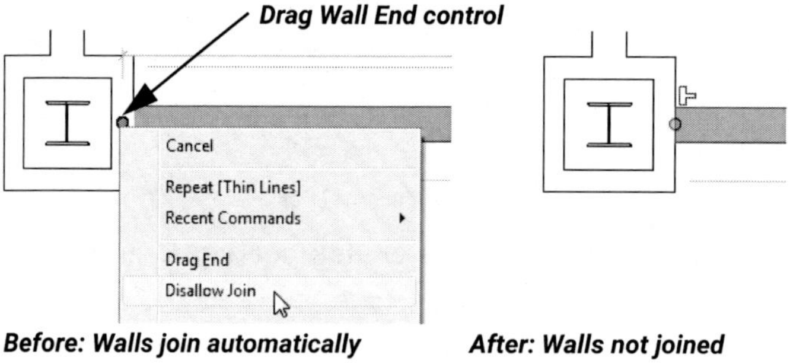

Figure 7–25

- To rejoin the walls, right-click on the **Drag Wall End** control and select **Allow Join**. Manually drag the wall back to where you want it to touch the target wall.

- If you select a wall, you can change the **Allow Join/Disallow Join** option by clicking on the icon that displays next to the wall's end, as shown in Figure 7–26. Click (Allow Join) to join the walls together or click (Disallow Join) to unjoin them.

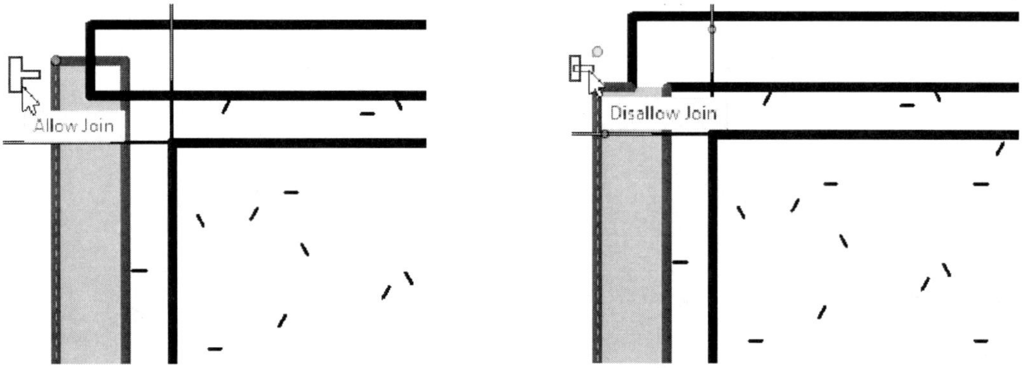

Figure 7–26

Editing Wall Joins

Use **Wall Joins** to modify the configuration of the intersections, as shown in Figure 7–27. Do not use this command if you have complex wall joins; instead, modify the length of the wall in relation to the adjoining walls.

Figure 7–27

How To: Modify the Configuration of a Wall Join

1. In the *Modify* tab>*Geometry* panel, click (Wall Joins).
2. Click on the wall join that you want to edit. There is a square box around the join. Hold <Ctrl> to select multiple joins.
3. In the *Modify | Wall Joins* tab>*Configuration* panel, select the required configuration and display options, as shown in Figure 7–28.

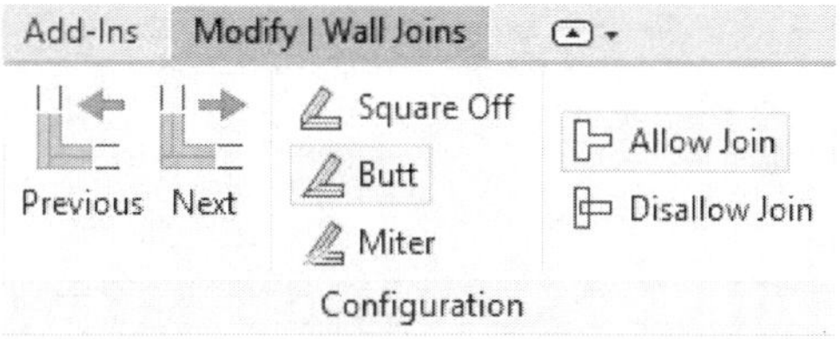

Figure 7–28

- Select from three configurations: (Butt), (Miter), or (Square Off), as shown in Figure 7–29.

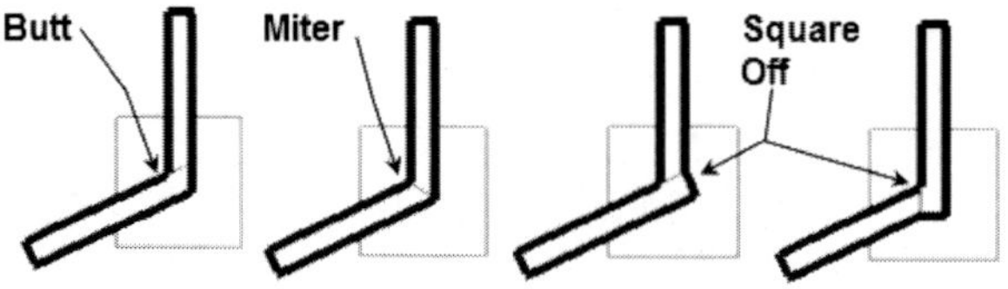

Figure 7–29

- Click (Previous) and (Next) to toggle the butt or squared-off corner configurations through the various intersection options.

How To: Modify Display Options of Wall Joins

1. In the *Modify* tab>*Geometry* panel, click (Wall Joins).
2. Click on the wall join that you want to edit. To modify multiple joins at the same time, draw a window around several wall intersections (as shown in Figure 7–30), or hold <Ctrl> and pick additional intersections. A square box displays around each join.

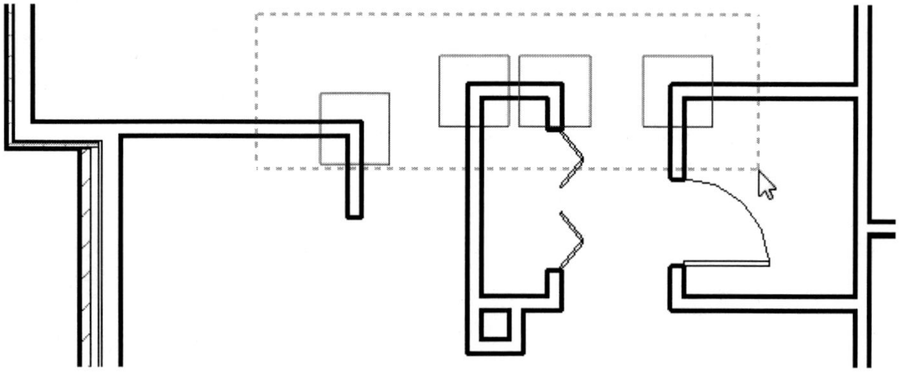

Figure 7–30

3. In the *Modify | Wall Joins* tab>*Display* panel, expand the (Display) drop-down list. This controls whether or not wall joins are displayed. The options are **Use View Setting** (set up in View Properties), **Clean Join**, and **Don't Clean Join**, as shown in Figure 7–31.

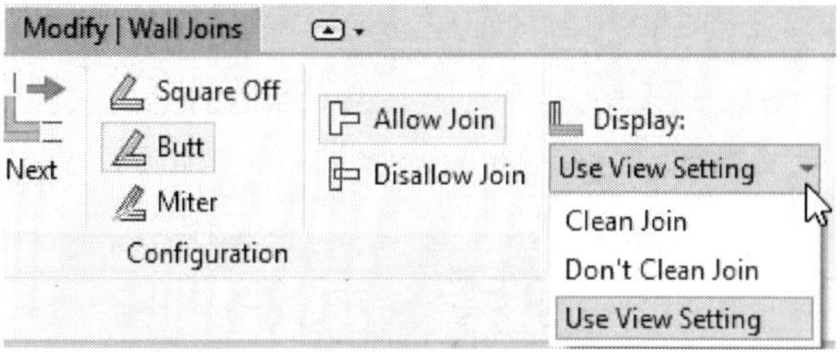

Figure 7–31

4. With any *Display* options selected, you can click (Allow Join) or (Disallow Join) in the *Modify | Wall Joins* tab>*Configuration* panel (shown previously in Figure 7–31). When you select one of these two options, the contextual tab options gray out. To bring back your options, click the wall's corner again.

Editing Wall Profiles

Walls often follow the contours of a site or an angle, such as following a line of stairs, as shown in Figure 7–32. If needed, you can edit the profile of a wall.

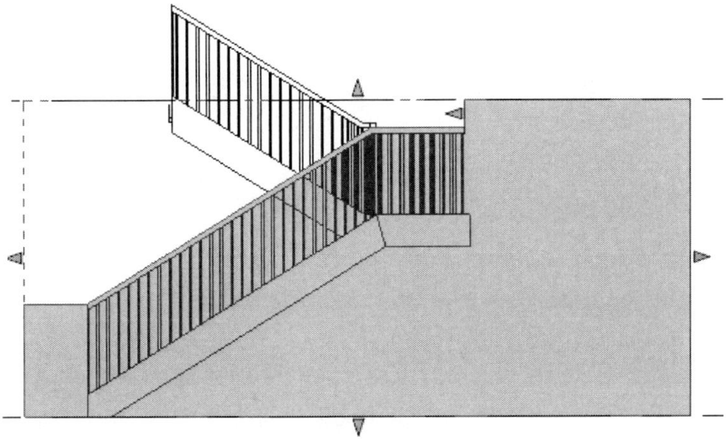

Figure 7–32

How To: Edit the Profile of a Wall

1. Open an elevation or section view in which you can see the face of the wall that you want to edit.
2. Select the wall (by highlighting the wall boundary). You can also double-click on a wall to edit the profile.
   - You cannot edit the profile of a tapered wall.
3. In the *Modify | Walls* tab>*Mode* panel, click (Edit Profile). The wall is outlined in magenta, indicating the profile of the wall.

4. In the *Modify | Walls > Edit Profile* tab>*Draw* panel, use the tools to modify the profile sketch of the wall, as shown on the top in Figure 7–33.

   Note: *The sketch must form a continuous loop. Verify that the lines are clean without any gaps or overlaps. Use any of the tools in the Modify panel to clean up the sketch.*

5. Once the profile is complete, click (Finish Edit Mode). The wall now follows the new profile, as shown on the bottom in Figure 7–33.

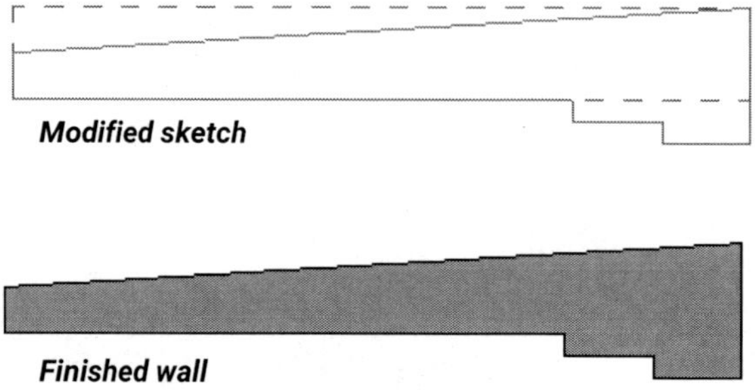

Figure 7–33

- After you adjust the sketch, you can add isolated footings to create the appropriate shape.

Editing Wall Layer Elevations

Individual layers of walls can have their height modified to better control elevations of finishes, such as brick veneer extending to a foundation (as shown in Figure 7–34), while the other layers rest on the floor slab.

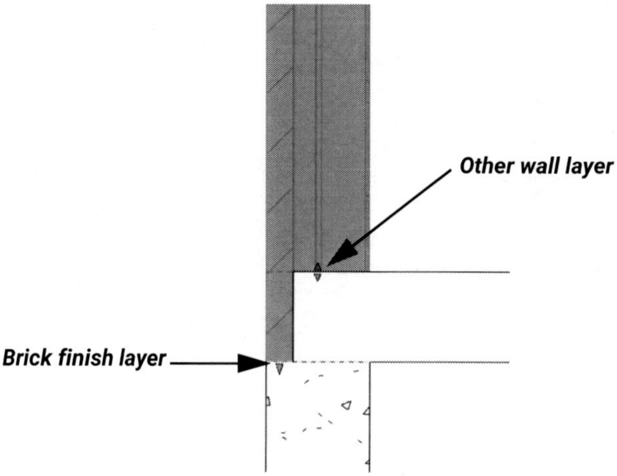

Figure 7–34

How To: Edit Wall Layers

1. In any view, select a wall. In Properties, click **Edit Type**.
2. In the *Type Properties* dialog box, click the **Edit...** button next to *Structure* in the *Construction* section.
3. In the *Edit Assembly* dialog box, click the **<<Preview** button, as shown in Figure 7–35, to expand the preview window.

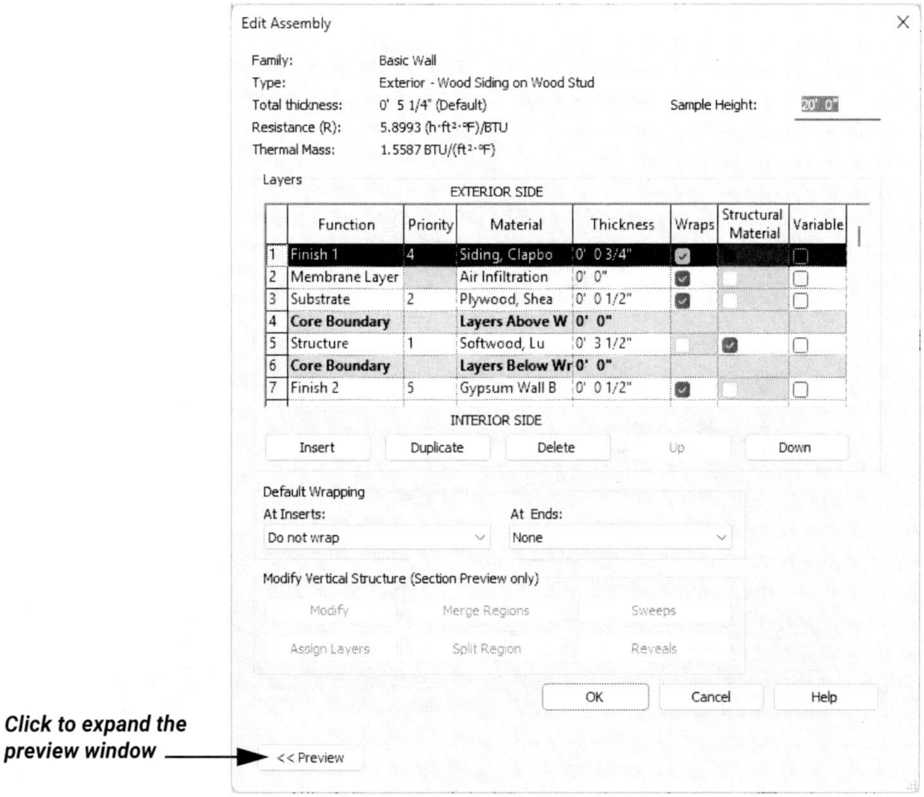

Figure 7–35

4. Set the *View* to **Section: Modify type attributes**, as shown in Figure 7–36.

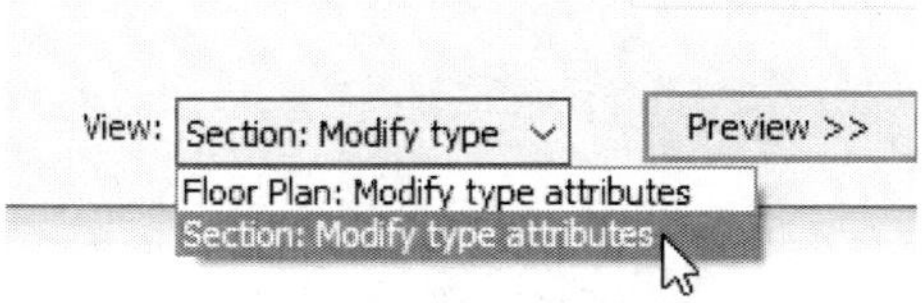

Figure 7–36

5. In the preview window, zoom in to the bottom edge of the wall, as shown in Figure 7–37, and in the *Modify Vertical Structure* area, click **Modify**. The selected layer will turn from blue to red.

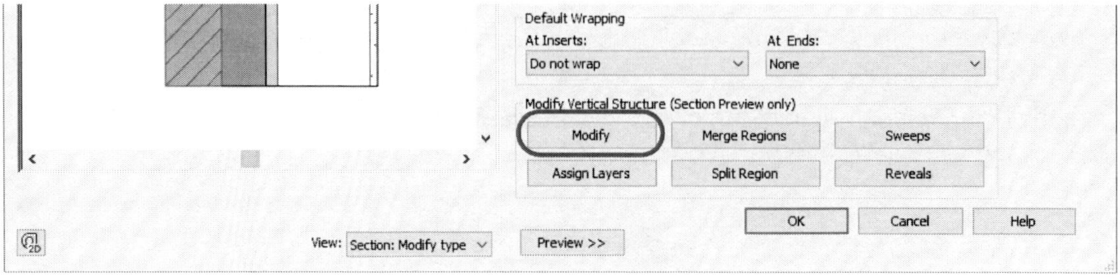

Figure 7–37

Note: If doing this to multiple layers in a wall, all the layers must be adjacent to each other.

6. Click on the outer boundary at the bottom of the selected layer, as shown on the right in Figure 7–38. A lock will display, as shown on the left in Figure 7–38.

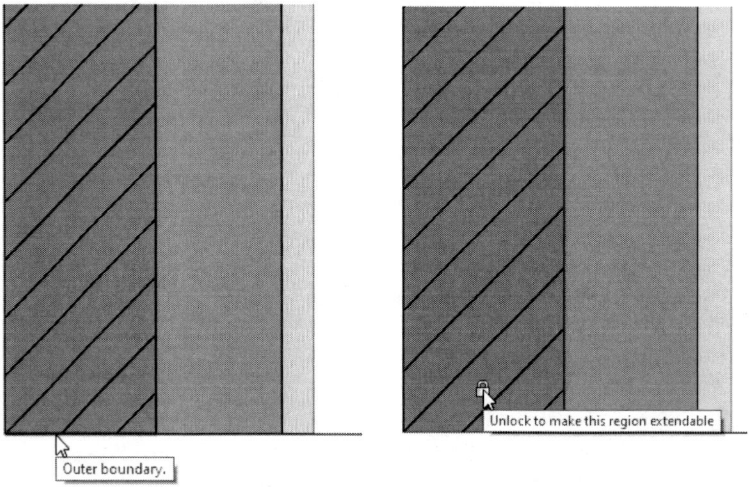

Figure 7–38

7. Click the lock to make the selected layer or region extendable.

Note: Make sure the lock displayed shows as unlocked, as shown in Figure 7–39, before you proceed.

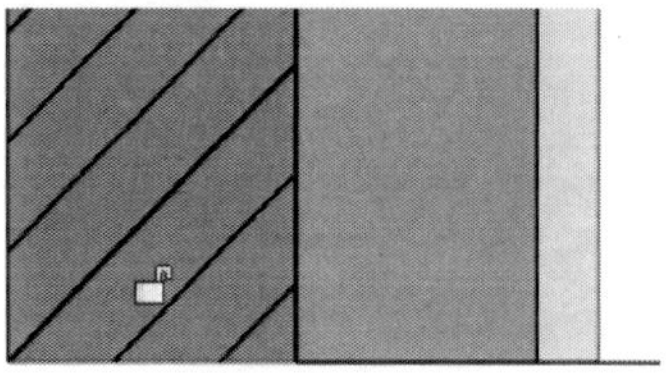

Figure 7–39

8. Click **OK** twice.
9. In a section view, you can select the wall and use the grips to extend the layer, as shown in Figure 7–40.

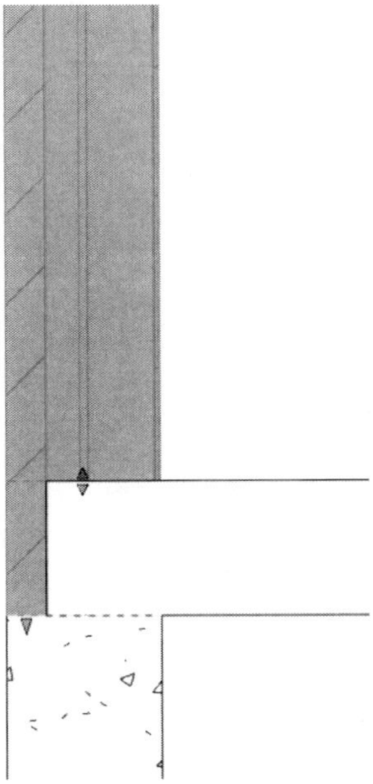

Figure 7–40

- An alternative option for adjusting the extension is in the instance properties of the wall. Set the *Base Extension Distance* to adjust unlocked layers, as shown in Figure 7–41.

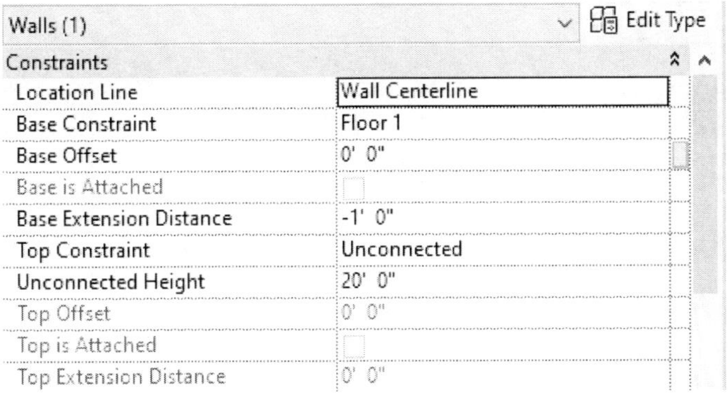

Figure 7–41

- If the layers were unlocked at the top instead of the bottom, you would be able to adjust the top extension distance in Properties or by dragging grips in a section view.

Wall Openings

You can add openings in walls that are not windows or doors by using the **Wall Opening** tool. This creates rectangular openings for both straight and curved walls, as shown in Figure 7–42.

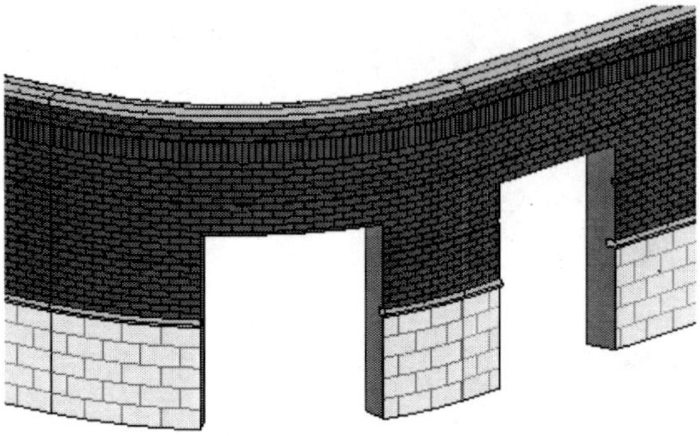

Figure 7–42

How To: Add Wall Openings

1. Open a plan, elevation, section, or 3D view.
2. In the *Architecture* tab>*Opening* panel, click (Wall Opening).
3. Select the wall.
4. If in a 3D view or a view that displays the face of the selected wall, pick two points on the diagonal to determine the opening size. If you are in a plan view or a view that displays the wall's edge, you need to pick the start and stop points for the wall opening.

- You can use temporary dimensions to size the opening while in the command and both temporary dimensions and shape handles to modify the opening when it is selected, as shown in Figure 7–43.

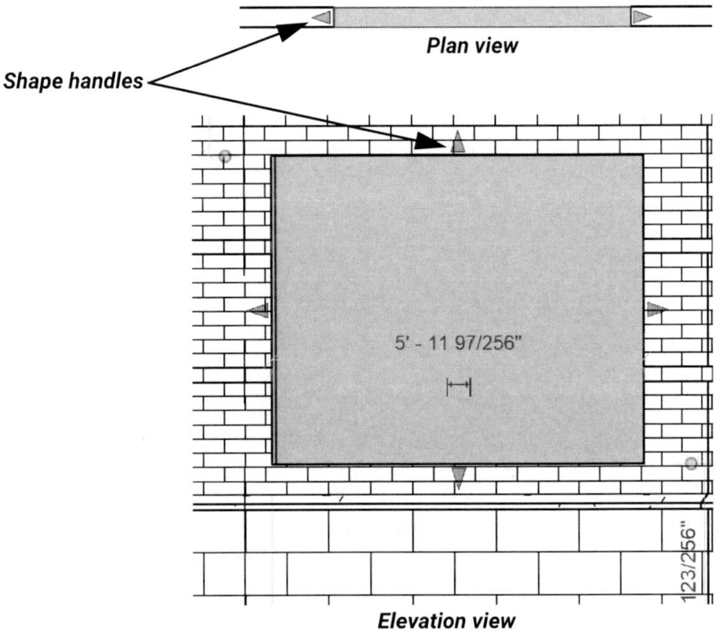

Figure 7–43

Hint: Matching Properties

You can select an existing wall and use it to assign the wall type and instance properties to other walls by using the **Match Type** command. This command also works with all elements that have types.

1. In the *Modify* tab>*Clipboard* panel, click (Match Type), or type **MA**. The cursor changes to an arrow with a clean paintbrush.
2. Select the source element that you want all of the others to match. The paintbrush changes to look as if it has been dipped in black paint, as shown in Figure 7–44.

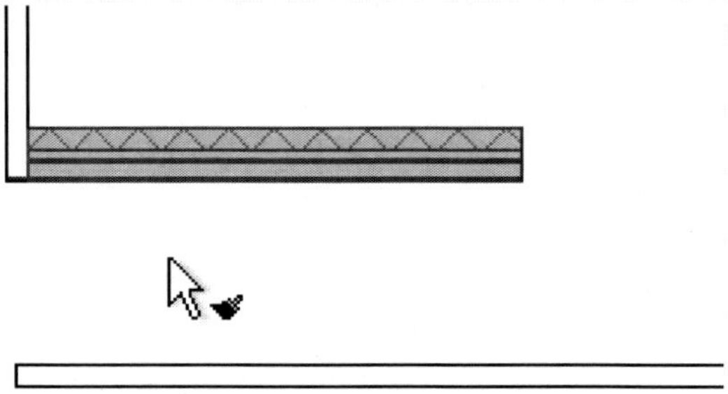

Figure 7–44

3. To select more than one element, in the *Modify | Match Type* tab>*Multiple* panel, click (Select Multiple). You can then use windows, crossings, <Ctrl>, and <Shift> to create a selection set of elements to change.
4. Click (Finish) to apply the type to the selection.

- Click in an empty space in the view to empty the brush so that you can repeat the command with a different element.
- Elements to be matched must be of the same type (e.g., all walls, all doors, etc.).

5. Click (Modify) to end the command.

7.3 Adding Wall Footings

Footings are appended to the bottom of a wall, which means that any change to the base of the host wall influences the footing. This occurs for lateral movement and horizontal movement. For the example shown in Figure 7–45, when the wall profile changes based on a sloped site (as shown on the left), the footing breaks and follows the modified profile (as shown on the right). This is accomplished by editing the profile of the foundation wall.

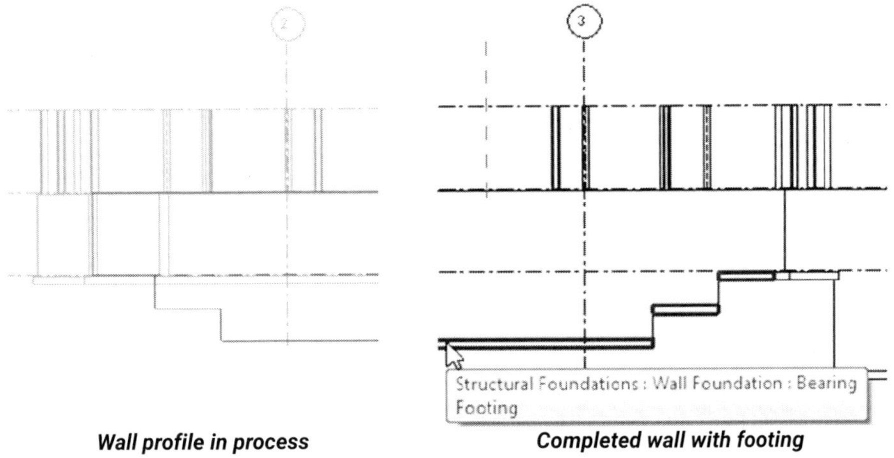

Figure 7–45

- Once a footing is in place, you can add reinforcement in a section view, as shown in Figure 7–46. With the advantages of having a true foundation in place, you can accurately tag and schedule the footings.

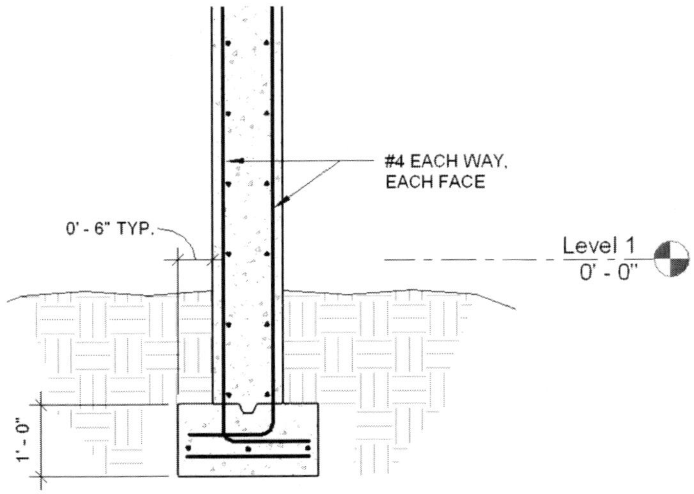

Figure 7–46

- You can edit a footing's profile the same way you would edit a wall profile.
- You can apply two types of continuous footing systems, as shown in Figure 7–47. You must have walls in your model to add a footing system.
  - **Retaining footings:** A footing with one side offset to accommodate additional lateral loads and reinforcement.
  - **Bearing footings:** A footing with an equal distance on either side of the bearing wall.

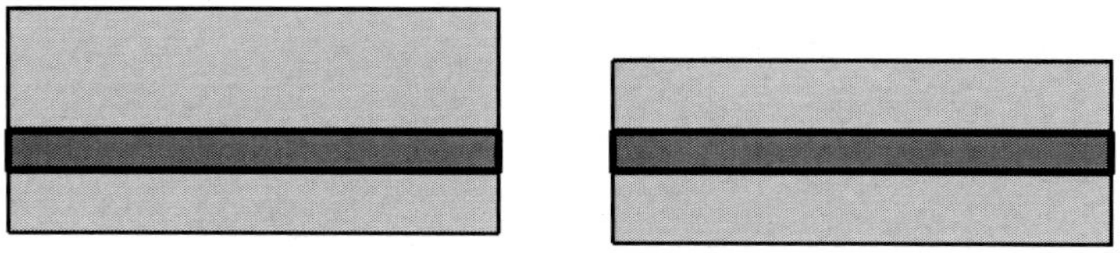

Retaining footing ***Bearing footing***

Figure 7–47

How To: Place a Bearing or Retaining Footing

1. Create or use existing walls in a 3D, section, or elevation view.
   - A wall must be in place to add a bearing or retaining footing.
2. Create a foundation plan and, if needed, edit the *View Range* (in Properties or type **VR**) so that the walls display and you can select them.
3. In the *Structure* tab>*Foundation* panel, click (Wall) to start the **Structural Foundations: Wall** command, or type **FT**.
4. In the Type Selector, select a type, as shown in Figure 7–48.

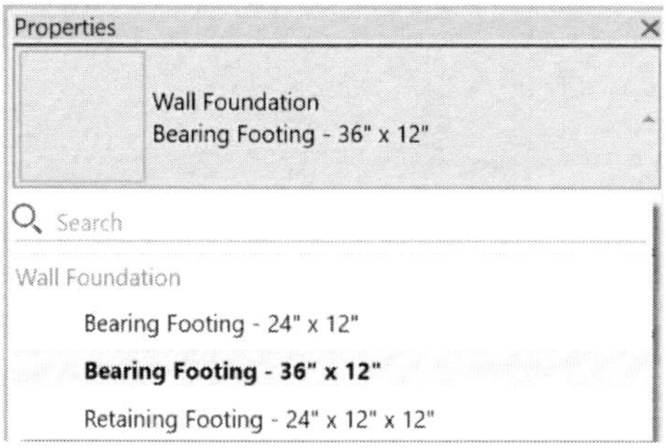

Figure 7–48

5. Select a wall. The footing is placed beneath the wall, as shown in Figure 7–49.

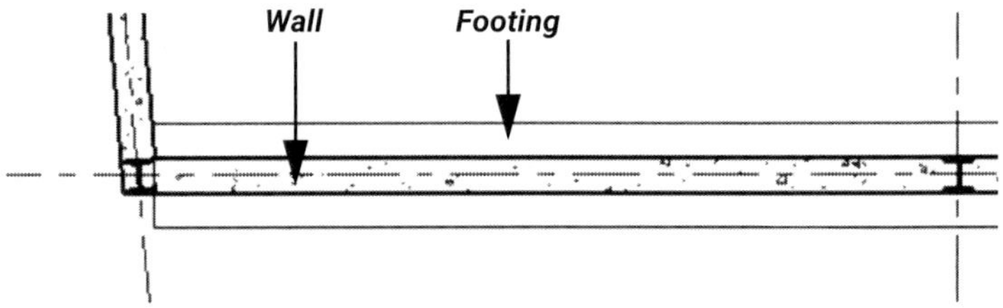

Figure 7–49

- To select multiple walls, hover over one wall and then press <Tab> to select all connected walls. Alternatively, in the *Modify | Place Wall Foundation* tab>*Multiple* panel, click (Select Multiple). Select the walls using any selection method and click (Finish) to place the footings.

- You can flip retaining footings using the Flip control, as shown in Figure 7–50.

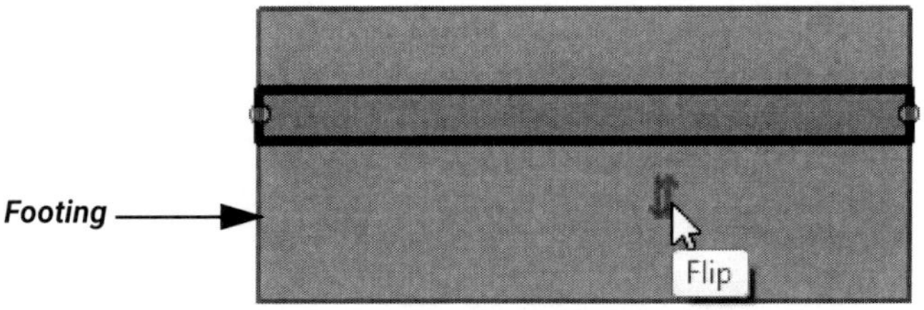

Figure 7–50

Hint: Materials

When you are creating some types, such a wall footings, one option is to set the *Structural Material*. In the *Type Properties* dialog box, in the *Materials and Finishes* section, click in the *Value* column and then click (Browse), as shown in Figure 7–51.

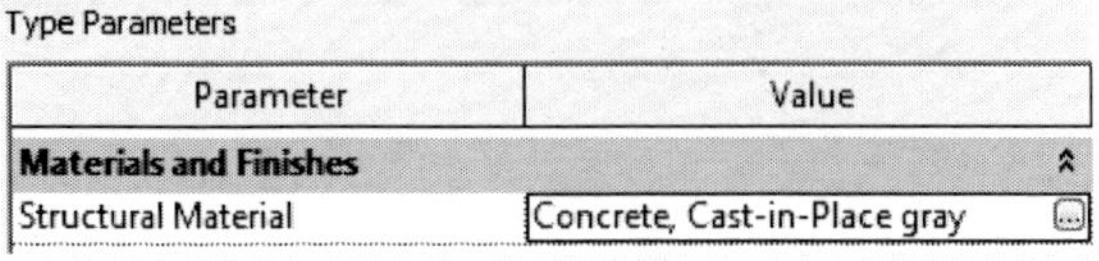

Figure 7–51

In the Material Browser (shown in Figure 7–52), specify the material you want to use and click **OK.**

Figure 7–52

Practice 7a
Model the Exterior Shell

Practice Objectives

- Add walls by tracing over lines in an imported DWG file.
- Add curtain walls.

In this practice, you will add exterior walls, including a curtain wall, to create the exterior shell of the project. You will use an imported file to help establish the location of the walls. The completed practice model is shown in Figure 7–53.

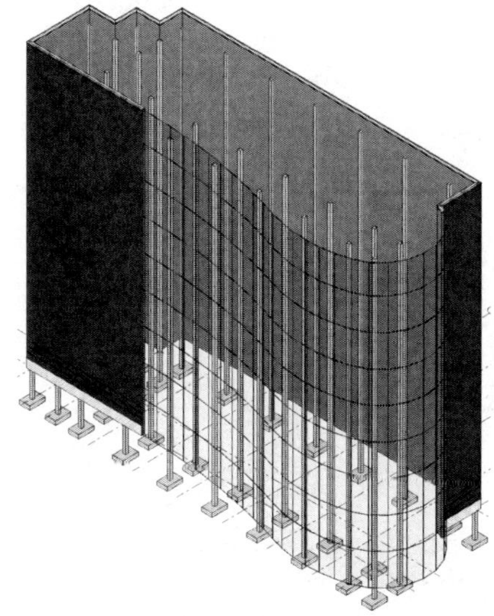

Figure 7–53

Task 1: Add walls by picking lines.

1. Open the project **Arch-WallsExt.rvt** from the practice files folder.
2. Verify that you are in the **Floor Plans: Floor 1** view.
3. In the View Control Bar, set the *Detail Level* to (Medium). Doing so will display wall layers as you draw walls in this current view only.
4. In the *Architecture* tab>*Build* panel, click (Wall).
5. In the Type Selector, select **Basic Wall: Exterior - Brick and CMU on MTL. Stud**.
6. In the *Modify | Place Wall* tab>*Draw* panel, click (Pick Lines), then verify (Offset) is set to **0'-0"**.

7. In the *Modify | Place Wall* tab, verify that (Join Status) is toggled on (highlighted) in the *Draw* panel and (Auto Join) is toggled off (not highlighted) in the *Constraint* panel. In the *Levels* panel, verify (Height) is selected, then in the drop-down list, select **Parapet**.
8. In Properties, set or verify the following options:
    - *Location Line:* **Finish Face: Exterior**
    - *Base Offset:* **0'-0"**
    - *Top Offset:* **0'-0"**
    - *Cross-Section:* **Vertical**
9. Pan and zoom over to the west stairwell. Along grid line 5, select the horizontal exterior wall in the imported DWG file, as shown in Figure 7–54. Ensure that the dashed line displays inside the wall and the highlighted edge is the on the exterior side of the wall. This wall is a compound wall and you want the brick to display on the outside.

    Note: *A visual indicator that the wall's exterior side is facing the correct way is that (Change wall's orientation) will display on the outside or exterior side of the wall in the view. As you draw each wall, you can click the icon to flip the wall as needed.*

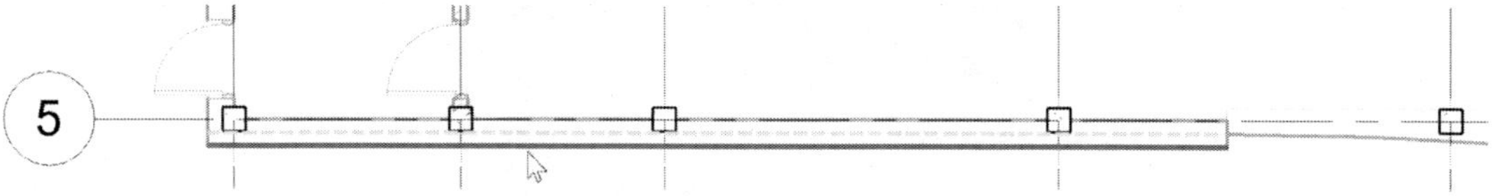

Figure 7–54

10. Still in the **Wall** command, select the west vertical exterior wall (next to the west stairs), as shown on the left in Figure 7–55.
11. Click (Modify), then select the wall and click and drag the lower **Drag Wall End** grip down past the door, as shown on the right in Figure 7–55.

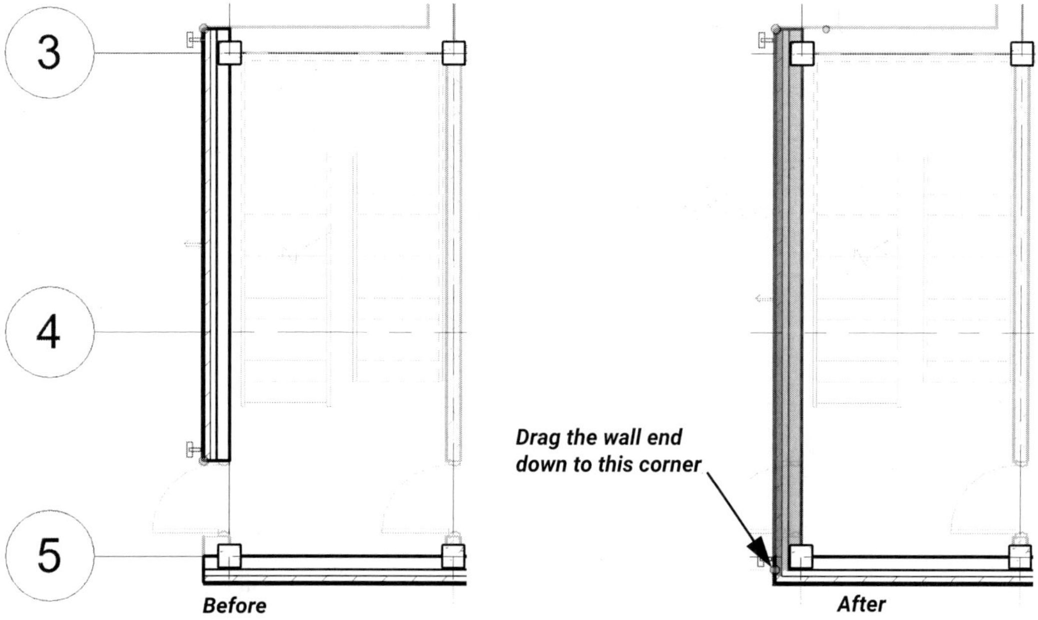

Figure 7–55

12. Click (Modify). Start the **Wall** command again and select **Pick Lines** from the *Draw* panel. Verify the options are the same and continue selecting lines working left to right around the exterior of the building.
    - Do not select the small section of wall below the east stairwell's exterior door.
    - Make sure you select the small curved portion of the wall between the curtain wall and the east stairwell door, as shown in Figure 7–56.
    - Do not select the curved curtain wall lines.

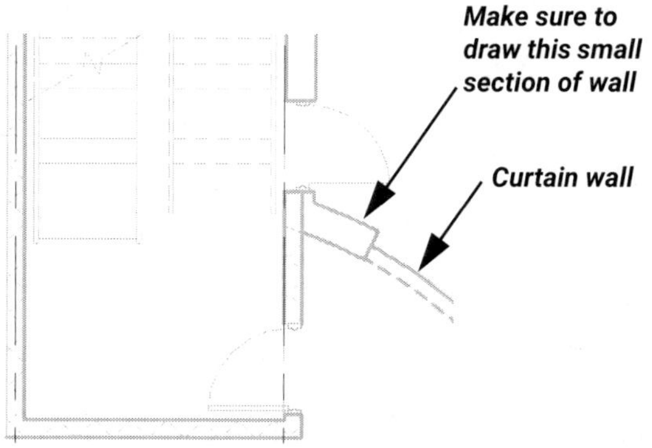

Figure 7–56

13. Click (Modify).
14. Zoom in to the east stairwell. In the *Modify* tab>*Modify* panel, click (Trim/Extend to Corner) and select the vertical wall on grid line J, then select the curved wall below the door. Figure 7–57 shows the before and after for the wall trim. (The grid lines have been modified in the figure for clarity.)

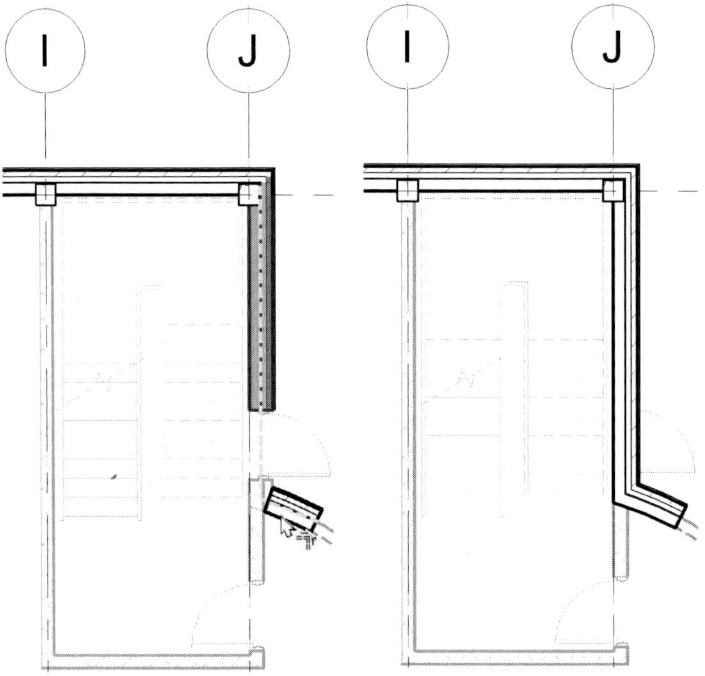

Before Trim ***After Trim***

Figure 7–57

15. Click (Modify).
16. Zoom out to see the entire hotel.
17. Save the project.

Task 2: Add basic curtain walls.

1. In the *Architecture* tab>*Build* panel, click (Wall).
2. In the *Modify | Place Wall* tab>*Draw* panel, click (Pick Lines) and verify (Join Status) is toggled on. In the *Levels* panel, verify (Height) and **Parapet** are selected.
3. In the Type Selector, scroll down to the *Curtain Wall* section and select **Curtain Wall: Exterior Glazing**, then verify the following properties:
   - *Base Offset:* **0'-0"**
   - *Top Offset:* **0'-0"**
4. Select the curved lines at the southeast end of the building (you will create three curtain walls along this curved wall), as shown in Figure 7–58.

   Note: *When you hover over the areas shown in Figure 7–58, the segments will highlight.*

   As you place the walls, verify that (Change wall's orientation) displays on the outside or exterior side of the curtain wall in the view.

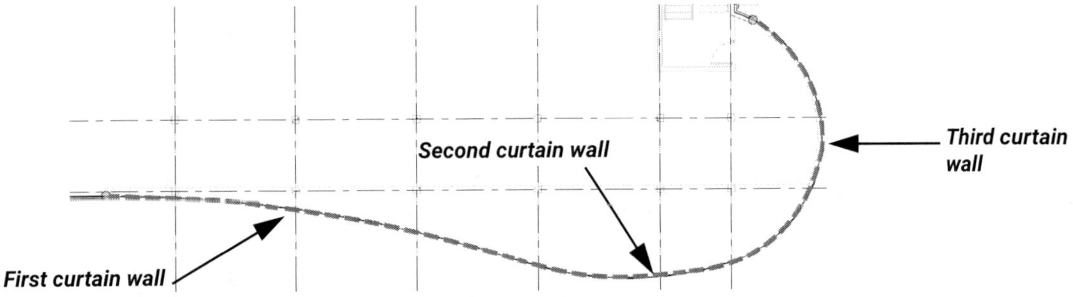

Figure 7–58

5. Click (Modify).

6. In the Quick Access Toolbar, click (Default 3D View). The model displays as shown in Figure 7–59.

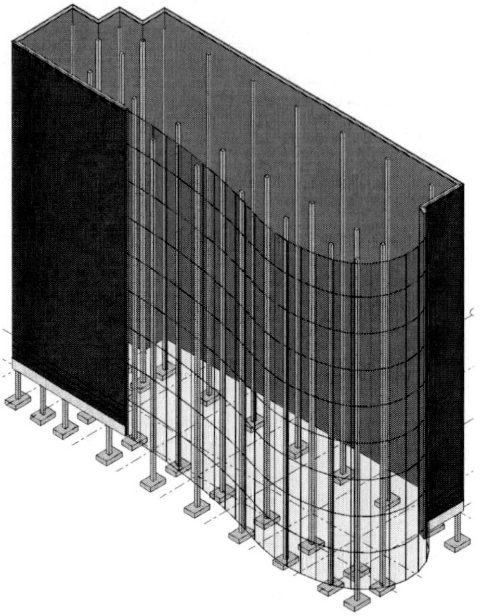

Figure 7–59

7. Save and close the project.

End of practice

Practice 7b
Add Interior Walls

Practice Objectives

- Model and modify walls.
- Use modify tools, including Align, Offset, Trim/Extend, Copy, and Mirror.

In this practice, you will add interior walls to the first floor plan, using **Offset**, **Split Element**, **Trim**, and **Align** to help create them. Figure 7–60 shows the completed first floor plan (the DWG is turned off in figure for clarity). Review the figure below and become familiar with the different areas of the hotel.

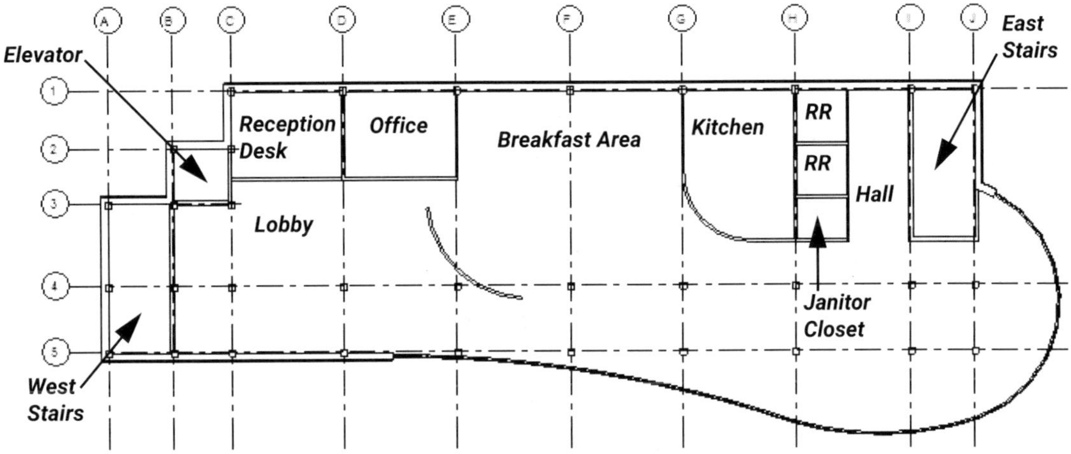

Figure 7–60

Task 1: Add and align the stair and elevator walls.

1. Open the project **Arch-WallsInt.rvt** from the practice files folder.
2. Open the **Floor Plans: Floor 1** view.
3. Zoom in on the stair and elevator area on the west side of the building.
4. In the *Architecture* tab>*Build* panel, click (Wall).
5. In the *Modify | Place Wall* tab>*Draw* panel, click (Line), if not already selected. Click (Chain) to toggle it off (not highlighted) and verify (Join Status) is toggled on.

   *Note: If you leave the **Chain** option on, the wall will snap to other walls rather than the columns.*

6. In Properties, verify or set the following:
   - *Wall Type:* **Basic Wall: Generic 8" Masonry**
   - *Location Line:* **Wall Centerline**
   - *Base Constraint:* **Floor 1**
   - *Base Offset:* **0'-0"**
   - *Top Constraint:* **Up to level: Roof**
   - *Top Offset:* **0'-0"**
   - *Cross-Section:* **Vertical**
7. Draw the walls around the stairwell and elevator, drawing each wall separately from column to column, as shown in Figure 7–61. (The walls in the image have been enhanced for clarity.)
   - If needed, you can use the **Align** command to ensure that the walls are aligned with the DWG walls.

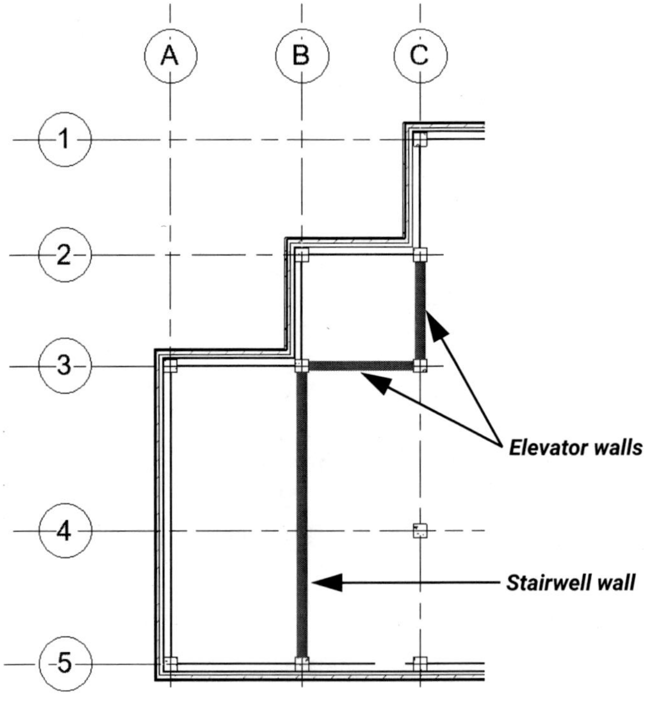

Figure 7–61

8. Still in the **Wall** command, pan over to the east stairwell. Using the same wall type and settings, add the walls shown in Figure 7–62 using the DWG as a guide for placement. (The walls in the image have been enhanced for clarity.) Remember that **Chain** is toggled off so you will need to draw each wall.

   Note: *Grid line bubbles have been modified in the image for clarity.*

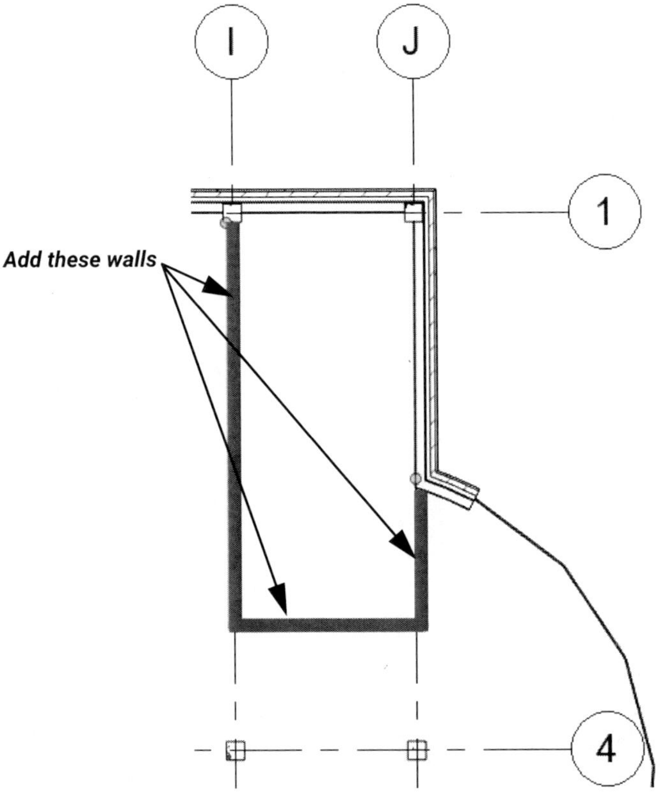

Figure 7–62

9. Click (Modify).
10. Zoom out or type **ZF** to display the entire building floor plan.
11. Save the project.

Task 2: Add the reception and office walls.

1. Pan and zoom over to the grid C1, D1, and E1 area to create the reception and office walls.
2. Start the **Wall** command and in the *Modify | Place Wall* tab>*Draw* panel, click (Line), if not already selected. Verify (Chain) is still toggled off and (Join Status) is toggled on.

3. In Properties, set the following:
   - *Wall type:* **Basic Wall: Interior - 4 7/8" Partition (1-hr)**
   - *Location Line:* **Wall Centerline**
   - Base Constraint: **Floor 1**
   - *Base Offset:* **0'-0"**
   - *Top Constraint:* **Up to level: Floor 2**
   - *Top Offset:* (negative) **-1'-0"**
   - *Cross-Section:* **Vertical**

   Note: *Setting the Top Offset to a negative number leaves room for the floor above.*

4. Draw the walls shown in Figure 7–63. Start at the column on grid intersection E1 and draw down **13'-0"**, then draw a wall down from grid intersection D1 the same distance. Finally, draw a bottom horizontal wall from grid line E to C.

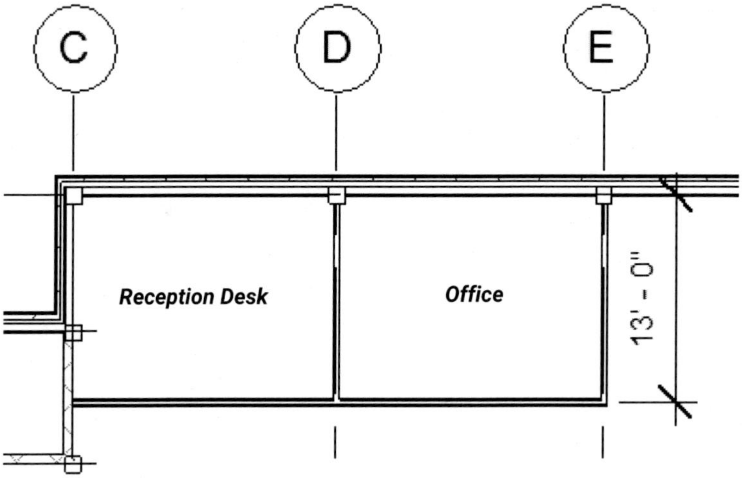

Figure 7–63

5. Click (Modify).
6. Zoom in to the interior wall connection on grid line D and select the bottom horizontally drawn wall.
7. In the *Modify | Walls* tab>*Modify* panel, click (Split Element).

8. Click the horizontal wall at the edge of the vertical wall, as shown in Figure 7–64. (The blue dashed line displays if you are hovering over the wall's centerline but this is not required when splitting the wall.)

   Note: *Click*  *(Thin Lines) to toggle on and off to display the line thickness in the drawing area.*

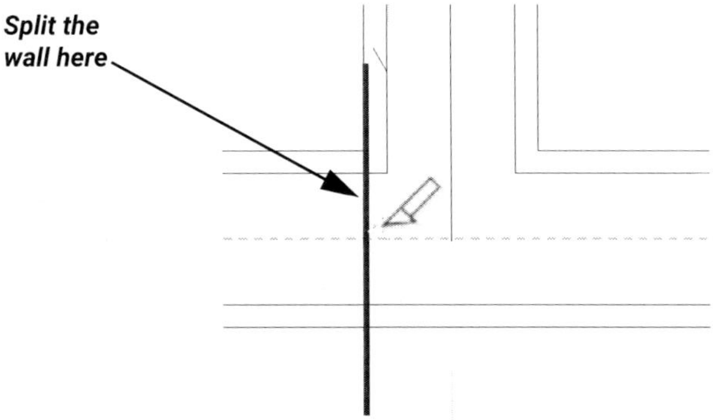

Figure 7–64

9. Click  (Modify).
10. Select the left part of the split wall.
11. In Properties, set the following:
    - *Top Constraint:* **Unconnected**
    - *Unconnected Height:* **4'-0"**

This split wall will now become the base for the reception desk.

12. Click  (Modify).

13. In the *Modify* tab>*Modify* panel, select (Trim/Extend to Corner). Select the right piece of the split wall and then the vertically drawn wall on grid line D, as shown in Figure 7–65, to join them. (Your walls may look different than in the figure depending on where you split the wall.)

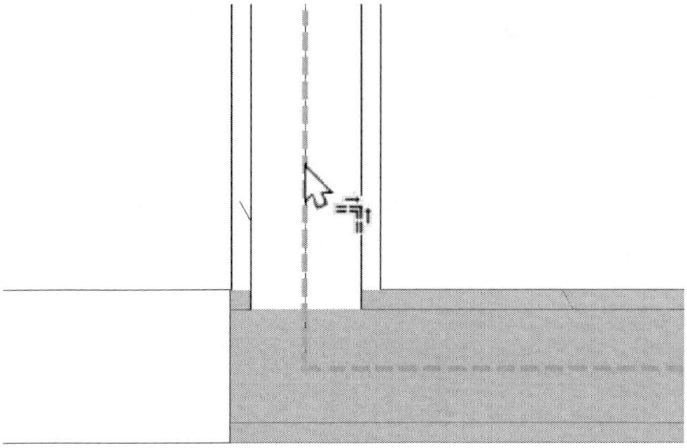

Figure 7–65

14. Click (Modify).

15. Modify the reception counter wall to butt up against the middle vertically drawn wall. Select the split wall on the left, right-click on the wall end control (shown in Figure 7–66), and select **Disallow Join** (you can also click the **Disallow Join** icon).

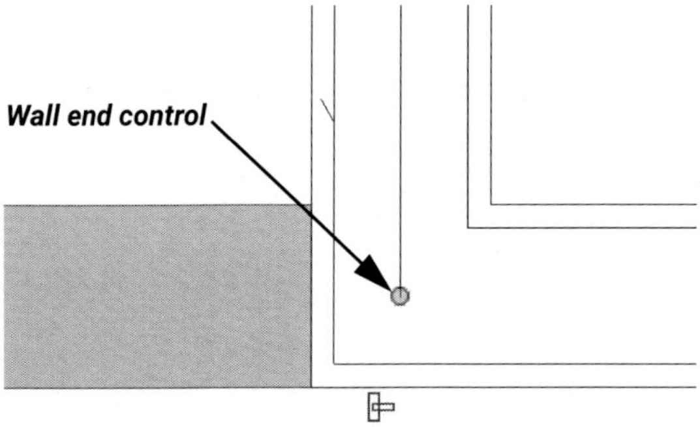

Figure 7–66

16. Select the wall end control and drag it so it butts up against the edge of the wall, as shown in Figure 7–67.

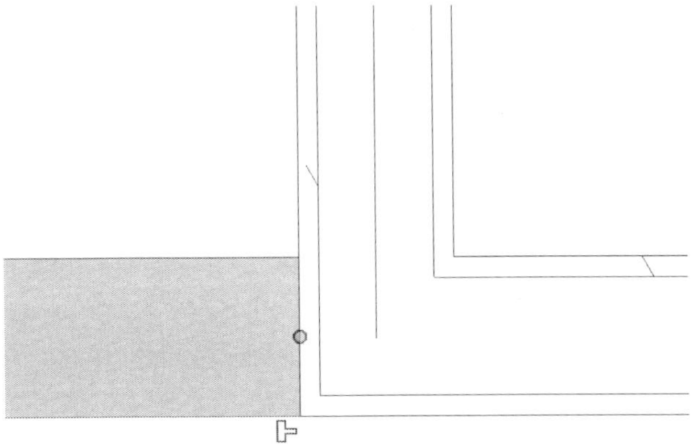

Figure 7–67

17. Click (Modify).

Task 3: Add the reception desk.

1. Zoom and pan over to the grid 2C area (Reception Desk), as shown in Figure 7–68.

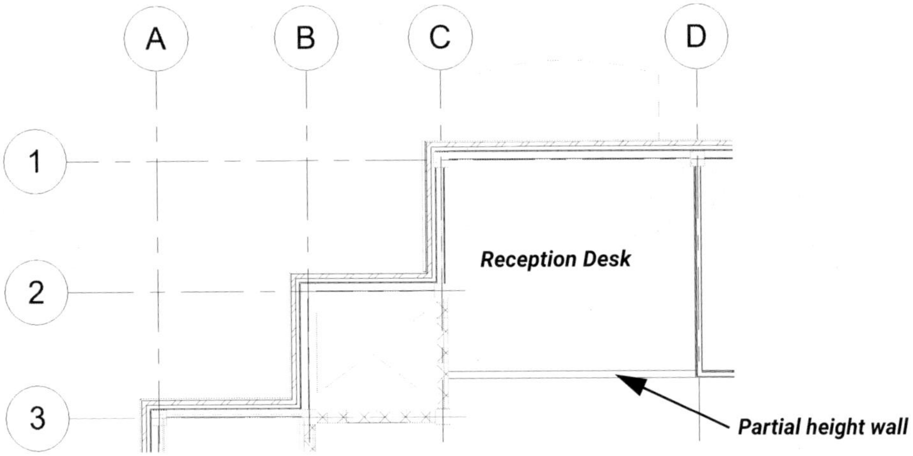

Figure 7–68

2. In the *Architecture* tab>*Build* panel, expand (Component) and click (Place a Component). In the Type Selector, select **Counter-Top-Lobby 24" Depth**, if not already selected.

   Note: Place a Component *is the default command for Component.*

3. In Properties, set the *Offset from Host* to **1'-1-5/8"**.
   - You need to set the *Offset from Host* because the countertop family's default height is **3'-0"** above the level. (This *Dimensions* parameter can be viewed by selecting the countertop and clicking **Edit Type** in Properties.) The partial height wall in the project is **4'-0"** high and the countertop thickness is about **1-1/2"**.
4. Place the countertop component over the partial height wall.
5. Click (Modify).
6. Select the countertop. Move it, if needed, and modify its length using the control grips on each end, as shown in Figure 7–69. Extend it so that it touches the vertical walls on both ends. Click (Modify) when done.

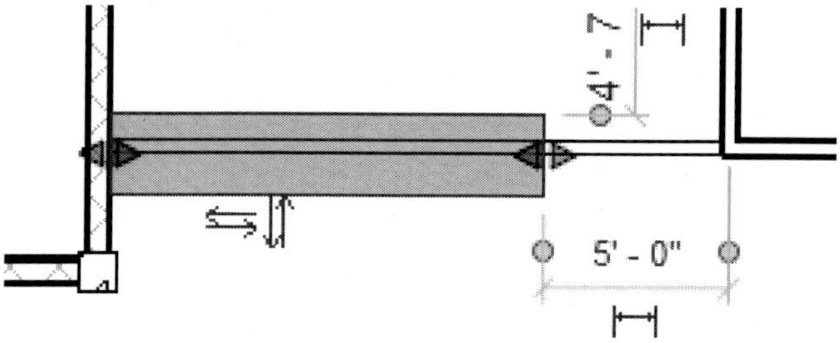

Figure 7–69

   - To get a better view of this offset, place a section through the countertop and open the section view. Adjust the crop region, if needed.
7. Save the project.

Task 4: Add the kitchen walls.

1. In the **Floor Plan: Floor 1** view, pan over to the east stairwell so you can see grid lines G, H, and I.
2. In the *Architecture* tab>*Work Plane* panel, click (Ref Plane) and draw a reference plane from the exterior face of the stairwell wall over to grid line G, as shown in Figure 7–70.

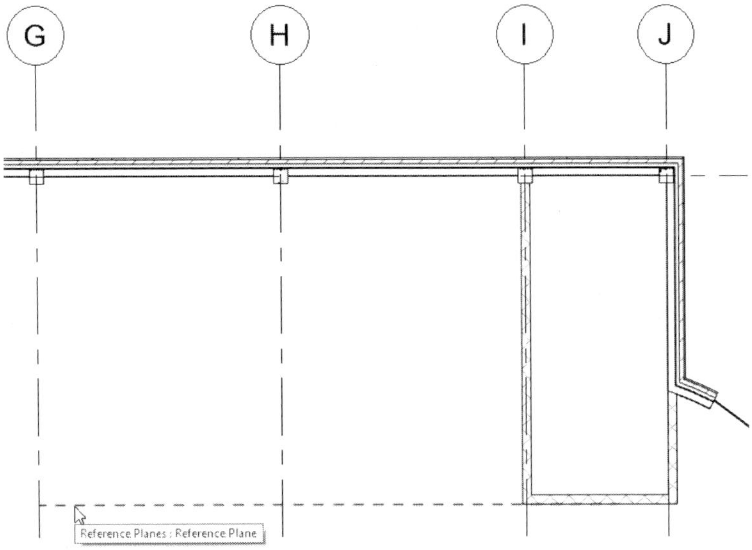

Figure 7–70

3. Click (Modify).
4. Start the **Wall** command and verify or set the following properties:
   - *Wall type:* **Basic Wall: Interior - 4 7/8" Partition (1-hr)**
   - *Location Line:* **Wall Centerline**
   - *Base Constraint:* **Floor 1**
   - *Base Offset:* **0'-0"**
   - *Top Constraint:* **Up to level: Floor 2**
   - *Top Offset:* (negative) **-1'-0"**
   - *Cross-Section:* **Vertical**
5. In the *Modify | Place Wall* tab>*Draw* panel, toggle (Chain) on.

6. Draw a wall along grid line H down to the reference plane, then over to grid line G and up to the exterior wall column, as shown in Figure 7–71.

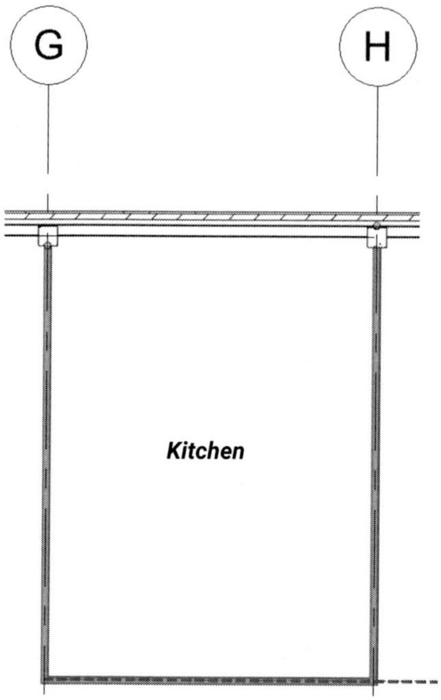

Figure 7–71

7. Click (Modify).
8. Zoom in on the bottom wall and the horizontal reference plane.
9. In the *Modify* tab>*Modify* panel, click (Align).
10. Align the exterior face of the wall (as shown in Figure 7–72) with the reference plane (select the reference plane first, followed by the face of the wall).

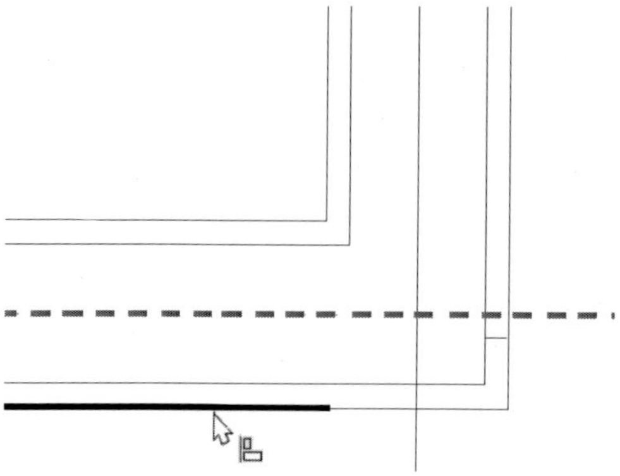

Figure 7–72

11. Click (Modify).
12. Start the **Wall** command. In the *Modify | Place Wall* tab>*Draw* panel, select (Fillet Arc). Click (Radius), then set the value to **10'-0"** and press <Enter>.

Note: Hover over the Draw panel icons to display the sketch tools' tooltips.

13. For the first selection, select the wall along grid line G, and for the second selection, select the wall along the reference plane to create the arc at the corner, as shown in Figure 7–73.

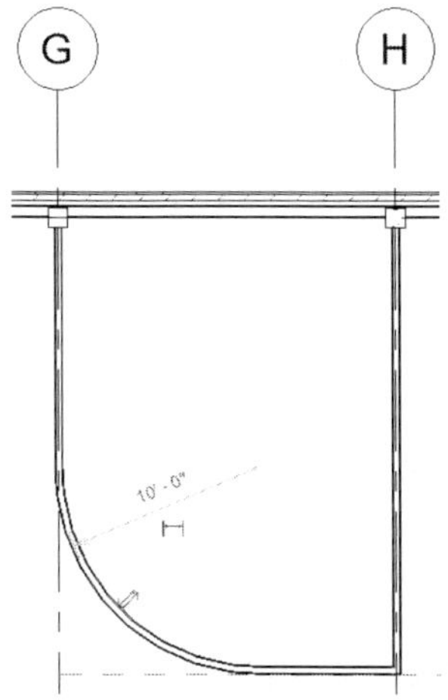

Figure 7–73

14. Click (Modify).

Task 5: Add the restroom and janitor closet walls.

Note: Use (Trim/Extend to Corner), (Trim/Extend Single), and (Trim/Extend Multiple) as needed to get the walls in place.

1. Start the **Wall** command and use the same wall properties as before (**Interior - 4 7/8" Partition (1-hr)**). In the *Modify | Place Wall* tab>*Draw* panel, set the (Offset) to **8'-0"**.

2. Use the (Pick Lines) sketch tool and hover over the wall on grid line H. When you see the dashed preview line to the right of grid line H (as shown in Figure 7–74), click to place the wall. (The preview line has been enhanced in the image for clarity.)

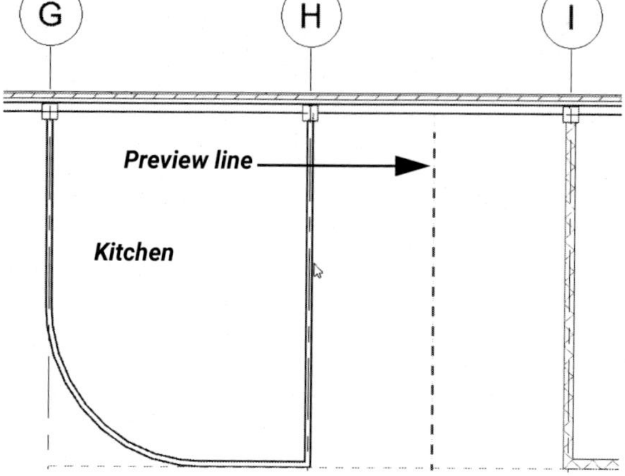

Figure 7–74

3. Click (Modify).
4. Start the **Trim/Extend to Corner** command and trim the lower kitchen wall to the newly offset wall, as shown in Figure 7–75.

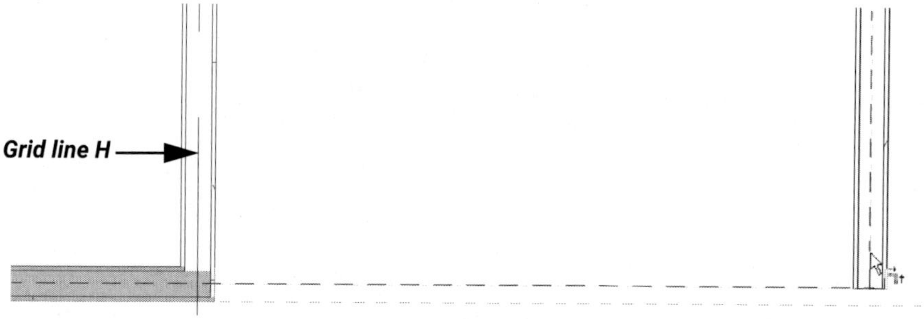

Figure 7–75

5. Click (Modify).

6. In the *Modify* tab>*Modify* panel, select (Trim/Extend Single). Select the exterior wall first, then select the newly drawn vertical wall. The interior wall is now joined to the exterior wall, as shown in Figure 7–76.

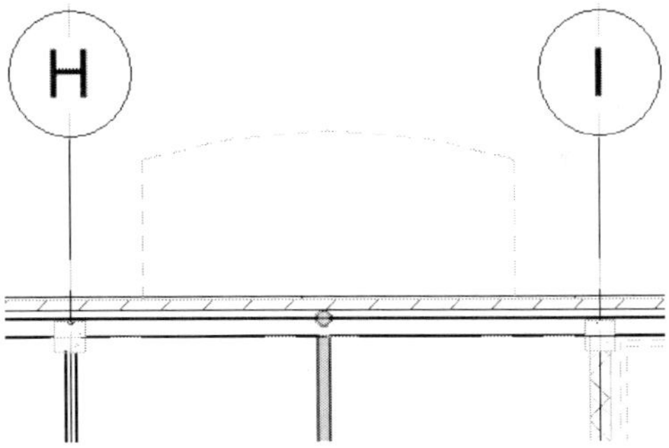

Figure 7–76

7. Click (Modify).
8. Draw a partition wall **5'-6"** above the bottom wall, as shown in Figure 7–77.

   Note: *Use temporary dimensions to get the wall into the correct position. You may need to move the temporary dimension witness lines.*

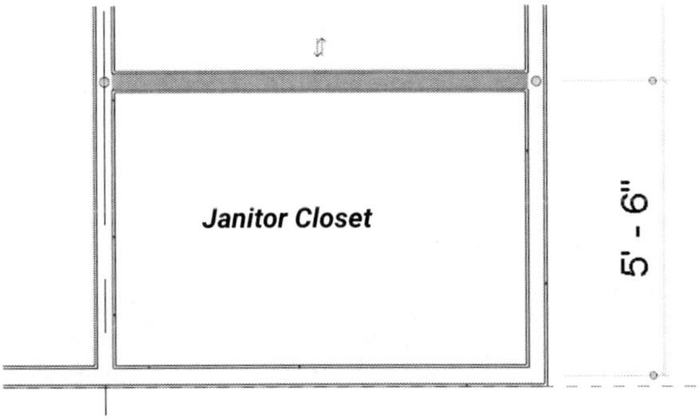

Figure 7–77

9. Click (Modify).
10. Select the new wall. In the *Modify | Walls* tab>*Modify* panel, click (Offset). In the *Modify | Offset* tab>*Offset* panel, verify that (Copy) and (Numerical) are selected and set the (Offset) to **8'-8"**.

11. Hover your cursor over the wall (as shown in Figure 7–78), and when you see the dashed preview line above the janitor closet wall, click to place the wall.

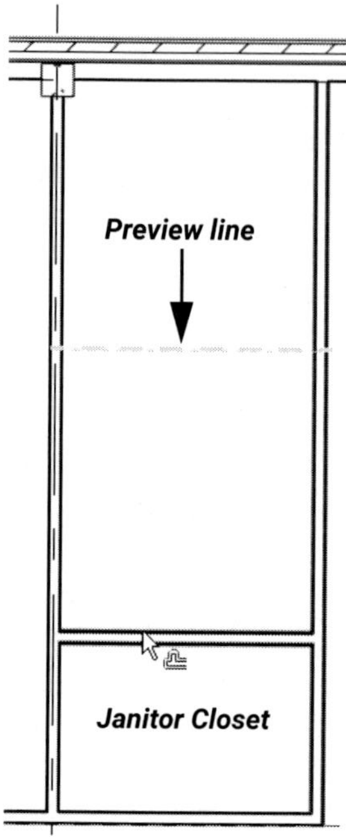

Figure 7–78

12. Click (Modify) and delete the reference plane.

    Note: *Reference planes will display in all other plan views and can cause confusion for others.*

Task 6: Draw a curved wall.

In this task, you need to create a curved slanted wall to separate the breakfast area from the lobby. The curved wall's placement does not need to be precise but drawing reference planes will help guide you while drawing the wall.

1. Zoom and pan below the reception desk and office area (between grid lines D and E).
2. Start the **Reference Plane** command.
3. Starting at grid line E and the corner of the office walls, draw reference planes intersecting each other, as shown in Figure 7–79. To quickly offset the reference planes, use (Pick Lines) and set the (Offset) value in the *Draw* panel according to the dimensions shown in the image below. Select the exterior face of the wall and grid line E for the offsets. Hint: If you let your cursor hover over a grid line, the tooltip will tell you which grid line you are offsetting from.
   - You do not need to draw the dimensions; they are for reference only.

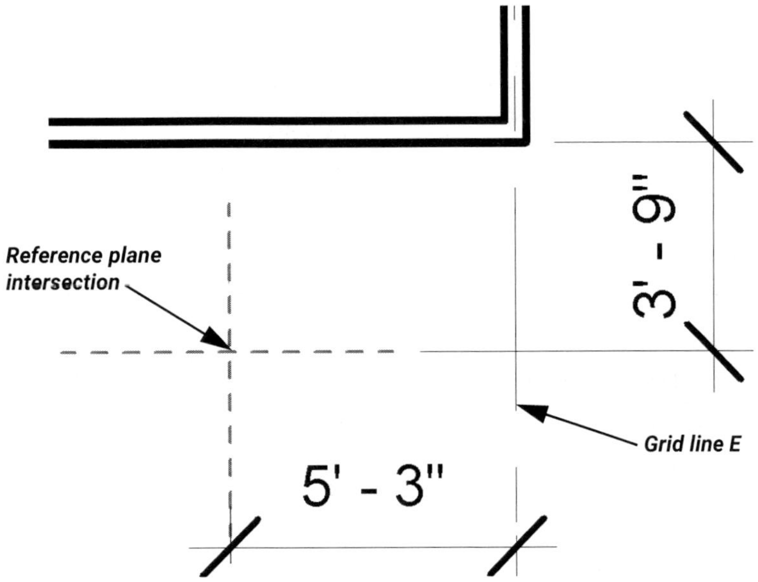

Figure 7–79

4. Click (Modify).
5. If needed, stretch the reference planes so that they intersect each other, as shown above in Figure 7–79.
6. Start the **Reference Plane** command again.

7. Offset from grid line E and grid line 4 and draw reference planes intersecting each other, as shown in Figure 7–80.

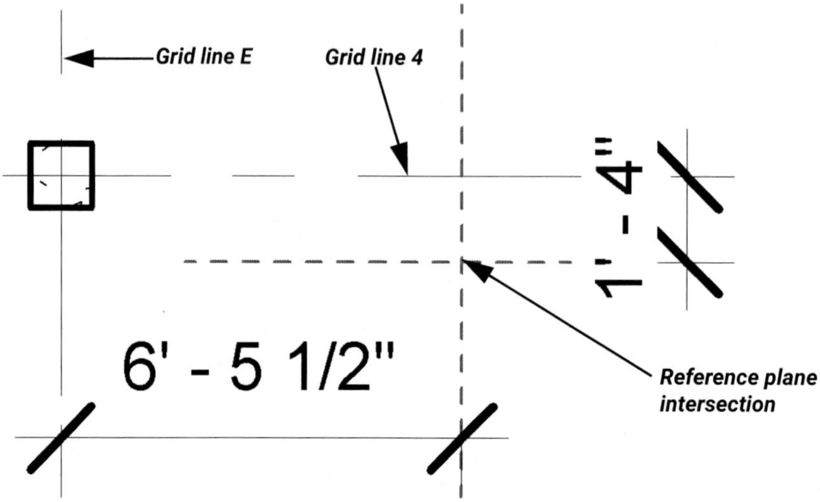

Figure 7–80

8. Start the **Wall** command, select the (Start-End-Radius Arc) sketch tool, and toggle off (Chain).
9. In Properties, verify or set the following:
   - *Wall type:* **Basic Wall: Interior - 4 7/8" Partition (1-hr)**
   - *Location Line:* **Wall Centerline**
   - *Base Constraint:* **Floor 1**
   - *Top Constraint:* **Unconnected**
   - *Unconnected Height:* **8'-0"**
   - *Cross-Section:* **Slanted**
   - *Angle From Vertical:* **4.00°**

10. Draw the slanted curved wall starting with selecting the top reference lines' intersection for the first pick, then the bottom reference lines' intersection as the second pick. For the last pick, select a point so that it creates a slight arc to the left, as shown in Figure 7–81.

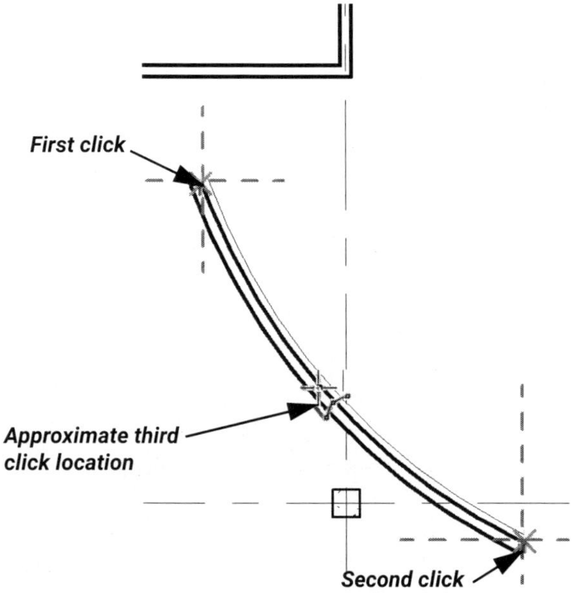

Figure 7–81

11. Click (Modify).

12. Delete the reference planes that you created.

13. Zoom out, then save and close the project.

End of practice

Practice 7c
Model Additional Walls

Practice Objective

- Model and modify additional walls.

If time permits, you can add a parapet above the curtain walls (as shown in Figure 7–82), as well as walls to the second floor, basement, and footings.

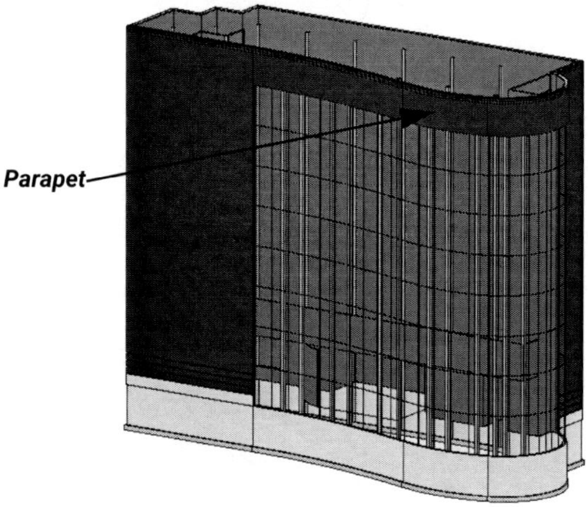

Figure 7–82

Task 1: Add a parapet.

1. Open the project **Arch-WallsOpt.rvt** from the practice files folder.
2. In the Quick Access Toolbar, click  (Default 3D View).
3. From the tabs along the top of the view, click the X next to **Floor 1** to close it.
4. Open the **Floor Plans: Roof** view.
5. Type **WT** to tile the Roof and 3D view, then type **ZA** to zoom both views. You will work in the Roof view and use the 3D view to see the changes happen in real-time.
6. In the **Roof** view, select the three curtain walls in the southeast area of the building. Ensure you are selecting the curtain walls, which will display as dashed lines.
7. In Properties, set the *Top Constraint* to **Up to Level: Roof** and the *Top Offset* to (negative) **-2'-0"**. This will give you room to draw the parapet walls.
8. Click  (Modify).
   - The curtain walls display in halftone because the tops of the curtain walls are now below the Roof level.

9. Zoom in to the east stairwell corner and start the **Wall** command. In the *Modify | Place Wall* tab>*Draw* panel, click (Start-End-Radius Arc), then verify that (Chain) is toggled off.
10. In the Type Selector, select **Basic Wall: Exterior - Brick on MTL. Stud - parapet**, then verify or set the following properties:
    - *Location Line:* **Wall Centerline**
    - *Base Constraint:* **Roof**
    - *Base Offset:* (negative) **-2'-0"**
    - *Top Constraint:* **Up to level: Parapet**
    - *Top Offset:* **0'-0"**
    - *Cross-Section:* **Vertical**
11. Starting at the exterior wall of the east stairs, the first selection point is at the end of the existing wall. The second selection point is at the intersection of grid line J and the curtain wall (not the curtain panel). The third selection point is at the tangent point along the curtain wall. Select the points in the order shown in Figure 7–83. Ensure that you select the endpoints before selecting the tangent point on the arc.

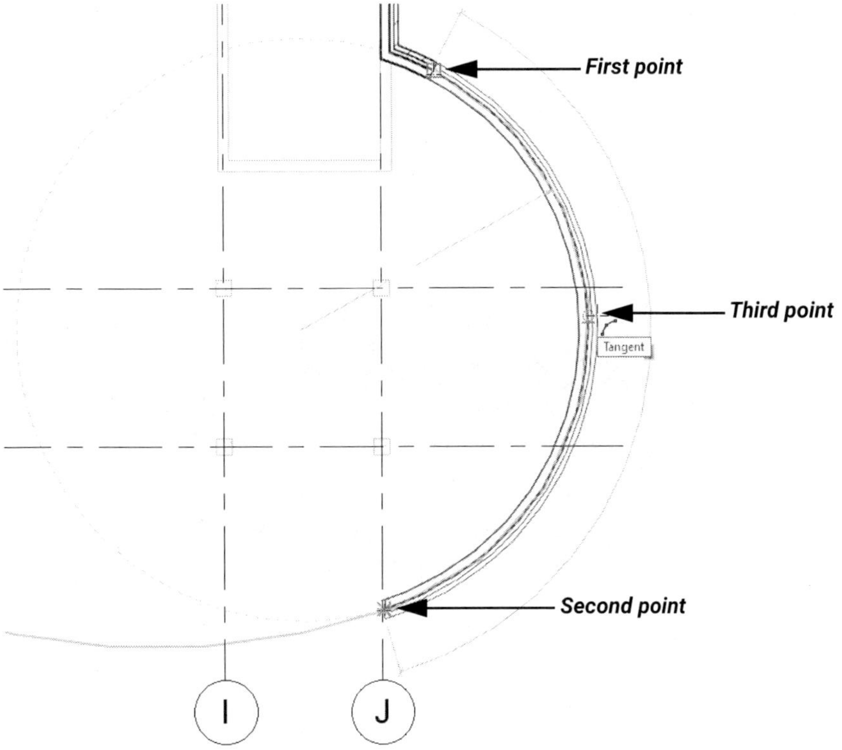

Figure 7–83

12. Still in the **Wall** command, draw another arc wall from grid line J to grid line H, then again from grid line H to the end of the existing exterior wall, as shown in Figure 7–84.

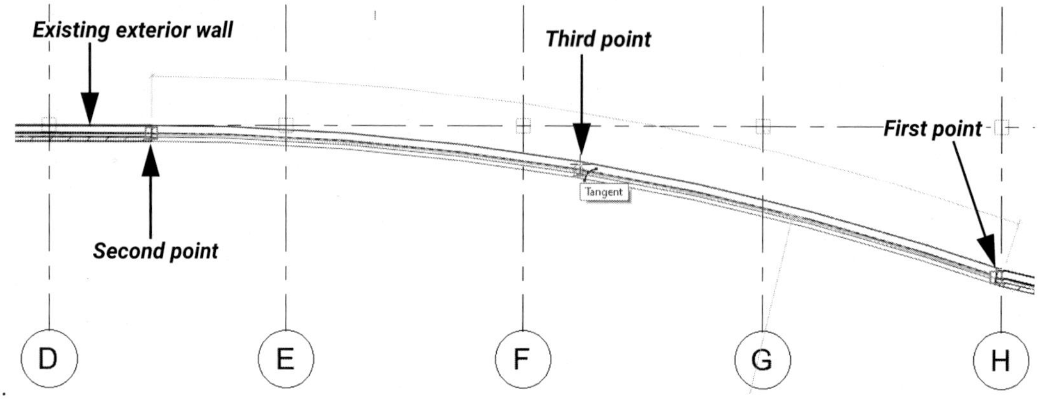

Figure 7–84

- Creating the wall this way solves some issues because the center line of the curtain wall is at a slight offset from the main wall.
- If a warning displays about a wall sweep, you can ignore it.

13. Click (Modify).
14. Type **ZA** to display the full floor plan.
15. Review the 3D view. The new parapet wall over the curtain wall displays, as shown in Figure 7–85.

Figure 7–85

16. Type **TW** to set the views back to tab view.
17. Save the project.

Task 2: Add Floor 2 walls.

1. Open the **Floor Plans: Floor 2** view. The view displays the walls created in the project and the linked drawing of the second floor.
2. Add walls for the guest rooms, as shown in Figure 7–86, using the following options:
   - *Wall type:* **Interior - 4 7/8" Partition (1-hr)**
   - *Location Line:* **Wall Centerline**
   - *Base Constraint:* **Floor 2**
   - *Top Constraint:* **Up to level: Floor 3**
   - *Top Offset:* (negative) **-1'-0"**
   - *Cross-Section:* **Vertical**
   - Align the center of the vertical walls to the grid lines.
   - Ignore all of the door openings.
   - You can use the **Copy** and **Mirror** tools to duplicate the walls once you have modeled one guest room layout.

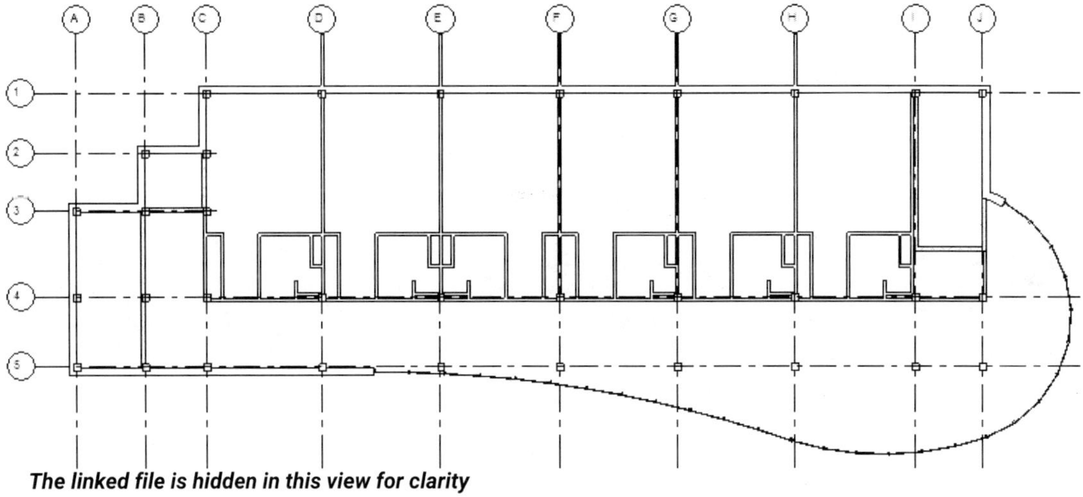

Figure 7–86

3. Save the project.

Task 3: Add basement walls.

1. Open the **Floor Plans: T.O. Footing** view.
2. With nothing selected, in Properties, in the *Underlay* section, set the *Range: Base Level* to **Floor 1** to see where the walls must be placed.
3. In the *Architecture* tab>*Build* panel, click (Wall).
4. In the *Modify | Place Wall* panel>*Draw* tab, verify that (Chain) is toggled off.
5. In Properties, verify or set the following options:
    - *Wall type:* **Basic Wall: Generic - 12" Masonry**
    - *Location Line:* **Core Centerline**
    - *Base Constraint:* **T.O. Footing**
    - *Base Offset:* **0'-0"**
    - *Top Constraint:* **Up to level: Floor 1**
    - *Top Offset:* **0'-0"**
6. Starting at the west stairwell, draw the interior foundation walls between columns, then the two walls around the east stairwell, as shown in Figure 7–87.

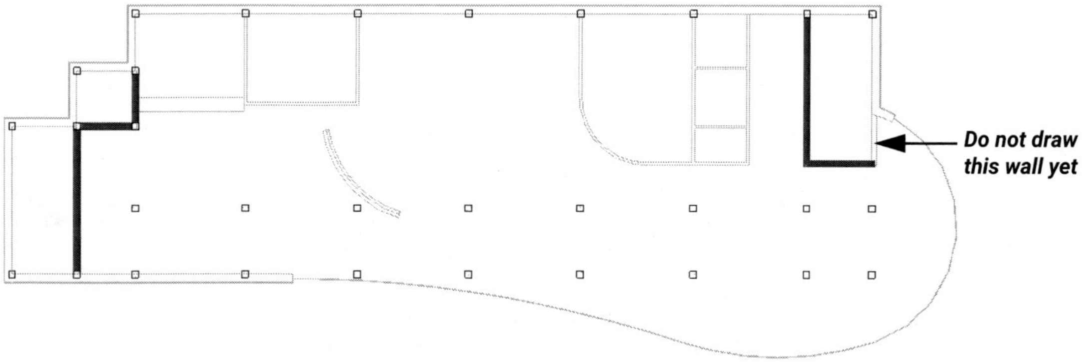

Figure 7–87

7. Click (Modify).
8. Zoom out so you can see the entire building.

9. Start the **Wall** command again. The settings should all be the same. Click (Pick Lines). At the exterior wall of the west stairwell, draw the walls around the exterior of the hotel by selecting the centerline of the walls (you might need to zoom in and use <Tab> to highlight the core centerline). Figure 7–88 shows the exterior walls highlighted.
   - Alternatively, you can hover your cursor over the exterior wall of the west stairwell and press <Tab> until you see all the walls' centerlines highlight . Once the walls are highlighted, including the curved curtain walls, click to select them.

Figure 7–88

10. Click (Modify).
11. Extend the east stairwell's wall to intersect with the stairwell wall, as shown in Figure 7–89.

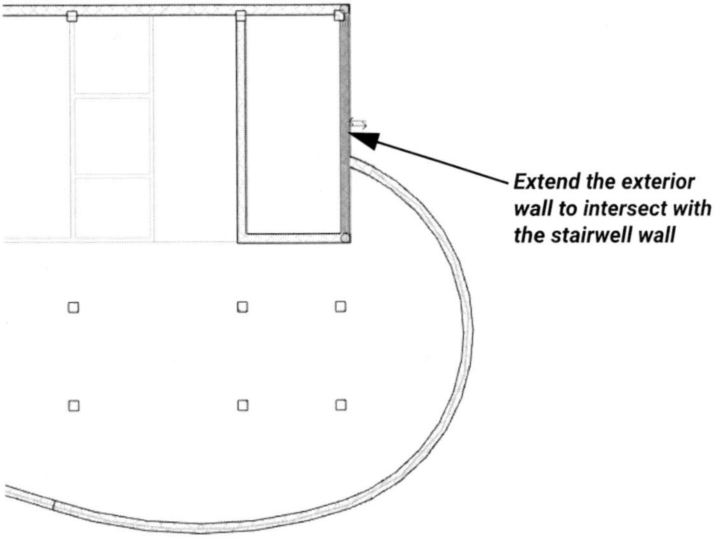

Figure 7–89

   - Use the modify tools to get them in place if needed.

12. Click (Modify).
13. Save the project.

Task 4: Add footings to the basement walls.

1. Still in the **Floor Plans: T.O. Footing** view, with nothing selected, in Properties, in the *Underlay* section, set the *Range: Base Level* to **None** to not display Floor 1.
2. Start the **Wall** command and click (Pick Lines) in the *Draw* panel.
3. In Properties, verify or set the following options:
   - *Wall type:* **Basic Wall: Generic - 24" Concrete**
   - *Location Line:* **Core Centerline**
   - *Base Constraint:* **T.O. Footing**
   - *Base Offset:* (negative) **-1'-6"**
   - *Top Constraint:* **Up to level: T.O. Footing**
   - *Top Offset:* **0'-0"**
4. Starting at the exterior wall of the west stairwell, draw the footings around the exterior of the hotel, then add footings to the interior walls around the east and west stairs and elevator by selecting the centerline of the walls (you might need to zoom in and use <Tab> to highlight the centerlines). The completed footings are shown in Figure 7–90.

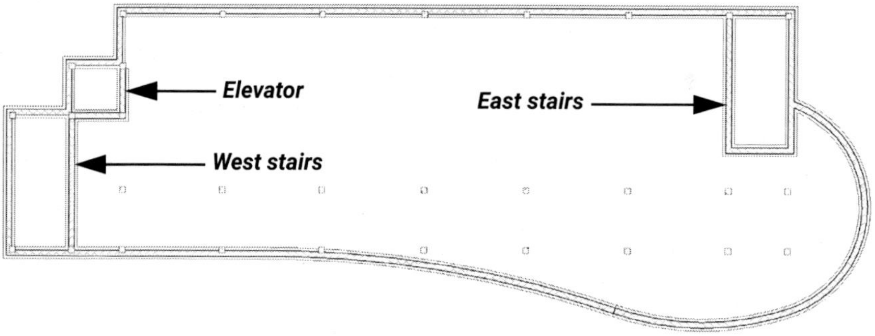

Figure 7–90

5. Open the 3D view and orbit to view the foundation walls and footings.
6. Save and close the project.

End of practice

7.4 Adding Room Elements

Rooms are model elements and are important for subdividing spaces within a building based on room-bounding elements like walls (as shown in Figure 7–91), by separation lines, or by a combination of both. Rooms contain parameter information like room name, number, area perimeter, and volume that can be used in tags and schedules. You can place rooms one at a time and with or without a tag. You can also place several rooms at one time in all appropriate bounded areas. If needed, you can use the **Highlight Boundaries** command to visually see all room-bounding elements in the current view.

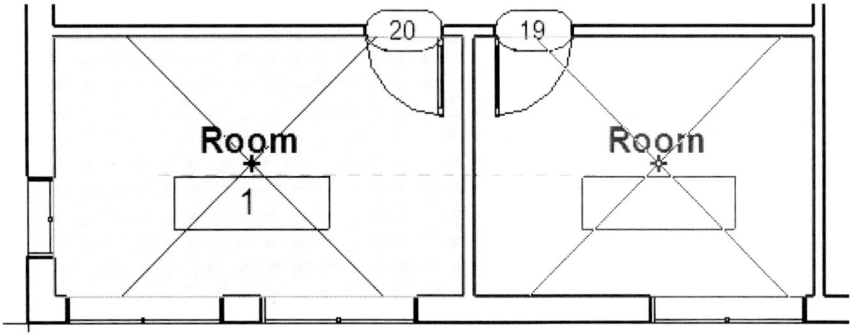

Figure 7–91

By default, rooms do not display in views and only the room tags display. To help visually aid in placing rooms in a model, open the *Visibility/Graphic Overrides* dialog box. On the *Model Categories* tab, in the *Visibility* column, expand **Rooms** and select one or all of the following, as shown in Figure 7–92:

- **Color Fill:** When turned on, rooms are colored in according to a selected color scheme if one is applied to the view.
- **Interior Fill:** When turned on, rooms are colored in to give a visual of where the room boundaries are located. By default, a light blue color is used.
- **Reference:** When turned on, a visual X is added through each room.

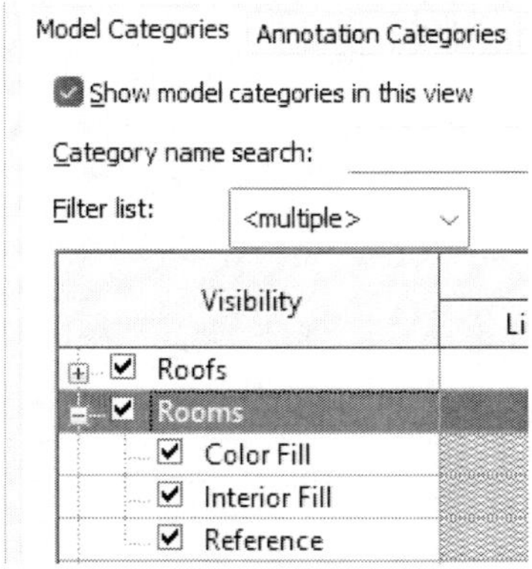

Figure 7–92

How To: Add Rooms

1. In the *Architecture* tab>*Room & Area* panel, click (Room), or type **RM**.
2. Move the cursor inside a boundary and click to place a room element. If you have (Tag on Placement) toggled on in the *Modify | Place Room* tab>*Tag* panel, it also places the tag.
   - Rooms are inserted with the default name of *Room*. Numbers increment automatically as you place rooms. You can select the first room on a floor and change the number, and any room tags placed thereafter will increment using the last tag's number. For example, if you change a room tag's number to 101, the next tag will be 102, and so on.
3. If needed, you can drag the room tag outside of the room boundary and a leader will automatically be added. Figure 7–93 shows the before and after of placing a room with a tag and then dragging it outside of the room boundary.

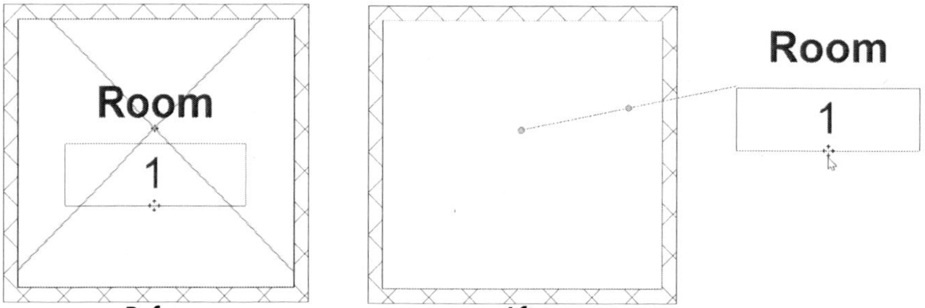

Before ***After***

Figure 7–93

4. Continue clicking inside boundaries to add other rooms.

- To add multiple rooms at once, in the *Modify | Place Room* tab>*Room* panel, click (Place Rooms Automatically). Rooms are added in every bounded area that does not already have a room, and a dialog box displays indicating how many rooms were created automatically.

Modifying Rooms

To select a room, hover the cursor near the room tag or move the cursor around slowly until you find the room's reference lines or X to highlight the room element, as shown in Figure 7–94. Click to select the room.

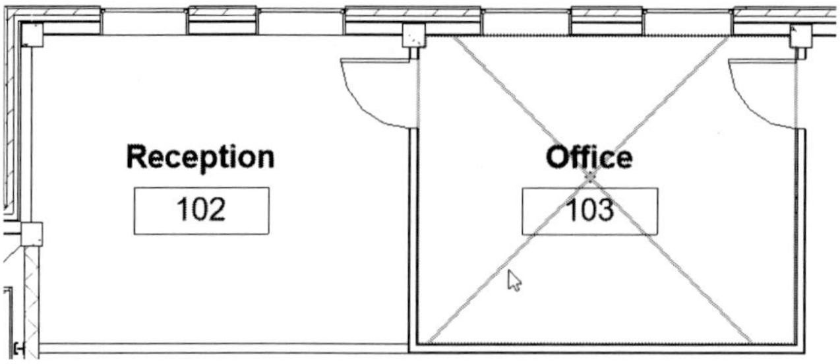

Figure 7–94

To change the name of one room, select the tag, then select the tag name and type the name of the room. The tag updates, as shown in Figure 7–95. You can also click on the room number and type a new number.

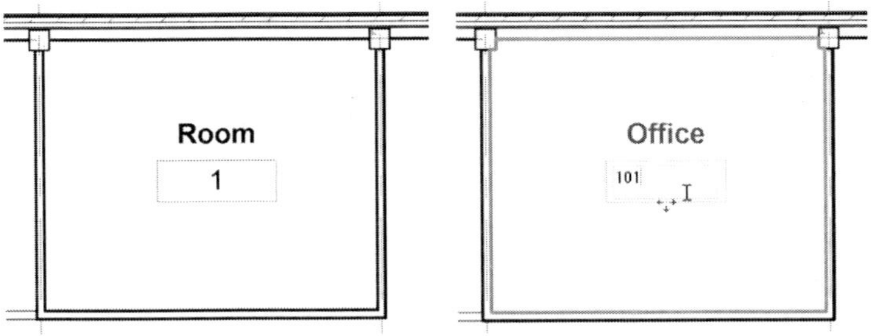

Figure 7–95

To change the names of several rooms, select the room elements and in Properties, change the *Name* parameter, as shown in Figure 7–96. All the rooms that were selected will update to show the same name. Other information, such as finishes, can also be added in the room properties. This information is made available to schedules.

Figure 7–96

If several of the room reference lines in a view have been shifted, as shown on the left in Figure 7–97, you can reset them to the center of their respective rooms by going to the *Architecture* tab>*Room & Area* panel, expanding (Room), and selecting (Re-center Reference). A dialog box will display indicating how many room references have been re-centered.

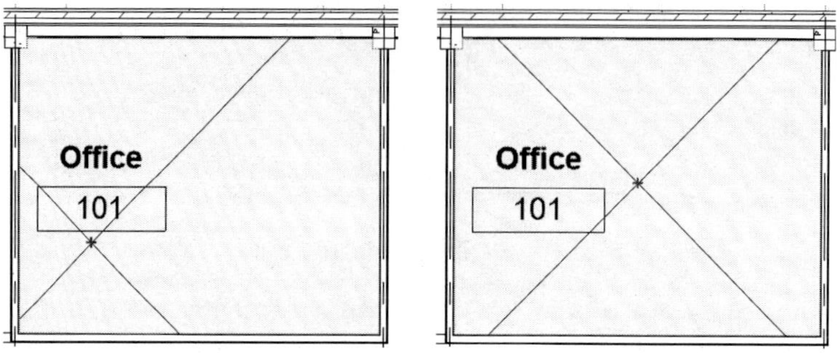

Before ***After***

Figure 7–97

- To only re-center one room reference, select the room reference lines, then in the *Modify | Rooms* tab>*Room* panel, click (Re-center Reference). The selected room reference is re-centered.

To re-center the tag to the center of the room reference lines, select one or more tags, then in the *Modify | Room Tags* tab>*Tag* panel, select (Move to Room Reference). The tags move to the center of each room, as shown in Figure 7–98.

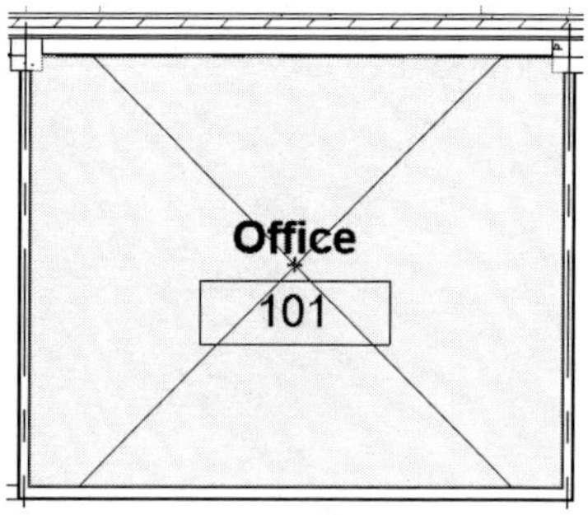

Figure 7–98

Adding Room Separation Lines

Room separation lines enable you to divide an open space into more rooms. Separation lines are model elements, so they will appear not only in the view you draw them in, but in any duplicate views, sections, and 3D views.

How To: Add Room Separation Lines

1. In the *Architecture* tab>*Room & Area* panel, click (Room Separator).
2. Use the *Draw* panel tools to place lines that divide the spaces.
3. After creating the room separation lines, use the **Room** command to add the rooms, as shown in Figure 7–99.

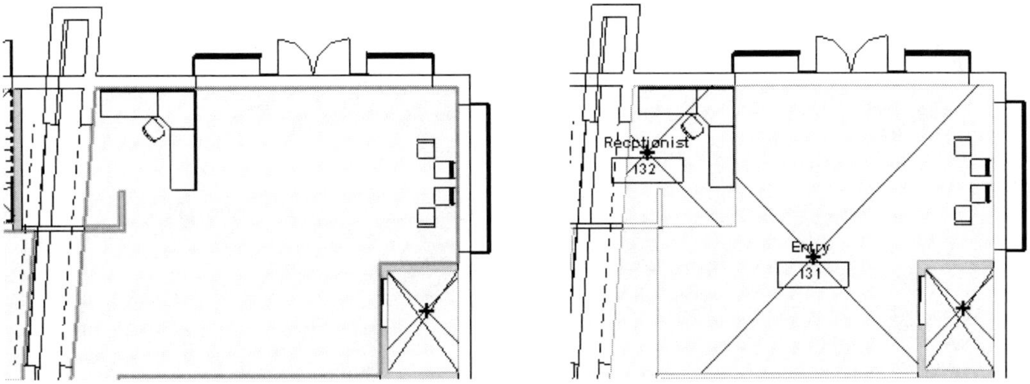

Before room separation lines ***With room separation lines***

Figure 7–99

- To hide a room separation line in the current view only, you can select it, right-click, and select **Hide in View>Element**. Select **Category** to hide all separation lines in the view.

  Note: *If you use the Hide in View>Category, if you need to continue to draw more separation lines in the view, they will disappear once drawn.*

- To unhide the separation lines hidden using the **Hide in View>Element** method, use (Reveal Hidden Elements) in the View Control Bar.

- To hide all separation lines in the current view only, open the *Visibility/Graphic Overrides* dialog box by typing **VV**, expand **Lines**, and uncheck the **<Room Separation>** checkbox, as shown in Figure 7–100. To unhide the separation lines, open the *Visibility/Graphic Overrides* dialog box, expand **Lines**, and check the checkbox.

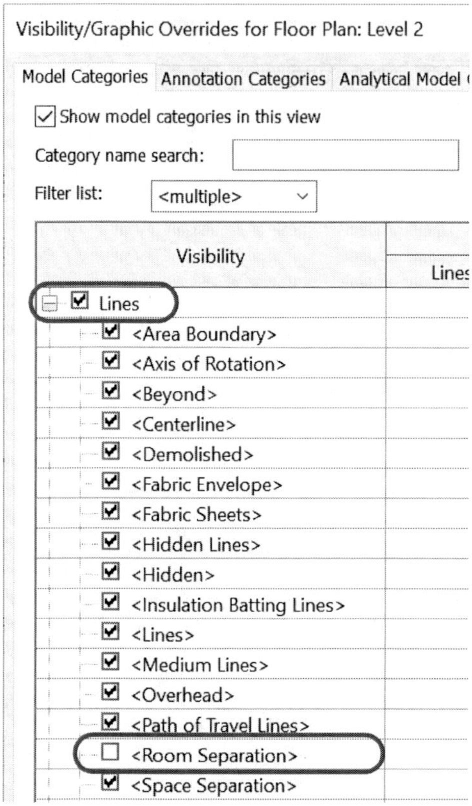

Figure 7–100

Practice 7d
Add Room Elements

Practice Objectives

- Set up a view that displays rooms.
- Add rooms and room separation lines.

In this practice, you will add rooms to the model. You will change the names and numbers of rooms using tags and Properties. You will add room separation lines to break up the larger open areas, as shown in the completed first floor plan in Figure 7–101. Review the figure below and become familiar with the different areas of the hotel.

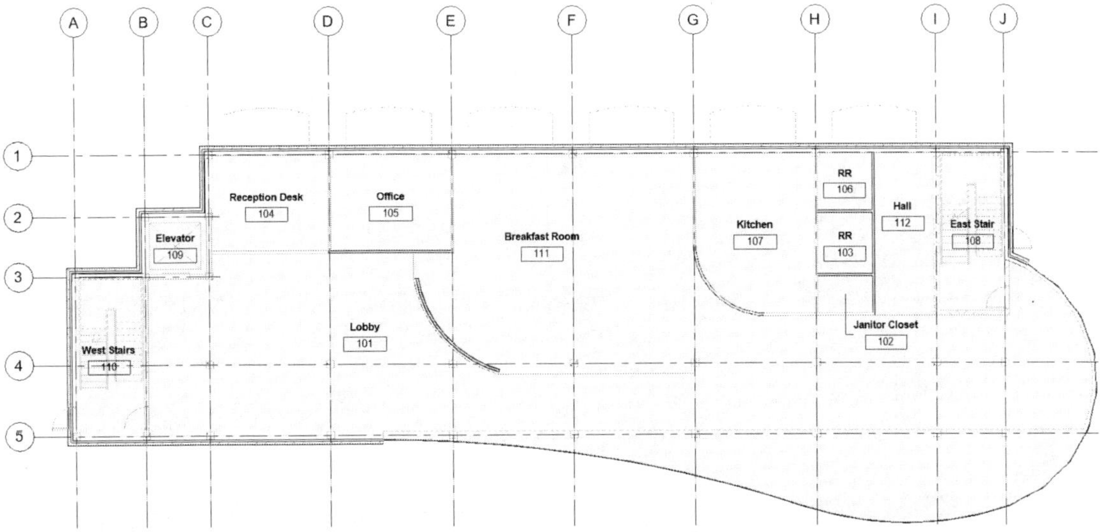

Figure 7–101

Task 1: Add rooms and room tags.

1. Open the project **Arch-Rooms.rvt**.
2. Verify that you are in the **Floor Plans: Floor 1** view.
3. In the *View* tab>*Graphics* panel, select (Visibility/Graphics), or type **VV**.
4. In the *Visibility/Graphic Overrides* dialog box, on the *Model Categories* tab, verify that only **Architecture** is selected in the *Filter list:* drop-down list.

5. In the *Category name search* field, type **room**. The *Visibility* column's categories will filter. Select the checkbox for **Interior Fill**, as shown in Figure 7–102, so that you can see the room color as you place rooms.

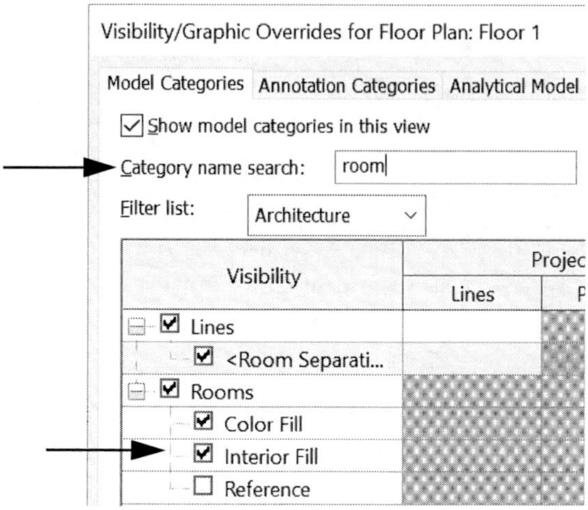

Figure 7–102

6. Click **OK**.
7. In the *Architecture* tab>*Room & Area* panel, click (Room).
8. In the *Modify | Place Room* tab>*Tag* panel, verify that (Tag on Placement) is toggled on, then place a room element inside the lobby area (to the left of the curved wall).
9. Click (Modify) and zoom in on the room tag.

10. Click on the tag and then click on the room name and change the room name to **Lobby**. Click on the room number to change it to **101**, as shown in Figure 7–103, and press <Enter>.

    - Changing this first room number ensures that the rest of the numbers increment correctly.

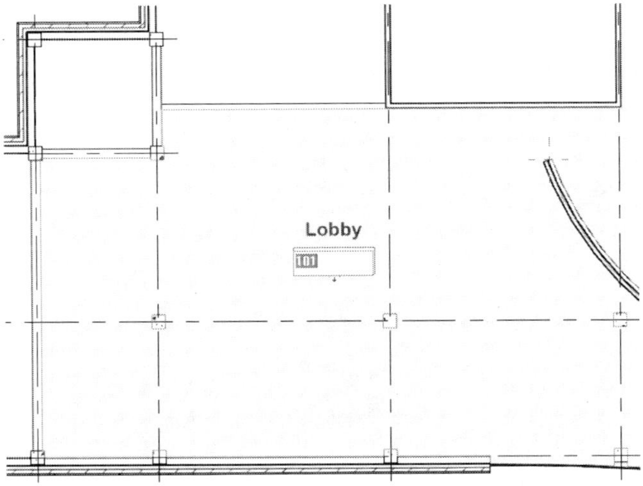

Figure 7–103

11. Click (Modify) and zoom out, then start the **Room** command again.
12. In the *Modify | Place Room* tab>*Room* panel, click (Place Rooms Automatically). The rest of the rooms are added to the model, as shown in Figure 7–104. Your room numbers might differ from what is shown in the figure, but you can renumber them after they are all added. Click **Close** in the dialog box.

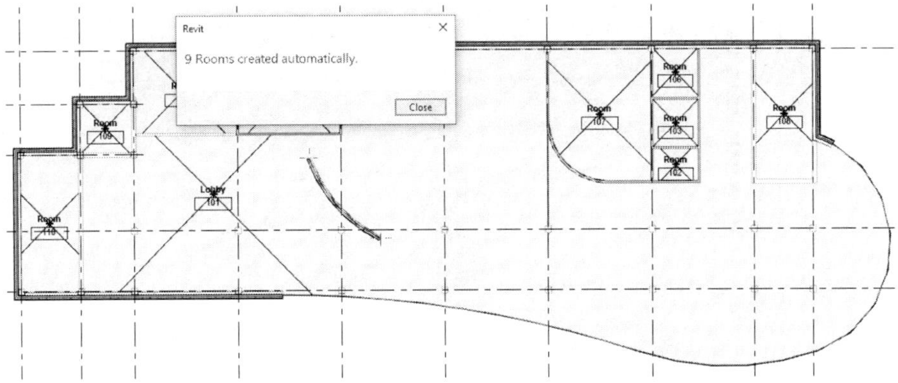

Figure 7–104

13. Select the room (the X and not the tag) above the Lobby between grid lines C and D, as shown in Figure 7–105. Hint: Press <Tab> to cycle through selectable objects that are close together or on top of each other.
14. In Properties, in the *Identity Data* section, note that the *Number* is automatically incremented. Set the *Name* to **Reception Desk** and verify the *Number* is **104** (as shown in Figure 7–105).

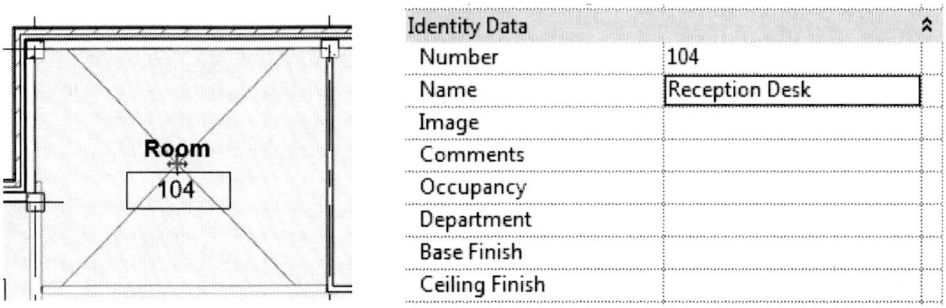

Figure 7–105

Note: *Your room numbers might differ from this example.*

15. Click **Apply** or move your cursor into the view window area to see the tag update, as shown in Figure 7–106.
16. If a warning dialog box displays indicating that elements have duplicate "Number" values, read it and click **OK** to continue working.
17. Click on the room tag in the room beside the Reception Desk room. Change the name to **Office** and, if needed, the room number to **105**, as shown in Figure 7–106.
    - If a warning displays, read it and continue working.

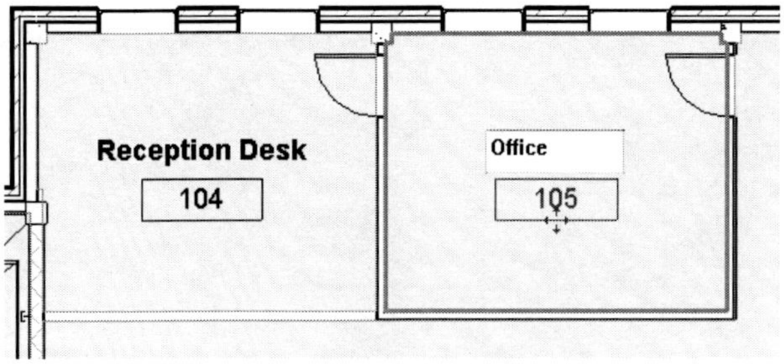

Figure 7–106

18. Rename and renumber the rest of the rooms (shown in Figure 7–107) by selecting the tag and changing the information in the view; alternatively, you can select the room (the X and not the tag) and change the name in Properties.

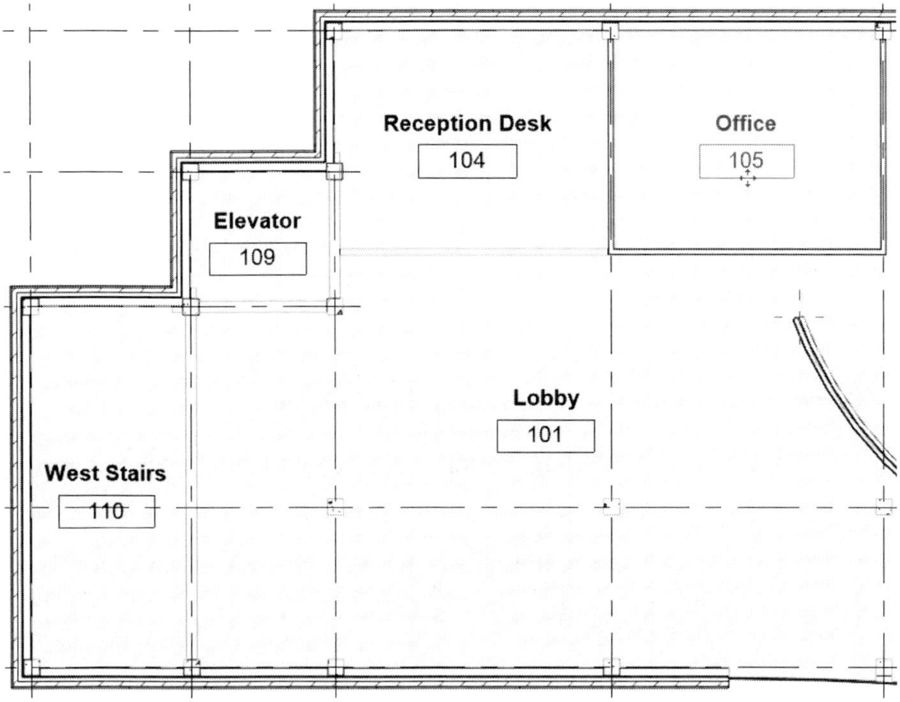

Figure 7–107

19. Pan and zoom over to the east side of the hotel and rename the rooms similarly to what is shown in Figure 7–108.

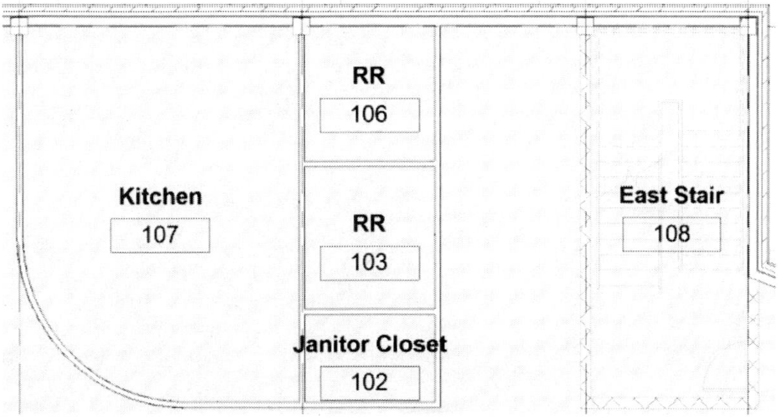

Figure 7–108

20. Note that the **Janitor Closet** text does not fit inside the room. Select the tag and drag it outside of the room. A leader is automatically added, as shown in Figure 7–109. Use the controls to adjust the leader as needed.

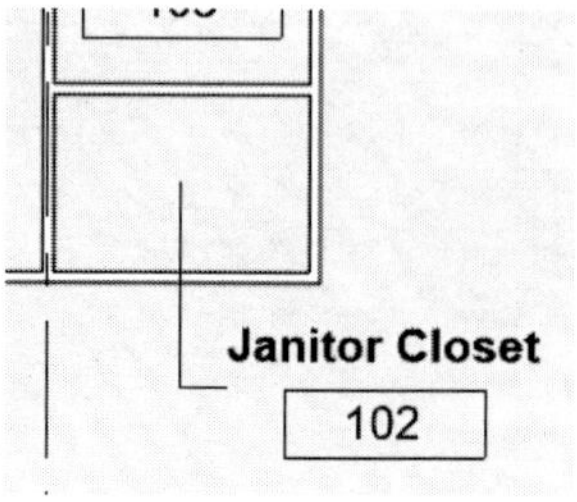

Figure 7–109

21. Save the project.

Task 2: Add room separation lines and additional rooms.

In this task, you will separate the breakfast area and hallway from the lobby.

1. In the *Architecture* tab>*Room & Area* panel, click (Room Separator).
2. Draw room separation lines to separate the breakfast area and hallway from the main lobby, as shown in Figure 7–110. For the breakfast area, draw the separation lines to include the curved slanted wall.

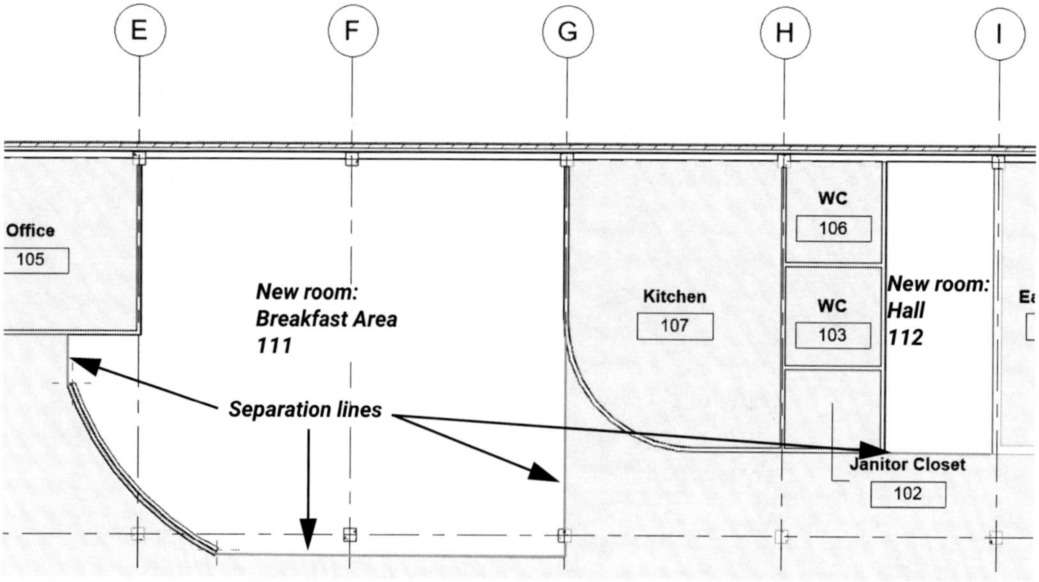

Figure 7–110

3. Start the **Room** command and verify that **Tag on Placement** is on. In Properties, in the *Name* field, type **Breakfast Area**, and then place the room in the location shown previously in Figure 7–110.
4. While still in the **Room** command, in Properties, change the *Name* value to **Hall** and place a room in the hallway, as shown previously in Figure 7–110.
5. Move tags around, as needed.
6. Type **VV** to open the *Visibility/Graphic Overrides* dialog box and under *Rooms*, turn off **Interior Fill**.

Task 3: Add rooms and room tags to Floor 2.

1. Open **Floor 2** and add a room and room tag in the first guest room. Modify the room number to be **201**.
2. Continue adding rooms and room tags to the other guest rooms, then select the six rooms, as shown in Figure 7–111. In Properties, under the *Identity Data* section, change the *Name* value to **Guest Room**.

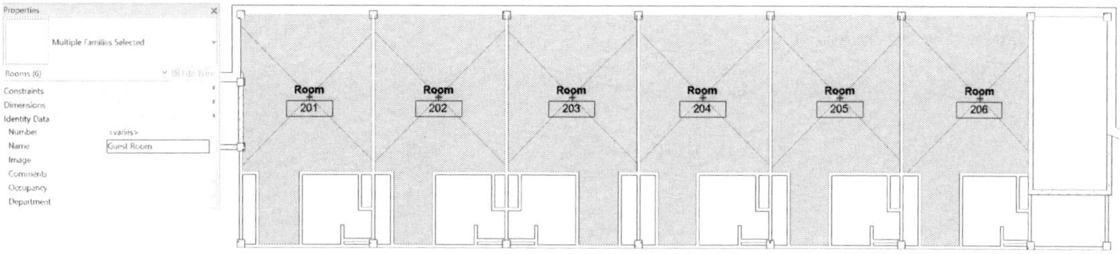

Figure 7–111

3. Continue adding rooms and room tags to the other areas, as shown in Figure 7–112. Modify the room tags' names and numbers to match what is shown in the image.

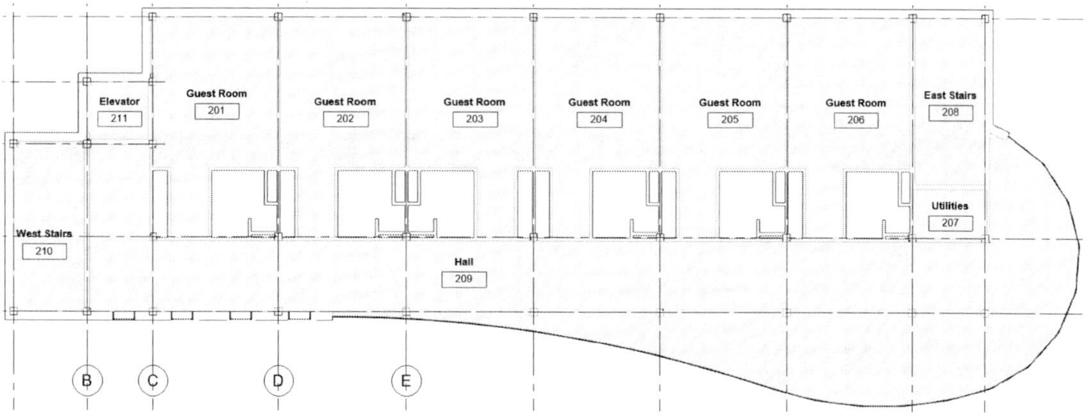

Figure 7–112

4. Zoom in to room 201. Select the walls for the closet, bathroom, and bathroom closet that are just inside guest room 201.
   - Do not select any of the separating walls (as shown in Figure 7–113), such as:
     - The wall that separates the guest rooms from each other
     - The wall that separates the guest room from the hallway
     - The wall that separates the room from the utilities room
     - The walls around the elevator or the walls around the east stairs
5. In Properties, in the *Constraints* section, uncheck **Room Bounding**.
6. Click in an empty space in the view to clear the selection. The entire guest room 201 is now included in the room tag, as shown in Figure 7–113.

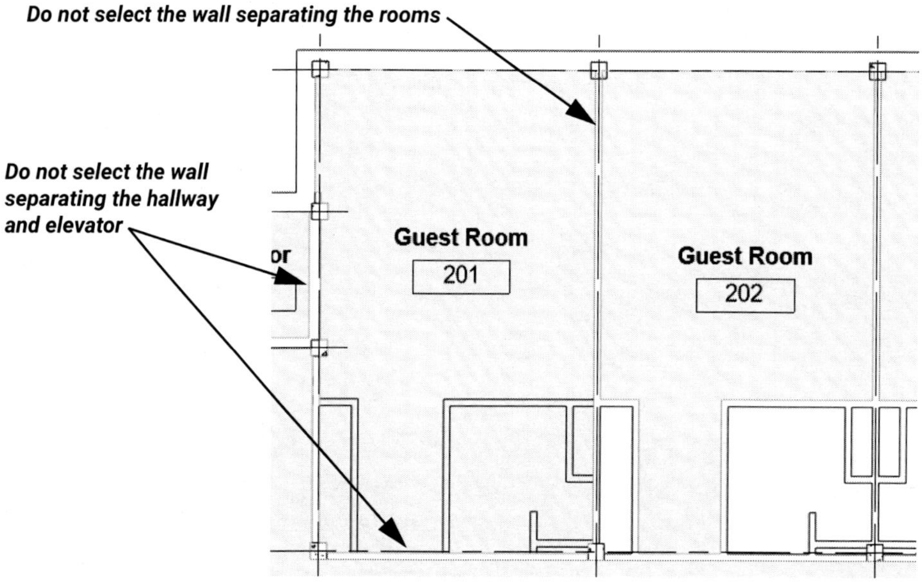

Figure 7–113

7. Save and close the project.

End of practice

Chapter Review Questions

1. Where do you specify the height of a wall before you start modeling it? (Select all that apply.)
    a. In the *Modify | Place Wall* tab.
    b. In Properties.
    c. In the Status Bar.
    d. In the Quick Access Toolbar.

2. Some walls are made from multiple layers of materials, such as brick, block, and drywall, as shown on the bottom in Figure 7–114. If the hatching for these materials is not displayed (as shown at the top in Figure 7–114), how do you change this?

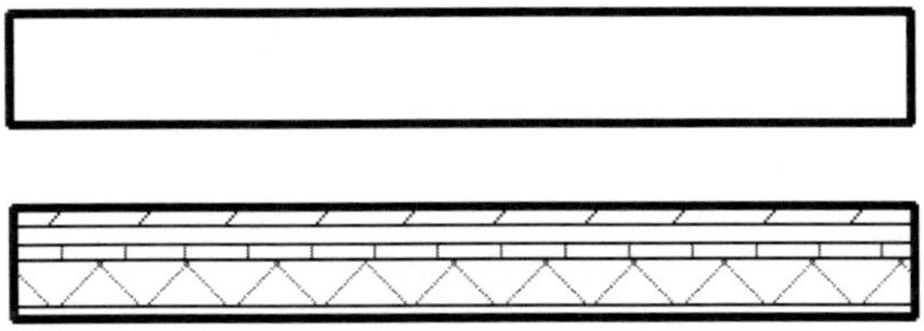

Figure 7–114

    a. Set the *Visual Style* to **Realistic**.
    b. Set the *Detail Level* to **Medium**.
    c. Set the *View Scale* to be higher.
    d. Set the *Phase* to **New**.

3. Which of the following tools enables you to change a wall from one made out of studs and brick to one made out of concrete?
    a. Properties
    b. Change Wall
    c. Type Selector
    d. Edit Wall

4. Match the names for the following controls with the numbers shown in Figure 7–115.

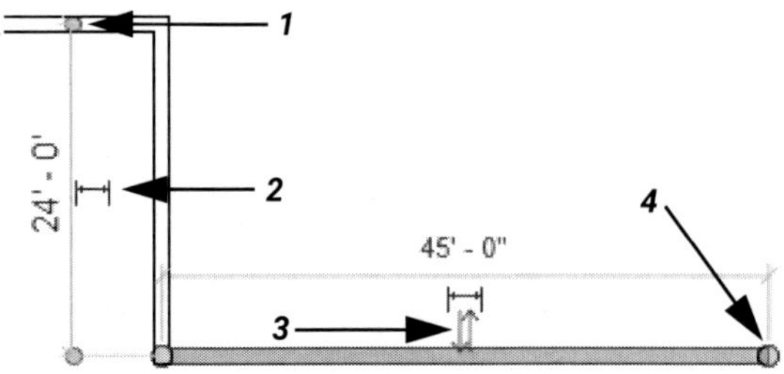

Figure 7–115

Control	Number
Drag wall end	
Flip	
Move witness line	
Make this temporary dimension permanent	

5. Which of the following are potential differences between the column surround wall and the associated walls, as shown in Figure 7–116? (Select all that apply.)

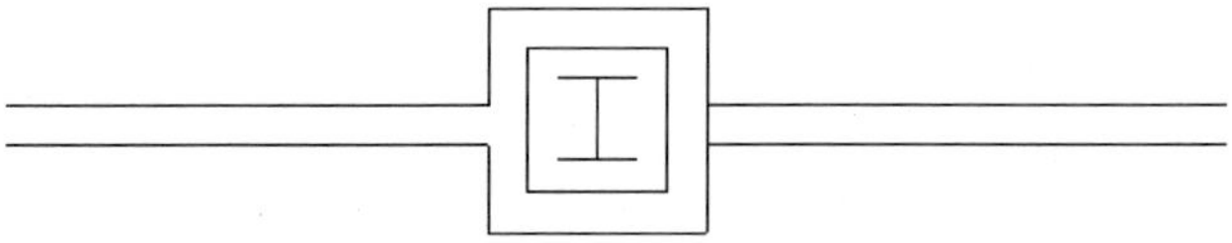

Figure 7–116

a. The column surround and wall on the left are made with the same wall type, while the wall type on the right is a different wall type.

b. The wall on the left has been joined together with the column surround, while the wall on the right was set to **Disallow Join**.

c. The wall on the left was trimmed against the column surround.

d. The wall on the right was extended to the column surround.

6. Which of the following would be true if you changed the top constraint of one wall from an unconnected height to a level?
    a. All walls of that type would also change height.
    b. Only that wall would change height.
    c. You cannot change just one walls height.

7. When you want to add rooms with the same name (as shown in Figure 7–117), you need to modify each one separately.

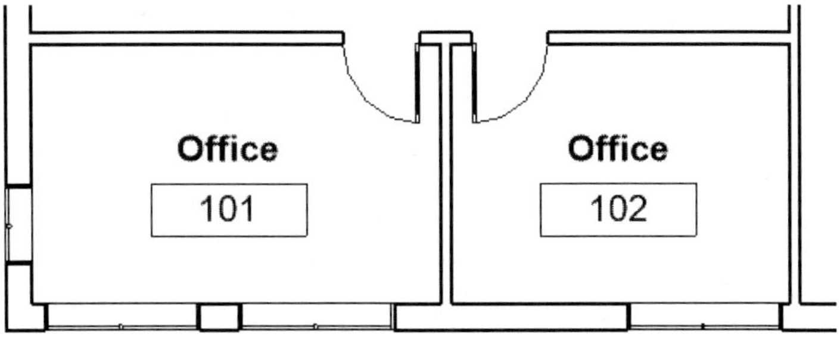

Figure 7–117

    a. True
    b. False

Command Summary

Button	Command	Location
	**Detail Level: Coarse**	• **View Control Bar**
	**Detail Level: Fine**	• **View Control Bar**
	**Detail Level: Medium**	• **View Control Bar**
	**Edit Profile**	• **Ribbon:** (when a wall is selected) *Modify | Walls* tab>*Mode* panel
	**Match Type**	• **Ribbon:** *Modify* tab>*Clipboard* panel • **Shortcut:** MA
	**Properties**	• **Ribbon:** *Modify* tab>*Properties* panel • **Shortcut:** PP
	**Room**	• **Ribbon:** *Architecture* tab>*Room & Area* panel • **Shortcut: RM**
	**Room Separator**	• **Ribbon:** *Architecture* tab>*Room & Area* panel
N/A	**Type Selector**	• **Properties** • **Ribbon:** *Modify* tab (*Optional*) • **Quick Access Toolbar** (*Optional*)
	**Wall**	• **Ribbon:** *Architecture* tab>*Build* panel
	**Wall Opening**	• **Ribbon:** *Architecture* tab>*Opening* panel

Chapter 8

Working with Doors and Windows

Doors and windows are hosted elements that are placed in walls. There are many different types of doors and windows available in the Revit® libraries, and you can easily create additional sizes of the types that come with the software to meet your design requirements.

Learning Objectives

- Insert doors and windows in walls.
- Modify door and window locations and properties that can be referenced in schedules.
- Create additional door and window sizes of a selected type.

8.1 About Doors and Windows

Doors and windows in Revit are designed to be hosted by walls. You can use temporary dimensions (as shown in Figure 8–1), alignment and preview lines, and snaps to help place the openings exactly where you need them in the walls.

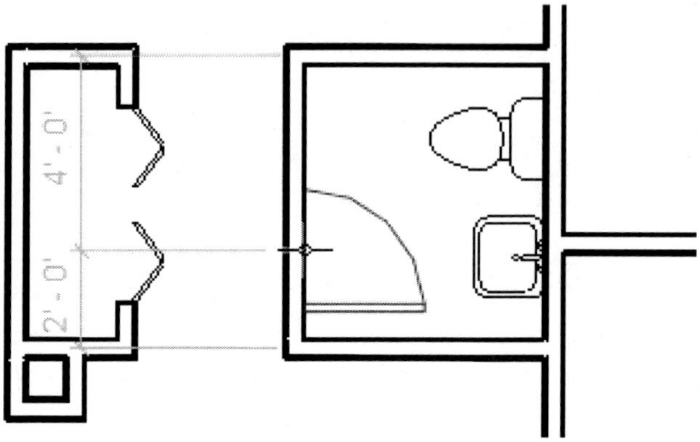

Figure 8–1

- You can add doors and windows in slanted and tapered walls.

How To: Add a Door or Window

1. In the *Architecture* tab>*Build* panel, click  (Door) or  (Window). The keyboard shortcuts are **DR** for doors and **WN** for windows.
2. To insert a tag with each door or window, in the *Modify | Place Door* or *Place Window* tab>*Tag* panel, select  (Tag on Placement). You can also specify the tag options, like *Orientation*, *Leader Line*, and *Leader Length*, as shown in Figure 8–2.
    - When **Tag on Placement** is selected, you can select  (Loaded Tags And Symbols) to see what is currently loaded, as well as load in tags for other element types, not just for doors or windows.

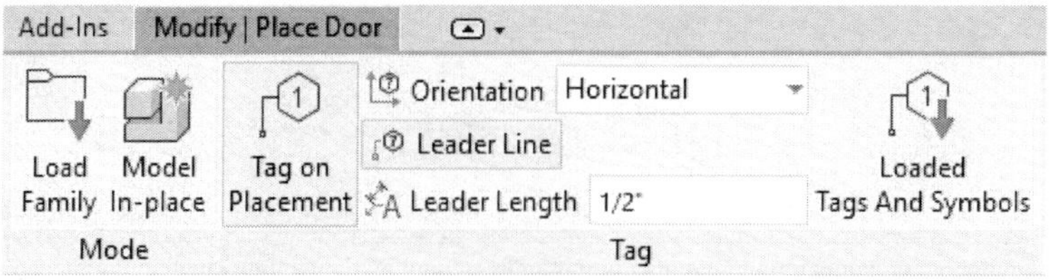

Figure 8–2

3. In the Type Selector, select the type of door or window.

4. Hover over the wall that you want to place the door or window. Use the temporary dimensions and/or other drawing aids to properly locate where you want the door.
    - Press <Spacebar> to change the swing of the door before placing it.
5. Click on the wall to insert the door or window.
6. Continue adding other doors or windows as needed.

- While placing a door or window, you can adjust its position using temporary dimensions. With doors, you can use the **Flip the instance facing** and **Flip the instance hand** controls to change the swing and hinge locations, as shown in Figure 8–3. With windows, you can flip the interior and exterior using the **Flip the instance facing** control.

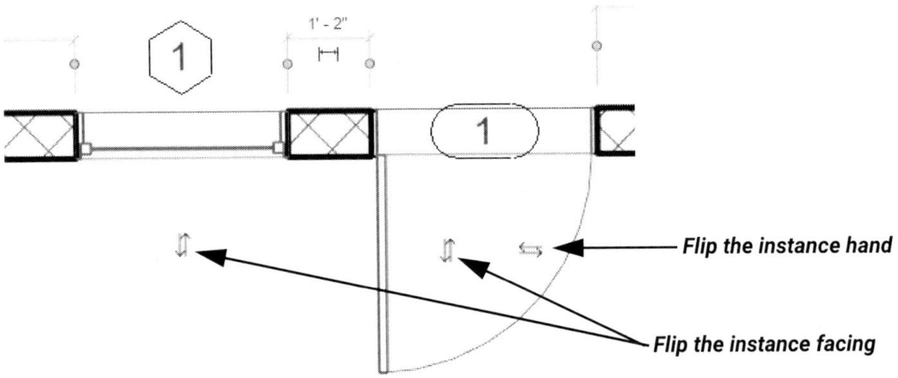

Figure 8–3

- If you are including window tags, select a point close to the outside of the wall when inserting the window so that the tag is placed on the outside.
- To move a door or window tag, select the tag. A control displays, as shown in Figure 8–4, which enables you to drag the tag to a new location.

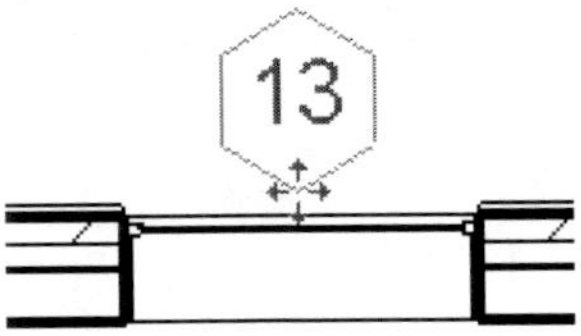

Figure 8–4

Modifying Door and Window Properties

The door or window types control most of their properties. To change the property information, you change the type in the Type Selector. You can also change instance parameters (as shown in Figure 8–5) that impact the specific door or window in the associated schedule. Instance parameters include things such as the *Swing Angle, Masonry, Drywall Frame, Sill Height, Frame Type, Frame Material,* etc.

> **Note:** *The exact properties vary according to the door or window selected.*

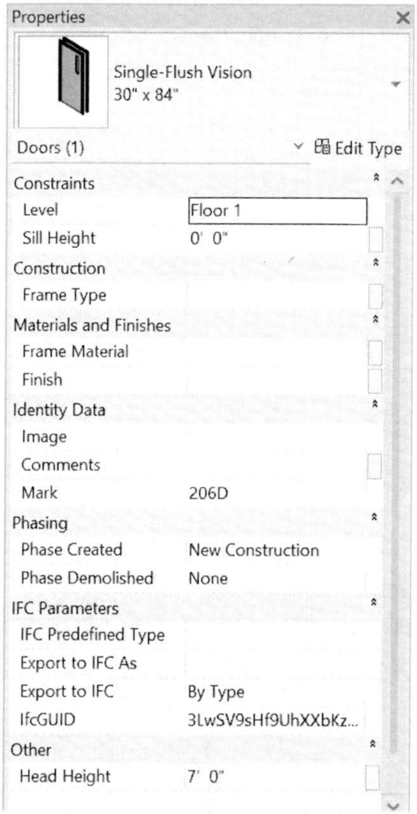

Figure 8–5

- The *Type Properties* dialog box includes type parameters such as *Function*, *Door Material*, *Frame Material*, and *Dimensions*, as shown in Figure 8–6. The *Identity Data* section is where you will want to add the manufacturer, model, keynote, and other information that will be pertinent in the door or window schedule.

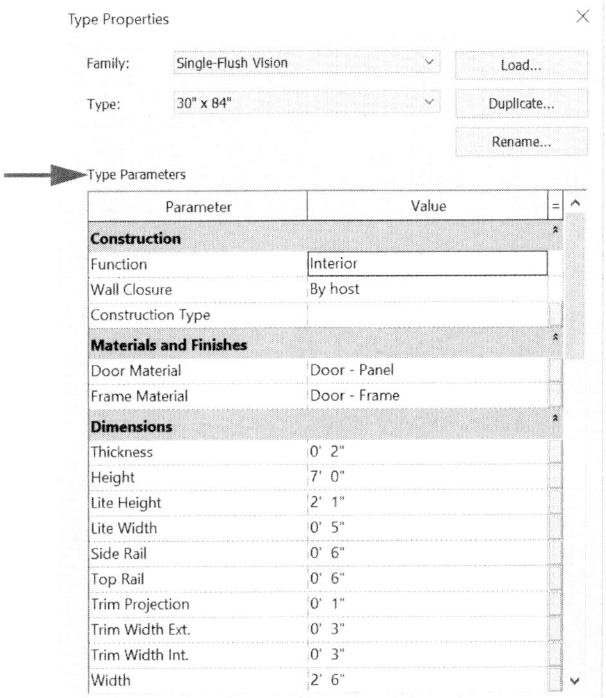

Figure 8–6

If a door (or window) has been inserted into a slanted wall, you have the option to select the door in the view and modify the *Orientation* to either **Vertical** or **Slanted**, as shown on the left in Figure 8–7. If it has been inserted into a tapered wall, you can set the *Orientation* to **Vertical**, **Slant along exterior**, or **Slant along interior**, as shown on the right.

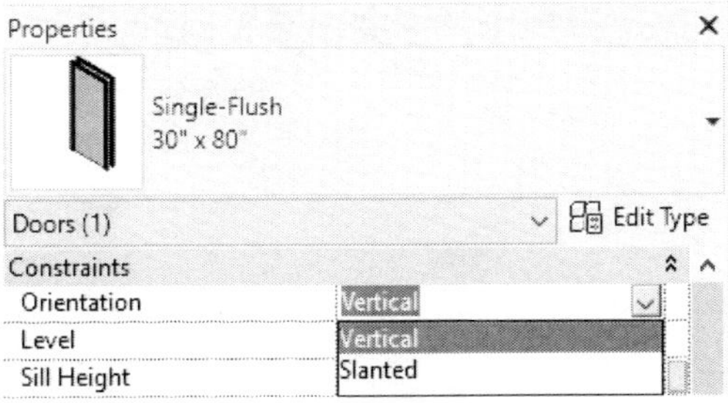

Properties for door inserted into slanted wall

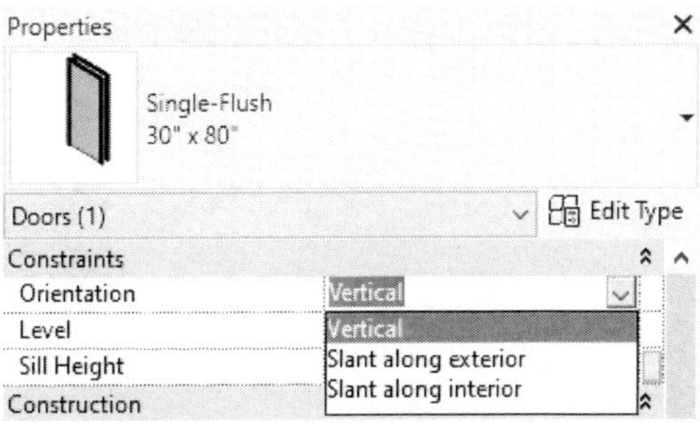

Properties for door inserted into tapered wall

Figure 8–7

Hint: Transferring Project Standards

Some elements (such as wall types) are not accessible from a specific library. However, you can copy them from other projects.

- Transferring project standards does not transfer loadable families like custom families or families from the Revit Library.

1. Open the project from which you want to copy information.
2. Open the project to which you want to copy the information.
3. In the *Manage* tab>*Settings* panel, click (Transfer Project Standards).
4. In the *Transfer Project Standards* dialog box, select an option in the *Copy from:* drop-down list and then select the settings you want to copy into the current file, as shown in Figure 8–8. Click **OK**.

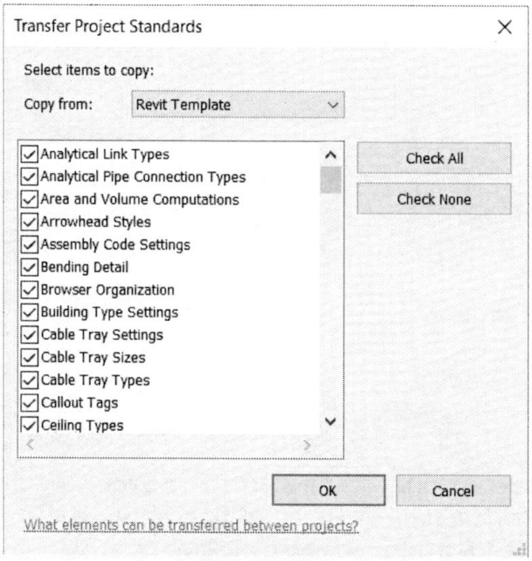

Figure 8–8

5. In the *Duplicate Types* dialog box, click either **Overwrite** or **New Only** to apply the settings to the current project.

8.2 Creating Additional Door and Window Sizes

You can easily add additional sizes to existing families of doors or windows that have been loaded into a project. To do this, you create a new type of the needed size based on an existing type, as shown in Figure 8–9.

- You can specify materials for door and window sub-elements in the *Type Properties* dialog box.
- The parameters might be different depending on the door or window you selected.

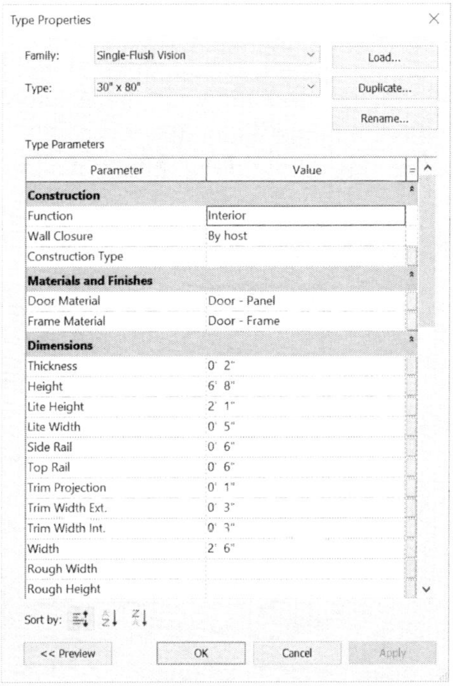

Figure 8–9

How To: Create Additional Door and Window Sizes

1. Start the **Door** or **Window** command.
2. In the Type Selector, select the type you want to modify. In Properties, click (Edit Type) or in the *Modify* tab>*Properties* panel, click (Type Properties).
3. In the *Type Properties* dialog box, click **Duplicate**.
4. In the *Name* dialog box, enter a new name for the element and click **OK**.
5. In the *Type Properties* dialog box, change the *Height* and *Width* parameters to match the size.
6. Click **OK** to close the dialog box. The new window or door type is now available for use.

Practice 8a
Add Doors and Windows

Practice Objectives

- Load door types.
- Add doors and windows to a model.
- Create a new door type.
- Copy elements to multiple levels.

In this practice, you will load door types and add doors and windows to a model, as shown in the completed practice for Floor 1 in Figure 8–10. You will use controls and temporary dimensions to help you place the doors and windows, then will copy them to multiple levels.

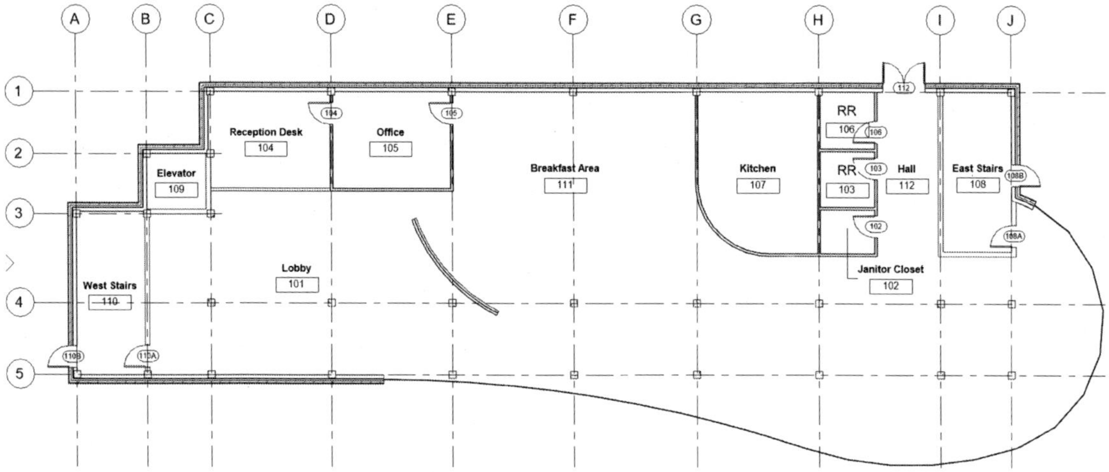

Figure 8–10

Task 1: Add doors.

1. Open the project **Arch-Doors.rvt** from the practice files folder.
2. Open the **Floor Plans: Floor 1** view.
3. Pan and zoom over to the west stairs.
4. In the *Architecture* tab>*Build* panel, click  (Door), or type **DR**.
5. In the *Modify | Place Door* tab>*Tag* panel, toggle on  (Tag on Placement), if not already on.
6. In the Type Selector, select **Door-Single-Panel: 36" x 80"**.

7. Using the linked CAD file as a guide, place the door near the lower corner of the building at grid A5, as shown in Figure 8–11. Use the flip arrows to make it swing in the right direction and use temporary dimensions to place it **3'** from the face of the wall. Click the tag and change the number to **101**.

   ***Note:** The Revit door sizes may differ from the CAD file. The CAD file is just a guide to place elements in the approximate location.*

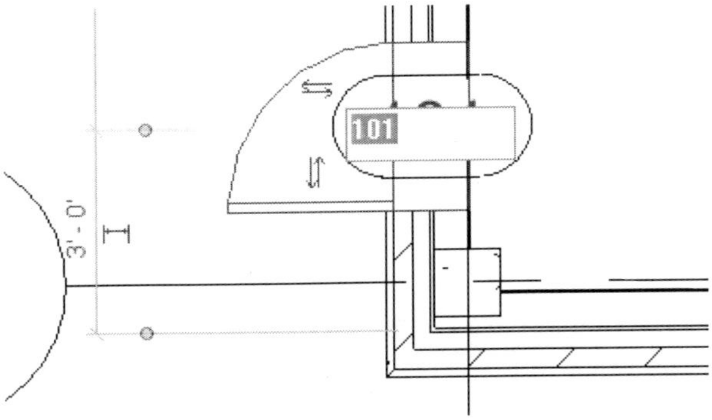

Figure 8–11

8. Continue adding single panel doors in the project, similar to the locations shown in Figure 8–12. Use the same door type. The tag number automatically increments.

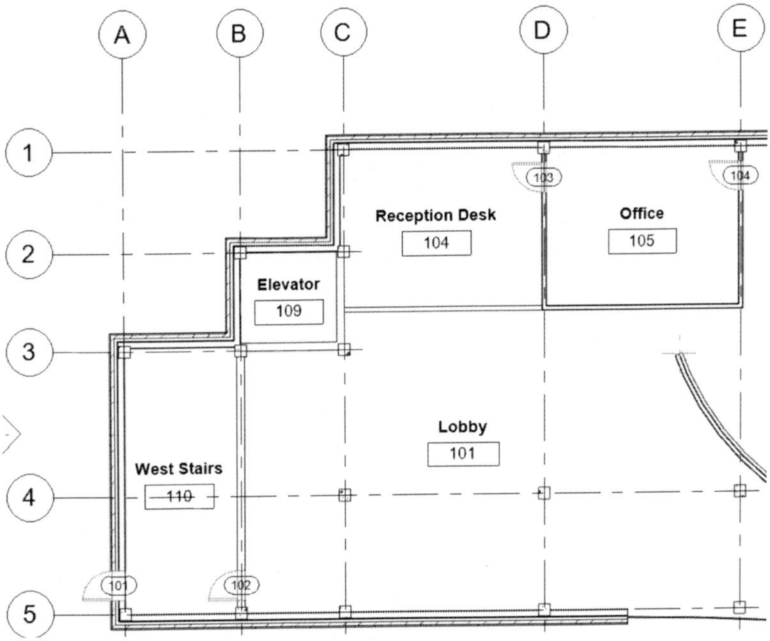

Figure 8–12

9. Zoom and pan over to the east stairs and place the **Door-Single-Panel: 36" x 80"** doors in the rooms, as shown in Figure 8–13. (Your numbering may differ from that in the figure below based on the sequence in which you placed the doors.)

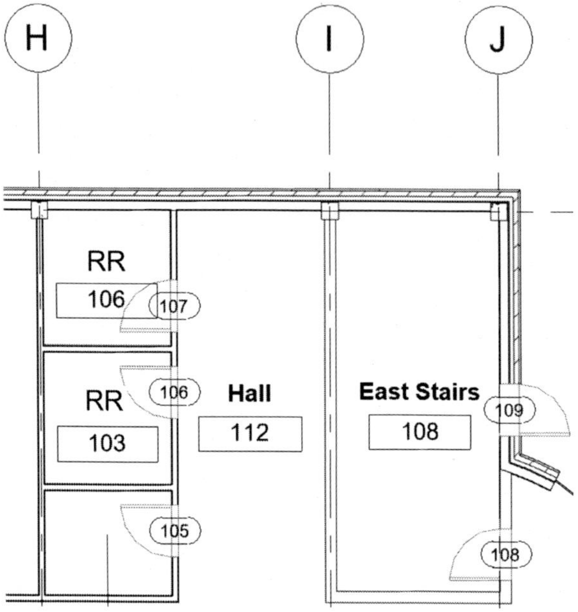

Figure 8–13

10. Still in the **Door** command, in the Type Selector, select **Door-Double-Glass: 72" x 84"**.
11. Place the door at the end of the hallway between grid lines H and I.
12. Zoom out to see the full floor plan.
13. Click (Modify).
14. Select the two sets of stairwell doors (the two doors in the west and east stairwells).
    - If you select multiple categories, use (Filter) to help select only the doors.
15. In the Type Selector, select **Single-Flush Vision: 36" x 84"**.
16. Click in an empty space in the view to clear the selection.

17. (Optional) You can modify the door numbers to match the room numbers similar to the pattern shown in Figure 8–14, or using your office standard if you have one.

- You may get a warning telling you that elements have duplicate mark values, just ignore it and keep renumbering all the door tags on Floor 1 to match their room number. For the stairwells' two doors, change them to the same number as their stairwell but add an A and B after it.

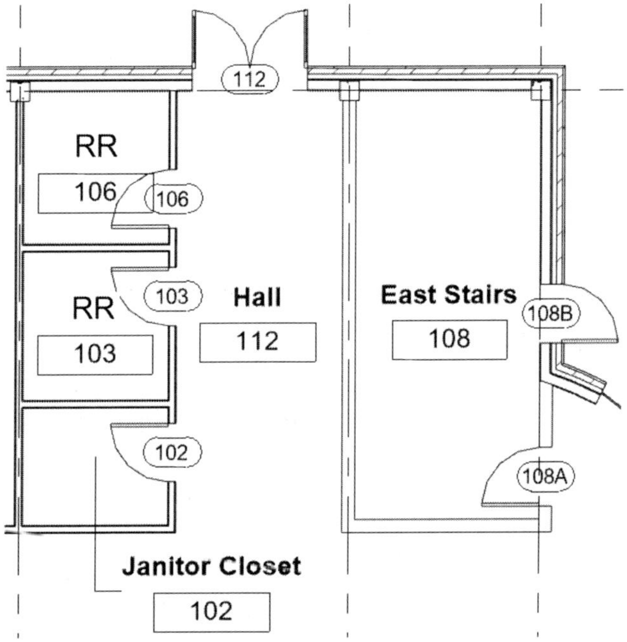

Figure 8–14

18. Save the project.

Task 2: Load door types.

1. Still in the **Floor 1** view, zoom in on the kitchen area.
2. In the *Architecture* tab>*Build* panel, click (Door).
3. In the *Modify | Place Door* tab>*Mode* panel, click (Load Family).
4. In the *Load Family* dialog box, navigate to the practice files *Families>Doors* folder and select **Door-Double-Flush_ Panel-Double-Acting.rfa**. Click **Open**.

5. In the *Specify Types* dialog box, select **72" x 80"** from the *Types* list, as shown in Figure 8–15, and click **OK**.

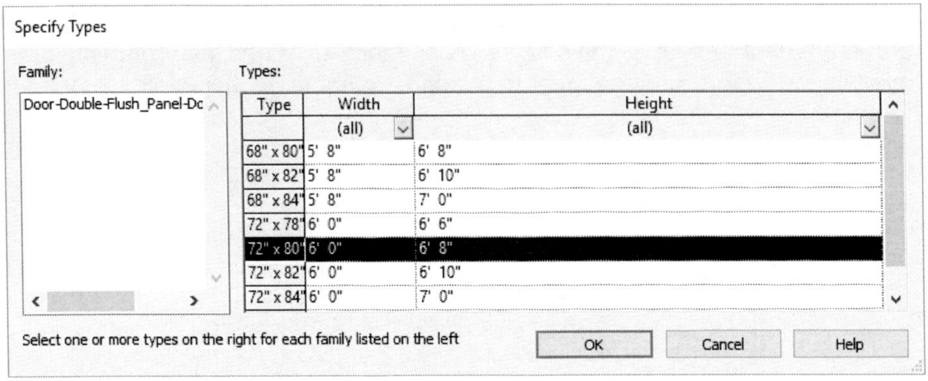

Figure 8–15

6. Start the **Load Family** command again. (Hint: Press <Enter> to repeat the last command.)
7. In the *Load Family* dialog box, navigate to the practice files *Families>Doors* folder and select **Single-Panel 4.rfa**. Click **Open**.
8. In the *Specify Types* dialog box, select **36" x 80"** from the *Types* list and click **OK**.
9. In the Type Selector, select **Door-Double-Flush_Panel-Double-Acting: 72" x 80"** and place an instance of it in the wall between the kitchen and breakfast area, as shown in Figure 8–16.
10. If needed, change the door tag to match the kitchen's room number, as shown in Figure 8–16.

    Note: *The order the doors are placed will determine the door tag number.*

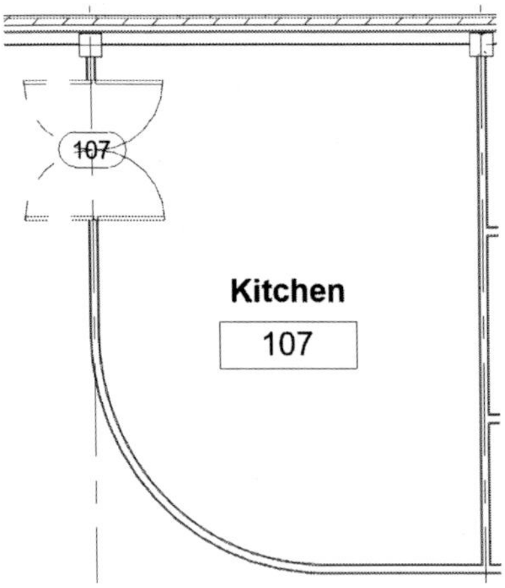

Figure 8–16

11. Click (Modify).
12. Zoom to the extents of the view and save the project.

Task 3: Add doors to Floor 2.

1. Open the **Floor Plans: Floor 2** view.
2. In the *Architecture* tab>*Build* panel, click (Door).
3. In the Type Selector, change the door type to **Single-Flush-Vision: 36" x 84"**.
4. Place the first door in the lower-left west stairwell and change the tag number to **210** to match the room tag number.
5. Add another door of the same type to the other east stairs at the opposite end of the building and modify the door tag to match the room tag number.
6. Still in the **Door** command, pan over to the first guest room next to the west stairs.
7. In the Type Selector, change the door type to **Single-Panel 4: 36" x 80"** and place a door at the entrance of guest room **201**. Change the door number to **201**.
8. Continue placing doors at the entrance of each guest room and the utilities room, allowing the numbers to increment. Press <Spacebar> to flip the door swing when needed.
9. Use the same type to add doors to the bathrooms and bathroom closets. This door size is too large for the bathroom closet door but you will modify it later.
10. Continue adding other doors using different door styles (e.g., **Bifold-4 Panel 72" x 84"** for the closets and **Double-Glass 72" x 84"** for the balconies). The rooms should look similar to the layout shown in Figure 8–17, though the numbering might be different.

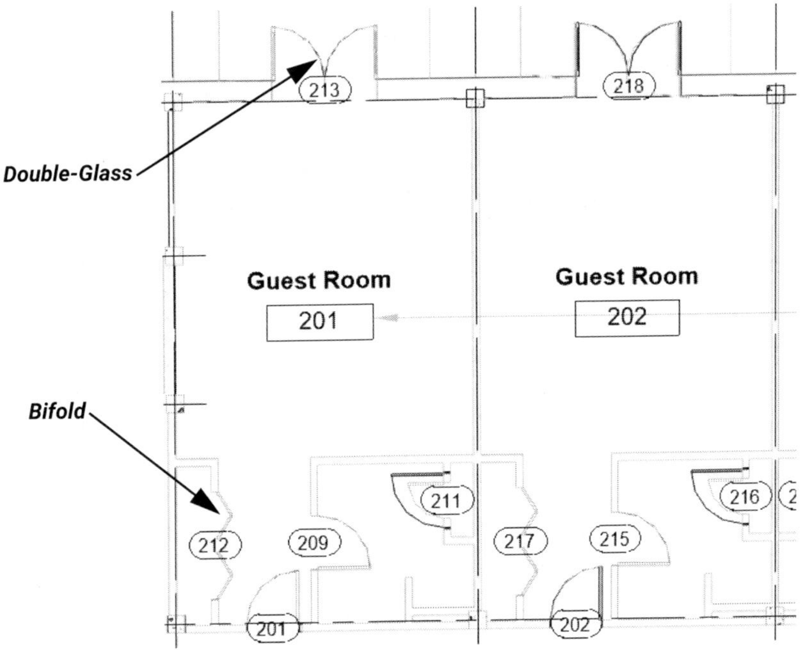

Figure 8–17

11. Click (Modify).
12. Renumber the doors in the guest rooms based on the room number if you have time (e.g., the doors in room 201 would become 201A, 201B, 201C, and 201D).
13. Save the project.

Task 4: Create a new door size.

1. Select one of the bathroom closet doors.
2. In Properties, click (Edit Type).
3. In the *Type Properties* dialog box, verify that **Single-Panel 4** is selected, as shown in Figure 8–18, and click **Duplicate...**.

Figure 8–18

4. In the *Name* dialog box, type **24" x 80"** and click **OK**.
5. In the *Dimensions* section, change the *Width* value to **2'-0"**.
   - Hint: You can type either **2** or **24"**, but you must add the " symbol to the value if you are using inches.
6. Click **OK** to close the dialog box.
7. Select the bathroom closet doors and change the type to the new door size.

Task 5: Add windows to Floor 2.

1. In the *Architecture* tab>*Build* panel, click (Window).
2. In the *Modify | Place Window* tab>*Tag* panel, toggle on (Tag on Placement), if not already on.
3. In the Type Selector, select **Casement 3x3 with Trim: 48" x 48"**, if not already selected.

4. Add the window close to the west stairs and grid B, as shown in Figure 8–19.
5. Click (Modify) and select the window. You might need to drag the witness line grip over to the grid line so that it references the grid, as shown in Figure 8–19, rather than a wall.
6. Use temporary dimensions to move the window **5'-0"** from grid B, as shown in Figure 8–19. (The door tags are turned off in the figure for clarity.)

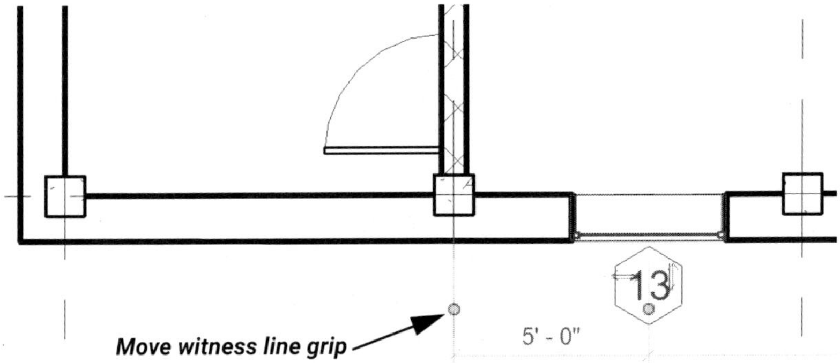

Figure 8–19

7. Click (Modify) and select the window and the window tag.
8. In the *Modify | Multi-Select* tab>*Modify* panel, click (Copy).
9. In the *Modify | Copy* tab>*Copy* panel, toggle on (Multiple), if not already on.
10. Select a point on the window as the move start point.
11. Move the cursor to the right, type **8** for the distance, and press <Enter>. Move the cursor past the new window to the right, type **8** again, and press <Enter>. Move the cursor over one last time, type **8 10**, as shown in Figure 8–20, and press <Enter>.

    Note: *Revit interprets 8 10 as 8'-10".*

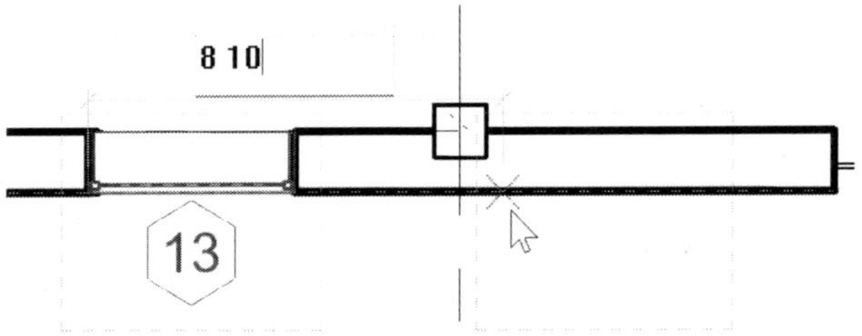

Figure 8–20

12. Click (Modify).

13. Select the linked DWG. In Properties, set the *Draw Layer* to **Foreground**. Zoom in to the group of windows and use the **Align** or **Move** tool to get the windows into the correct position.

14. Click (Modify).

15. Save the project.

Task 6: Copy windows to multiple levels.

1. Select the *3D* view tab to activate the view and verify that the front of the building where the windows are located is displayed, as shown in Figure 8–21. Change the visual style to **Consistent Colors**, if needed.

Figure 8–21

2. Select all four windows by holding <Ctrl> and selecting each one.

3. In the *Modify | Windows* tab>*Clipboard* panel, click (Copy to Clipboard).

4. In the *Clipboard* panel, expand (Paste) and click (Aligned to Selected Levels).

5. In the *Select Levels* dialog box, select the floors between and including **Floor 3** and **Floor 8**, as shown in Figure 8–22.

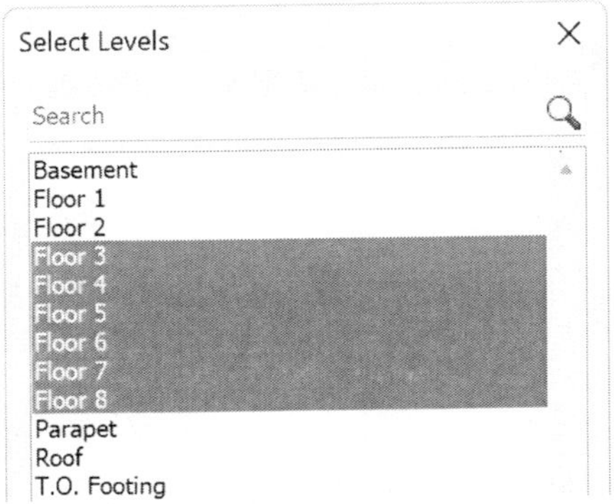

Figure 8–22

6. Click **OK**. The windows are copied up the side of the building, as shown in Figure 8–23.

   Note: *Additional doors and windows will be placed using storefront curtain walls in the next chapter.*

Figure 8–23

7. Save and close the project.

End of practice

Chapter Review Questions

1. How do you change the swing direction of a door? (Select all that apply.)
   a. When placing the door, press <Spacebar>.
   b. When placing the door, right-click and select **Change Swing**.
   c. Select an existing door and click the flip arrows.
   d. Select an existing door, right-click, and select **Change Swing**.

2. How do you add additional window or door families to a project?
   a. Find the window or door family using File Explorer, right-click, and select **Import into Revit Project**.
   b. Import them from the Window or Door Catalog.
   c. Load them from the Revit Library.
   d. Use the Window/Door tool to create new families.

3. How do you include a tag with a door or window?
   a. Select a door or window family that includes a tag.
   b. Select the *Tag* option in Properties before placing the door or window.
   c. Tags can only be used after placing the door or window.
   d. Toggle on **Tag on Placement** in the contextual tab.

4. Where are the door and window sizes located?
   a. In Properties
   b. In Type Properties
   c. In Door/Window Settings
   d. In the template file

5. How do you create additional door or window sizes?

a. Select the required door or window and use the **Size** tool to specify a new size.

b. In Properties, select the required door or window and click **Edit Type**, then select **Duplicate** and modify it.

c. Find the existing door or window family in the Project Browser, right-click, and select **New Size**.

d. Select the door or window in the view and edit it using size controls to the needed size.

Command Summary

Button	Command	Location
Clipboard		
	**Copy to Clipboard**	• **Ribbon:** *Modify* tab>*Clipboard* panel • **Shortcut:** <Ctrl>+<C>
	**Paste - Aligned to Selected Levels**	• **Ribbon:** *Modify* tab>*Clipboard* panel, expand Paste
	**Paste from Clipboard**	• **Ribbon:** *Modify* tab>*Clipboard* panel • **Shortcut:** <Ctrl>+<V>
Doors and Windows		
	**Door**	• **Ribbon:** *Architecture* tab>*Build* panel • **Shortcut:** DR
	**Edit Type/Type Properties**	• **Properties palette:** Edit Type • **Ribbon:** *Modify* tab>*Properties* panel
	**Measure**	• **Quick Access Toolbar** • **Ribbon:** *Modify* tab>*Measure* panel
	**Window**	• **Ribbon:** *Architecture* tab>*Build* panel • **Shortcut:** WN

Chapter 9

Working with Curtain Walls

Curtain walls are often used to create complex windows and storefronts. Curtain walls are created based on a curtain wall type to which additional curtain wall grids and mullions can be added and individual panels swapped out to create the needed pattern.

Learning Objectives

- Create basic curtain walls and storefronts using curtain wall types.
- Modify the curtain wall grid pattern.
- Switch out curtain wall panels with other panel types, doors, or windows.
- Add mullions to curtain wall grids.

9.1 Creating Curtain Walls

Curtain walls consist of panels laid out in a horizontal and vertical grid pattern. They can encase an entire building like a membrane or, as shown in Figure 9–1, fill a cutout in a standard wall, often called a storefront.

Figure 9–1

- You can create slanted curtain walls but not tapered.

How To: Create a Curtain Wall

1. In a plan view, model a wall using a curtain wall type.
2. In an elevation or 3D view, add curtain wall grids to the curtain wall.
3. Modify the panels of the curtain wall.

   Note: *Panels can be a specific material (such as glass or stone) or can incorporate doors, windows, or other wall types.*

4. Add mullions to separate the panels.

The components of a curtain wall are shown in Figure 9–2.

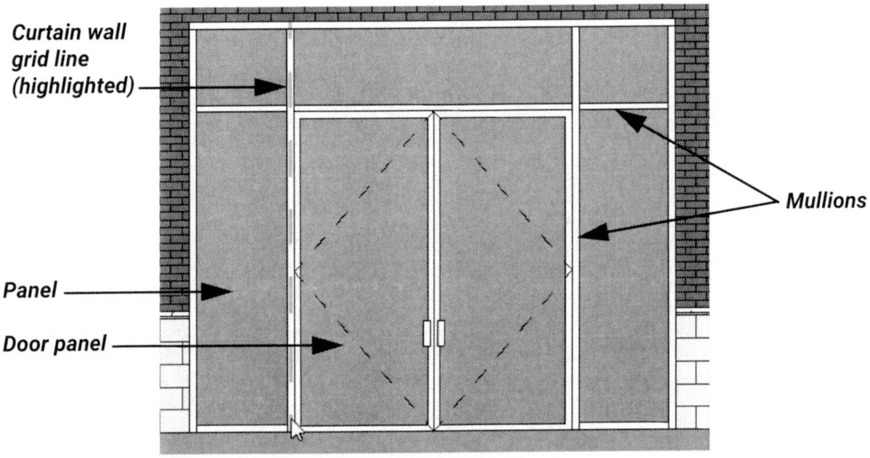

Figure 9–2

- The simplest way to create a curtain wall is to use a curtain wall type with a preset uniform curtain wall grid already applied to it, such as the three types that come with the software, as shown in Figure 9–3.

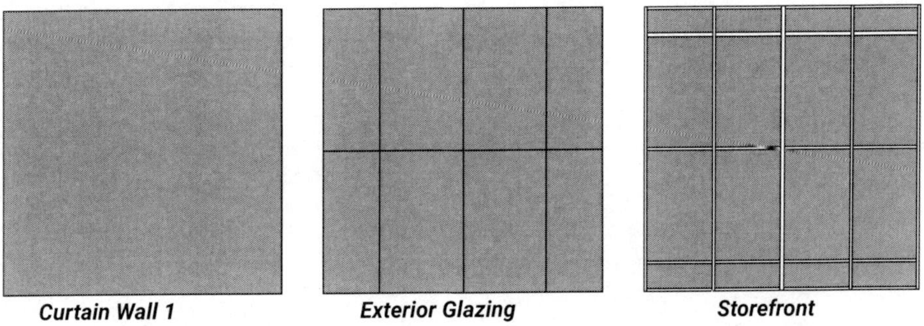

Figure 9–3

- Many curtain walls do not have a uniform pattern of exact distances between curtain wall grids, as shown in Figure 9–4. Therefore, you need to create these designs directly on the curtain wall. You can start with a curtain wall type that has a basic uniform curtain wall grid, if applicable.

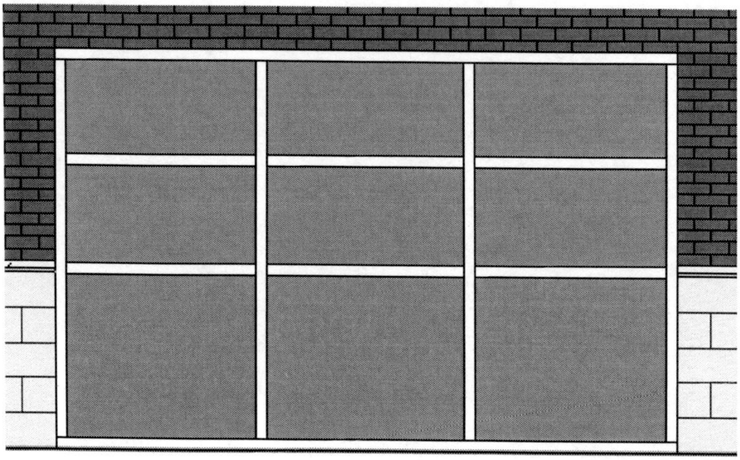

Figure 9–4

Some curtain walls are embedded into other walls, as shown in Figure 9–5. They can also be used to create what looks like a complex set of windows. The **Storefront** curtain wall type is designed to be embedded in another wall and can be used to create interior glazed walls.

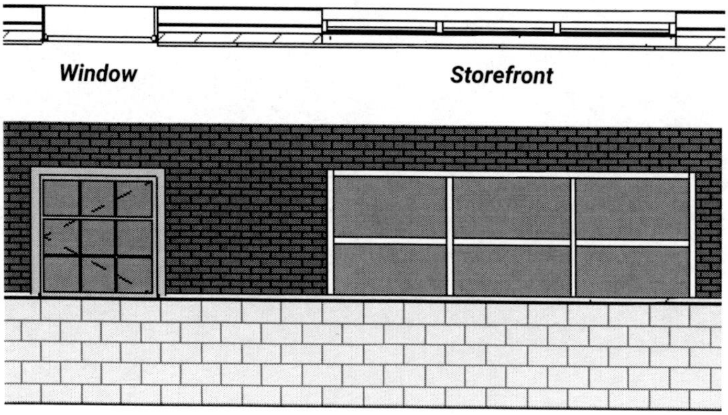

Figure 9–5

How To: Add a Storefront Wall in an Existing Wall

1. In the *Architecture* tab>*Build* panel, click (Wall).
2. In the Type Selector, select **Curtain Wall: Storefront**. In Properties, set the *Base Constraint*, *Top Constraint*, and *Offsets* as needed. The height can be less than the height of the wall in which you are embedding.
3. Select a point on the existing wall, as shown in Figure 9–6.

Figure 9–6

4. Select the second point along the wall. (Hint: Press <Tab> to cycle from the default Horizontal and Nearest snap to the dynamic dimension and then type the distance for the embedded curtain wall.) The wall displays, as shown in Figure 9–7.

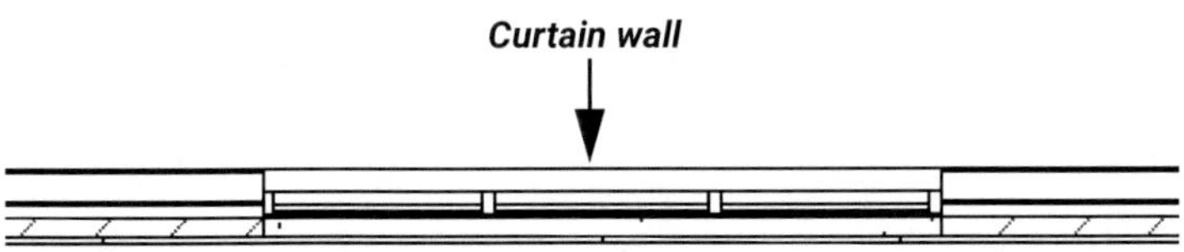

Figure 9–7

5. Open the appropriate elevation view. Select the outside edge of the curtain wall and use the shape handles and dynamic dimensions to modify the size of the storefront, as shown in Figure 9–8.

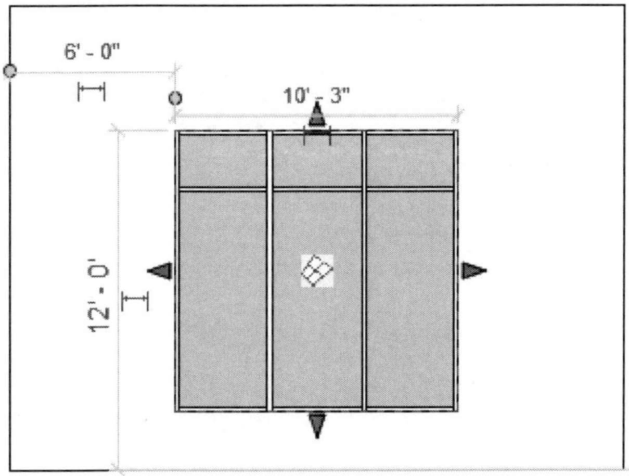

Figure 9–8

9.2 Adding Curtain Wall Grids

Once you have a curtain wall in place with at least one panel, you need to separate it into multiple panels for the design. Each curtain wall grid line divides a panel into two or more smaller panels, as shown in Figure 9–9.

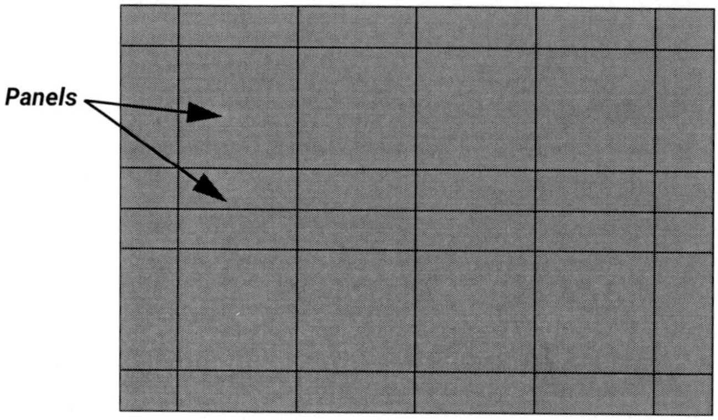

Figure 9–9

How To: Create a Curtain Wall Grid

1. After you have drawn the base curtain wall in a plan view, switch to an elevation or 3D view.
2. In the *Architecture* tab>*Build* panel, click (Curtain Grid).
3. In the *Modify | Place Curtain Grid* tab>*Placement* panel, select an insertion method, as described below.

(All Segments)	Creates a curtain wall grid line through the entire curtain wall height or width.
(One Segment)	Creates a curtain wall grid line between only the selection point and the next line. The entire curtain wall grid line is established, but only one segment displays. You can add other segments later.
(All Except Picked)	Creates a curtain wall grid line through the entire curtain wall and permits you to go back and remove segments of the curtain wall grid line. The removed segment displays as a dashed line until you add another curtain wall grid line or start another command.

4. Move the cursor over an edge of the curtain wall or an existing curtain wall grid line. Dynamic dimensions are displayed, as shown in Figure 9–10. The new curtain wall grid line is perpendicular to the edge at the point you select. Click at the required location.

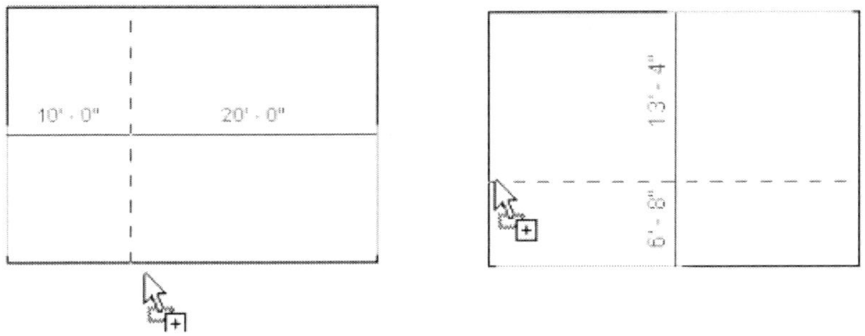

Figure 9–10

- Curtain wall grids automatically snap to the midpoint or 1/3 point of the panel. They also snap to levels, column grids, and reference planes.
- You can (Copy) and (Array) curtain wall grid lines. This method can be the fastest way of creating curtain wall grids across the length of a wall.

Modifying Curtain Wall Grids

Once you have placed the curtain wall grid lines, they might not be exactly where you want them or overlap other lines where you do not want them to overlap. You can modify the location of curtain wall grid lines in the curtain wall and add or remove segments from the lines, as shown in Figure 9–11.

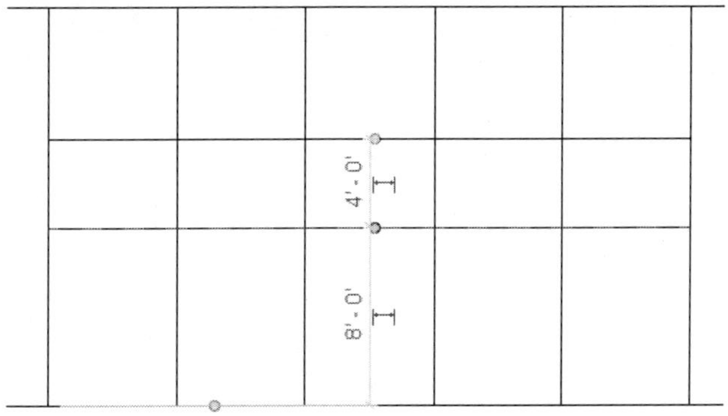

Figure 9–11

- To modify the curtain wall grid, you must select a curtain wall grid line, not a wall or the mullion. Hover your cursor over the area and press <Tab> to cycle through elements. Watch the tooltip or Status Bar as you cycle through the elements and click when you see **Curtain Wall Grids : Curtain Wall Grids : Grid Line**, as shown in Figure 9–12.

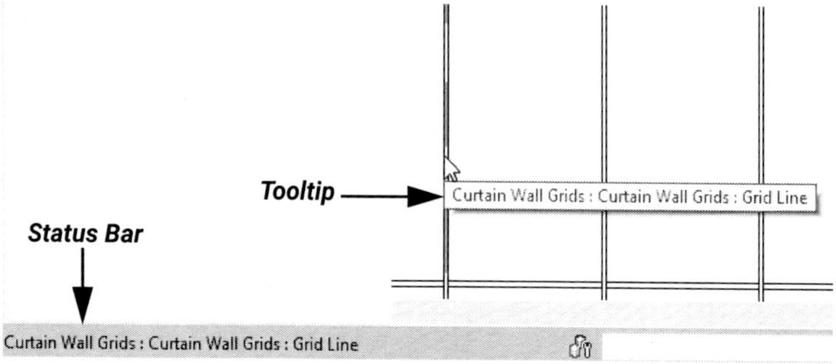

Figure 9–12

- To move a curtain wall grid line, select it and use dynamic dimensions or (Move).
- If you select a curtain wall grid line that was created using the **Curtain Wall** wall style, (Prevent or allow change of element position) is displayed, indicating that the element is constrained to a host element. Click the icon to enable you to move the line.

How To: Add or Remove Segments of Curtain Wall Grids

1. Select a curtain wall grid line to modify.
2. In the *Modify | Curtain Wall Grids* tab>*Curtain Grid* panel, click (Add/Remove Segments).
3. Click the part of the curtain wall grid that you want to add or remove. The line displays as dashed when you click to remove a segment, as shown in Figure 9–13. You must select curtain wall grid lines one at a time with this command.

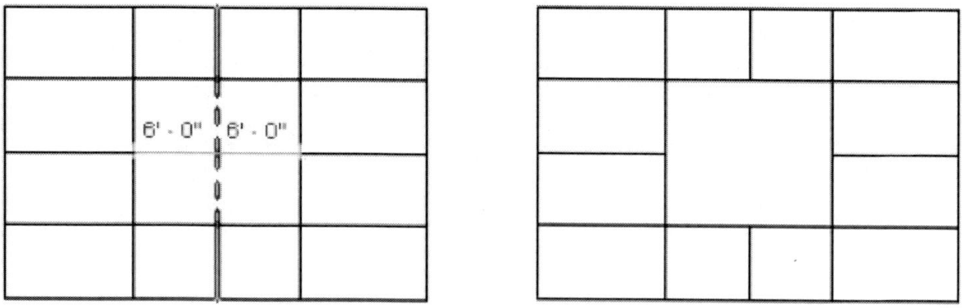

Figure 9–13

4. Click in an empty space in the drawing area to finish the command.

- You can create non-rectangular panels by removing individual curtain wall grid segments.

Hint: Aligning and Locking

When you use the **Align** command, you can also lock the lines together so if one moves, the other does as well. However, locking also causes the software to slow down. Therefore, be careful how much you use the **Lock** option and apply it only when you expect to make a lot of modifications.

Practice 9a
Work with Curtain Walls

Practice Objectives

- Modify curtain wall properties.
- Add curtain wall grid lines.

In this practice, you will modify a curtain wall using Properties to ensure that the lines match up with other elements. You will also add curtain wall grid lines that follow the pattern of a nearby wall. The finished elevation is shown in Figure 9–14.

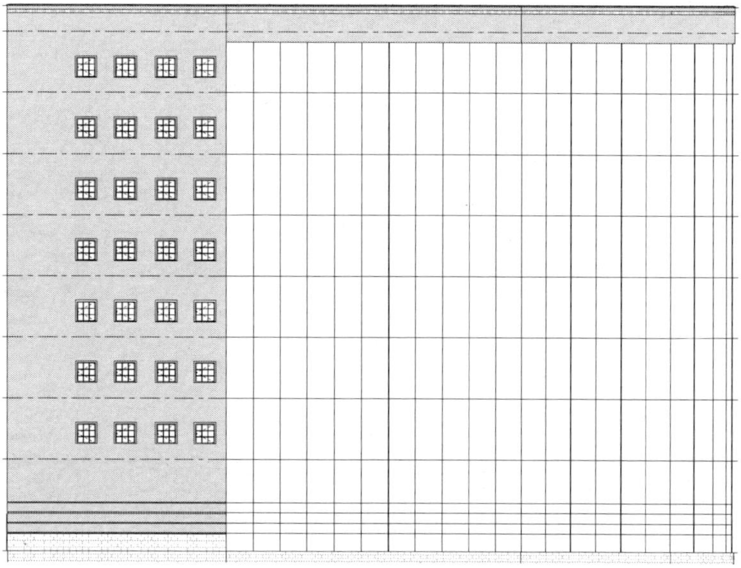

Figure 9–14

1. Open the project **Arch-CrtWall.rvt** from the practice files folder.
2. Verify you are in the **Elevations (Building Elevation): South** view.
3. In order to select the entire curtain wall, verify in the Status Bar that (Select Elements by Face) is toggled on (i.e., there is no red X over the icon).
4. To be able to see the brick reveals clearly, in the Quick Access Toolbar, toggle off (Thin Lines). When Thin Lines is on it is highlighted and looks like this: .
5. Select the entire curtain wall closest to the exterior brick wall, as shown outlined with dashed lines in Figure 9–15 (the curtain wall selection in the figure is exaggerated for clarity). Note that when you hover your cursor over a panel in a section of a curtain wall, the entire curtain wall boundary will highlight.

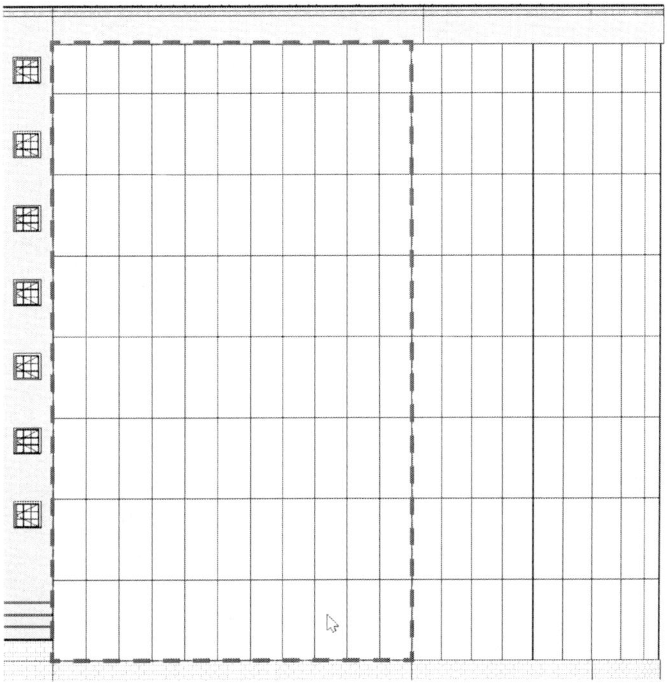

Figure 9–15

6. In Properties, in the *Horizontal Grid* section, change the *Offset* to **6'-0"**. Note that the curtain wall grid lines shift up and are now aligned with the levels.
7. Repeat Steps 5 and 6 for the second and third curtain walls.
8. Zoom in to the lower left of the building and ensure that the brick/CMU and the curtain wall are displayed. Press <Tab> to cycle through the curtain wall elements until you see the dashed line and the tooltip that displays *Curtain Wall Grids : Curtain Wall Grids : Grid Line*, as shown in Figure 9–16, and click it.

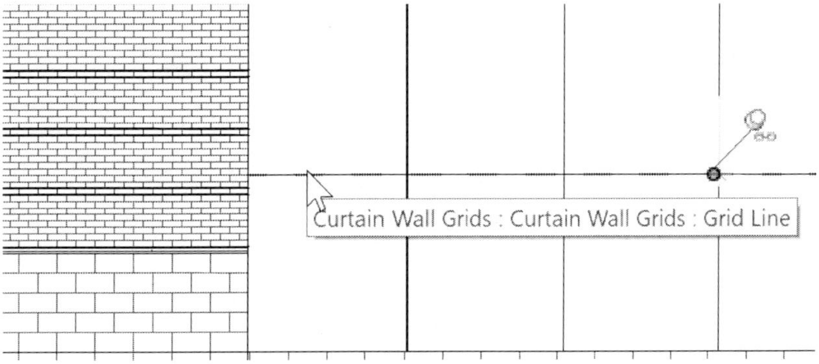

Figure 9–16

9. Along the curtain wall grid line, click (Prevent or allow change of element position) or type **UP** to unpin the curtain wall grid line. Alternatively, in the *Modify | Curtain Wall Grids* tab>*Modify* panel, select (Unpin).

   Note: *The curtain wall grid lines that get unpinned need to stay unpinned to maintain their new position.*

10. In the *Modify | Curtain Wall Grids* tab>*Modify* panel, click (Align), then verify that **Lock** is unchecked in the *Align* panel. Align the curtain wall grid line so it matches with the top of the CMU sill, as shown in Figure 9–17, by selecting the top of the CMU as the first pick and then the curtain wall grid as the second pick.

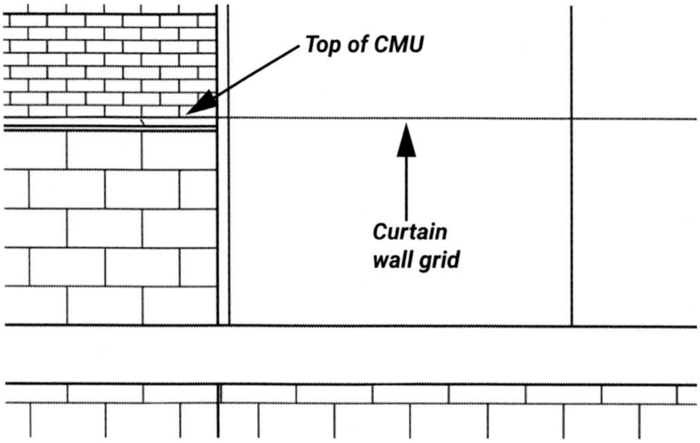

Figure 9–17

11. Click (Modify).
12. In the *Architecture* tab>*Build* panel, click (Curtain Grid). In the *Modify | Place Curtain Grid* tab>*Placement* panel, verify **All Segments** is selected.

13. Hover your cursor along the edge of the curtain wall and brick. When the curtain wall grid line displays horizontally, as shown in Figure 9–18, click to place the curtain wall grid.

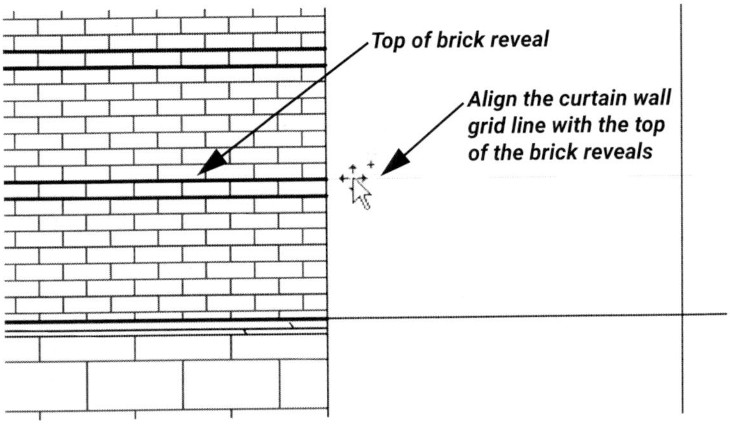

Figure 9–18

14. Add two more curtain wall grid lines and align them (if needed) with the top of the reveals in the brick, as shown in Figure 9–19.

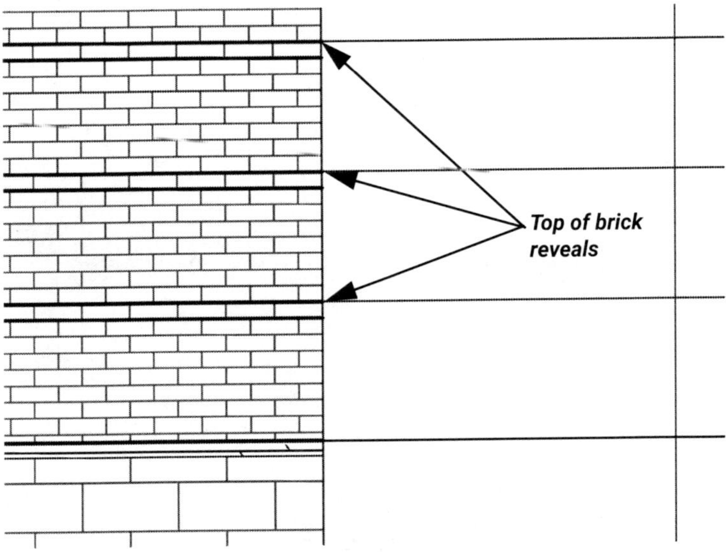

Figure 9–19

15. Click (Modify).
16. Select the four curtain wall grid lines (hold <Ctrl> and select each line individually).
    - Note: Properties will show **Curtain Wall Grids (4)** under the Type Selector.
17. In the *Modify | Curtain Wall Grids* tab>*Modify* panel, click (Move).

18. Click one of the curtain wall grid lines for the first selection point and move your cursor down. Type **1 1/4"** (make sure to add a space between 1 and 1/4 and type the inches symbol) and press <Enter>. Ensure that you move the cursor down before entering the move value. This places them correctly for the mullions, that are added later.

19. Click (Modify).

Pan over to the second curtain wall. Note that this curtain wall also needs three curtain wall grid lines and the fourth curtain wall grid line needs to be aligned.

20. Select the bottom curtain wall grid line and click (Prevent or allow change of element position) to unpin the curtain wall grid line, as shown in Figure 9–20.
21. With the curtain wall grid line still selected, in the contextual tab, start the (Align) tool.
22. Align the curtain wall grid lines by first selecting the bottommost curtain wall grid line on the left and then selecting the curtain wall grid line on the right.

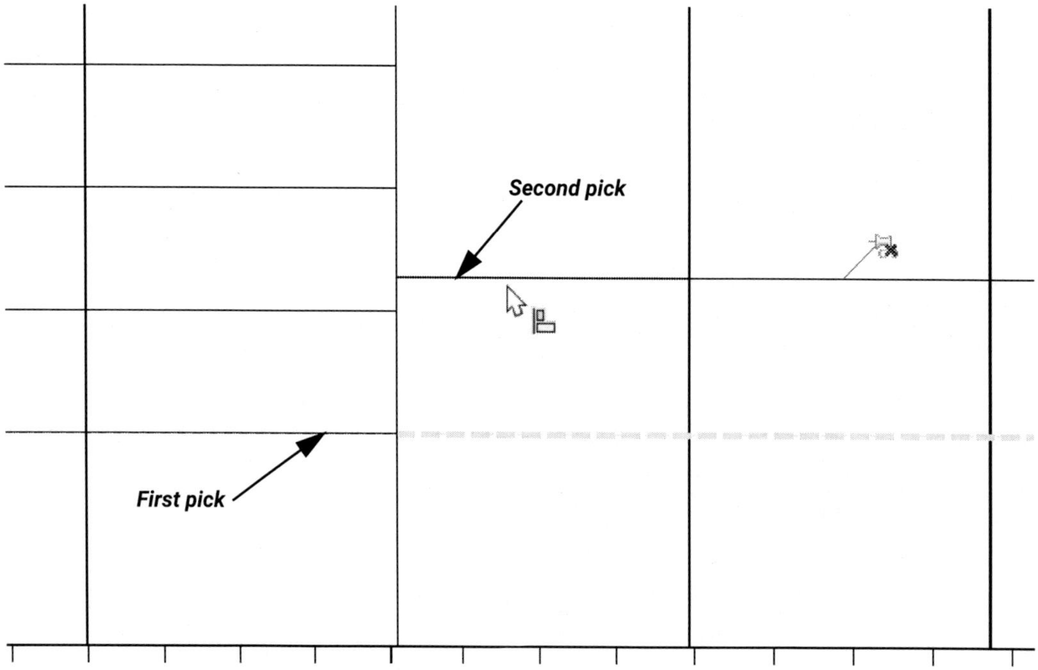

Figure 9–20

23. Click (Modify).

24. Pan over to the third curtain wall and note that its grid line is off, as shown in Figure 9–21. Unpin the grid line and use the **Align** tool to align it as well.

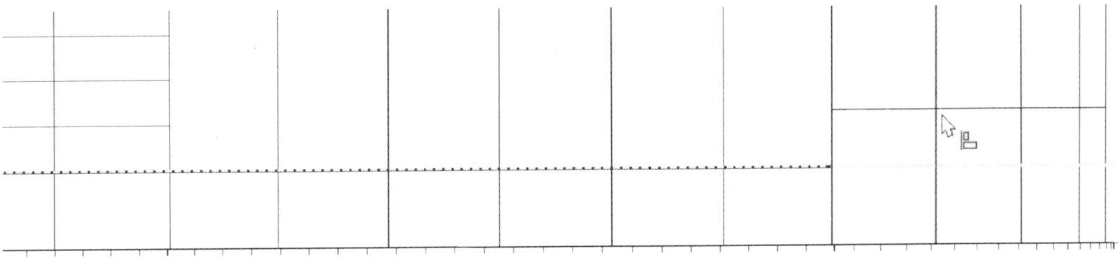

Figure 9–21

25. Click (Modify).
26. In the *Architecture* tab>*Build* panel, click (Curtain Grid) and add three horizontal curtain wall grid lines to the two curtain walls to match the first curtain wall, as shown in Figure 9–22 (the three grid lines have been darkened in the image for clarity).

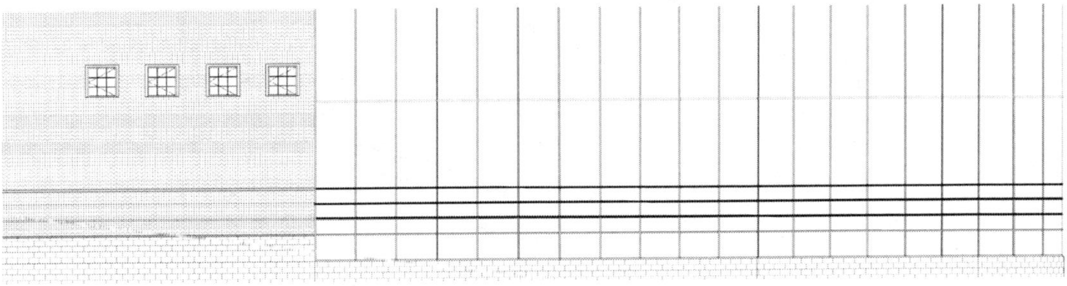

Figure 9–22

27. Zoom out until the entire front of the building is displayed.
28. Save and close the project.

End of practice

9.3 Working with Curtain Wall Panels

The default panel for a curtain wall is typically a glazed panel. As you create the curtain wall grid and refine the wall design, you might want to use other materials for some of the panels, as shown in Figure 9–23. You can select the existing panels and in the Type Selector, select a panel type with the material you want to use.

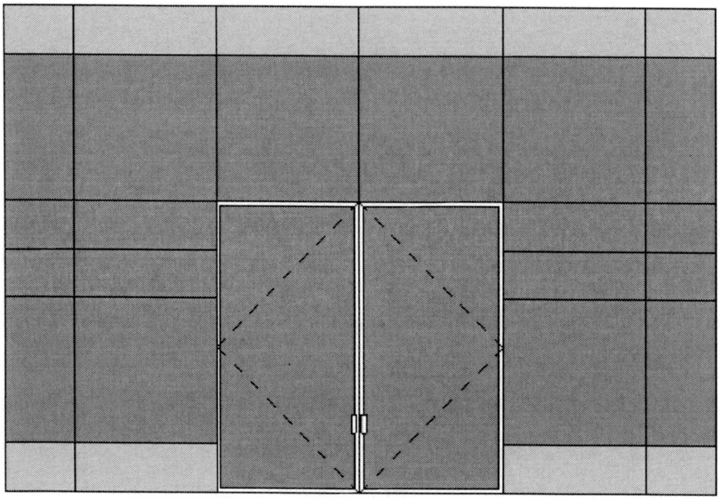

Figure 9–23

- Additionally, the panel type controls the thickness and can define a door or window for the panel.
- To select a panel, hover the cursor over its edge, press <Tab> until it highlights, and then click to select it.
- To select all of the panels, select the edge of the curtain wall, right-click, and select **Select Panels on Host.**
- If  (Prevent or allow change of element position) displays (as shown in Figure 9–24), it indicates that the panel is locked and that changes to the element are not permitted. Click the icon to toggle off the lock and modify the panel.

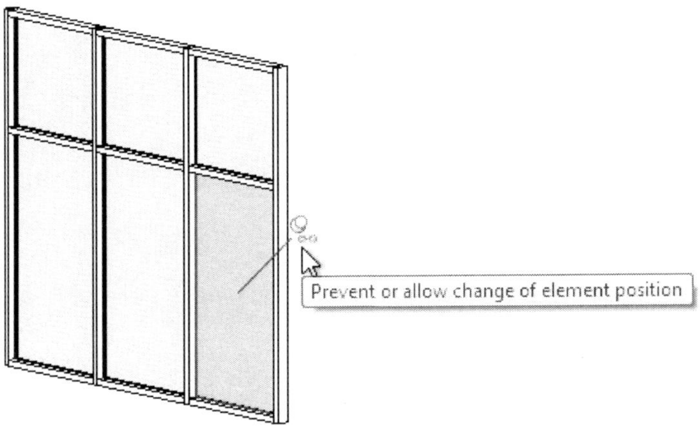

Figure 9–24

- To unpin multiple panels, select them and type **UP** (for **Unpin**).

Default Panel Types

Three panel types come with the default project template:

Empty Panel	You cannot delete a panel in a curtain wall, but you can change the panel type to an empty panel.
Glazed Panel	A typical panel type with glass as its material.
Solid Panel	A panel type using a solid material. You can create variations of this type with other materials.

- You can use any other wall type (including other curtain wall types) to fill in a panel.
- Door and window panels are available through the Revit Library. Similar to other panel types, door and window panels fill the size of the panel to which they are applied. Adjust the curtain wall grid for the correct sizes, as shown in Figure 9–25.

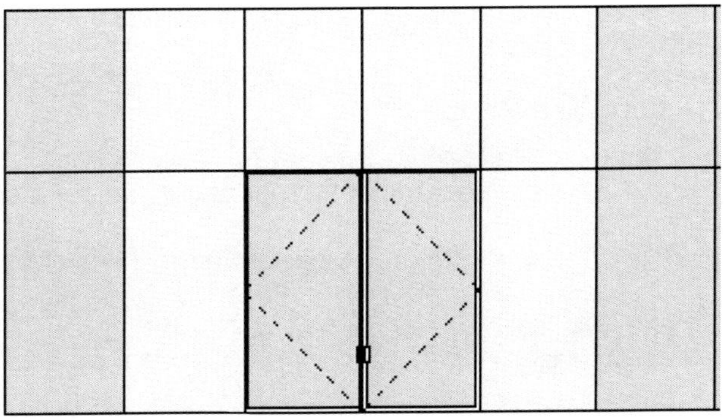

Figure 9–25

How To: Place Doors and Windows in Curtain Wall Panels

1. Load the door or window type that can be used as a curtain wall panel, such as **Door-Curtain-Wall-Double-Glass.rfa**.
2. Modify the curtain wall grid layout to ensure that the size of the opening in the curtain wall matches the size of the door you want to use.
3. Select the curtain wall panel.
4. In the Type Selector, select the type that you want to use as the panel.
5. The door or window fills the panel area.

Creating a Curtain Wall Panel

While you can create curtain wall panels in many complex ways, a basic technique is to specify a material for a flat system panel, as shown in Figure 9–26.

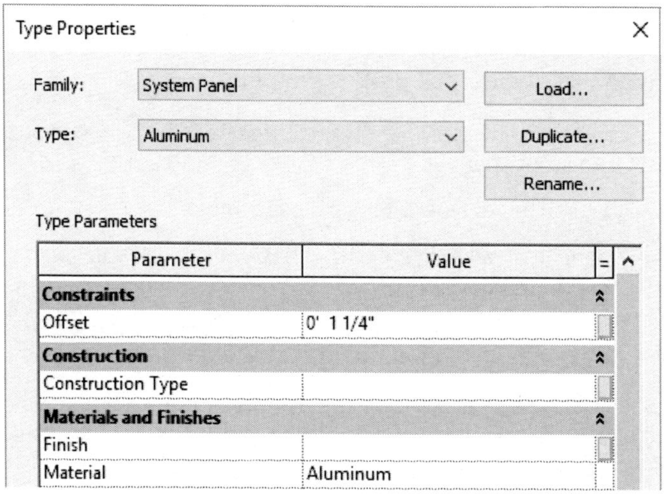

Figure 9–26

How To: Create a Curtain Wall Panel

1. Select a panel and use <Tab> to select the entire panel (i.e., select a solid panel to create a new solid panel type). If it is pinned, unpin it by clicking (Prevent or allow change of element position).
2. In Properties, click (Edit Type), or in the *Modify | Curtain Panels* tab>*Properties* panel, click (Type Properties).

3. In the *Type Properties* dialog box, click **Duplicate** to create a copy of the existing family type.
4. Give the panel a new name that describes its purpose (e.g., **Brick** or **Aluminum**). The new name automatically includes the family name, such as **System Panel**.
5. Set the *Thickness, Offset, Material,* and any other parameters as needed. Many materials are available in the Material Browser that opens when you click [...] (Browse)next to *Material*.
6. Click **OK** to close the dialog box and finish the panel. It is automatically applied to the panel you selected for modification.

- The *Thickness* of the material is centered on the curtain wall grid if you did not specify an *Offset*. If you want the panel to be recessed in the wall, use a negative offset. If you want the panel to stand out from the wall, use a positive offset.
- Materials with patterns, such as the brick shown in Figure 9–27, do not display the pattern when the view is zoomed out far. Zoom in to view the material.

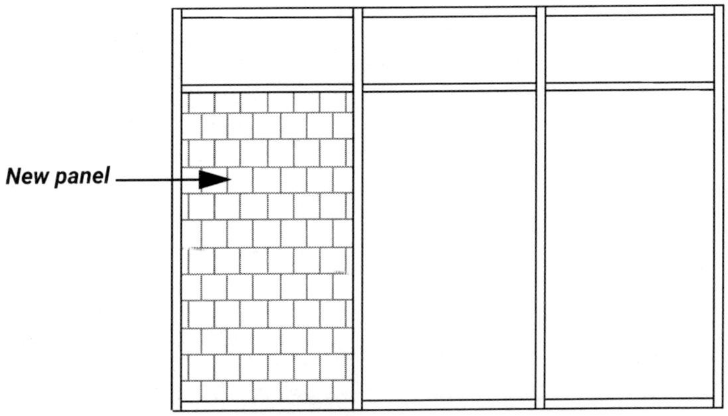

Figure 9–27

9.4 Attaching Mullions to Curtain Wall Grids

Mullions are the frameworks for curtain wall panels, as shown in Figure 9–28. They can be many sizes, shapes, and materials. Add them as the final step in your curtain wall design after you have placed the curtain wall grid lines.

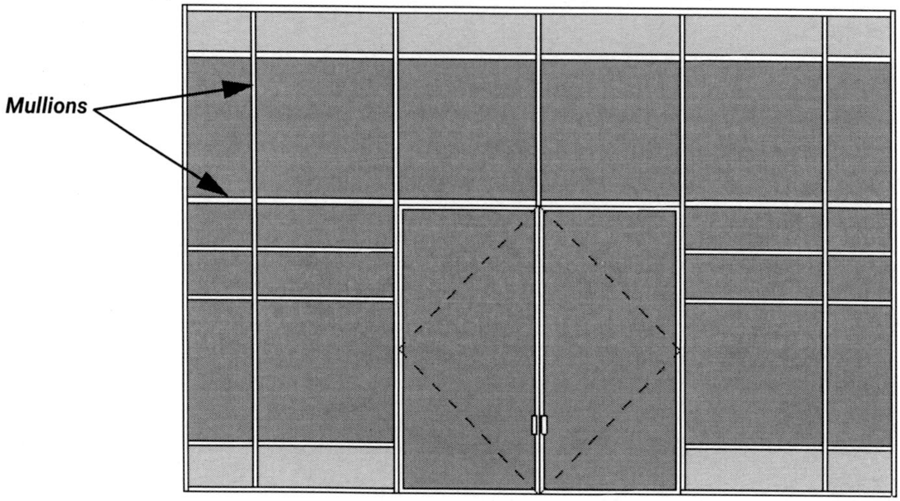

Figure 9–28

How To: Add Mullions

1. In the *Architecture* tab>*Build* panel, click (Mullion).
2. In the Type Selector, select the mullion style. There are no modifiable properties when you insert a mullion.
3. In the *Modify | Place Mullion* tab>*Placement* panel, select a *Create Mullion on* method: (Grid Line), (Grid Line Segment), or (All Grid Lines).
4. Select the curtain wall grid line on which you want to place the mullion. If the curtain wall grid line is inside a curtain wall, the mullion is placed on the curtain wall grid's center line. If it is on the edge of the wall, the mullion is placed so that its exterior is flush with the outside of the wall.

   Note: *Mullions must be placed individually; they cannot be copied or arrayed.*

   - Hold <Shift> to place a mullion only on the selected segment.
   - Hold <Ctrl> to place the mullion on all empty curtain wall grid segments (i.e., all without mullions).

- Corner mullion types are designed for the intersection of two curtain walls. They adjust to fit the angle of the intersection.

Modifying Mullions

To quickly select mullions, hover your cursor over a curtain wall or mullion, right-click, and select **Select Mullions**. The mullion options include **On Vertical Grid** or **On Horizontal Grid**, **Inner Mullions**, **Border Mullions**, or **Mullions on Host**, as shown in Figure 9–29.

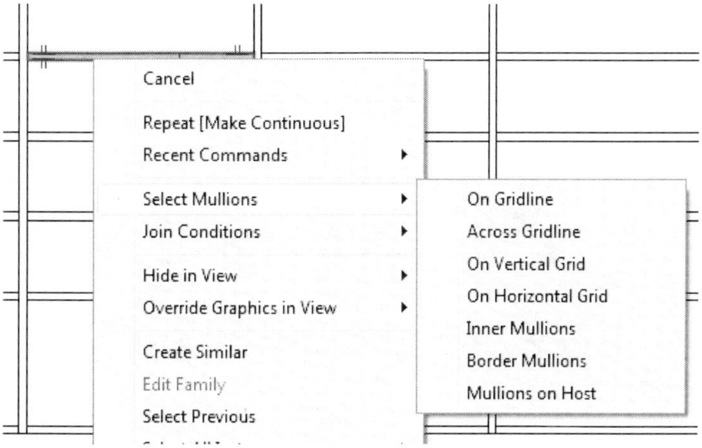

Figure 9–29

- Modify mullion styles by changing their type in the Type Selector.
- To move mullions, you need to hover your cursor over the mullion and use <Tab> to select the curtain wall grid, then move the curtain wall grid line and the mullions will move with it.
- If you delete a curtain wall grid line, the mullion is also deleted. However, if you delete a mullion, the curtain wall grid line is not deleted.
- You can change the way mullions intersect. Select the mullion and in the *Modify | Curtain Wall Mullions* tab>*Mullion* panel, click (Make Continuous) or (Break at Join). Alternatively, select the mullion and click the **Toggle Mullion Join** control, as shown in Figure 9–30.

Figure 9–30

Practice 9b
Add Mullions and Panels to Curtain Walls

Practice Objectives

- Add and modify mullions.
- Add a storefront entrance and door panel.

In this practice, you will add and modify mullions along the three curtain walls. You will also create a storefront that includes a door panel as the front entrance of the building. The finished elevation is shown in Figure 9–31.

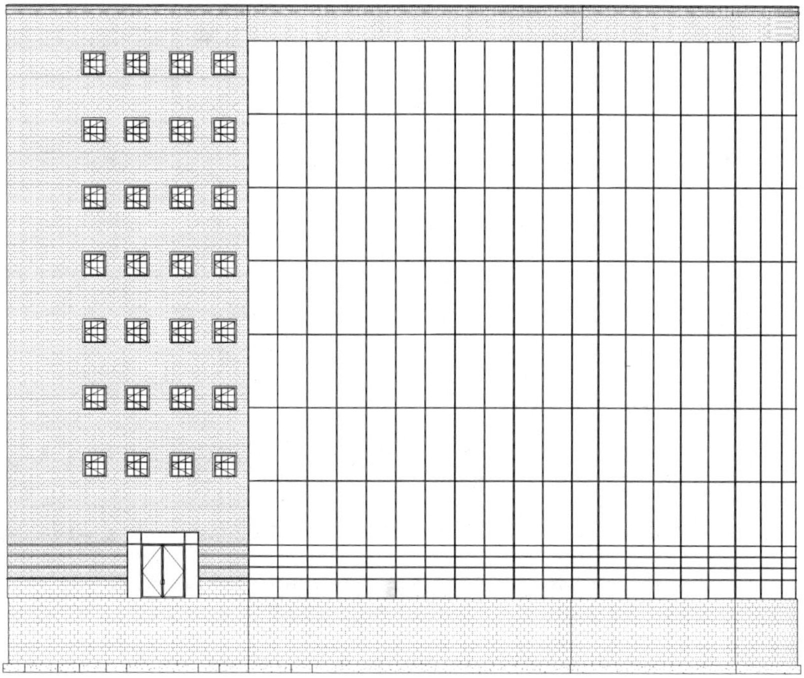

Figure 9–31

Task 1: Add and modify mullions.

1. Open the project **Arch-CrtMullions.rvt** from the practice files folder.
2. Verify that you are in the **Elevations (Building Elevations): South** view. Note that the levels have been hidden in the view.
3. Verify in the Status Bar that  (Select Elements by Face) is toggled on (i.e., there is no red X over the icon).

4. In the *Architecture* tab>*Build* panel, click (Mullion).
5. In the *Modify | Place Mullion* tab>*Placement* panel, click (All Grid Lines).
6. In the Type Selector, select **Rectangular Mullion: 2.5" x 5" rectangular**, if not already selected.
7. Select the first curtain wall. Mullions are placed on all of the curtain wall grid lines. If a warning message displays, read and ignore it. Repeat this process for the next two curtain walls.
8. Click (Modify).

Task 2: Modify mullions.

1. Zoom in to the bottom of the curtain wall where two curtain walls meet. Note that there are two mullions side by side, as shown in Figure 9–32, and the second mullion is not needed.

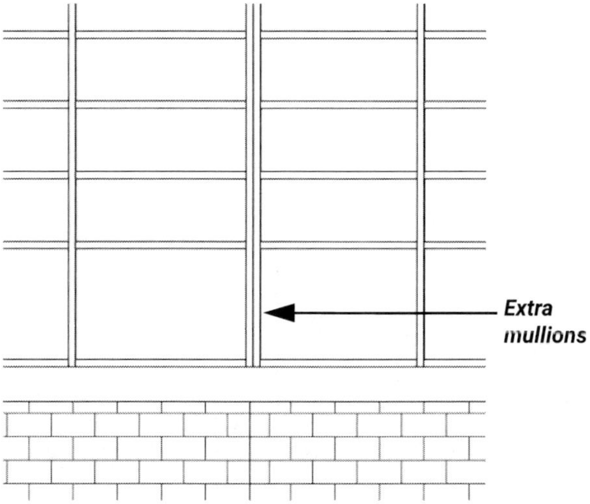

Figure 9–32

2. To make it easier to edit the mullions, select one of the mullions, then in the View Control Bar, click (Temporary Hide/Isolate) and select **Isolate Category**.
3. Click in an empty space in the view to clear the selection.
4. Select one of the vertical mullions where the two curtain walls meet. Right-click and select **Select Mullions>On Gridline**. All the mullions on the grid line are selected. Press <Delete>.
5. Pan over to where the next curtain walls meet and repeat the steps to delete the extra set of mullions.
6. Zoom out until you can see the bottom of all the curtain walls.

7. Draw a selection window (left to right) around the entire bottom row, so only the bottom row is selected, as shown in Figure 9–33.

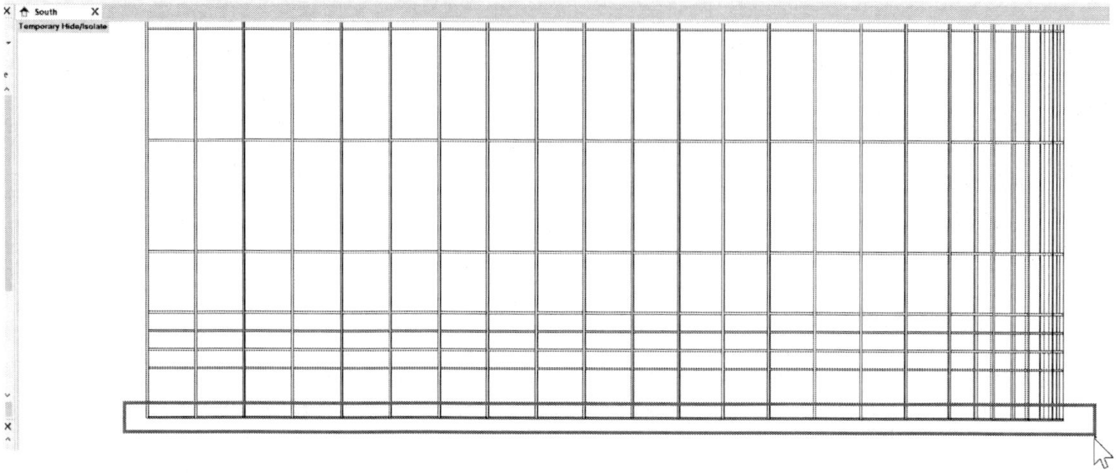

Figure 9–33

8. In the *Modify | Curtain Wall Mullions* tab>*Mullion* panel, click (Make Continuous). This changes how the mullions join, as shown in Figure 9–34. Note that there are two places where the mullions ignored the action.

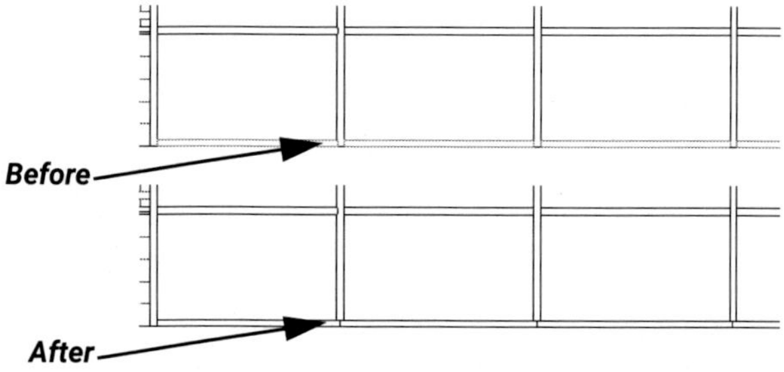

Figure 9–34

9. Click (Modify).

10. Zoom and pan along the bottom mullions to where the mullion ignored the **Make Continuous** command (the vertical mullion still extends past the bottom horizontal mullion). Select the horizontal mullion and click the **Toggle Mullion Join** icon, as shown in Figure 9–35. Pan to the next one and repeat the steps to join the mullions.

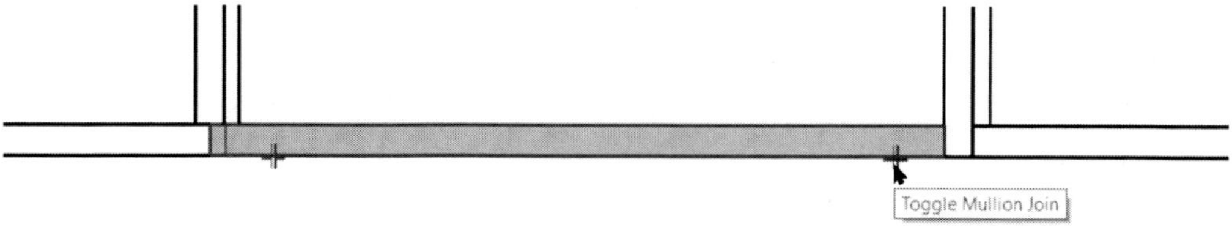

Figure 9–35

11. In the View Control Bar, click (Temporary Hide/Isolate) and select **Reset Temporary Hide/Isolate**.
12. Save the project.

Task 3: Add the storefront entrance.

1. Open the **Floor Plans: Floor 1** view.
2. Zoom to the lower-left exterior wall along grid 5C. You will add a storefront between grids 5C and 5D.
3. In the *Architecture* tab>*Build* panel, click (Wall).
4. In the Type Selector, select **Curtain Wall: Storefront**.
5. In Properties, verify or set the following values:
    - *Base Constraint:* **Floor 1**
    - *Base Offset:* **0'-0"**
    - *Top Constraint:* **Up to level: Floor 2**
    - *Top Offset:* (negative) **-6'-0"**
6. Working from right to left, draw the storefront **14'-6"** between grids 5C and 5D, along the existing wall's centerline. If needed, use temporary dimensions to shift the storefront so the edge is **1'-3"** off of the right column grid line, as shown in Figure 9–36.

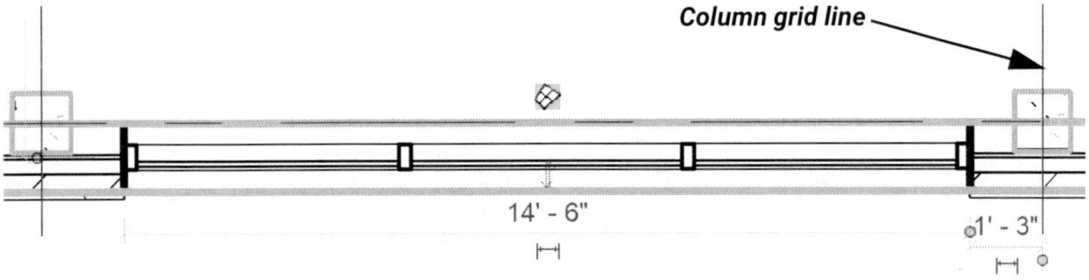

Figure 9–36

7. Click (Modify).
8. Click the *South* view tab to activate the view, then zoom in on the storefront.
9. In the Quick Access Toolbar, toggle on (Activate Controls and Dimensions).
10. In the lower-right corner of the Status Bar, click (Drag Elements on Selection) so the icon has a red X on it ( ).

11. With nothing selected, use a window selection (left to right) around the storefront to select the panels and mullions.

   - Because this curtain wall was created as a preset type, all of the curtain wall grids, mullions, and panels are pinned, as shown in Figure 9–37.

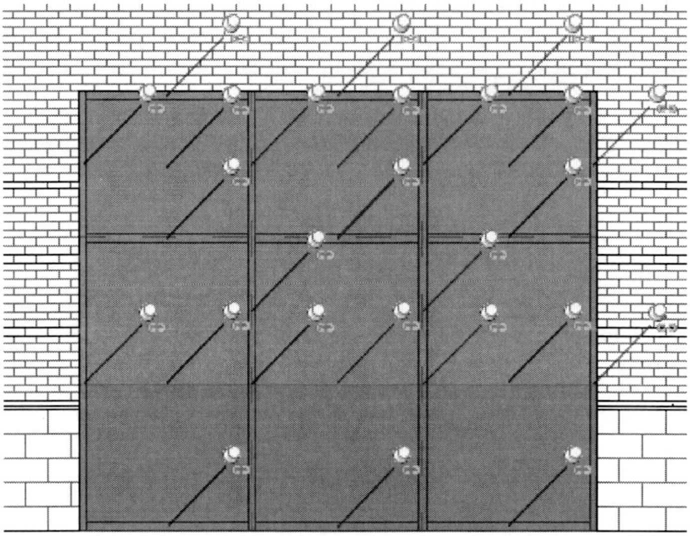

Figure 9–37

12. Type **UP** to unpin the elements, as shown in Figure 9–38.

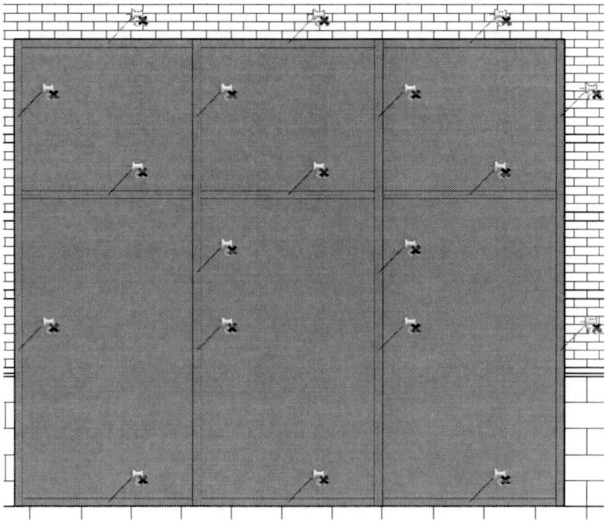

Figure 9–38

13. Click (Modify).

14. Modify the storefront, as shown in Figure 9–39, by starting the **Align** tool and aligning the horizontal storefront curtain wall grid line with the curtain wall grid line in the main curtain wall (shown in Figure 9–39).

    Note: *When aligning, the first pick is the reference or point for alignment. The second pick is what you want to align or move into alignment with the reference.*

15. Click (Modify).
16. Select the vertical curtain wall grid lines by pressing <Tab> to cycle through the elements and use temporary dimensions to make the two outer panels **3'-0"**. This will make the center panel **8'-6"**, as shown in Figure 9–39.

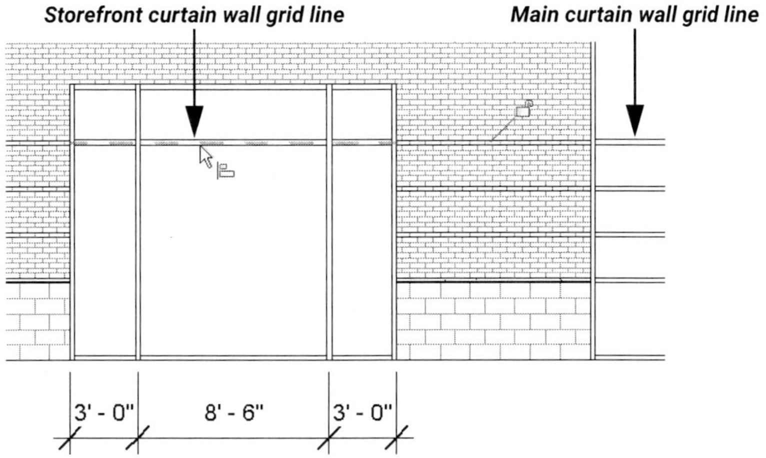

Figure 9–39

17. Click (Modify).

18. Select the three horizontal mullions at the top of the storefront, as shown on the top in Figure 9–40, then in the *Modify | Curtain Wall Mullions* tab>*Mullion* panel, click (Make Continuous) so that the mullion runs straight across, as shown on the bottom.

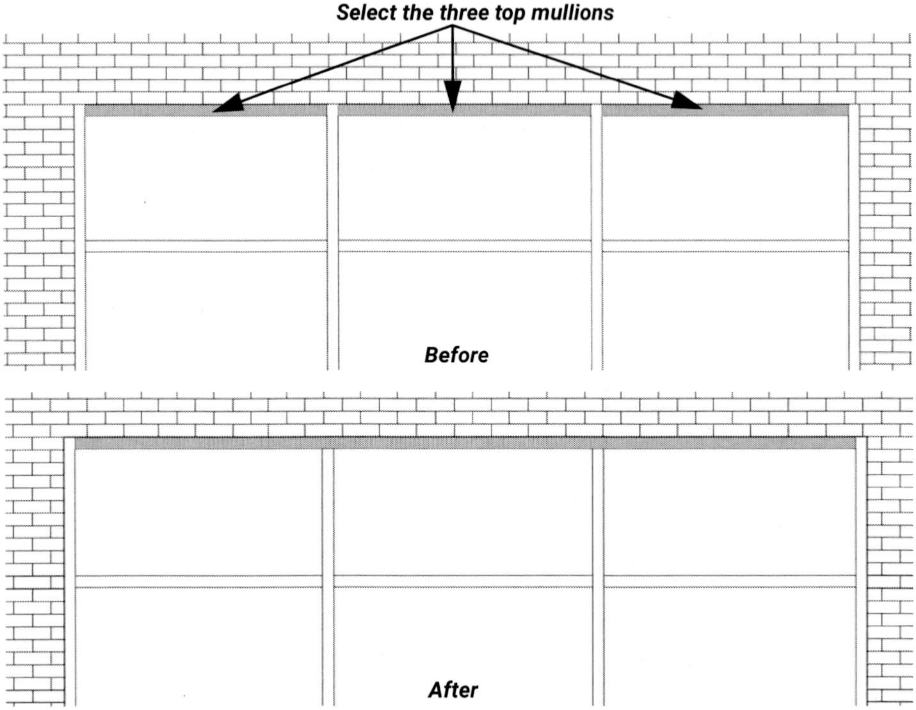

Figure 9–40

19. Click (Modify).

20. Save the project.

Task 4: Add a door in the storefront.

1. In the *Insert* tab>*Load from Library* panel, click (Load Family).
2. In the *Load Family* dialog box, navigate to the practice files *Families>Doors* folder, select **Door-Curtain-Wall-Double-Storefront.rfa**, and click **Open**.
3. Select the large panel, as shown in Figure 9–41. (Use <Tab> to cycle through the selections, then click to select it.)

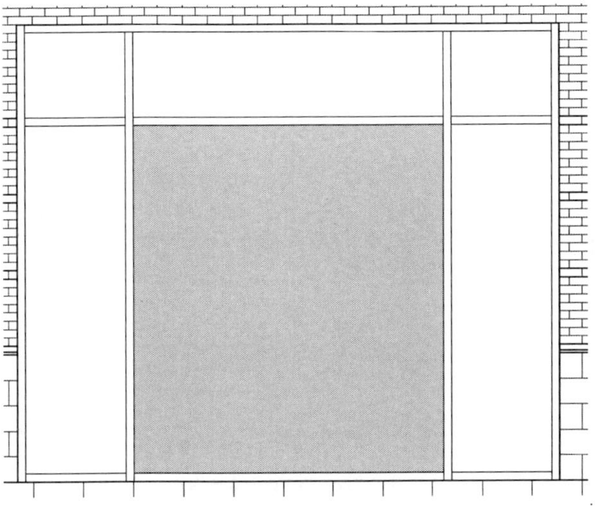

Figure 9–41

4. In the Type Selector, select **Door-Curtain-Wall-Double-Storefront**. The panel changes to the door.
5. Click (Modify).

6. Below the door, select the mullion (as shown in Figure 9–42) and press <Delete>.
   - If you cannot delete the mullion, select it and verify that it is unpinned.

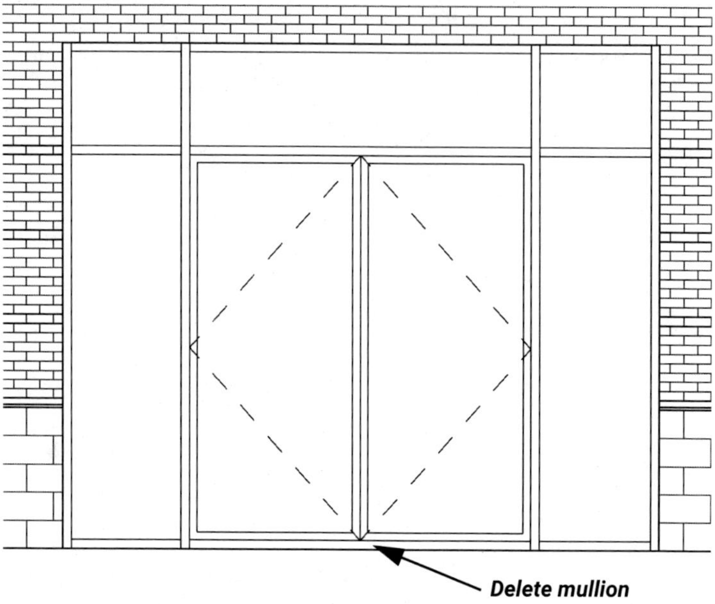

Figure 9–42

7. Change the *Detail Level* to **Fine** to see the door handles.
8. Zoom out until the entire front elevation is displayed.
9. View the project in 3D.
10. Save and close the project.

End of practice

Chapter Review Questions

1. Which command do you start with to create a curtain wall?

    a.  (Wall)

    b.  (Curtain Grid)

    c.  (Curtain System)

2. You are placing a curtain wall grid and it keeps snapping to one dimension, such as the TWO-THIRDS OF CURTAIN PANEL shown in Figure 9–43, when you want it to be another. What should you do?

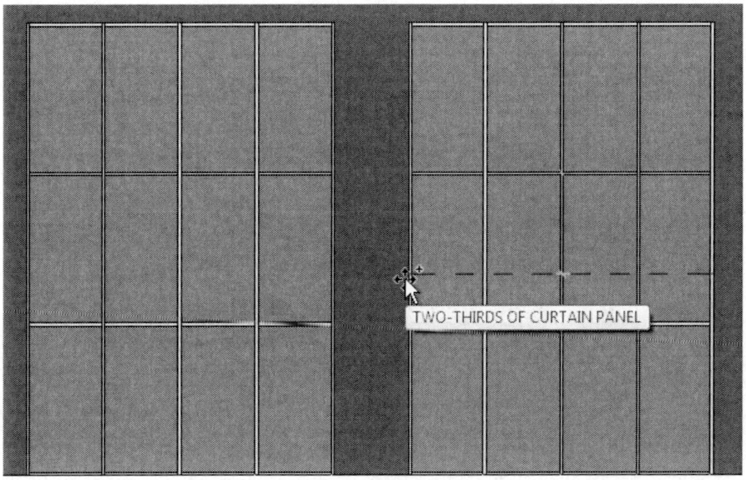

Figure 9–43

    a. Change the snap settings.
    b. Edit the curtain wall type to permit manual curtain wall grid placement.
    c. Use a non-uniform curtain wall type instead of a uniform one.
    d. Place the curtain wall grid anyway, select the temporary dimension, and change it to the required value.

3. How do you select one panel to modify it?

a. Select the middle of the panel.

b. Hover your cursor over the edge of the panel and press <Tab> until its boundary highlights, then click to select it.

c. Select the curtain wall, right-click, and select **Panel Select**.

d. In the *Selection Priority* drop-down list, select **Curtain Panel**.

4. Once you select a panel, what can you swap it for? (Select all that apply.)

a. Empty system panel

b. Storefront door

c. Blank panel

d. Wall type

5. How do you change the way in which two mullions intersect, as shown in Figure 9–44? (Select all that apply.)

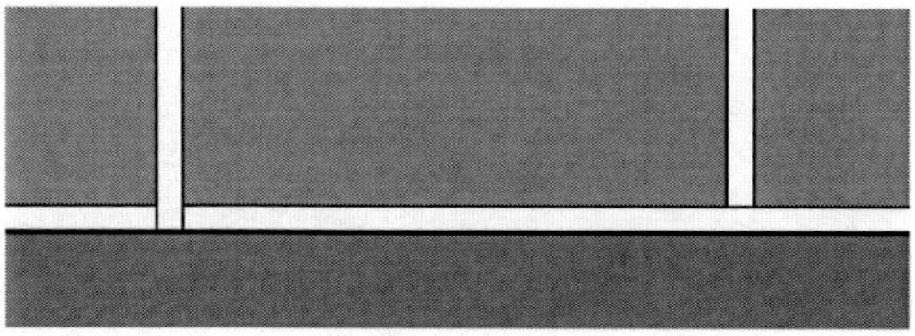

Figure 9–44

a. Select one of the mullions and press <Tab> until the correct intersection displays.

b. Select one of the mullions and click **Make Continuous** or **Break at Join** in the contextual tab.

c. Select one of the mullions and click the **Toggle Mullion Join** control.

d. Select both mullions and select the **Intersect** box in the contextual tab.

Command Summary

Button	Command	Location
	**Add/Remove Segments**	• **Ribbon:** *Modify | Curtain Wall Grids* tab>*Curtain Grid* panel
	**Curtain Grid**	• **Ribbon:** *Architecture* tab>*Build* panel
	**Curtain Grid: All Except Picked**	• **Ribbon:** *Modify | Place Curtain Grid* tab>*Placement* panel
	**Curtain Grid: All Segments**	• **Ribbon:** *Modify | Place Curtain Grid* tab>*Placement* panel
	**Curtain Grid: One Segment**	• **Ribbon:** *Modify | Place Curtain Grid* tab>*Placement* panel
	**Mullion**	• **Ribbon:** *Architecture* tab>*Build* panel
	**Mullion: All Grid Lines**	• **Ribbon:** *Modify | Place Mullion* tab>*Placement* panel
	**Mullion: Break at Join**	• **Ribbon:** *Modify | Curtain Wall Mullions* tab>*Mullion* panel • **Right-click:** (with mullion selected) Join Conditions> Break at Join
	**Mullion: Grid Line**	• **Ribbon:** *Modify | Place Mullion* tab>*Placement* panel
	**Mullion: Grid Line Segment**	• **Ribbon:** *Modify | Place Mullion* tab>*Placement* panel
	**Mullion: Make Continuous**	• **Ribbon:** *Modify | Curtain Wall Mullions* tab>*Mullion* panel • **Right-click:** (with mullion selected) Join Conditions> Make Continuous

Chapter

10

Modeling Floors

Floors in Revit® can be used as full depth floors or as a thin veneer that shows floor material placed on an underlying floor. You can customize floors by creating slopes for drainage, cutting holes, or creating shafts that cut through multiple floors. Adding floors and applying materials adds to the aesthetics of a floor plan layout.

Learning Objectives

- Sketch and modify floor boundaries.
- Join geometry between floors and walls for a cleaner visual presentation.
- Add a shaft opening that cuts through multiple floors.
- Slope a floor in one or more directions for drainage.

10.1 Modeling Floors

The **Floor** command can generate any flat or sloped surface, such as floors, patios, decks, and balconies, as shown in Figure 10–1. Typically created in a plan view, the floor can be based either on bounding walls or on a sketched outline.

Figure 10–1

- Floors are a system family component that can contain several different types within the style. The floor type controls the thickness of a floor.
- You can model the floor finish on top of the linked architectural or structural floor, or floors can be copy/monitored from a linked Revit model.
- Floors can be placed on top of floors. For example, a structural floor can have a finish floor of tile or carpet placed on top of it, as shown in Figure 10–2. These floors can then be scheduled separately.

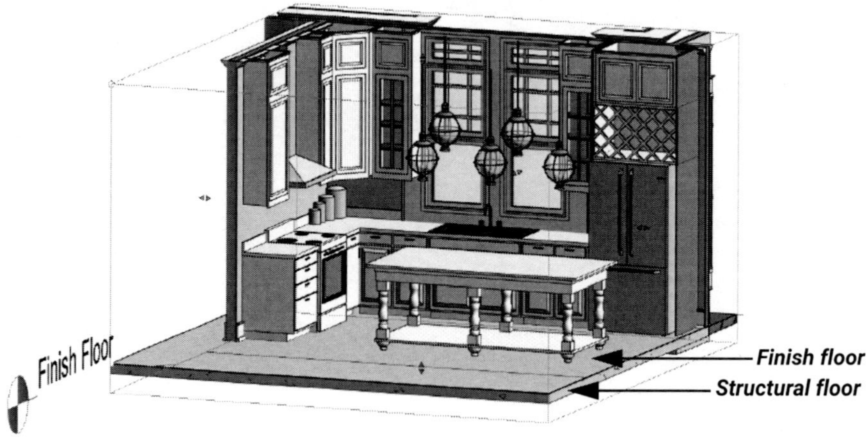

Figure 10–2

How To: Add a Floor

1. In the *Architecture* tab>*Build* panel, expand (Floor) and click (Floor: Architectural) or (Floor: Structural). You are placed in sketch mode where other elements in the model are grayed out.
2. In the Type Selector, set the type of floor you want to use. In Properties, set any constraints as needed.
3. In the *Modify | Create Floor Boundary* tab>*Draw* panel, click (Boundary Line).

   Note: *The lines in the sketch must form a closed loop. Use tools in the Modify panel to adjust intersections.*

   - Click (Pick Walls) and select the walls, setting either the inside or outside edge. If you have selected a wall, you can click (Flip) to switch the inside/outside status of the boundary location, as shown in Figure 10–3.
   - Click (Line) or one of the other sketch tools and sketch the boundary edges.
   - Use the modify tools to align, move, or trim the boundary lines.
4. Click (Slope Arrow) to define a slope for the entire floor.
5. Click (Span Direction), as shown in Figure 10–3, to modify the direction of the structural elements in the floor.

   Note: *The span direction is automatically placed on the first sketch line.*

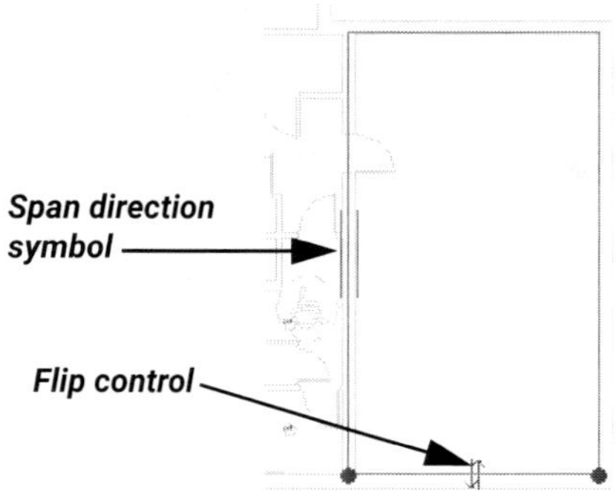

Figure 10–3

6. Click (Finish Edit Mode) to create the floor.

- If your floor boundary lines are not enclosed correctly, an error that cannot be dismissed will be shown. Two error messages are illustrated in Figure 10–4 to indicate floor boundary line issues. The problematic floor boundary lines will be highlighted in orange within the drawing area. Click **Continue** to resolve the issues using the modify tools.

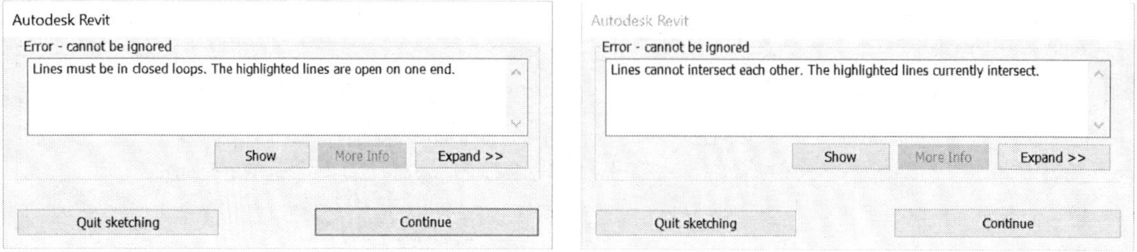

Figure 10–4

- If you create a floor on an upper level, an alert box displays asking if you want the walls below to be attached to the underside of the floor and its level, as shown in Figure 10–5. If you have a variety of wall heights, it is better to click **Don't attach** and attach the walls separately.

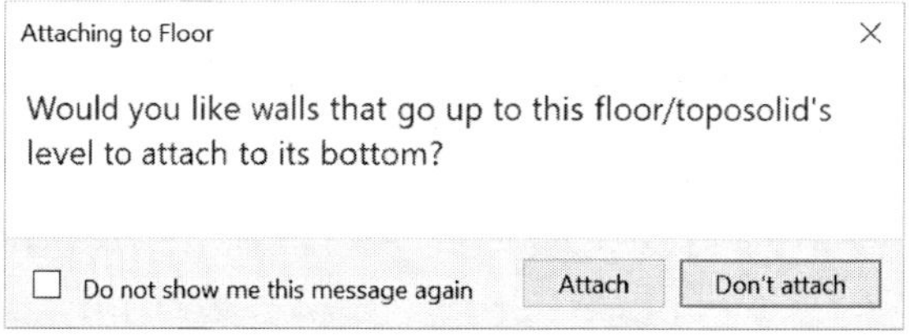

Figure 10–5

- Another alert box might open, as shown in Figure 10–6. You can automatically join the geometry by clicking **Yes** or you can do so at a later time.

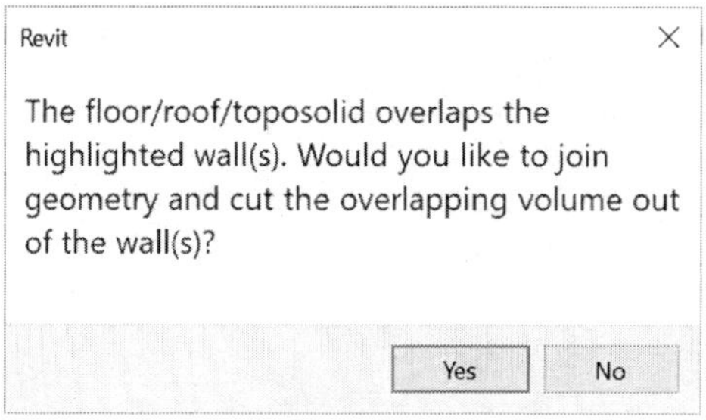

Figure 10–6

Options While in the Floor Command

- If you are using (Pick Walls), select (Extend Into Wall) in the *Set Offset* panel if you want the floor to cut into the wall. For example, the floor would cut through the gypsum wall board and the air space but stop at a core layer such as CMU.
- If you select one or more of the boundary sketch lines, you can also set the *Concrete Cantilever* or *Steel Cantilever* in the *Other* section in Properties. (You will need to click (Modify) first before selecting a boundary sketch line to access these properties.)
- To create an opening inside the floor, create a separate closed loop inside the first one, as shown in Figure 10–7.

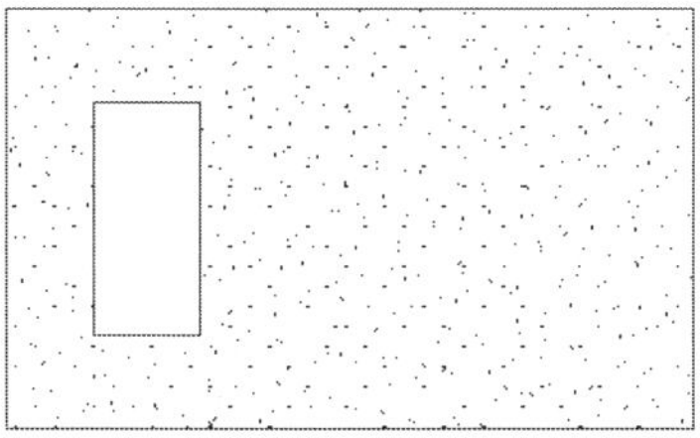

Figure 10–7

Hint: Sketched Arcs and Tangent Lock

If you are adding arcs or ellipses to a sketch that are tangent to other lines, you can lock the geometry in place by clicking the tangency lock (Toggle Join Tangency), as shown in Figure 10–8.

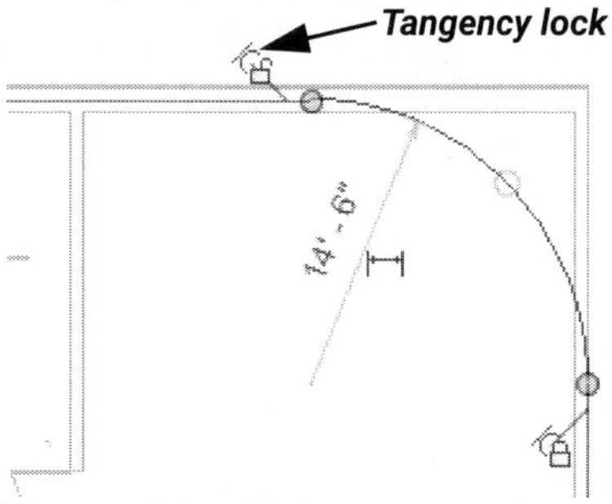

Figure 10–8

- This lock is available whenever you are in sketch mode.

Modifying Floors

You can change a floor to a different type by selecting the floor and changing the type in the Type Selector. In Properties, you can modify parameters including the *Height Offset From Level*, as shown in Figure 10–9. When you have a floor selected, you can also edit the boundaries.

> ***Note:** Many of the parameters in Properties are used in schedules, including Elevation at Top/Bottom and Elevation at Top/Bottom Core for multi-layered floors.*

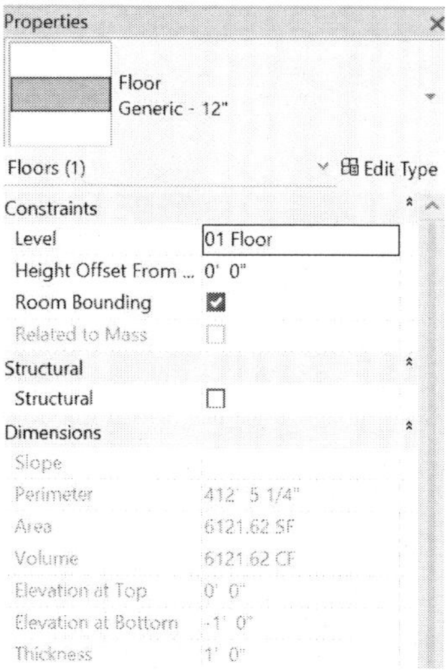

Figure 10–9

How To: Modify the Floor Sketch

1. Select a floor. You might need to hover your cursor over an element near the floor and press <Tab> until the floor type displays in the Status Bar or in a tooltip, as shown in Figure 10–10.

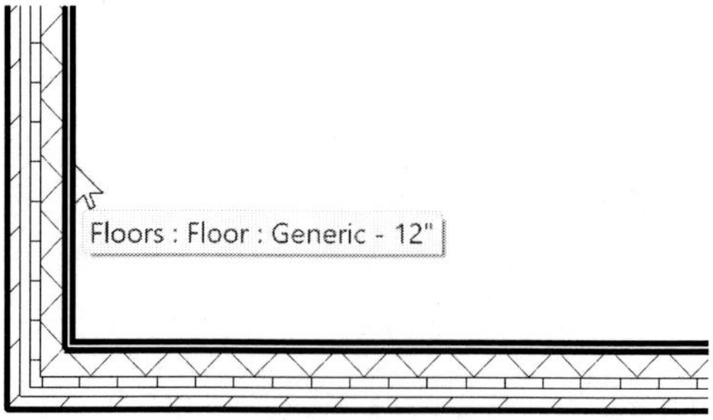

Figure 10–10

2. In the *Modify | Floors* tab>*Mode* panel, click (Edit Boundary). You are placed into Edit Boundary mode.
   - Alternatively, select a floor, then double-click on it to be placed directly into Edit Boundary mode.
3. Modify the sketch lines using the sketch tools, controls, and the various modify tools.
4. Click (Finish Edit Mode).

- Floor sketches can be edited in plan and 3D views, but not in elevations. If you try to edit in an elevation view, you are prompted to select another view in which to edit.

Hint: Selecting Floor Faces

If it is difficult to select the floor edges, toggle on (Select Elements by Face) in the Status Bar. This will enable you to select the floor face and not just the edges.

How To: Attach Walls to the Floor

1. Select the wall or walls that you want to attach to the floor.
2. In the *Modify | Walls* tab>*Modify Wall* panel, expand (Attach Top) and select either (Attach Top) or (Attach Base), as shown in Figure 10–11.

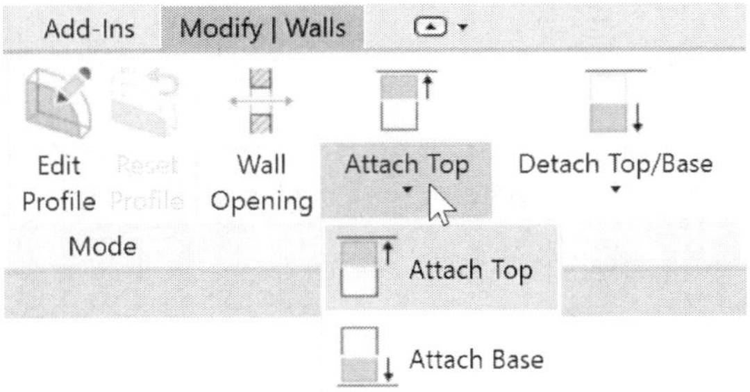

Figure 10–11

3. Select the floor. The wall will now be attached to the floor. If there are any changes to the floor's level or height offset from level, the wall's base level will adjust accordingly within the constraints.

Joining Geometry

Join Geometry is a versatile command used to clean up intersections. The elements remain separate, but the intersections are cleaned up. It can be used with many types of elements, including floors, walls, and roofs. In Figure 10–12, the wall on the left has not been joined with the floor and therefore the wall's layers are not cleaned up based on the floor's boundary. The wall and floor on the right have been joined

Note: *Cutting a section through the objects you want to join helps to display them more clearly.*

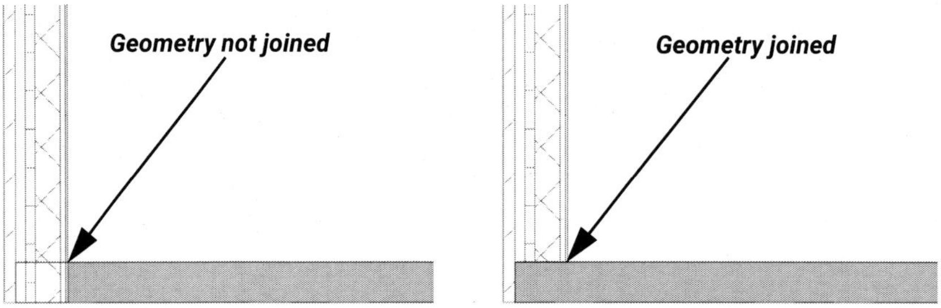

Figure 10–12

How To: Join Geometry

1. In the *Modify* tab>*Geometry* panel, expand (Join) and click (Join Geometry).
2. Select the elements to join.
    - If you toggle on the (Multiple Selection) option in the *Modify | Join Geometry* tab> *Multiple Selection* panel, you can select several elements to join to the first selection.

- To remove the join, expand (Join), click (Unjoin Geometry), and select the elements to unjoin them.

Hint: Selection Sets

If there are elements in the model that you know you will need to select multiple times, you can create a selection set by selecting all the elements in the view and in the contextual tab> *Selection* panel, selecting (Save). When you need to select that group of elements again, in the *Manage* tab>*Selection* panel, click (Load). Once a selection set is created, you have to ability to select (Edit) to edit the selection.

- To switch the join order, expand  (Join), click  (Switch Join Order), and select the elements to switch the join order, as shown in Figure 10–13.

Figure 10–13

Practice 10a
Model Floors

Practice Objectives

- Add floors.
- Copy a floor to multiple levels.

In this practice, you will create and modify floors in the basement, first floor, and second floor of a project. You will then copy the floor on the second floor to other related levels and clean up connections between the floors and wall. The completed practice for the second floor with balconies is shown in Figure 10–14.

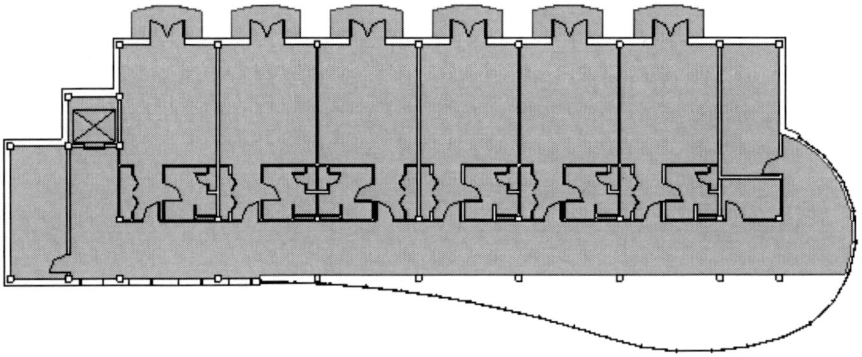

Figure 10–14

Task 1: Add the basement floor.

1. Open the project **Arch-Floors.rvt** from the practice files folder.

   Note: *More components have been added to this file and may differ from what you added in the previous practice.*

2. Open the **Floor Plans: Basement** view.
3. In the View Control Bar, click (Hide Crop Region).
4. In Properties, in the *Underlay* section, change the *Range: Base Level* to **Floor 2** and *Range: Top Level* to **Unbounded**. This allows you to see the levels above.
5. In the *Architecture* tab>*Build* panel, click (Floor).
6. In the Type Selector, select **Floor: Concrete-1'-0"**.
7. In Properties, set the *Height Offset From Level* to **0'-0"**.

8. In the *Modify | Create Floor Boundary* tab>*Draw* panel, click (Pick Walls) and select the inside face of the exterior foundation walls. Use the modify tools to ensure that the boundary is a closed loop.
9. Click (Finish Edit Mode).
10. When the alert box about joining geometry opens, click **Yes**. The floor pattern displays as shown in Figure 10–15.

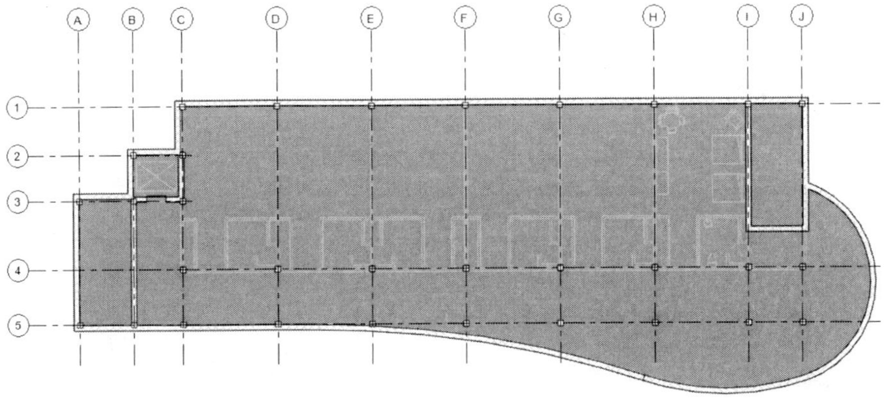

Figure 10–15

11. Click in an empty space in the view to release the floor selection.
12. Start the **Floor** command again. Hint: Press <Enter> to repeat the last command.
13. In the Type Selector, select **Floor: Tile**. In Properties, set the *Height Offset From Level* to **1/4"** to match the thickness of the tile.
14. Draw the boundary around the stairwells and hallway, as shown in Figure 10–16.

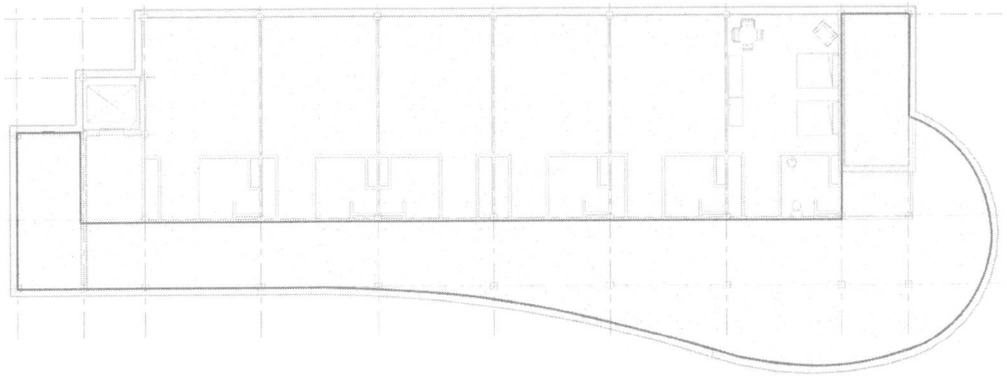

Figure 10–16

15. Click (Finish Edit Mode).

16. If prompted to join overlapping geometry, click **Yes**.

    Note: *If an error appears that cannot be dismissed, the floor boundary lines that either intersect or fail to form a closed loop will be highlighted in orange. To address this, select* ***Continue*** *to resolve the issue with the floor boundary lines, and then click* ***Finish Edit Mode****.*

17. Click in an empty space in the view to release the selection, then zoom in to the west stairs to display the different floorings, as shown in Figure 10–17.

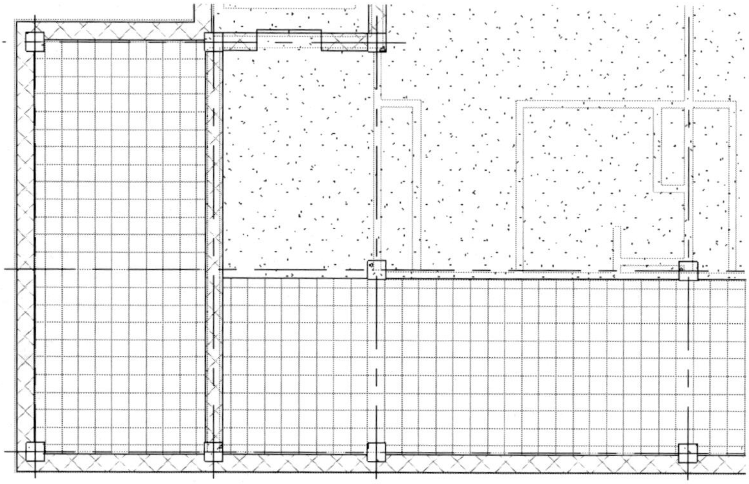

Figure 10–17

18. Double-click on the tile flooring to start Edit Boundary mode, then select and drag the sketch boundary line or align it to the face of the wall (shown in Figure 10–18) so it includes the hall that leads to the elevator.

Figure 10–18

19. Click (Finish Edit Mode).
    - If prompted to join overlapping geometry, click **Yes**.
20. Save the project.

Task 2: Add the second floor and balconies.

1. Open the **Floor Plans: Floor 2** view.
2. In the View Control Bar, click (Reveal Hidden Elements).
3. Select the DWG by selecting on the DWG's note. In the *Modify | Hotel-Level-2.dwg* tab> *Reveal Hidden Elements* panel, click (Unhide Category).
4. In the *Reveal Hidden Elements* panel, click (Toggle Reveal Hidden Elements Mode).
5. In the View Control Bar, click (Hide Crop Region) to hide the crop region in the view.
6. Select a door tag and a room tag, and type **VH** to hide them in the view.
7. In the *Architecture* tab>*Build* panel, click (Floor).
8. In Properties, select **Floor: Generic - 12"** in the Type Selector and set the *Height Offset From Level* to **0'-0"**.

9. In the *Modify | Create Floor Boundary* tab>*Set Offset* panel, verify that (Extend Into Wall) is toggled on and that the (Offset) is **0'-0"**.

10. Use (Pick Walls) and select the inside of the main exterior walls. Do not select the three curved curtain walls.

11. Change to (Pick Lines) and select the lines of the hallway in the linked CAD (DWG) file, as shown in Figure 10–19.

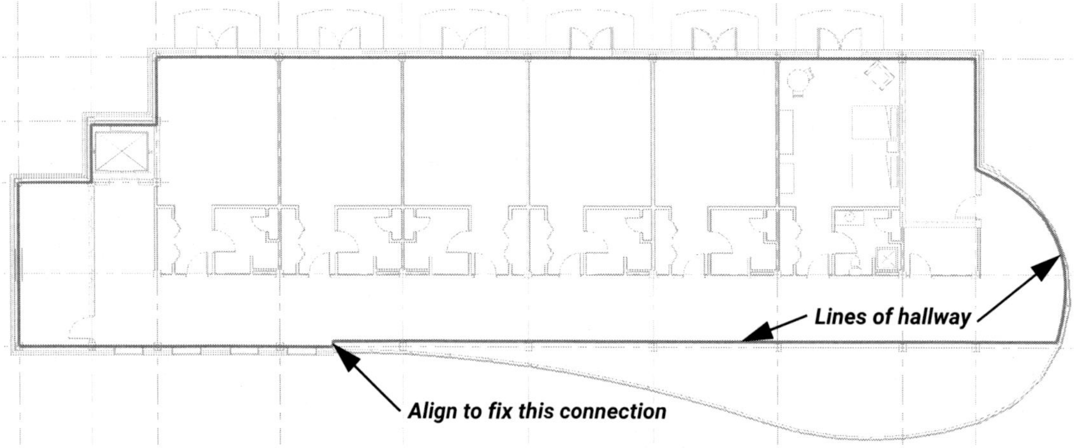

Figure 10–19

12. Zoom in and fix the connection at the front wall and hallway. Delete the vertical line. Use the **Align** tool to align the hallway line to the front wall line, as shown in Figure 10–20, and check the other connections.

Note: *For accuracy, you need to modify the floor in Revit even though the linked CAD file (DWG) has the floor jogged out.*

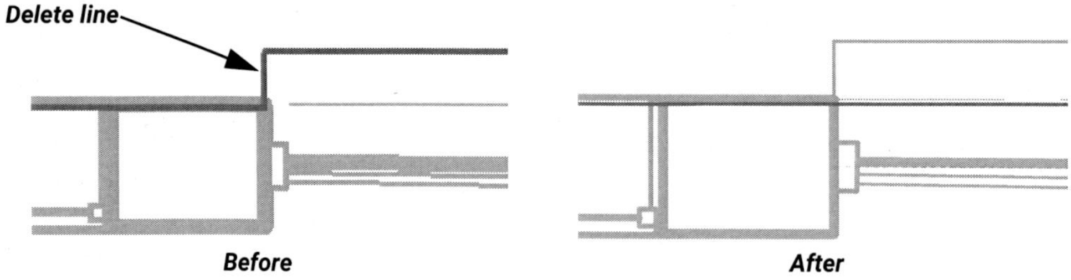

Figure 10–20

13. Click (Finish Edit Mode).

- If the *Attaching to Floor* alert box displays, click **Don't attach**. You do not want to attach the walls to this floor.
- If the Revit alert box about joining geometry displays, click **Yes** to cut overlapping geometry out of the walls.

14. The floors are placed, as shown in Figure 10–21.

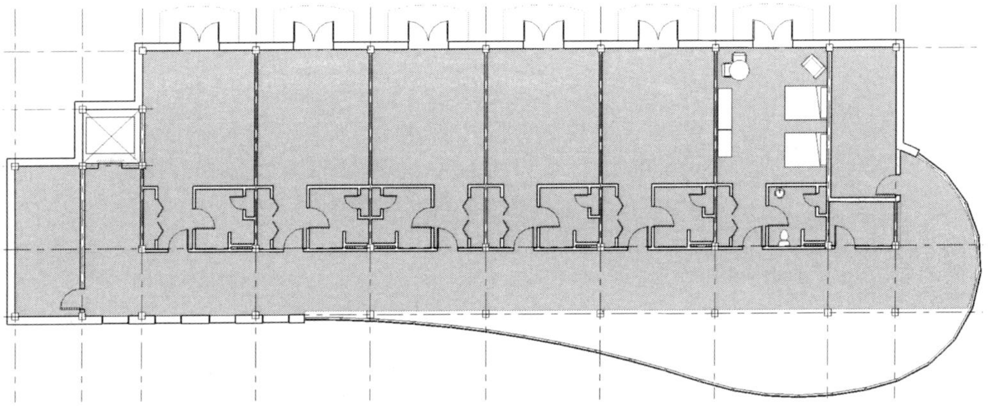

Figure 10–21

15. Click in an empty space in the view to release the floor selection.

16. Pan to the upper-left balcony.

17. In the *Architecture* tab>*Build* panel, click (Floor) and set the following options:

- In the Type Selector, select **Floor: Generic - 12" Balcony**.
- In Properties, set the *Height Offset From Level* to (negative) **-0'-4"**.

18. Use (Pick Lines) to create the outline of the balcony, as shown in Figure 10–22. You want the balcony floor to meet the Floor 2 floors. Verify that the boundary lines create a closed loop.
    - Use the **Trim/Extend to Corner** tool, if needed, to clean up any lines.

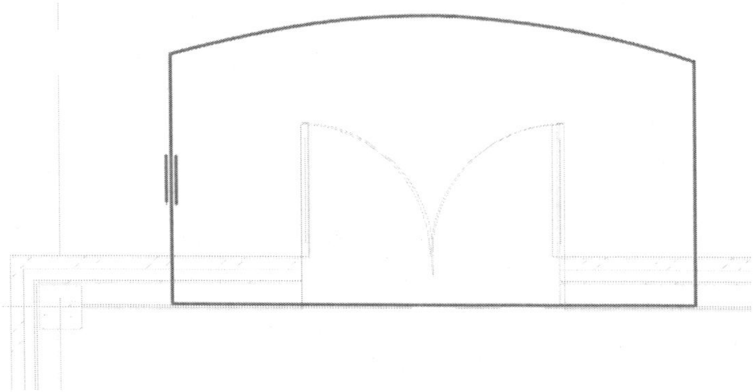

Figure 10–22

19. Click (Modify).
20. Select the balcony boundary lines.
21. Start the **Copy** command and in the *Copy* panel, verify that (Multiple) and (Constrain) are toggled on. Copy the elements to the other balconies.
22. Click (Finish Edit Mode).
    - If the alert box displays, click **Don't attach**.
23. In the *Modify* tab>*Geometry* panel, expand (Join) and click (Join Geometry), then select the balcony floor and Level 2's floor.
24. Click (Modify).
25. Select the imported CAD file and type **VH** to hide it in the view.
26. Save the project.

Task 3: Copy the floor and balcony floors to the other floors.

1. Close any open view or projects except for **Floor Plans: Floor 2**. Open the Default 3D view, then use the ViewCube to rotate the 3D view to display the back of the hotel.
2. Set **Floor 2** to be the active view, then type **WT** to tile the views and **ZA** to zoom all in both views.
3. In the **Floor Plans: Floor 2** view, select the new floor and balcony floors.
4. In the *Modify | Floors* tab>*Clipboard* panel, click (Copy to the Clipboard).
5. In the *Clipboard* panel, expand (Paste) and click (Aligned to Selected Levels).
6. In the *Select Levels* dialog box, select **Floor 3** through **Floor 8**, as shown in Figure 10–23. Click **OK**.

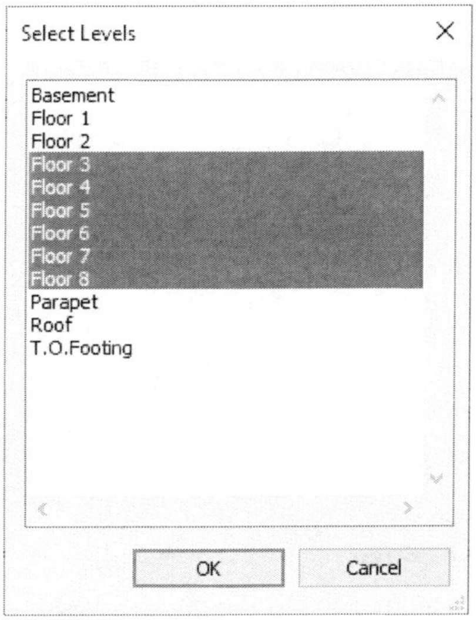

Figure 10–23

7. Click (Modify).
8. Save and close the project.

End of practice

10.2 Creating Shaft Openings

Openings can be added to floors (as well as roofs and ceilings) by drawing a closed sketch in an existing floor, roof, or ceiling. When you have elevator shafts or other floor openings that span more than one floor, create a shaft opening and specify the depth to cut through the required levels, then place symbolic lines to represent a shaft opening in plan view, as shown in Figure 10–24.

> ***Note:*** *Shaft openings only cut floors, roofs, and ceilings. They do not cut walls, beams, or other objects. Shafts are their own element so they can be deleted without affecting the host.*

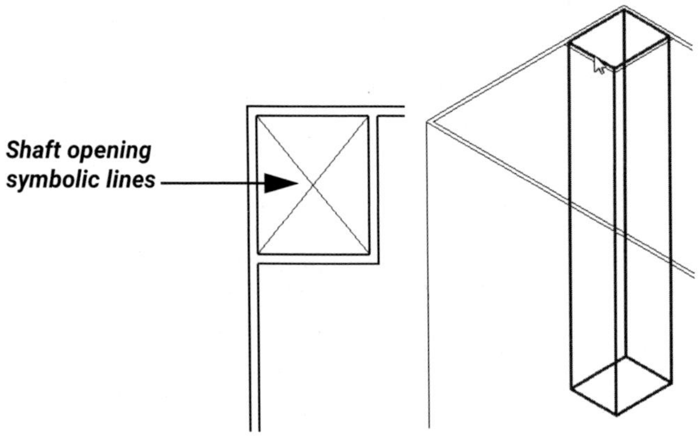

Figure 10–24

How To: Add a Shaft Opening

1. In the *Architecture* tab>*Opening* panel, click (Shaft).
2. In the *Modify | Create Shaft Opening Sketch* tab>*Draw* panel, click (Boundary Line).
3. In the *Draw* panel, select one of the sketch tools. If needed, set the (Offset) and/or (Radius) and toggle on (Chain).
4. In Properties, set the following:
   - *Base Constraint* and *Base Offset*
   - *Top Constraint* and *Top Offset* (if a level is selected) or *Unconnected Height* (if **Unconnected** is selected)
5. Sketch lines to define the shaft opening. Make sure to draw a closed loop.
6. (Optional) In the *Draw* panel, click (Symbolic Line) and draw symbolic lines such as an opening symbol in plan view.

   Note: *Shaft symbolic lines repeat on each level.*

7. Click (Finish Edit Mode) to create the opening.

    - When using (Pick Walls) or other drawing tools to define the perimeter of the opening, you can select the **Flip** control to flip the lines to the outside, as shown in Figure 10–25.

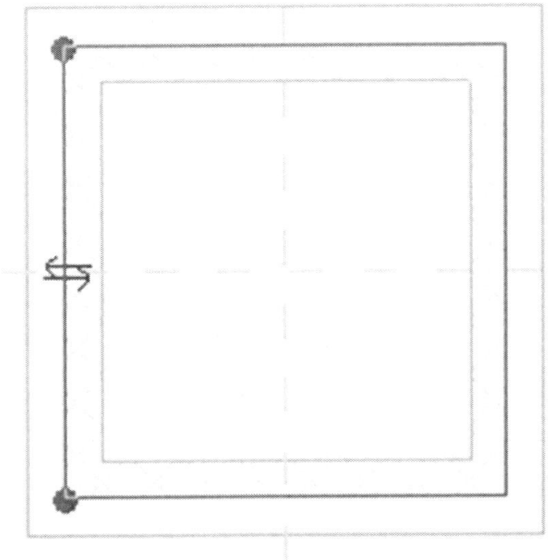

Figure 10–25

- A shaft is a separate element from the floor, roof, ceiling, or wall, and can be deleted without selecting a host element.

10.3 Creating Sloped Floors

Floors can have slopes applied to them. To make a floor slope in one direction, you place a *slope arrow* in the sketch of the floor, as shown in Figure 10–26.

> ***Note:*** *The slope arrow only displays while sketch mode is active.*

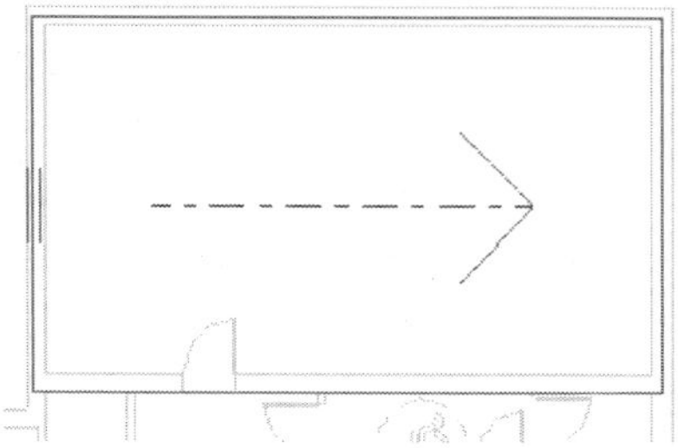

Figure 10–26

- Once the floor is created, you can add multiple drainage points and cause the floor to warp toward them.
- A floor can only have a slope arrow or be edited to have multiple drainage points; it cannot have both.
- These tools also work with roofs and structural slabs.

How To: Slope a Floor in One Direction

1. Select the floor you want to slope. In the *Modify | Floors* tab>*Mode* panel, click (Edit Boundary).
2. In the *Modify | Floors > Edit Boundary* tab>*Draw* panel, click (Slope Arrow).
3. Select two points to define the arrow. The first point is the tail and the second is the head. The tail and head locations are points at which you can specify heights. The direction of the arrow determines the orientation of the slope.
4. In Properties, you can choose to define the slope arrow by **Height at Tail** or **Slope** by setting the *Specify* value, as shown in Figure 10–27.

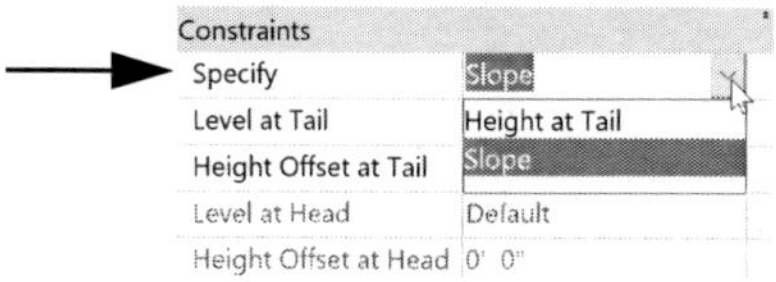

Figure 10–27

- If *Specify* is set to **Height at Tail**, you can modify the *Level at Tail*, *Height Offset at Tail*, *Level at Head,* and *Height Offset at Head*, as shown in Figure 10–28.

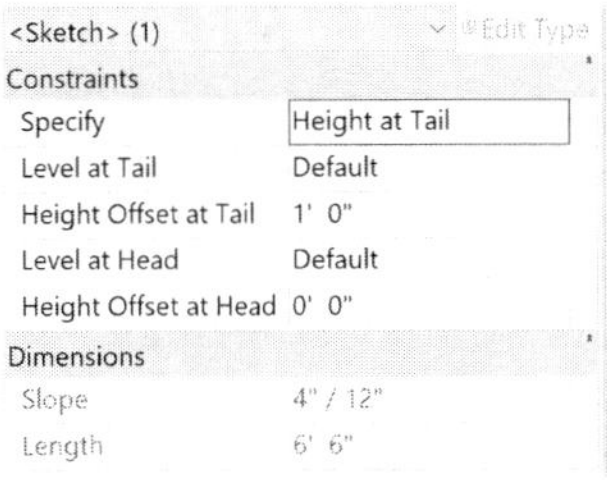

Figure 10–28

- If *Specify* is set to **Slope**, you can modify the *Level at Tail*, *Height Offset at Tail,* and *Slope,* as shown in Figure 10–29.

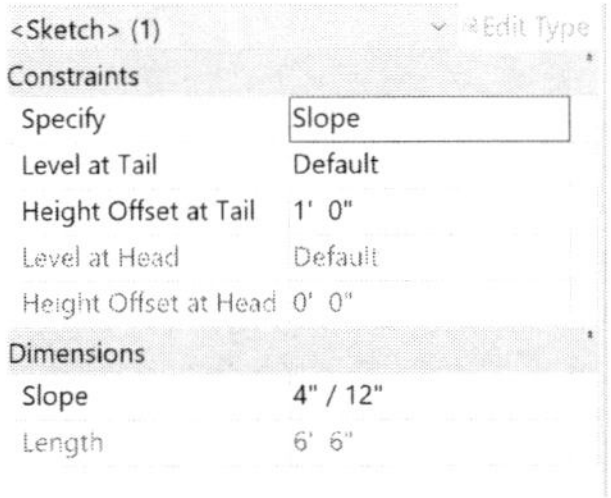

Figure 10–29

Creating Multiple Slopes for Drainage

Surfaces often need to have floors that slope towards drains, as shown in Figure 10–30. In addition, all flat roofs are not actually flat, but also slope towards drains. Several tools provide ways of creating points for the drain locations, as well as creating folding lines to define how the slope is going to drain.

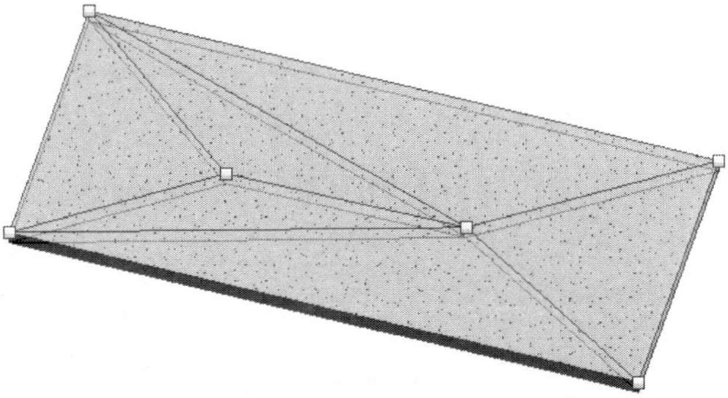

Figure 10–30

- These tools work with floors, roofs, structural floors, and toposolids.

- These tools cannot be combined with the slope arrow. If a floor or roof has a slope arrow, these tools will not be available.
- Set the *Elevation Base* setting when defining points during shape editing. Doing this defines the elevation of the point from one of the selected: **Current Level**, **Project Base Point**, **Survey Point**, or **Internal Origin**.
- Warping a floor also warps a floor pattern. Depending on the level of detail that you want to show, you might not want to actually model the points as outlined here but rather to annotate the plan view to show the location for drains.

How To: Create Multiple Slopes for Drainage

1. Select the flat floor, roof, or slab that you want to add a slope to.
2. In the *Modify | Floors* tab>*Shape Editing* panel (shown in Figure 10–31), select the tools that you want to use to define the slopes.

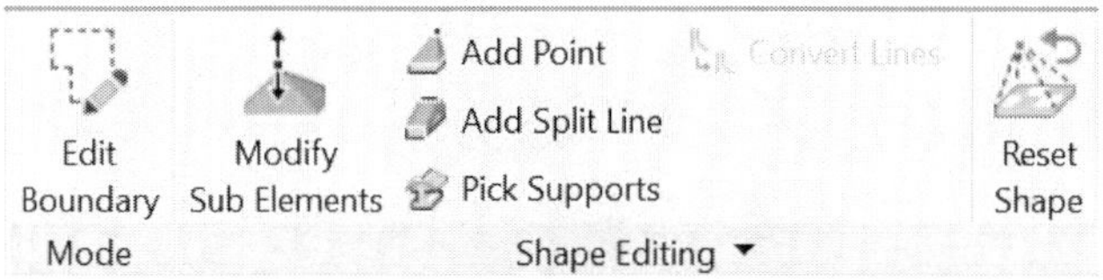

Figure 10–31

	Add Point: Allows you to place points on a surface to define the location of the low or high points. Additional settings can be specified in the contextual tab>*Modifier Elevation* panel, so the point being placed within the floor references the surface or coordinates in conjunction with a specified *Elevation Base*, *Offset from Surface*, *Elevation*, and *Snap XYZ*. • displays when you place the point along the surface boundary line and when placing a point within the surface boundary. Slope lines are automatically added from the corners and edges of the surface to the point.
	Add Split Line: Allows you to define sub-regions on the surface to be able to manipulate the areas independently. Toggle on (Chain) if you want to add more than one connected segment.
	Pick Supports: Select structural beams that define the split lines.
	Concert Lines: Converts a selected folding line to a split line.

Modify Sub-Elements: Change the elevation base as well as the elevation of edges and points from the *Modify Sub Elements* panel.

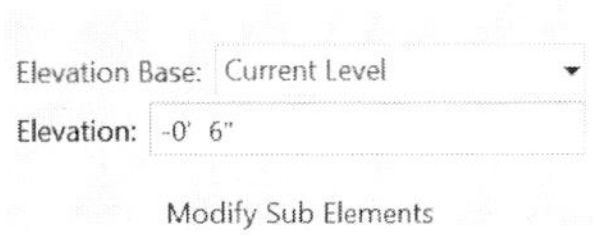

- While in the Modify Sub-Elements mode, you can select on a point and drag it to another location within the surface.
- To modify the elevation of a point, click on the point and then the elevation. Type the new elevation and press <Enter>. The point updates.

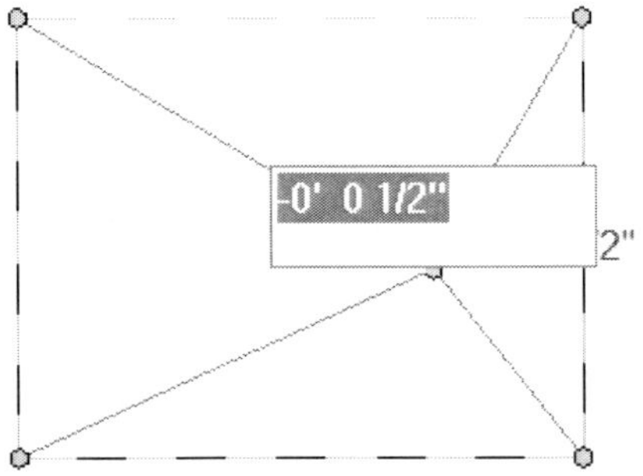

- You can also modify the elevation and move points or folding lines using shape handles without clicking  (Modify Sub-Elements), as shown in the figure below. Press <Tab> to cycle through the options to reach the element you want to modify.

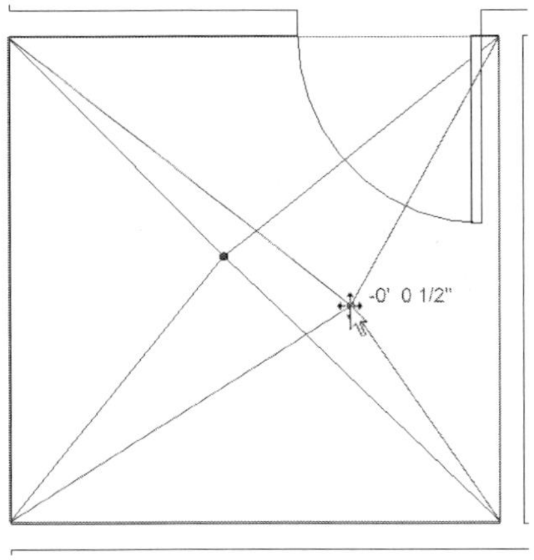

Reset Shape: Reset a selected surface to its original shape, discarding any modifications made.

- Floors, roofs, and slabs use styles set to a constant thickness (where the entire element slopes) or to a variable thickness (where only the top layer slopes), as shown in Figure 10–32.

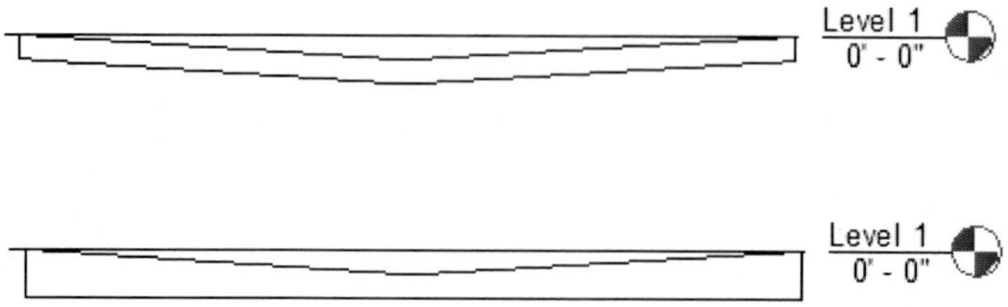

Figure 10–32

Practice 10b
Create Shaft Openings and Sloped Floors

Practice Objectives

- Create a shaft opening.
- Slope floors.

In this practice, you will add a shaft opening for the elevator, as shown on the left in Figure 10–33. You will also slope floors for drainage in the restrooms and janitor closet, as shown on the right in Figure 10–33, using the *Shape Editing* tools.

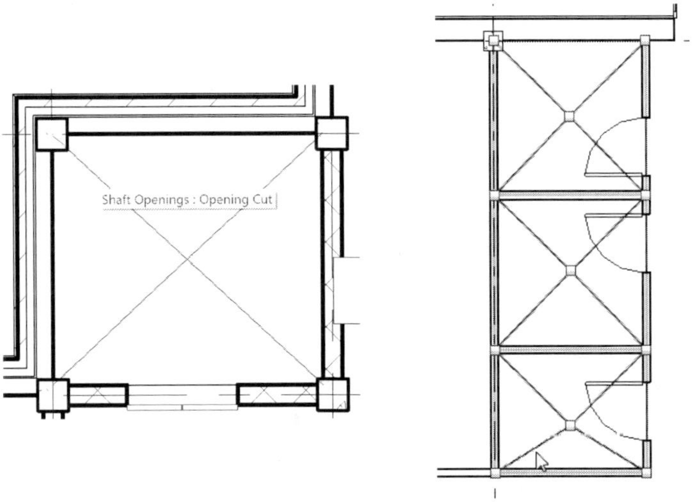

Figure 10–33

Task 1: Create a shaft opening.

1. Open the project **Arch-Slope.rvt** from the practice files folder.
2. Verify you are in the **Floor Plans: Floor 1** view and zoom in to the elevator area.
3. In the *Architecture* tab>*Opening* panel, click (Shaft).
4. In the *Modify | Create Shaft Opening Sketch* tab>*Draw* panel, verify that (Boundary Line) is selected.

5. Use (Pick Walls) and select the walls within the elevator to create the boundary, as shown in Figure 10–34. If needed, use (Trim/Extend to Corner) to ensure that the boundary is closed.
   - Shafts do not cut through structural elements.

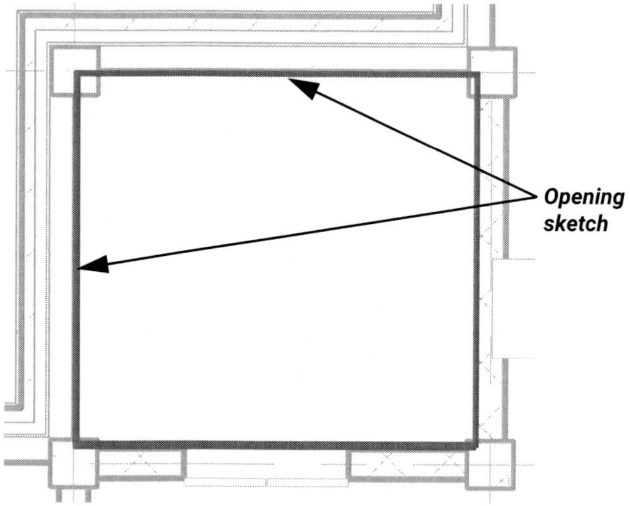

Figure 10–34

6. In Properties, verify that the shaft opening's *Base Constraint* is **Floor 1**. Set the *Base Offset* to (negative) **-1'-0"** and the *Top Constraint* to **Up to level: Roof**.
7. In the *Modify | Create Shaft Opening Sketch* tab>*Draw* panel, select (Symbolic Line) and toggle off (Chain). In the *Line Style* panel, set (Line Style) to **<Thin Lines>**, if not already set.

8. Draw an X in the shaft opening from corner to corner, as shown in Figure 10–35.

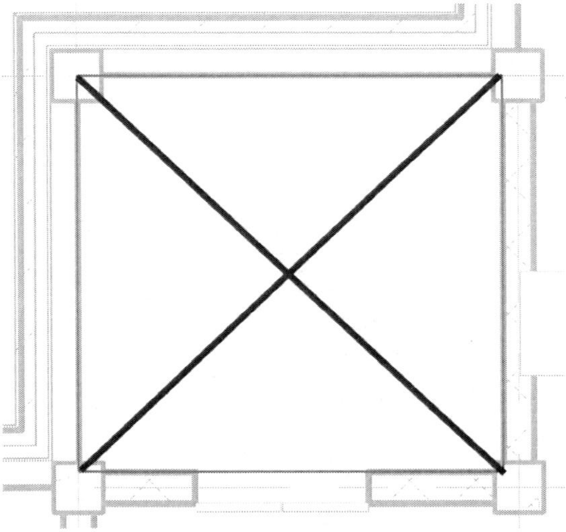

Figure 10–35

9. Click (Finish Edit Mode).
10. Click (Modify).
11. Save the project.

Task 2: Slope floors for drainage.

1. Open the **Floor Plans: Floor 1 - Restrooms** view.
2. In the View Control Bar, verify **Show Crop Region** is toggled on, then expand the size of the crop region so the janitor closet below is also included in the plan.

3. Click on the face of the floor to select it. Figure 10–36 shows the floor selected. In Properties, you should see **Floor: Generic - 12"** as the selected floor.

   Note: *If you cannot select the floor, verify (Select Elements by Face) is toggle on.*

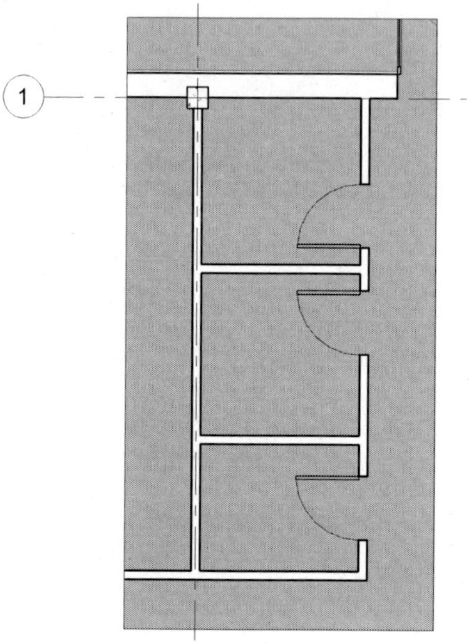

Figure 10–36

4. In the *Modify | Floors* tab>*Shape Editing* panel, click (Add Split Line). In the *Modifier Elevation* panel, verify (Along Surface) is selected, and in the *Draw* panel, toggle on (Chain).

5. Draw the outside edges, as shown in Figure 10–37.
6. When you have finished drawing the outside edges, right-click and select **Cancel**. Alternatively, you can press <Esc>.
7. Select (Add Split Line) and toggle off (Chain) in the *Draw* panel, then draw the two internal lines, as shown in Figure 10–37.

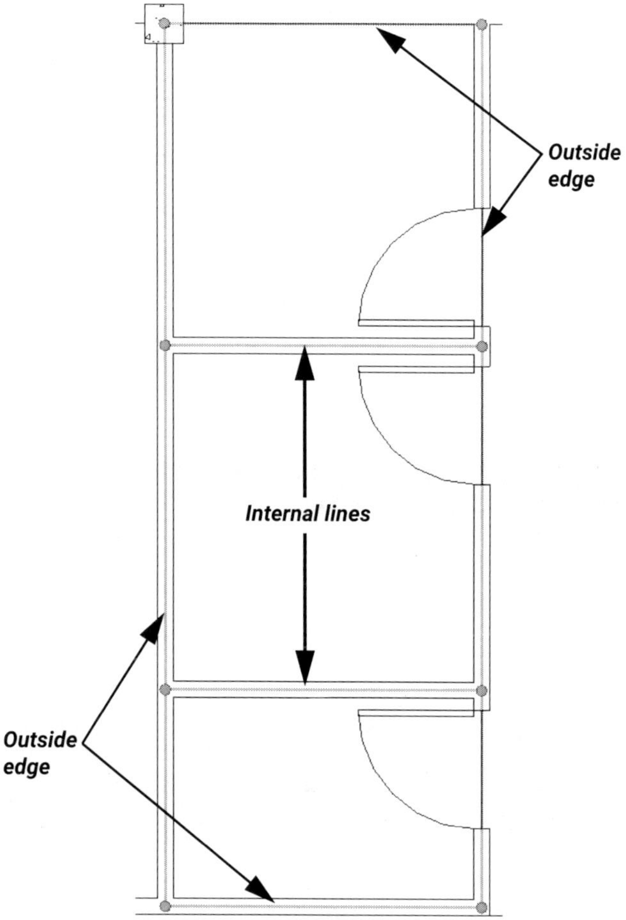

Figure 10–37

8. In the *Shape Editing* panel, click (Add Point). In the *Modifier Elevation* panel, verify (Along Surface) is selected and set the *Elevation Base* to **Project Base Point** and the *Offset from Surface* to (negative) **-1/2"**. Place a point approximately in the center of each room, as shown for one of them in Figure 10–38.

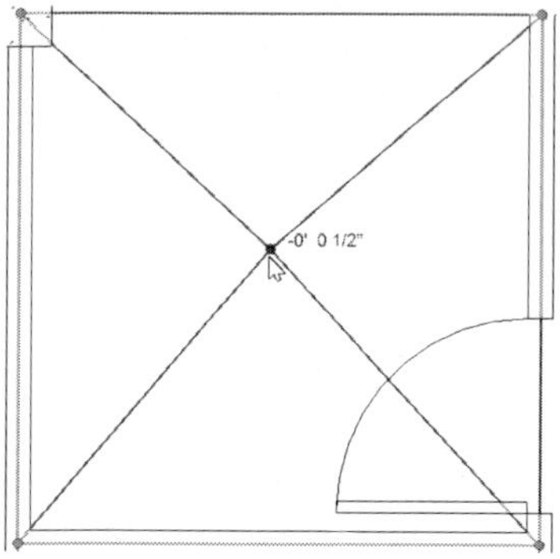

Figure 10–38

9. Click (Modify).
10. Save and close the project.

End of practice

10.4 Creating Floor Types

Another way to specify the correct top material for a floor and to assign the layers of materials that make up a floor (as shown in Figure 10–39) is to create floor types.

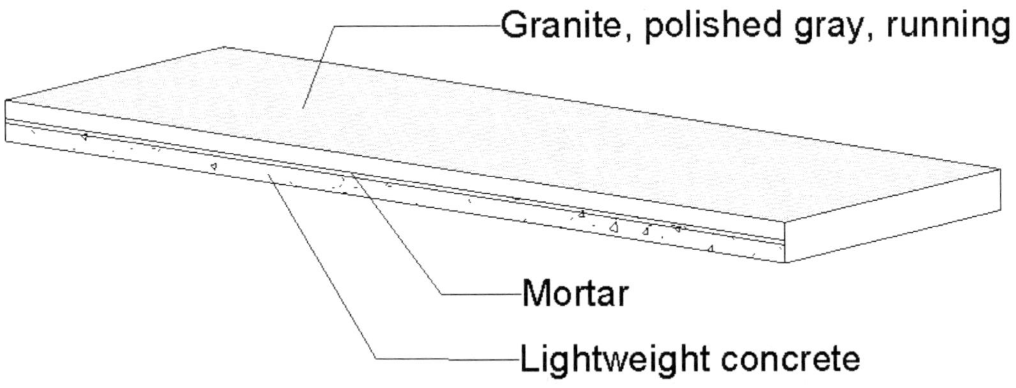

Figure 10–39

- This method is also used to create and modify wall, ceiling, and roof types.
- You can create as many layers as required to define the structure.
- You can use floor types to create area plantings.

How To: Create a Compound Floor Type

1. Start the **Floor** command.
2. In Properties, select a type similar to the one you want to create and click (Edit Type).
3. In the *Type Properties* dialog box, click **Duplicate...**.
4. In the *Name* dialog box, enter a name for the new type and click **OK**.
5. In the *Type Properties* dialog box, next to the *Structure* parameter, click **Edit...**.
6. In the *Edit Assembly* dialog box, modify the layers of the assembly as required, and click **OK**.
7. Modify any type parameters in the *Type Properties* dialog box.
8. Click **OK** to close the dialog box.

Editing Floor Assemblies

In the *Edit Assembly* dialog box, you can define the layers that make up the compound structure, as shown in Figure 10–40.

> ***Note:*** *To better visualize the wall or floor, click* ***<< Preview*** *to open a view of the layers in the structure. You can preview the structure in a plan or section view, and zoom or pan in the preview screen.*

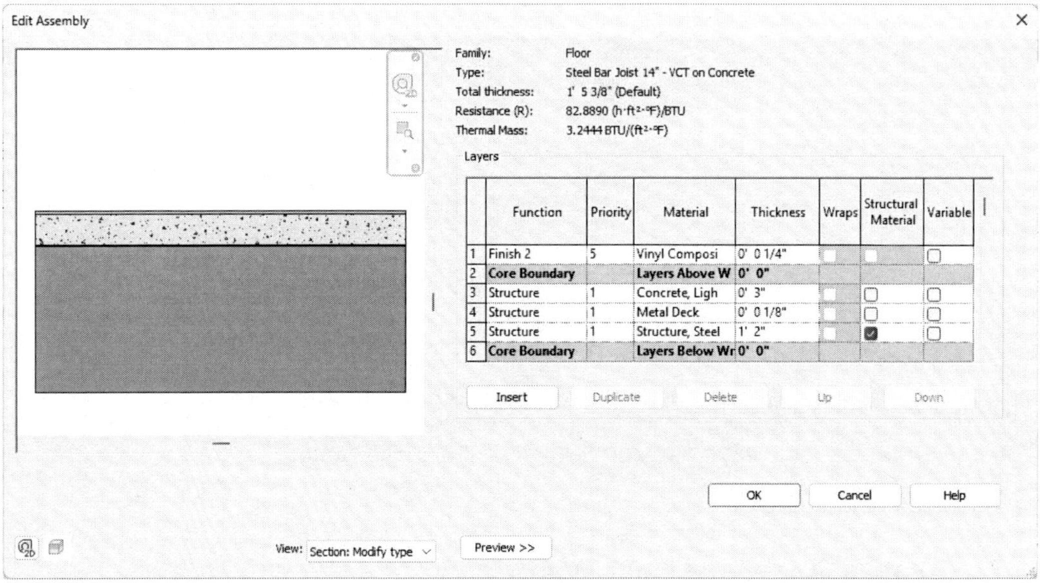

Figure 10–40

Assembly Information

The top of the dialog box lists the *Family* (such as **Basic Wall** or **Floor**), the *Type* that you gave to the new type, and the *Total thickness* (the sum of the layers), as shown in Figure 10–41. It also includes *Resistance (R)* and *Thermal Mass*, which are automatically calculated from the materials assigned to the layers. You can also set a *Sample Height* if you are creating a floor type.

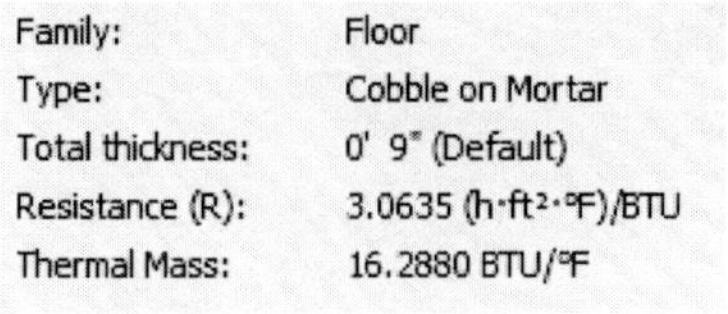

Figure 10–41

Layers

When you specify the layers for the compound element, you assign them a *Function*, *Priority*, *Material*, and *Thickness*, as shown in Figure 10–42.

Layers

	Function	Priority	Material	Thickness	Wraps	Structural Material	Variable
1	Finish 2	5	Vinyl Composit	0' 0 1/4"			☐
2	**Core Boundary**		**Layers Above Wr**	**0' 0"**			
3	Structure	1	Concrete, Light	0' 3"		☐	☐
4	Structure	1	Metal Deck	0' 0 1/8"		☐	☐
5	Structure	1	Structure, Steel	1' 2"		☑	☐
6	**Core Boundary**		**Layers Below Wr**	**0' 0"**			

Figure 10–42

- Use the buttons to insert additional layers and to rearrange them in the layer list. You can also delete layers from the list.
- The *Core Boundary* function defines the layers above and below the wrapping; a heavier line is displayed when a plan or section view is cut.
- Editing an assembly works from the exterior side at the top of the list to the interior side at the bottom. For floors and roofs, you can work around the layers above and below the wrap of the *Core Boundary*.

Options

Function	Select from a set list of functions in the drop-down list, then set the *Priority* from highest (1) to lowest (5). High priority layers connect before low priority layers.
Structure	The structural support for the wall, floor, or roof.
Substrate	A material that acts as a foundation for another material, such as plywood or gypsum board.
Thermal/ Air Layer	An open layer for air space.
Finish 1	The exterior finish layer, such as brick for a wall.
Finish 2	The interior finish layer, such as drywall for a wall.
Membrane Layer	A vapor barrier. Typically, this is set to a zero thickness. Therefore, it does not have a priority code.

Structural Deck	(Floors only) A structural support based on a *Deck Profile*. You can also specify the *Deck Usage* with a **Bound Layer Above** or a **Standalone Deck**. 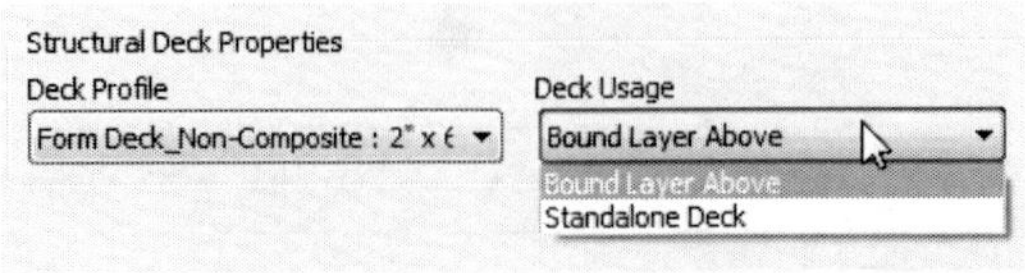
Material	Select from a list of available materials. Layers clean up if they share the same material. If they do not, a line displays at the join.
Thickness	Set the thickness of the particular layer.

Wall Only Options

Sample Height	Displays the height of a wall in section when you are creating it. It does not impact the height of the wall in the project.
Default Wrapping	Set up how the heavy line style wraps around openings in walls: *at Inserts* (**Do not wrap**, **Interior**, **Exterior**, or **Both**) and *at Ends* (**None**, **Exterior**, or **Interior**). Wrapping is only visible in plan view.
Wraps	Set up individual layers to wrap – select the **Wraps** option at the end of each layer.

- Roofs, floors, and structural slabs have an additional parameter that relates to sloping for drains. When *Variable* is not selected, the slab is set to a constant thickness and the entire element slopes, as shown on the top in Figure 10–43. When *Variable* is selected, only the top layer slopes, as shown on the bottom in Figure 10–43.

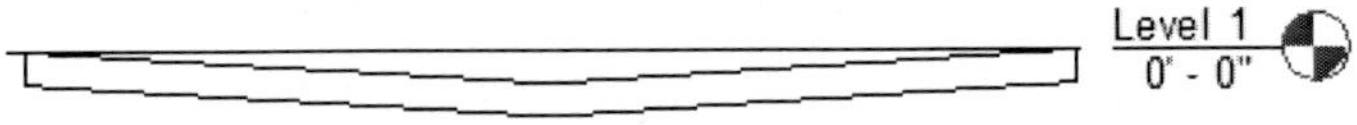

Variable not checked

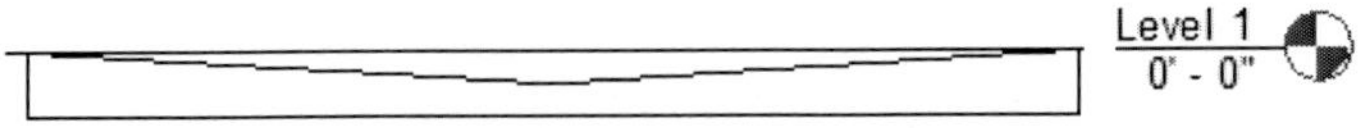

Variable checked

Figure 10–43

- Retaining walls are a specific wall type whose *Function* is set to **Retaining** in the *Type Properties* dialog box, as shown in Figure 10–44.

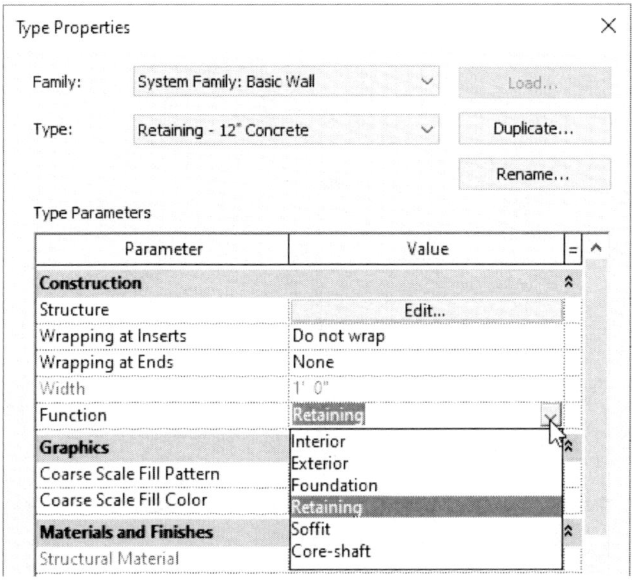

Figure 10–44

Chapter Review Questions

1. When creating a floor, the boundary sketch must be a closed loop to finish the sketch.
   a. True
   b. False

2. How do you change the thickness of a floor, such as those shown in Figure 10–45?

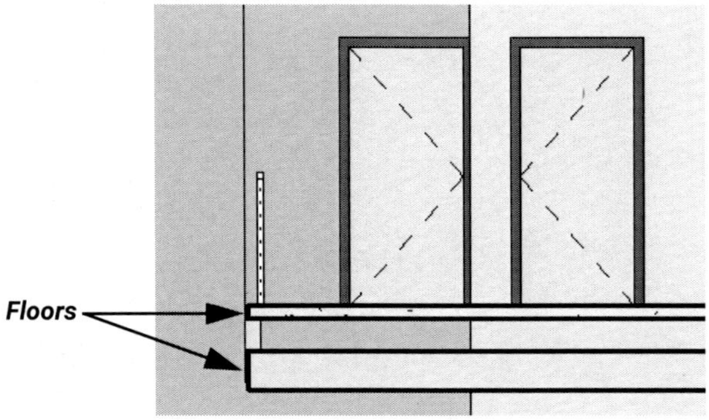

Figure 10–45

   a. In the Type Selector, change the *Floor Type*.
   b. In the contextual tab, change the *Floor Thickness*.
   c. In Properties, change the *Floor Thickness*.
   d. In the contextual tab, change the *Floor Type*.

3. Which of the following *Opening* commands cuts an opening in multiple floors at the same time?
   a. By Face
   b. Shaft
   c. Wall
   d. Vertical

4.  (Add Point) allows you to place points on a surface to define the location of the low or high points.

a. True

b. False

Command Summary

Button	Command	Location
	**Floor: Architectural**	• **Ribbon:** *Architecture* tab>*Build* panel, expand Floor
	**Floor: Structural**	• **Ribbon:** *Architecture* tab>*Build* panel, expand Floor
	**Shaft**	• **Ribbon:** *Architecture* tab>*Opening* panel
Shape Editing Tools		
	**Add Point**	• **Ribbon:** *Modify | Floors* tab>*Shape Editing* panel
	**Add Split Line**	• **Ribbon:** *Modify | Floors* tab>*Shape Editing* panel
	**Modify Sub Elements**	• **Ribbon:** *Modify | Floors* tab>*Shape Editing* panel
	**Pick Supports**	• **Ribbon:** *Modify | Floors* tab>*Shape Editing* panel
	**Reset Shape**	• **Ribbon:** *Modify | Floors* tab>*Shape Editing* panel

Chapter 11

Modeling Ceilings

In Revit®, ceilings are modeled using reflected ceiling plans. You can add ceilings by selecting a room boundary or by sketching ceilings that do not fill an entire room. You can create basic ceilings made of acoustical tile grids, or you can create custom ceilings of different heights with a soffit wall added between. In addition to creating a ceiling, you can also place ceiling fixtures directly onto ceiling elements.

Learning Objectives

- Add automatic ceilings that fill an entire room boundary and sketched ceilings that are customized to suit a design.
- Modify ceiling boundaries and the grid locations for acoustical tiles to ensure that the tiles fit the room correctly.
- Add ceiling components, including lighting and mechanical fixtures.
- Add soffit walls in the gap between ceilings of different heights.

11.1 Modeling Ceilings

Adding ceilings to Revit models is a straightforward process that is similar to adding floors. To place a ceiling, click inside areas that are bounded by walls, as shown in the large room on the right in Figure 11–1, and the ceiling is created. You can also sketch custom ceilings when required. Any fixtures you attach to a ceiling display in reflected ceiling plans, as well as in sections and 3D views.

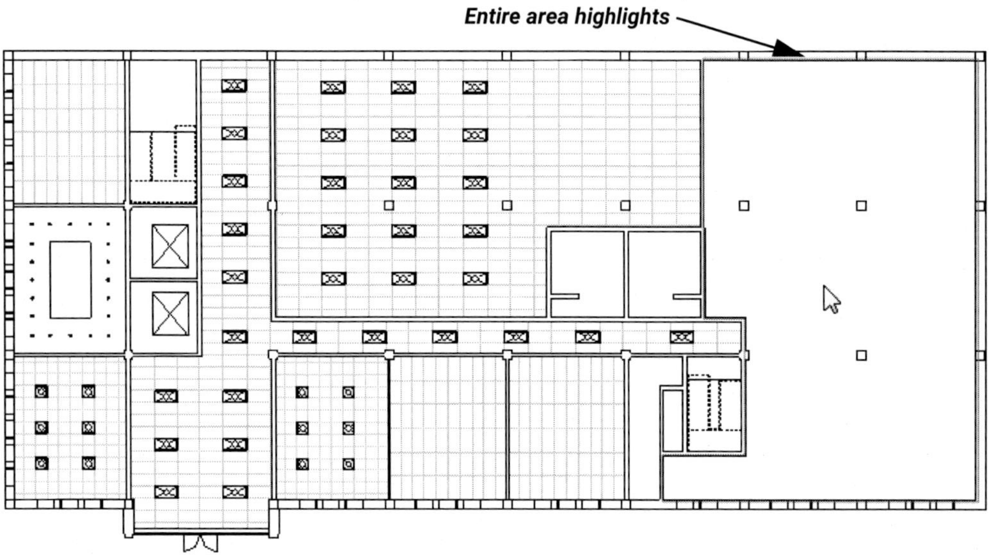

Figure 11–1

- If the walls are lower than what your ceiling properties *Height Offset From Level* is set to, **Automatic Ceiling** will not work and you will see a icon. You will have to either lower the ceiling height offset or use the **Sketch Ceiling** tool.
- If multiple ceilings are sketched in a room, you can add a slope to create vaulted or cathedral ceilings.

How To: Create an Automatic Boundary Ceiling

1. Open a ceiling plan view.
2. In the *Architecture* tab>*Build* panel, click (Ceiling).
3. In the Type Selector, select the ceiling type. In Properties, set the *Height Offset From Level*.
4. In the *Modify | Place Ceiling* tab>*Ceiling* panel, verify that (Automatic Ceiling) is selected. Click inside a room to create a ceiling, as shown in Figure 11–2.

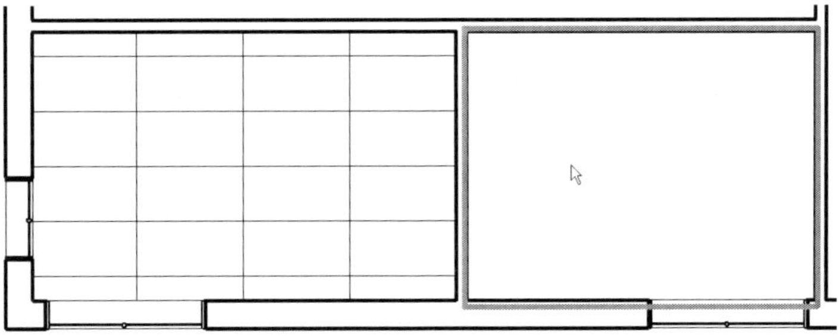

Figure 11–2

5. Continue adding ceilings to other rooms, as needed, or click (Modify) to end the command.

Hint: Room Bounding Status

Elements such as walls, floors, ceilings, and roofs have a *Room Bounding* property set in Properties. In most cases, this is toggled on by default as these elements typically define areas and volumes.

The **Automatic Ceiling** tool uses this property to identify walls that set the outline of a ceiling. If you toggle off this property for a wall (such as a partial height wall), the **Automatic Ceiling** tool ignores the wall.

Ceilings can also be used as a room bounding for volume calculations.

- To modify a ceiling boundary, select a ceiling and either:
  - in the *Modify | Ceilings* tab>*Mode* panel, click (Edit Boundary), or
  - double-click on the ceiling to enter Edit Boundary mode.

Sketching Ceilings

To add a ceiling to part of a room, as shown in Figure 11–3, or to have two different ceiling types at separate levels, you need to sketch a ceiling.

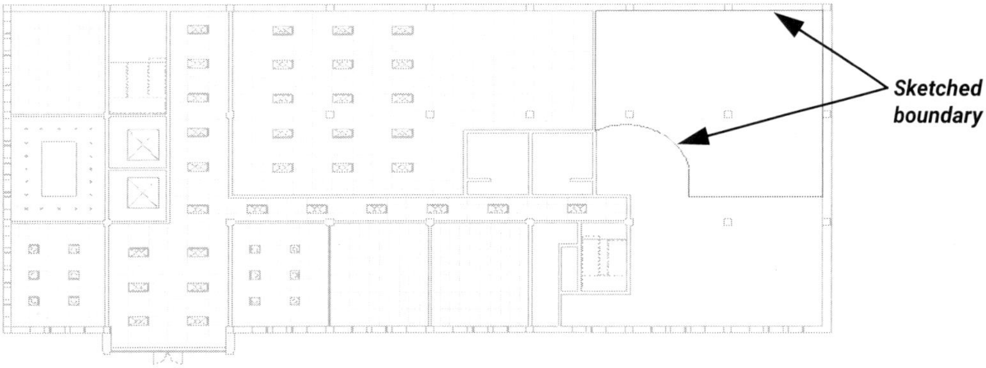

Figure 11–3

How To: Sketch a Ceiling

1. In the *Architecture* tab>*Build* panel, click (Ceiling).
2. In the *Modify | Place Ceiling* tab>*Ceiling* panel, click (Sketch Ceiling).
3. In the *Draw* panel, click (Line) or (Pick Walls) and define a closed loop for the ceiling boundary, similar to sketching a floor boundary.

- To create a sloped ceiling, in the *Modify | Ceilings > Edit Boundary* tab>*Draw* panel, click (Slope Arrow) and draw the arrow in the direction you want the slope. In Properties, specify **Height at Tail** or **Slope**, as shown in Figure 11–4, and set the other parameters as needed.

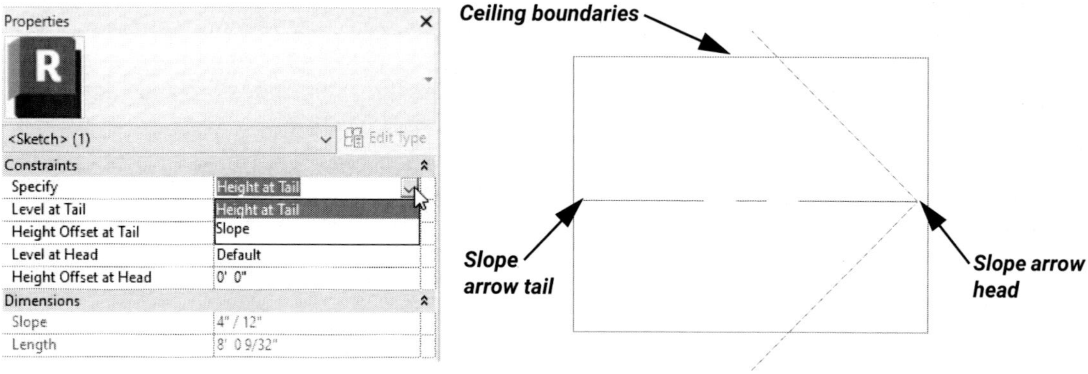

Figure 11–4

4. Click (Finish Edit Mode) to create the ceiling.

- To include a hole in a ceiling, include the hole as part of the sketch. The hole must be a closed loop completely inside the ceiling boundary.
- In the *Architecture* tab>*Opening* panel, you can also use (Opening By Face), (Shaft Opening), or (Vertical Opening) to cut a hole in a ceiling that is separate from the sketch. This can often be used for fireplaces or skylights.

Modifying Ceiling Grids

When using acoustical tile ceiling types, you can reposition the ceiling grid locations by moving or rotating the grid lines, as shown in Figure 11–5.

> ***Note:*** *To change a rectangular ceiling tile pattern from horizontal to vertical, select a ceiling grid line and rotate it 90°.*

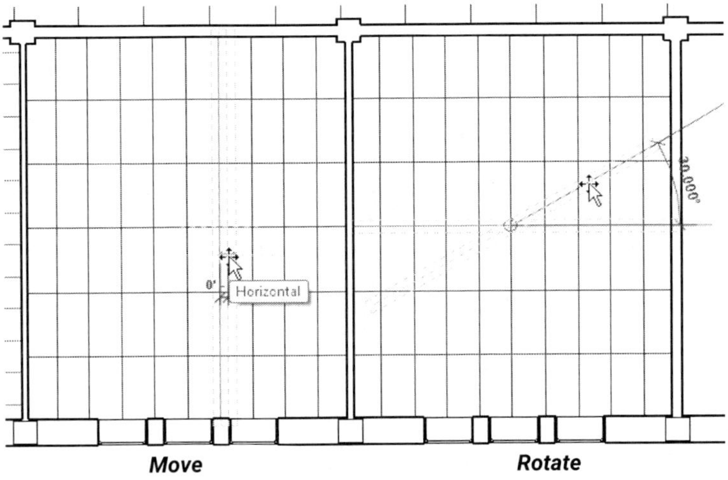

Figure 11–5

How To: Move a Ceiling Grid

1. Select a ceiling grid line in the ceiling that you want to modify.
2. In the *Modify | Ceilings* tab>*Modify* panel, click (Move).
3. Move the cursor to one side and type a distance, typically an increment of the ceiling grid size.

How To: Rotate a Ceiling Grid

1. Select a ceiling grid line in the ceiling that you want to modify.
2. In the *Modify | Ceilings* tab>*Modify* panel, click (Rotate).
3. In the *Modify | Rotate* tab>*Rotate* panel, select either (Place) or (Center). Once the center of rotation is placed, you can manually click to rotate or enter an (Angle) in the *Rotate* panel, as shown in Figure 11–6.

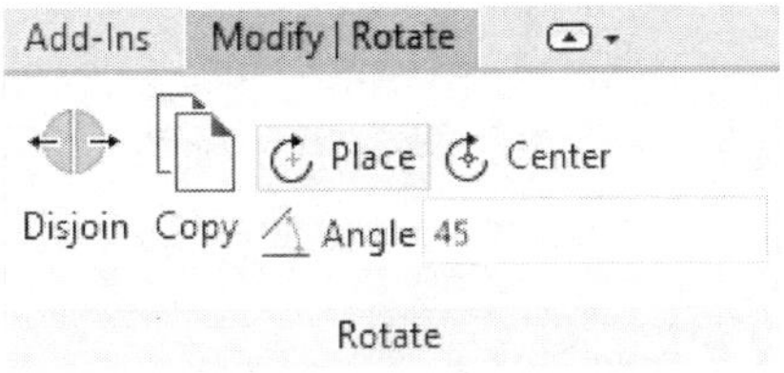

Figure 11–6

11.2 Adding Ceiling Fixtures

Several groups of components are commonly used with ceilings, such as:

- Lighting fixtures (shown in Figure 11–7)
- Mechanical equipment (for registers and diffusers)
- Specialty equipment (such as exit signs or sprinklers)

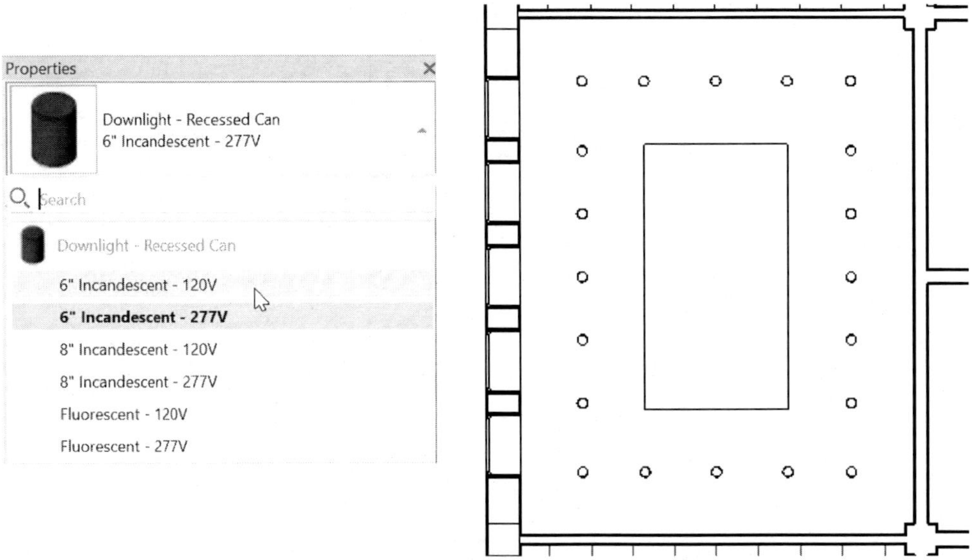

Figure 11–7

- Use  (Component) to place ceiling fixtures in the ceiling view.

  Note: *After placing a component, press <Spacebar> to rotate it in 90° increments.*

- The Revit Library contains a variety of lighting fixtures and mechanical ceiling fixtures.
- Many lighting fixtures include types that specify the voltage of the lamp, as shown above in Figure 11–7.
- Some lighting fixtures are wall-based, instead of ceiling-based, and need to be placed on a wall in a floor plan view. These include items such as sconces.
- When you delete a ceiling, the associated components (such as lighting fixtures) are also deleted.
- Components come in based on their center point and respond to the nearby walls, not to the ceiling grid. Place an instance of the component and use **Move** or **Align** to get it to the correct location on the ceiling grid, then use **Copy** to place additional instances on the ceiling grid.

- Some lighting fixtures can display the light source, as shown in the section on the right in Figure 11–8. To display the light source, in the *Visibility/Graphic Overrides* dialog box, on the *Model Categories* tab, expand **Lighting Fixtures** and select **Light Source**, as shown on the left in Figure 11–8.

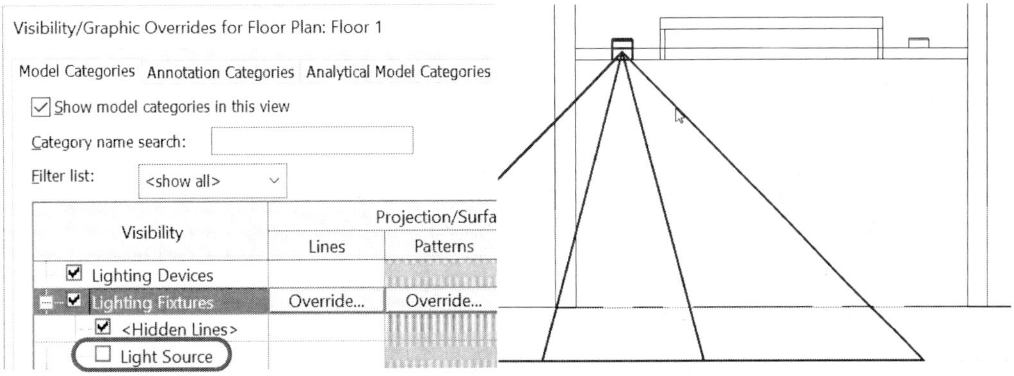

Figure 11–8

- The light sources display their true strength in renderings.

Practice 11a
Model Ceilings and Add Ceiling Fixtures

Practice Objectives

- Create automatic ceilings with ceiling grids.
- Add ceiling components.

In this practice, while working in a reflected ceiling plan, you will add acoustical tile ceilings to several support spaces. You will then add light fixtures and air terminals. Figure 11–9 shows the light fixtures and air terminals placed in the kitchen and restrooms area.

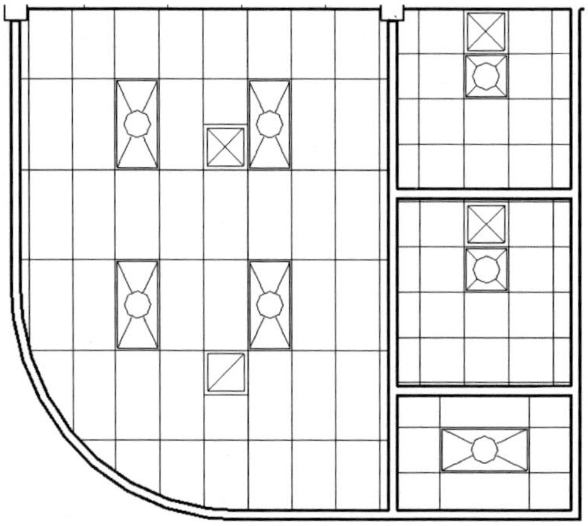

Figure 11–9

Task 1: Create ceilings with ceiling grids.

1. Open the project **Arch-Ceilings.rvt** from the practice files folder.
2. Open the **Ceiling Plans: Floor 1** view. (Make sure you are opening the ceiling plan and not the floor plan view.)
   - To clarify the view, you might want to hide the grids and section marker categories by selecting the elements and typing **VH**.
3. Pan and zoom in to the kitchen and restrooms area.
4. In the *Architecture* tab>*Build* panel, click (Ceiling).
5. In the *Modify | Place Ceiling* tab>*Ceiling* panel, verify that (Automatic Ceiling) is selected.
6. In the Type Selector, select **Compound Ceiling: 2' x 4' ACT System**, if not already selected.
7. In Properties, set the *Height Offset From Level* to **9'-0"**.

8. Click inside the kitchen, in each of the two restrooms (as shown in Figure 11–10), and in the janitor closet to add a ceiling to all four rooms.

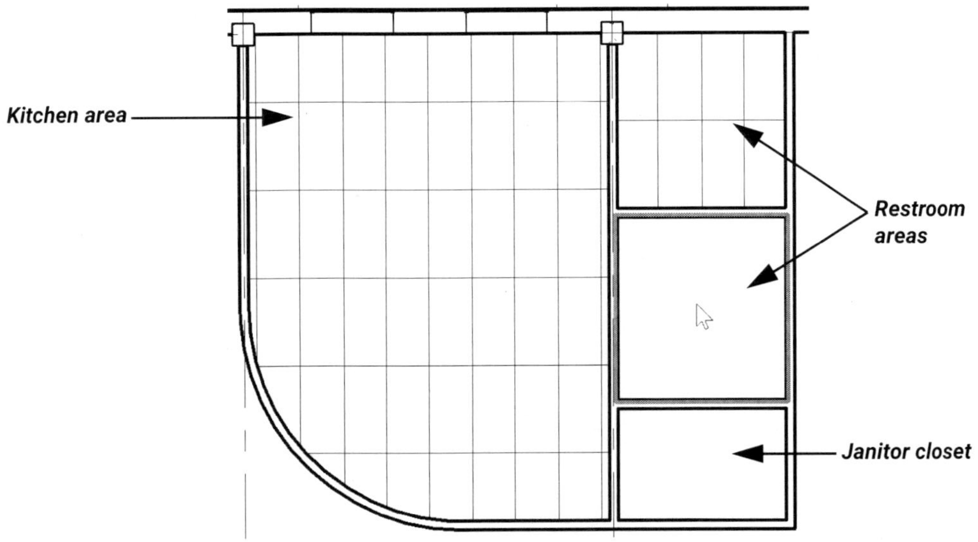

Figure 11–10

9. Click (Modify).
10. Select a ceiling grid line in each of the restrooms.
11. In the Type Selector, select **Compound Ceiling: 2' x 2' ACT System**. In Properties, set the *Height Offset From Level* to **10'-0"**.
12. Both restrooms' ceiling grids change. Click (Modify).
13. Save the project.

Task 2: Add and modify ceiling-hosted components.

1. In the *Architecture* tab>*Build* panel, click (Component).
2. In the *Modify | Place Component* tab>*Mode* panel, click (Load Family) and load the following components from the practice files *Families>Lighting* folder:
   - **Troffer Light 2x2 Parabolic.rfa**
   - **Troffer Light 2x4 Parabolic.rfa**
3. In the Type Selector, select **Troffer Light 2x2 Parabolic2'x2'(2Lamp) - 277V** .

4. Place one light fixture in each of the restrooms, as shown in Figure 11–11. Accuracy is not necessary as you will fix the placement in the next steps.
   - Note that when you are not hovering over a ceiling, your cursor changes from the light fixture to the cannot place icon ( ), indicating that you cannot place the element in the area your cursor is currently in as the light fixture belongs to a ceiling-based family.

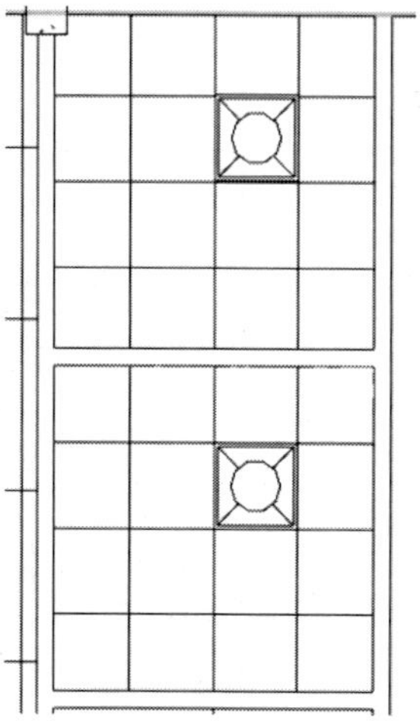

Figure 11–11

5. Click (Modify).
6. Zoom in to the top restroom.
7. In the *Modify* tab>*Modify* panel, click (Align).
8. In the *Modify | Align* tab>*Align* panel, verify **Multiple Alignment** is unchecked and check the checkbox for **Lock**.
9. Select the ceiling grid line first and then the edge of the light fixture second, as shown in Figure 11–12. Do this to both horizontal and vertical grid lines.

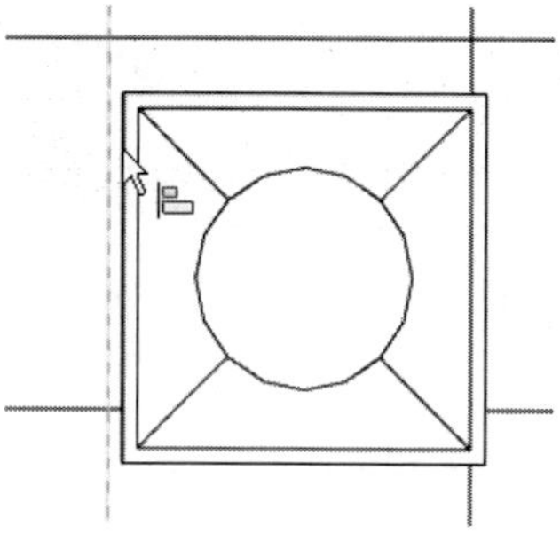

Figure 11–12

10. Repeat the alignment in the second restroom.
11. Click (Modify).

12. In the top restroom, select a ceiling grid line.

13. In the *Modify | Ceilings* tab>*Modify* panel, click (Move).

14. In the *Modify | Move* tab>*Move* panel, verify that (Constrain) is toggled off.

15. Move the grids either vertically or horizontally so that the lighting fixture is approximately in the center of the room, as shown in Figure 11–13. Repeat for the bottom restroom.

    - Hint: You can use your arrow keys to move the ceiling up or down. Use **Align** to align the two ceiling grids vertically.

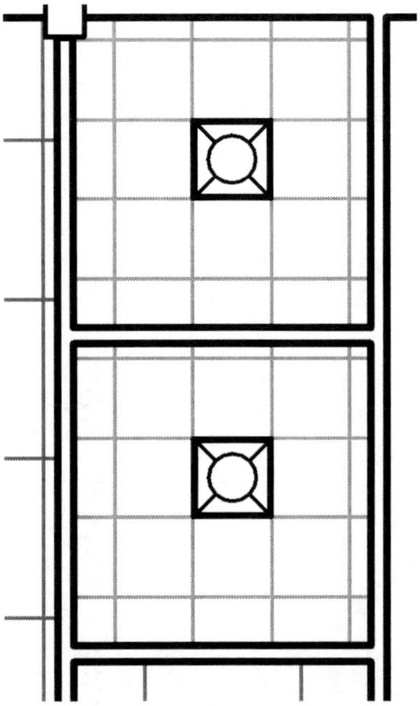

Figure 11–13

16. Click (Modify).

17. Zoom in to the janitor closet. Select a horizontal ceiling grid line (it does not matter which one) and, using your keyboard's arrow keys, move the grid line so the horizontal grid lines are similar to what is shown in Figure 11–14. Repeat this for the vertical ceiling grid lines.

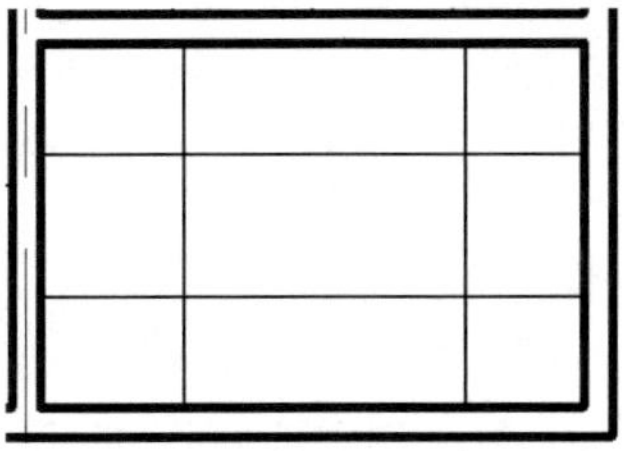

Figure 11–14

18. Pan and zoom out so you can see the kitchen and the janitor closet.

19. Start the **Component** command again.

20. In the Type Selector, select **Troffer Light 2x4 Parabolic 2'x4'(2 Lamp) - 277V** and place four light fixtures in the kitchen and another one in the janitor closet. Place them horizontally at the approximate locations shown in Figure 11–15.

21. Click (Modify).

22. Select any light fixtures that need to be rotated and press <Spacebar> to rotate the light fixtures 90° so they match the ceiling grid shown in Figure 11–15.

23. Click (Modify).

24. Use the **Align** and **Move** commands, as well as the arrow keys, to position the light fixtures and ceiling grids as shown in Figure 11–15.

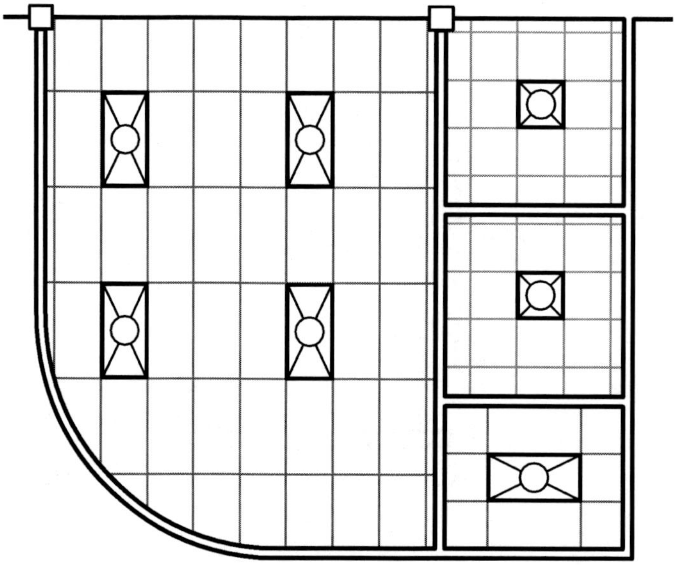

Figure 11–15

25. Click (Modify).

26. Start the **Component** command again.

27. In the *Modify | Place Component* tab>*Mode* panel, click **Load Family** and load the following components from the practice files *Families>Air Terminals* folder:

- **Square Return Register.rfa**
- **Square Supply Diffuser.rfa**

28. In the Type Selector, select the supply or return diffuser.

29. Place a 24" x 24" supply diffuser in each room (excluding the janitor closet) and a return register in the kitchen, as shown in Figure 11–16. Use the **Align** tool to align the diffusers and register into place on the ceiling grid.

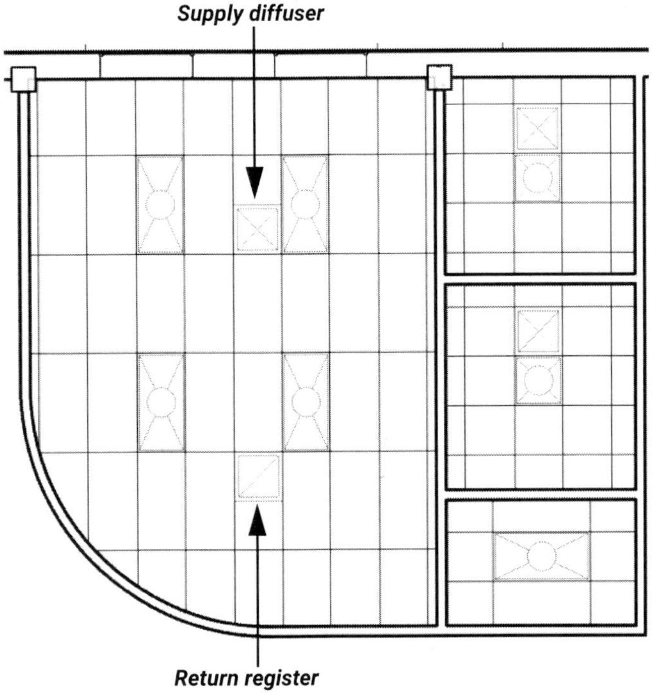

Figure 11–16

30. Save and close the project.

End of practice

11.3 Creating Ceiling Soffits and Raised Ceilings

Ceiling soffits are parts of a ceiling that have been lowered, as shown in Figure 11–17, or that connect two ceilings of different heights. Creating a ceiling soffit takes two steps. First, you create a ceiling, and then you model walls using a soffit wall type. This is how you would create waffle and raised ceilings.

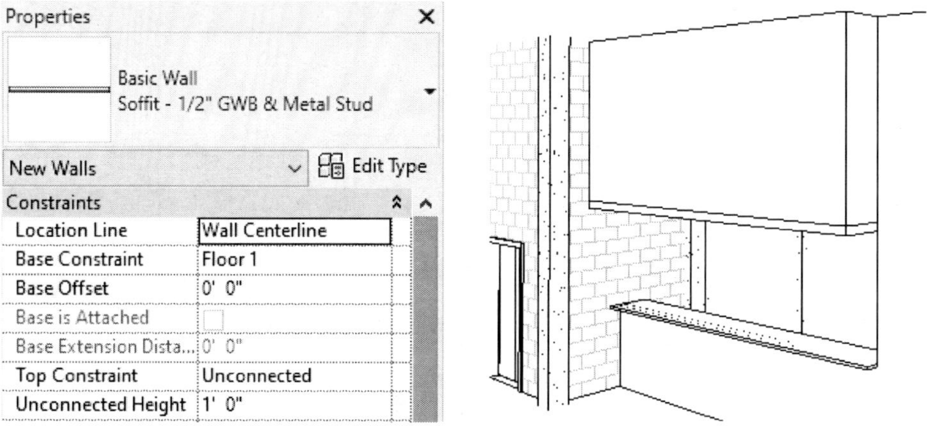

Figure 11–17

How To: Create a Ceiling with a Soffit

1. Open a ceiling plan.
2. In the *Architecture* tab>*Build* panel, click (Ceiling).
3. In the Type Selector, select the ceiling type. In Properties, set the *Height Offset From Level*.
4. In the *Modify | Place Ceiling* tab>*Ceiling* panel, click (Sketch Ceiling).
5. Draw the ceiling outline, such as the example shown in Figure 11–18.

Figure 11–18

6. Click (Finish Edit Mode).
7. In the *Architecture* tab>*Build* panel, click (Wall) to create the soffit wall.
8. In the Type Selector, select a soffit wall type. In Properties, set the *Base Offset* from the floor and set the *Top Constraint/Unconnected Height* as required to establish the height of the soffit.
   - Sometimes it is easier to set the height of the soffit walls by extending or trimming elements in a section view.
9. In the *Modify | Place Wall* tab>*Draw* panel, click (Pick Lines). Select the edges of the ceiling to create the walls, as shown in Figure 11–19.

   Note: If the wall is on the outside of the ceiling, flip it using the Flip control and create the rest of the walls using the opposite ***Location Line*** *option.*

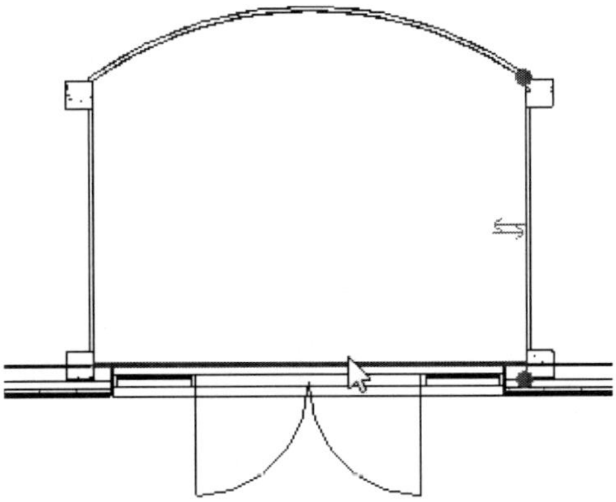

Figure 11–19

10. Display the ceiling in a 3D or section view to verify that it is displayed correctly.

Hint: Joining Geometry

When you are working with elements that are next to each other, they might need additional modification so that they display as expected. For example, one way to fix connections between walls and ceilings is to join the geometry.

In the *Modify* tab>*Geometry* panel, click (Join Geometry) and then select the elements to join.

Practice 11b
Create Ceiling Soffits

Practice Objective

- Create ceiling soffits.

In this practice, you will sketch a ceiling, add fixtures, and create a soffit wall in the hallway. Figure 11–20 shows what the ceiling soffit will look like when completed in plan view. Optionally, you will also add a recessed ceiling and soffit to the breakfast area.

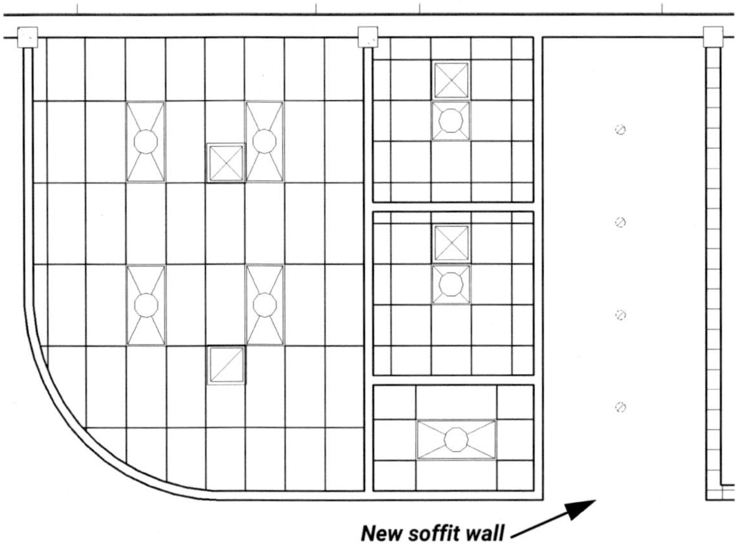

Figure 11–20

Task 1: Sketch a ceiling.

1. Open the project **Arch-CeilingSoffits.rvt** from the practice files folder.
2. Verify that you are in the **Ceiling Plans: Floor 1** view and zoom in on the hallway by the restrooms.
3. In the *Architecture* tab>*Build* panel, click (Ceiling).
4. In the *Modify | Place Ceiling* tab>*Ceiling* panel, click (Sketch Ceiling).
5. In the Type Selector, select **Compound Ceiling: GWB on Mtl.Stud**, and in Properties, set the *Height Offset From Level* to **10'-0"**.
6. Sketch the outline of the ceiling (as shown in Figure 11–21) in the hallway using the sketch tools.

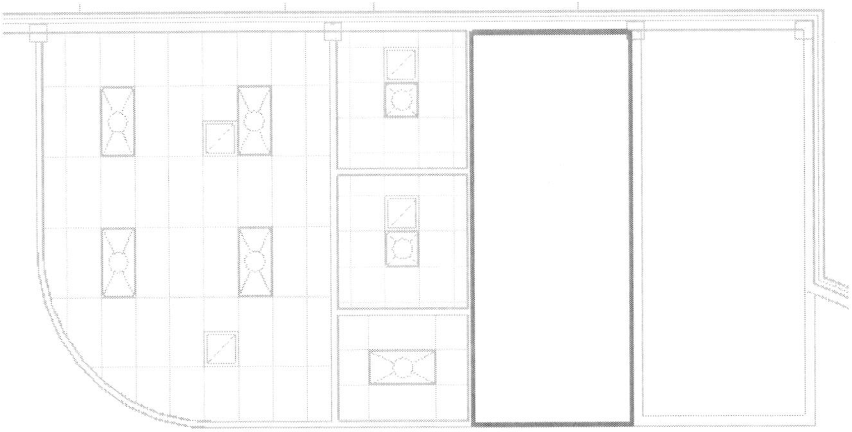

Figure 11–21

7. Click (Finish Edit Mode).
8. In the *Architecture* tab>*Build* panel, click (Component).
9. In the Type Selector, select **Downlight - Recessed Can: 6" Incandescent - 277V**.
10. Add four lights down the hallway, as shown in Figure 11–22. Because the lights are being placed on the ceiling, their elevation from level is automatically set to the appropriate height. Hint: You can place the lighting fixtures and use temporary dimensions to space them out, or use a reference plane or the **Array** command to space them equally in the hallway.

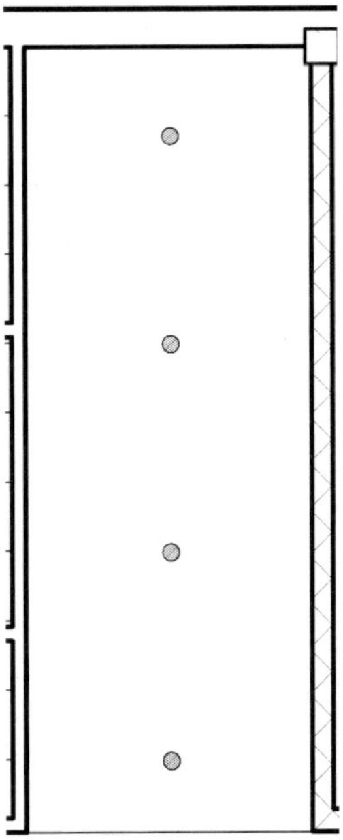

Figure 11–22

11. Save the project.

Task 2: Add a ceiling soffit.

1. Open the **Sections (Wall Section): Lobby Hall - Ceiling Soffit** view and zoom in on the hallway area between levels Floor 1 and Floor 2 and grid lines H and I, as shown in Figure 11–23.

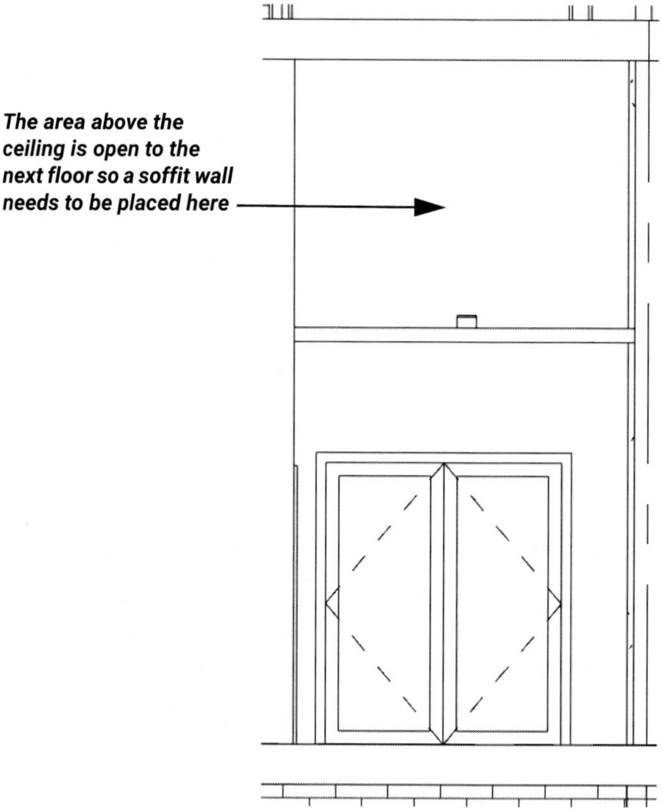

Figure 11–23

2. Return to the **Ceiling Plans: Floor 1** view and zoom in to the hallway next to the restrooms.
3. In the *Architecture* tab>*Build* panel, click (Wall). In the Type Selector, select **Basic Wall: Soffit 1/2" GWB & Metal Stud**.
4. In Properties, verify or set the following:
    - *Location Line*: **Finish Face: Interior**
    - *Base Constraint*: **Floor 1**
    - *Base Offset*: **10'-0"**
    - *Top Constraint*: **Up to level: Floor 2**
    - *Top Offset*: (negative) **-1'-0"**

5. Draw the wall across the face of the ceiling (from left to right), as shown in Figure 11–24.

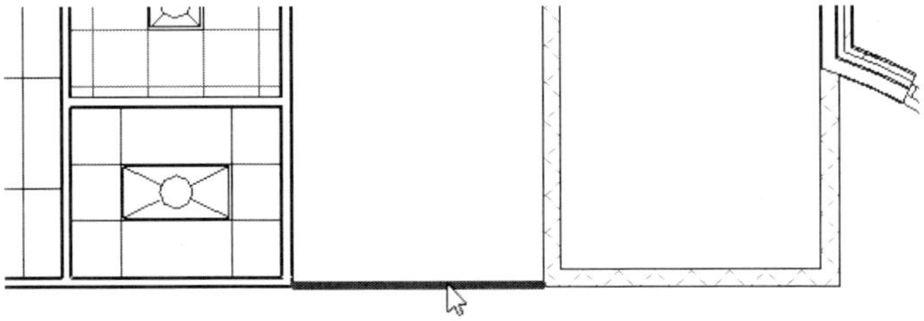

Figure 11–24

6. Click (Modify).
7. Activate the **Lobby Hall - Ceiling Soffit** view.
8. In the *Modify* tab>*Geometry* panel, click (Join Geometry).
9. Select the soffit wall above the ceiling and then select the ceiling, as shown on the left in Figure 11–25.
10. Select the ceiling again, and then the edge of the wall to the left. The elements clean up, as shown on the right in Figure 11–25.
11. Click (Modify).

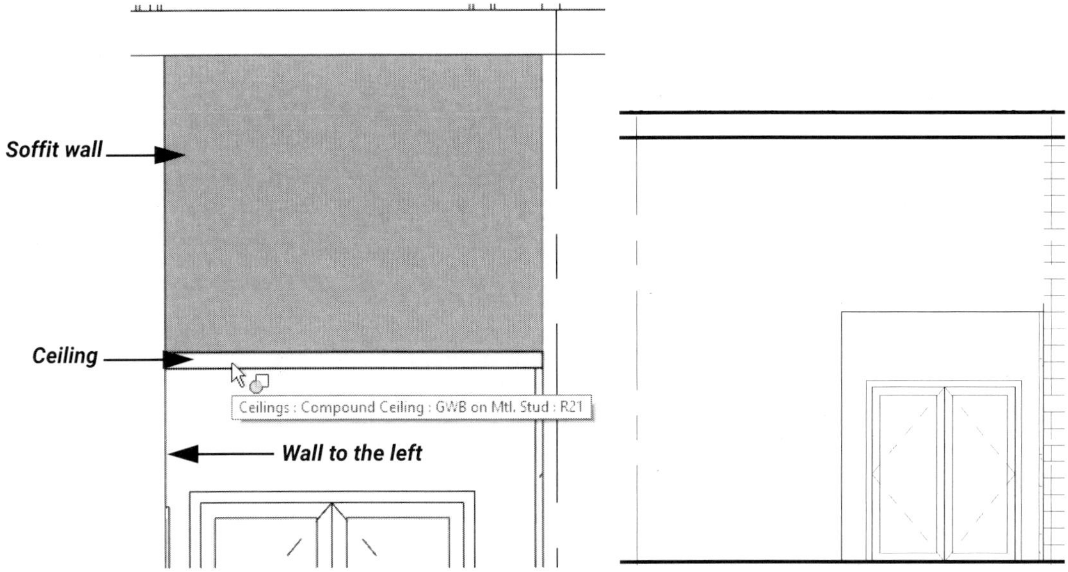

Figure 11–25

12. Save and close the project.

End of practice

Chapter Review Questions

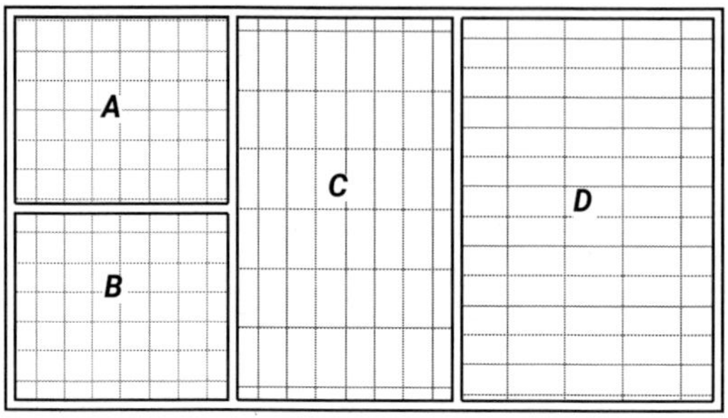

Figure 11–26

1. For the rooms labeled A and B in Figure 11–26, which command do you use to change the position of the ceiling grid?

   a.  (Offset)

   b.  (Move)

   c.  (Rotate)

   d.  (Copy)

2. For the rooms labeled C and D in Figure 11–26, which command do you use to change the direction of the ceiling grids?

   a.  (Align)

   b.  (Move)

   c.  (Rotate)

   d.  (Copy)

3. Which of the following component types can be hosted by ceiling elements? (Select all that apply.)

a. Mechanical diffusers and returns

b. Lighting fixtures

c. Curtain wall grids

d. Columns

4. Which of the following commands would you use to create a ceiling with a soffit around the edges? (Select all that apply.)

a. (Automatic Ceiling)

b. (Sketch Ceiling)

c. (Wall)

d. (Component)

5. Which of the following commands can you use to get a lighting fixture fitted exactly in a ceiling grid, as shown in Figure 11–27? (Select all that apply.)

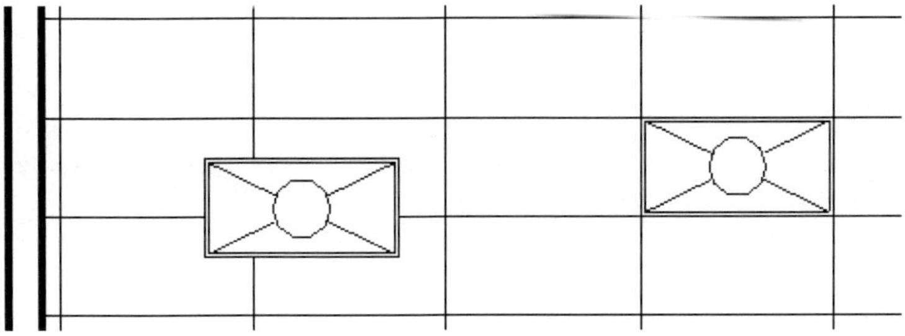

Figure 11–27

a. (Trim/Extend to Corner)

b. (Align)

c. (Join)

d. (Move)

Command Summary

Button	Command	Location
	**Automatic Ceiling**	• **Ribbon:** *Modify | Place Ceiling* tab>*Ceiling* panel
	**Ceiling**	• **Ribbon:** *Architecture* tab>*Build* panel
	**Join**	• **Ribbon**: *Modify* tab>*Geometry* panel
	**Place a Component**	• **Ribbon:** *Architecture* tab>*Build* panel
	**Sketch Ceiling**	• **Ribbon:** *Modify | Place Ceiling* tab>*Ceiling* panel

Chapter

12

Modeling Roofs

You can create simple or very complex roofs in Revit® using two different methods. The footprint method enables you to create roofs using a process that is similar to that for creating a floor. You can also use the extrusion method, which is based on a profile that controls the shape of the roof.

Learning Objectives

- Sketch roofs using the footprint method for flat, shed, gable, or hip roofs.
- Set work planes to help you create extruded roof profiles.
- Sketch a profile for the roof that can then be extruded.

12.1 Modeling Roofs

Revit provides two main ways of creating roofs:

- **By Footprint:** The roof is created in a floor plan view by defining the area to be covered.
- **By Extrusion:** The roof is created in an elevation or section view by defining a profile sketch or using a reference plane drawn in a view to set the work plane.

The footprint method can generate most common roof types, including flat, shed, gable, mansard, and hip roofs. The extrusion method is required for an odd-shaped roof, a roof with two slopes on the same face, or a curved roof, as shown in Figure 12–1.

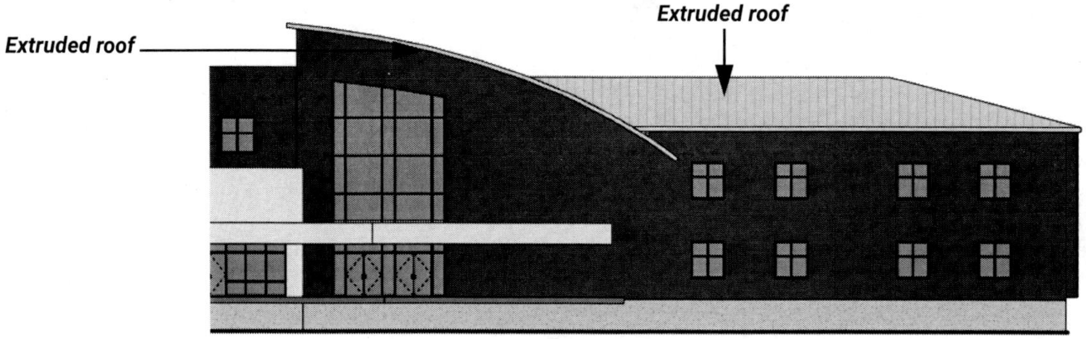

Figure 12–1

- Other roof options, found in the **Roof** drop-down list, are the following:
  - **Roof by Face** can be used with massing elements to create irregular shapes.
  - **Roof: Soffit** connects the edge of the roof to the wall with a flat footprint.
  - **Roof: Fascia** places a profile, whether flat or built-up board, on the outside edge of the roof and can be used for friezes.
  - **Roof: Gutter** adds a gutter on the edge of the roof, but does not include downspouts.

Roof Types

The following are examples of roof types that would typically be created using **Roof by Footprint** or **Roof by Extrusion**.

Flat Roof

A flat roof is simply a roof in which none of the edges define a slope. Specify an overhang distance to extend the roof beyond the walls or define the profile along the inside of the wall to create a roof behind a parapet, as shown in Figure 12–2.

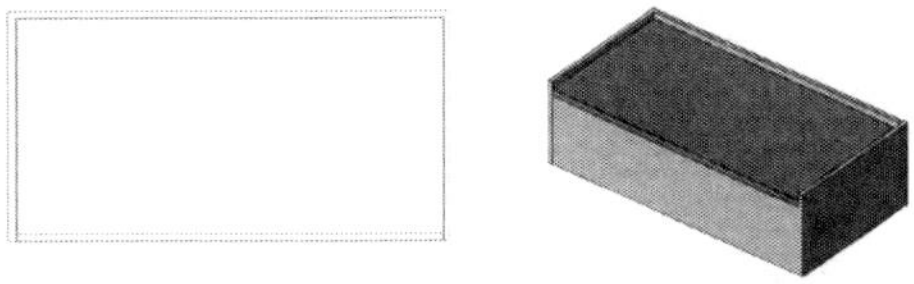

Figure 12–2

Shed Roof

For shed roofs, only the edge at the low eave line is slope defining, as shown in Figure 12–3.

Figure 12–3

Hipped Roof

With hipped roofs, all four edges are the roof are slope defining. Vary the slope to create different types of hips, as shown in Figure 12–4. Half-hip (or jerkinhead) roof types are also created this way.

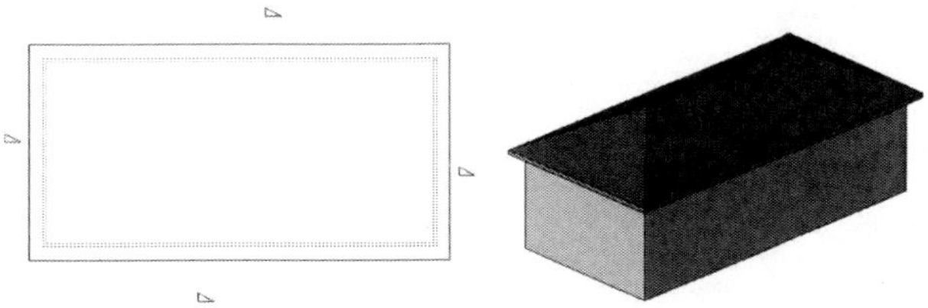

Figure 12–4

Mansard Roof

A mansard roof is generally constructed as two roofs, the first steeply sloped and the second either flat or sloping at a much shallower angle, as shown in Figure 12–5. This type of roof can be created using two separate roofs, the first ending at a cutoff level and the second filling the opening in the first. Before starting this process, create a level at the elevation corresponding to where the roof slopes change.

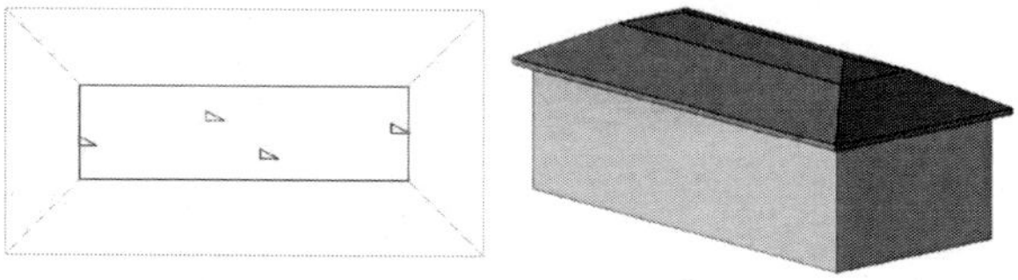

Figure 12–5

- Remember to cut a section through the roof and then use the **Move** tool to adjust the starting height of the upper roof so that it matches the ending height of the lower roof.

Hip Gable/Dutch Gable/Bonnet Roof

This type of roof is also created by constructing two roofs: a hip and a gable. In this case, rather than using a cutoff level, create the roof by sketching the perimeter of the first roof (the hip roof) and then sketch another closed perimeter inside the first. This second perimeter will form a hole in the hip roof and will then be used to draw the sketch for the gable roof, as shown in Figure 12–6.

Figure 12–6

- When creating this type of roof, add walls to fill in the open end of the gable and attach the wall to the upper gable and lower hip roof.

Gambrel Roof

A gambrel roof consists of two roofs: a lower portion with a steep slope angle and an upper portion with a shallower slope angle, but with gable ends. Creating it as an extrusion works better because the roof maintains a consistent fascia along the gable end, as shown in Figure 12–7.

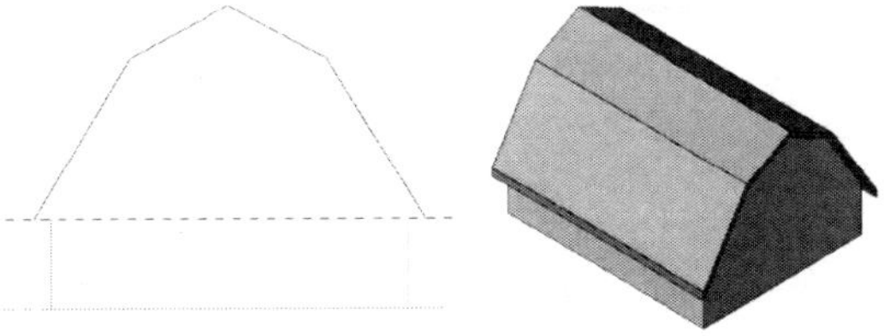

Figure 12–7

Barrel Vault Roof

A barrel vault roof, by definition, is a roof that is an extrusion of a curve, whether cylindrical or elliptical, along a given distance (as shown in Figure 12–8). This is also true for bow roofs.

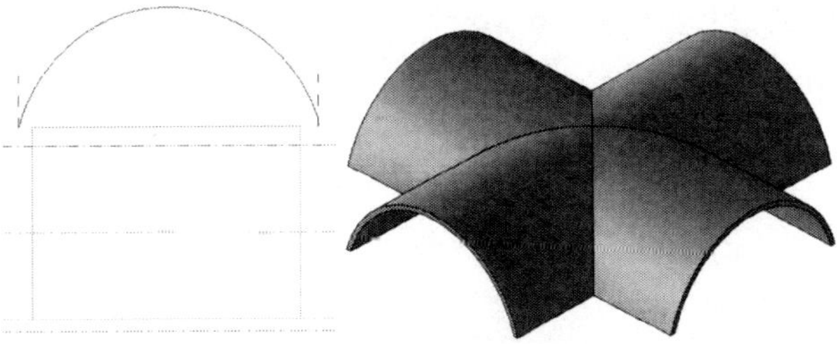

Figure 12–8

Complex Roofs

Revit will automatically create complex roofs that follow the shape of the roof footprint. For example, Revit will automatically create valleys for roofs that follow L-shaped footprints or create conical roofs when following an arc footprint, as shown in Figure 12–9.

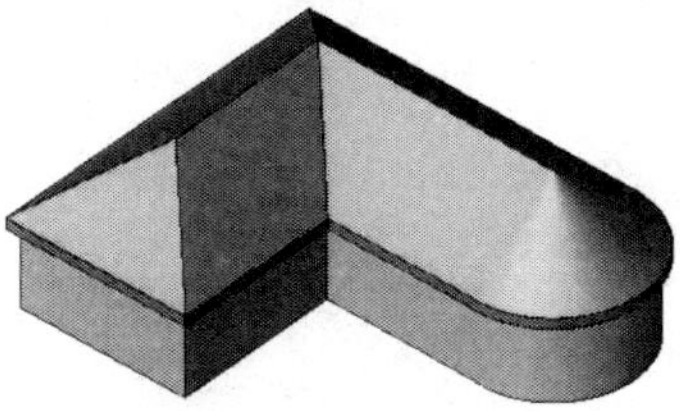

Figure 12–9

12.2 Creating Roofs by Footprint

To create a flat roof or any basic single-sloped roofs (hip, shed, or gable), start with a plan view and define a sketch or "footprint" around the area that you want the roof to cover, as shown in Figure 12–10.

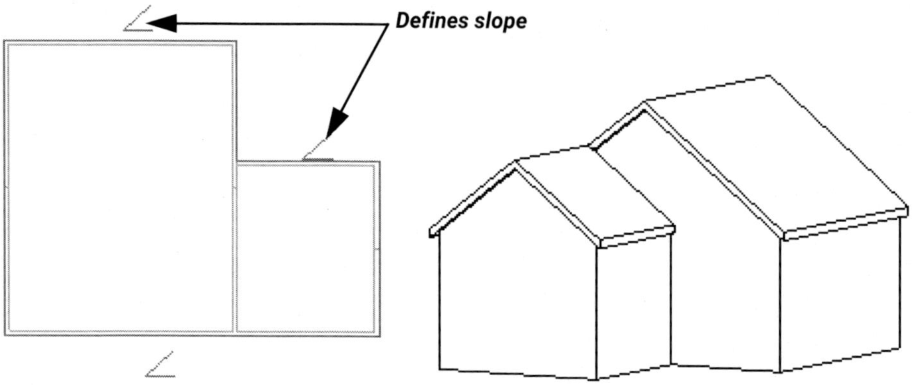

Figure 12–10

You control the type of roof by specifying which edge(s) define the slope:

- No edges sloped = flat roof
- One edge sloped = shed roof
- Two opposing edges sloped = gable roof
- All edges sloped = hip roof

How To: Add a Roof by Footprint

1. Open a plan view at the roof level of the building.
2. In the *Architecture* tab>*Build* panel, expand (Roof) and click (Roof by Footprint).
3. In the *Draw* panel, ensure that (Boundary Line) is toggled on. Click (Pick Walls), (Line), or any other sketch tool to create the roof footprint. You can include arcs in the sketch. The options on the ribbon differ depending on which sketch tool is selected.
    - The lines must form a closed boundary with no overlapping lines. If they do not, use (Trim/Extend to Corner) to modify the lines, as needed.

4. Additional options that can be set on the *Modify | Create Roof Footprint* tab (shown in Figure 12–11) are:

   - (Offset): Enter the distance at which a roof line is drawn from the selection or sketch.
   - (Radius): Add a curve of a specified radius to the sketch line.
   - (Sides): Enter the number of sides when sketching a polygon.
   - (Chain): When toggled on, enables you to model multiple connected sketch lines.
   - (Define Slope): This option toggles the slope-defining property of the sketch line on and off. When toggled on, the sketch line you create will display an adjacent angle symbol and a value specifying the slope. You can change the slope by editing this value. When toggled off, the perimeter line you sketch will not define a slope. Note that lines representing gable ends do not define a slope.
   - (Extend Into Wall): When toggled on, the overhang dimension is measured from the roof edge to the exterior core of the wall. When toggled off, the overhang is measured from the exterior finish face of the wall.
   - (Overhang): When (Pick Walls) is selected, you can enter an overhang value to specify how far the roof extends beyond the face of the wall.

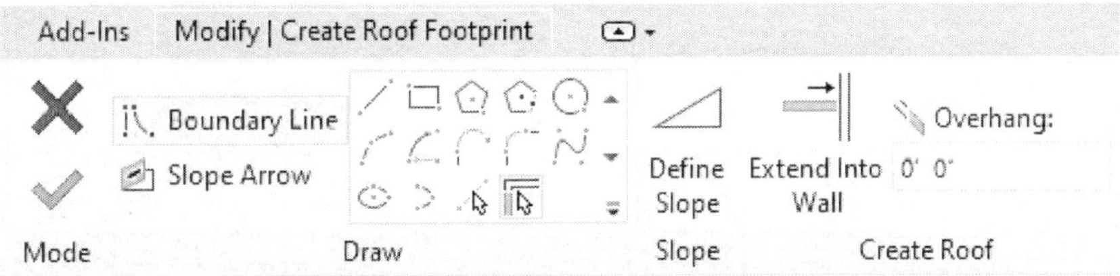

Figure 12–11

5. As you are drawing your footprint, you can select and modify each segment of the sketch as needed using Properties (as shown in Figure 12–12), temporary dimensions, or controls to create different roof types.

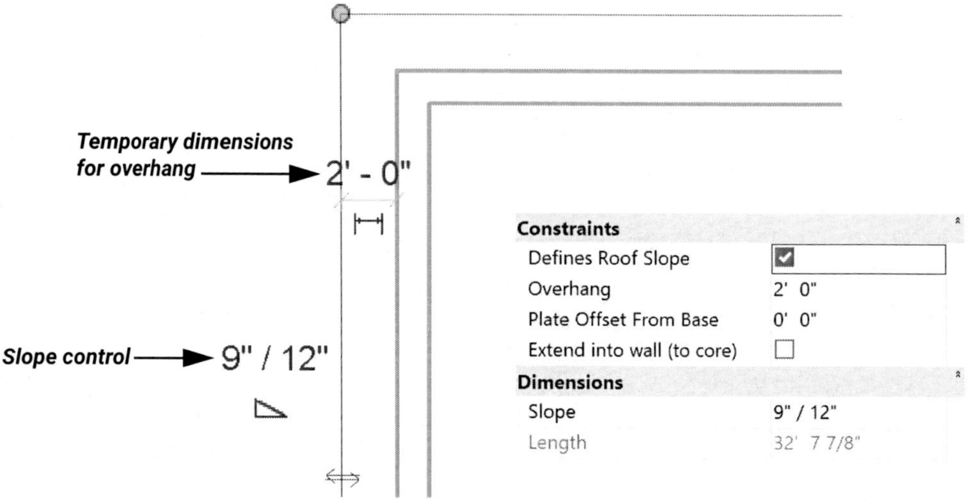

Figure 12–12

6. Click (Finish Edit Mode).
7. An alert box might open, as shown in Figure 12–13. You can attach the highlighted walls to the roof now or later.
   - You have the option to check the box for **Do not show me this message again**. Revit will remember your last selection and do this for every instance this occurs.

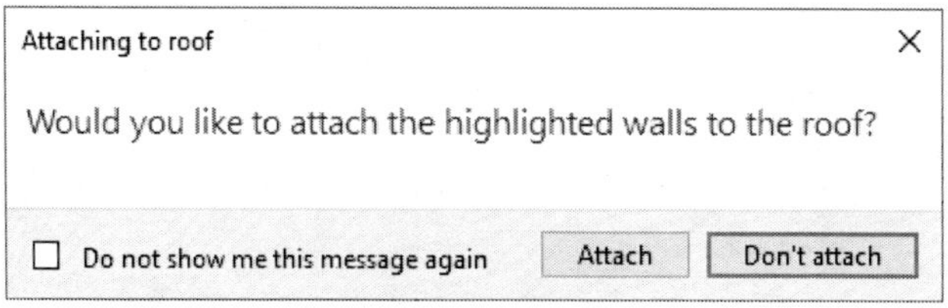

Figure 12–13

8. The roof is still selected and, in Properties, you can set the properties for the entire roof. These include roof type, *Base Offset From Level*, *Rafter Cut*, and *Cutoff Level*. To edit a roof sketch, either:
   - double-click on the edge of the roof, or
   - with the roof selected, click (Edit Footprint).

Attaching Walls to Roofs

Attaching walls to the roof extends the walls up to the roof, as shown in Figure 12–14. Attach walls while still in the **Roof** command, or you can use the **Attach Top/Base** command later in the design process.

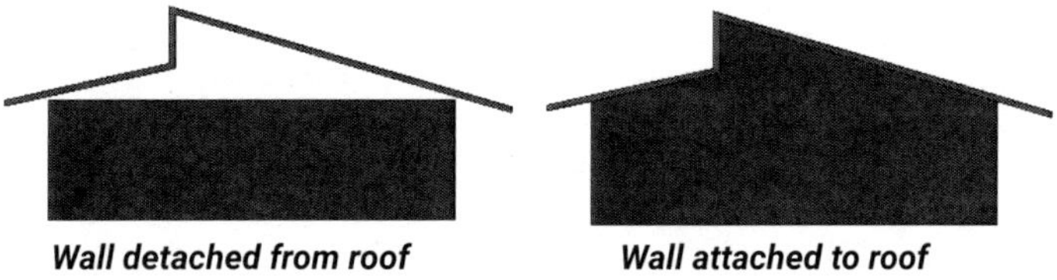

Figure 12–14

- **Attach Top/Base** can also be used with walls that are against sloping floors or topographic site features.

How To: Attach Walls to Roofs

1. Select the wall or walls that you want to attach to the roof.
2. In the *Modify | Walls* tab>*Modify Wall* panel, expand (Attach Top) and select (Attach Top), as shown in Figure 12–15. The last command used will be the default tool that displays in the ribbon.

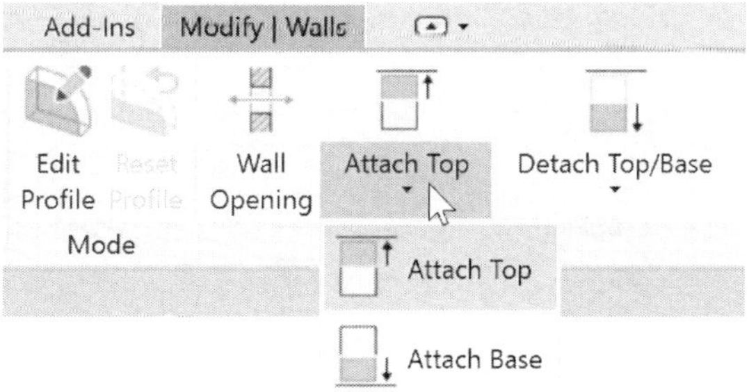

Figure 12–15

3. Select the roof. The walls are trimmed or extended to the roof line.

Walls will typically need to be attached to the roof in order to match the elevation profile of the roof element. If the walls you previously created extend above the roof, Revit will ask you if you want to attach the highlighted walls to the roof. If you say **Yes**, the profile of the walls will be changed to follow the slope of the roof. If the walls end below the roof, you can select the walls and then attach them to the roof.

How To: Detach Walls from Roofs

1. Select the wall or walls that you want to detach from the roof.
2. In the *Modify | Walls* tab>*Modify Wall* panel, expand (Detach Top/Base) and select (Detach Top/Base) or (Detach All). **Detach All** will automatically detach all selected walls from the roofs and floors they are attached to. The last command used will be the default tool that displays in the ribbon.
3. Select the roof. The walls' top constraint height is restored.

Modifying the Footprint of a Roof

Once your roof is created, you can modify it by selecting the roof and changing its parameters in Properties. You can also modify the roof footprint sketch or extruded profile of a roof.

Roof by Footprint Properties

Base Level	Sets the level for the roof.
Base Offset From Level	Sets the height of the roof above or below the level where it is being sketched (allows for raised heel truss designs).
Cutoff Level	Specifies the level at which the roof should be cut off. Typically, another roof will be created to fill the hole created by cutting off the first roof. This property and the *Cutoff Offset* apply to the first roof, not the second roof.
Cutoff Offset	Specifies the height of the cutoff above or below the level specified by the *Cutoff Level*.
Rafter Cut	Defines the rafter cut on an eave by selecting from a drop-down list: • **Plumb Cut:** Cuts the roof fascia at a 90° vertical. • **Two Cut - Plumb:** Cuts the roof fascia 90° vertically and horizontally at the *Fascia Depth*. • **Two Cut - Square:** Cuts the roof fascia at 90° relative to the face of the roof and horizontally at the *Fascia Depth*.
Fascia Depth	Sets the length of the lines defining the fascia. Does not affect the size of additionally applied fascia profiles.

Rafter or Truss	Select either **Rafter** or **Truss** for the roof construction method to control how the roof sits on the walls. If **Rafter** is selected, the *Plate Offset From Base* is measured from the inside of the wall. If **Truss** is selected, the *Plate Offset From Base* is measured from the outside of the wall, as shown in Figure 12–16. 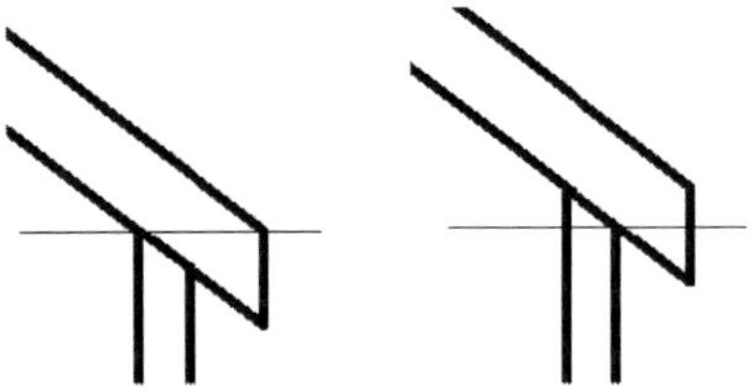 **Figure 12–16**
Maximum Ridge Height	A read-only value that displays the maximum height of the top of the roof above the base level of the building.
Slope	Controls the value of the slope-defining line.

How To: Modify the Footprint of a Roof

1. To edit a roof sketch, double-click on the edge of the roof. Alternatively, with the roof selected, in the *Modify | Roofs* tab>*Mode* panel, click (Edit Footprint).
2. In the *Modify | Roofs > Edit Footprint* tab>*Draw* panel, use the tools to edit the roof's sketch lines.
3. To finish editing the roof, click (Finish Edit Mode).

Setting Up a Roof Plan View

When creating a roof, add a level with a floor plan view where the bottom of the roof should be located. If there are roofs at different heights, create a level for each location.

Most plan views are typically cut at **3'-0" to 4'-0"** above the bottom of the level, as shown in Figure 12–17. However, this does not work with pitched roofs, whose structures can reach **20'-0"** high or more. To change the height of the area shown in the roof plan, change the *View Range*.

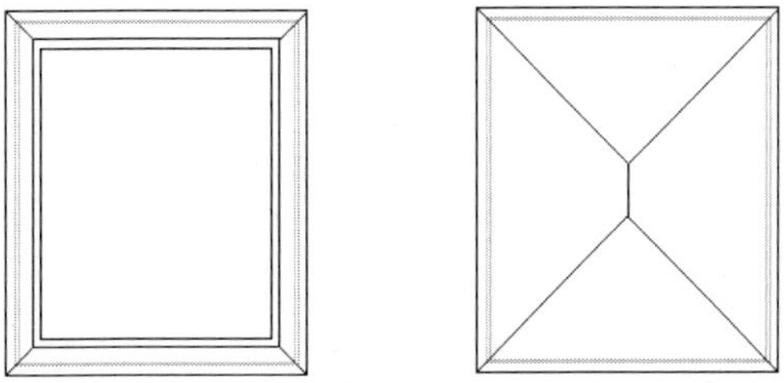

View Range Cut Plane @ 4'-0" ***View Range Cut Plane @ 30'-0"***

Figure 12–17

Practice 12a
Create Roofs by Footprint

Practice Objectives

- Create flat and sloped roofs using Roof by Footprint.
- Create a roof plan view.

In this practice, you will create a flat roof on the main part of the hotel, and flat and sloped roofs over the poolhouse. Figure 12–18 shows the completed practice. The pool curtain wall, soffit, and parapet walls have been added to this practice file.

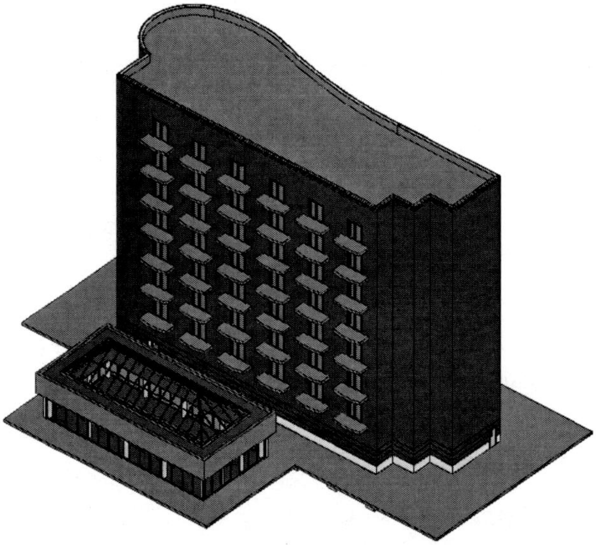

Figure 12–18

Task 1: Create a flat roof.

1. Open **Arch-RoofFP.rvt** from the practice files folder.
2. Verify that you are in the **Floor Plans: Roof** view, and in Properties, set the *Underlay>Range: Base Level* to **None**.
3. Hide the grid lines, section, and elevation markers.
4. Open the **3D Views: {3D}** view. Make the **Roof** view the active view, then type **WT** to tile the views. Type **ZA** to zoom all.
5. In the *Architecture* tab>*Build* panel, expand (Roof) and click (Roof by Footprint).
6. In the *Modify | Create Roof Footprint* tab>*Slope* panel, verify that (Define Slope) is toggled off.

7. In the *Create Roof* panel, verify that the (Overhang) is set to **0'-0"**.
8. In the *Draw* panel, click (Pick Walls) and select the inside of the walls around the building, as shown in Figure 12–19.

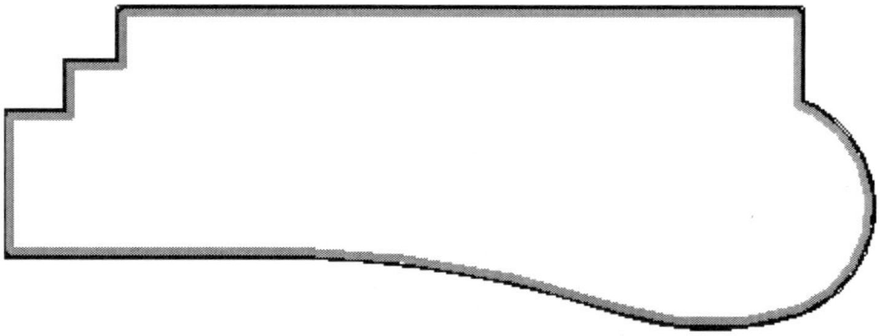

Figure 12–19

9. In the Type Selector, select **Basic Roof: Steel Truss - Insulation on Metal Deck - EPDM**.
10. Click (Finish Edit Mode). The roof is created and still selected.
11. Click in an empty space in the view to clear the selection.
12. Close the **Roof** view so the **{3D}** view is the only one active.
13. Save the project.

Task 2: Create a poolhouse roof plan view.

1. Orbit the 3D view until the poolhouse at the back of the building displays by either holding <Shift> and the mouse wheel to orbit in the 3D view or clicking on the northwest corner of the ViewCube to rotate the model. Several features are in place, including the parapet walls, as shown in Figure 12–20.

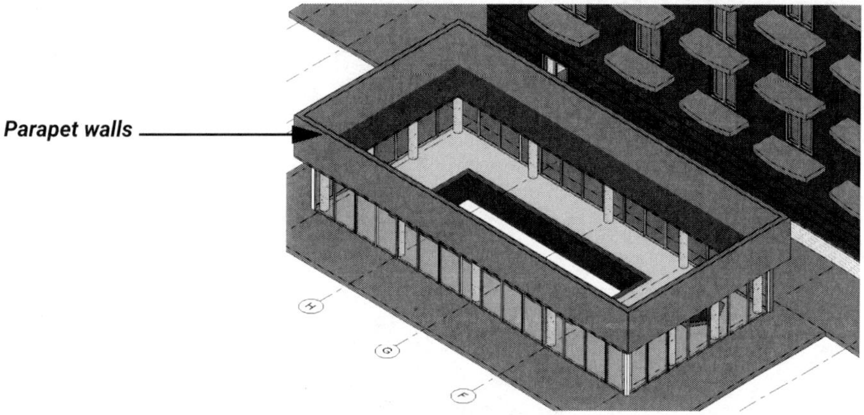

Figure 12–20

2. Zoom in to the poolhouse. Select the four poolhouse parapet walls. Hold down <Ctrl> to select more than one element.
3. In the *Modify | Walls* tab>*View* panel, click (Selection Box).
4. Click in an empty space in the view to clear the selection. The parapet walls are within a section box, as shown in Figure 12–21.

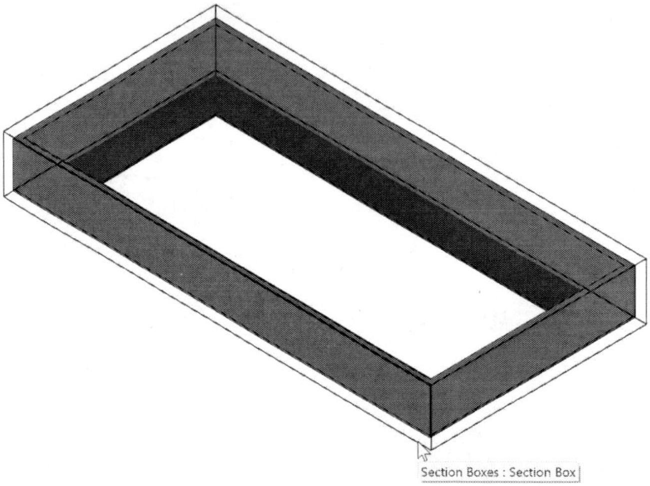

Figure 12–21

5. Select the section box and use the control grips to stretch the section box to show the entire poolhouse. Make sure to stretch the top control grip up so you can see the roof that will be created.
6. With the section box still selected, right-click on it and select **Hide in View>Elements**.
7. In the Project Browser, rename the {3D} view to **3D - Poolhouse** and press <Enter>.
8. Duplicate the **Floor Plans: Floor 1 - Poolhouse** view.
9. The new view opens and is the active view. Rename the copy as **Roof - Poolhouse**.
10. In the View Control Bar, change the *Scale* to **1/4" = 1'-0"**.

11. In Properties, in the *Extents* section, click **Edit...** next to *View Range*, or type **VR**. In the *View Range* dialog box, set the following (as shown in Figure 12–22):

    Primary Range:

    - *Top*: **Floor 4**, *Offset:* **7'-6"**
    - *Bottom*: **Unlimited**
    - *Cut plane, Offset:* **40'-0"**

    View Depth:

    - *Level*: **Unlimited**

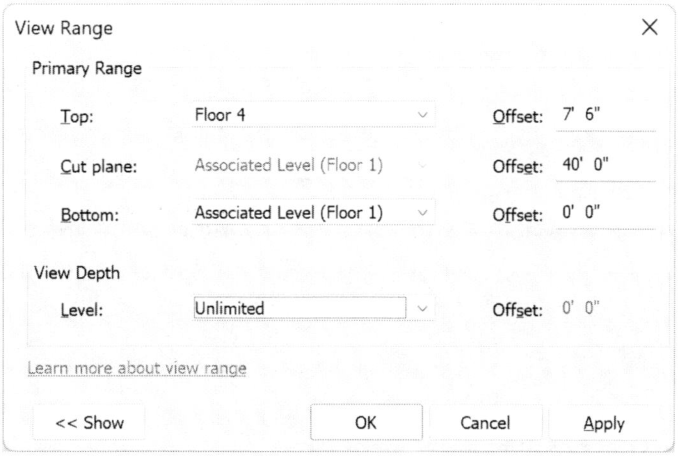

Figure 12–22

12. Click **Apply** and **OK**.
13. With the **Roof - Poolhouse** view as the active view, type **WT** to tile the two views and **ZA** to zoom all views.
14. Save the project.

Task 3: Create roofs on the poolhouse.

1. In the **Roof - Poolhouse** view, in the *Architecture* tab>*Build* panel, click (Roof). **Roof by Footprint** is the default roof command.
2. In the *Modify | Create Roof Footprint* tab>*Draw* panel, click (Pick Walls). In the *Slope* panel, verify that (Define Slope) is toggled off, then in the *Create Roof* panel, verify that the *Overhang* is set to **0'-0"**. Do not set the roof type (it will be done later).

3. Select the inside of the parapet walls, as shown in Figure 12–23.
4. Click (Pick Lines) and select the soffit opening, as shown in Figure 12–23. This creates a flat roof with an opening in it.

Figure 12–23

5. Click (Finish Edit Mode). If prompted, click **Don't attach** in the *Attaching to Roof* dialog box.
6. With the roof still selected, in Properties, set the following:
   - *Type:* **Basic Roof: Generic - 12"**
   - *Base Level:* **Floor 2**
   - *Base Offset From Level:* (negative) **-2'-0"**
7. Move your cursor into the drawing area.
8. The roof is now in the correct location, as shown in Figure 12–24.

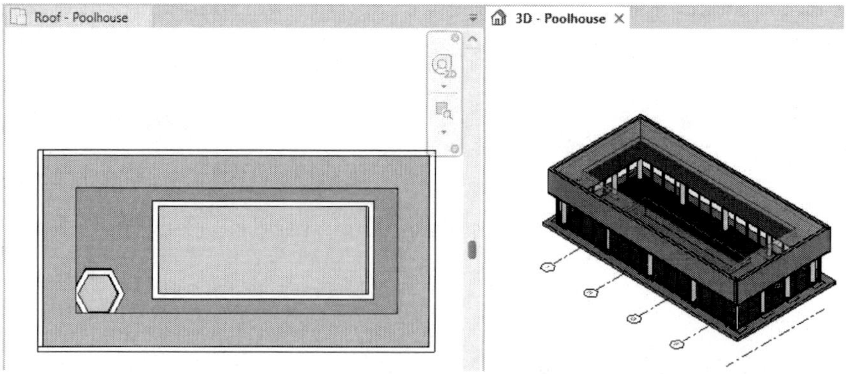

Figure 12–24

9. Click in the view to release the roof.
10. Start the **Wall** command.

11. In the *Draw* panel, select (Pick Lines).
12. In Properties, set the following:
    - *Wall Type:* **Basic Wall: Exterior - EIFS on Mtl.Stud**
    - *Location Line:* **Finish Face: Interior**
    - *Base Constraint:* **Floor 2**
    - *Base Offset:* (negative) **-1'-0"**
    - *Top Constraint:* **Unconnected**
    - *Unconnected Height:* **1'-0"**
13. Draw a short wall around the soffit opening (as shown on the left in Figure 12–25), making sure that the preview lines (dashed lines) display on the soffit side (as shown on the right in Figure 12–25).

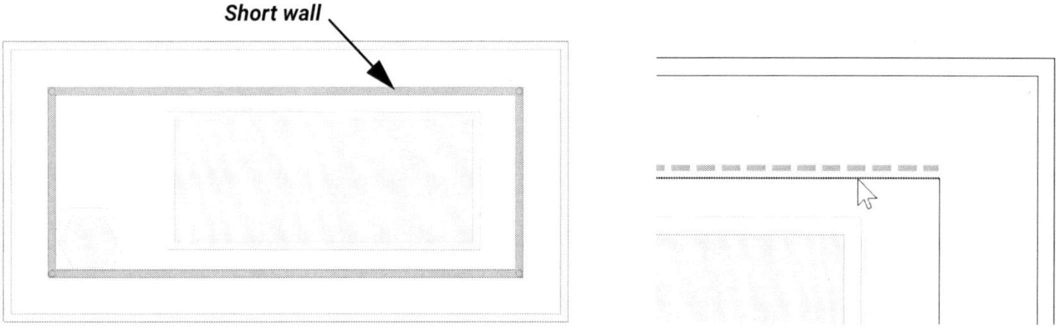

Figure 12–25

14. Click (Modify).
15. Start the (Roof) command.
16. In the *Draw* panel, select (Pick Walls).
17. In the *Slope* panel, click (Define Slope) to toggle it on. Verify there is no overhang and that (Extend Into Wall) is toggled off.
18. In the Type Selector, select **Sloped Glazing: Sloped Glazing Pool Roof** and set the following properties:
    - *Base Level:* **Floor 2**
    - *Base Offset from Level:* **0'-0"**
    - *Grid 1 Justification*: **Center**

19. Select the outside of the new walls you just created, as shown in Figure 12–26.

Figure 12–26

20. Click (Finish Edit Mode). If the message dialog box displays, click **Don't attach** to not attach any walls to the roof.

- If a warning message displays, read and close the warning dialog box.

21. The new roof displays, as shown in Figure 12–27. Click (Modify).

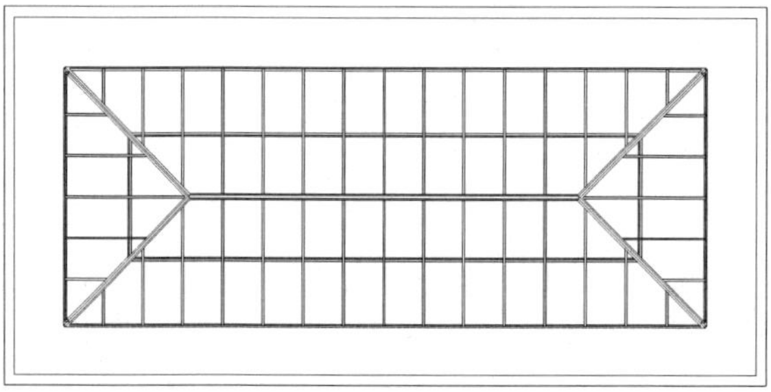

Figure 12–27

22. In the Quick Access Toolbar, click (Default 3D view) to open a default 3D view. Orbit the view to see the poolhouse and hotel. Change the visual style to view the elements better, if needed.

23. Save and close the project.

End of practice

12.3 Creating Roofs by Extrusion

Extruded roofs enable you to create complex roof forms, such as the curved roof shown in Figure 12–28. Extruded roofs are based on a sketch of the roof profile in an elevation or section view and do not need to be a closed sketch. The profile is extruded between a start and end point. From there you can modify the roof by adding openings or joining it to other roofs.

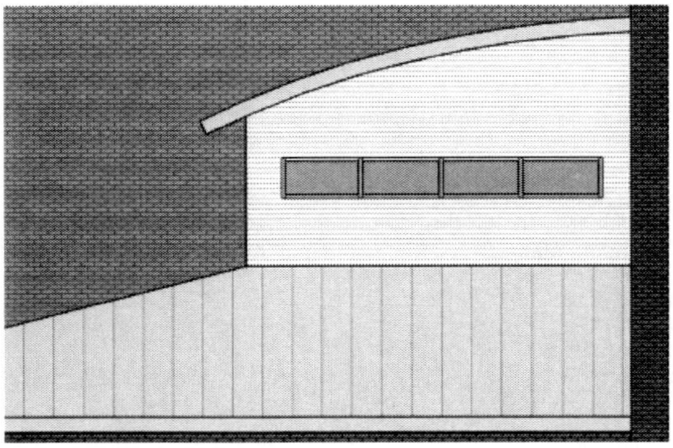

Figure 12–28

Establishing Work Planes

When creating a roof by extrusion, you are prompted to specify a work plane. A work plane is the surface you sketch on or extrude from.

- In a plan view, the work plane is automatically parallel to the level.
- In an elevation or 3D view, you need to specify the work plane before you start sketching.

To see the active work plane, in the *Architecture* tab>*Work Plane* panel, click (Show Work Plane). Alternatively, you can click (Viewer). This opens the Workplane Viewer, a separate window showing the current work plane, as shown in Figure 12–29.

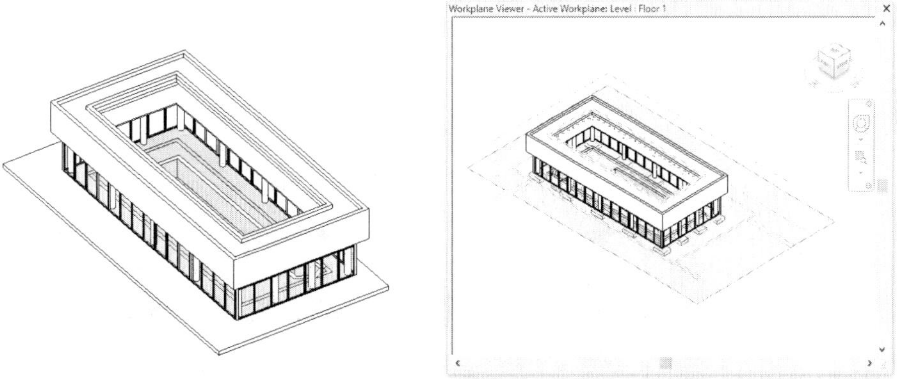

Figure 12–29

- Named reference planes can be used to specify a work plane that would otherwise not be displayed in a view. This is especially helpful when creating extruded roofs.
- You can set the work plane by selecting **Set Work Plane**, which opens the *Work Plane* dialog box with additional options, or **Pick a Plane**, which enables you to select a linear or horizontal plane in the view.

How To: Pick a Plane

1. In the *Architecture* tab>*Work Plane* panel, expand (Set) and select (Pick a Plane), or type **PK**.
2. Select a work plane in the view.

How To: Set the Work Plane

1. Start a command that requires a work plane, or in the *Architecture* tab>*Work Plane* panel, click (Set).
2. In the *Work Plane* dialog box, select one of the options.
    - **Name:** Select an existing level, grid, or named reference plane, as shown in Figure 12–30, and click **OK**.

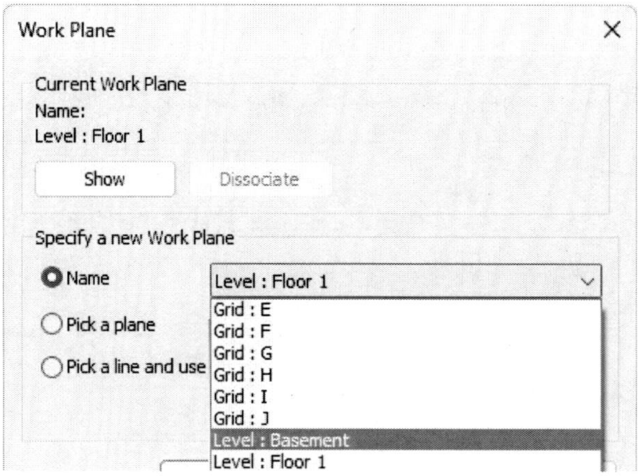

Figure 12–30

- **Pick a plane:** Click **OK** and select a plane in the view, such as a wall face. Ensure that the entire plane is highlighted before you select it.
- **Pick a line and use the work plane it was sketched in:** Click **OK** and select a model line such as a room separation line.

- If you are in a view in which the sketch cannot be created, the *Go To View* dialog box opens, as shown in Figure 12–31. Select one of the views and click **Open View**.

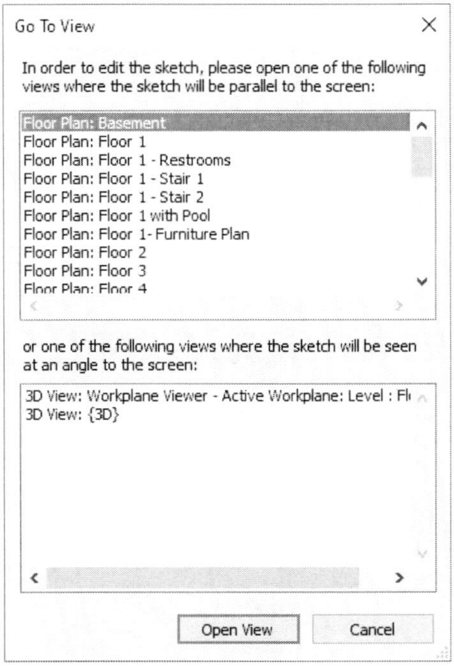

Figure 12–31

How To: Create an Extruded Roof

1. Open an elevation or a section view.
2. In the *Architecture* tab>*Build* panel, expand (Roof) and click (Roof by Extrusion).
3. If needed, in the *Work Plane* dialog box, select the work plane on which you want to sketch the roof profile and click **OK.**

4. In the *Roof Reference Level and Offset* dialog box, specify the base *Level* and *Offset* (if any), as shown in Figure 12–32.

   ***Note:** By default, this level is set to the highest one in the project. The offset creates a reference plane at that distance.*

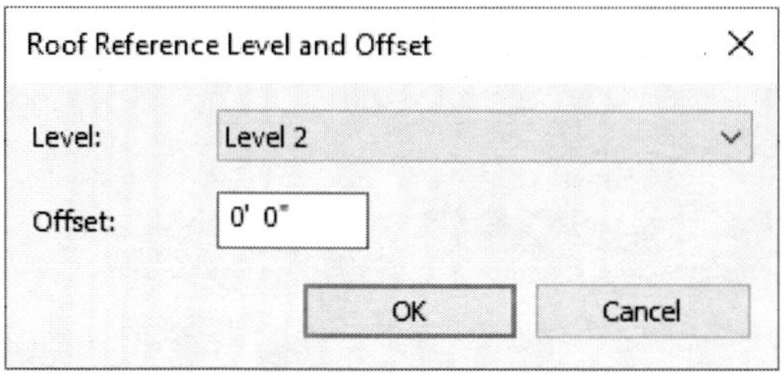

Figure 12–32

   - Use reference planes to help you create the roof profile. Reference planes created in sketch mode do not display once the roof is finished.

5. Use the sketch tools to create the profile, as shown in Figure 12–33. Sketch only the shape of the roof in profile, not the thickness.

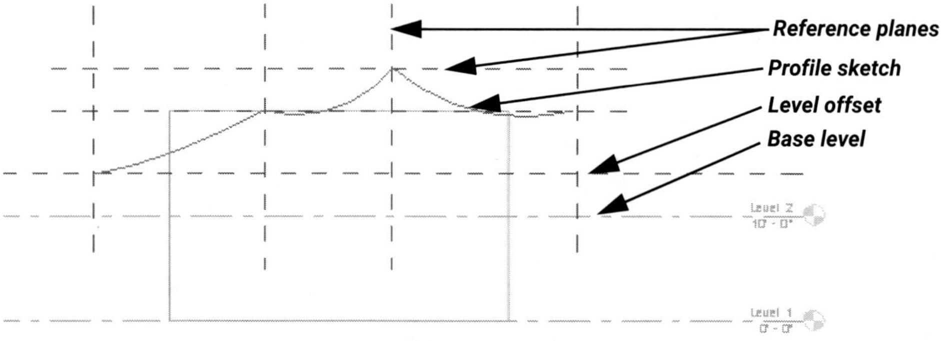

Figure 12–33

6. In Properties, set the *Extrusion Start* and *End*.
   - The direction in which the roof profile extrudes is known as the extrusion direction. The extrusion of a roof can extend in either direction along a line perpendicular to the plane in which the profile is created. To adjust the extrusion distance, use the *Extrusion Start* and *Extrusion End* values to adjust the length of the extrusion. You can extend the extrusion towards or away from the view.
   - Extrusion directions that are up or towards the view are positive, and extrusion directions that are down or away from the view are negative.

7. Click (Finish Edit Mode).

8. In the Type Selector, select the roof type.
    - The thickness, which is determined by the roof type, is added below the profile sketch line.
9. View the roof in 3D and make any other needed modifications. For example, you can use the controls on the ends of the roof to extend the overhang (as shown in Figure 12–34), as well as modify the roof using temporary dimensions and Properties.

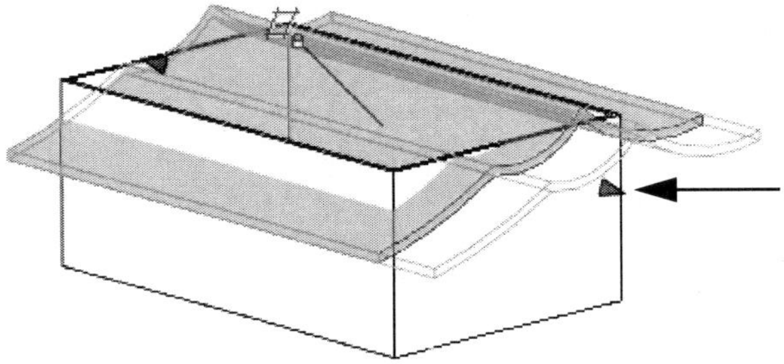

Figure 12–34

10. Attach the walls to the roof.

Modifying Extruded Roofs

You can make changes to the roof's profile in one of the following ways:

- Double-click on the edge of the roof.
- Select the roof. In the *Modify | Roofs* tab>*Mode* panel, click  (Edit Profile).

Roof by Extrusion Properties

Extrusion Start	Sets the extrusion start point for the roof.
Extrusion End	Sets the extrusion end point for the roof.
Reference Level	Specifies the reference level for the roof.
Level Offset	Specifies the offset from the reference level for the roof.
Rafter Cut	Defines the rafter cut on an eave by selecting from a drop-down list: • **Plumb Cut:** Cuts the roof fascia at a 90°vertical. • **Two Cut - Plumb:** Cuts the roof fascia 90° vertically and horizontally at the *Fascia Depth*. • **Two Cut - Square:** Cuts the roof fascia at 90° relative to the face of the roof and horizontally at the *Fascia Depth*.

How To: Modify the Profile of an Extruded Roof

1. Double-click on the edge of the roof. Alternatively, select the roof and in the *Modify | Roofs* tab>*Mode* panel, click (Edit Profile).
2. In the *Modify | Create Extrusion Roof Profile* tab>*Draw* panel, use the tools to create a closed boundary. The boundary can be entirely inside the roof or touching the roof boundaries.
3. Click (Finish Edit Mode).

How To: Modify the Plan View of an Extruded Roof

1. Open a plan view where the entire roof displays.
2. Select the roof.
3. In the *Modify | Roofs* tab>*Opening* panel, click (Vertical).
4. In the *Modify | Create Extrusion Roof Profile* tab>*Draw* panel, use the tools to create a closed boundary.The boundary can be entirely inside the roof or touching the roof boundaries.
5. Click (Finish Edit Mode). The extruded view now has a cutout, as shown in Figure 12–35.

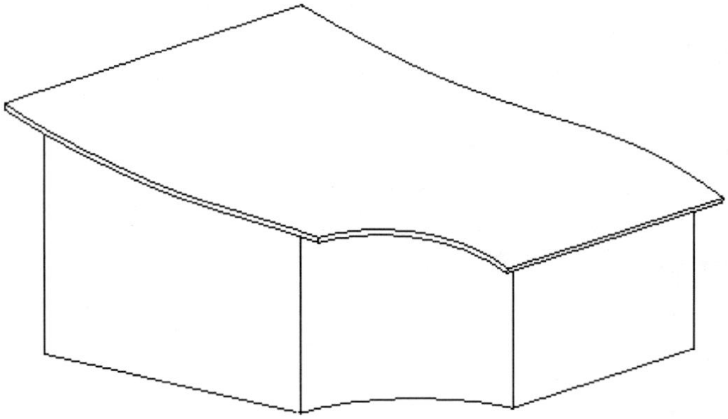

Figure 12–35

Joining Roofs

When you want to join a roof to another roof, or a wall face that is taller than the roof, you can use the **Join/Unjoin Roof** command. An example is shown in Figure 12–36. When using the command, watch the Status Bar in the lower-left corner to see what action needs to be taken.

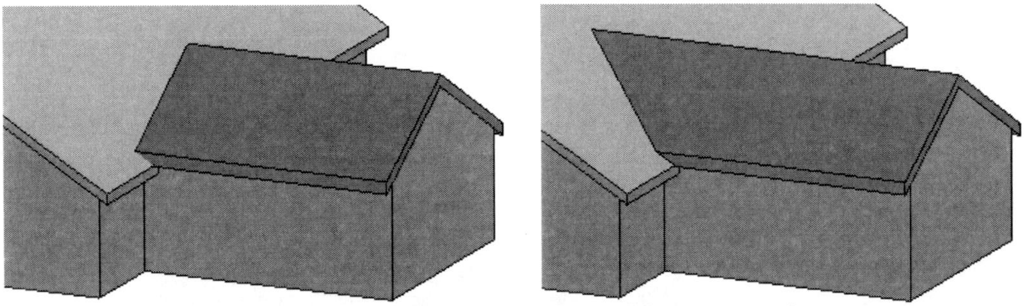

Before joining roofs ***After joining roofs***

Figure 12–36

How To: Use Join/Unjoin Roof

1. In the *Modify* tab>*Geometry* panel, click (Join/Unjoin Roof).
2. Select one of the roof edges.
3. Select the other roof or the wall.

Hint: Join Geometry

Where roofs overlap walls or other roofs, use **Join Geometry** to clean up the intersections. The elements remain separate, but the intersections are cleaned up, as shown in Figure 12–37.

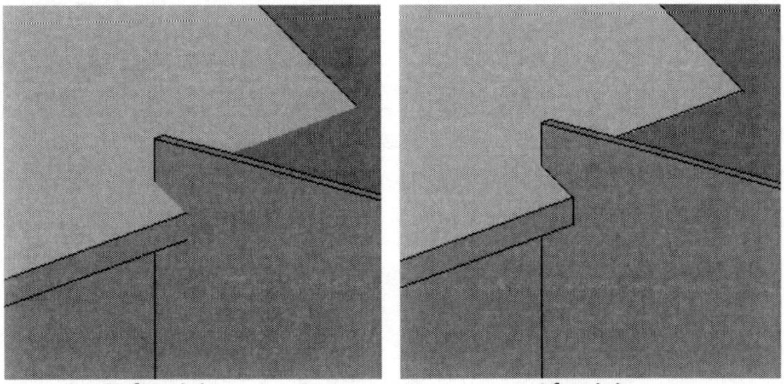

Before join ***After join***

Figure 12–37

Practice 12b
Create Roofs by Extrusion

Practice Objectives

- Create an extruded roof.
- Modify the plan profile of a roof.

In this practice, you will create a curved extruded roof to cover the main entrance of the building and modify its plan profile to cover the side entrance. Figure 12–38 displays an example of the finished extruded roof.

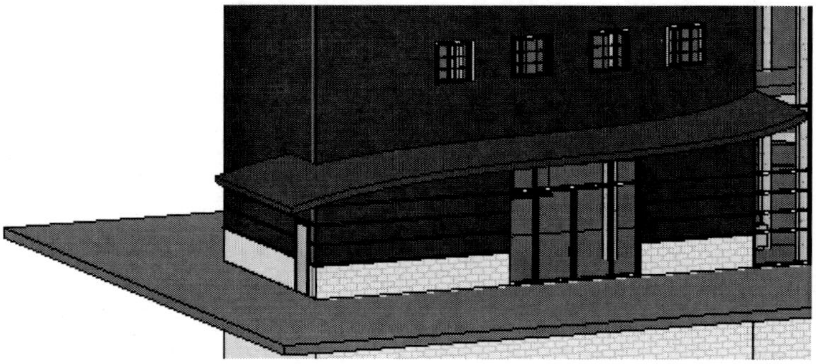

Figure 12–38

Task 1: Create a roof by extrusion.

1. Open **Arch-RoofExtrd.rvt** from the practice files folder.
2. Verify that you are in the **Elevations (Building Elevation): South** view.
3. Zoom in on the area around the front entrance.
4. In the *Architecture* tab>*Build* panel, expand (Roof) and click (Roof by Extrusion).
5. In the *Work Plane* dialog box, verify that **Pick a plane** is selected and click **OK**.
6. Select the front face of the exterior brick wall.
7. In the *Roof Reference Level and Offset* dialog box, set the *Level* to **Floor 2** and *Offset* to **0'-0"**, then click **OK**. A reference plane is set at this level and the model is grayed out.

8. In the *Draw* panel, select (Spline). Sketch the profile of a roof similar to the one shown in Figure 12–39. It should extend beyond the building to the left but finish at the end of the brick wall on the right and no higher than the reference plane.
   - After the spline is sketched, click **Modify** to end the sketch, then select the spline. You can adjust the curves of the spline by clicking and dragging the spline controls.

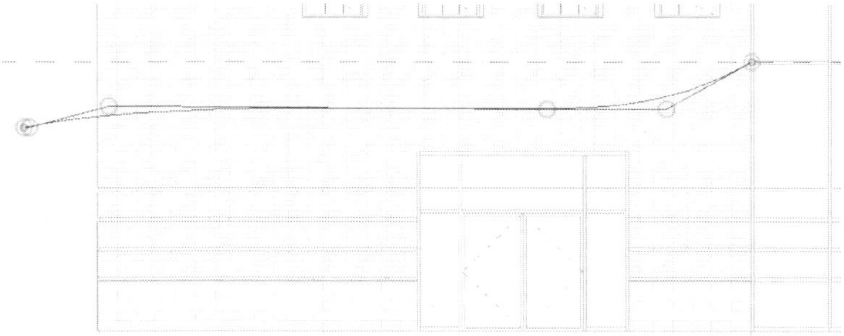

Figure 12–39

9. Click (Finish Edit Mode).
10. With the extruded roof still selected, in the Type Selector, select **Basic Roof: Generic - 9"**.
11. In Properties, set the *Extrusion End* to (negative) **-6'-0"**. This sets the roof inside the wall.
12. Click (Modify).
13. View the new roof in 3D. It is mostly inside the building at this point.
14. Save the project.

Task 2: Modify the extruded roof.

1. Open the **Floor Plans: Site** view. This view displays the entire building in plan including all of the roofs.
2. Select the entrance roof and using controls, widen the roof towards the outside of the front of the building until it is **20'-0"** wide, as shown in Figure 12–40. When finished, the *Extrusion Start* should be **14'-0"** and the *Extrusion End* should be (negative) **-6'-0"** in Properties.

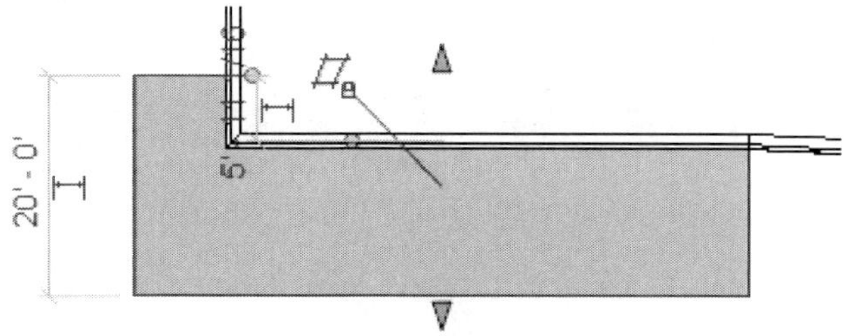

Figure 12–40

3. With the extruded roof selected, in the *Modify | Roofs* tab>*Opening* panel, click (Vertical).
4. Draw a rectangular cutout of the roof for the portion that passes through the building, as shown in Figure 12–41.

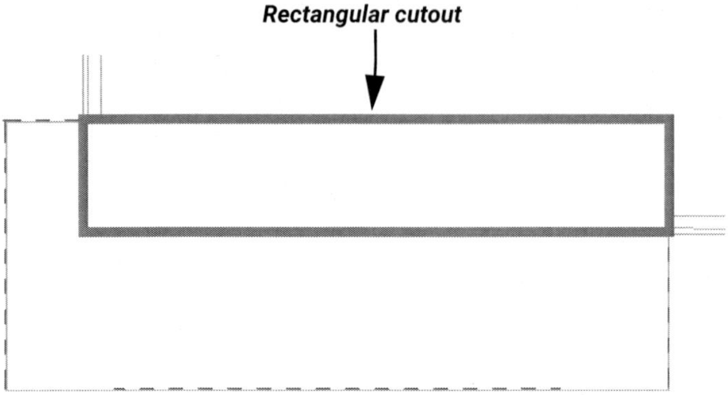

Figure 12–41

5. Click (Finish Edit Mode).
6. View the modified roof in 3D. It now wraps around the side of the building to cover the side entrance, as shown in Figure 12–42.

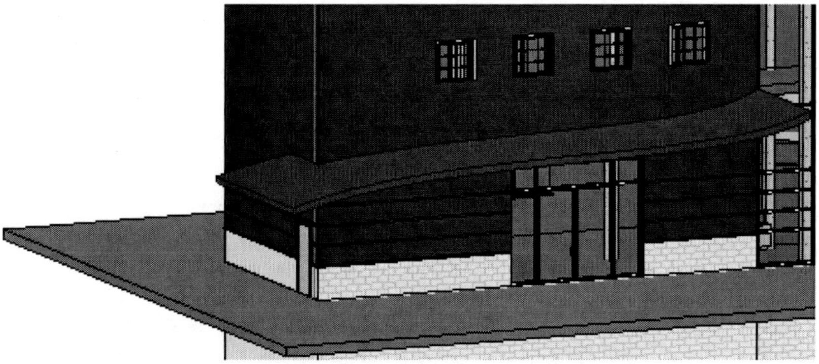

Figure 12–42

7. Save and close the project.

End of practice

Chapter Review Questions

1. How would you create a roof sloping in one direction only?
   a. By extrusion and rotate the roof to the correct angle.
   b. By footprint and use **Define Slope** to define a slope along one side.
   c. By extrusion and use **Define Slope** to define the overall slope of the roof.
   d. By footprint and use the **Shape Editing** tools to create the slope.

2. To create a flat roof, which of the following commands would you use to sketch the boundary of the roof and to set its thickness?
   a. **Roof by Footprint** with **Define Slope** toggled off and the thickness set by the roof type.
   b. **Roof by Extrusion** with **Define Slope** toggled off and the thickness extruded from the sketch.

3. Which of the following methods makes a wall touch the underside of a roof?
   a. Select the wall and use **Attach Top**.
   b. Select the roof and use **Attach Base**.
   c. Select the wall and edit the profile.
   d. Select the roof and use **By Face**.

4. Which roof type and view should you use to create a curved roof?
   a. Roof by Footprint, plan view
   b. Roof by Footprint, elevation or section view
   c. Roof by Extrusion, plan view
   d. Roof by Extrusion, elevation or section view

5. A work plane can be assigned using a named reference plane.
   a. True
   b. False

Command Summary

Button	Command	Location
	**Attach Top/Base**	• **Ribbon:** *Modify | Walls* tab>*Modify Wall* panel
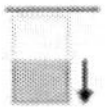	**Detach Top/Base**	• **Ribbon:** *Modify | Walls* tab>*Modify Wall* panel
	**Join Geometry**	• **Ribbon:** *Modify* tab>*Geometry* panel, expand Join
	**Join/Unjoin Roof**	• **Ribbon:** *Modify* tab>*Geometry* panel
	**Reference Plane**	• **Ribbon:** *Architecture* tab>*Work Plane* panel
	**Roof by Extrusion**	• **Ribbon:** *Architecture* tab>*Build* panel, expand Roof
	**Roof by Footprint**	• **Ribbon:** *Architecture* tab>*Build* panel, expand Roof
	**Set Work Plane**	• **Ribbon:** *Architecture* tab>*Work Plane* panel
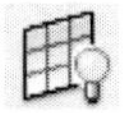	**Show Work Plane**	• **Ribbon:** *Architecture* tab>*Work Plane* panel
	**Unjoin Geometry**	• **Ribbon:** *Modify* tab>*Geometry* panel, expand Join
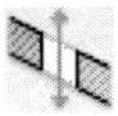	**Vertical (Opening)**	• **Ribbon:** *Modify | Roofs* tab>*Opening* panel
	**Viewer**	• **Ribbon:** *Architecture* tab>*Work Plane* panel

Chapter 13

Modeling Stairs, Railings, and Ramps

When modeling in Revit®, you can easily create basic stairs in straight, U-shaped, and multi-landing configurations. To create more complex shapes, you can convert runs and landings to sketches. Ramps can also be created by specifying runs and landings. Railings can be added automatically with the Stair and Ramp commands, or you can sketch railings on stairs and add them to balconies and decks. Railings are also sometimes used for fence lines.

Learning Objectives

- Create and modify component-based stairs made of runs, landings, supports, and railings.
- Convert runs and landings to sketches.
- Add and modify railings that are connected to stairs, as well as free-standing railings.
- Create ramps to make your design accessible.

13.1 Creating Component Stairs

As with other Revit elements, stairs are *smart* parametric elements. With just a few clicks, you can create stairs of varying heights and designs, complete with railings. Stairs can be created by assembling stair components (as shown on the left in Figure 13–1) or by sketching a custom layout (as shown on the right in Figure 13–1).

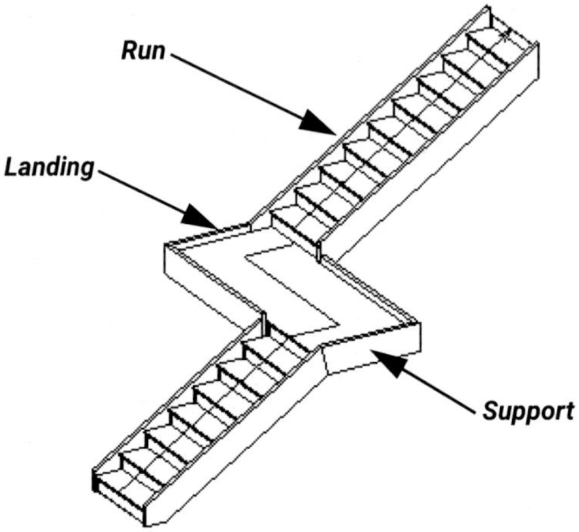

Figure 13–1

When creating component-based stairs, Revit defines three parts of a stair that can be assembled, as shown in Figure 13–1:

- **Runs:** The actual stair tread and riser elements. These include straight runs which can be combined for multi-landing stairs, spiral stairs, and L-shaped and U-shaped winders.
- **Landings:** The platform between runs. These are typically created automatically and then modified if needed. They can also be created independently of the assembly for grand staircases.
- **Supports:** The stringer or carriage that structurally holds the stair elements. These can be created automatically or you can pick the edges where you want the different types to go. These can be placed on either side of the stairs or in the center of the stairs.

- Railings are typically added in the **Stair** command. They display after you complete the stair. Railings can also be created for independent use, such as fencing.
- You can select and edit each of the components while you are in Stair Edit mode or after the stair has been created.

- Each component of the stair is independent but also has a relationship to the other components. For example, if steps are removed from one run they are added to connected runs to maintain the overall height, as shown in Figure 13–2.

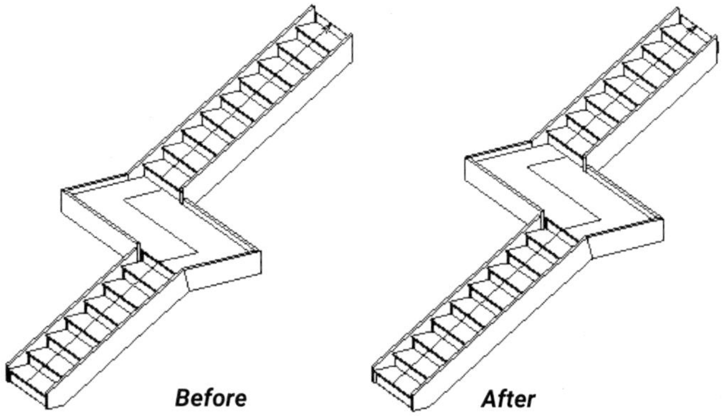

Figure 13–2

Creating Runs

To create a component stair, you must first place the run elements. There are six different options available in the *Components* panel, as shown in Figure 13–3 and described in the following table.

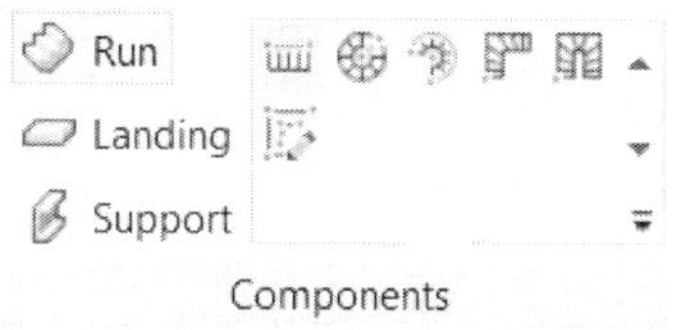

Figure 13–3

	Straight	Draws a straight run by selecting the start and end points of the run.
	Full-Step Spiral	Draws a spiral run based on a start point and radius.
	Center-Ends Spiral	Draws a spiral run based on a center point, start point, and end point.
	L-Shape Winder	Draws an L-shaped winder based on the lower end.
	U-Shape Winder	Draws a U-shaped winder based on the lower end.
	Create Sketch	Opens additional tools where you can sketch stair boundary and risers individually.

Note: *Component stairs can include a mix of the different types of runs.*

Hint: Stairs and Views

When creating stairs you can work in either plan or 3D views. It can help to have the plan view and a 3D view open and tiled side by side. Only open the views in which you want to work and type **WT** to tile the views.

How To: Create a Component-Based Stair

1. In the *Architecture* tab>*Circulation* panel, click (Stair).
2. In the Type Selector, select the stair type, as shown in Figure 13–4.

   Note: *The stair type can impact all of the other settings. Therefore, it is important to select it first.*

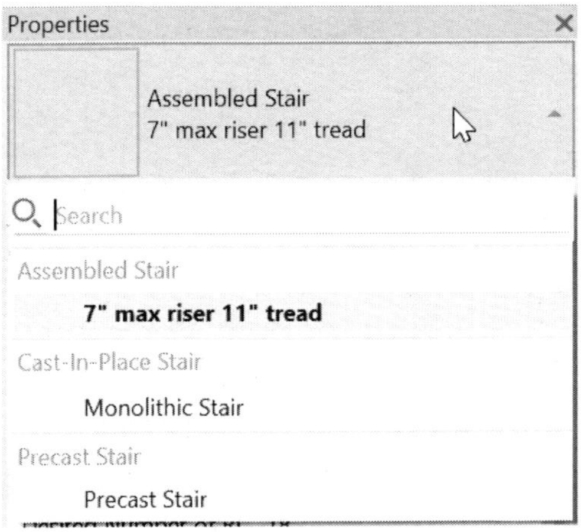

Figure 13–4

3. In Properties (shown in Figure 13–5), set the *Base Level*, *Top Level*, and any other information that is needed.

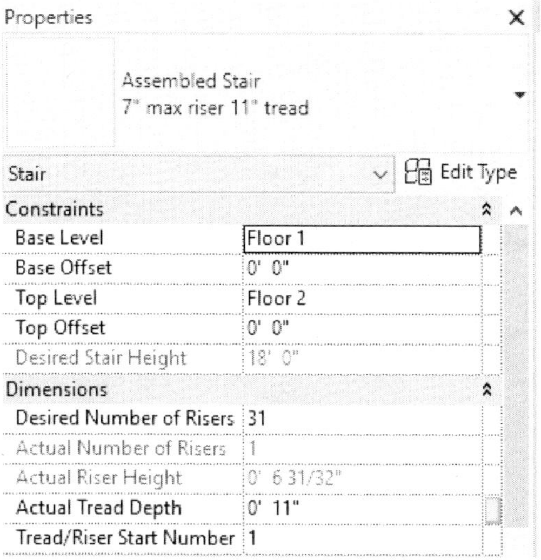

Figure 13–5

4. In the *Modify | Create Stairs* tab>*Tools* panel, click (Railing), select a railing type in the *Railing* dialog box (as shown in Figure 13–6), and specify whether the *Position* is on the **Treads** or **Stringer**. Click **OK**.

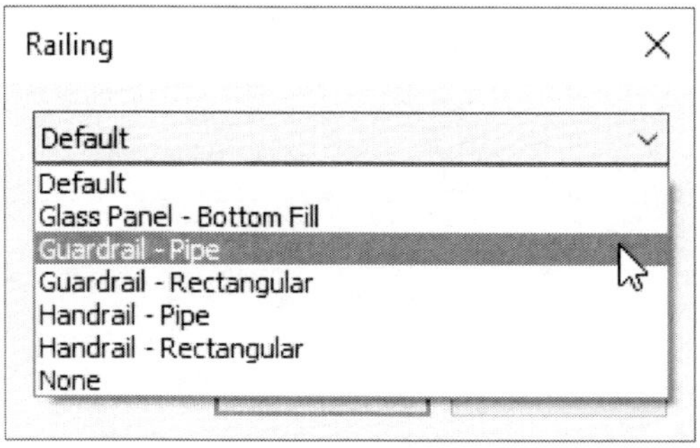

Figure 13–6

***Note:** Railings can also be added and modified after the stair has been placed.*

5. In the *Modify | Create Stair* tab>*Components* panel, click (Run) and then click (Straight).

6. In the *Create Stairs* panel (shown in Figure 13–7), specify the following options:

   - (Location Line): Select **Exterior Support: Left**, **Run: Left**, **Run: Center**, **Run: Right**, or **Exterior Support: Right**.
   - (Offset): Specify a distance from the *Location Line*. This is typically used if you are following an existing wall but do not need to have the stairs directly against them.
   - (Actual Run Width): Specify the width of the stair run (not including the supports).
   - (Automatic Landing): Creates landings between stair runs (recommended).

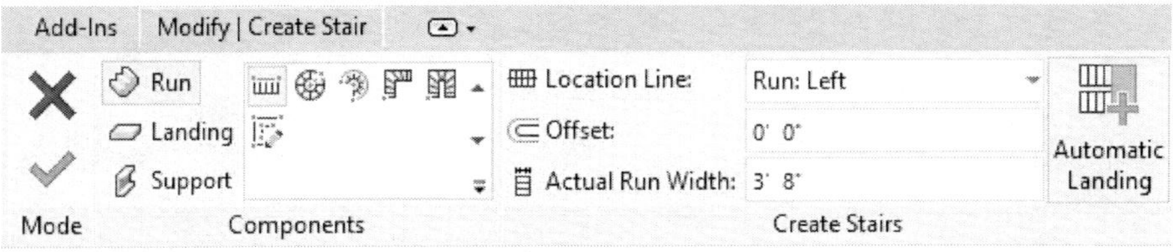

Figure 13–7

7. Click on the screen to select a start point for the run. A box displays, indicating the stair orientation and the number of risers created and remaining, as shown in Figure 13–8.

   Note: *If you are creating a complex stair pattern, sketch reference planes in the* ***Stairs*** *command to help you select the start and end points of each run.*

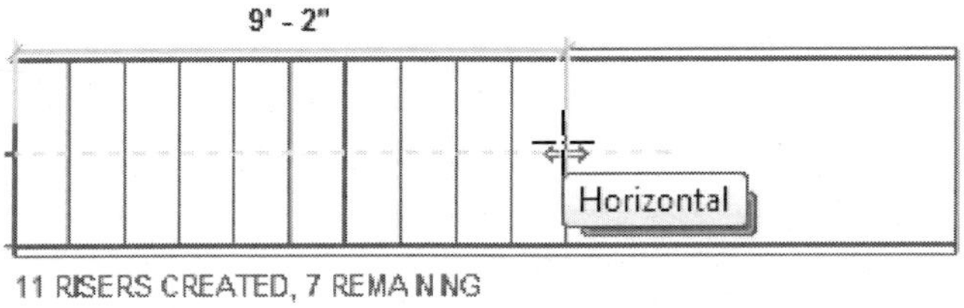

Figure 13–8

   - For straight stairs of a single run, select a second point anywhere outside the box to create the run.
   - For multi-landing or u-shaped stairs, select a second point inside the box for the length of the first run, move the cursor in the direction of the turn, then select a start point and an end point for the next run.
   - If the stair is going in the wrong direction, click (Flip) in the *Modify | Create Stair* tab> *Tools* panel.

8. Click (Finish Edit Mode) to create the stairs, complete with railings.

Creating Other Types of Runs

While most stairs are created using straight runs, there are times when you need to create specialty runs, such as spirals and winders, or when you need to sketch a stair such as that shown in Figure 13–9.

Figure 13–9

How To: Create a Full-Step Spiral Run

1. Start the **Stair** command and set up the properties as needed.
2. In the *Components* panel, click  (Full-Step Spiral).
3. Select the center point of the spiral.
4. Select (or type) the radius of the spiral. The run is created, as shown in Figure 13–10.

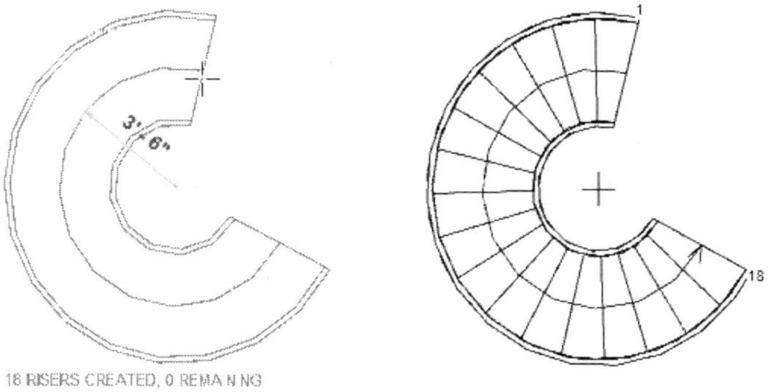

In process *Completed*

Figure 13–10

How To: Create a Center-Ends Spiral Run

1. Start the **Stair** command and set up the properties as needed.
2. In the *Components* panel, click (Center-Ends Spiral).
3. Select the center of the spiral.
4. Select (or type) the radius of the spiral, as shown on the left in Figure 13–11.
5. Drag the cursor to display the number of risers, as shown on the right in Figure 13–11.

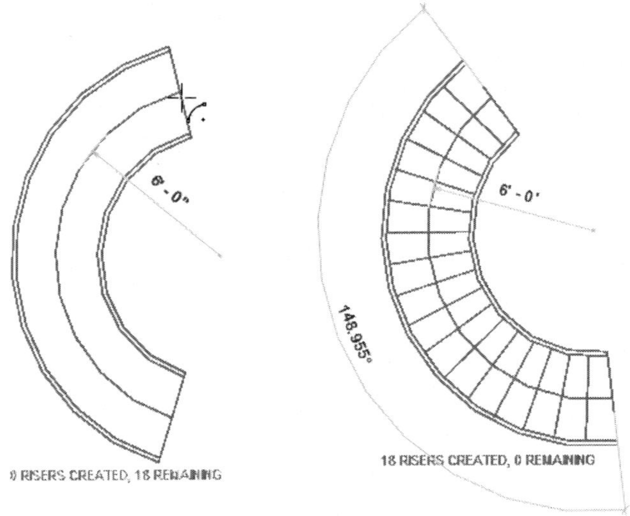

Select the radius ***Select the end of the run***

Figure 13–11

Note: *You can create spiral stairs with landings with this option.*

How To: Create Winder-Based Stairs

1. Start the **Stair** command and set up the properties as needed.
2. In the *Components* panel, click (L-Shape Winder) or (U-Shape Winder).
3. Click a start point to place the overall stair.

4. Select the stair and use the arrow controls to modify the length, as shown in Figure 13–12.

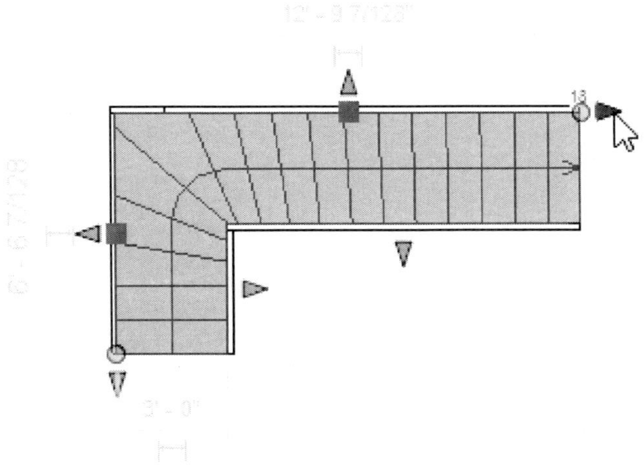

Figure 13–12

How To: Sketch a Stair

1. Start the **Stair** command and set up the properties as needed.
   - In many cases, a custom stair is shorter and should be set using a base and top offset from the same level, as shown in Figure 13–13. By default, a stair height is from level to level.

   Note: *Change the level offsets before starting to sketch the stair.*

Constraints	
Base Level	Level 1
Base Offset	0' 0"
Top Level	Level 1
Top Offset	2' 0"
Multistory Top Level	None

Figure 13–13

2. In the *Modify | Create Stair* tab>*Components* panel, click (Run) and then click (Sketch).

3. In the *Modify | Create Stair > Sketch Run* tab, use (Boundary), (Riser), and (Stair Path) to draw the parts of the stair, as shown in Figure 13–14.

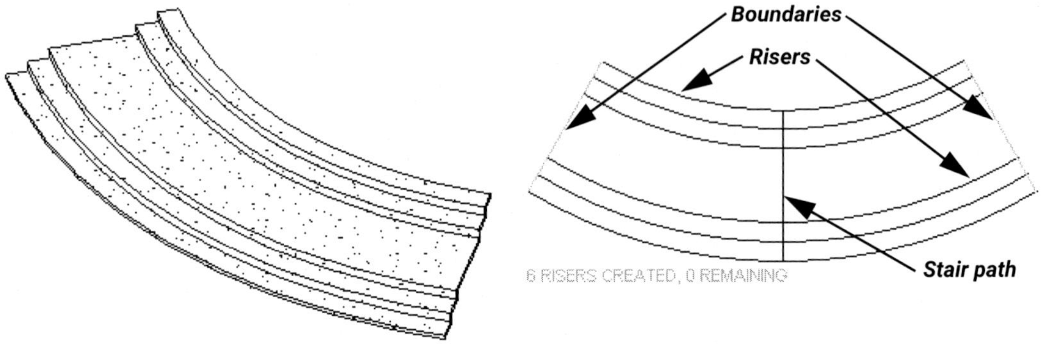

Figure 13–14

4. Click (Finish Edit Mode).
5. If you want to add a landing, you can sketch one.
6. Click (Finish Edit Mode) to complete the final assembly.

Creating Landings

Landings are typically created automatically between any breaks in runs. Once finishing the stair, you can easily modify the landings to create custom designs. There are two additional options to create landings, as shown in Figure 13–15:

- **Pick Two Runs:** Places the landing at the correct height between the runs.
- **Create Sketch:** Enables you to sketch the shape of the landing, but you must place it at the correct height.

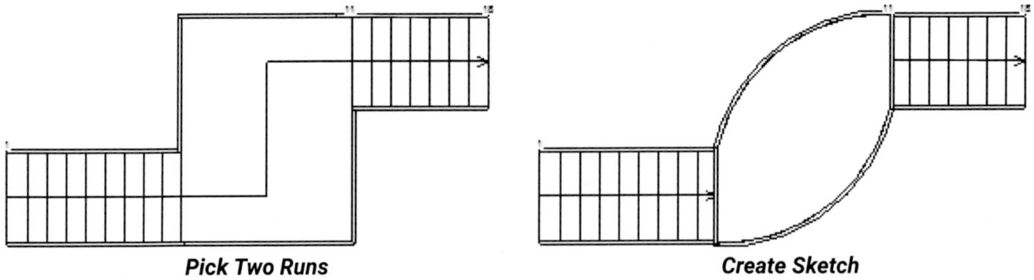

Figure 13–15

- You can connect runs with a landing as long as the start level and end level of the runs are at the same height.

Adding Supports

Stair supports are included in the stair type if needed. However, you might want to delete them and add them later. Note that this only works if the stair type has supports that are specified in the type properties.

How To: Add Stair Support Components

1. If there are no supports, double-click on the stair and in the *Modify | Create Stair* tab> *Components* panel, click (Support) and then click (Pick Edges).
2. Select the edge on which you want to place the support. Hover your cursor over the first support and press <Tab> if you have more than one connected edge on which you want to place the supports.
3. Finish the stair as needed.

Hint: Troubleshooting

When working with stairs and other elements, *Warnings* (such as the one shown in Figure 13–16) display when something is wrong, but you can keep on working. In many cases, you can close the dialog box and fix the issue or wait and do it later.

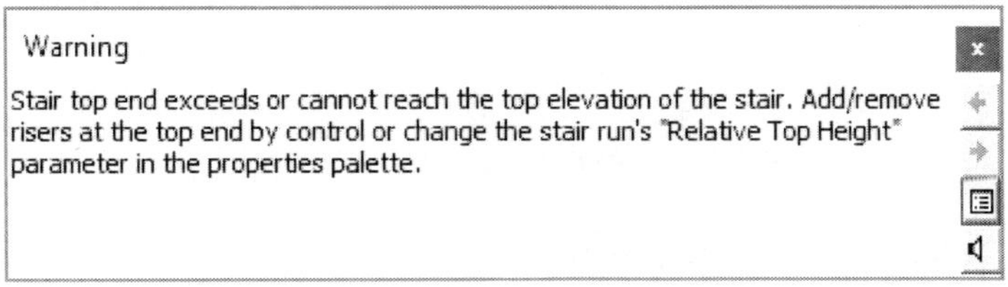

Figure 13–16

Sometimes *Errors* display where you must take action. These force you to stop and fix the situation.

When you select an element that has a related warning, (Show Related Warnings) displays in the ribbon. When selected, it opens a dialog box in which you can review the warning(s) related to the selected element. You can also display a list of all of the warnings in the project by clicking (Review Warnings) in the *Manage* tab>*Inquiry* panel.

Practice 13a
Create Component Stairs

Practice Objectives

- Create a component stair.
- Model a custom sketch stair.

In this practice, you will create U-shaped stairs in each of the stairwells. Figure 13–17 shows the completed practice. You will also create a sketched stair at the entrance to the building.

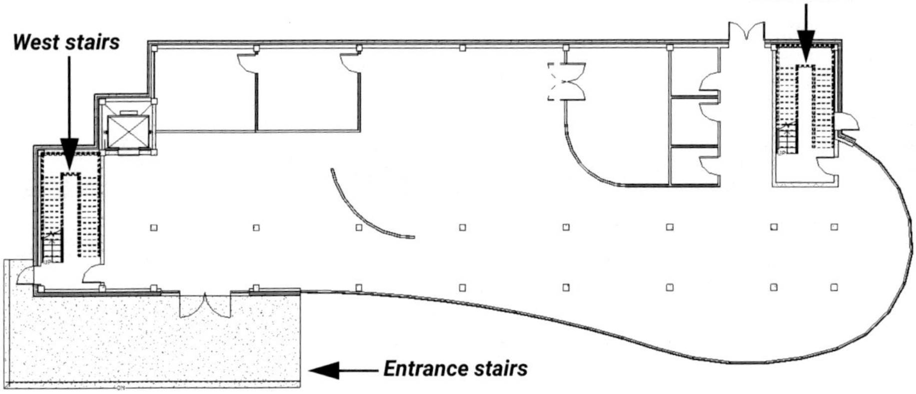

Figure 13–17

Task 1: Create Stair 1 on the first floor.

1. Open the project **Arch-Stairs.rvt** from the practice files folder.
2. Open the **Floor Plans**: **Floor 1 - Stairs-West** view. This is a callout view from the main floor plan.
3. Hide the grid lines and sections, and turn off the crop region.
4. Open the **3D - West Stairs** view. The walls have been set to transparent so you can see the stairs.
5. Close any other views except for **Floor 1 - Stairs-West** and **3D - West Stairs**.
6. Click on the *Floor 1 - Stairs-West* tab to make it the active view. Tile the views by typing **WT** and then type **ZA** to zoom all.
7. Working in the **Floor 1 - Stairs-West** view, in the *Architecture* tab>*Circulation* panel, click  (Stair).

8. In Properties, verify or set the following properties:
   - *In the Type Selector:* **Assembled Stair: Hotel Stairs**
   - *Base Level:* **Floor 1**
   - *Base Offset:* **0'-0"**
   - *Top Level:* **Floor 2**
   - *Top Offset:* **0'-0"**

   Note the *Desired Number of Risers* is **31**.
9. In the *Modify | Create Stair* tab>*Tools* panel, click (Railing). In the *Railing* dialog box, select **Hotel Stair Guardrail**, as shown in Figure 13–18. Verify that the *Position* is set to **Treads** and click **OK**.

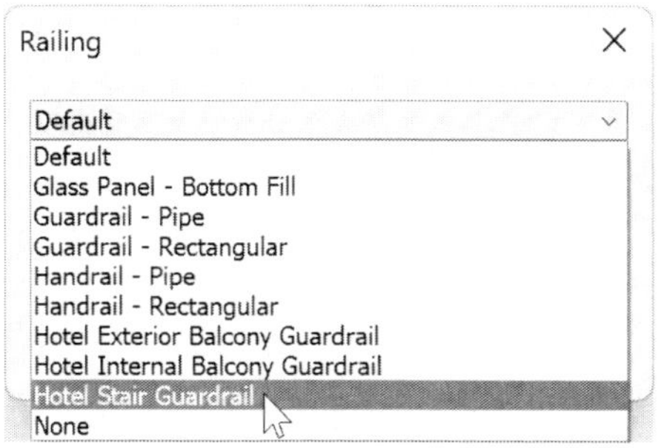

Figure 13–18

10. In the *Modify | Create Stair* tab>*Work Plane* panel, click (Ref Plane). In the *Place Reference Plane* tab>*Draw* panel, select (Pick Lines) and set the (Offset) to **4'-0"**. Create a horizontal reference plane by selecting the interior side of the top wall of the stairwell.

11. Create another reference plane offset **13'-9"** from the first reference plane to indicate the start of the run, as shown in Figure 13–19.

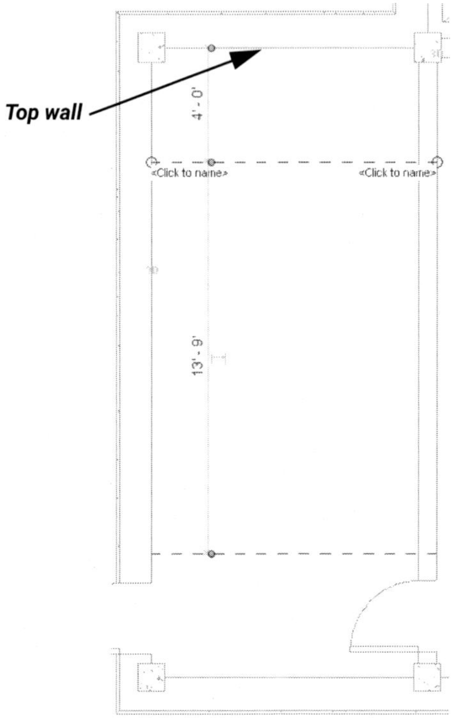

Figure 13–19

12. In the *Modify | Create Stair* tab>*Components* panel, click (Run).
13. In the *Create Stairs* panel, set (Location Line) to **Run: Left**, (Offset) to **0'-0"**, and (Actual Run Width) to **3'-8"**. Toggle on (Automatic Landing).

14. Pick the start point of the first run at the lower reference line on the interior side of the exterior wall, as shown in Figure 13–20. Pick the second point at the upper reference plane and the interior side of the exterior wall.
15. Move your cursor to the opposite side of the stairwell to start the second run.
16. Pick the start point for the second run at the intersection of the wall and the reference plane, as shown in Figure 13–20. Pick the second point past the completed number of stairs.

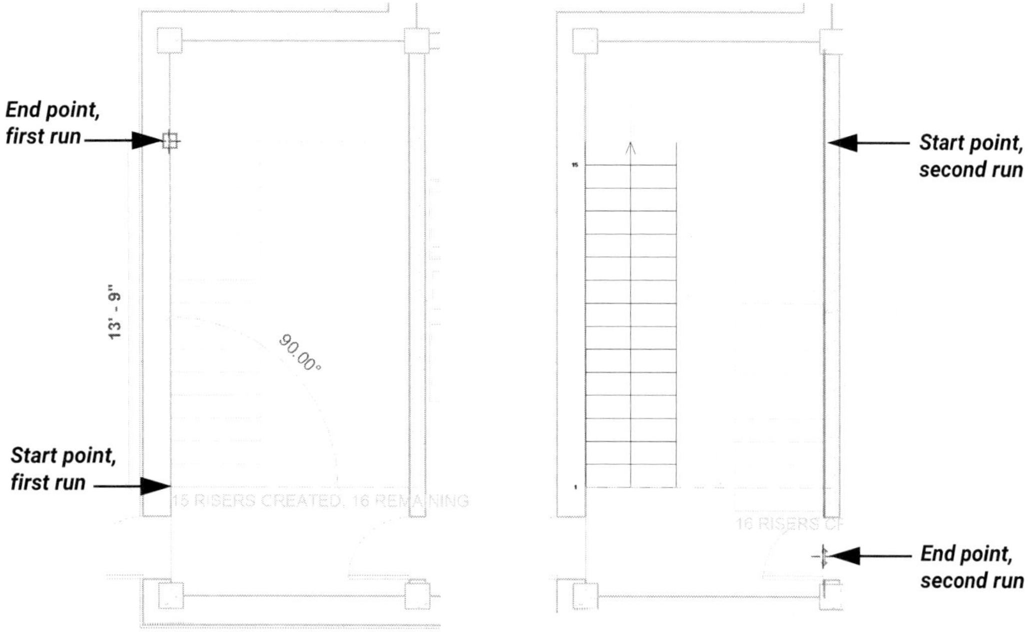

Figure 13–20

17. Click (Finish Edit Mode). The stairs with railing display.
18. Type **TW** to tab the views and **ZF** to zoom to fit.
19. Save the project.

Task 2: Create the east stairs on the first floor.

1. Open the **Floor Plans**: **Floor 1 - Stairs-East** view and type **ZF** to zoom to fit.
2. Repeat the process outlined above to create a stair in this stairwell, using the same stair and railing type and the same settings and Properties.
3. Save the project.

Task 3: Sketch entrance stairs.

1. Open the **Floor Plans: Floor 1** view.
2. Hide the grid lines and sections by selecting one of each and typing **VH**.
3. Click (Modify).
4. In Properties, in the *Underlay* section, set the *Range: Base Level* to **Floor 1** and *Range: Top Level* to **Unbounded**. This displays the outline of the entrance roof that you will use as a guide to create custom stairs.
5. In the *Architecture* tab>*Circulation* panel, click (Stair).
6. In Properties, verify or set the following:
    - *In the Type Selector:* **Cast-In-Place Stair: Monolithic Stair - Hotel**
    - *Base Level:* **Floor 1**
    - *Base Offset*: (negative) **-1'-0"**
    - *Top Level*: **Floor 1**
    - *Top Offset:* **0'-0"**
    - *Desired Number of Risers:* **2**
7. In the *Modify | Create Stairs* tab>*Tools* panel, click (Railing). In the *Railing* dialog box, select **None** and click **OK**.
8. In the *Components* panel, click (Run), then click (Create Sketch).
9. In the *Draw* panel, click (Boundary), then click (Pick Lines). Verify (Offset) is set to **0'-0"**. Select the ends of the roof outline that are labeled "Boundary lines" in Figure 13–21. (The sketch lines in the following images have been widened for emphasis.)

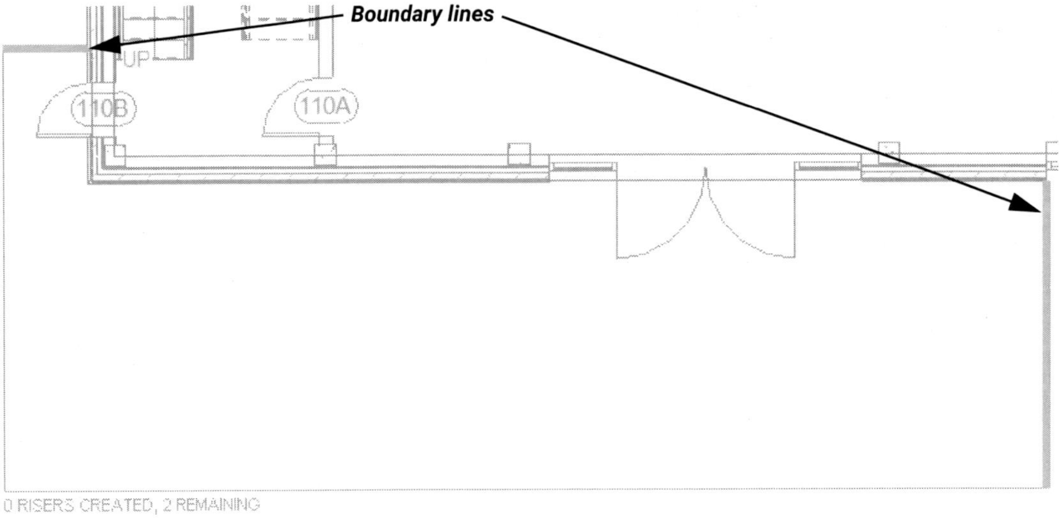

Figure 13–21

10. Click (Riser). Use (Pick Lines) to select the other sides of the roof outline (labeled "First set of riser lines" in Figure 13–22).

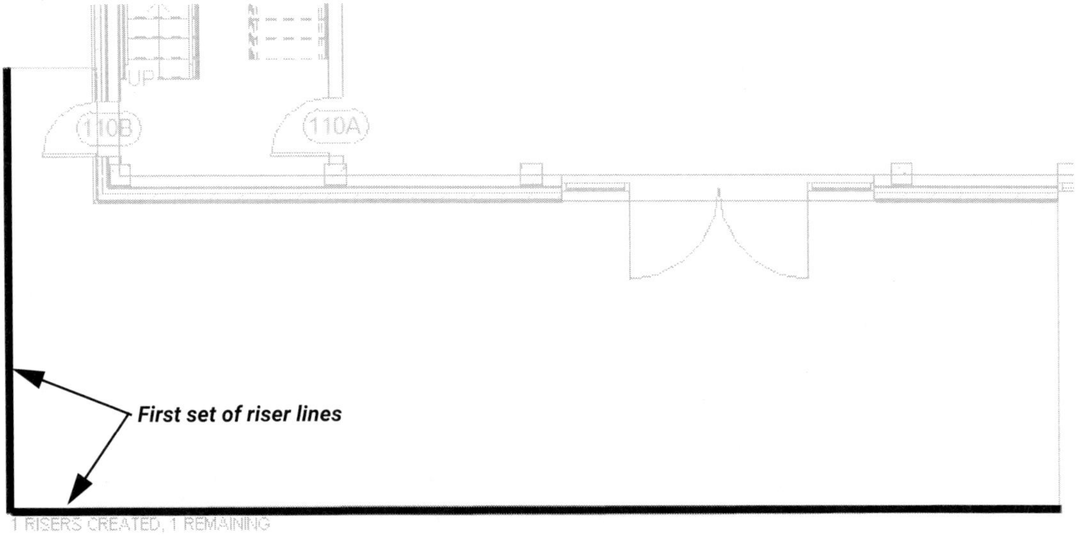

Figure 13–22

11. With (Pick Lines) still selected, set (Offset) to **1'-0"**. Offset another set of risers on the outside of the existing riser lines, as shown in Figure 13–23.

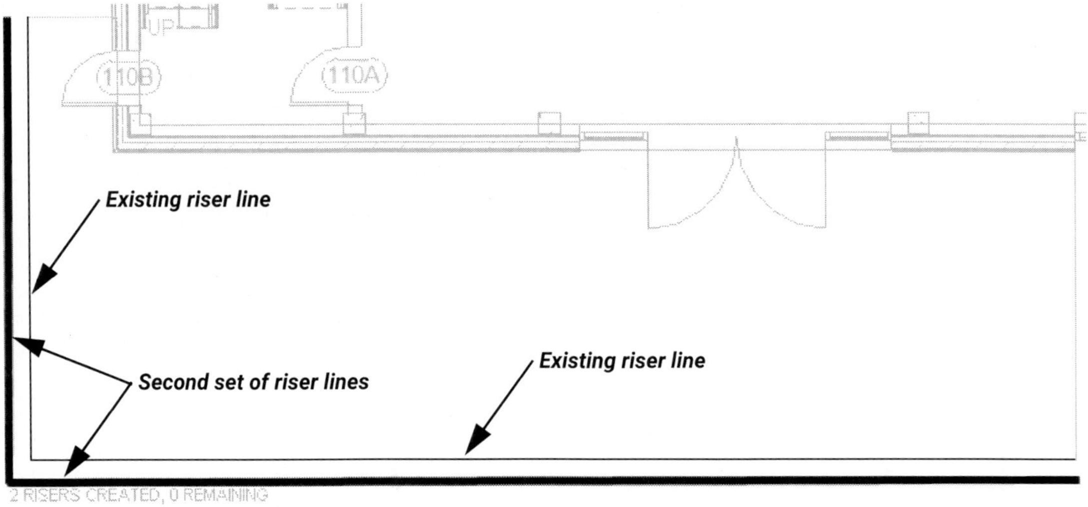

Figure 13–23

12. Click (Modify).

13. Use (Trim/Extend to Corner) to clean up the intersections of the boundary lines and outside risers, as shown in Figure 13–24.

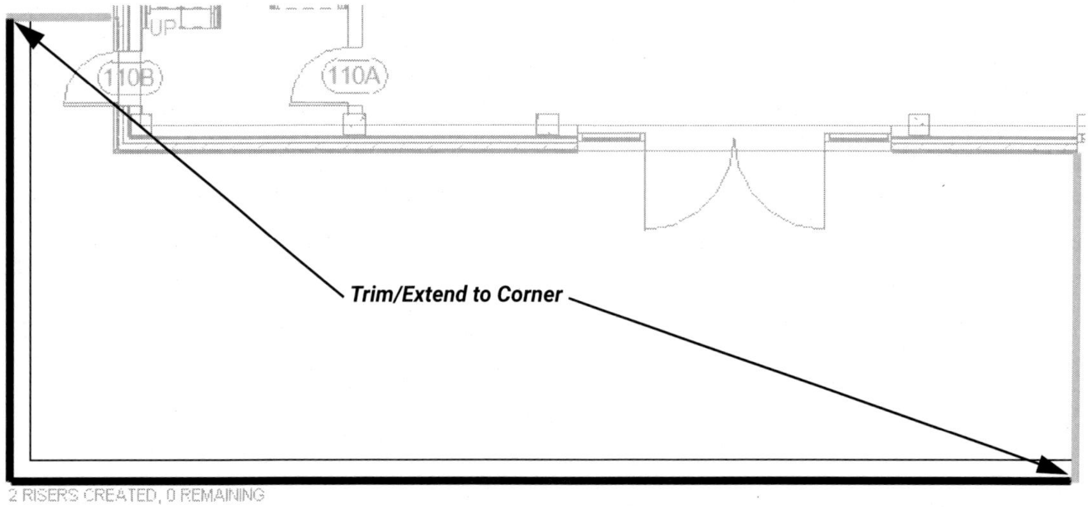

Figure 13–24

14. Click (Finish Edit Mode) to complete the stair portion of the assembly.
15. In the *Modify | Create Stair* tab>*Tools* panel, click (Flip). This will flip the risers to the correct direction.
16. In the *Modify | Create Stair* tab>*Components* panel, click (Landing) and then (Create Sketch).
17. Use **Pick Lines** to create the boundary for the landing, as shown in Figure 13–25. If needed, use (Trim/Extend to Corner) to clean up all the intersections of the boundary lines.

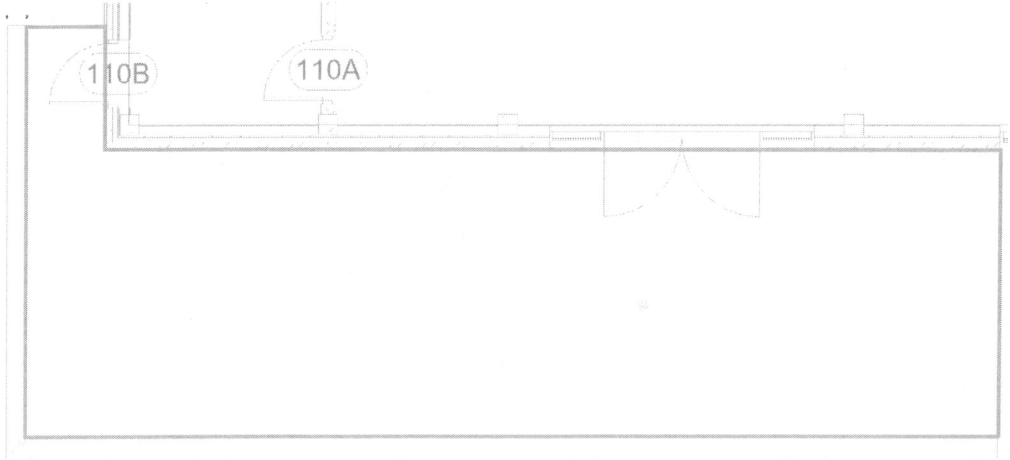

Figure 13–25

18. Click (Finish Edit Mode) twice to create the full stair assembly. Ignore any warnings that display.
19. Select the **DN** stair tag if it displays on the stairs, as shown in Figure 13–26.

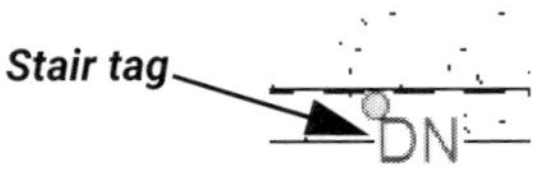

Figure 13–26

20. In Properties, uncheck *Show Up Text* and *Show Down Text*, as shown in Figure 13–27.

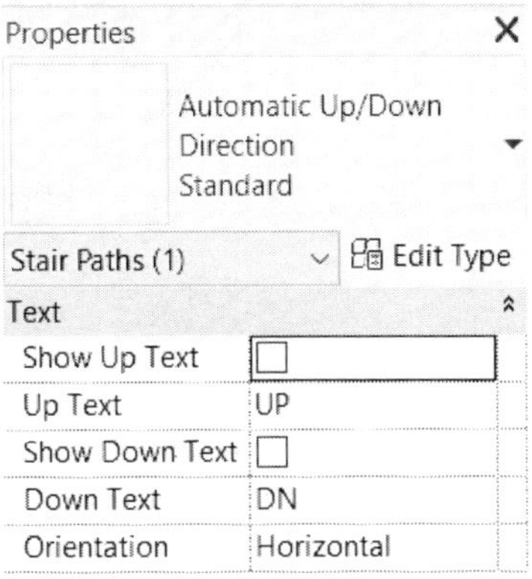

Figure 13–27

21. Click (Modify).
22. In Properties, set the *Underlay>Range: Base Level* to **None**.
23. View the stairs in 3D, as shown in Figure 13–28.

Figure 13–28

24. Save and close the project.

End of practice

13.2 Modifying Component Stairs

Stairs can be modified in a variety of ways. For example, in Figure 13–29, a straight stair with a landing has been modified to make one run wider than the other and the landing wider than both runs, creating a balcony. The landing has been further customized by sketching a curved feature.

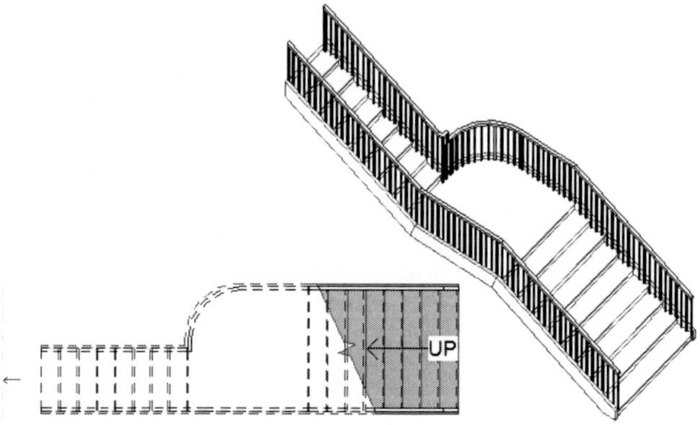

Figure 13–29

- Modifying stair components can be done when you first create the stair or later when you edit a stair.
- When working with a finished stair, you can change the type and properties, as well as flip the stair direction, as shown on the left in Figure 13–30. You can select a stair run and use temporary dimensions to modify the length and width, as shown on the right.

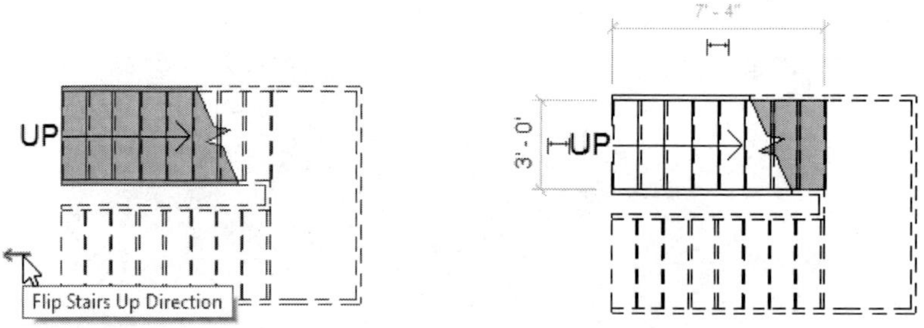

Full stair selected ***One run selected***

Figure 13–30

- To select a stair run, hover your cursor over the stair and press <Tab> to cycle through until the one you want highlights.

Editing Individual Stair Components

Within Stair Edit mode, you can make more significant modifications to individual components using temporary dimensions and shape handles, as shown in Figure 13–31. Numerous snaps and alignment and preview lines are also available as you modify the components.

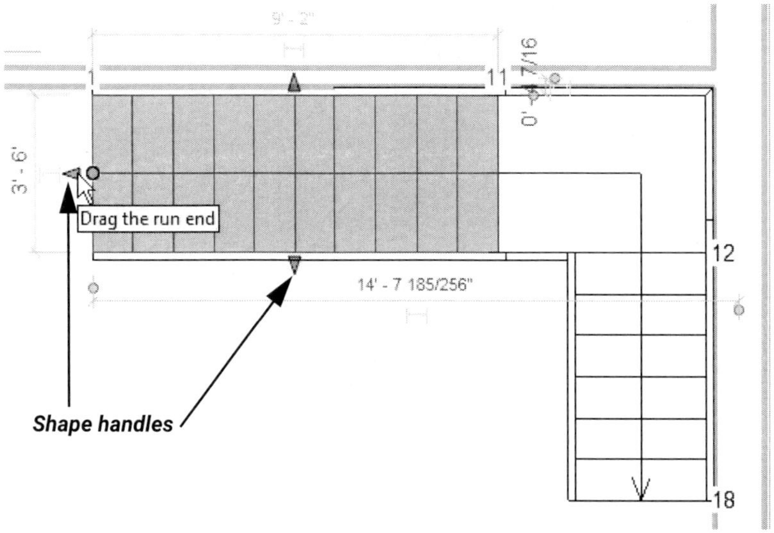

Figure 13–31

- To edit stairs, double-click on the stairs or, in the *Modify | Stairs* tab>*Edit* panel, click (Edit Stairs).
  - The arrow shape handle at the end of a run lengthens or shortens the run and modifies the other run so that the overall number of steps stays consistent and retains the start and end level.
  - The circle shape handle at the end of a run lengthens or shortens the run, does not modify any other runs, but changes the start and end level.
  - The arrow shape handle on the sides of the runs or landings can be used to modify the width.
  - You can use temporary dimensions for the run width and connections to other elements, but not for run lengths. Use the shape handles instead.
  - When you have finished modifying the stair, click (Finish Edit Mode).

Converting Components to Sketches

To customize a run or landing with more options, convert it into a sketch and modify the outline of the sketch, as shown for a curved landing in Figure 13–32.

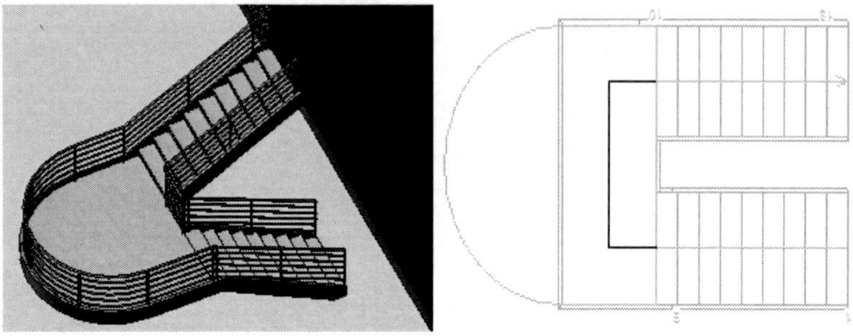

Figure 13–32

How To: Turn a Stair Component into a Sketch

1. Select a stair.
2. In the *Modify | Stairs* tab>*Edit* panel, click (Edit Stairs).
3. Select the run or landing that you want to customize.
4. In the *Tools* panel, click (Convert to sketch-based). Doing so turns the component into a custom sketched element.
5. In the *Tools* panel, click (Edit Sketch).
6. Use the options in the *Modify | Create Stair > Sketch Landing* (or *Run*) tab>*Draw* panel to modify the boundary, riser, or stair path, as needed. The boundary of a landing is shown in Figure 13–33.

   Note: *Editing an existing landing is the easiest way to create a custom landing.*

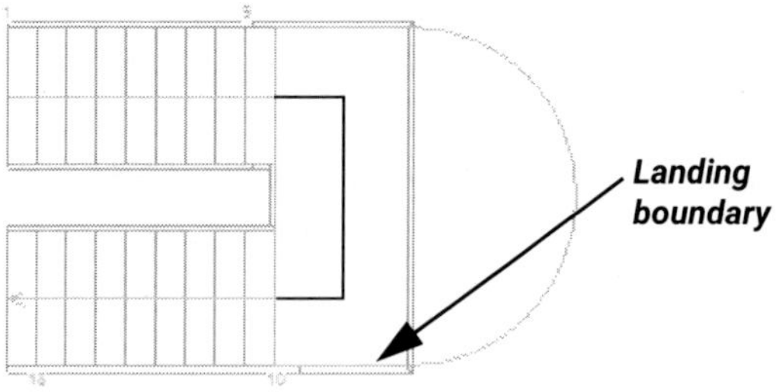

Figure 13–33

7. Click (Finish Edit Mode) to complete the sketch. Click again to return to the stair.

Multistory Stairs

Once you have created a component stair that runs from one level to another, you can expand that stair to extend to multiple stories. You can select which levels the multistory stairs extend to and skip levels as needed, as shown in Figure 13–34.

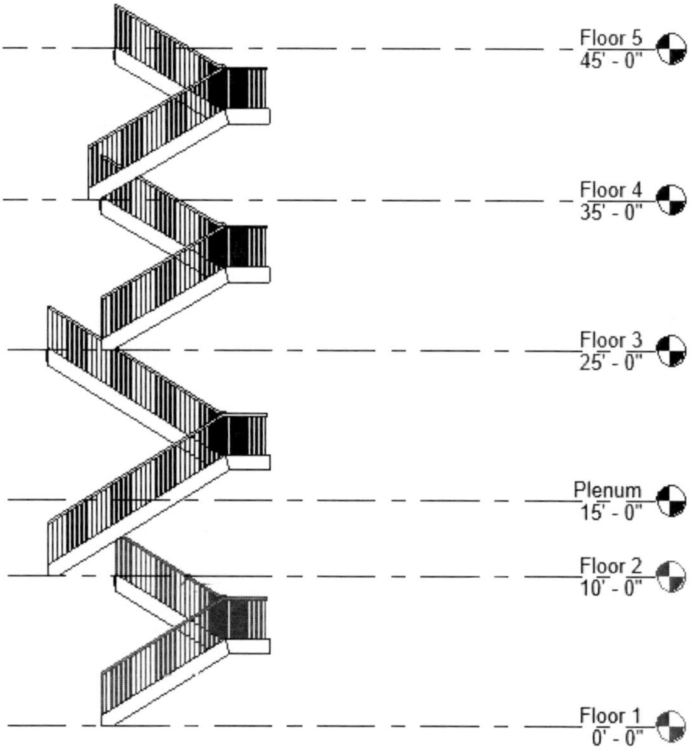

Figure 13–34

How To: Create Multistory Stairs

Note: *You can also create multistory stairs while you are in the* ***Create Stair*** *command.*

1. Open an elevation or section view where the base stairs and levels are displayed.
2. Select the stair that you want to turn into a multistory stair.
3. In the *Modify | Stairs* tab>*Multistory Stairs* panel, click (Select Levels).
4. In the *Modify | Multistory Stairs* tab>*Multistory Stairs* panel, click (Connect Levels).
5. Select the levels you want to connect. Hold <Ctrl> to select multiple levels.
   - If you need to remove any levels, click (Disconnect Levels) and select the levels you want to remove.

6. Click (Finish).

- If you are not in an elevation or section view when you start the **Multistory Stair** command, the *Go To View* dialog box displays, enabling you to select and open a view by clicking **Open View**.
- To edit multistory stairs, ensure that you are selecting the full multistory stair element, as shown in Figure 13–35. Press <Tab> to cycle through the various components of the stairs as needed. In the *Modify | Multistory Stairs* tab>*Multistory Stairs* panel, click (Connect/ Disconnect Levels) and select either **Connect Levels** or **Disconnect Levels** to modify the levels that are selected.

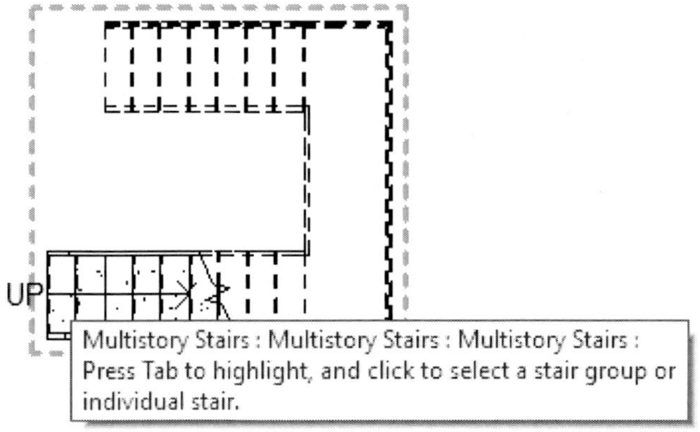

Figure 13–35

- If you change the height of a level, the stair components in the multistory stair are updated to match the new distance.
- If you change the type of a railing after a multistory stair has been placed, any runs of the same height (i.e., grouped together) are also updated. Runs of different heights would need to be modified separately.

Practice 13b
Modify Component Stairs

Practice Objectives

- Expand a set of stairs to multistory stairs.
- Cut out floors where stairs penetrate them.
- Create shafts.

In this practice, you will modify stairs and turn them into multistory stairs. You will also modify the floors for stair openings and add shafts to create openings for the upper floors. Figure 13–36 shows the completed multistory stairs in a building section view.

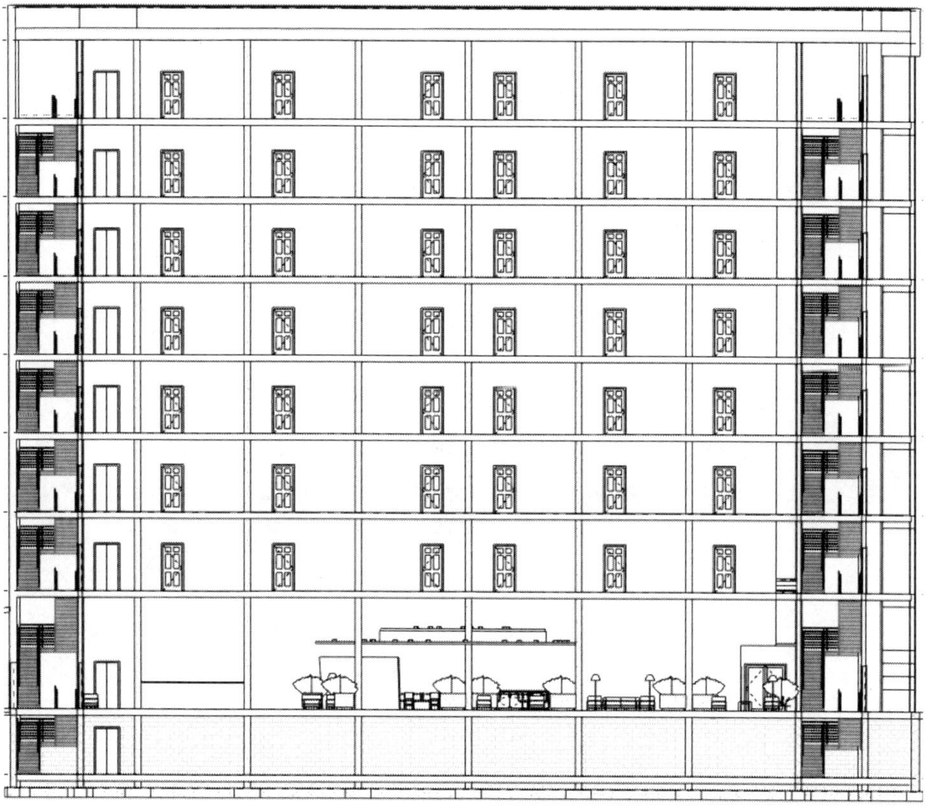

Figure 13–36

Task 1: Create multistory stairs.

1. Open the project **Arch-StairsModify.rvt** from the practice files folder.
2. Open the **Sections (Building Section): E/W Building Section** view. You will see the west stairs.
3. Select the assembled stair shown in Figure 13–37.

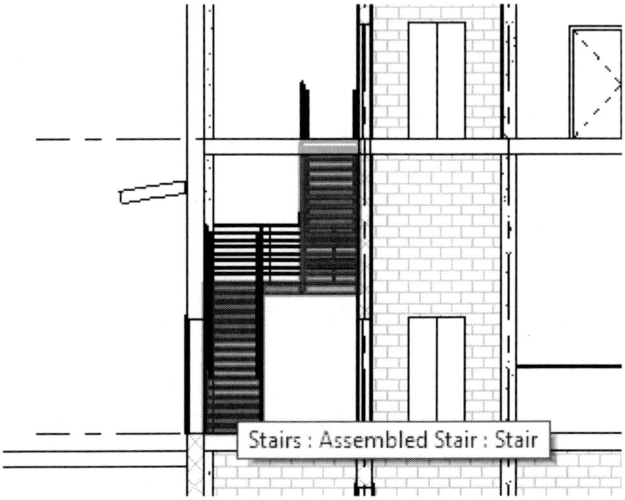

Figure 13–37

4. In the *Modify | Stairs* tab>*Multistory Stairs* panel, click (Select Levels). In the *Modify | Multistory Stairs* tab>*Multistory Stairs* panel, verify that (Connect Levels) is selected.
5. Hold <Ctrl> and select the level lines for **Floor 3** to **Floor 8**. (Do not select the **Roof** or **Parapet** levels.)

6. Click (Finish). The stairs are added between the rest of the floors, as shown in Figure 13–38.

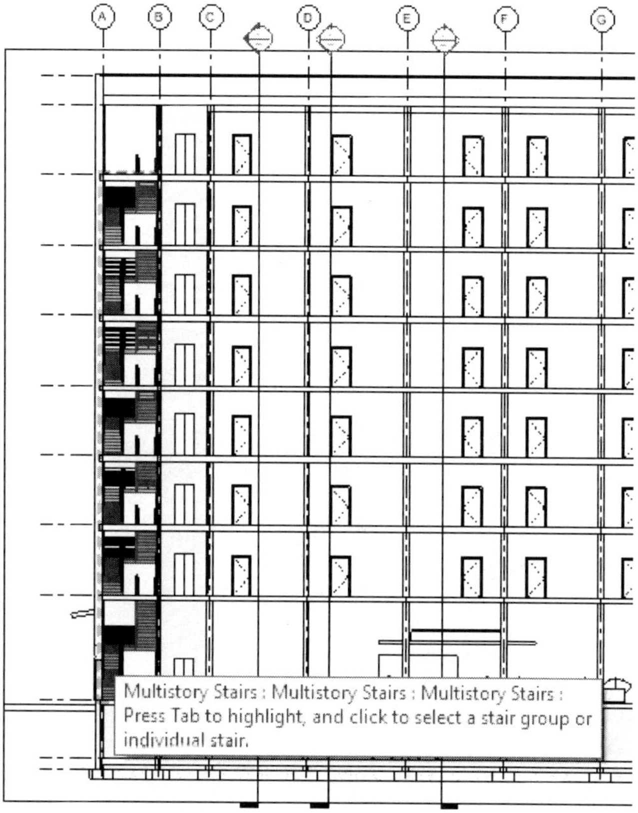

Figure 13–38

7. With the new multistory stairs still selected, in the *Modify | Multistory Stairs* tab>*Multistory Stairs* panel, click (Connect/Disconnect Levels).

8. Click (Connect Levels) and select the **Basement** level line, then click (Finish). The stairs to the basement are added.
   - If needed to see the stairs on all of the floors, set the *Visual Style* to (Consistent Colors).

9. Save the project.

You need to do this to the east stairs, but they are not visible in the building section view so you will need to modify the section in plan view.

10. Return to the **Floor 1** view.
11. Select the E/W Building Section line (do not select on the section marker head).
12. Pan over to the east stairs area.
13. In the *Modify | Views* tab>*Section* panel, click (Split Segment).
14. Split the section close to the stairs; you will then click inside the east stairwell to place the split section, as shown in Figure 13–39.

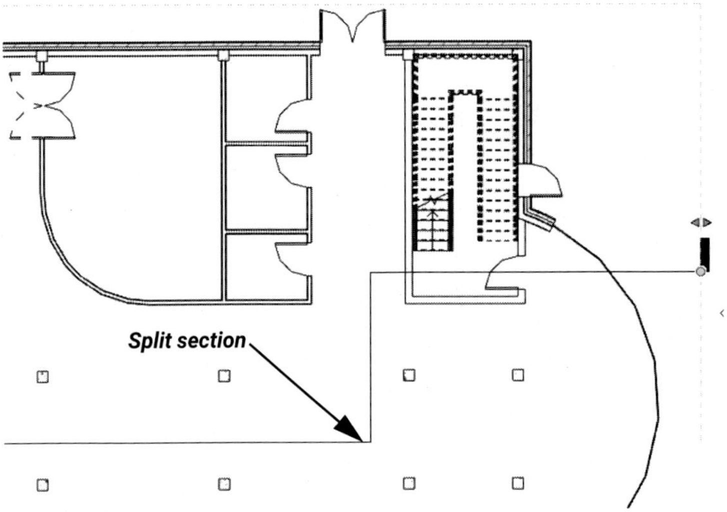

Figure 13–39

15. Click (Modify).
16. Activate the **E/W Building Section**. You are now able to see the east stairs. Repeat the process of turning the east stairs into a multistory stair and adding stairs to the basement.
17. Save the project.

Task 2: Modify the second floor stair openings.

1. Open the **Floor Plans: Floor 2** view.

   Note: *If needed, toggle on (Select Elements by Face).*

2. Select the floor.
3. In the *Modify | Floors* tab>*Mode* panel, click (Edit Boundary).
4. Zoom in to the west stairs.

5. Modify the floor boundary line so that it creates an opening for the west stairs, as shown in Figure 13–40.

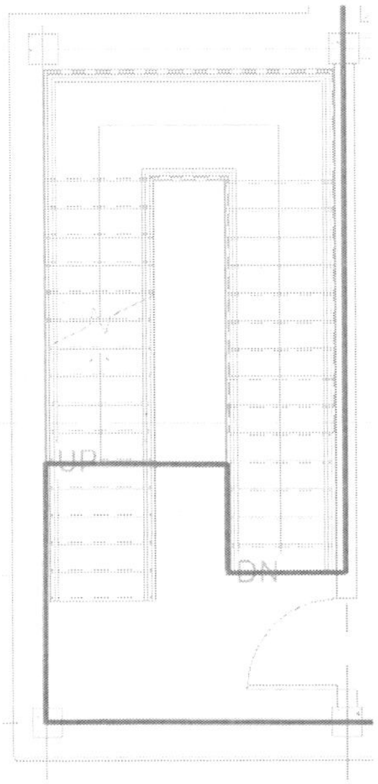

Figure 13–40

6. Pan over to the east stairwell and modify the floor boundary there as well, as shown in Figure 13–41.

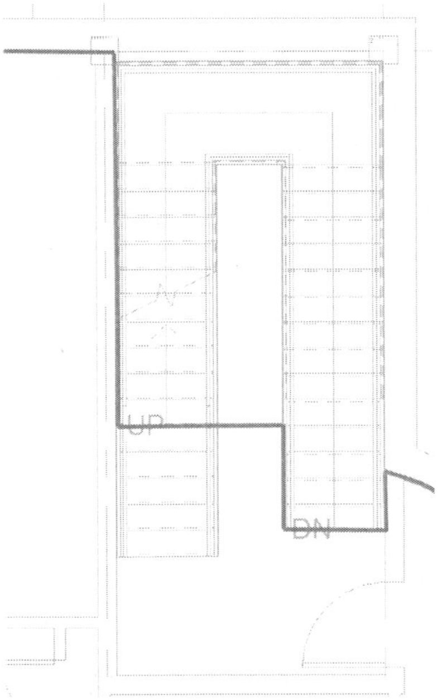

Figure 13–41

7. Use (Trim/Extend to Corner) to clean up the intersections of the boundary lines.
8. Click (Finish Edit Mode). If prompted, click **Yes** to overlap the highlighted floor and click **Don't attach** in the *Attaching to floor* dialog box.
9. Zoom out to display the entire second floor, as shown in Figure 13–42.

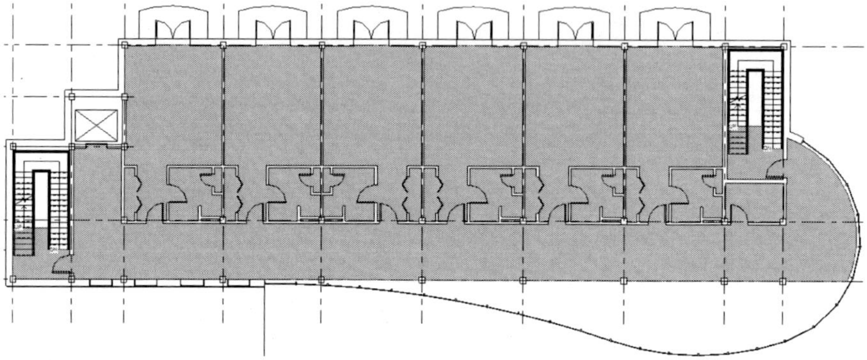

Figure 13–42

10. Click (Modify).
11. Save the project.

Task 3: Add shafts in the stairwells.

1. Open the **Floor Plans: Floor 3** view.
2. In Properties, set the *Underlay>Range: Base Level* to **None**.
3. Pan and zoom in to the west stairs.
4. In the *Architecture* tab>*Opening* panel, click (Shaft).

5. Draw the sketch of the shaft similar to that shown in Figure 13–43.

   Note: *You can use a shaft here because the openings are the same on all of the floors.*

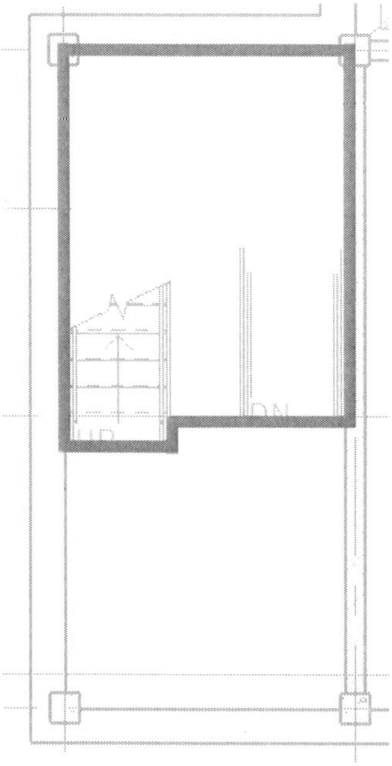

Figure 13–43

6. Click (Modify).
7. In Properties, set the *Base Constraint* to **Floor 3** with a *Base Offset* of (negative) **-1'-0"** and the *Top Constraint* to **Up to level: Floor 8** with a *Top Offset* of **0'-0"**.
8. Click (Finish Edit Mode) to create the shaft.

9. Repeat the process on the east stairwell, as shown in Figure 13–44.

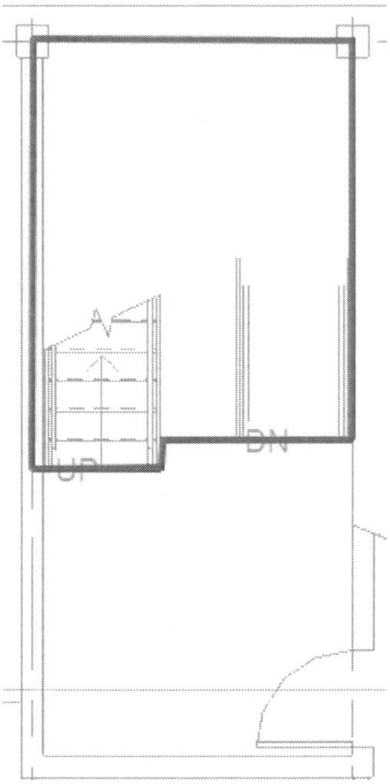

Figure 13–44

10. Save and close the project.

End of practice

13.3 Working with Railings

Railings can be automatically created with stairs, but you can modify or delete them independently of the stair element. You can also add railings separately from the stairs for other locations, as shown in Figure 13–45.

> ***Note:*** *Hosts for sketched railings include floors, slabs, slab edges, the tops of walls, and roofs. You can also add railings to toposolids.*

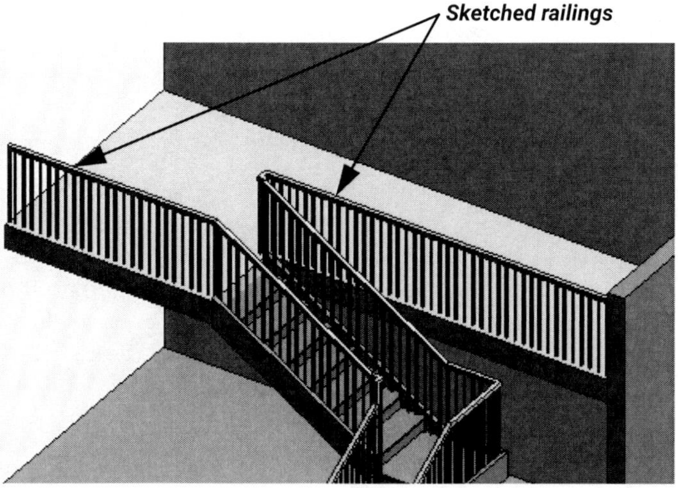

Figure 13–45

- You can also add railings to existing stairs and ramps if they were not included when the stairs/ramps were created.

How To: Add Railings by Sketching

1. Open a plan or 3D view.
2. In the *Architecture* tab>*Circulation* panel, expand (Railing) and click (Sketch Path).
3. In the Type Selector, specify the railing type.
4. In the *Modify | Create Railing Path* tab>*Tools* panel, click (Pick New Host) and select the element that you want the railing to associate to, such as a stair, floor, or top of a wall.
    - If you are working in a 3D or section view, you can select **Preview** in the *Modify | Create Railing Path* tab>*Options* panel and the railing displays while you are still in edit mode. This only works if you have selected a host.

- If the host is sloped, the railing will follow the slope, as shown in Figure 13–46. The sketch displays at the host's level.

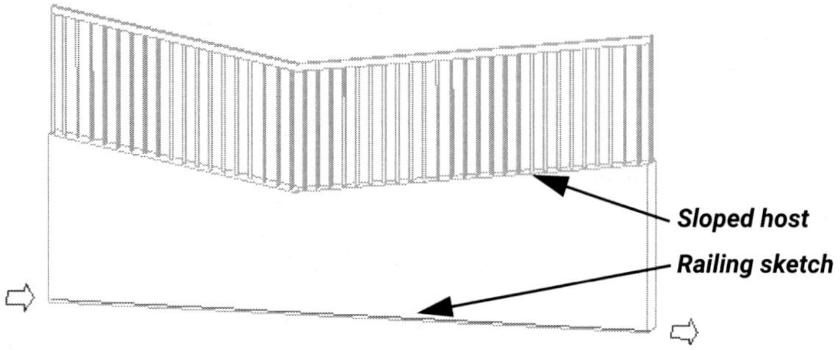

Figure 13–46

5. Use the sketch tools to sketch the lines that define the railings.
6. Click (Finish Edit Mode) to create the railing.

- The railing must be a single connected sketch. If it is not, you are prompted with a warning, such as the one shown in Figure 13–47.

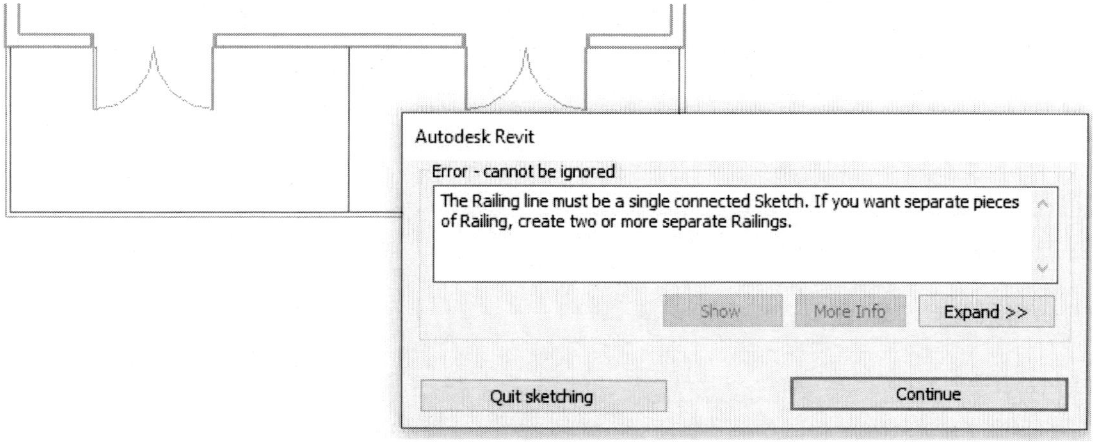

Figure 13–47

How To: Add Railings Using Place on Stair/Ramp

1. In the *Architecture* tab>*Circulation* panel, expand (Railing) and click (Place on Stair/ Ramp).
2. In the *Modify | Place Railing on Stair/Ramp* tab>*Position* panel, click (Treads) or (Stringer).
3. Select the stair or ramp where you want to add the railings.

- (Place on Stair/Ramp) only works if there are no railings on the stair. If you want to add an additional railing (e.g., down the middle of a wide stair), you need to sketch the railing.

Modifying Railings

Modifying railings can be as simple as changing their type, as shown in Figure 13–48. You can also edit the path of a railing.

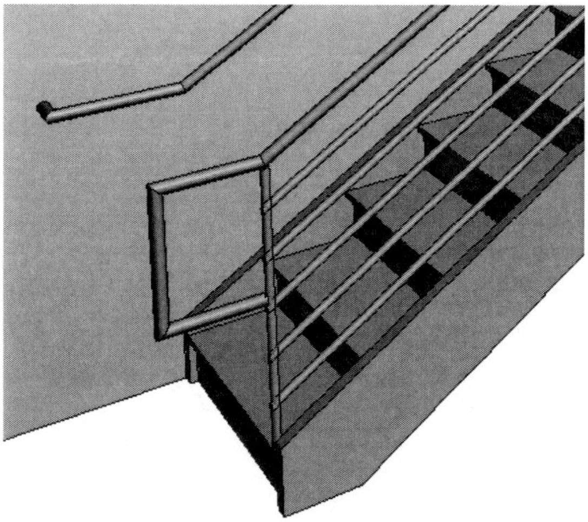

Figure 13–48

- You can delete railings separately from stairs or ramps. However, deleting a stair or ramp automatically deletes related railings.
- You can use the (Split Element) command on railings. Doing so results in separate railings, as shown in Figure 13–49.

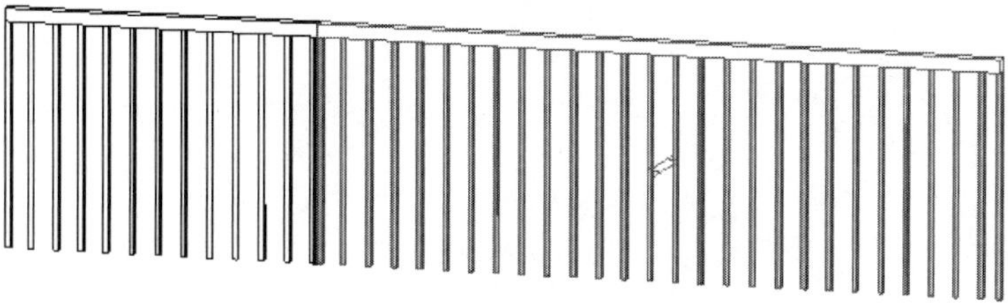

Figure 13–49

Editing the Path of a Railing

To edit the path of a railing, double-click on the railing, or select the railing and in the *Modify | Railings* tab>*Mode* panel, click (Edit Path). This places you in edit mode, in which you can modify the individual lines that define the railing, as shown in Figure 13–50. You can create additional lines, but they must be connected to the existing lines.

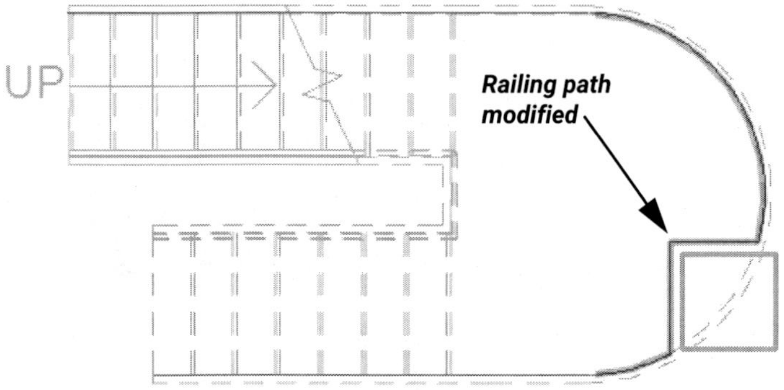

Figure 13–50

> ***Note:*** *Unlike many other elements in edit mode, railings do not have to be in a closed loop.*

Practice 13c
Work with Railings

Practice Objectives

- Modify railings and handrails.
- Add stand-alone railings.

In this practice, you will modify the railings in the stairwells by changing the railings against the wall to a new type. You will add stand-alone railings to connect the railing for Level 8 to the stairwell wall. You will also add railings to the interior balconies (shown in the completed practice in Figure 13–51) and to the exterior balconies.

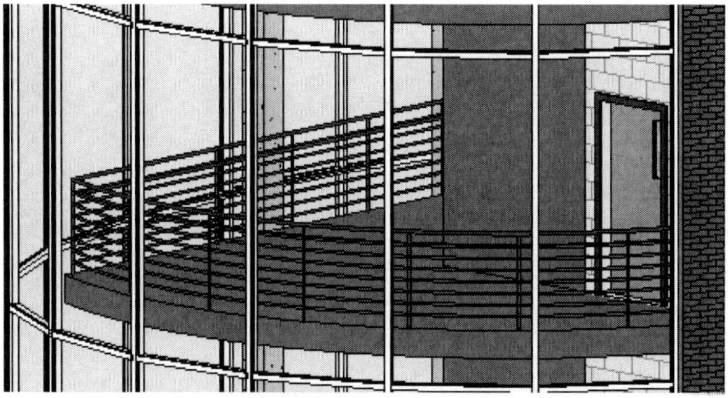

Figure 13–51

Task 1: Modify the railing type.

1. Open the project **Arch-Railings.rvt** from the practice files folder. Verify that you are in the **Floor Plans: Floor 1 - Stairs-West** view.

2. In the Quick Access Toolbar, expand (Default 3D view) and select (Camera). Create a camera view looking from the door into the stairwell to display the new stairs and railings, as shown in Figure 13–52. (Your 3D view may differ from the image depending on your camera and target placement.) In the camera view, modify the crop region controls as needed to show the first run of the stair. Set the *Visual Style* to (Shaded).

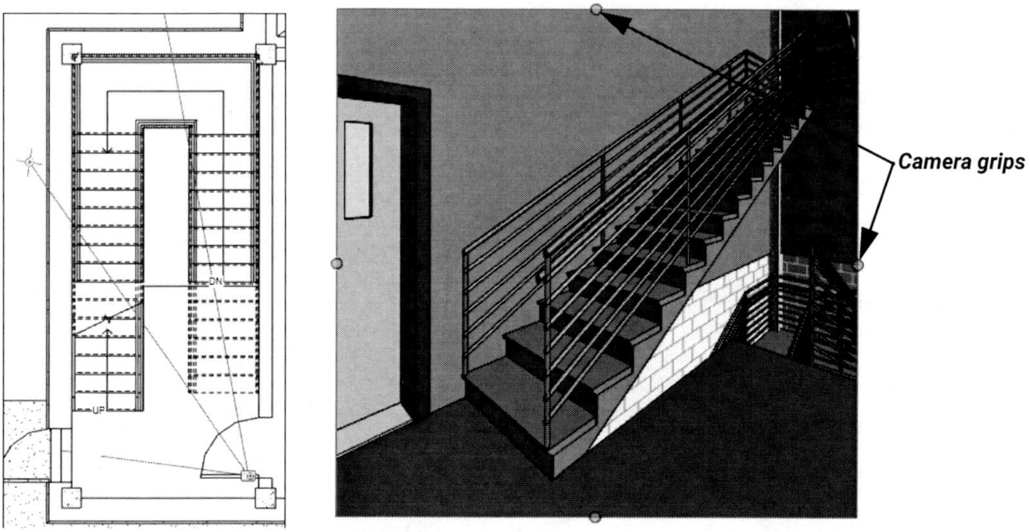

Figure 13–52

3. In the Project Browser, in the *3D Views* section, right-click on the new 3D view and rename it as **CAM - Floor 1 West Stairs**.

   Note: *Press <Ctrl>+<Tab> to move between the* ***3D Camera*** *view and the* ***Floor Plan*** *view or use the view tabs at the top of the window.*

4. Select the railing that is against the wall and in the Type Selector, select **Railing: Hotel Stair Handrail - Wall**. The railing type changes, as shown in Figure 13–53. In Properties, set the *Offset from Path* to **0'-0"**. Note this changes the handrails only for this level.

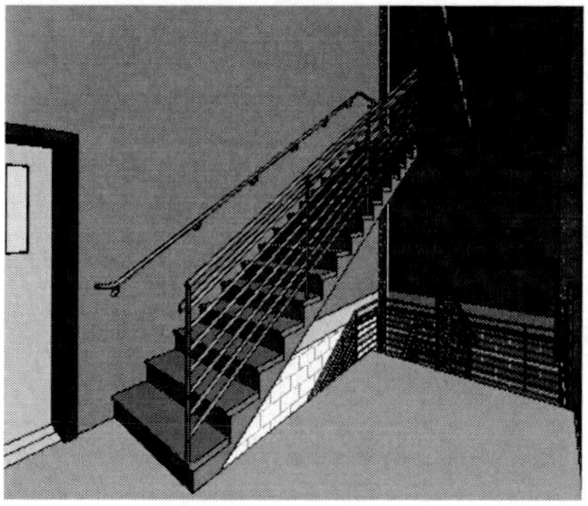

Figure 13–53

5. Repeat this on the east stairs.
6. Save the project.

Task 2: Modify the existing railing and connect a new railing.

1. Open the **Floor Plan: Floor 8** view and zoom in to the west stairwell. Close any other open views.
2. Select the railing that is against the wall and in the Type Selector, select **Railing: Hotel Stair Handrail - Wall**. The railing type changes. In Properties, set the *Offset from Path* to **0'-0"** .
3. Create a camera view (the same way you did in Floor 1) looking into the stairwell. Rename the new 3D view **CAM - Floor 8 West Stairs**.
4. Tile the **Floor 8** and **CAM - Floor 8 West Stairs** views.
5. In the **Floor 8** view, select the railing that is against the wall. In the Type Selector, select **Railing: Hotel Stair Handrail - Wall**. In Properties, change the *Offset from Path* to **0'-0"**.
6. Select the inside railing, as shown in Figure 13–54.

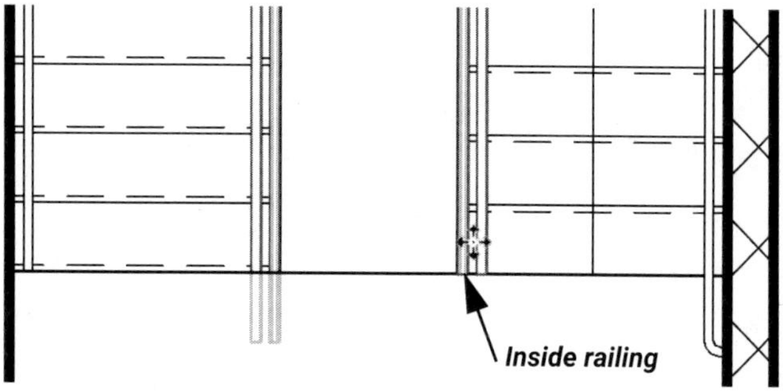

Figure 13–54

7. In the *Modify | Railings* tab>*Mode* panel, click (Edit Path), or double-click on the railing.
8. In the *Modify | Railings > Sketch Path* tab>*Options* panel, select **Preview**. This allows you to see the changes in the camera view as you make them in the floor plan view.
9. In the *Modify | Railings > Sketch Path* tab>*Work Plane* panel, click (Ref Plane).

10. To draw a reference plane, use the **Pick Lines** sketch tool, set the (Offset) to **4"**, and hover your cursor over the edge of the floor (as shown in Figure 13–55), then click to place the reference plane. (The DN text will display depending on how zoomed in to the stairs you are.)

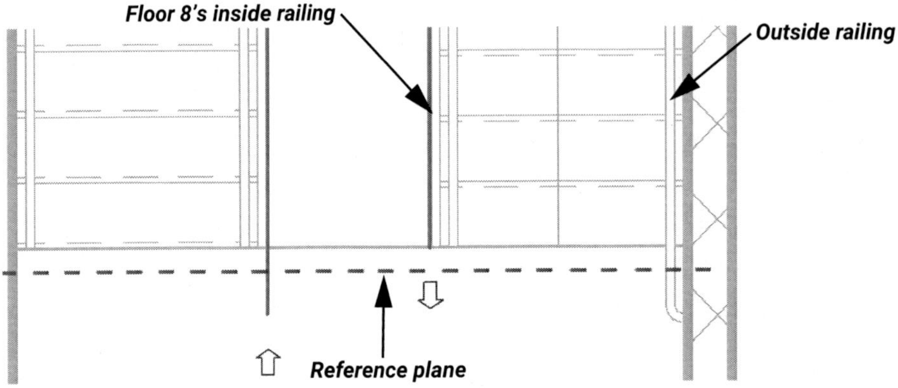

Figure 13–55

11. Click (Modify).
12. Select and drag just the end of the inside railing on the right stairs to meet the reference plane, as shown in Figure 13–56. (The dimension in the figure is for reference only.)

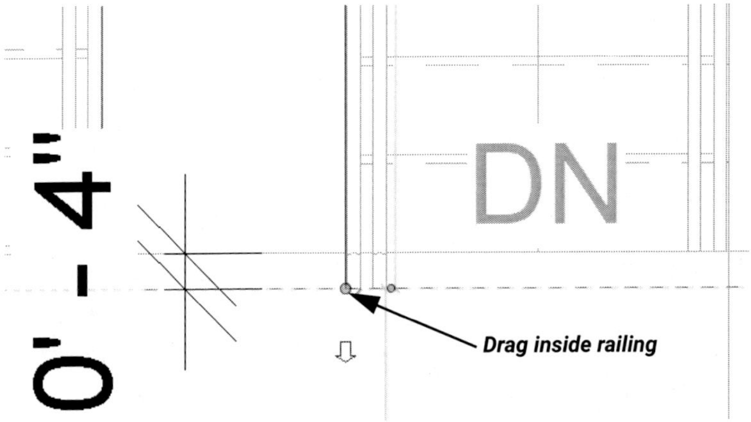

Figure 13–56

13. Click (Finish Edit Mode).
14. Click (Modify).
15. Pan and zoom so you can see the exterior wall of the stairwell and the inside railing. You will need to add a railing from the wall, connecting to the stair railing.

16. In the *Architecture* tab>*Circulation* panel, expand (Railing) and select (Sketch Path). Note that **Sketch Path** is the default tool when selecting **Railing**.
17. In Properties, select the **Hotel Stair Guardrail** railing type in the Type Selector, then set the *Base Offset* to **0'-0"**.
18. In the *Modify | Create Railing Path* tab>*Work Plane* panel, select (Ref Plane). Draw a horizontal reference plane **6"** from the edge of the floor and a vertical reference plane passing through the midpoint of the inside railing, as shown in Figure 13–57. (The dimension in the image is for reference only.)
    - **Hint:** Type **SM** to force a snap to the midpoint of the end of the railing.

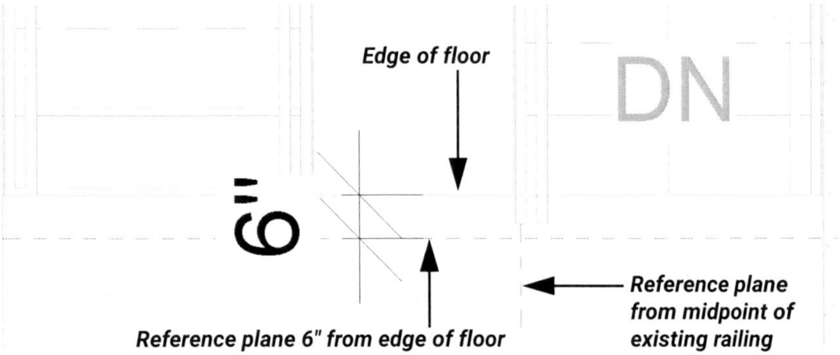

Figure 13–57

19. Click (Modify).
20. In the *Modify | Create Railing Path* tab>*Draw* panel, select (Line) and (Chain).
21. Sketch the railing path from the midpoint of the inside railing to the reference plane and then over to the wall, as shown in Figure 13–58. (You must start at the railing and draw over to the wall.)

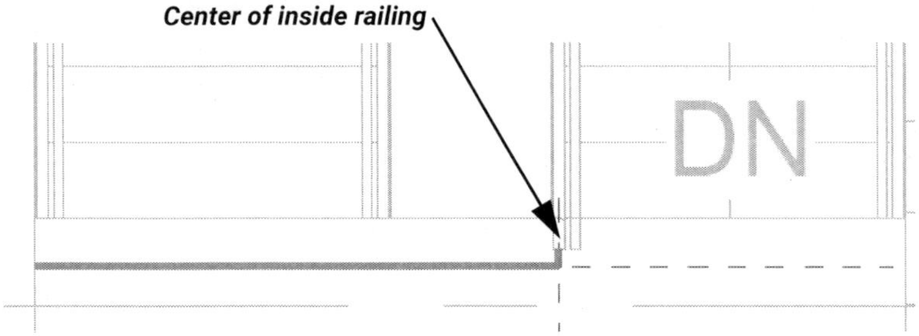

Figure 13–58

22. Click (Modify).
23. Click (Finish Edit Mode).

24. Click (Modify).
25. In the **CAM - Floor 8 West Stairs** view, review the new railing, as shown in Figure 13–59.

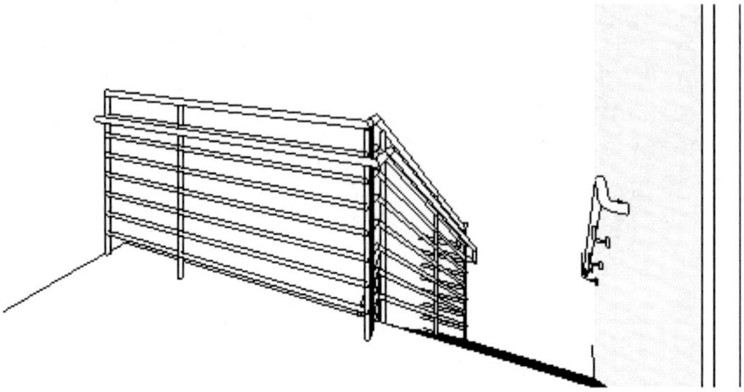

Figure 13–59

*Note: If needed, select the new railing and click the **Flip Railing Direction** control so the guardrail and handrails match.*

26. Type **TW** to tab the views.
27. Save the project.

Task 3: Add balcony railings.

1. Open the **Floor Plans: Floor 2** view and pan and zoom to the south of the building to the hallway and interior balcony.
2. In the *Architecture* tab>*Circulation* panel, select (Railing).
3. In the Type Selector, select **Railing: Hotel Interior Balcony Guardrail**. In Properties, set the *Base Offset* and *Offset from Path* to **0'-0"**.
4. In the *Modify | Create Railing Path* tab>*Draw* panel, select (Pick Lines), then set the (Offset) to **0'-11"**.
5. Select the edge of the balcony floor, as shown in Figure 13–60. Make sure that the preview dashed line is on the inside of the balcony floor.

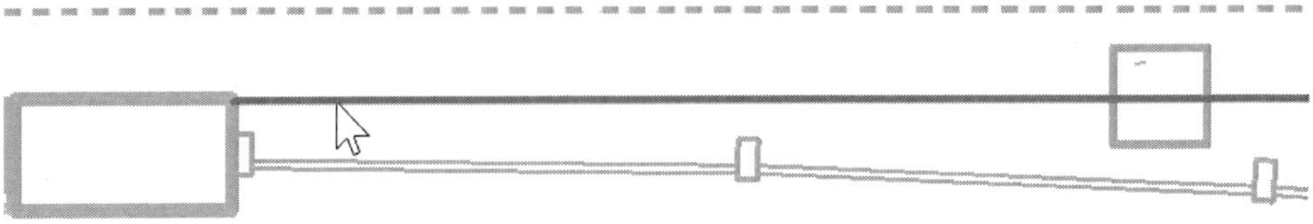

Figure 13–60

6. Continue adding railing with an **11"** offset until you get to the east stairwell (include the curved section), as shown in Figure 13–61.

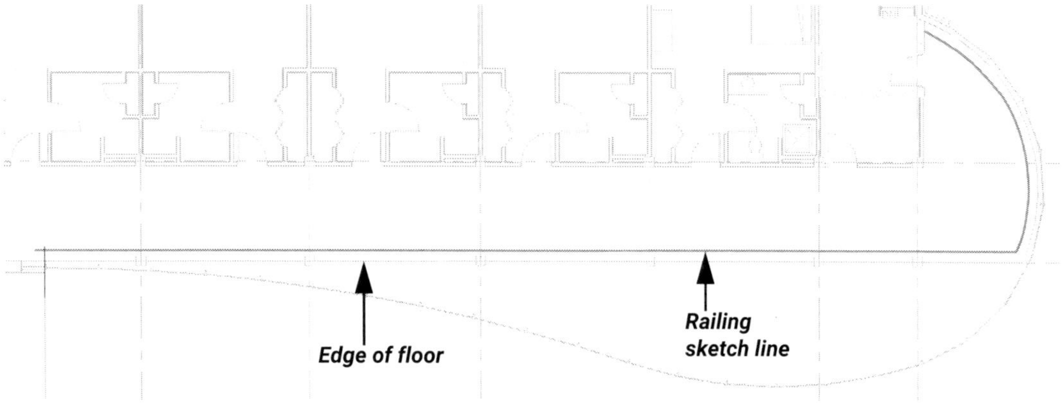

Figure 13–61

7. In the *Draw* panel, click **Line** and set the (Offset) to **0'-0"**. Add a railing that returns back to the wall, **11"** from the edge of the brick exterior wall, as shown in Figure 13–62. (The dimension in the figure is for reference only.)

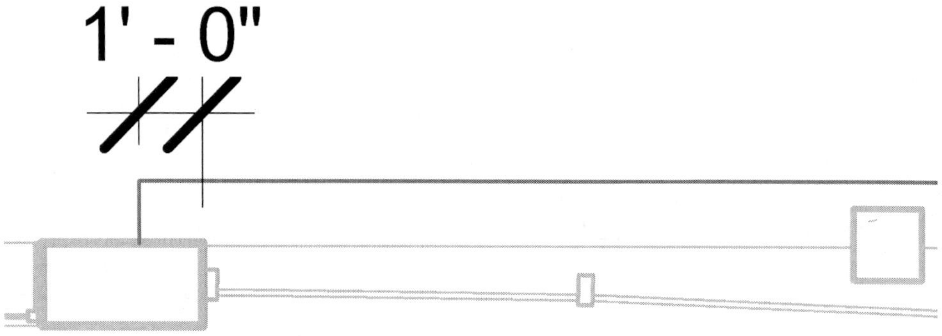

Figure 13–62

- If needed, use the **Trim/Extend to Corner** command and railing control grips to modify the sketch lines.

8. Click (Finish Edit Mode).
9. Zoom in and pan to one of the outdoor balconies on the back of the building.
10. Start the **Railing** command again. In the Type Selector, select **Railing: Hotel Exterior Balcony Guardrail**.
11. In the *Modify | Create Railing Path* panel>*Draw* tab, set the (Offset) to **0'-3"**.

12. In Properties, set the *Base Offset* to (negative) **-0'-4"** and select the inside of the balcony floor edge to add railings to the balcony, as shown in the sketch in Figure 13–63. Just draw railings on one balcony.

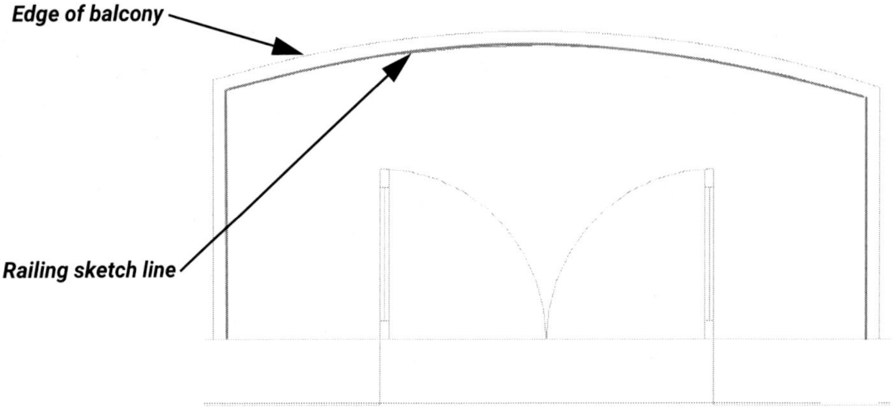

Figure 13–63

13. Click (Finish Edit Mode).
14. Copy the completed balcony railing to the other balconies on **Floor 2**.
15. Select all the interior and exterior balcony railings.
    - Hint: Select one exterior balcony railing, right-click, and select **Select All Instances>Visible in View**, then press <Ctrl> to select the hallway railing as well.
16. In the *Modify | Railings* tab>*Clipboard* panel, select (Copy to Clipboard).
17. In the *Clipboard* panel, expand (Paste) and select (Aligned to Selected Levels).
18. In the *Select Levels* dialog box, select **Floor 3**, then press and hold <Ctrl> and continue selecting each floor up to **Floor 8**.
19. Click **OK**.

20. Open the Default 3D view, orbit around to the back of the hotel, and verify the placement of all the railings, as shown in Figure 13–64.

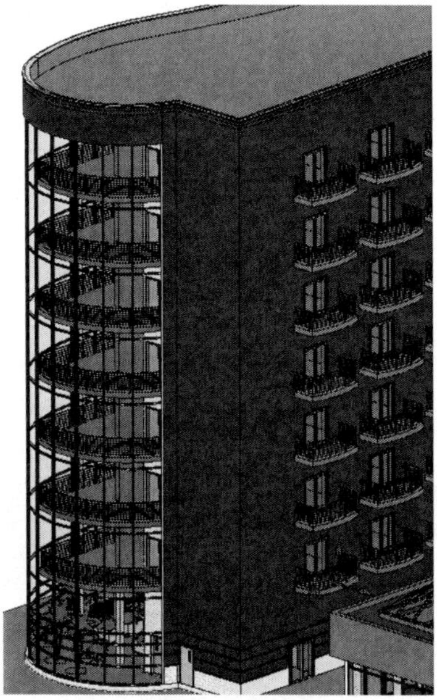

Figure 13–64

21. Save and close the project.

End of practice

13.4 Creating Ramps

The process of creating ramps is similar to that of creating stairs with runs and automatic landings. You can also sketch a boundary with risers at the start and end of each slope. Ramps are most often used for short vertical distances, as shown in Figure 13–65, as they require a lot of space for their runs. Check the local building codes to determine the maximum length of a run before a landing is required.

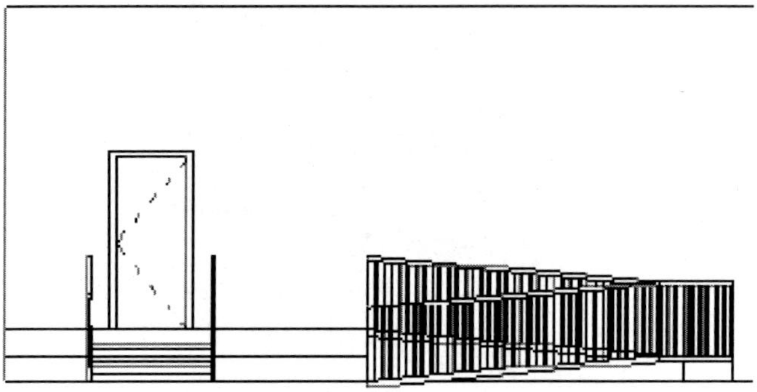

Figure 13–65

After a ramp has been created, you can add a spot slope annotation. A spot slope can be added to a ramp in elevation, 3D, plan, and section views.

- For more information on annotations, see ***Chapter 15 Working with Annotations***.

How To: Create a Ramp Using Runs

1. In the *Architecture* tab>*Circulation* panel, click (Ramp).
2. In the Type Selector, select the ramp type.
3. In the *Modify | Create Ramp Sketch* tab>*Tools* panel, click (Railing), then select a railing type in the *Railing Types* dialog box and click **OK**.
4. In Properties, specify the *Constraints*, especially *Base Level* and *Top Level* and their offsets (as shown in Figure 13–66), and other properties. The *Width* of the ramp is set in the *Dimensions* section.

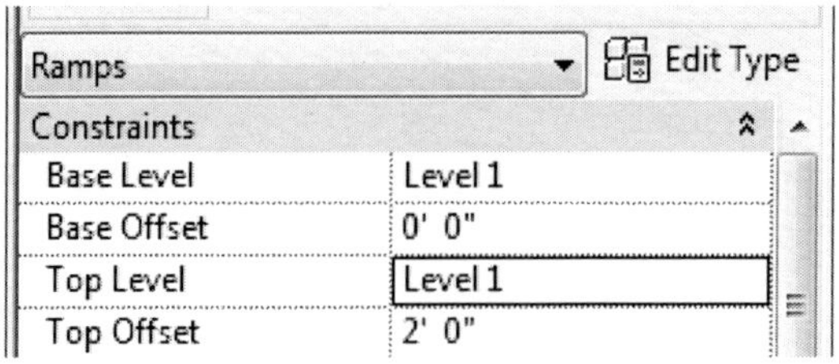

Figure 13–66

5. Draw reference planes to specify the locations of the run start and end points before creating the ramp. The run is based on the centerline of the ramp.
6. In the *Draw* panel, click (Run) and select a start point for the run. A preview box displays the ramp's orientation and length. Click (Line) or (Center-ends Arc) to switch between linear and curved runs.
    - Landings are automatically created between runs, as shown in Figure 13–67.

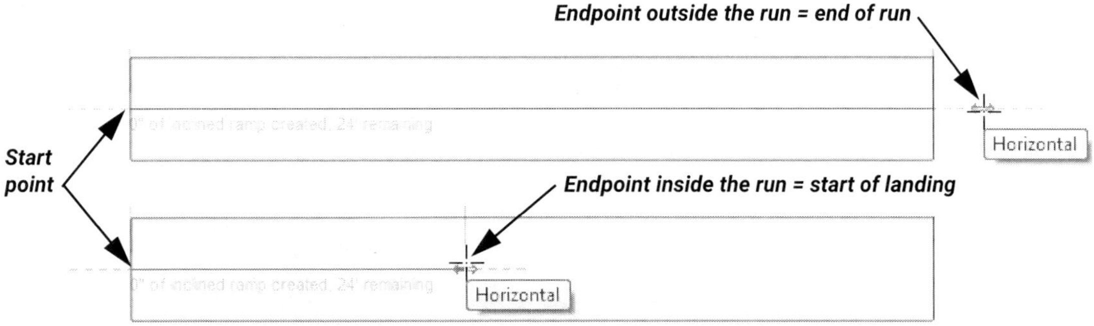

Figure 13–67

7. Click (Finish Edit Mode). The ramp (including railings) is created.

How To: Sketch a Ramp Using Boundary and Riser

1. Click (Ramp) and set up the ramp type and properties.
2. In the *Modify | Create Ramp Sketch* tab>*Draw* panel, click (Boundary).
3. Use the sketch tools to outline the sides (not the ends) of the ramp, as shown by the green lines in Figure 13–68.
4. In the *Modify | Create Ramp Sketch* tab>*Draw* panel, click (Riser).
5. Use the sketch tools to specify the ends of the slope of each ramp, as shown by the black lines in Figure 13–68.

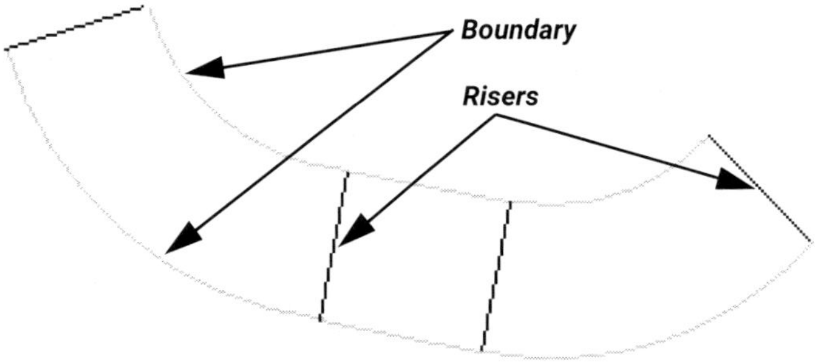

Figure 13–68

6. Click (Finish Edit Mode).

Practice 13d
Create Ramps

Practice Objectives

- Add a ramp.
- Modify ramp railings.

In this practice, you will create a ramp with railings and then modify placement of the railings. Figure 13–69 shows the completed ramp and railings.

Figure 13–69

Task 1: Add a ramp.

1. Open the project **Arch-Ramp.rvt** from the practice files folder.
2. Verify that you are in the **Floor Plans: Floor 1** view, then zoom in to the right side of the entrance stairs.
3. In the *Architecture* tab>*Circulation* panel, click  (Ramp).
4. In the Type Selector, select **Ramp: Hotel Ramp**.
5. In Properties, set the following:
    - *Base Level*: **Floor 1**
    - *Base Offset*: (negative) **-1'-0"**
    - *Top Level*: **Floor 1**
    - *Top Offset*: **0'-0"**
    - *Width*: **6'-0"**

6. In the *Modify | Create Ramp Sketch* tab>*Tools* panel, click (Railing). In the *Railing Types* dialog box, select the **Hotel Ramp Guardrail** railing type and click **OK**.
7. In the *Work Plane* panel, click (Ref Plane).
8. Draw the reference planes shown in Figure 13–70.

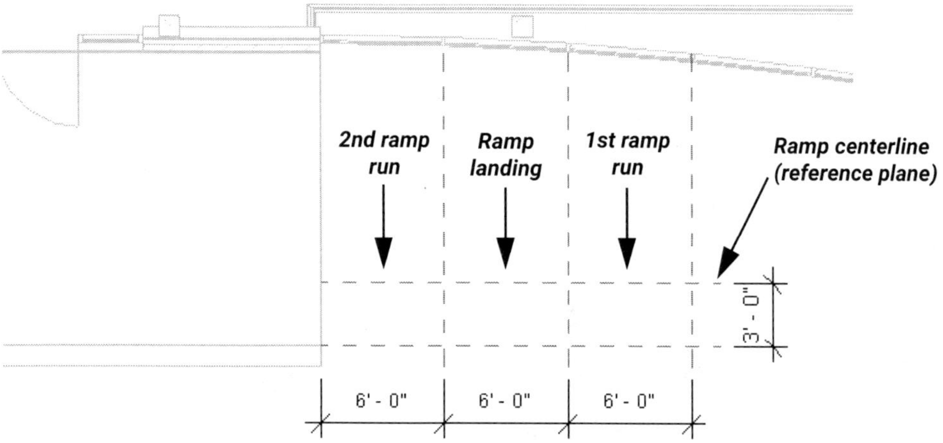

Figure 13–70

9. Click (Modify) to return to the *Modify | Create Ramp Sketch* tab in the ribbon.
10. In the *Draw* panel, click (Run).
11. Starting from the rightmost reference plane, pick the vertical and top horizontal reference plane intersection as the start point. Move the cursor to the left and pick the next intersection as the second point, as shown in Figure 13–71.

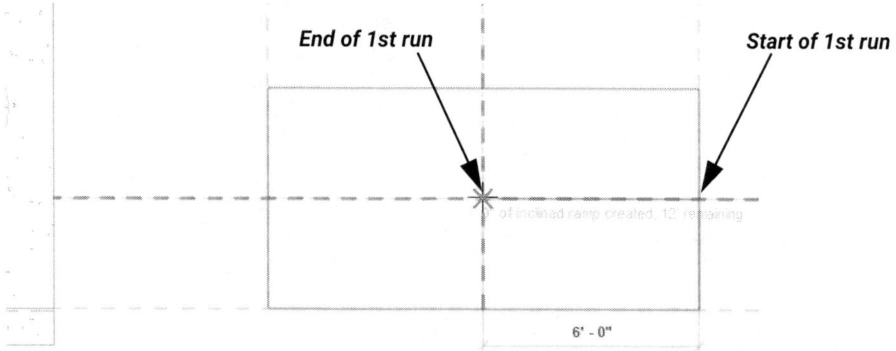

Figure 13–71

12. Still in the **Ramp** command, pick the next intersection to start the second run and then the last point at the entrance stairs, as shown in Figure 13–72.

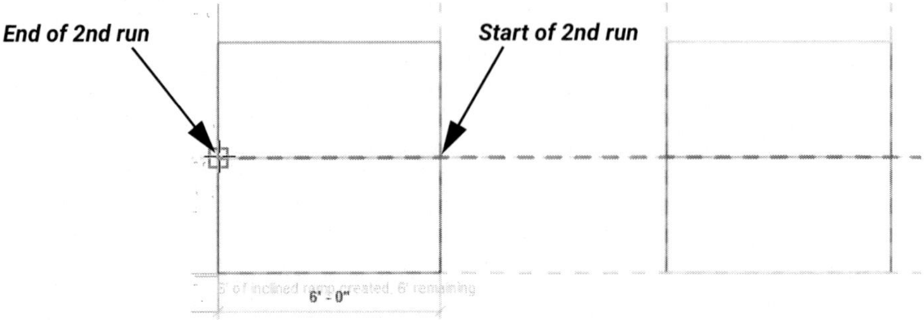

Figure 13–72

13. Click (Finish Edit Mode).
14. Click (Modify).

Task 2: Modify ramp railings.

In this task, the railings need to be moved so that they are fixed on the ramp.

1. Select both of the railings and in Properties, change the *Offset from Path* to (negative) **-0'-2"**.
2. Click (Modify).
3. Open the default 3D view and check that the ramp displays, as shown in Figure 13–73.
4. Zoom in to the railings, as shown in Figure 13–73.

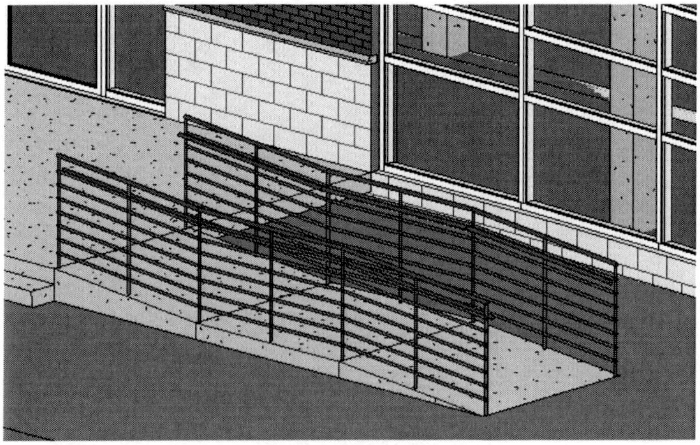

Figure 13–73

5. Save and close the project.

End of practice

Chapter Review Questions

1. Which of the following is NOT a stair component within Revit?

a. Runs

b. Landings

c. Treads

d. Supports

2. To edit a stair, you can double-click on it.

a. True

b. False

3. When do you need to use the (Railing) command? (Select all that apply.)

a. When you want an extra railing in the middle of very wide stairs.

b. When you create a stair or ramp.

c. When you create railings that are not attached to stairs or ramps.

d. When you use the **Stair by Sketch** command.

4. To create a stair that covers multiple floors (as shown in Figure 13–74), what needs to be done after you create the stair?

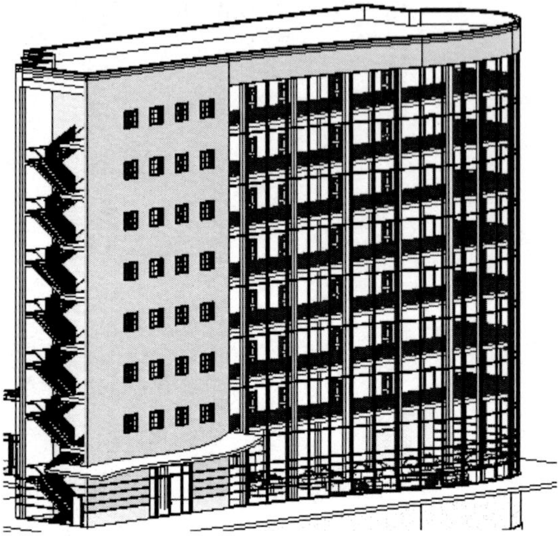

Figure 13–74

a. Select a stair and select **Multistory Top Level** from the drop-down list of levels in Properties.
b. Select a stair created at the top level of the floors, right-click, and select **Multistory Stair**.
c. Select a stair and copy it to the clipboard, then use **Paste Aligned to Selected Levels** and specify the levels where you want the stairs.
d. Select the stairs, select **Connect Levels** in the ribbon, and then select the levels where you want stairs.

5. Which of the following elements is most helpful in specifying the start and end runs of ramps?
a. Walls
b. Stairs
c. Sketch lines
d. Reference planes

Command Summary

Button	Command	Location
Stairs and Ramps		
	**Connect Levels**	• **Ribbon:** *Modify | Multistory Stairs* tab>*Multistory Stairs* panel
	**Convert to sketch-based**	• **Ribbon:** *Modify | Create Stair* tab>*Tools* panel
	**Disconnect Levels**	• **Ribbon:** *Modify | Multistory Stairs* tab>*Multistory Stairs* panel
	**Edit Sketch**	• **Ribbon:** *Modify | Create Stair* tab>*Tools* panel
	**Edit Stairs**	• **Ribbon:** *Modify | Stairs* tab>*Edit* panel
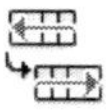	**Flip**	• **Ribbon:** *Modify | Create Stair* tab>*Tools* panel
	**Landing (Stair)**	• **Ribbon:** *Modify | Create Stair* tab>*Components* panel
	**Ramp**	• **Ribbon:** *Architecture* tab>*Circulation* panel
	**Run (Stair)**	• **Ribbon:** *Modify | Create Stair* tab>*Components* panel
	**Select Levels**	• **Ribbon:** *Modify | Stairs* tab>*Multistory Stairs* panel
	**Stair**	• **Ribbon:** *Architecture* tab>*Circulation* panel
	**Support (Stair)**	• **Ribbon:** *Modify | Create Stair* tab>*Components* panel

Button	Command	Location
Railings		
	**Edit Path (Railings)**	• **Ribbon:** *Modify | Railings* tab>*Mode* panel
	**Railing**	• **Ribbon:** *Modify | Create Stair (Create Stairs Sketch) (Create Ramp)* tab>*Tools* panel
	**Railing>Place on Stair/ Ramp**	• **Ribbon:** *Architecture* tab>*Circulation* panel, expand Railing
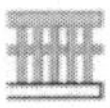	**Railing>Sketch Path**	• **Ribbon:** *Architecture* tab>*Circulation* panel, expand Railing
	**Pick New Host**	• **Ribbon:** *Modify | Create Railing Path (Railings)* tab> *Tools* panel

Construction Documentation

The third section of this guide continues to teach the Autodesk® Revit® tools, focusing on tools that help you to create accurate construction documents for a design.

This section includes the following chapters:

- Chapter 14: Creating Construction Documents
- Chapter 15: Working with Annotations
- Chapter 16: Adding Tags and Schedules
- Chapter 17: Creating Details

Chapter

14

Creating Construction Documents

The accurate creation of construction documents in Revit® ensures that the design is correctly communicated to downstream users and other stakeholders. Construction documents are created primarily in special views call sheets. Selecting title blocks, assigning title block information, placing views, and printing the sheets are essential steps in the construction documentation process.

Learning Objectives

- Add sheets with title blocks and views of a project.
- Enter the title block information for individual sheets and for an entire project.
- Place and organize views on sheets.
- Print sheets using the default *Print* dialog box.

14.1 Setting Up Sheets

While you are modeling a project, the foundations of the working drawings are already in progress. Any view (such as a floor plan, section, callout, or schedule) can be placed on a sheet, as shown in Figure 14–1.

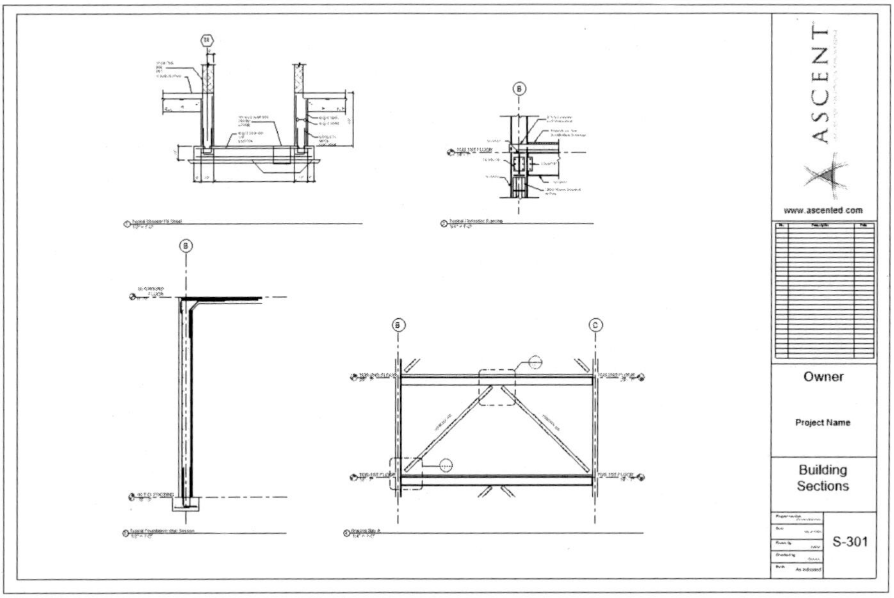

Figure 14–1

- Company templates can be created with standard sheets using the company (or project) title block and related views already placed on the sheet.
- The sheet size is based on the selected title block family.
- Sheets are listed in the *Sheets* section in the Project Browser.
- Most information on sheets is included in the views. You can add general notes and other non-model elements directly to the sheet, though it is better to add them using drafting views or legends, as these can be placed on multiple sheets.

How To: Set Up Sheets

1. In the Project Browser, right-click on **Sheets (all)** and select **New Sheet...**, or in the *View* tab>*Sheet Composition* panel, click (Sheet).

2. In the *New Sheet* dialog box, select a title block from the list, as shown in Figure 14–2.

   *Note: Click **Load...** to load a title block from the Revit Library or your company's custom title block.*

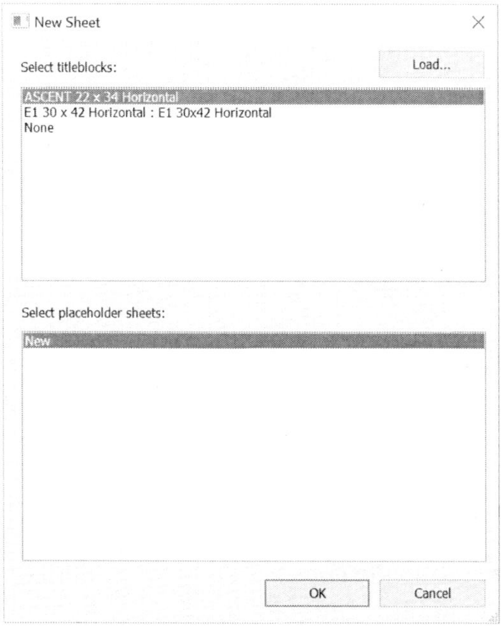

Figure 14–2

3. Click **OK**. A new sheet is created using the selected title block.
4. Fill out the information in the title block as needed.
5. Add views to the sheet.

- When you create sheets, the next sheet is incremented numerically.
- Double-click on the sheet name to change the name and number in the *Sheet Title* dialog box.
- When you change the *Sheet Name* and/or *Number* in the title block, it automatically changes the name and number of the sheet in the Project Browser.
- The plot stamp on the side of the sheet automatically updates according to the current date and time. The format of the display uses the regional settings of your computer.
- The scale is automatically entered when a view is inserted onto a sheet. If a sheet has multiple views with different scales, the scale displays **As Indicated** by default.

Sheet (Title Block) Properties

Each new sheet includes a title block. You can change the title block information in Properties, as shown on the left in Figure 14–3, or by selecting any blue label you want to edit (*Sheet Name*, *Sheet Number*, *Drawn by*, etc.), as shown on the right.

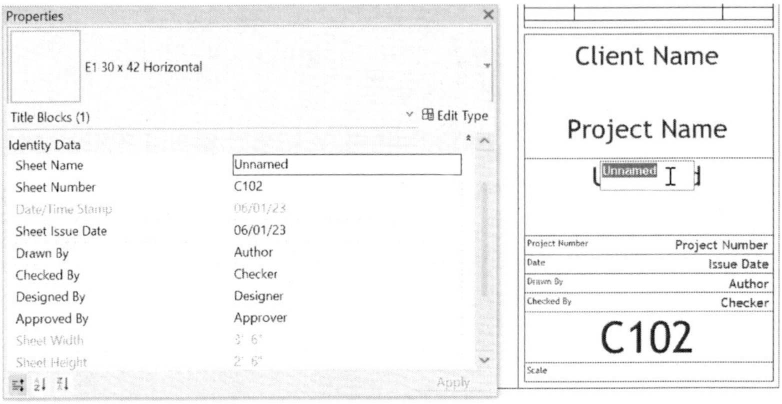

Figure 14–3

Properties that apply to all sheets can be entered in the *Project Information* dialog box (shown in Figure 14–4). In the *Manage* tab>*Settings* panel, click (Project Information).

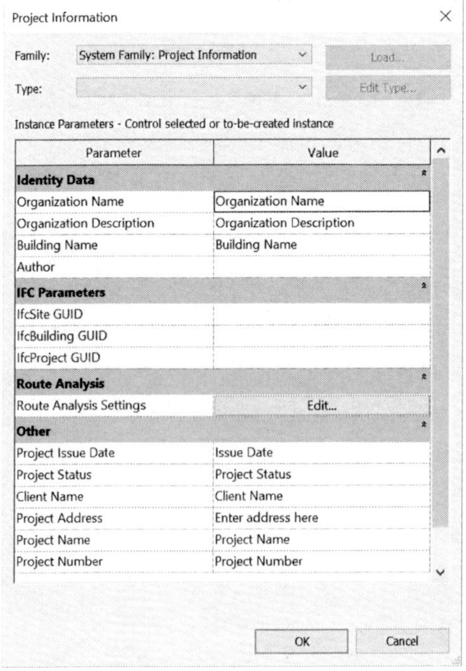

Figure 14–4

14.2 Placing Views on Sheets

The process of adding views to a sheet is simple. Drag and drop a view from the Project Browser onto the sheet, as shown in Figure 14–5. The new view on the sheet is displayed at the scale specified in the original view and the title block displays the view's scale. When multiple views are added that have different scales, by default the title block displays **As Indicated**. The view title displays the name, number, and scale of the view, as shown in Figure 14–5. Once the view has been placed on a sheet, the icon next to the view name in the Project Browser is filled in.

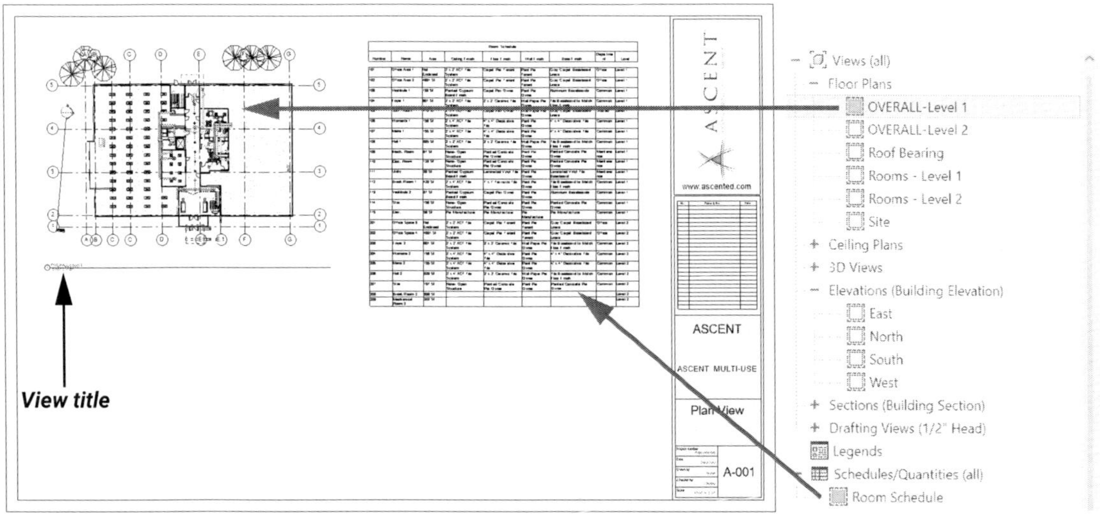

Figure 14–5

How To: Place Views on Sheets from the Project Browser

1. Set up the view as you want it to display on the sheet, including the scale and visibility of elements.
2. Create or open the sheet where you want to place the view.
3. Select the view in the Project Browser and drag and drop it onto the sheet. Alternatively, use <Shift> or <Ctrl> to select multiple views, then drag them to the sheet.

   Note: *Alignment lines from existing views display to help you place additional views.*

- Views can only be placed on a sheet once. If a view has already been placed on a sheet, the *Placing Views* dialog box will display, indicating what you can do, as shown in Figure 14–6.

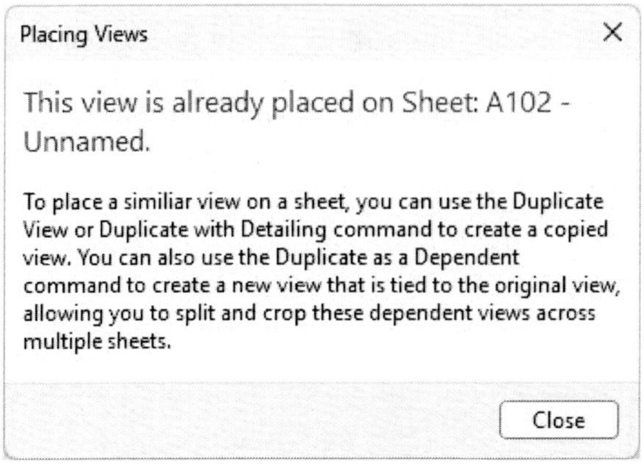

Figure 14–6

- Views on a sheet are associative. They automatically update to reflect changes to the project.
- Each view on a sheet is listed under the sheet name in the Project Browser, as shown in Figure 14–7.

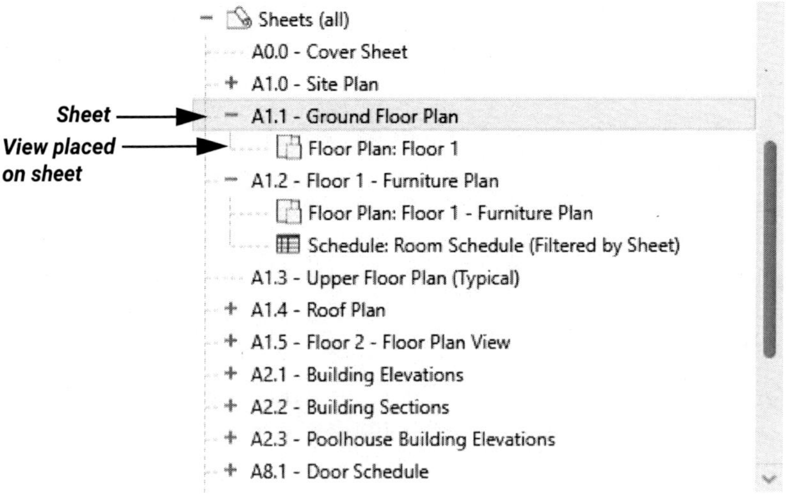

Figure 14–7

How To: Add Multiple Views to a Sheet

1. Open a sheet that you want to place views on.
2. In the *View* tab>*Sheet Composition* panel, click  (Place View). Alternatively, in the Project Browser, right-click on the sheet name and select **Add View...**.
3. In the *Select View* dialog box (shown in Figure 14–8), you can use the search at the top of the dialog box to narrow down the views in the list, then use <Shift> or <Ctrl> to select multiple views you want to use and click **OK**.

Note: *This method lists only those views which have not yet been placed on a sheet.*

Figure 14–8

4. The views will be attached to your cursor, as shown in Figure 14–9. Click to place the views on the sheet.

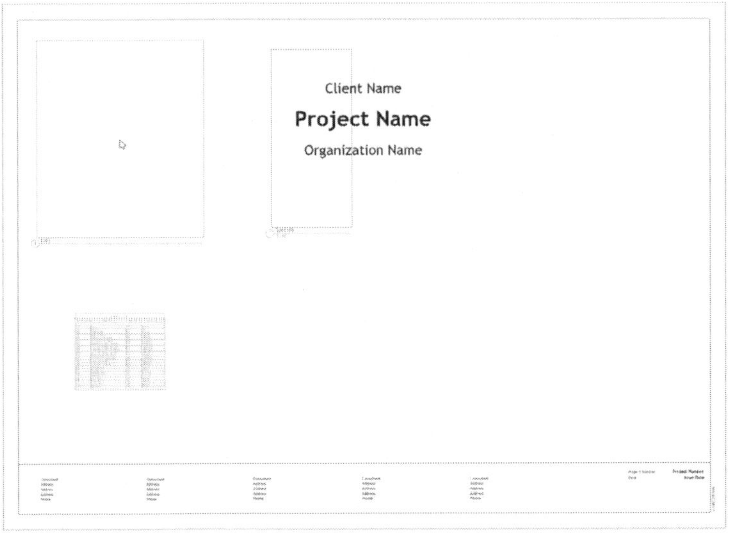

Figure 14–9

Opening Sheets

To open sheets from the Project Browser, you can double-click on a sheet from the *Sheets (all)* section. As the project gets larger, you can easily open a sheet by right-clicking on a view in the Project Browser or right-clicking in the view area.

- In the Project Browser, right-click on a view that displays the blue show view placement on sheet status icon and select **Open Sheet**, as shown on the left in Figure 14–10.
- In an open view with nothing selected, right-click and select **Open Sheet**, as shown on the right in Figure 14–10.

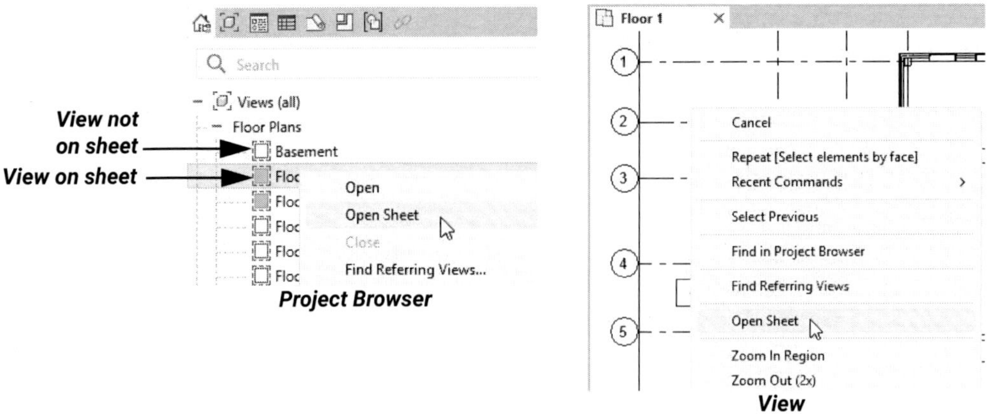

Figure 14–10

14.3 Modifying Views on a Sheet

You can reduce the time it takes to modify the views that are placed on a sheet by activating the view directly on the sheet and editing it there, or by opening the view from the sheet if more detailed changes are needed. You can also swap a view on a sheet with a view that is already on another sheet from the ribbon or Properties. After placing a view onto a sheet, you can also save the position of the view, edit its position, and manage saved positions, as shown in Figure 14–11. When multiple views of different scales are placed on a sheet, you can modify the *Scale* parameter to display a custom value.

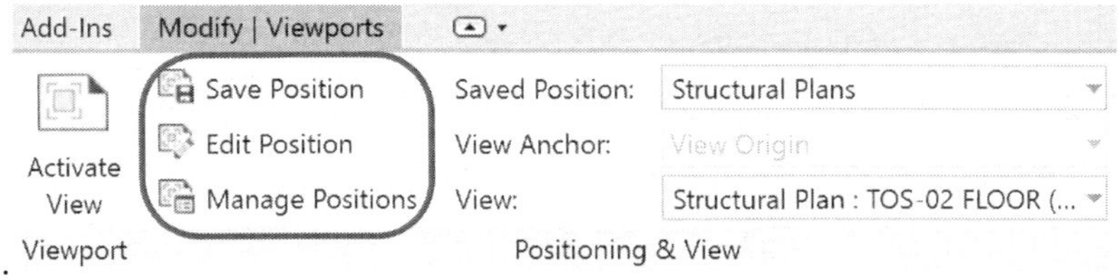

Figure 14–11

How To: Open a View on a Sheet

1. Select one or more views on a sheet.
2. Right-click and select **Open**, as shown in Figure 14–12.

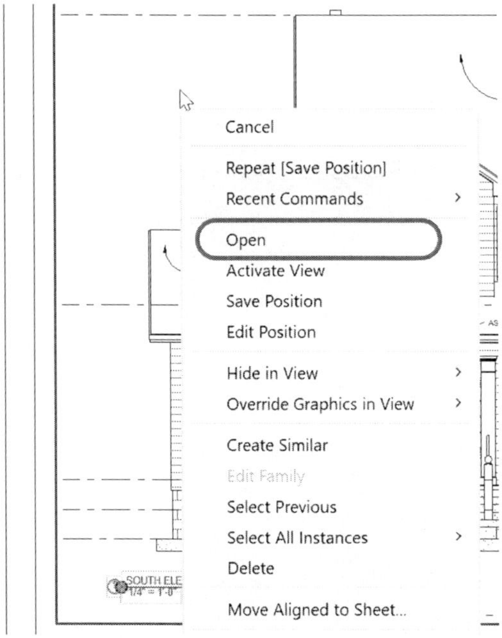

Figure 14–12

- If more than one view was selected, click **OK** in the *Open View* dialog box to open them.

How To: Activate a View on a Sheet

1. Select one or more views on a sheet.
2. Right-click and select **Activate View**.
   - You can also activate the view by selecting (Activate View) in the *Modify | Viewports* tab>*Viewport* panel.

How To: Save a View Position

1. Open a sheet view and select a view on the sheet.
2. In the *Modify | Viewports* tab>*Positioning & View* panel, click (Save Position).
   - Alternatively, you can select the view, right-click, and select **Save Position**.
3. In the *Save View Position* dialog box, enter a name and click **OK**.

How To: Edit a Saved View Position

1. Select a view on a sheet that is using a saved position.
2. In the *Modify | Viewports* tab>*Positioning & View* panel, click (Edit Position).
3. Modify the viewport's position.
4. In the *Edit View Position* panel, click (Finish).

How To: Manage Saved Positions

1. Select a view on a sheet that is using a saved position.
2. In the *Modify | Viewports* tab>*Positioning & View* panel, click (Manage Positions).

3. In the *Manage Positions* dialog box, click (Rename) to rename the saved position (as shown in Figure 14–13) or (Delete) to delete the saved position.

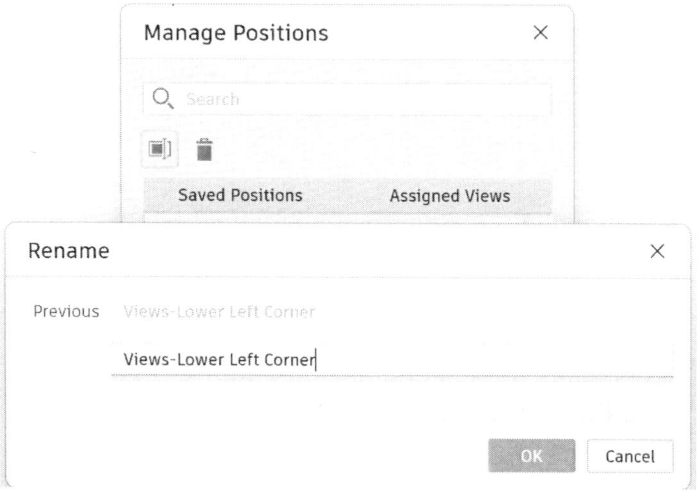

Figure 14–13

How To: Swap a View on a Sheet

1. In the Project Browser, open a sheet view from the *Sheets* section.
2. Select the view that is on the sheet.
3. In the *Modify | Viewports* tab>*Positioning & View* panel, expand the *View* drop-down list, as shown in Figure 14–14, and select a new view from the list (views will have suffixes at the end of their names with the sheet number if they are already placed on a sheet). You can use the search bar to filter the list.

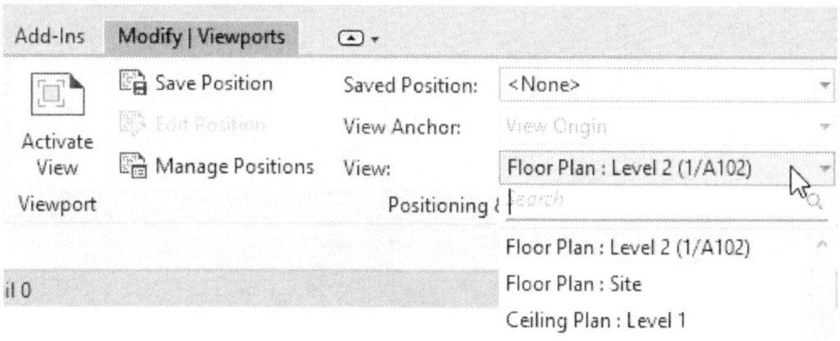

Figure 14–14

4. If you select a view that is already on a sheet, the *View Already Placed* dialog box will display, as shown in Figure 14–15.

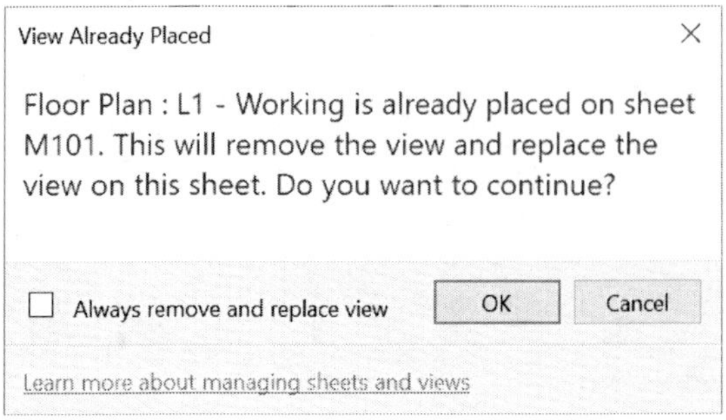

Figure 14–15

5. Click **OK** to swap the view.
   - Alternatively, with the viewport selected, in Properties, in the *Identity Data* section, change the *View* on the sheet by expanding the parameter's drop-down list and selecting a different view, as shown in Figure 14–16. If you select a view that is already on another sheet, the *View Already Placed* dialog box will display.

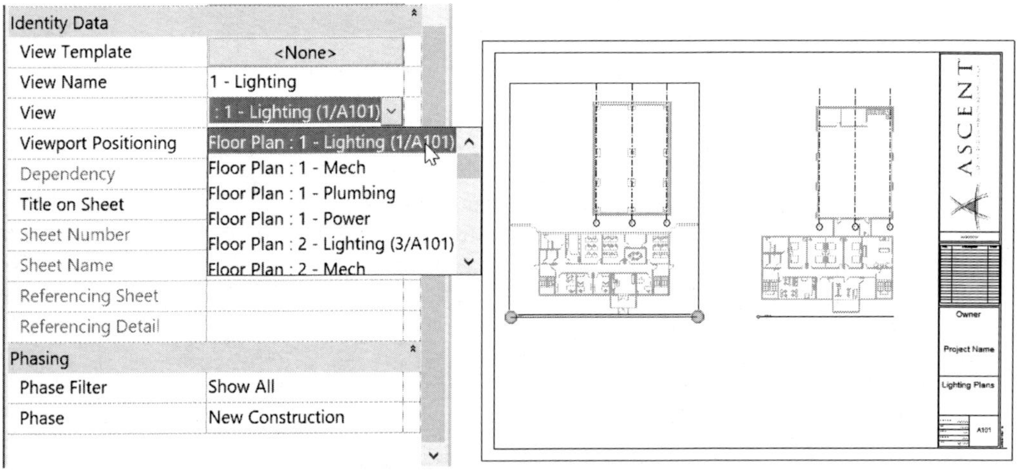

Figure 14–16

- When swapping views, you can specify if you want to retain the view title's position from a viewport's type properties, as shown in Figure 14–17. When the checkbox for *Preserve Title Position* is checked, the view title will resize to the viewport when a different size view is swapped.

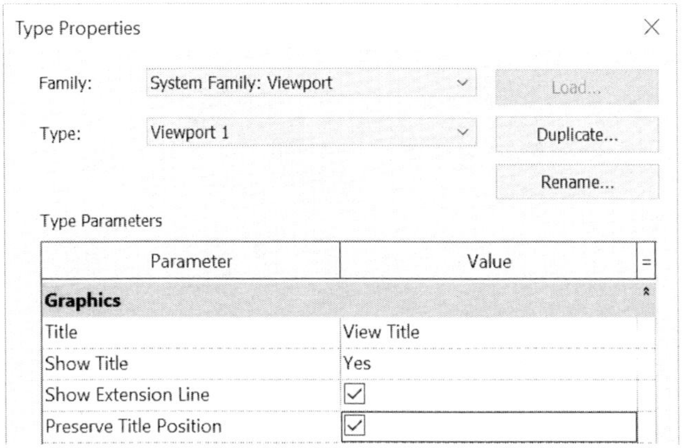

Figure 14–17

You can move a view and keep its alignment to the sheet it is on from the Project Browser or the right-click menu of the view.

How To: Move Views to Another Sheet

1. Open a sheet, then select the views you want to move, right-click, and select **Move View Aligned to Sheet....** Alternatively, in the Project Browser, select a view that has been placed on a sheet, right-click, and select **Move View Aligned to Sheet...**, as shown in Figure 14–18. You can also right-click on the view and select **Move Aligned to Sheet....**

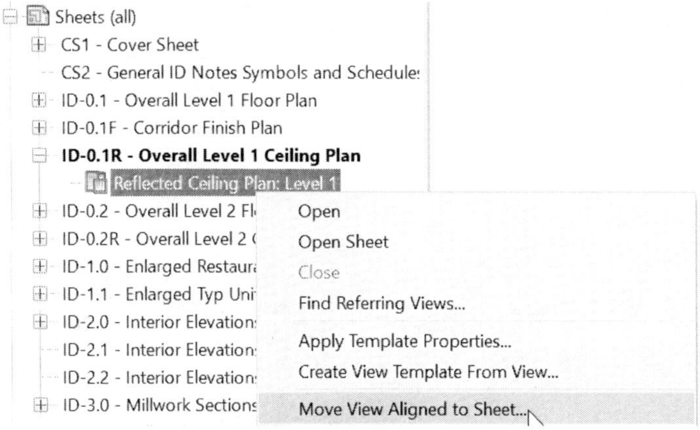

Figure 14–18

2. In the *Select Sheet* dialog box, select a sheet, as shown in Figure 14–19, and click **OK**. The view moves to the sheet, keeping its original alignment.
   - To quickly find a sheet from the list, use the search bar at the top of the dialog box.

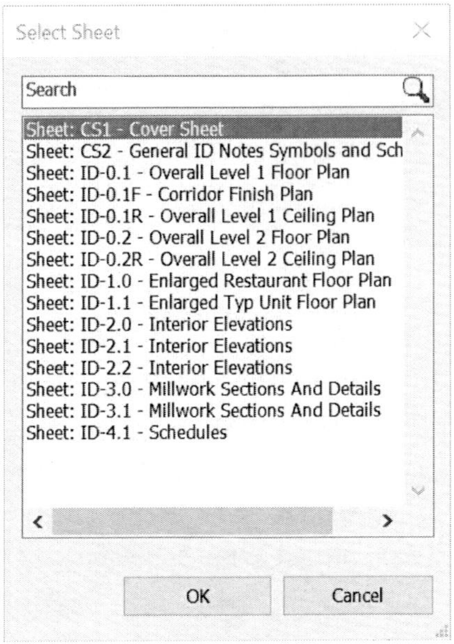

Figure 14–19

- Alternatively, in the *Sheet* section in the Project Browser, expand a sheet and manually drag a view to another sheet. The view is moved and keeps its original alignment.

How To: Customize the Sheet Scale with Multiple Views

1. Select the title block.
2. In Properties, click **Edit Type...**.
3. Enter a custom value for the *Scale Override (Multiple Values)* parameter, as shown in Figure 14–20.

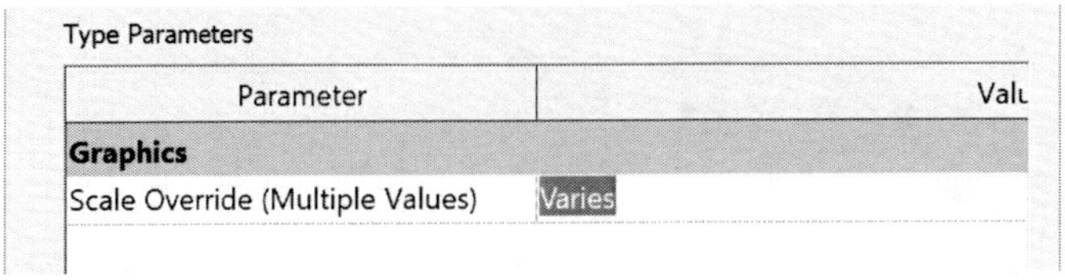

Figure 14–20

   - If views are removed and only one view remains, the sheet scale will display the scale of the view.

Removing Views from Sheets

There are three ways to remove a view from a sheet:

- In the Project Browser, right-click on a view and select **Remove From Sheet**, as shown in Figure 14–21.
    - You can select multiple views to remove as long as they are on the same sheet. If they are not, the **Remove From Sheet** option will be grayed out in the right-click menu.

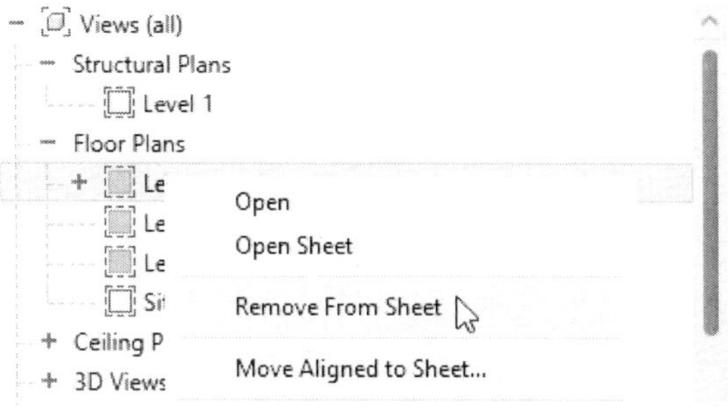

Figure 14–21

- If multiple views are selected, click **OK** in the *Remove From Sheet* dialog box, as shown in Figure 14–22.

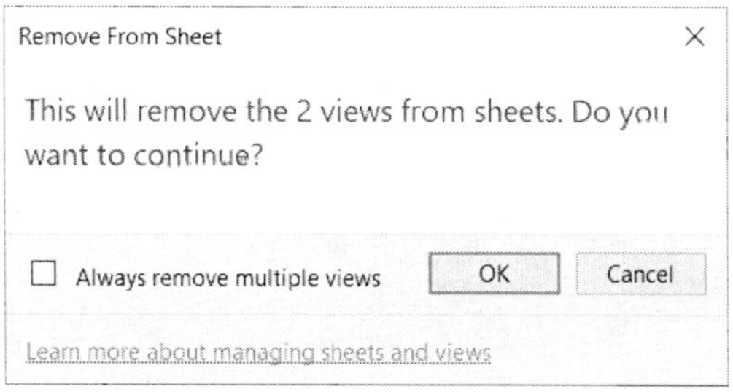

Figure 14–22

- In the Project Browser under the *Sheets* section, you can expand the sheet, select the views, right-click, and select **Remove From Sheet**, as shown in Figure 14–23. If multiple views are selected, click **OK** in the *Remove From Sheet* dialog box.

Figure 14–23

- You can remove a view directly from a sheet by selecting the view and pressing <Delete>.

Duplicating Sheets

Duplicating a selected sheet will automatically generate a copy with the same name and sheet number, followed by a number in parentheses, as shown in Figure 14–24.

Figure 14–24

How To: Duplicate Sheets

1. In the Project Browser>*Sheets* section, right-click on a sheet and select **Duplicate Sheet**.
2. Select one of the following options:
   - **Duplicate Empty Sheet:** Creates a new sheet with the same title block and project information.
     - No model or annotation elements on the sheet are duplicated.
   - **Duplicate with Sheet Detailing:** Creates a new sheet with the same title block, project information, and any legends, keynotes, schedules, and annotations.

- **Duplicate with Views:** Before a sheet gets created, you are prompted to specify how you would like the views on the sheet to be duplicated, as shown in Figure 14–25.

Figure 14–25

Note: *To review duplicating view types, refer to* ***Chapter 3 Working with Views****.*

- In the *Duplicate with Views* dialog box, select **Duplicate**, **Duplicate with Detailing**, or **Duplicate as a Dependent**.
- If you are duplicating a sheet that has drafting views and want to duplicate the view with the model and annotation elements, you need to use the **Duplicate with Detailing** option.

Sheet Collections

A sheet collection is a way to create various construction document submission sets or groupings, for example construction document submittals, within the *Sheets* section in the Project Browser. After sheets have been created, you can create sheet collections and add desired sheets to the collection by dragging and dropping the sheet into the collection or by selecting the sheet and setting the *Sheet Collection* in Properties.

How To: Create a Sheet Collection

1. In the Project Browser>*Sheets* section, right-click on a sheet and select **New Sheet Collection**.
2. Name the new sheet collection using one of the following methods:
   - In Properties, click in the *Name* value and type the desired name.
   - In the Project Browser, click on the newly created sheet collection and type the desired name.
   - Right-click on the newly created sheet collection and select **Rename...**.

3. Drag the sheet to the new collection. Alternatively, select the sheet and in Properties next to *Sheet Collection*, expand the drop-down list and select the sheet collection you would like to add the sheet to.
    - It may be necessary to duplicate the sheet. You can keep the same sheet number to create the various sheet collections.

Modifying Views and View Titles

After you have the desired views on a sheet, you can modify their locations and titles. You can use some of the modify tools, like **Move** and **Rotate**, as well as the arrow keys.

- You cannot use any tools that utilize the copy feature, like **Copy**, **Mirror**, and **Offset**.

How To: Move a View on a Sheet

1. Open a sheet view.
2. Select and drag a view to another location on the sheet. When selecting the view, the view title moves with the view.

How To: Modify the Viewport's View Title

1. Open a sheet view.
2. Select only the view title and drag it to the new location.

- To modify the length of the line under the title name, select the viewport and drag the controls, as shown in Figure 14–26.

Figure 14–26

- To change the title of a view on a sheet without changing its name in the Project Browser, select either the viewport or the view title, then in Properties, in the *Identity Data* section, type a new title for the *Title on Sheet* parameter, as shown in Figure 14–27.

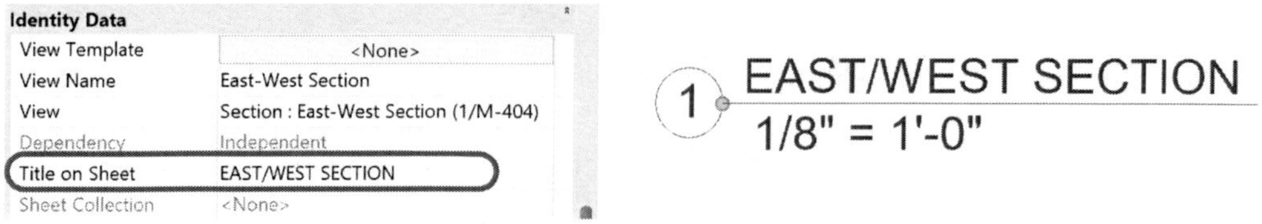

Figure 14–27

Rotating Views

When creating a vertical sheet, you can rotate the view on the sheet by 90° counterclockwise or clockwise. Select the view on the sheet and set the direction of rotation in the *Rotation on Sheet* drop-down list in Properties, as shown in Figure 14–28.

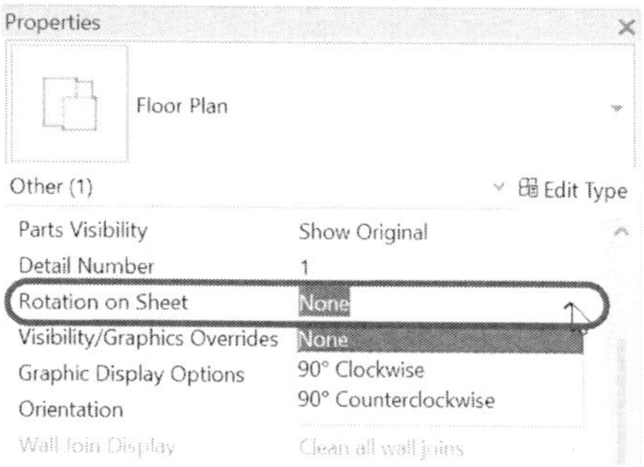

Figure 14–28

Note: *For more information about rotating the project or individual views to angles other than 90°, refer to the ASCENT guide Autodesk Revit: Site Planning and Design.*

Working Inside Views

To make small changes to a view while working on a sheet:

- Double-click *inside* the view to activate it.
- Double-click *outside* the view to deactivate it.

Only elements in the viewport are available for modification. The rest of the sheet is grayed out, as shown in Figure 14–29. Use this method only for small changes. Significant changes should be made directly in the view.

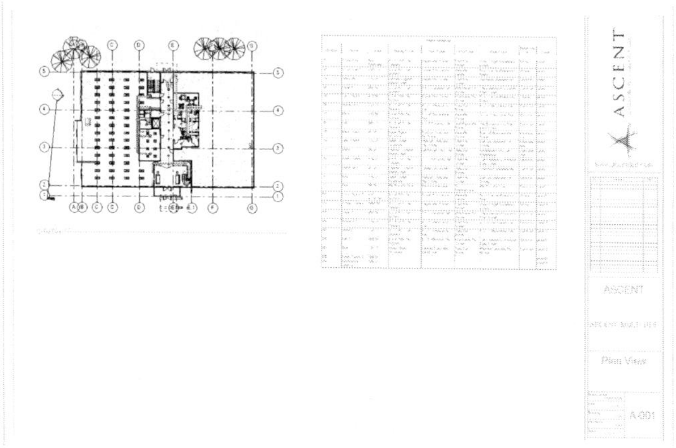

Figure 14–29

- You can activate and deactivate views by selecting the viewport, right-clicking, and selecting from the menu, or by using the tools found in the *Modify | Viewports* or *Views* tab>*Sheet Composition* panel.
- Changes you make to elements when a view is activated also display in the original view.
- If you are unsure which sheet a view is on, right-click on the view in the Project Browser and select **Open Sheet**. This is not available for schedules and legends, which can be placed on more than one sheet.

Resizing Views on Sheets

Each view displays the extents of the model or the elements contained in the crop region. If the view does not fit on a sheet (as shown in Figure 14–30), you might need to crop the view or move the elevation markers closer to the building.

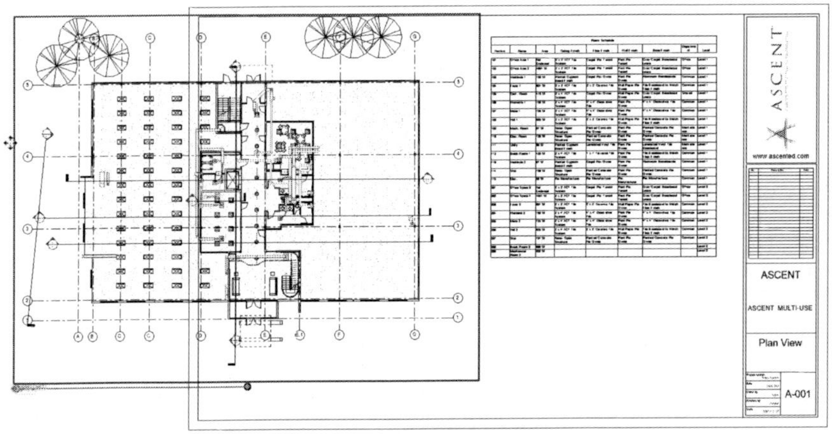

Figure 14–30

Note: *If the extents of the view change dramatically based on a scale change or a crop region, it is easier to delete the view on the sheet and drag it over again.*

How To: Add an Image to a Sheet

Company logos and renderings saved to image files (such as .JPG and .PNG) can be added directly on a sheet or in a view.

1. In the *Insert* tab>*Import* panel, click (Image).
2. In the *Import Image* dialog box, select and open the image file. The extents of the image display, as shown in Figure 14–31.

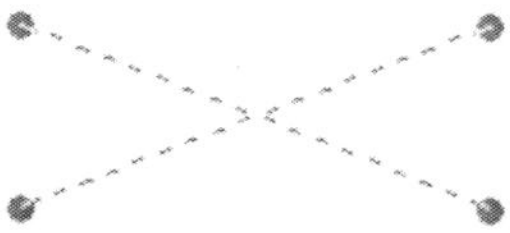

Figure 14–31

3. Place the image where you want it.
4. The image is displayed. Pick one of the grips and extend it to modify the size of the image.

- In Properties, you can adjust the height and width and also set the *Draw Layer* to either **Background** or **Foreground**, as shown in Figure 14–32.

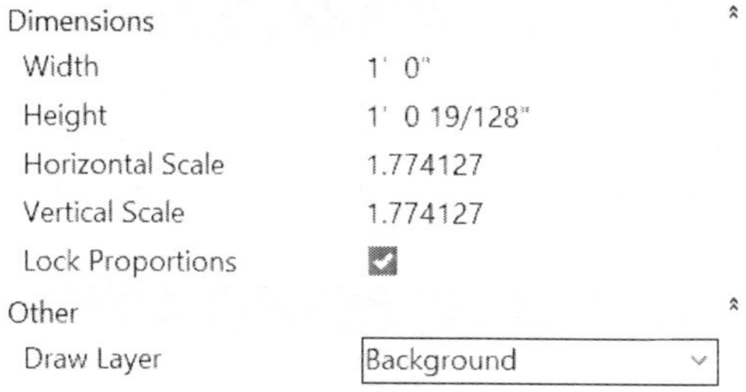

Figure 14–32

- You can select more than one image at a time and move them as a group to the background or foreground.
- In the *Modify | Raster Images* tab (shown in Figure 14–33), you can access the *Arrange* options and the **Manage Links** command.

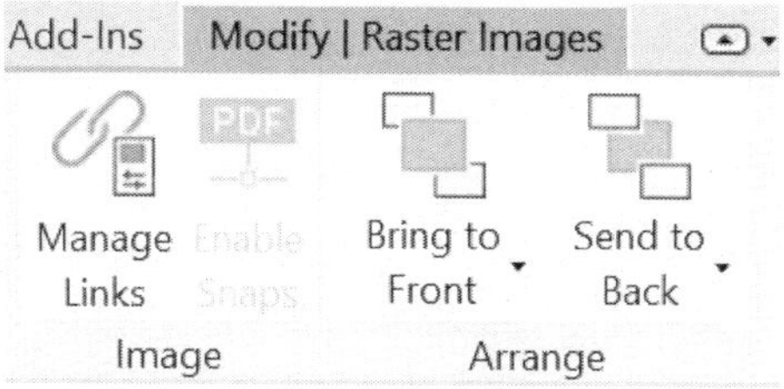

Figure 14–33

Practice 14a
Set Up Sheets

Practice Objectives

- Set up project properties.
- Create sheets individually.
- Modify views to prepare them to be placed on sheets.
- Place views on sheets.

In this practice, you will complete the project information, create new sheets, and then add views to the sheets, such as the completed sheet with building elevations shown in Figure 14–34. You will also fill in title block information and import an image for the cover sheet. Complete as many sheets as you have time for.

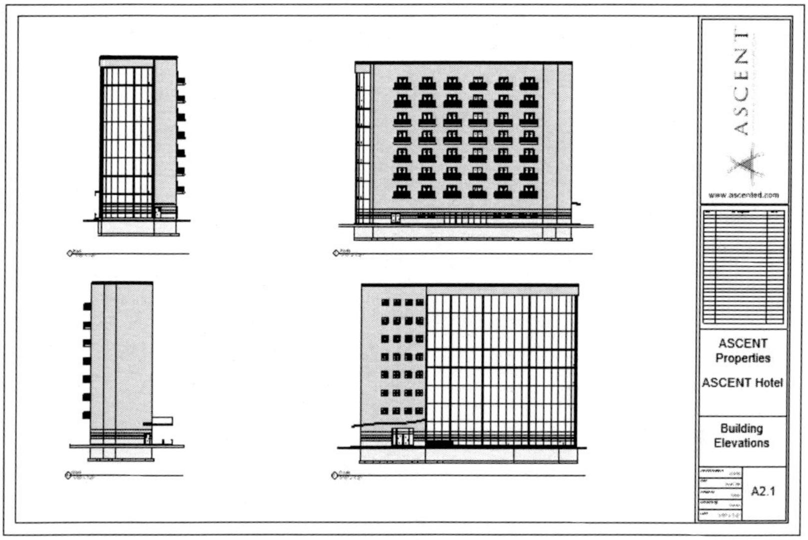

Figure 14–34

Task 1: Complete the project information.

1. Open the project **Arch-Sheets.rvt** from the practice files folder.
2. In the *Manage* tab>*Settings* panel, click (Project Information).

3. In the *Project Information* dialog box, in the *Other* section, set the following parameters:
   - *Project Issue Date:* Enter a date
   - *Project Status:* **Design Development**
   - *Client Name:* **ASCENT Properties**
   - *Project Address:* Click ⋯ (Browse)and enter your address
   - *Project Name:* **ASCENT Hotel**
   - *Project Number:* **1234-567**

   Note: *These properties are used across the entire sheet set and do not need to be entered on each sheet.*

4. Click **OK**.
5. Save the project.

Task 2: Create a sheet.

1. In the *View* tab>*Sheet Composition* panel, click (Sheet).
2. In the *New Sheet* dialog box, select the **ASCENT_22 x 34 Horizontal** title block and click **OK**.
3. Zoom in on the lower-right corner of the title block. The project properties filled out earlier are automatically added to the sheet (e.g., *Project Number*, *Project Status*, etc.).
4. In the Project Browser, scroll down to the *Sheets (all)* section and expand it. Note that the sheet number and name displays the same information as the title block.
5. Select the title block. Click on the sheet number, then change it to **A0.0** and press <Enter>. Click *Unnamed*, type **Cover Sheet** (as shown in Figure 14–35), and press <Enter>.

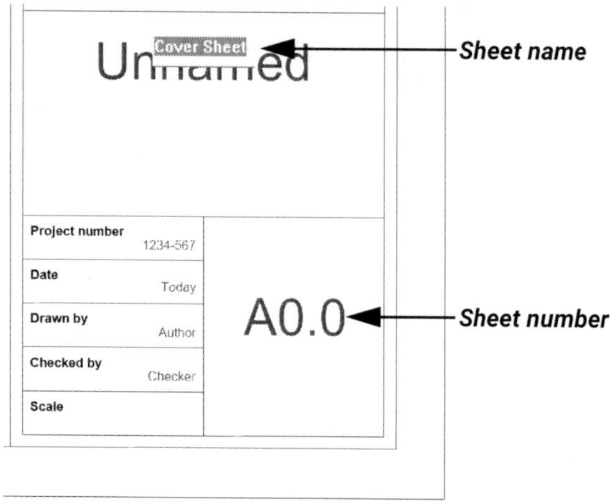

Figure 14–35

6. Click (Modify). Note that in the Project Browser, the sheet number and name have updated to reflect the changes made in the title block.
7. Zoom back out to display the whole sheet.
8. In the *Insert* tab>*Import* panel, click (Import Image).
9. In the *Import Image* dialog box, navigate to the practice files *Images* folder, select **Exterior Front Perspective.jpg** or **Exterior Front Perspective 2.jpg**, and click **Open**.
10. Your cursor will have an X shape (indicating the size of your image), as shown in Figure 14–36. Click to place the image on the sheet.

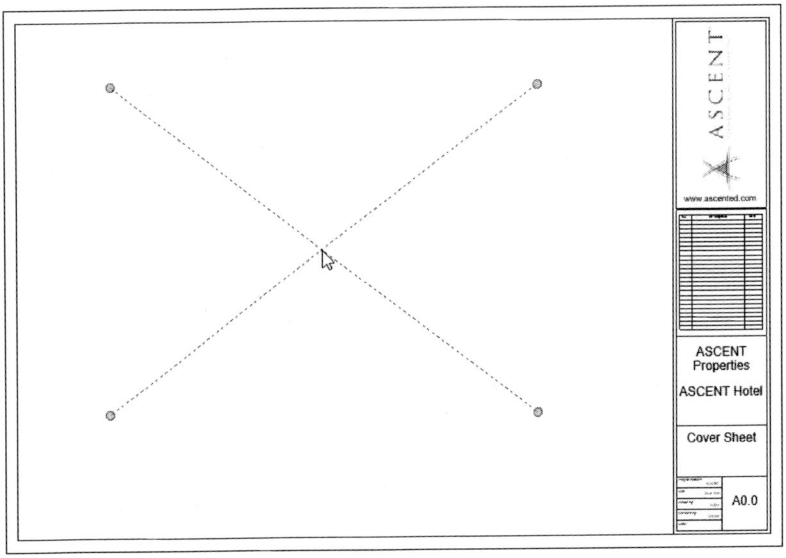

Figure 14–36

11. Use the grips to adjust the size of the image to make room for notes.
12. Click (Modify).

Task 3: Duplicate a sheet and add views.

1. In the Project Browser, right-click on the cover sheet and select **Duplicate Sheet>Duplicate Empty Sheet**.
2. In the Project Browser, right-click on the new sheet and select **Rename...**.
3. In the *Sheet Title* dialog box, set the *Number* to **A9.1** and the *Name* to **Poolhouse Perspective View**. Click **OK**. The sheet updates with the information.
4. From the Project Browser, drag and drop the **3D - Poolhouse** view onto the sheet, as shown in Figure 14–37, then click (Modify).

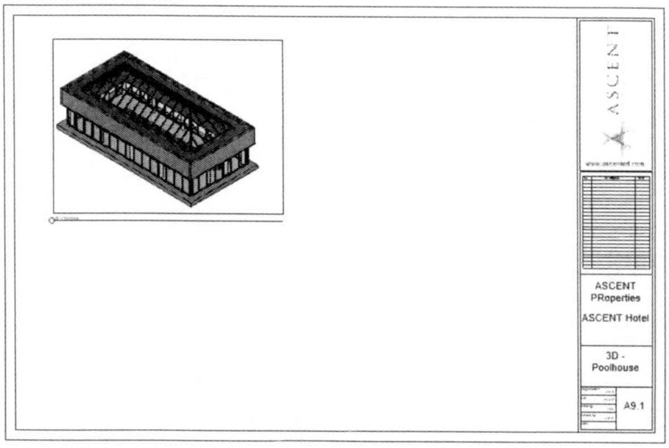

Figure 14–37

5. Select the the viewport. In the Type Selector, select **Viewport: NoTitle**.
6. Double-click inside the viewport; the titleblock grays out and you can modify the actual view.
7. In Properties, in the *Extents* section, clear the checkmark from **Crop Region Visible**. (This could also be toggled off in the View Control Bar.)
8. Double-click outside and away from the viewport to deactivate the view and return to the sheet.
9. In the Project Browser, right-click on the **A9.1 Poolhouse Perspective View** sheet and select **Duplicate Sheet>Duplicate Empty Sheet**. A new copy of the sheet is created.
10. In Properties, in the *Identity Data* section, change the *Sheet Number* to **A9.2** and the *Sheet Name* to **Poolhouse Building Elevations**.
11. In the Project Browser, in the *Elevations (Building Elevation)* section, select **Pool-East**, **Pool-North**, **Pool-South**, and **Pool-West**.

12. Drag and drop them onto the **Poolhouse Building Elevations** sheet. They are placed onto the sheet. Do not worry about the arrangement of the views as you will fix it later in the practice.
13. Using the ASCENT title block, create the following new sheets. (Try creating new sheets using the different ways you have learned.)

Sheet Number	Sheet Name
A1.1	Ground Floor Plan
A1.2	Floor 1 - Furniture Plan
A1.3	Upper Floor Plan (Typical)
A1.4	Roof Plan
A2.1	Building Elevations
A2.2	Building Sections

14. Save the project.

Task 4: Set up and add views to sheets.

1. Open sheet **A1.1 - Ground Floor Plan** and drag and drop the **Floor 1** view onto the sheet.
2. In the Project Browser, right-click on **A1.1 - Ground Floor Plan** and select **Duplicate Sheet>Duplicate with Views**.
3. In the *Duplicate with Views* dialog box, select **Duplicate**.
4. The new copied sheet opens. Note that this also creates a copy of the Floor 1 view called **Floor 1 Copy 1**, which is listed in the Project Browser under both the sheet and in the *Floor Plans* section.
5. In Properties, change the *Sheet Number* to **LS1.1** and the *Sheet Name* to **Floor 1 - Life Safety Plan**.
6. Select the view on the sheet. In Properties, in the *Identity Data* section, change the *View Name* to **Floor 1 - Life Safety Plan**.
7. In the sheet, double-click on the view and do the following:
    - Hide all elements except the actual building elements.
    - Toggle on the crop region and ensure that it is tight up against the building.

    Note: *The crop region defines the extent of the view on the sheet.*

    - Toggle **Show Crop Region** off.
8. Double-click outside the view to deactivate the view.

9. In the Project Browser, right-click on the **Floor 2** view and select **Duplicate View>Duplicate**. Rename it to **Floor 2 - Life Safety Plan**.
10. In the Project Browser, right-click on the **LS1.1 - Floor 1 - Life Safety Plan** sheet and select **Duplicate Sheet>Duplicate Empty Sheet**. Rename it to **LS1.2 - Floor 2 - Life Safety Plan**.
11. In the Project Browser, right-click on the **LS1.2 - Floor 2 - Life Safety Plan** sheet and select **Add View...**.
12. In the *Select View* dialog box, scroll down and select **Floor Plan: Floor 2 - Life Safety Plan**, as shown in Figure 14–38. Click **OK** and place the view on the sheet.

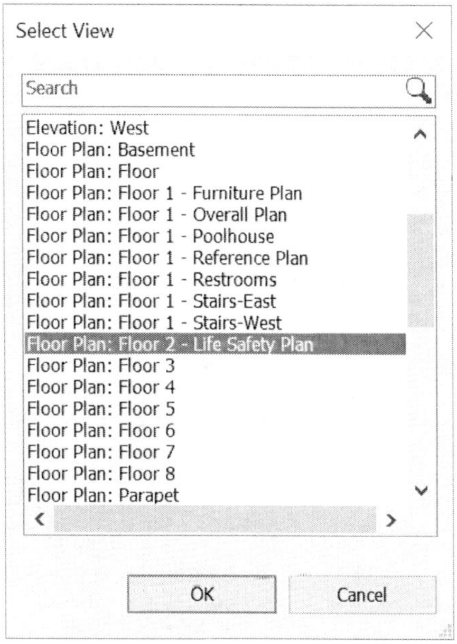

Figure 14–38

Task 5: Modify views on sheets.

1. Open the **A9.2 - Poolhouse Building Elevations** sheet.

2. Move the views around using alignment lines to help align the views, then modify crop regions and hide unnecessary elements in the views. Toggle off crop regions after you have modified them similar to Figure 14–39.

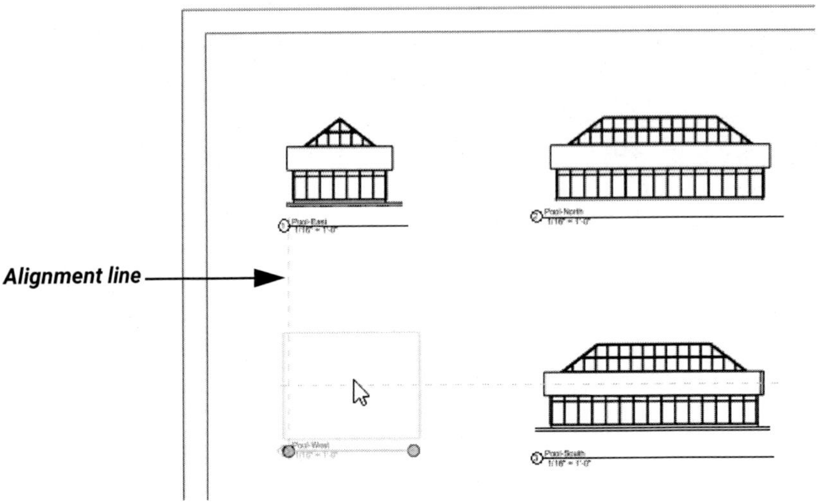

Figure 14–39

3. Place the following views on the corresponding sheets:

View Name	Sheet Number and Name
Floor 1 - Furniture Plan	A1.2: Floor 1 - Furniture Plan
Typical Guest Room Plan	A1.3: Upper Floor Plan (Typical)
Roof	A1.4: Roof Plan
E/W Building Section N/S Building Section	A2.2: Building Sections

- Once you have added a view to a sheet, the corresponding elevation marker will display the sheet number, as shown in Figure 14–40.

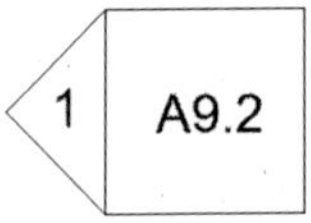

Figure 14–40

4. Save and close the project.

End of practice

14.4 Printing Sheets

With the **Print** command, you can print individual sheets or a list of selected sheets. You can also print an individual view or a portion of a view for check prints or presentations. To open the *Print* dialog box (shown in Figure 14–41), in the *File* tab, click (Print), or press <Ctrl>+<P>.

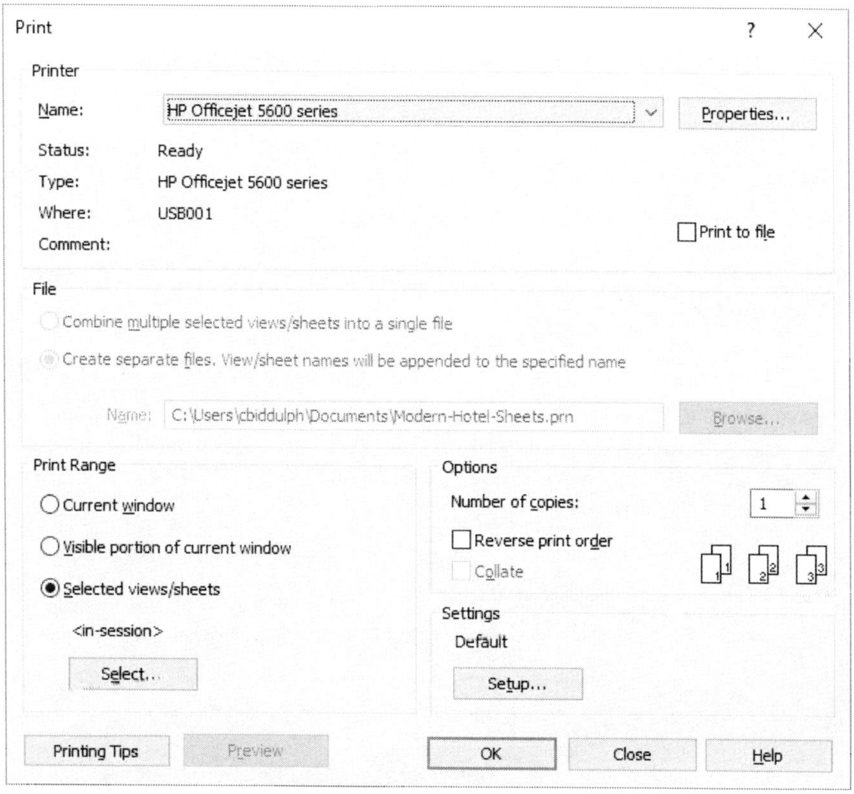

Figure 14–41

Printing Options

The *Print* dialog box is divided into the following areas: *Printer*, *File*, *Print Range*, *Options*, and *Settings*. Modify them as needed to produce the plot you want.

- **Printing Tips:** Opens Autodesk WikiHelp online, in which you can find help with troubleshooting printing issues.
- **Preview:** Opens a preview of the print output so that you can see what is going to be printed.

Printer

Select from the list of available printers, as shown in Figure 14–42. Click **Properties...** to adjust the properties of the selected printer. The options vary according to the printer. Select the **Print to file** option to print to a file rather than directly to a printer. You can create .PLT or .PRN files.

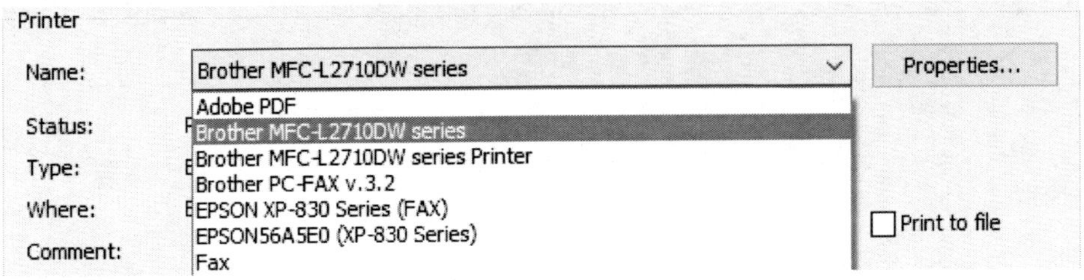

Figure 14–42

- You must have a PDF print driver installed on your system to print to PDF, or you can export views and sheets to PDF.

File

The *File* area is only available if the **Print to file** option has been selected in the *Printer* area or if you are printing to an electronic-only type of printer. You can create one file or multiple files depending on the type of printer you are using, as shown in Figure 14–43. Click **Browse...** to select the file location and name.

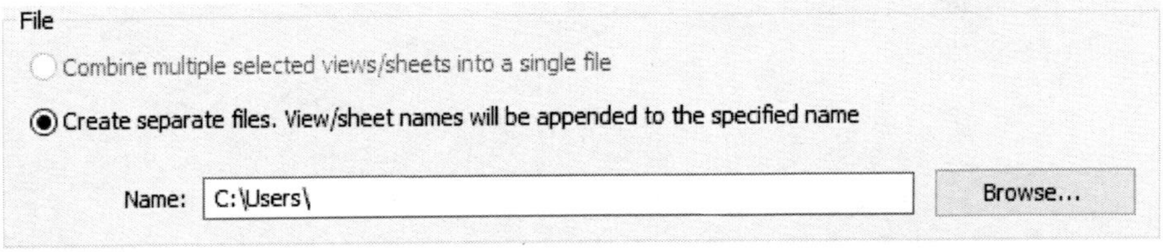

Figure 14–43

Print Range

The *Print Range* area enables you to print individual views/sheets or sets of views/sheets, as shown in Figure 14–44.

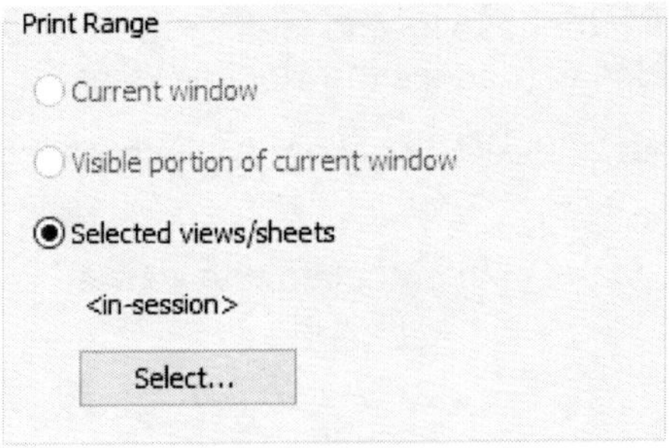

Figure 14–44

- **Current window:** Prints the entire current sheet or view you have open.
- **Visible portion of current window:** Prints only what is displayed in the current sheet or view.
- **Selected views/sheets:** Prints multiple views or sheets. Click **Select...** to open the *Select Views/Sheets* dialog box (shown in Figure 14–45) to choose what to include in the print set. You can save these sets by name so that you can more easily print the same group again.

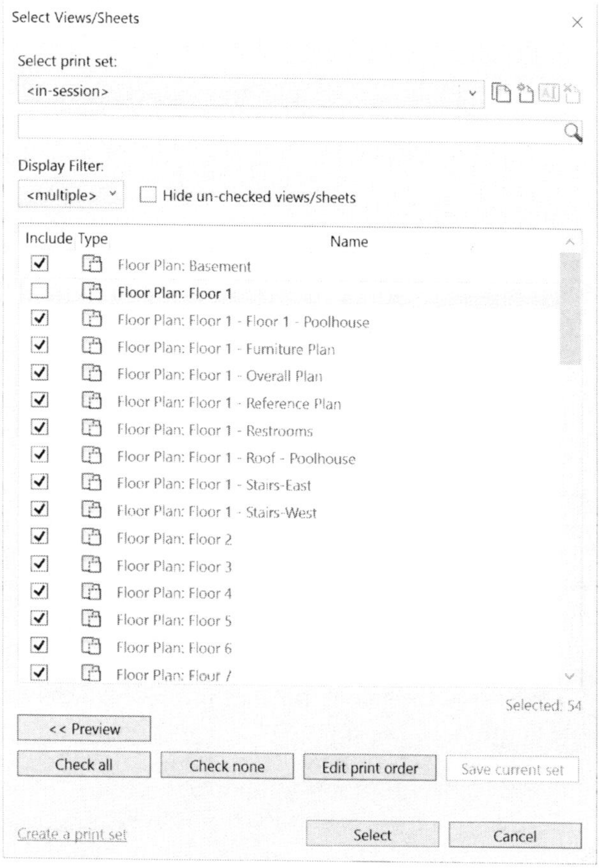

Figure 14–45

- Click **Edit print order** to open the *Edit Print Order in* dialog box. You can edit the selected views and sheets by **Browser organization**, **Sheet Number (Ascending)**, or **Manual order**. If you select **Manual order**, you can drag the views and sheets to put them in a custom order, as shown in Figure 14–46.

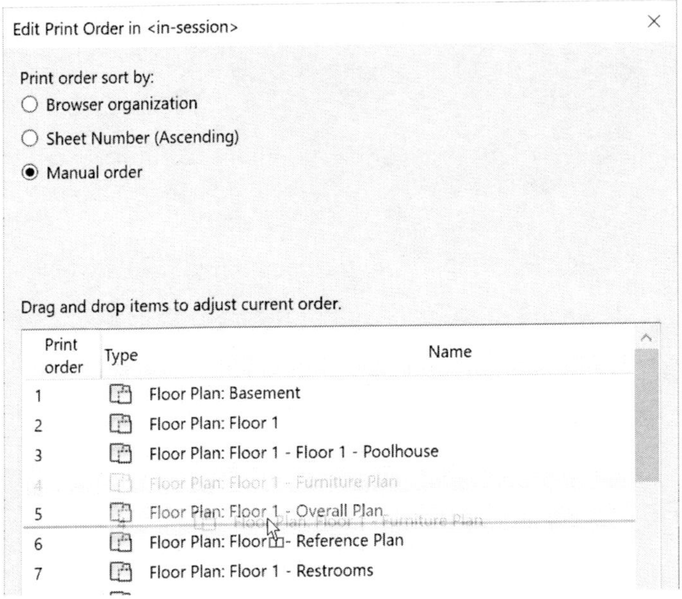

Figure 14–46

Options

If your printer supports multiple copies, you can specify the number in the *Options* area, as shown in Figure 14–47. You can also reverse the print order or collate your prints. These options are also available in the printer properties.

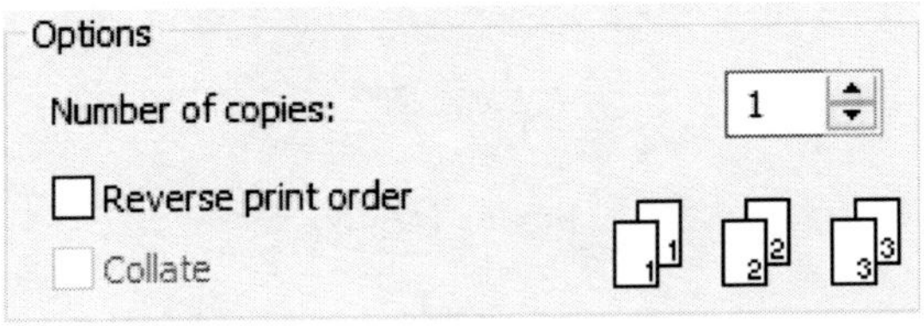

Figure 14–47

Settings

Click **Setup...** to open the *Print Setup* dialog box, as shown in Figure 14–48. Here, you can specify the *Orientation* and *Zoom* settings, among others. You can also save these settings by name.

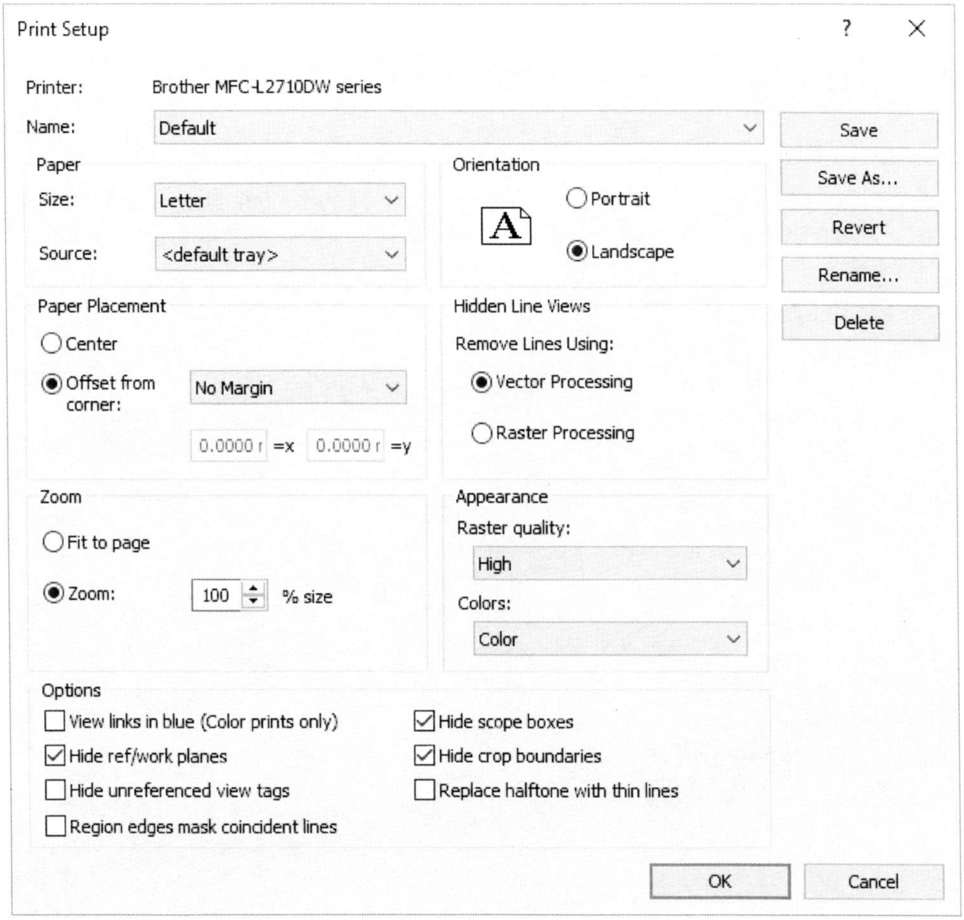

Figure 14–48

- In the *Options* area, specify the types of elements you want to print or not print. Unless specified, all of the elements in a view or sheet print.
- Sheets should always be printed at **Zoom** set to **100%** size unless you are creating a quick markup set that does not need to be exact.

Exporting Views and Sheets to PDF

If you do not have a PDF driver to utilize in the *Print* dialog box, you can export your views or sheets to PDF. If you set the *Export Range* to **Selected views/sheets**, you have the ability to edit the print order of the views/sheets by **Browser organization**, **Sheet Number (Ascending)**, or **Manual order**.

How To: Export Views and Sheets to PDF

1. In the *File* tab, select (Export)> (PDF).
2. In the *PDF Export* dialog box (shown in Figure 14–49), enter a *File Name* and the *Location* you would like the PDF to be exported to, and select the other settings, as needed.
   - The *PDF Export* settings are similar to those found in the Revit *Print* dialog box.

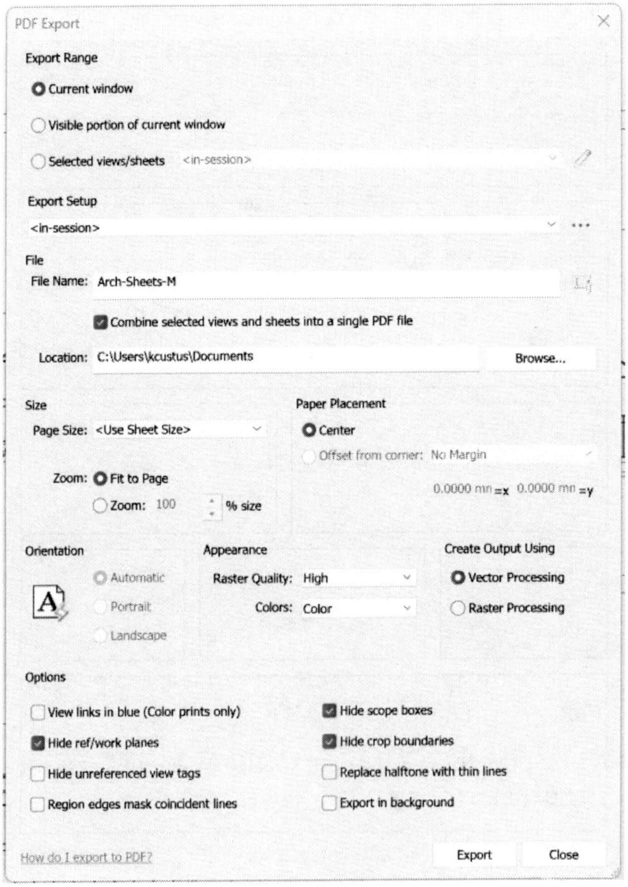

Figure 14–49

3. Click **Export**.

Chapter Review Questions

1. How do you specify the size of a sheet?
   a. In the Sheet Properties, specify the *Sheet Size*.
   b. In the contextual tab, specify the *Sheet Size*.
   c. In the *New Sheet* dialog box, select a titleblock to control the sheet size.
   d. In the sheet view, right-click and select **Sheet Size**.

2. How is the title block information filled in, as shown in Figure 14–50? (Select all that apply.)

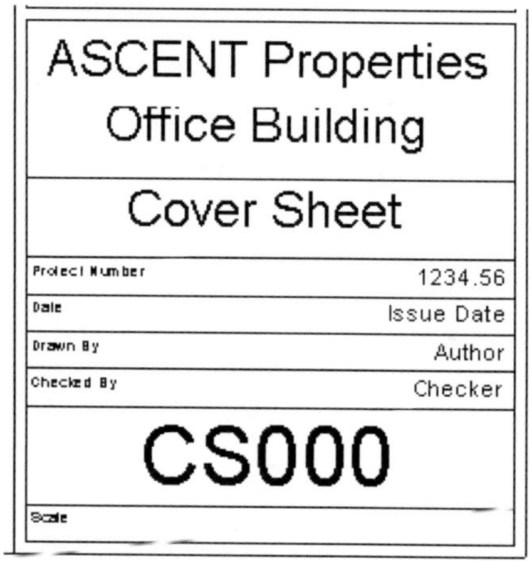

Figure 14–50

   a. Select the title block and select the label that you want to change.
   b. Select the title block and modify it in Properties.
   c. Right-click on the sheet in the Project Browser and select **Information**.
   d. Some of the information is filled in automatically from the Project Information.

3. On how many sheets can a floor plan view be placed?
   a. 1
   b. 2-5
   c. 6+
   d. As many as you want

4. Which of the following is the best method to use if the size of a view is too large for a sheet, as shown in Figure 14–51?

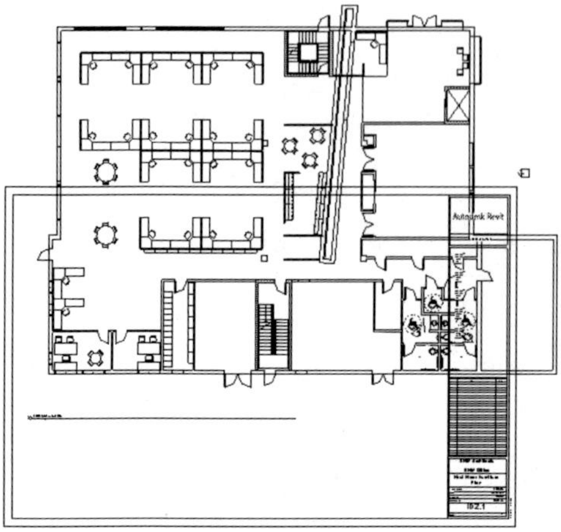

Figure 14–51

a. Delete the view, change the scale, and place the view back on the sheet.

b. Change the scale of the sheet.

5. How do you swap a view that has already been placed on a sheet?

a. Select the title block and change the view using the *View* drop-down list in the ribbon.

b. Select the view on the sheet, then right-click and select a different view.

c. Select the view on the sheet and change the view using the *View* drop-down list in the ribbon.

d. Select the view in the Project Browser and change the view using the *View* drop-down list in the ribbon.

6. Images can be placed on sheets.

a. True

b. False

7. You can only export sheets to PDF.

a. True

b. False

Command Summary

Button	Command	Location
	Activate View	• **Ribbon:** (*select the view*) *Modify | Viewports* tab>*Viewport* panel • **Double-click:** *(in viewport)* • **Right-click:** (*on view*) Activate View
	Deactivate View	• **Ribbon:** *View* tab>*Sheet Composition* panel, expand Viewports • **Double-click:** *(on sheet)* • **Right-click:** (*on view*) Deactivate View
	PDF	• ***File* tab**>Export
	Place View	• **Ribbon:** *View* tab>*Sheet Composition* panel
	Print	• ***File* tab**
	Sheet	• **Ribbon:** *View* tab>*Sheet Composition* panel

Chapter 15

Working with Annotations

When you create construction documents, annotations are essential for showing the design intent. Annotations such as dimensions and text can be added to views at any time during the creation of a project. Detail lines and symbols can also be added to views as you create the working drawing, while legends can be created to provide a place to document any symbols that are used in a project.

Learning Objectives

- Add dimensions to the model as a part of the working drawings.
- Add text to a view and use leaders to create notes pointing to a specific part of the model.
- Create text types using different fonts and sizes to suit your company standards.
- Draw detail lines to further enhance the documentation view and create a key plan.
- Add view-specific annotation symbols for added clarity.
- Create legend views and populate them with symbols of elements in the project.

15.1 Working with Dimensions

You can create permanent dimensions that are view-specific using aligned, linear, angular, radial, diameter, and arc length dimensions. These dimensions can be placed in views, with the exception of schedules and sheets. These can be individual or a string of dimensions, as shown in Figure 15–1. With aligned dimensions, you can also dimension entire walls with openings, grid lines, and/or intersecting walls.

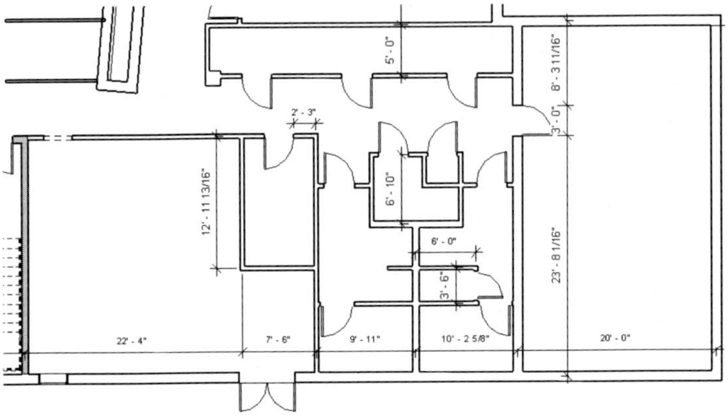

Figure 15–1

- Dimensions reference elements; therefore, they must be added to the model in a view for accuracy. You can dimension on sheets, but would need to draw elements like detail lines in order to use a dimension command in a sheet view.
- When adding dimensions in 3D views, whether they are locked or not, proceed with caution when selecting the items to dimension. You can set the work plane or use <Tab> to cycle through elements.
- You cannot change a dimension's numerical value because the measurement is a reflection of the modeled geometry. To change the value, you must modify the elements that the dimension is attached to.

How To: Add Dimensions

1. In the *Annotate* tab>*Dimension* panel, select one of the following dimension commands.

   Alternatively, click (Aligned Dimension) in the Quick Access Toolbar or type **DI**, then select a command in the *Modify | Place Dimensions* tab>*Dimension* panel if needed.

Aligned	Most commonly used dimension type. Select individual elements or entire walls to dimension.
Linear	Used when you need to specify certain points on elements.
Angular	Used to dimension the angle between two elements.
Radial	Used to dimension the radius of circular elements.
Diameter	Used to dimension the diameter of circular elements.
Arc Length	Used to dimension the length of the arc of circular elements.

2. In the Type Selector, select a dimension style.
3. In the *Modify | Place Dimensions* tab>*Dimension* panel, expand the *Prefer* drop-down list and select the location line of the wall to dimension from, as shown in Figure 15–2.
   - This option can be changed as you add dimensions.

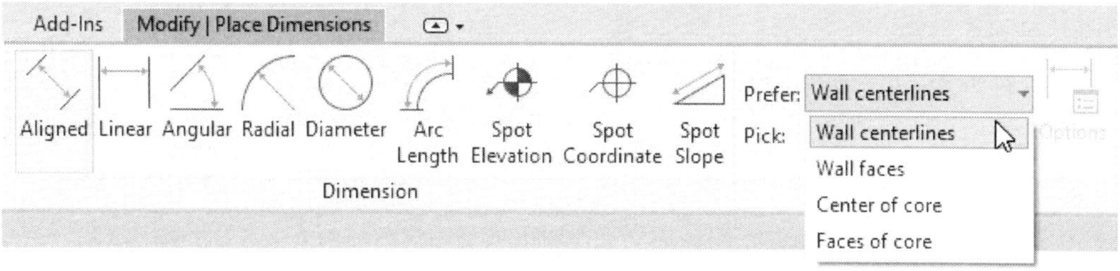

Figure 15–2

4. In the *Modify | Place Dimensions* tab>*Dimension* panel, expand the *Pick* drop-down list and select one of the following options:

   - **Individual References:** Select the elements in order (as shown in Figure 15–3) and then click in an empty space in the view to position the dimension string.

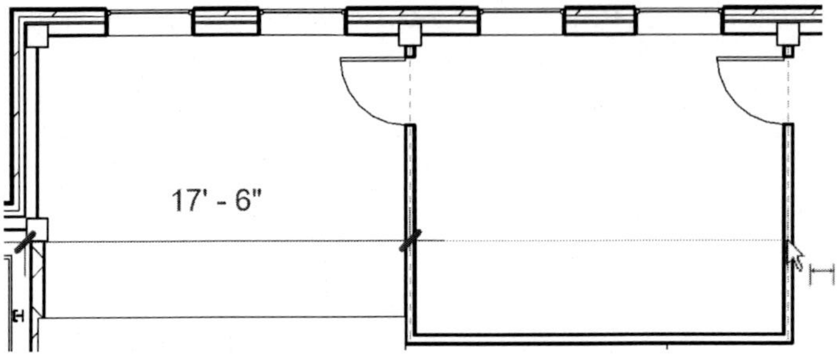

Figure 15–3

   - **Entire Walls:** Select the wall you want to dimension and then click the cursor to position the dimension string, as shown in Figure 15–4.

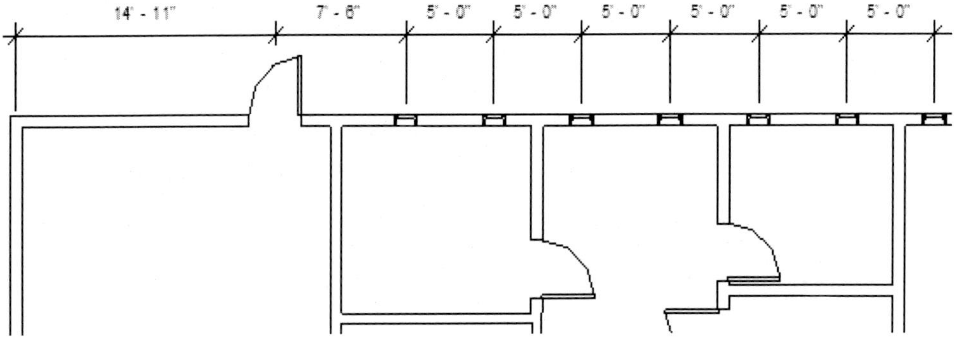

Figure 15–4

- When dimensioning entire walls, you can specify how you want *Openings*, *Intersecting Walls*, and *Intersecting Grids* to be treated by the dimension string. In the *Modify | Place Dimensions* tab>*Place Dimensions* panel, click (Options). In the *Auto Dimension Options* dialog box (shown in Figure 15–5), select the references you want to have automatically dimensioned.

  Note: *If the* ***Entire Wall*** *option is selected without additional options, it places an overall wall dimension.*

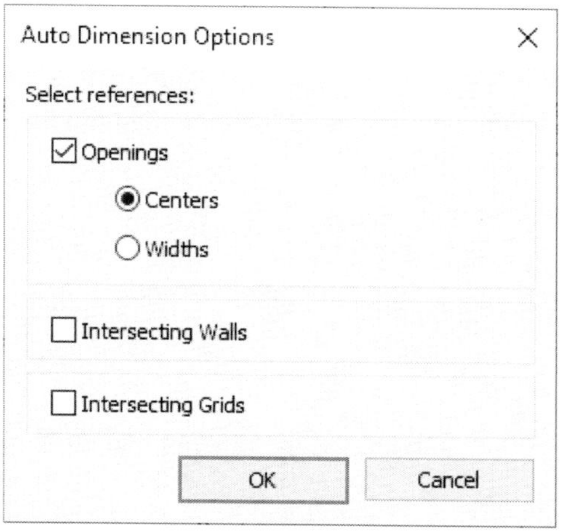

Figure 15–5

Spot Slope

You can add a spot slope dimension to a surface that has a slope to it, like ramps, floors, or slabs. They can be added in a plan (as shown in Figure 15–6), section, elevation, or 3D view.

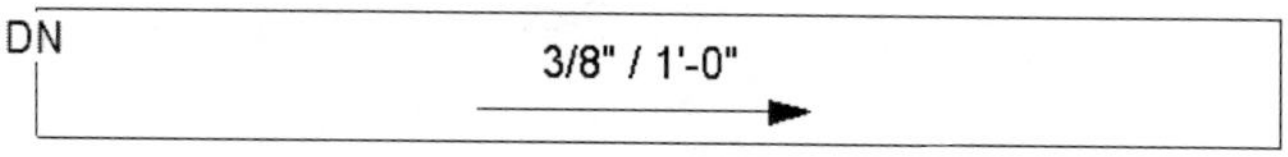

Figure 15–6

How To: Add a Spot Slope Dimension

1. In the *Annotate* tab>*Dimension* panel, click (Spot Slope).
2. Click on the sloped surface to place the spot slope.

Modifying Dimensions

When you move elements that are dimensioned (e.g., a wall), the dimensions automatically update. You can also modify dimensions by selecting a dimension or dimension string and making changes. Figure 15–7 shows the various parts of dimensions that aid in modifying.

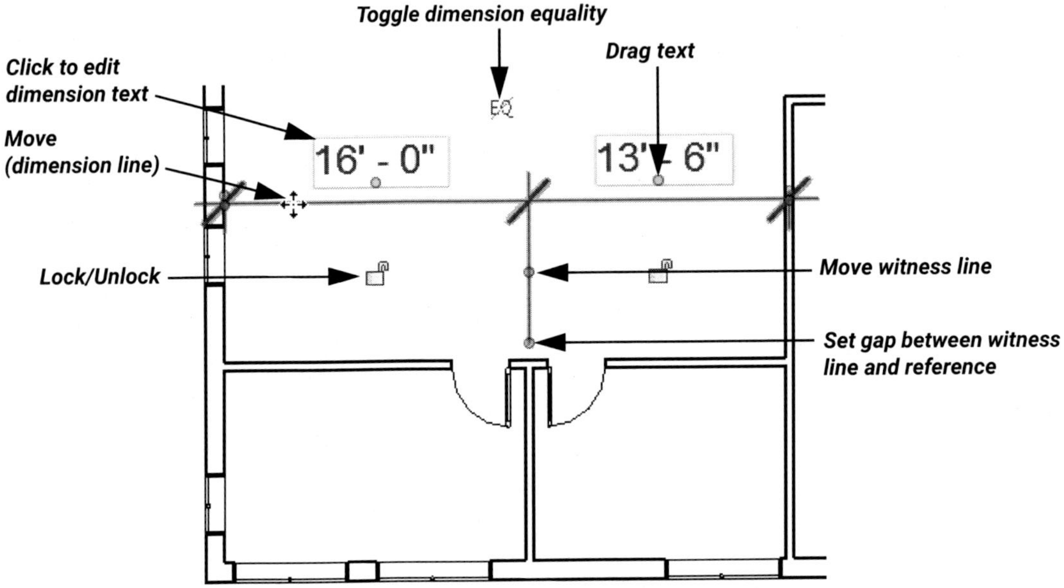

Figure 15–7

- To move the dimension value, select the **Drag text** control under the value and drag it to a new location. It automatically creates a leader from the dimension line if you drag it away. The style of the leader (arc or line) depends on the dimension style.
- To move the dimension line (the line parallel to the element being dimensioned), simply drag the line to a new location, or select the dimension and drag the ✥ (Drag to new position) control.
- To change the gap between the witness line and the element being dimensioned, drag the control at the end of the witness line.
- To move the witness line (the line perpendicular to the element being dimensioned) to a different element or face of a wall, use the **Move Witness Line** control in the middle of the witness line. While moving the witness line, you can hover your cursor over an element or component and press <Tab> repeatedly to cycle through the various options. You can also drag this control to move the witness line to a different element, or right-click on the control and select **Move Witness Line**.

Adding and Deleting Dimensions in a String

- To add a witness line to a string of dimensions, select the dimension and, in the *Modify | Dimensions* tab>*Witness Lines* panel, click  (Edit Witness Lines). Select the element(s) you want to add to the dimension. Click in an empty space in the view to finish.
- To delete a witness line, drag the **Move Witness Line** control to a nearby witness line's element. Alternatively, you can hover the cursor over the control, right-click, and select **Delete Witness Line**.
- To delete one dimension in a string and break the string into two separate dimensions, select the string, hover your cursor over the dimension that you want to delete, and press <Tab>. When it highlights (as shown on the top in Figure 15–8), pick it and press <Delete>. The selected dimension is deleted and the dimension string is separated into two elements, as shown on the bottom in Figure 15–8.

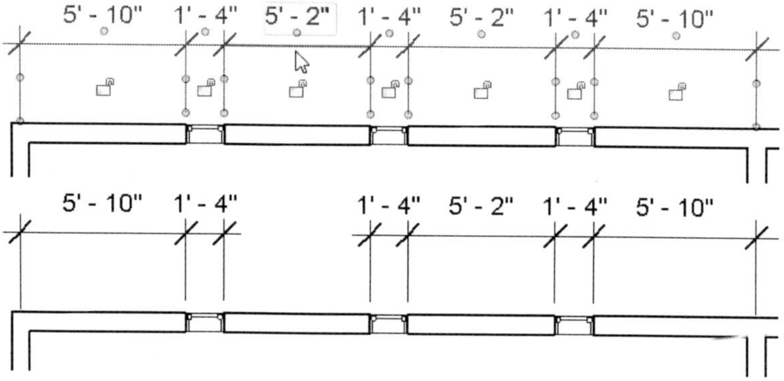

Figure 15–8

Modifying the Dimension Text

Because Revit is parametric, changing the dimension text without changing the elements dimensioned would cause problems throughout the project. These issues could cause problems beyond the model if you use the project model to estimate materials or work with other disciplines.

You can append the existing dimension text with prefixes and suffixes (as shown in Figure 15–9), or create a dimension style that has a prefix or suffix preset in the type properties. This can help you in renovation projects.

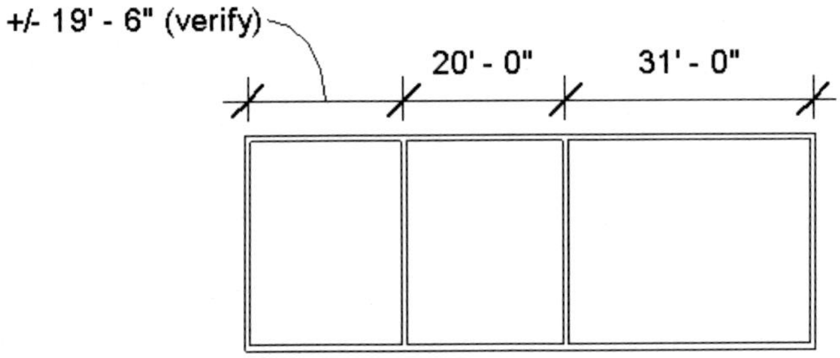

Figure 15–9

Double-click on the dimension text to open the *Dimension Text* dialog box, as shown in Figure 15–10, and make modifications as needed.

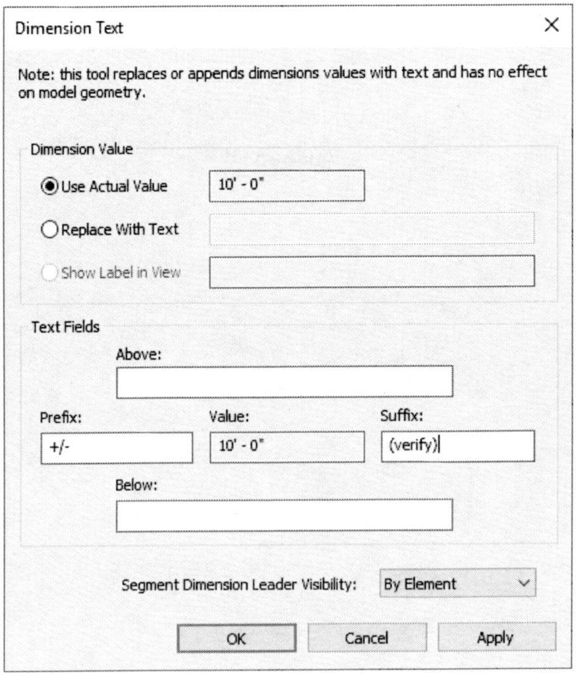

Figure 15–10

Hint: Multiple Dimension Options

If you are creating details that show one element with multiple dimension values, as shown in Figure 15–11, you can easily modify the dimension text.

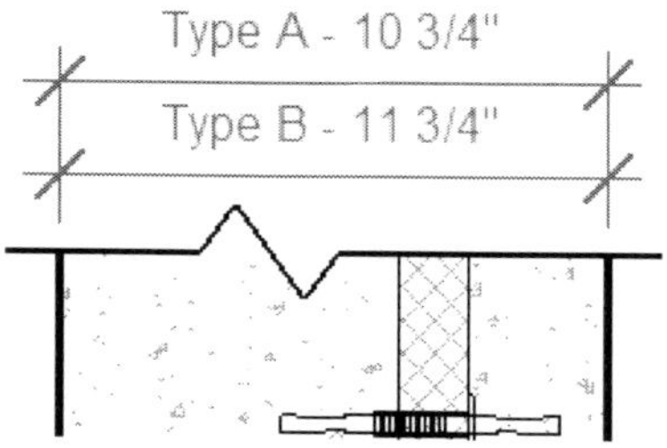

Figure 15–11

Select the dimension and then the dimension text. The *Dimension Text* dialog box opens. You can replace the text, as shown in Figure 15–12, or add text fields above or below, as well as a prefix or suffix.

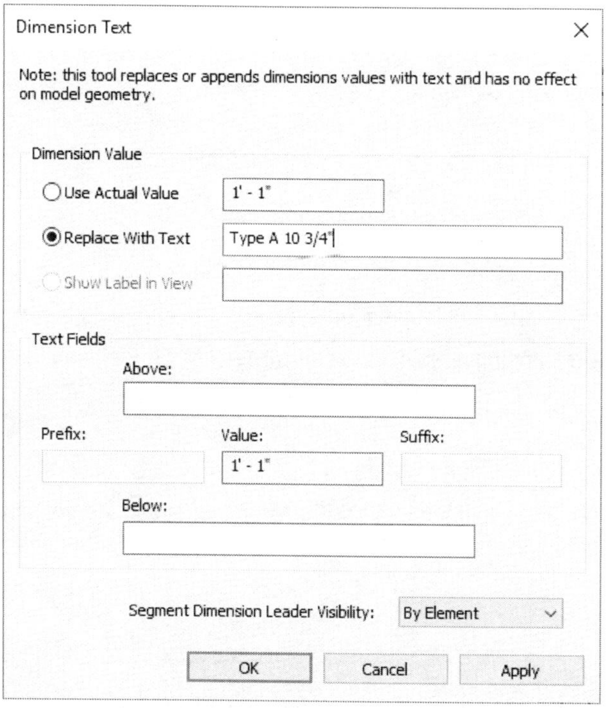

Figure 15–12

- This also works with Equality Text Labels.

If you find that you are always modifying dimensions manually, you can create a type-driven dimension style by duplicating the dimension style and specifying a set prefix and suffix within the type parameters, as shown in Figure 15–13.

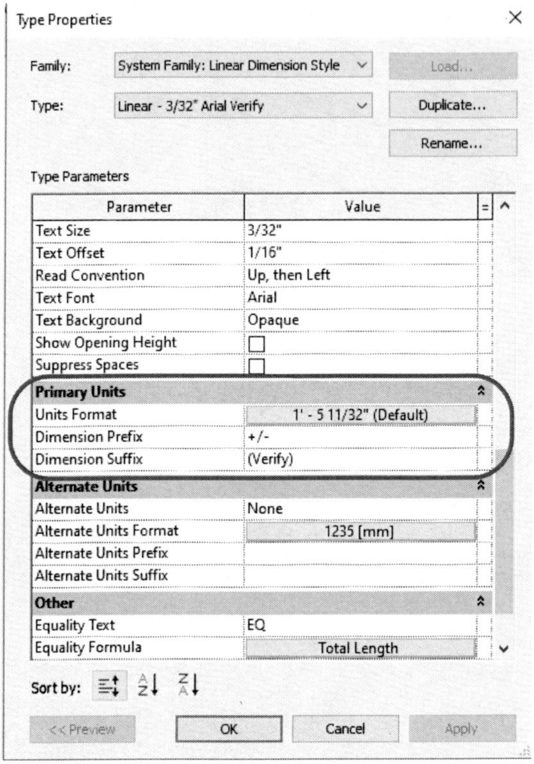

Figure 15–13

This eliminates the need to manually modify the dimension every time you need to add a prefix or suffix.

Setting Constraints

The three types of constraints you can use with dimensions are locks, equal settings (shown in Figure 15–14), and labels.

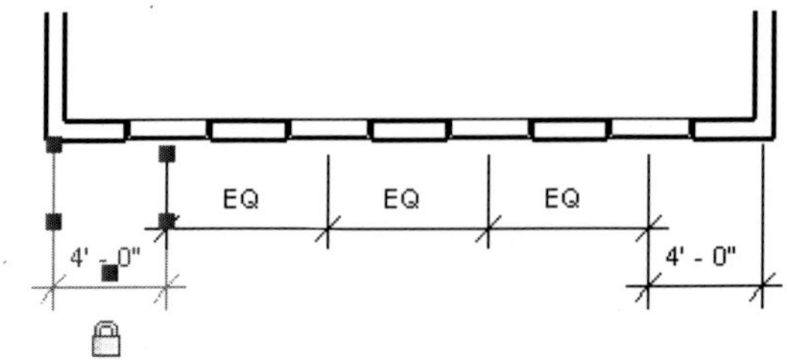

Figure 15–14

Locking Dimensions

When you lock a dimension, the value is set and you cannot make a change between it and the referenced elements. If it is unlocked, you can move it and change its value.

- Note that when you try to move an element that has locked dimensions, you will get an error dialog box indicating that you cannot keep the elements joined. This dialog box cannot be ignored, so you can either unjoin the elements or click **Cancel**.

Setting Dimensions Equal

For a string of dimensions, select the **EQ** symbol to constrain the elements to be at an equal distance apart. This actually moves the elements that are dimensioned.

- The equality text display can be changed in Properties, as shown in Figure 15–15. The style for each of the display types is set in the dimension type.

Figure 15–15

Labeling Dimensions

If you have a distance that needs to be repeated multiple times, such as the *Wall to Window* label shown in Figure 15–16, or one where you want to use a formula based on another dimension, you can create and apply a global parameter, also called a label, to the dimension.

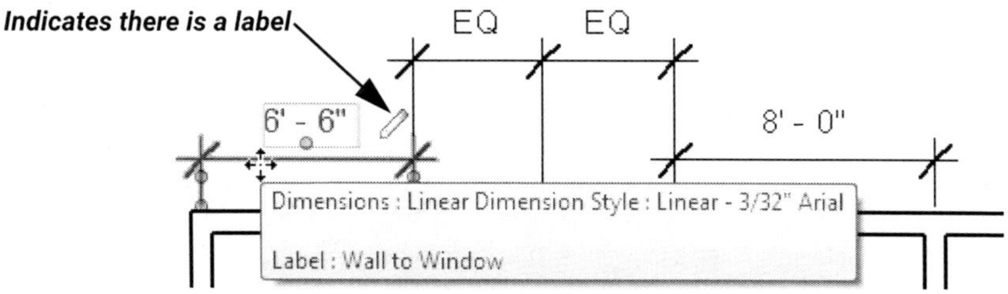

Figure 15–16

- To apply an existing label to a dimension, select the dimension and in the *Modify | Dimensions* tab>*Label Dimension* panel, select the label in the drop-down list, as shown in Figure 15–17.

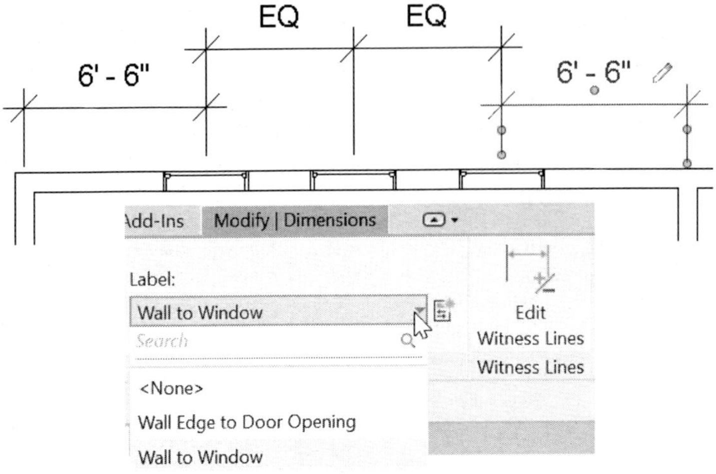

Figure 15–17

How To: Create a Label

1. Select a dimension.
2. In the *Modify | Dimensions* tab>*Label Dimension* panel, click (Create Parameter).
3. In the *Global Parameter Properties* dialog box, type in a *Name*, as shown in Figure 15–18, and click **OK**.

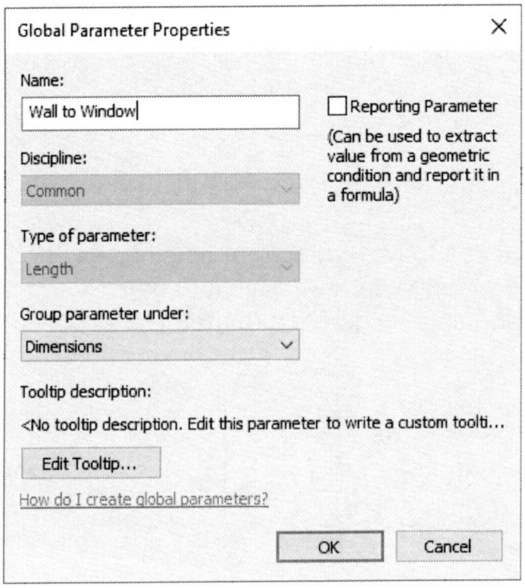

Figure 15–18

4. The label is applied to the dimension.

How To: Edit the Label Information

1. Select a labeled dimension.
2. Click (Global Parameters), as shown in Figure 15–19.

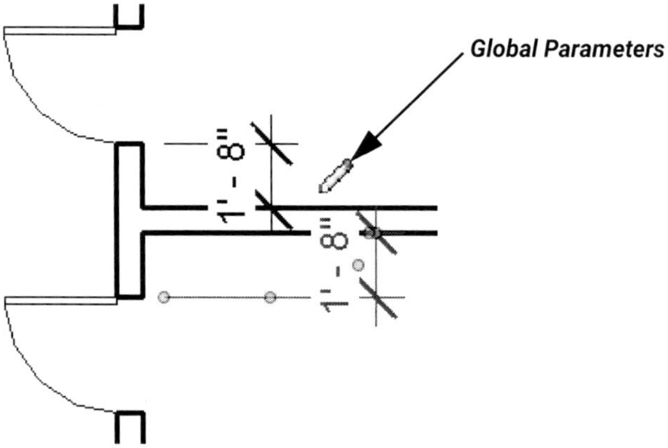

Figure 15–19

3. In the *Global Parameters* dialog box, in the *Value* column, type the new distance, as shown in Figure 15–20.

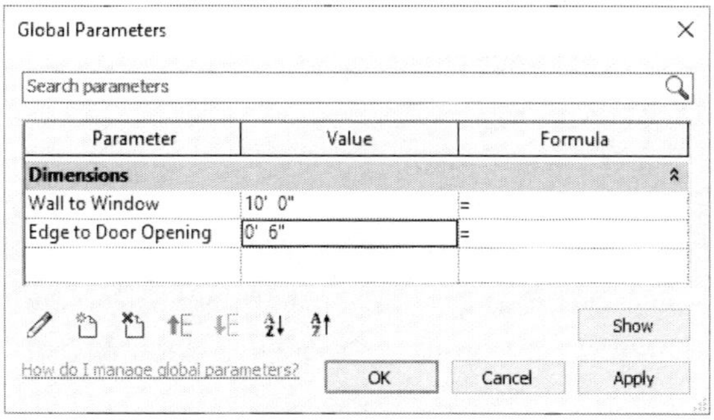

Figure 15–20

4. Click **OK**. The selected dimension and any other dimensions using the same label are updated.

- You can also edit, create, and delete global parameters in this dialog box.

Working with Constraints

To find out which elements have constraints applied to them, in the View Control Bar, click (Reveal Constraints). Constraints display as shown in Figure 15–21.

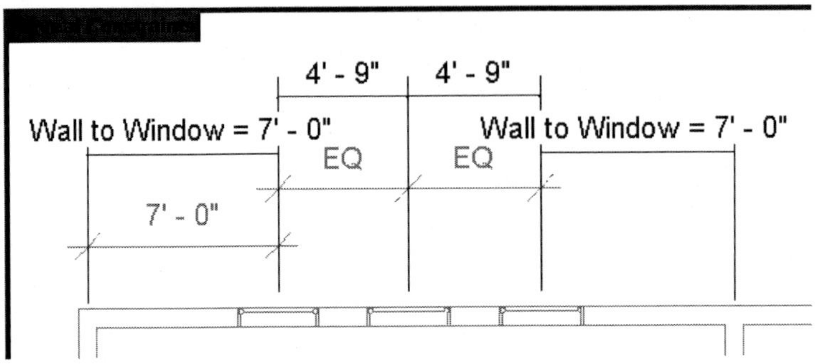

Figure 15–21

- If you try to move the element beyond the appropriate constraints, a warning dialog box displays, as shown in Figure 15–22.

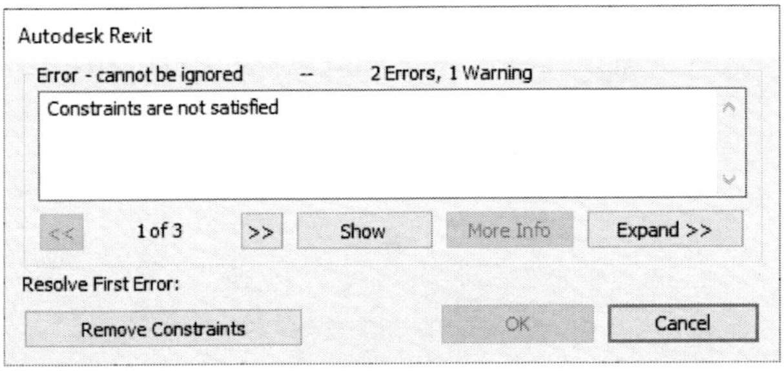

Figure 15–22

- If you delete dimensions that are constrained, a warning dialog box displays, as shown in Figure 15–23. Click **OK** to retain the constraint or click **Unconstrain** to remove the constraint.

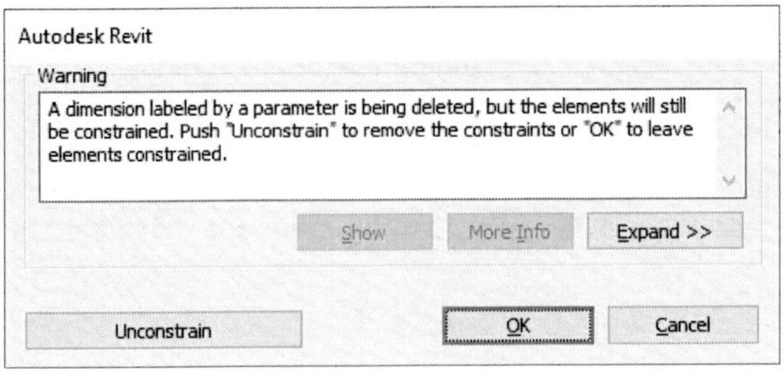

Figure 15–23

Practice 15a
Work with Dimensions

Practice Objectives

- Add a string of dimensions.
- Dimension using the **Entire Walls** option.
- Edit the witness lines of dimensions.

In this practice, you will add dimensions using several different methods to a floor plan view. You will also modify the dimensions so that they show what you are expecting. Note that some additional elements, including storefront curtain walls and windows, have been added at the back of the building. The completed floor plan is shown in Figure 15–24.

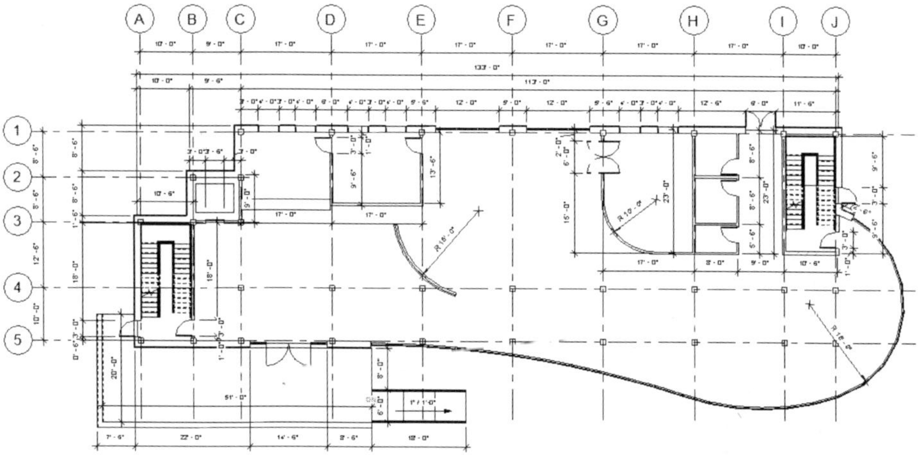

Figure 15–24

Task 1: Add dimensions to the column grid.

1. Open the project **Arch-Dimensions.rvt** from the practice files folder.
2. In the Project Browser, duplicate the **Floor Plans: Floor 1** view (without detailing so that the door and window tags do not display).
3. Rename the new view to **Floor 1 - Dimension Plan**.

4. In Properties, in the *Extents* section, check **Crop Region Visible** and **Annotation Crop**. Adjust the crop region in the view to only display the hotel and not the poolhouse. Adjust the outer annotation crop region so that the elevation markers are not displayed, as shown in Figure 15–25, but there is still room to add dimensions.

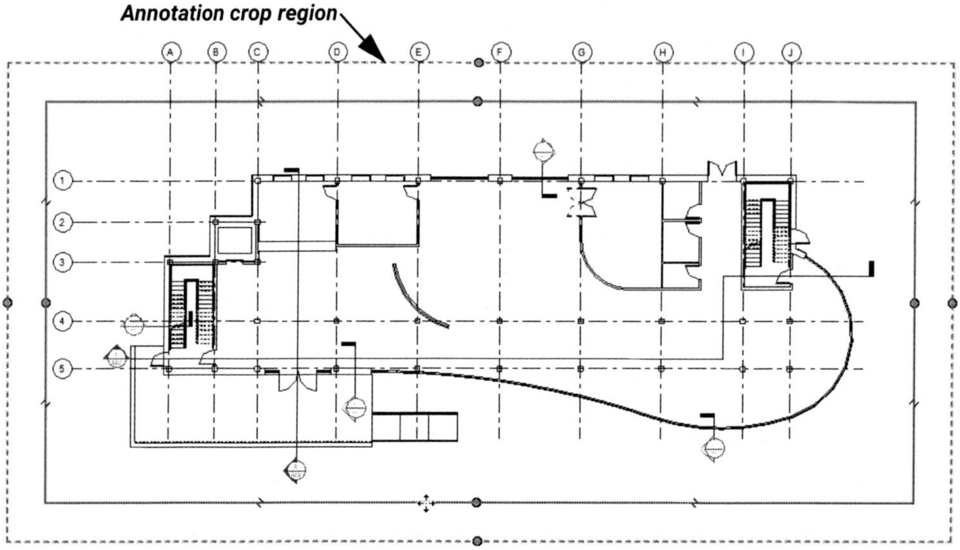

Figure 15–25

5. In Properties, uncheck **Crop Region Visible** and **Annotation Crop**. This needs to be done so you can dimension outside of the crop region area.
6. For clarity while dimensioning, select a section marker and type **VH** to hide it in the view.
7. In the Quick Access Toolbar, click (Aligned Dimension).
8. Dimension the column grid lines in each direction, as shown in Figure 15–26, by clicking the first grid line and then clicking each subsequent grid line in the same direction. Click in an empty space in the drawing after you dimension the last grid line.

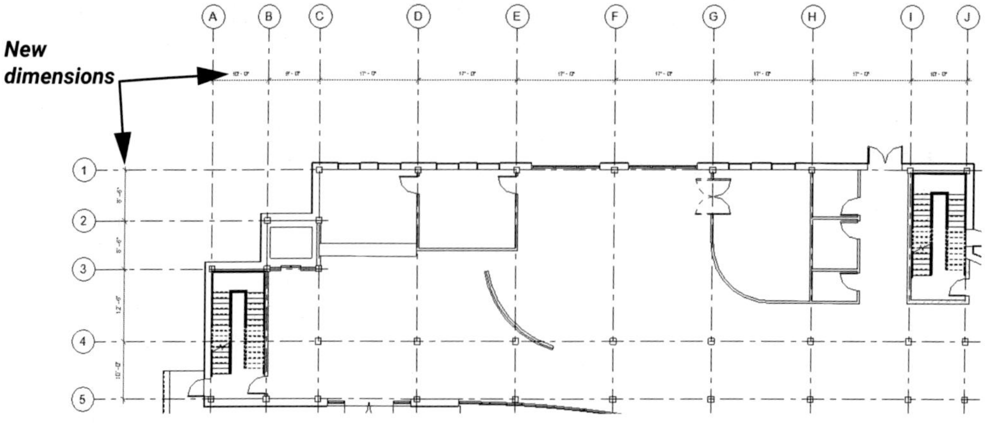

Figure 15–26

9. Click (Modify).
10. Save the project.

Task 2: Dimension the exterior and interior walls.

1. In the *Annotate* tab>*Dimension* panel, click (Aligned Dimension).
2. In the *Modify | Place Dimensions* tab>*Place Dimensions* panel, expand the *Prefer* drop-down list and select **Wall faces**, then expand the *Pick* drop-down list and select **Entire Walls**.
3. Click (Options).
4. In the *Auto Dimension Options* dialog box, check the checkbox for **Openings** (if not already checked) and select **Widths**, as shown in Figure 15–27. Click **OK**.

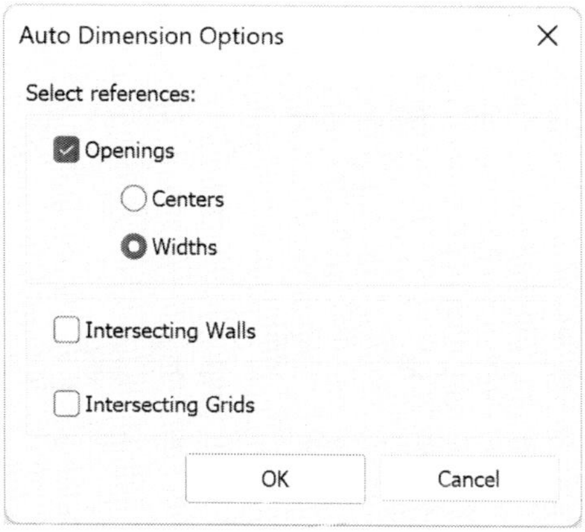

Figure 15–27

5. Select the back wall and click a location above the exterior wall to place the dimension.
6. Click (Modify) and select the dimension string.

7. Zoom in on the upper-left corner of the building. Use the **Move Witness Line** control to relocate the line from the end of the wall (as shown in Figure 15–28) to grid line C, which passes through the column.

   Note: *Use <Tab> to select different faces of a wall to dimension to. Hover the cursor over the different grips to see the tooltip describing what it is.*

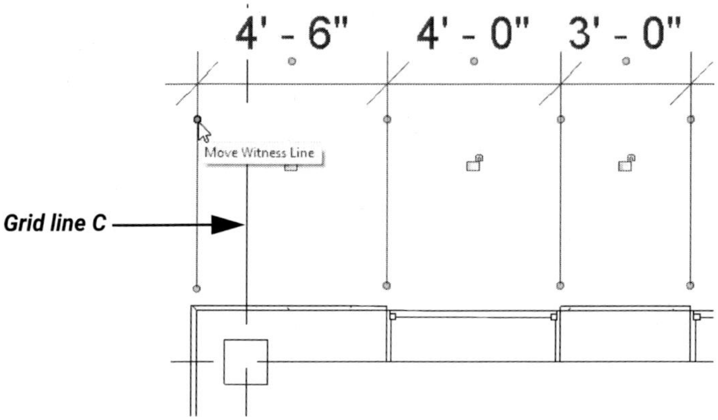

Figure 15–28

8. Click (Modify).
9. On the same wall, pan over to the curtain walls between grid lines E, F, and G, where the storefront openings are displayed. These were not dimensioned automatically.
10. Select the wall dimension line. In the *Modify | Dimensions* tab>*Witness Lines* panel, click (Edit Witness Lines).
11. Select the outside edges of each side of the storefront openings to add the witness lines, then click in an empty space in the view to apply the changes. The modified dimension string displays, as shown in Figure 15–29.

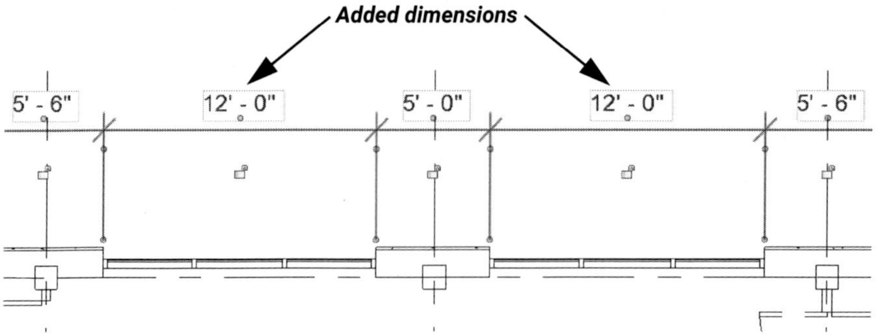

Figure 15–29

12. Click (Modify).

13. Pan over to the west side of the building to grids 1, 2, and 3.
14. Start the **Aligned Dimension** command and verify that **Entire Walls** is selected.
15. Click on the three walls to create a continuous string of dimensions and place them outside the exterior walls.
16. Note that at grid line 3, there are dimensions at the exterior core face and interior core face of the walls, as shown in Figure 15–30.

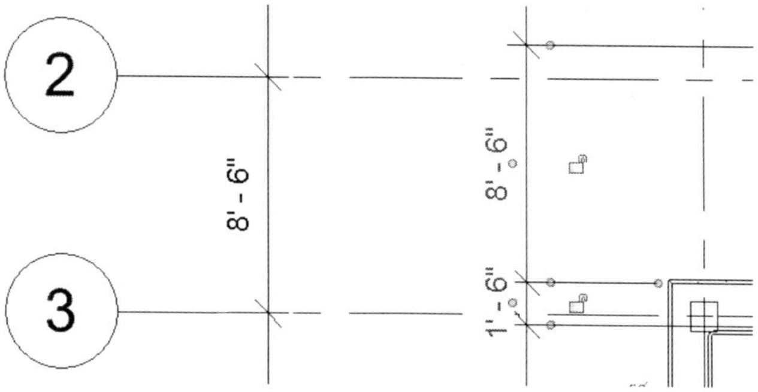

Figure 15–30

17. Click (Modify).
18. Select the dimension string, right-click on the interior core face witness line grip, and select **Delete Witness Line**, as shown in Figure 15–31.

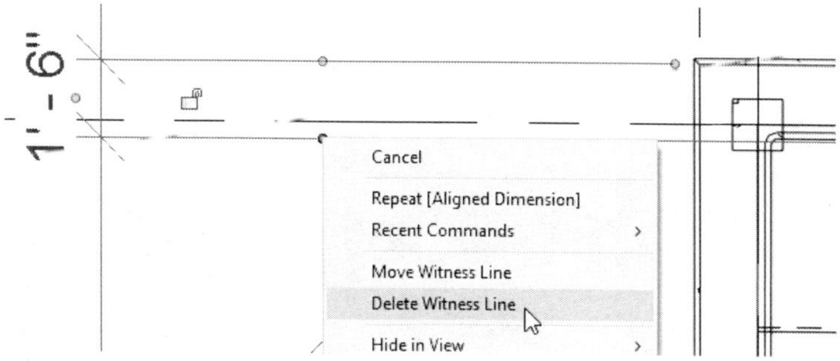

Figure 15–31

19. Pan down the same dimension string and note that the two dimensions are too close to each other and the bottom dimension is at the exterior core instead of the center of the column.
20. Modify the end dimension's witness line to be on the center of the column and not the exterior core.

21. Select the dimension's drag text grip (as shown in Figure 15–32) and drag it outside of the dimension's string. A leader will display.

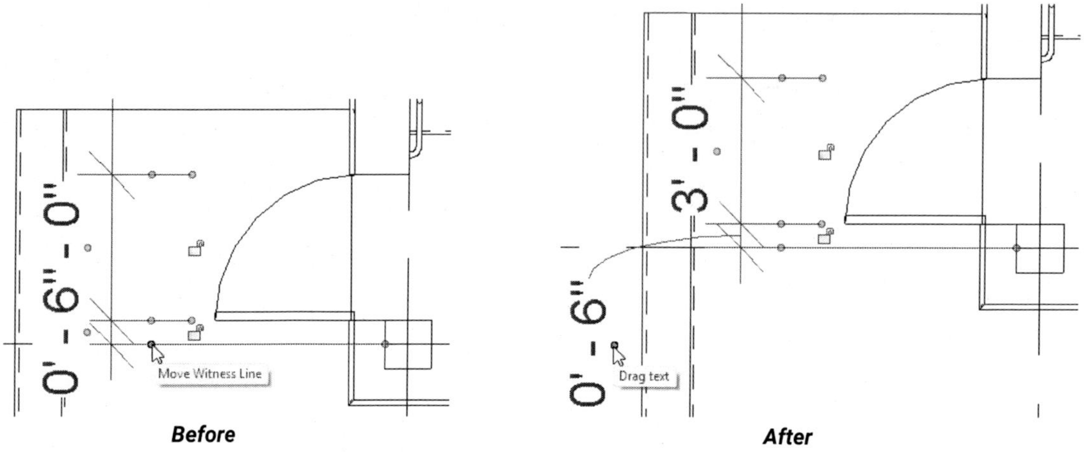

Figure 15–32

22. In the *Annotate* tab>*Dimension* panel, use the various dimensioning commands and methods to dimension the interior spaces, as shown in Figure 15–33, removing dimensions if needed. (Hint: Do not forget to change from *Pick:* **Entire Walls** to *Pick:* **Individual References**.) Your dimensions might not be exactly as shown in Figure 15–33 based on what part of the wall you dimension from.

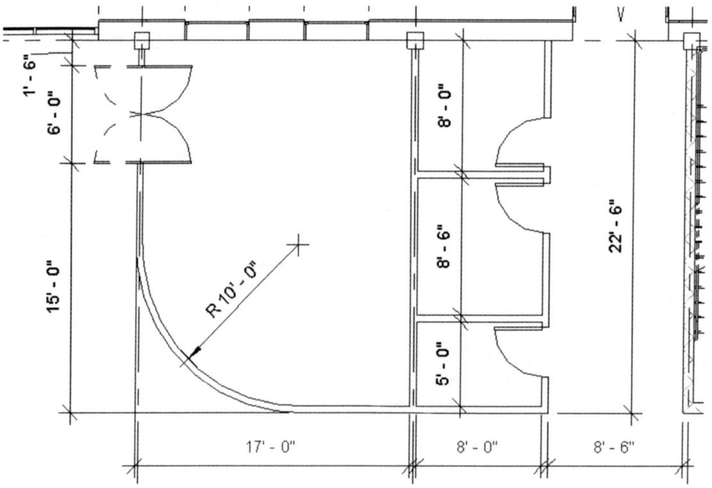

Figure 15–33

23. Pan over to the ramp at the south end of the building.
24. In the *Annotate* tab>*Dimension* panel, click (Spot Slope).

25. Hover your cursor over the ramp to see the slope dimension. Note that if you move your cursor over the middle portion of the ramp, your slope dimension displays **[No Slope]**.
26. Click on the ramp's surface to place the spot slope.
27. Click (Modify).
28. Save the project.

Task 3: Dimension the typical guest room.

1. Open the **Floor Plans: Typical Guest Room - Dimension Plan** view.
2. Start the **Aligned Dimension** command and set *Prefer* to **Wall faces** and *Pick* to **Individual References**.
3. In Properties, click **Edit Type...**.
4. Duplicate the **Linear Dimension Style: Linear - 3/32" Arial** dimension style and call it **Linear - 3/32" Arial (TYP)**.
5. In the *Primary Units* section, type **(TYP)** next to *Dimension Suffix* and click **OK**.
6. Dimension the guest room closet, as shown in Figure 15–34.

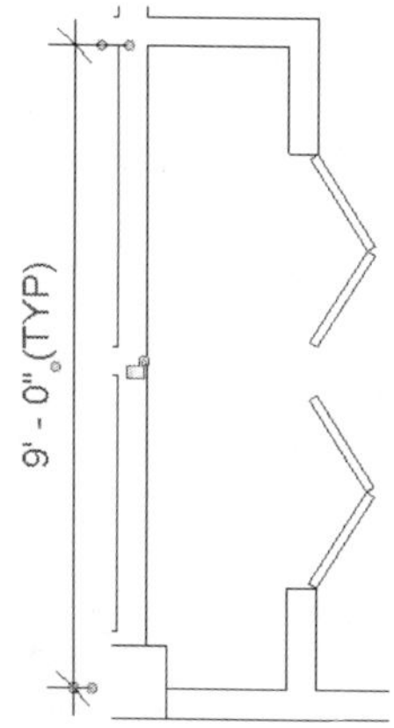

Figure 15–34

7. If time permits, dimension the rest of the typical guest room.
8. Save and close the project.

End of practice

15.2 Working with Text

The **Text** command enables you to add notes to views or sheets, such as the detail shown in Figure 15–35. The same command is used to create text with or without leaders.

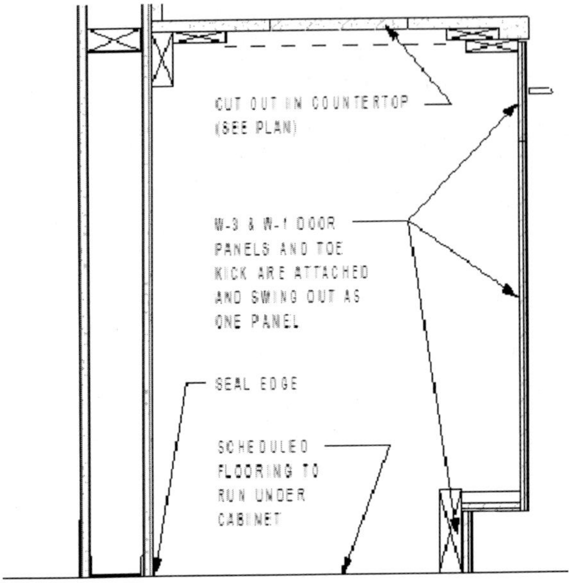

Figure 15–35

The text height is automatically set by the text type in conjunction with the scale of the view (as shown in Figure 15–36, using the same size text type at two different scales). Text types display at the specified height, both in the views and on the sheet.

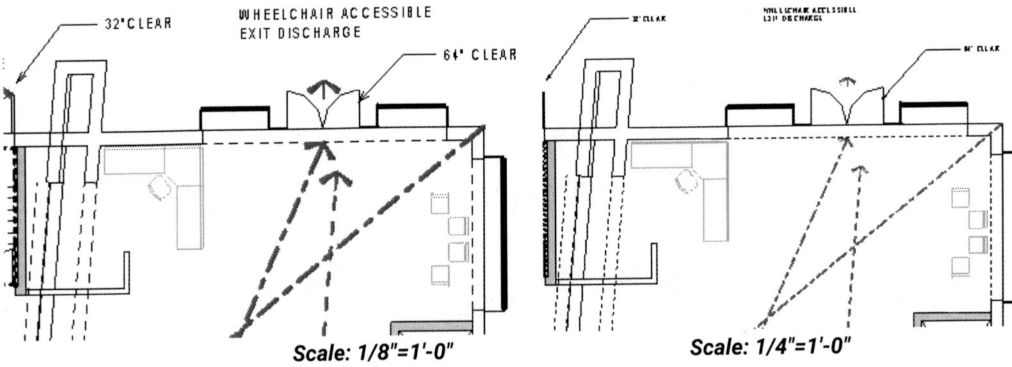

Figure 15–36

How To: Add Text

1. In the *Annotate* tab>*Text* panel, click A (Text).
2. In the Type Selector, set the text type.

   Note: The text type sets the font and height of the text.

3. In the *Modify | Place Text* tab>*Leader* panel, select the method you want to use: A (No Leader), A (One Segment), A (Two Segments), or A (Curved), as shown in Figure 15–37. You can set where the leader will attach to the text on the left and right using the **Leader at** options.
4. In the *Text* panel, set the justification for the text, as shown in Figure 15–37.

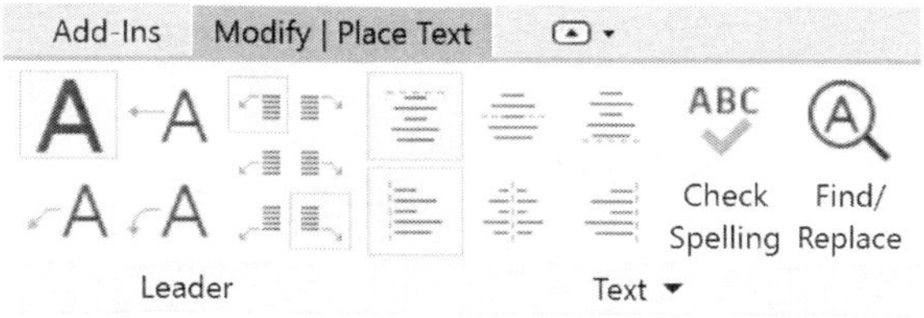

Figure 15–37

5. Select the location for the leader and text.
   - Use alignment lines to help you align the text with other text elements.
   - If **No leader** is selected, select the start point for the text and begin typing.
   - If using a leader, the first point places the arrow and you then select points for the leader. The text starts at the last leader point.
   - To set a word wrapping distance, click and drag the circle grip controls to set the start and end points of the text.
6. Type the needed text. In the *Edit Text* tab, specify additional options for the font and paragraph, as shown in Figure 15–38.

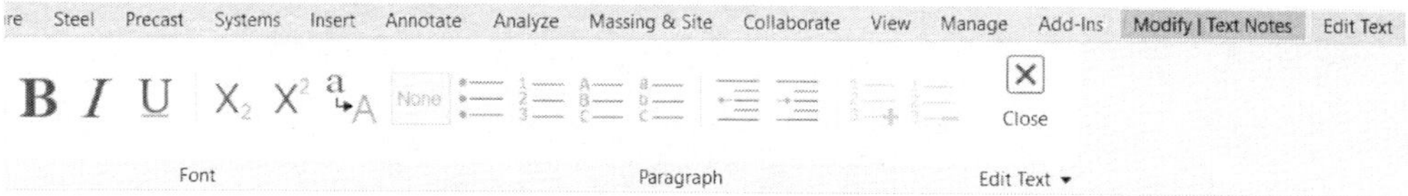

Figure 15–38

7. In the *Edit Text* tab>*Edit Text* panel, click (Close) or click outside the text box to complete the text element.
   - Pressing <Enter> after a line of text starts a new line of text in the same text window.

How To: Add Text Symbols

1. Start the **Text** command and click to place the text.
2. As you are typing text and need to insert a symbol, right-click and select **Symbols** from the shortcut menu. Select from the list of commonly used symbols, as shown in Figure 15–39.

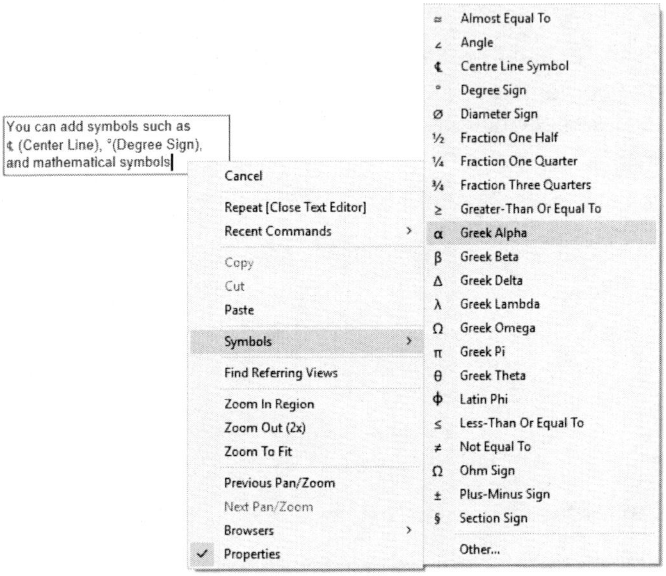

Figure 15–39

3. If the symbol you need is not listed, click **Other...**.
4. In the *Character Map* dialog box, click on a symbol and click **Select**, as shown in Figure 15–40.

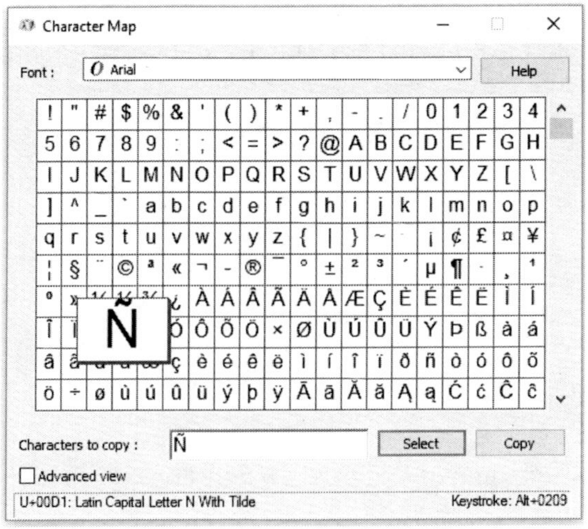

Figure 15–40

5. Click **Copy** to copy the character to the clipboard and paste it into the text box.

- The font in the *Character Map* should match the font used by the text type. You do not want to use a different font for symbols.

Modifying Text

After you have added text notes, you can begin editing. You can edit text notes to have leaders, change the text style that is being used, and change the positioning.

- You can modify the text note, including the **Leader** and **Paragraph** styles.
- You can edit the text, including changes to individual letters, words, and paragraphs in the text note.
- You can modify all text notes in a view so that they all align either left (as shown on the left in Figure 15–41), right, top, bottom, middle, or center justified within the text note bounding box, as well as distributing the text notes horizontally or vertically between all the text. These tools are also available for aligning tags and keynotes.

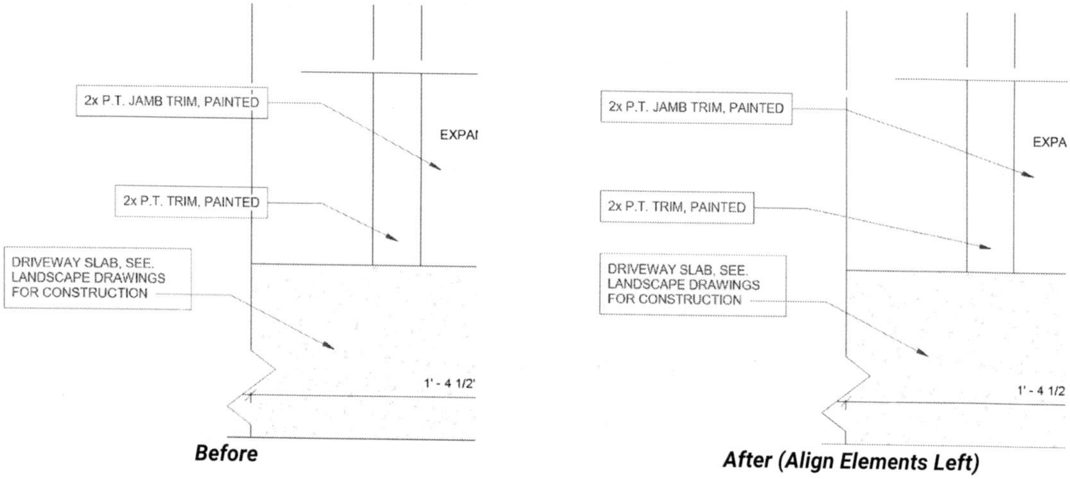

Figure 15–41

Modifying the Text Note Using Controls

Click once on the text note to modify the text box and leaders using controls, as shown in Figure 15–42, or using the tools in the *Modify | Text Notes* tab.

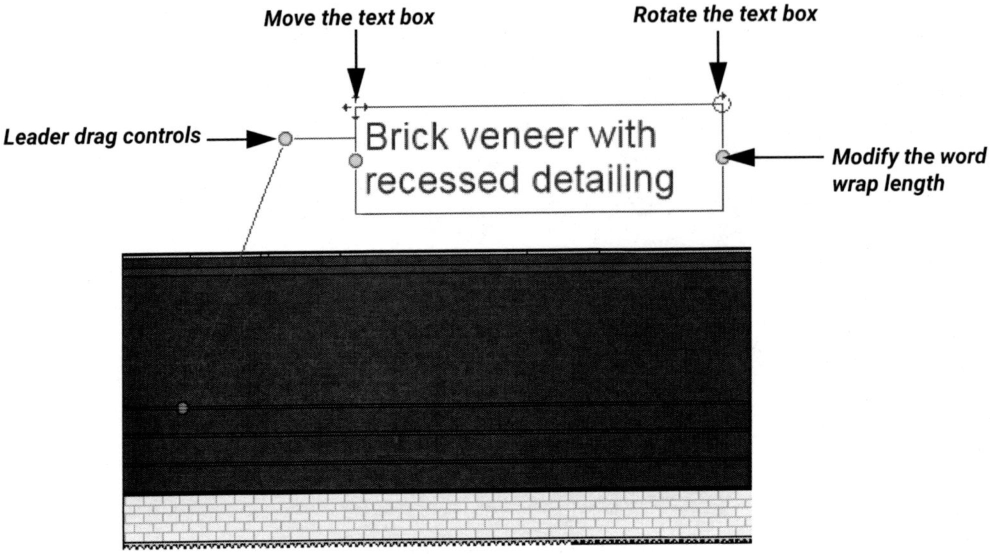

Figure 15–42

How To: Add a Leader to Text Notes

1. Select the text note.
2. In the *Modify | Text Notes* tab>*Leader* panel, select the direction and justification for the new leader, as shown in Figure 15–43.

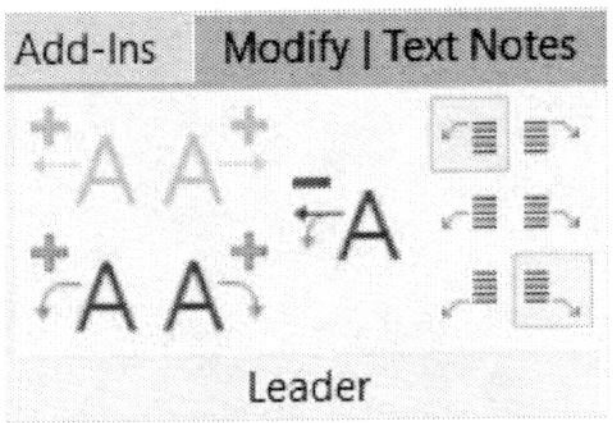

Figure 15–43

3. The leader is applied, as shown in Figure 15–44. Use the drag controls to place the arrow as needed.

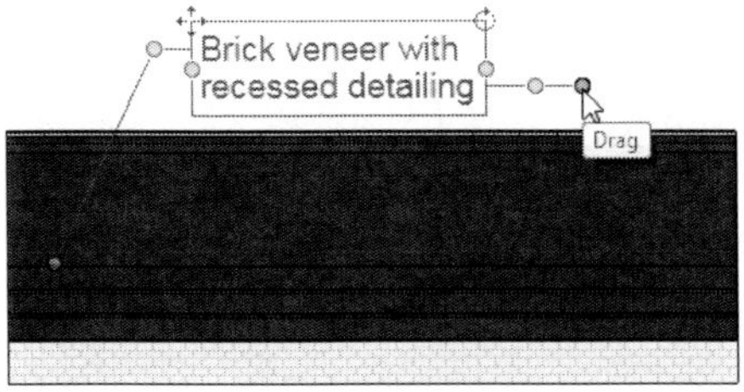

Figure 15–44

- You can remove leaders by clicking (Remove Last Leader).

Editing the Text

The *Edit Text* tab displays when you double-click on a text note. This tab enables you to make various customizations. These include modifying the font of selected words as well as creating bulleted and numbered lists, as shown in Figure 15–45.

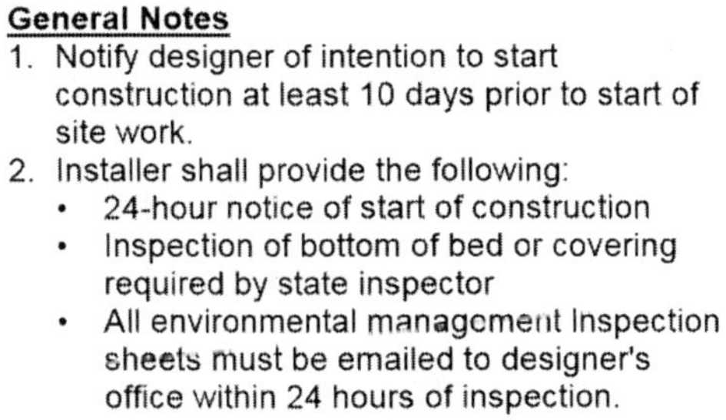

Figure 15–45

- You can **Cut**, **Copy,** and **Paste** text using the clipboard. For example, you can copy text from a document and then paste it into the text editor in Revit.
- To help you see the text better as you are modifying it, in the *Edit Text* tab, expand the *Edit Text* panel and select one or both of the options, as shown in Figure 15–46.

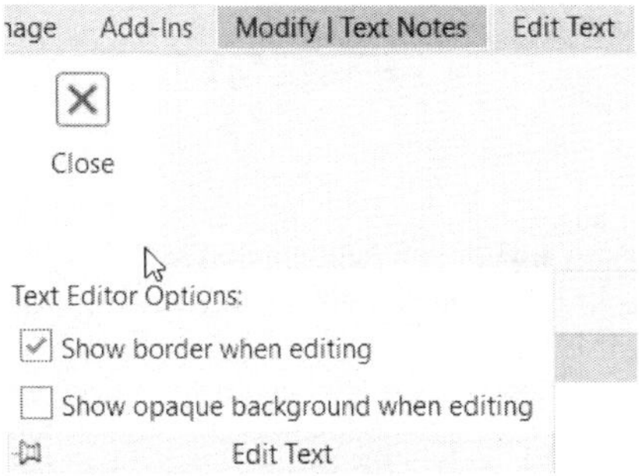

Figure 15–46

How To: Modify the Font

1. Select individual letters or words.
2. Click on the font modification you want to include:
   - B (Bold)
   - I (Italic)
   - U (Underline)
   - X_2 (Subscript)
   - X^2 (Superscript)
   - aA (All Caps)

- When pasting text from a document outside of Revit, font modifications (e.g, Bold, Italic, etc.) are retained.

How To: Create Lists

1. In Edit Text mode, place the cursor in the line where you want to add to a list.
2. In the *Edit Text* tab>*Paragraph* panel, click the type of list you want to create:
   - (Bullets)
   - (Numbers)
   - (Uppercase Letters)
   - (Lowercase Letters)
3. As you type, press <Enter> and the next line in the list is incremented.

   Note: *If you do not want a line to be a part of the list, select the line and click None (None) on the Paragraph panel.*

4. To include sub-lists, at the beginning of the next line, click (Increase Indent) or press <Tab>. This indents the line and applies the next level of lists, as shown in Figure 15–47.

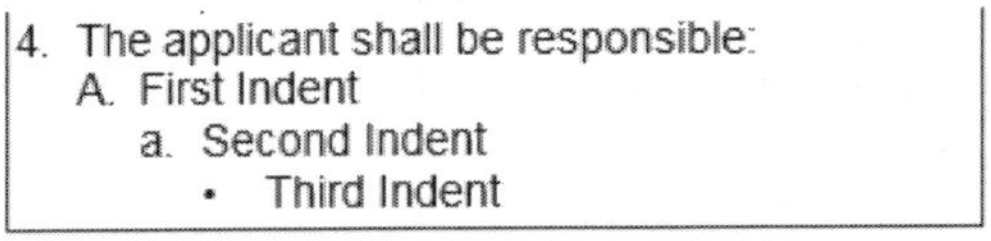

Figure 15–47

   Note: *The indent distance is set up by the text type Tab Size.*

   - You can change the type of list after you have applied the first increment. For example, you might want to use a list of bullets instead of letters, as shown in Figure 15–48.

5. Click (Decrease Indent) or press <Shift>+<Tab> to return to the previous list style.

- Press <Shift>+<Enter> to create a blank line in a numbered list.

- To create columns or other separate text boxes that build on a numbering system (as shown in Figure 15–48), create the second text box and list, then place the cursor on one of the lines and in the *Paragraph* panel, click (Increment List Value) until the list matches the next number in the sequence.

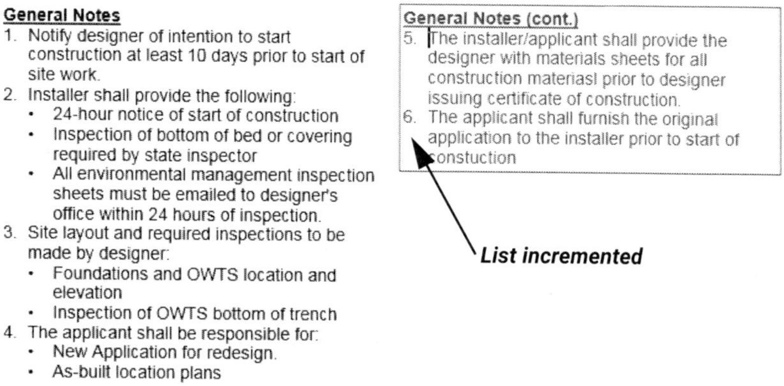

Figure 15–48

6. Click (Decrement List Value) to move back a number.

Hint: Model Text

Model text is different from annotation text. It is designed to create full-size text on the model itself. For example, you would use model text to create a sign on a door, as shown in Figure 15–49. One model text type is included with the default template. You can create other types as needed.

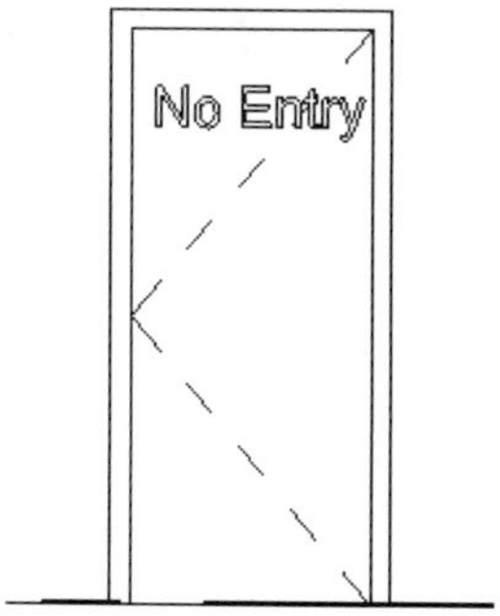

Figure 15–49

- Model text can be viewed in all views.
- Model text is added from the *Architecture* tab>*Model* panel by clicking (Model Text).

Multiple Alignment

After placing annotations, such as tags, text, or keynotes, you can align them either vertically and horizontally. You will want to verify that your text border is not stretched out too far and that it is as tight to the text as possible to get an accurate alignment. If there is a leader line, it will stretch with the annotation. You can manually adjust it after the alignment is done.

How To: Align Multiple Annotations

1. Select multiple annotations.
2. In the *Modify | Text Notes* tab>*Multiple Align* panel, select one of the following alignment types.

Vertical Alignment Types

- (Distribute Vertically): Spaces all selected text, tags, or keynotes vertically (as shown in Figure 15–50) based on the text border.

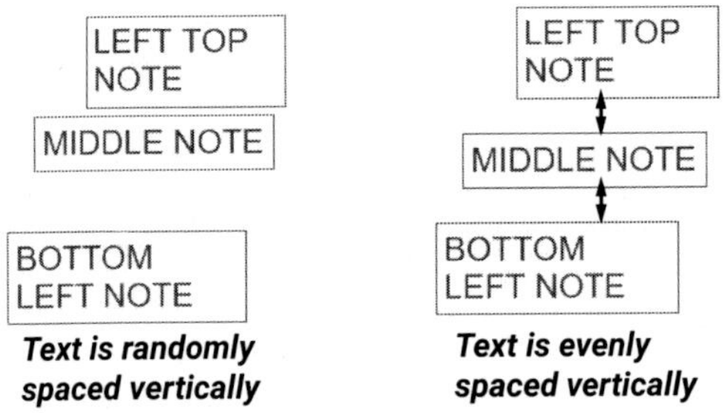

Figure 15–50

- (Align Elements Top): Aligns selected text to the topmost text border (as shown in Figure 15–51).

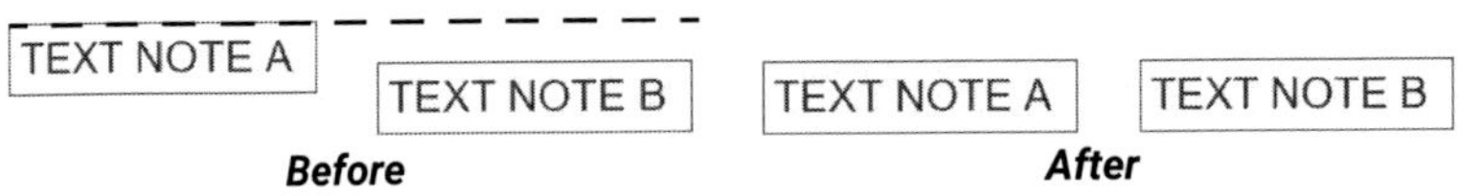

Figure 15–51

- (Align Elements Middle): Aligns selected text vertically to the middle of the text border (as shown in Figure 15–52).

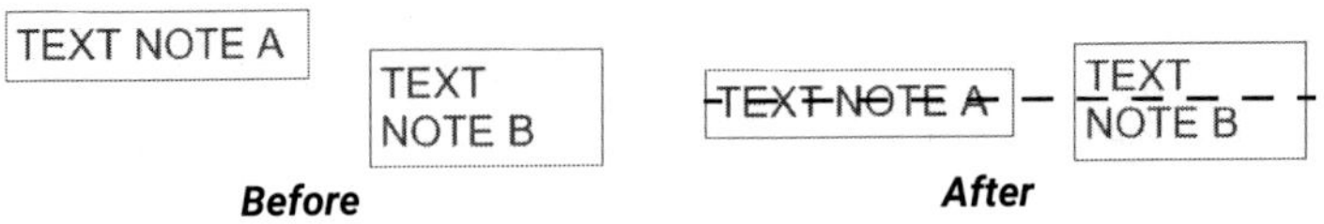

Figure 15–52

- (Align Elements Bottom): Aligns all selected text to the bottommost text border (as shown in Figure 15–53).

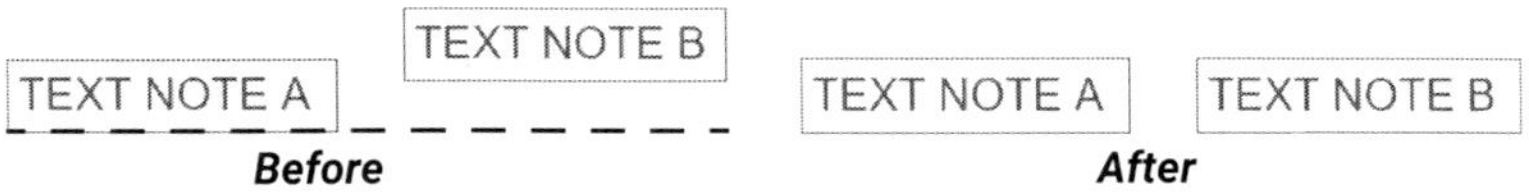

Figure 15–53

Horizontal Alignment Types

- (Distribute Horizontally): Aligns selected text by spacing them evenly horizontally between text borders (as shown in Figure 15–54). Best used with multiple columns of text notes that need to be spaced evenly.

Figure 15–54

- (Align Elements Left): Aligns all text to the leftmost edge of the text border (as shown in Figure 15–55).

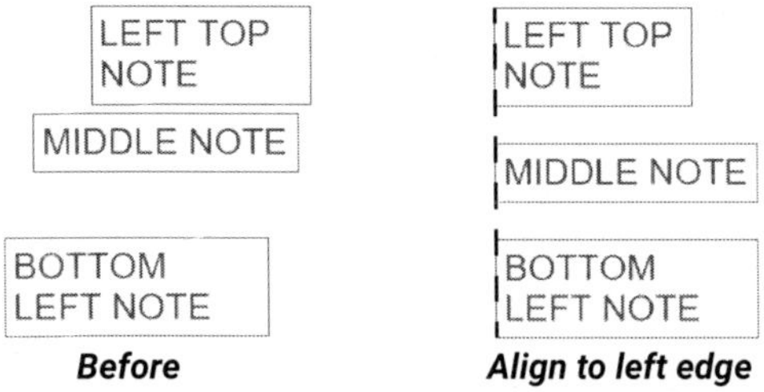

Figure 15–55

- (Align Elements Center): Adjusts the position of the selected text, ensuring that it is evenly centered horizontally within the combined borders of the selected text, tags, or keynotes (as shown in Figure 15–56).

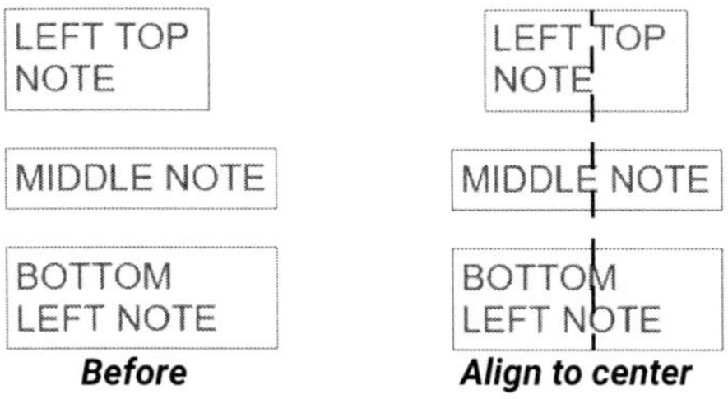

Figure 15–56

- (Align Elements Right): Aligns all text to the rightmost edge of the text border (as shown in Figure 15–57).

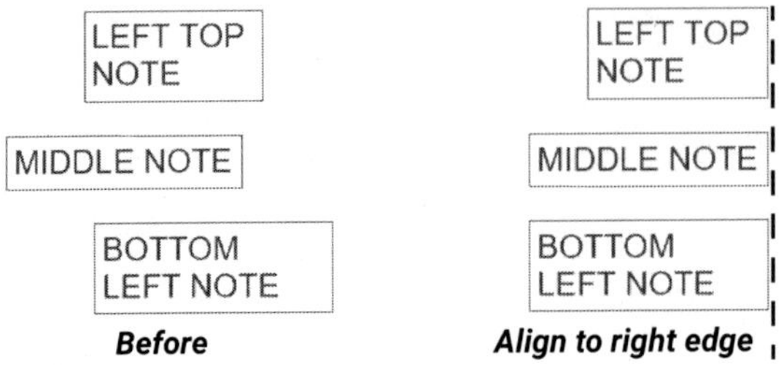

Figure 15–57

Spell Checking

The check spelling feature in Revit checks spelling of text notes while editing, in a selected text note, or in a view or sheet. As you are typing text, if Revit detects a misspelled word, it will underline it in red. Right-click on any highlighted text and select the correct spelling of the word or expand **More Suggestions** to see additional spelling suggestions, as shown in Figure 15–58. You can also select **Add to Dictionary** for Revit to learn the word.

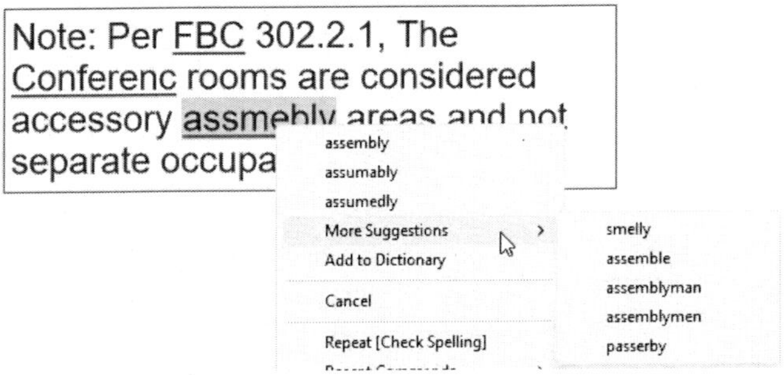

Figure 15–58

- Spell checking does not work on text in a tag, text in elements, text notes in groups, or text in schedules.

How To: Spell Check All Text in a View

1. To spell check all text in a view, in the *Annotate* tab>*Text* panel, click (Spelling), or press <F7>.
2. In the *Check Spelling* dialog box, shown in Figure 15–59, go through all spelling errors caught. As with other spell checkers, you can **Ignore**, **Add**, or **Change** the word.

- You can also check the spelling in selected text. With text selected, in the *Modify | Text Notes* tab>*Tools* panel, click (Check Spelling).

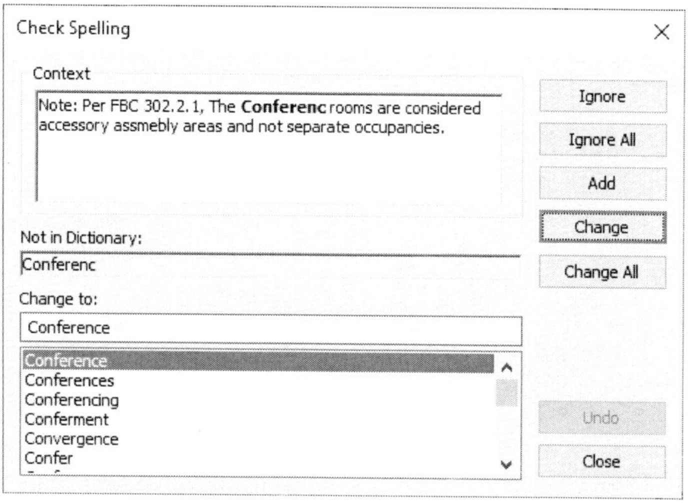

Figure 15–59

Creating Text Types

If you need new text types with a different text size or font (such as for a title or hand-lettering), you can create new ones, as shown in Figure 15–60. It is recommended that you create these in a project template so they are available in future projects.

Figure 15–60

- You can copy and paste text types from one project to another or use **Transfer Project Standards**.

How To: Create Text Types

1. In the *Annotate* tab>*Text* panel, click (Text Types). Alternatively, start the **Text** command.
2. In Properties, click **Edit Type**.
3. In the *Type Properties* dialog box, click **Duplicate**.
4. In the *Name* dialog box, type a new name and click **OK**.
5. Modify the text parameters, as needed. The parameters are shown in Figure 15–61.

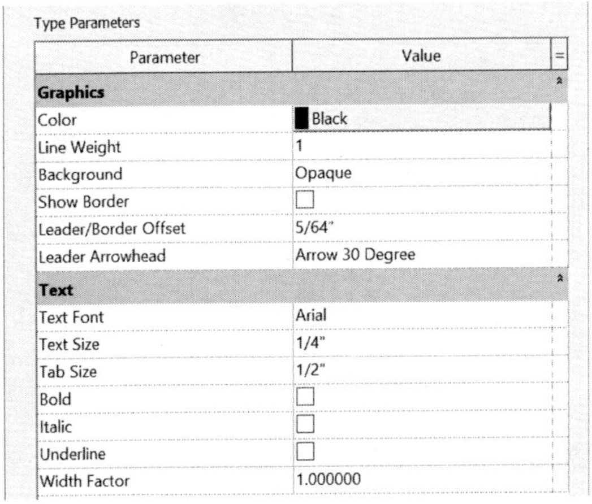

Figure 15–61

- The *Background* parameter can be set to **Opaque** or **Transparent**. An opaque background includes a masking region that hides lines or elements behind the text.
- In the *Text* area, the *Width Factor* parameter controls the width of the lettering, but does not affect the height. A width factor greater than **1** spreads the text out and a width factor less than **1** compresses it.
- The *Show Border* parameter, when selected, includes a rectangle around the text.

6. Click **OK** to close the *Type Properties* dialog box.

Practice 15b
Work with Text

Practice Objectives

- Create text types.
- Add text with and without leaders to a view.
- Add a numbered and bulleted list to a sheet.

In this practice, you will add text with and without leaders to a view. You will also add a text note with numbered and bulleted list on a site plan sheet. The completed sheet is shown in Figure 15–62.

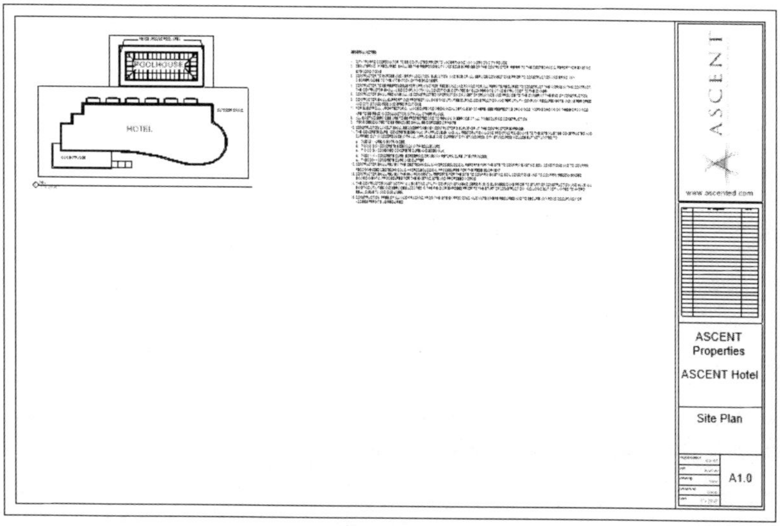

Figure 15–62

Task 1: Create text types.

1. Open the project **Arch-Text.rvt** from the practice files folder.
2. In the *Annotate* tab, at the bottom of the *Text* panel, click ↘ to open the *Type Properties* dialog box.

3. In the *Type Properties* dialog box, duplicate any existing text type and create new text types using the properties outlined in the following table. Click **Apply** in the *Type Properties* dialog box after each text style is created to start the next one.

Name	**1/8" Arial**	**1/8" Arial Narrow**	**1/8" Arial Narrow Italic**
Text Font	Arial	Arial Narrow	Arial Narrow
Text Size	1/8"	1/8"	1/8"
Tab Size	1/4"	1/4"	1/4"
Width Factor	1.0	0.9	0.9
Italic	No	No	Yes

4. When finished, click **OK**.
5. Save the project.

Task 2: Add text to a view.

1. Open the **Floor Plans: Site** view.
2. In the *Annotate* tab>*Text* panel, click A (Text).
3. In the Type Selector, select **Text: 1/4" Arial**.
4. Add the **HOTEL** and **POOLHOUSE** text, as shown in Figure 15–63, by clicking the location where you want the text to be located and then typing in the text box. When finished, click away from the text box. You will remain in the **Text** tool until you click (Modify).
5. Change the text type to **1/8" Arial Narrow** and add the **OUTDOOR DINING**, **MAIN ENTRANCE**, and **FENCE AROUND POOL AREA** text shown in Figure 15–63.
6. Click (Modify).
   - To modify the placement of the text, select the text and use the grip to move the text into position.
7. Select the **FENCE AROUND POOL AREA** text. In the *Modify | Text Notes* tab>*Leader* panel, click (Add Left Side Straight Leader) and (Add Right Side Straight Leader) twice each, then modify the leaders by clicking and dragging the **Drag** controls as needed.

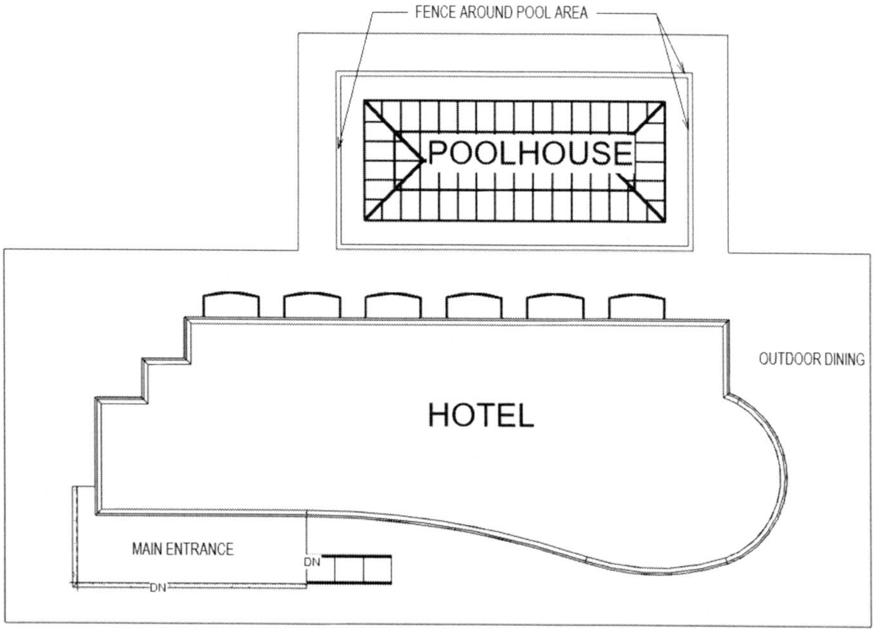

Figure 15–63

8. Save the project.

Task 3: Create a general note.

Note: In this task, you are placing the text directly on the sheet. Check your office standards, as using a Legend view for general notes might be preferred.

1. In the Project Browser, right-click on sheet **A0.0 - Cover Sheet** and select **Duplicate Sheet>Duplicate Empty Sheet**.
2. Change the sheet number to **A1.0** and the sheet name to **Site Plan**.

3. Add the **Floor Plans: Site** view to the sheet, as shown in Figure 15–64.

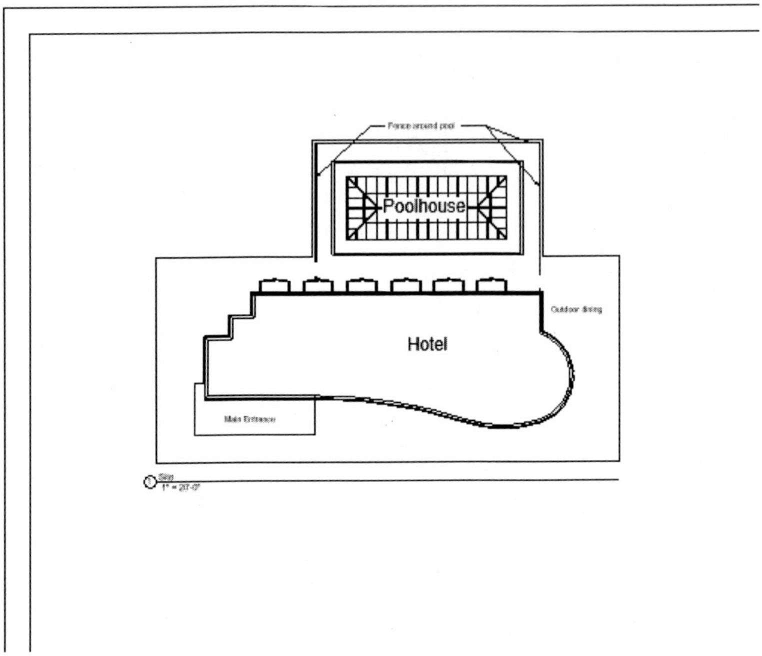

Figure 15–64

4. In a text editor (such as Word or Notepad), navigate to the practice files *Documents* folder and open either **General Notes.docx** or **General Notes.txt**. (If you open the .DOCX file, you may need to click **Enable Editing** at the top of the document.)

The rest of the steps below are referencing the text copied from the General Notes.txt file.

5. Copy the entire contents of the file to the clipboard.
6. In Revit, start the **Text** command.
7. Verify that no leader is selected, set the text type to **1/8" Arial**, and draw a text box similar to the one shown in Figure 15–65.

Figure 15–65

8. In the *Edit Text* tab>*Clipboard* panel, click (Paste).
9. Remain in Edit Text mode and zoom in on the text box. Note that there are numbered and lettered lists in the text, but the formatting is not quite correct.
10. Select all of the text and, in the *Edit Text* tab>*Paragraph* panel, click (List: Numbers).
11. The paragraphs are recognized and numbered but some of the existing numbers are still there, as shown in Figure 15–66 (the width of your text box will determine the line item return). You will need to delete the numbers that were copied in.

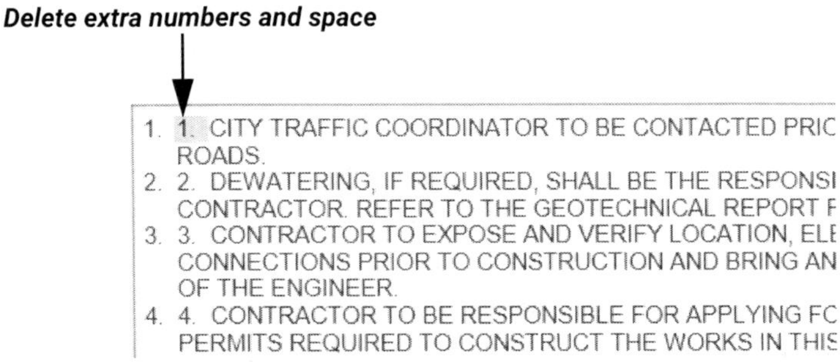

Figure 15–66

12. Select the lettered paragraphs that are shown highlighted in Figure 15–67. In the *Edit Text* tab>*Paragraph* panel, click (Increase Indent).

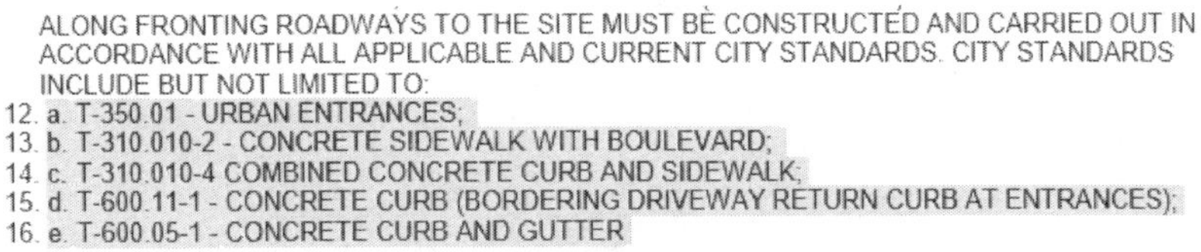

Figure 15–67

13. This changes them to uppercase letters, as shown in Figure 15–68.

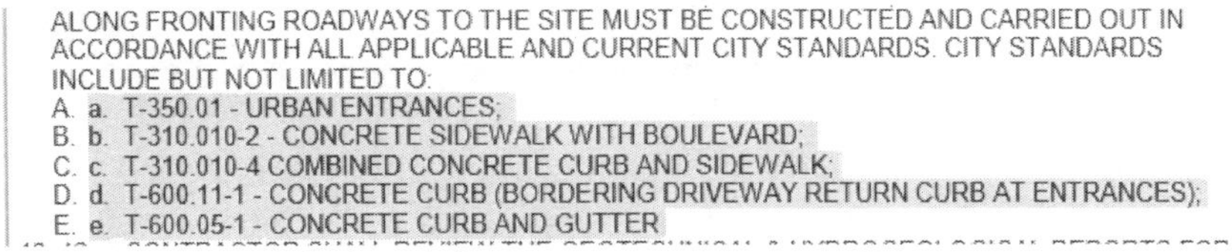

Figure 15–68

14. In the *Edit Text* tab>*Paragraph* panel, click (List: Lowercase letters).

15. Zoom in and remove the additional characters, as shown in Figure 15–69.

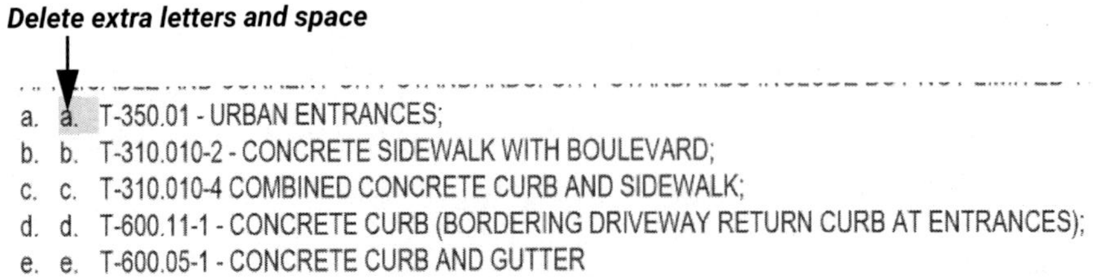

Figure 15–69

16. Continue fixing the rest of the numbers in the text note.

17. At the beginning of the list, select next to **1.** in the list and press <Enter> twice to make room for a title. This removes the 1. from the first list item.

18. Click on the first list item. In the *Edit Text* tab>*Paragraph* panel, click (List: Numbers). This corrects the numbering.

19. Click at the top of the text note or press the up arrow key twice and add the text **general notes:** in all lowercase.

20. Select the **general notes:** text and in the *Edit Text* tab>*Font* panel, click (All Caps), **B** (Bold), and U (Underline), so the text appears as shown in Figure 15–70.

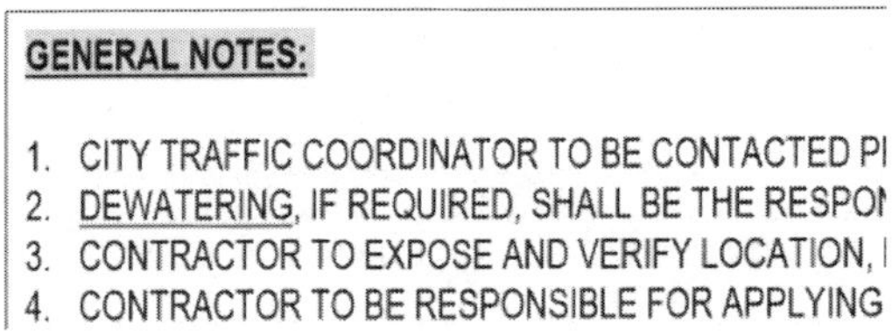

Figure 15–70

21. In the *Edit Text* tab>*Edit Text* panel, click (Close).

22. Click outside the text box and use the controls, if needed, to relocate or resize the text note.

23. Zoom out to see the full sheet.

24. Save and close the project.

End of practice

15.3 Adding Detail Lines and Symbols

While annotating views for construction documents, you might need to add detail lines and symbols to clarify the design intent or show information, such as the life safety plan exit information shown in Figure 15–71.

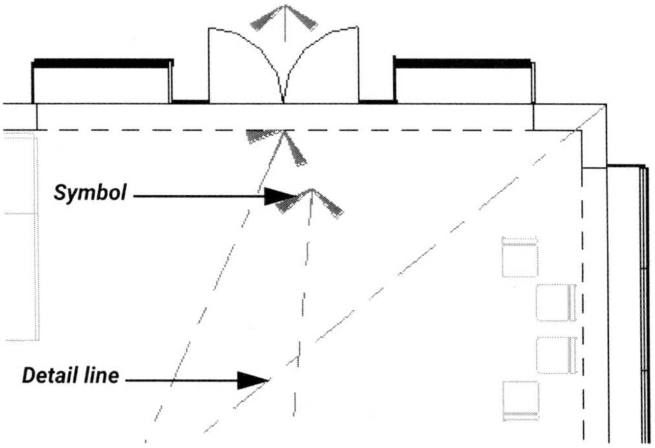

Figure 15–71

- Detail lines and symbols are view-specific, which means that they only display in the view in which they were created.
- You can add detail lines in a plan, elevation, or legend view, but not in a 3D view.

How To: Draw a Detail Line

1. In the *Annotation* tab>*Detail* panel, click (Detail Line).
2. In the *Modify | Place Detail Lines* tab>*Draw* panel, select a sketch tool. Additional options will display depending on the tool selected, as shown in Figure 15–72. Set them as needed.
3. In the *Line Style* panel, expand the *Line Style* drop-down list and select the type of line you want to use, as shown in Figure 15–72.

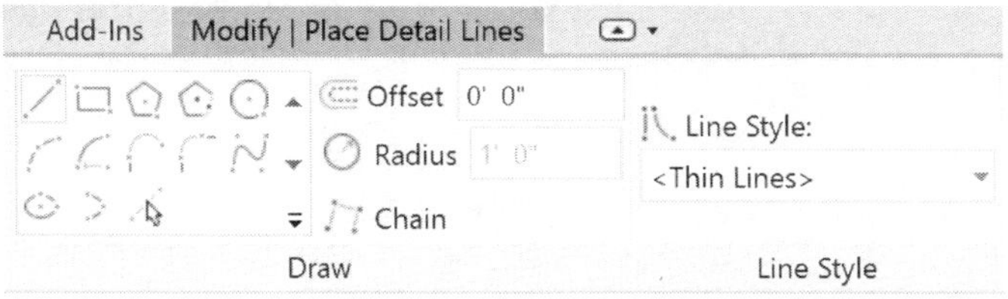

Figure 15–72

4. Draw the detail line.

Using Symbols

Many of the annotations used in working drawings are frequently repeated. Several of them have been saved as symbols in Revit, such as the North Arrow, Center Line, and Graphic Scale annotations shown in Figure 15–73.

> ***Note:*** *Symbols are 2D elements that only display in one view, while components can be in 3D and display in many views.*

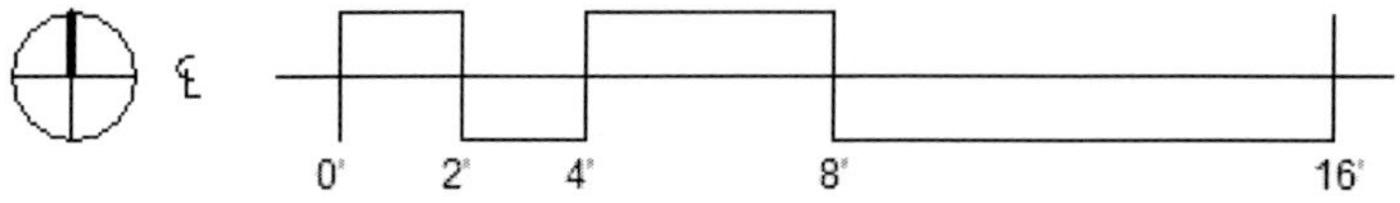

Figure 15–73

- You can also create or load custom annotation symbols.

How To: Place a Symbol

1. In the *Annotate* tab>*Symbol* panel, click (Symbol).
2. In the Type Selector, select the symbol you want to use.
3. If needed, in the *Modify | Place Symbol* tab>*Leader* panel (shown in Figure 15–74), enter a number in the (Number of Leaders) field. If you want to rotate the symbol as you insert it, toggle on (Rotate After Placement) in the *Rotate* panel.

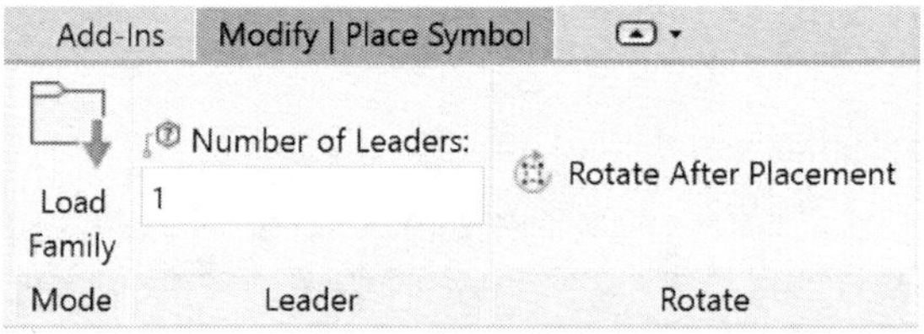

Figure 15–74

4. Place the symbol in the view. Rotate it if you toggled on **Rotate After Placement**. If you specified leaders, use the leader line grips to move them into place.

- In the *Annotate* tab>*Symbol* panel, click (Stair Path) to label the slope direction and walk line of a stair, as shown in Figure 15–75. In Properties, you can specify if you want to *Show Up/Down Text* and modify what text will display in the view.

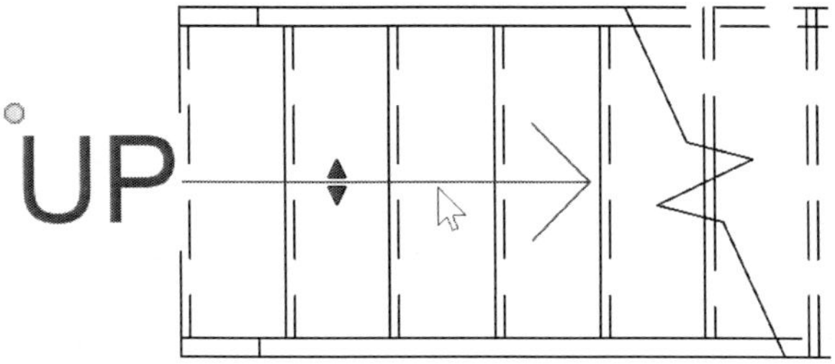

Figure 15–75

Practice 15c
Add Detail Lines and Symbols

Practice Objectives

- Add detail lines.
- Add symbols.

In this practice, you will modify a site plan by adding detail lines to lay out the utilities. You will also add symbols for a power pole and north arrow. Figure 15–76 shows the completed practice.

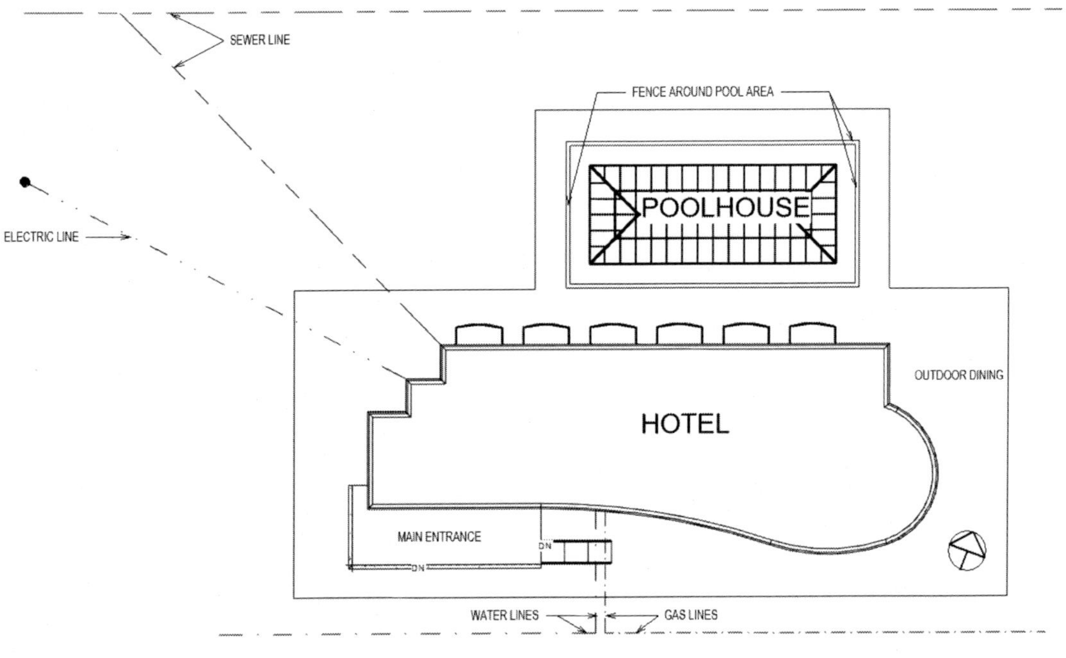

Figure 15–76

Task 1: Create a utilities plan using detail lines.

1. Open the project **Arch-Symbols.rvt** from the practice files folder.
2. Open the **Floor Plans: Site** view.
3. In the *Annotate* tab>*Detail* panel, click (Detail Line).
4. In the *Modify | Place Detail Lines* tab>*Line Style* panel, set the *Line Style* to **Sewer Lines**. In the *Draw* panel, toggle off (Chain).

5. Draw a diagonal line from the corner of the building, as shown in Figure 15–77.

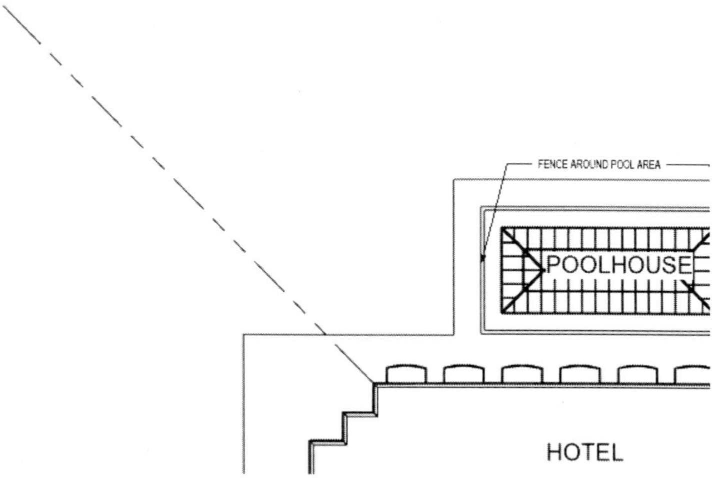

Figure 15–77

6. In the *Modify | Place Detail Lines* tab>*Draw* panel, select **Pick Lines**, then set (Offset) to **25'** and press <Enter>.
7. Hover your cursor over the edge of the floor above the poolhouse (as shown in Figure 15–78) and click when you see the dashed preview line above the poolhouse area.

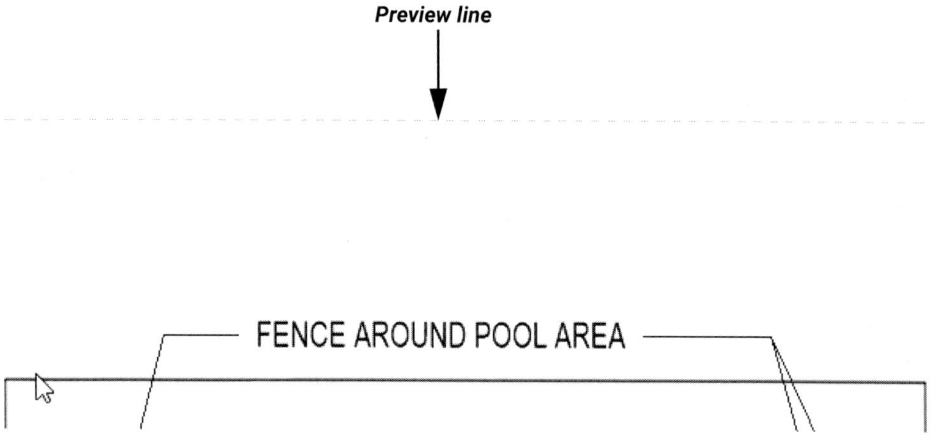

Figure 15–78

8. Click (Modify). Select the horizontal sewer line and stretch it out so that it intersects with the diagonal sewer line, as shown in Figure 15–79.
9. Start the **Detail Line** command again and draw the rest of the details, as shown in Figure 15–79. Change the *Line Style* to **Electric Lines**, **Water Lines**, and **Gas Lines**, as needed.
10. Click (Modify) and modify the detail lines as needed. Add text to label them as shown in Figure 15–79.

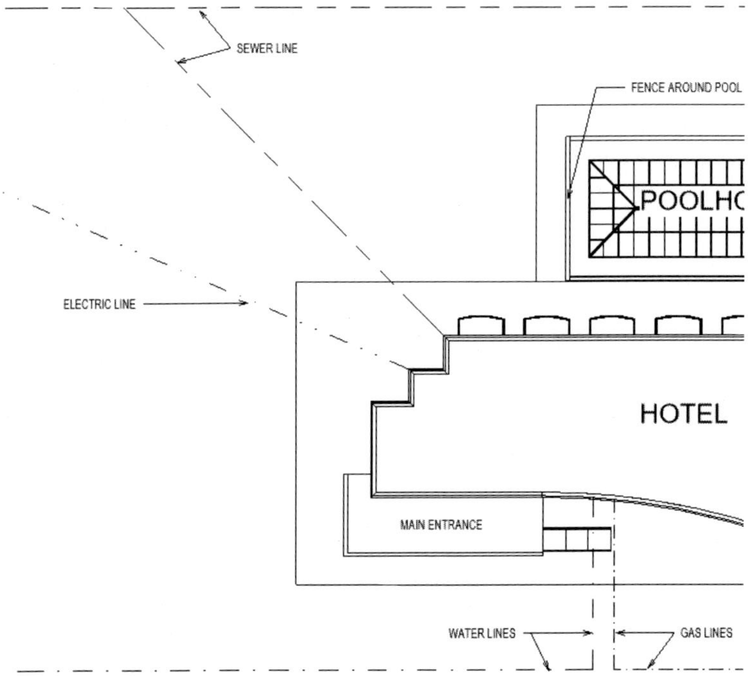

Figure 15–79

11. Save the project.

Task 2: Add symbols.

1. In the *Annotate* tab>*Symbol* panel, click (Symbol).
2. In the *Modify | Place Symbol* tab>*Mode* panel, click (Load Family).
3. In the *Load Family* dialog box, navigate to your practice files *Families>Annotation* folder. Select **Power Pole Symbol.rfa** and click **Open**.

4. Add a power pole at the end of the electric line, as shown in Figure 15–80.

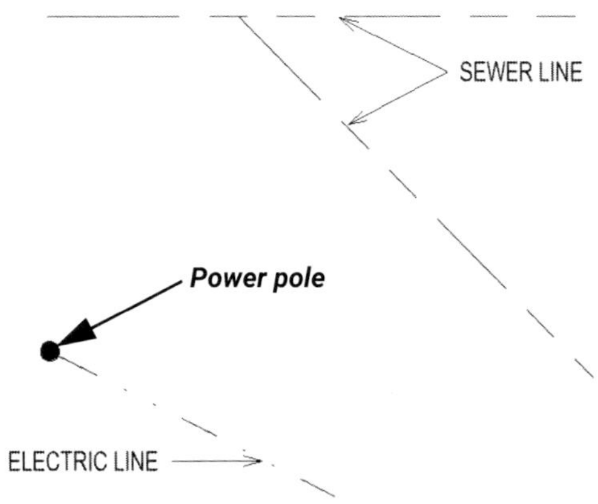

Figure 15–80

5. While still in the **Symbol** command, in the Type Selector, select **North Arrow 1** and place a north arrow to the lower-right side of the hotel.
6. Click (Modify).
7. Select the north arrow and, using the **Rotate** command, rotate it 20°, as shown in Figure 15–81.

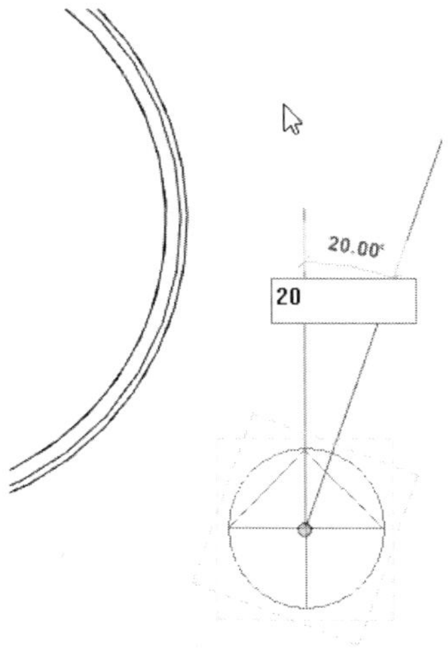

Figure 15–81

8. Open sheet **A1.0 - Site Plan**. Select the viewport and, in Properties, change the view scale to **1/16"=1'-0"**. Move the view on to the sheet.
9. Click (Modify).

10. Zoom in and select the view title, then move it below the view.
11. To make the view title line longer, click the viewport and use the view title line grip to adjust the length.
12. Save and close the project.

End of practice

15.4 Creating Legends

A legend is a separate view that can be placed on multiple sheets. Legends can be used to hold installation notes that need to be placed on a sheet with each floor plan, key plans, or any 2D items that need to be repeated. You can also create and list the annotations, line styles, and symbols that are used in your project, and provide explanatory notes next to the symbol, as shown in Figure 15–82. Additionally, legends can provide a list of materials or elevations of window types used in the project. Any components in a legend view will not be added to an instance count in the model's schedules.

> ***Note:*** *The elements in this figure are inserted using the* ***Symbol*** *command rather that the* ***Legend Component*** *or* ***Detail Component*** *commands. They are the nested generic annotation family inside of the electrical device family.*

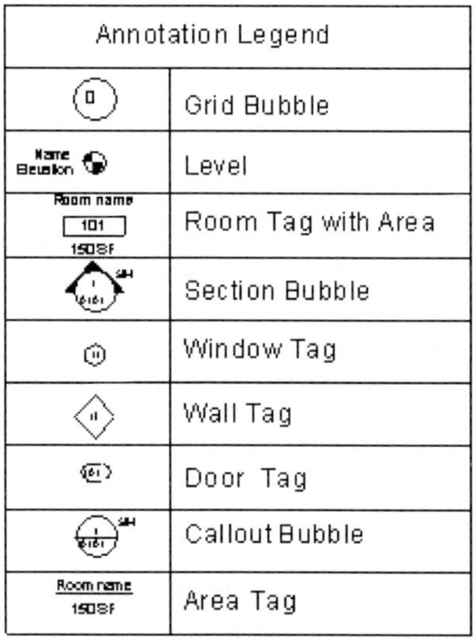

Figure 15–82

How To: Create a Legend

1. In the *View* tab>*Create* panel, expand (Legends) and click (Legend), or in the Project Browser, right-click on the *Legends* section title and select **New Legend...**.

2. In the *New Legend View* dialog box (shown in Figure 15–83), enter a name and select a scale for the legend, then click **OK**.

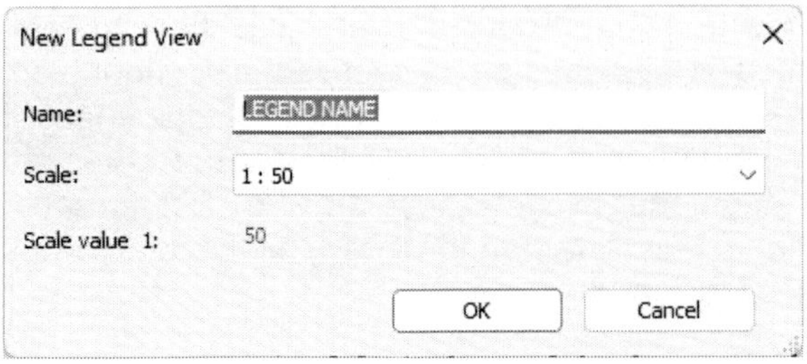

Figure 15–83

- You can modify a legend's scale in the View Control Bar after the legend view has been created.
- Use (Detail Line) and A (Text) to create the table and explanatory notes.
- Use the **Reference Plane** command to line up the components, then delete the reference planes when finished.

How To: Place Legend Components

1. In the *Annotate* tab>*Detail* panel, expand **Component** and select (Legend Component), as shown in Figure 15–84. Note that the last-used component command will be the icon you see in the ribbon.

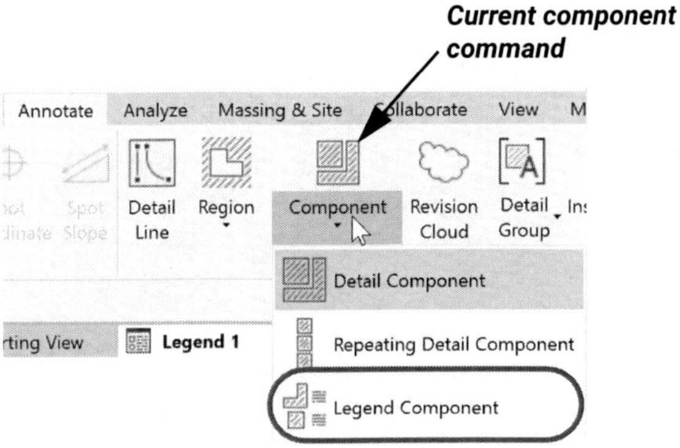

Figure 15–84

- You can also use commands such as (Symbol) to place generic annotations in the view.

2. In the *Modify | Place Legend Component* tab>*Placement* panel, expand **Component Type** and select the component type you want to use, as shown in Figure 15–85. This list contains all of the elements in the project that can be used in a legend.

Figure 15–85

3. Select the *View Direction* of the element that you want to place.

   Note: *If you expand the View Direction drop-down list and no other options display, click in the search bar and start typing the name of the direction you want, as shown in Figure 15–86.*

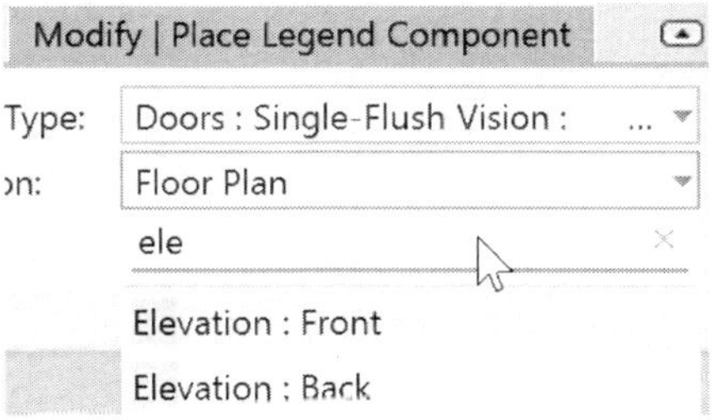

Figure 15–86

4. For section elements (such as walls, floors, and roofs), type a distance for the *Host Length*.

- Elements in legends can be dimensioned.
- Elements that are full size, such as planting components or doors, come in at their full size.
- Legends are views that can be placed on multiple sheets. You can use **Copy to the Clipboard** and **Paste** to copy legends from sheet to sheet.

Practice 15d
Create Legends

Practice Objective

- Create legends and add legend components, text, and dimensions.

In this practice, you will create door and window legends (as shown in Figure 15–87) by creating legend views, adding legend components, and labeling the door and window types with text.

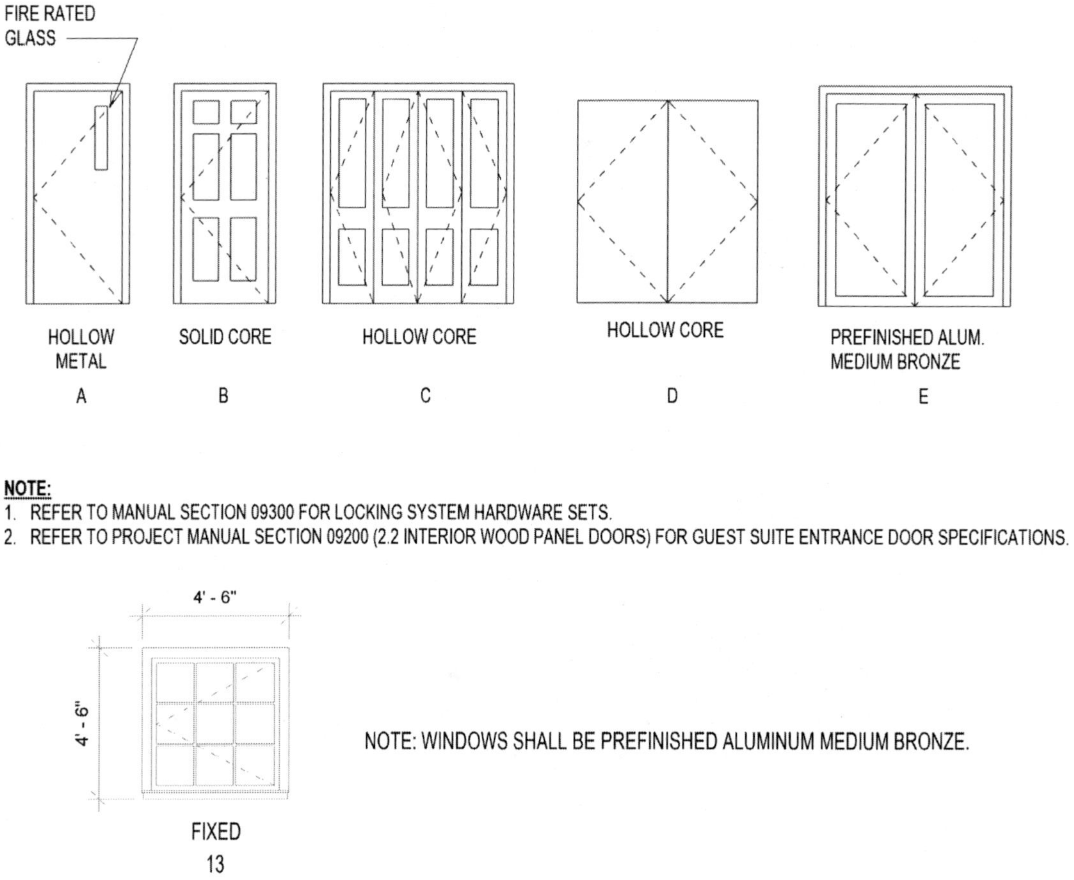

Figure 15–87

1. Open the project **Arch-Legends.rvt** from the practice files folder.
2. In the *View* tab>*Create* panel, expand (Legends) and click (Legend) to create a new legend view.
3. In the *New Legend View* dialog box, enter **Window Elevations** for the *Name* and set the *Scale* to **1/4" = 1'-0"**. Click **OK**.

4. In the *Annotate* tab>*Detail* panel, expand (Component) and click (Legend Component).
5. In the *Modify | Place Legend Component* tab>*Placement* panel, expand **Component Type** and select **Windows: Casement 3x3 with Trim: 48" x 48"**, then expand the *View Direction* drop-down list and select **Elevation: Front**. Place the component in the view. The window displays.

   Note: *If you do not have the* ***Elevation: Front*** *option in your View Direction drop-down list, type the name of the direction in the search bar, then select it from the list that displays.*

6. Click (Modify).
7. In the *Annotate* tab>*Text* panel, click (Text).
8. In the Type Selector, select **Text: 3/32" Arial**. Add **Fixed** and the window number **13** under the window, as shown in Figure 15–88.
9. Add dimensions and the note shown in Figure 15–88.
   - If needed, use the **Door and Window Notes.txt** or **Door and Window Notes.docx** found in the practice files *Documents* folder to quickly add the text notes.

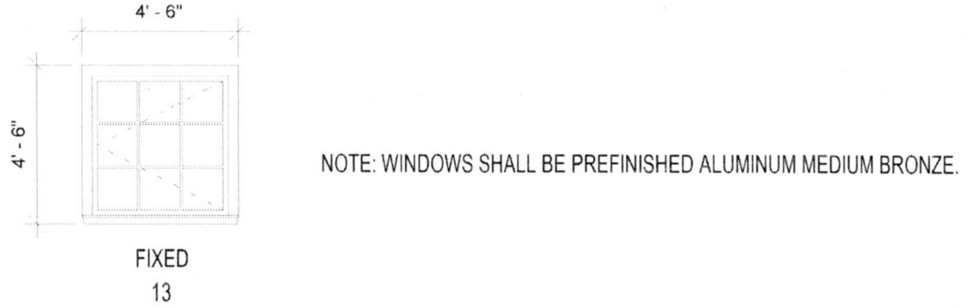

Figure 15–88

10. Create another legend view. Name it **Door Elevations** and set the *Scale* to **1/4" = 1'-0"**.
11. In the legend view, use the **Legend Component** command to add the **Elevation: Front** view direction of the following doors:
    - Doors : Single-Flush Vision : 36" x 84"
    - Doors : Single-Panel 4 : 36" x 84"
    - Doors : Bifold-4 Panel : 72" x 84"
    - Doors : Door-Double-Flush_Panel-Double-Acting : 72" x 84"
    - Doors : Double-Glass : 72" x 84"

    Note: *To align the doors, watch for the alignment line that displays before you place each door, then click to place it once you are lined up.*

12. Label the doors with the text shown in Figure 15–89.

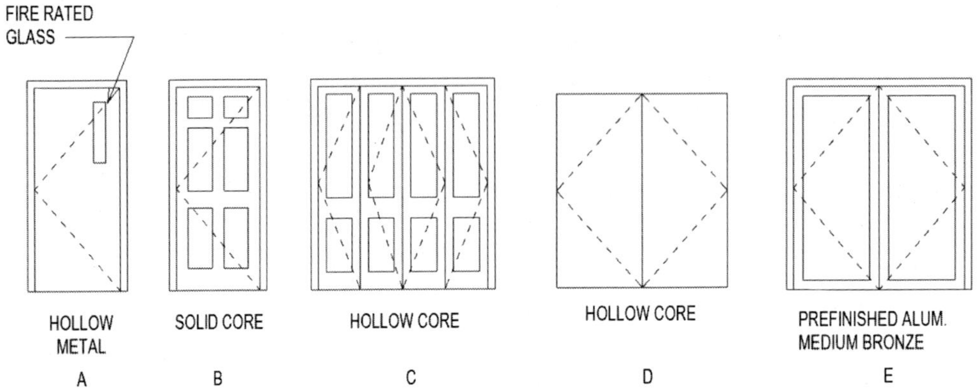

NOTE:
1. REFER TO MANUAL SECTION 09300 FOR LOCKING SYSTEM HARDWARE SETS.
2. REFER TO PROJECT MANUAL SECTION 09200 (2.2 INTERIOR WOOD PANEL DOORS) FOR GUEST SUITE ENTRANCE DOOR SPECIFICATIONS.

Figure 15–89

13. Save and close the project.

End of practice

Chapter Review Questions

1. When a wall is moved, how do you update the dimension?
   a. Edit the dimension and move it over.
   b. Select the dimension and then click **Update** in the contextual tab.
   c. The dimension automatically updates.
   d. Delete the existing dimension and add a new one.

2. How do you create new text styles?
   a. Using the **Text Styles** command.
   b. Duplicate an existing type.
   c. They must be included in a template.
   d. Using the **Format Styles** command.

3. When you edit text, how many leaders can be added using the leader tools?
   a. One
   b. One on each end of the text
   c. As many as you want at each end of the text

4. In which types of views can you add detail lines? (Select all that apply.)
   a. Plans
   b. Elevations
   c. 3D views
   d. Legends

5. Detail lines created in one view also display in the related view.
   a. True
   b. False

6. Which of the following describes the difference between a symbol and a component?
   a. Symbols are 3D and only display in one view. Components are 2D and display in many views.
   b. Symbols are 2D and only display in one view. Components are 3D and display in many views.
   c. Symbols are 2D and display in many views. Components are 3D and only display in one view.
   d. Symbols are 3D and display in many views. Components are 2D and only display in one view.

Command Summary

Button	Command	Location
Dimensions and Text		
	**Aligned Dimension**	• **Ribbon:** *Annotate* tab>*Dimension* panel • **Quick Access Toolbar** • **Shortcut:** DI
	**Angular Dimension**	• **Ribbon:** *Annotate* tab>*Dimension* panel
	**Arc Length Dimension**	• **Ribbon:** *Annotate* tab>*Dimension* panel
	**Diameter Dimension**	• **Ribbon:** *Annotate* tab>*Dimension* panel
	**Linear Dimension**	• **Ribbon:** *Annotate* tab>*Dimension* panel
	**Radial Dimension**	• **Ribbon:** *Annotate* tab>*Dimension* panel
	**Text**	• **Ribbon:** *Annotate* tab>*Text* panel • **Shortcut:** TX
Detail Lines and Symbols		
	**Detail Line**	• **Ribbon:** *Annotate* tab>*Detail* panel • **Shortcut:** DL
	**Stair Path**	• **Ribbon:** *Annotate* tab>*Symbol* panel
	**Symbol**	• **Ribbon:** *Annotate* tab>*Symbol* panel
Legends		
	**Legend (View)**	• **Ribbon:** *View* tab>*Create* panel, expand Legends
	**Legend Component**	• **Ribbon:** *Annotate* tab>*Detail* panel, expand Component

Chapter 16

Adding Tags and Schedules

Adding tags to your views helps you to identify elements such as doors, windows, or walls in the model. Tags are 2D annotation families with labels that extract information about the elements being tagged from their properties. Tags are typically added when you insert an element, but can also be added at any point in the design process.

Schedules are used to gather information stored in the various elements in the project and present them in a table format. In Revit®, you can create schedules specifically for architecture projects, such as building component schedules and material takeoff schedules. These schedules can then be added to sheets to create construction documentation.

Learning Objectives

- Add tags to elements in 2D and 3D views to prepare the views to be placed on sheets.
- Load tags that are required for projects.
- Understand schedules and their use in a project.
- Modify schedule content, including the instance and type properties of related elements.
- Add schedules to sheets as part of the construction documents.

16.1 Adding Tags

Tags are used to identify elements in a project. When placing certain elements, such as windows and doors, you can select **Tag on Placement** from the ribbon and a tag will be placed along with the element. Revit supplies tags for every category in the family library, which can then be placed on elements in the drawing anytime during the design process. Figure 16–1 shows elements that have been tagged.

Note: *Additional tags are stored in the Revit Library in the Annotations folder.*

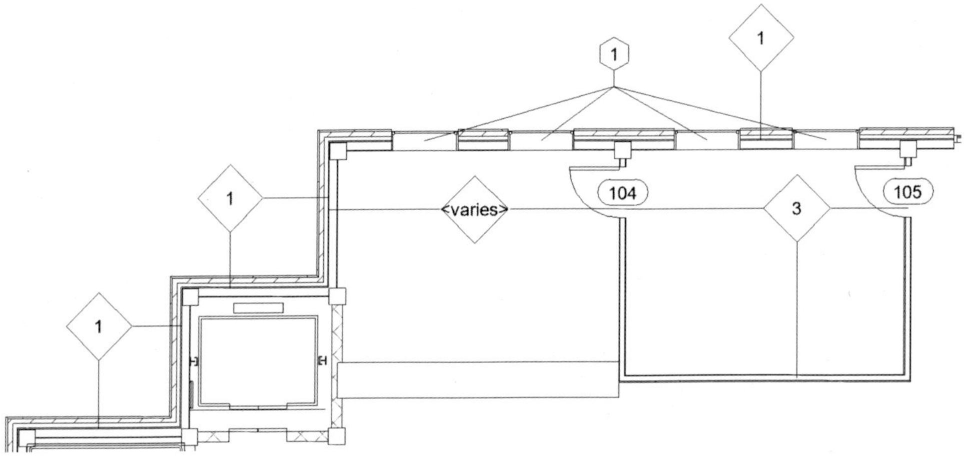

Figure 16–1

- The **Tag by Category** command works for most elements, except for a few that have separate commands (like rooms and spaces).
- Tags can be letters, numbers, or a combination of the two.

You can place three types of tags, as follows:

- (Tag by Category): Tags according to the category of the element. It places door tags on doors and wall tags on walls.
- (Multi-Category Tag): Tags elements belonging to multiple categories. The tags display information from parameters that they have in common.
- (Material Tag): Tags that display the type of material. They are typically used in detailing.

Tag Options

You can set tag options for leaders and tag orientation (as shown in Figure 16–2) in the *Modify | Tag* tab before placing a tag. You can also set other options in Properties either before or after placing a tag.

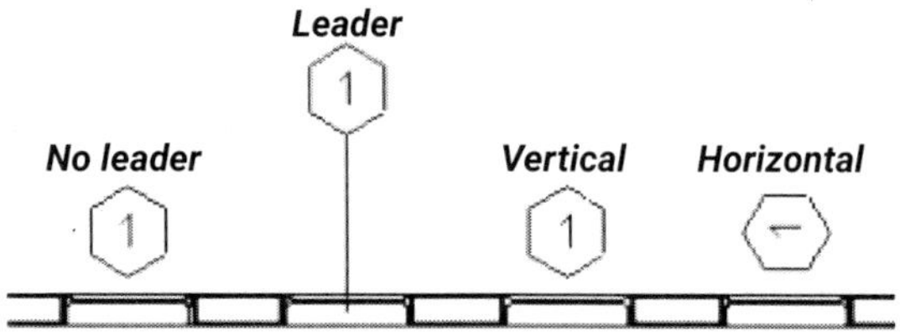

Figure 16–2

- Tag orientation can be set to the following. You can also press <Spacebar> to toggle the orientation while placing or modifying the tag.
    - **Horizontal:** Tag stays horizontal (0°) to the element it is tagging.
    - **Vertical:** Forces the tag to stay vertical (90°) to the element it is tagging no matter what.
    - **Model:** Tag rotates freely from the element, similar to room tags.
- When placing a tag, the (Leader End) can be set to be an **Attached End** or **Free End**, as shown in Figure 16–3, either in the *Modify | Tag* tab>*Leader* panel or in Properties. A free end has an additional drag control where the leader touches the element. When editing a tag, you also have the option to set the *Leader Start* to **Attached Start** or **Free Start**.
    - With **Attached End**, the tag and leader line stay attached to the element you are tagging. **Free End** allows you to move the tag and leader line away from the element.
    - Depending on which leader type was selected in the ribbon or Properties, when a tag is selected, its leader line will have either a (Change Leader Start/End to Free Start/End) or (Change Leader Start/End to Attached Start/End) icon on each end, allowing you to toggle between Attached Start/End and Free Start/End. These icons do not display when the tag is not selected.

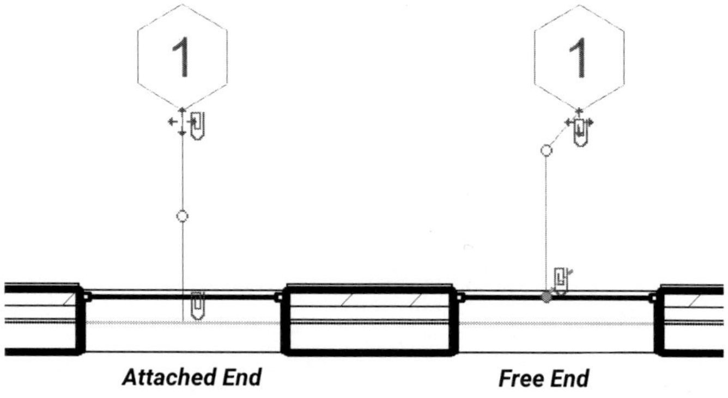

Figure 16–3

- If you change between **Attached End** and **Free End**, the tag does not move and the leader does not change location, and you will then move the tag manually.
- When  (Leader Line) is selected in the ribbon, you can specify the length of the leader in plotting units. It is grayed out if **Leader** is not selected or if a **Free End** leader is defined.
- If a tag is not loaded, a *No Tag Loaded* dialog box opens, as shown in Figure 16–4. Click **Yes** to open the *Load Family* dialog box in which you can select the appropriate tag.

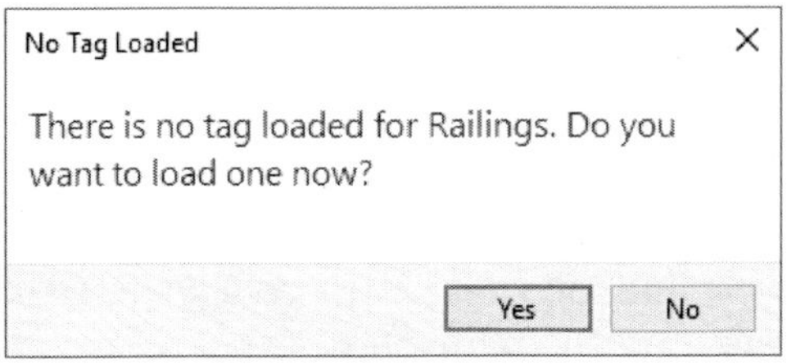

Figure 16–4

- Tags can be pinned so they stay in place if you move the element that is tagged. This is primarily used when tags have leaders, as shown in Figure 16–5.

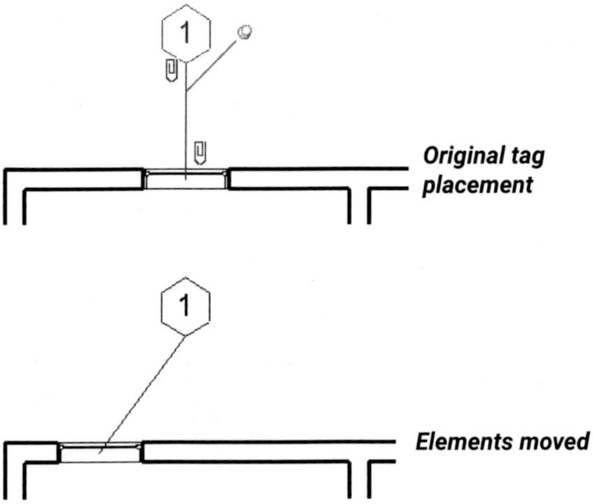

Figure 16–5

How To: Add Tags

1. In the *Annotate* tab>*Tag* panel, click (Tag by Category), (Multi-Category Tag), or (Material Tag), depending on the type of tag you want to place.
2. In Properties, specify the leader options, orientation, and angle, as needed, as shown in Figure 16–6. This can also be set in the *Modify | Tag* tab>*Placement* panel.

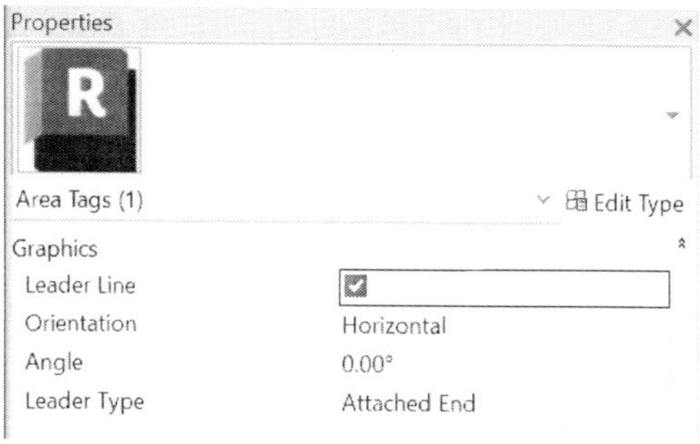

Figure 16–6

3. In the *Modify | Tag* tab>*Placement* panel, set the *Leader Length*.
4. Select the element you want to tag. If a tag for the selected element is not loaded, you are prompted to load it from the Revit Library.

Room Tags

If tags were not added to a room when they were created or you wish to add room tags to another view, you must to use a specific command. In the *Architecture* tab>*Room & Area* panel, click (Tag Room). Alternatively, in the *Annotate* tab>*Tag* panel, click (Room Tag), or type **RT**.

- You can change the name or number by clicking on the tag text to edit it, as shown in Figure 16–7.

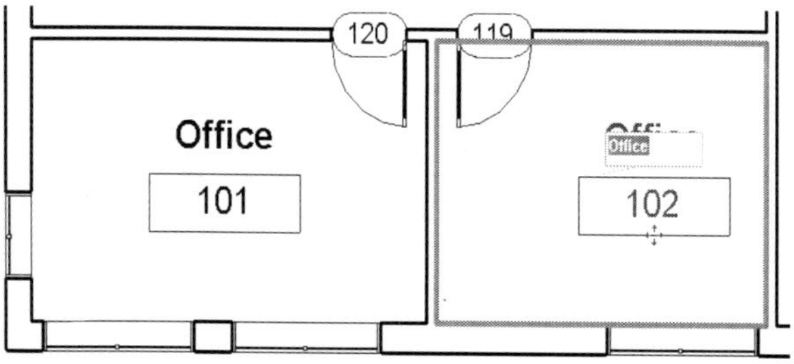

Figure 16–7

Multi-Leader Tags

If you have elements that need to be tagged that are in close proximity to one another, you can tag one element and then select other similar elements. This adds more leader lines from the elements to the tag, as shown with the windows in Figure 16–8. When selecting the tag, you can see how many host elements it is tagging in Properties (as shown on the left in Figure 16–8).

You cannot select elements that are of different categories, like a window and a door. You can only select similar elements to share a tag, like all windows or all doors.

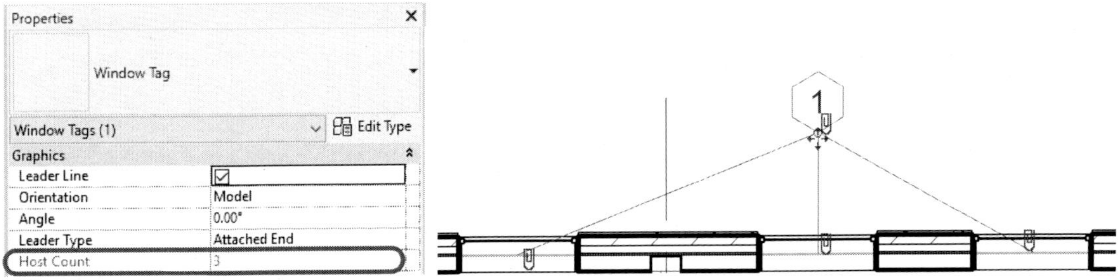

Figure 16–8

You can modify how the leaders are displayed when using the multi-leader tags. You can adjust how they will display in the view by showing all leaders, hiding select leaders, or hiding all leaders.

(Show All Leaders)	This turns on all leaders of any tag that is selected that used Multi-Leader tagging.
(Hide All Leaders)	This turns off all leaders of any tag that is selected that used Multi-Leader tagging.
(Show One Leader)	This turns off all leaders except for one leader of any tag that is selected that used Multi-Leader tagging.
(Select Leaders to Show)	This puts you into edit mode and enables you to select specific leaders to show or hide. When finished, you need to click (Finish).
(Merge Leaders)	Select to turn this feature on. This will merge all the leader line elbows to one location on the main leader line. You will not have the ability to adjust the leader lines individually. To get the leader line elbows back, select the **Merge Leaders** icon.

How To: Add a Multi-Leader Tag

1. In the *Annotate* tab>*Tag* panel, click (Tag by Category).
2. In the *Modify | Tag* tab>*Host* panel, verify (Add/Remove Host) is toggled on, as shown in Figure 16–9.
3. In the *Leaders* panel, set how multiple leaders will display.
4. Set the *Graphics* options in Properties or in the contextual tab (shown in the *Tags* and *Leader* panels in Figure 16–9).

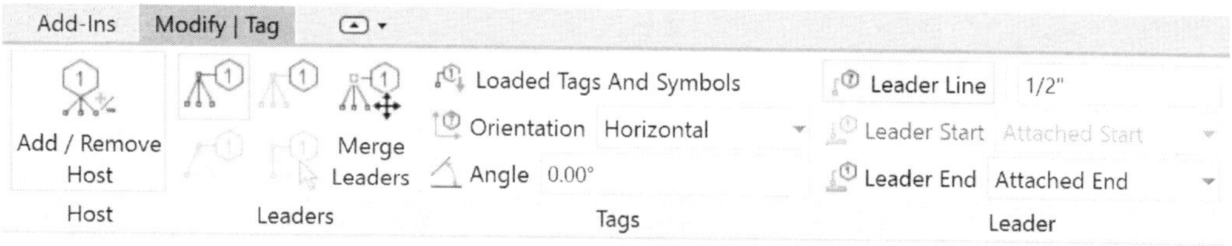

Figure 16–9

5. Select one element in the view to place a tag.
6. Select other similar elements to add to the tag. A leader line will be added for each element you select.

- Alternatively, if you have a tag already placed in the model and you want to add elements to the tag, select the tag, and in the contextual tab>*Host* panel, click (Add/Remove Host). In the *Leaders* panel, select how the leaders will display, then select the other elements in the view.

How To: Remove Elements from a Multi-Leader Tag

1. Select the tag.
2. In the contextual tab>*Host* panel, select (Add/Remove Host).
3. Select the element in the model. The leader line is removed.

How To: Add Multiple Tags

1. In the *Annotate* tab>*Tag* panel, click (Tag All).
2. In the *Tag All Not Tagged* dialog box (shown in Figure 16–10), select the checkbox beside one or more categories to tag. Selecting the checkbox beside the *Category* title selects all of the tags.

   ***Note:** To tag only some elements, select them before starting this command. In the Tag All Not Tagged dialog box, select **Only selected objects in current view**.*

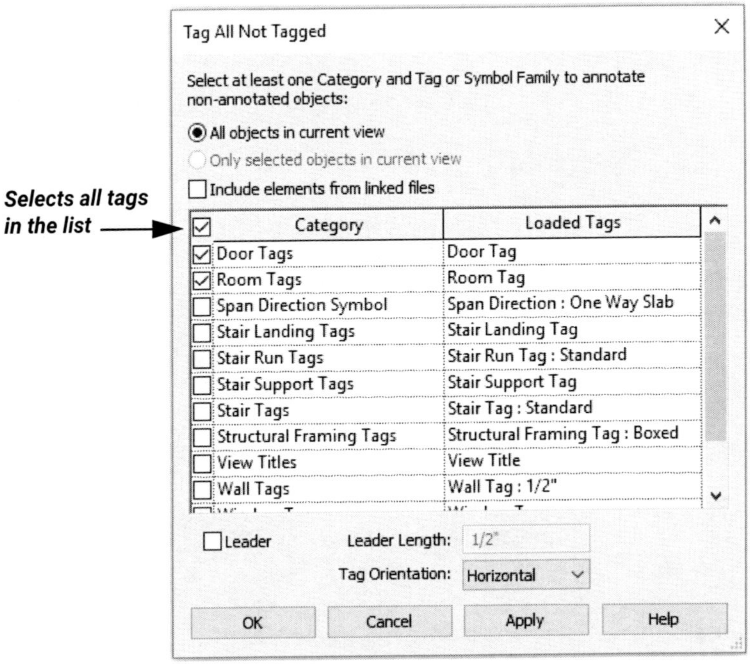

Figure 16–10

3. Set the *Leader* and *Tag Orientation* as needed.
4. Click **Apply** to apply the tags and stay in the dialog box. Click **OK** to apply the tags and close the dialog box.

- When you select a tag, the properties of that tag display.
  - To display the properties of the tagged element, in the *Modify* contextual tab>*Host* panel, click (Select Host).
- Rooms can be tagged using **Tag All Not Tagged**.

How To: Load Tags

1. In the *Annotate* tab, expand the *Tag* panel and click (Loaded Tags And Symbols) or, when a Tag command is active, in the *Modify | Tag* tab>*Tags* panel, click (Loaded Tags And Symbols).
2. In the *Loaded Tags And Symbols* dialog box (shown in Figure 16–11), click **Load Family...**.

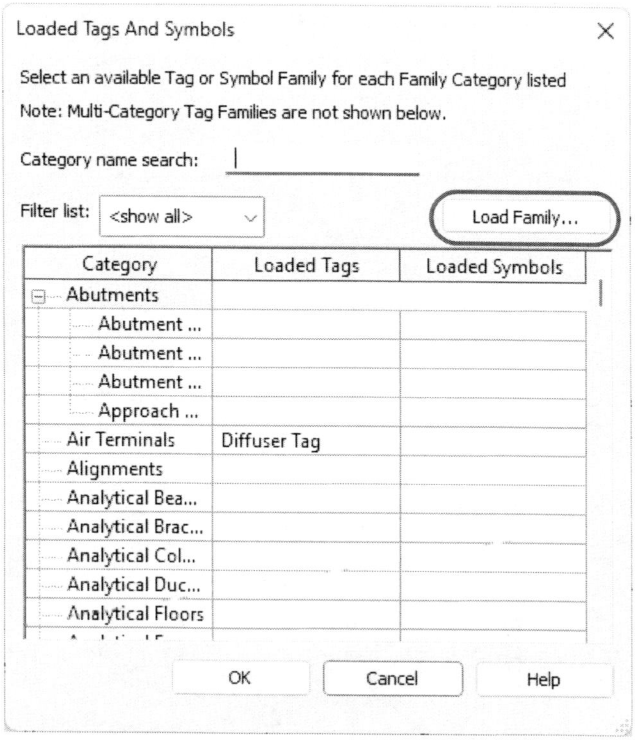

Figure 16–11

3. In the *Load Family* dialog box, navigate to the appropriate *Annotations* folder in the Revit Library, select the tag(s) needed, and click **Open**.
4. The tag is added to the category in the dialog box. Click **OK**.
   - The *Category name search* field can be used to search for the name of the element, if needed.

Instance vs.Type Tags

Many elements (such as doors) are tagged in a numbered sequence, with each instance of the door having a separate tag number. Other elements (such as windows and walls) are tagged by type, as shown in Figure 16–12. Changing the information in one tag changes all instances of that element.

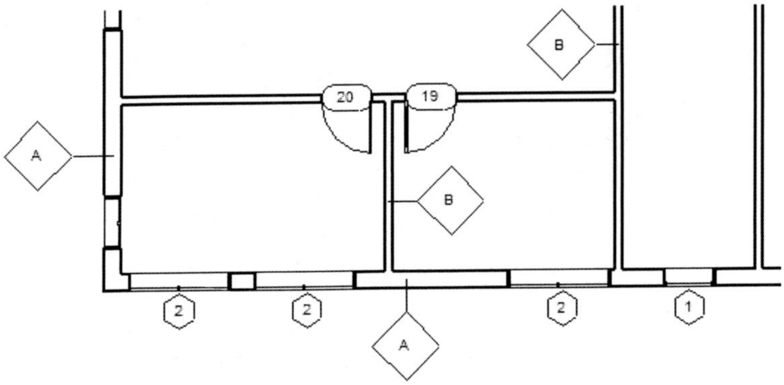

Figure 16–12

- To modify the number of an instance tag (such as a door or room), slowly click twice directly on the number in the tag and modify it, or you can modify the *Mark* property, as shown in Figure 16–13. Only that one instance updates.

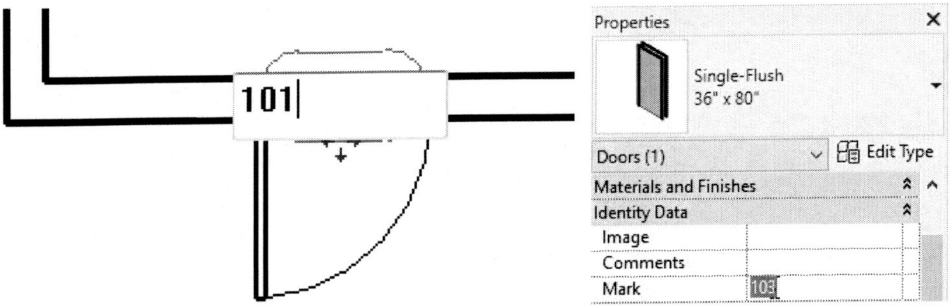

Figure 16–13

- To modify the number of a type tag, you can slowly click twice directly on the number or letter in the tag and modify it. Alternatively, you can select the element and in Properties, click (Edit Type). In the *Type Properties* dialog box, in the *Identity Data* section, modify the *Type Mark*, as shown in Figure 16–14. All instances of this element then update.

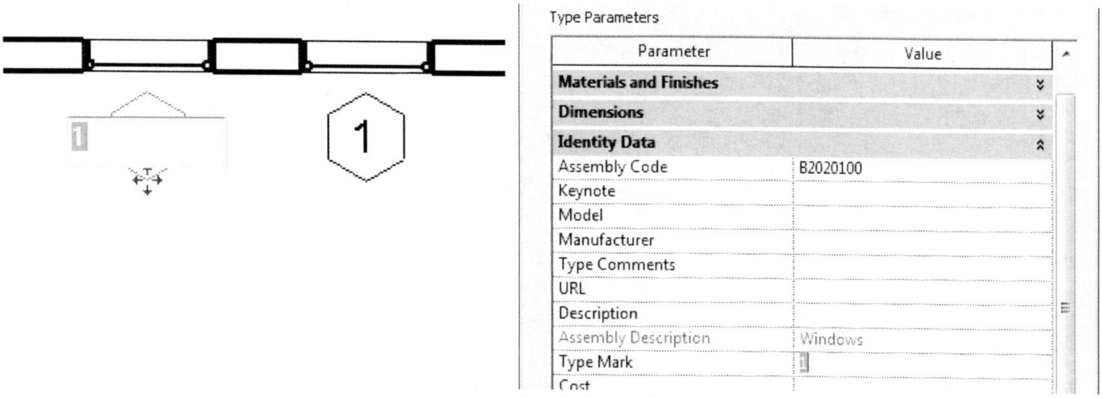

Figure 16–14

- When you change a type tag, an alert box opens to warn you that changing a type parameter affects other elements, as shown in Figure 16–15. If you want this tag to modify all other elements of this type, click **Yes**.

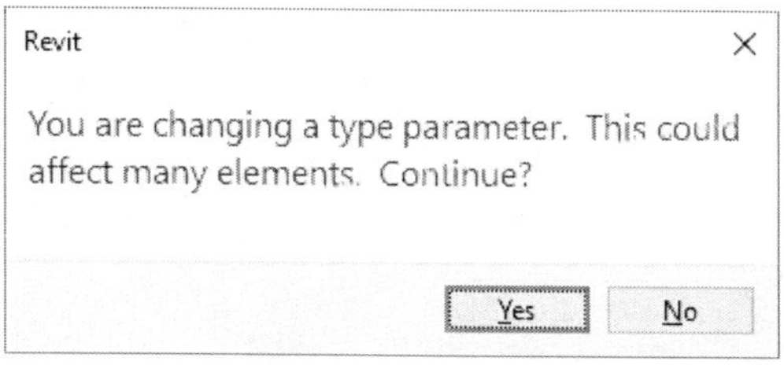

Figure 16–15

- If a tag displays with a question mark, it means that no information has been assigned to that element's parameter yet.

Tagging in 3D Views

You can add tags to isometric 3D views, as shown in Figure 16–16, as long as the views are locked first. Locking a 3D view enables you to create the view as you want it and then save it from being modified.

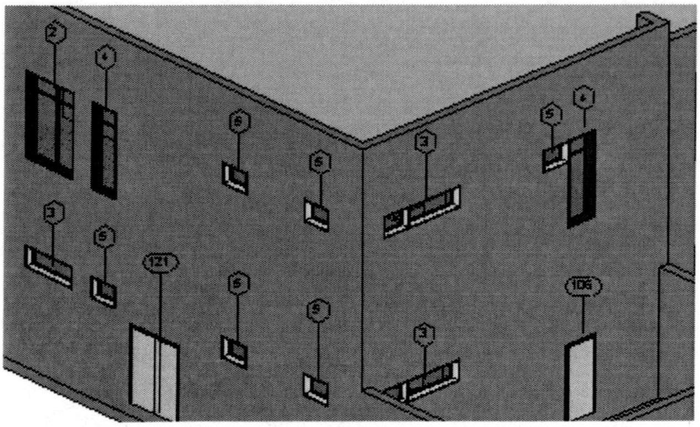

Figure 16–16

- You must lock an isometric 3D view in order to place tags. Dimensions can be added to isometric 3D views whether they are locked or not. Proceed with caution when selecting the items to dimension to ensure that the witness lines and text orient is snapping to and extending in the correct direction as intended.
- Locked views can be used with perspective views. This enables you to create the view as you want it and then save it from being modified. You cannot tag or add dimensions in a perspective view, as these are views created with the camera tool.

How To: Lock a 3D View

1. Open a 3D view and set it up as you want it to display.

   ***Note:** When adding text in a 3D view, you do not have to lock the view. When tagging in a 3D view, you have to lock the view.*

2. In the View Control Bar, click (Unlocked 3D View), then click (Save Orientation and Lock View).

- If you are using the default 3D view and it has not been saved, you are prompted to name and save the view first.
- You can modify the orientation of the view by clicking (Locked 3D View), then clicking (Unlock View). This also removes any tags you have applied.
- To return to the previous locked view, click (Unlocked 3D View), then click (Restore Orientation and Lock View).

Hint: Stair and Railing Tags

Tag by Category can be used to tag the overall stair, stair runs, landings, and railings, as shown in Figure 16–17. An additional type of tag, **Stair Tread/Riser Number**, creates a sequence of numbers for each tread or riser.

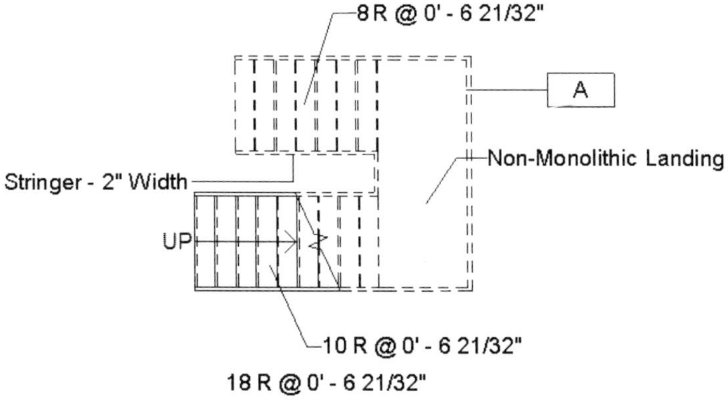

Figure 16–17

How To: Add Tread/Riser Number Tags to Stairs

1. Open a plan, elevation, or section view.
2. In the *Annotate* tab>*Tag* panel, click (Stair Tread/Riser Number).
3. In Properties, set up the *Tag Type*, *Display Rule*, and other parameters. These remain active for the project.
4. Select a reference line of a stair to place the numbers, as shown in Figure 16–18.

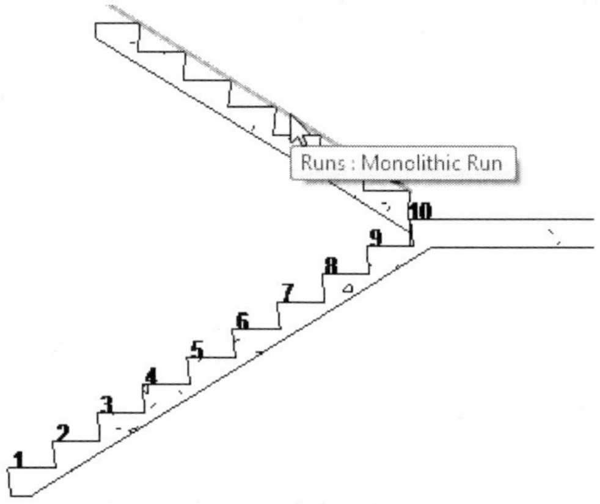

Figure 16–18

5. Continue selecting runs as needed.

Practice 16a
Add Tags

Practice Objectives

- Add tags to a model.
- Use the *Tag All Not Tagged* dialog box.
- Set the *Type Mark* parameter for tags.
- Add room tags.

In this practice, you will add wall tags in a floor plan and modify the *Type Mark* numbers for the walls. You will also tag all of the walls using the *Tag All Not Tagged* dialog box and tag the room elements in a separate view. Figure 16–19 shows the completed practice.

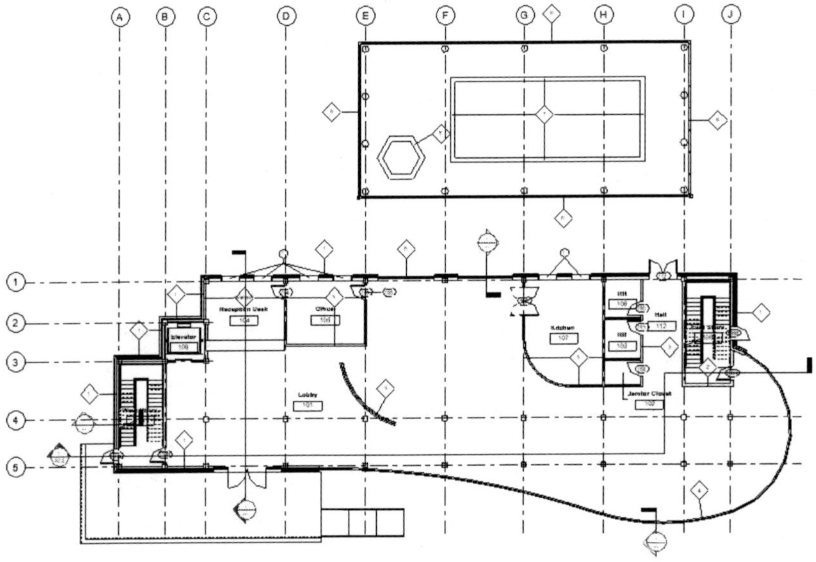

Figure 16–19

Task 1: Add tags to a floor plan.

1. Open the project **Arch-Tags.rvt** from the practice files folder.
2. Open the **Floor Plans: Floor 1** view, zoom in to the elevator and the west stairs area.
3. In the *Annotate* tab>*Tag* panel, click (Tag by Category). In Properties, select **Leader Line** and verify that *Orientation* is set to **Horizontal** and *Leader End* is set to **Attached End**.

4. Select the exterior wall of the west stairs, as shown in Figure 16–20.

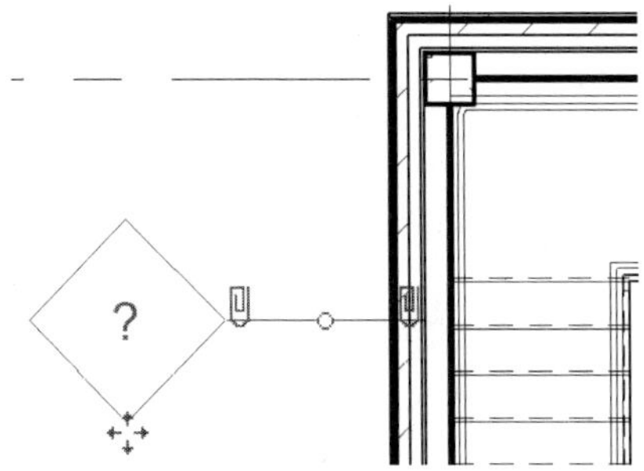

Figure 16–20

5. The tag comes in with a question mark because the wall does not have a *Type Mark* set yet. Click on the **?** in the tag, change the tag number to **1**, and press <Enter>.
6. When alerted that you are changing a type parameter, click **Yes** to continue.
7. You are still in the **Tag** command. Add a tag to the horizontal exterior wall above the stairs. This time, the tag number 1 comes in automatically as it is the same wall type as the first one, as shown in Figure 16–21.

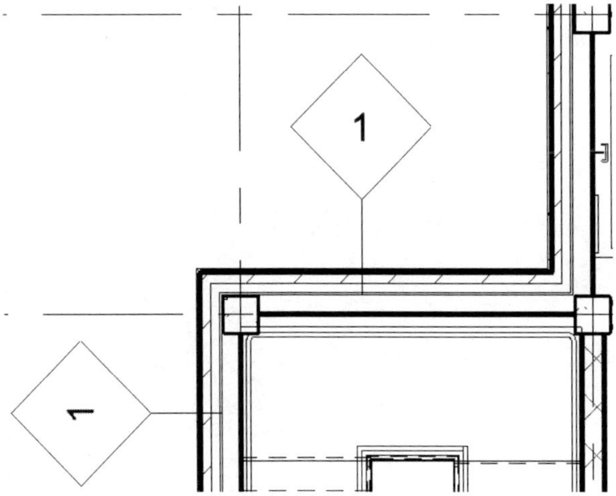

Figure 16–21

8. Click (Modify).
9. Select the interior wall dividing the stairs from the lobby.
10. In Properties, click (Edit Type).

11. In the *Type Properties* dialog box, in *Identity Data* section, set *Type Mark* to **2**, as shown in Figure 16–22. Click **OK**.

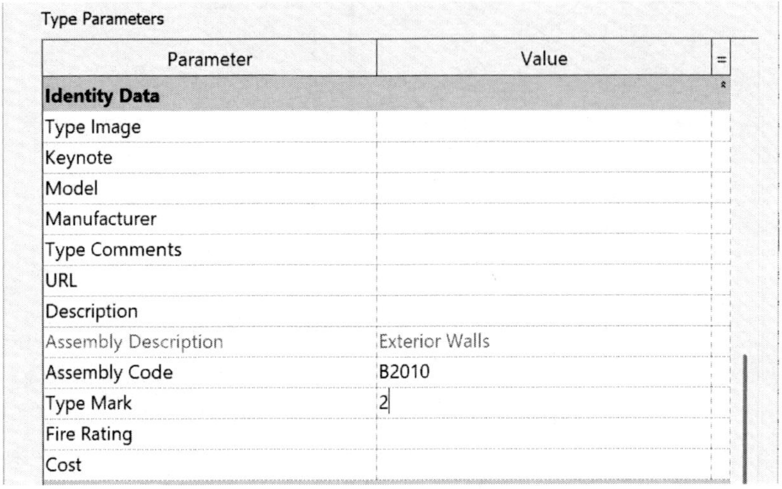

Figure 16–22

12. Select one of the interior partition walls in the office and set the *Type Mark* to **3**.
13. Click (Modify).
14. Select the wall tag that is above the stairs.
15. In the *Modify | Wall Tags* tab>*Leaders* panel, verify (Show All Leaders) is selected and (Merge Leaders) is toggled off, as shown in Figure 16–23. In the *Host* panel, click (Add/Remove Host).

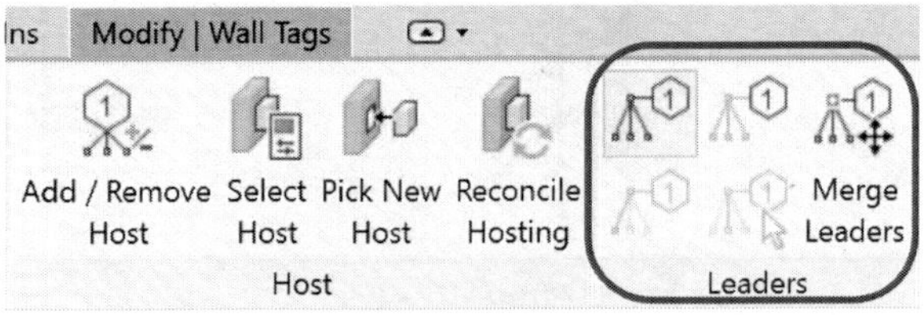

Figure 16–23

16. Select the wall that is to the right of the tag. A leader is added, as shown in Figure 16–24.

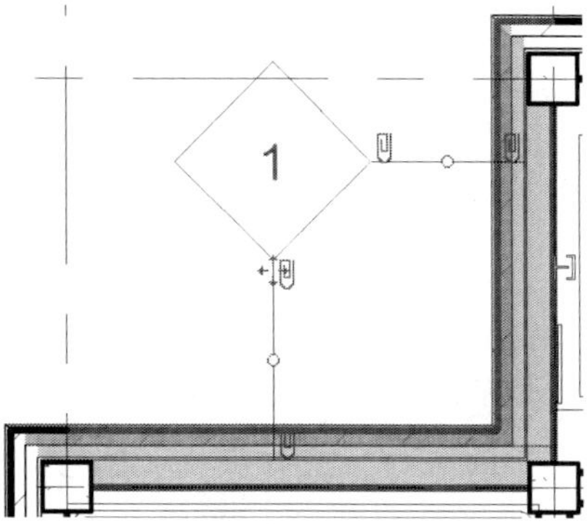

Figure 16–24

17. Click (Modify) twice.

18. Start the (Tag by Category) command and continue tagging the walls, using the **Add/ Remove Host** tool as needed.

- Note that when tagging a partition wall type, the type mark displays as set in the *Type Properties* dialog box. If you select two different walls, the tag will display **Varies** because there are two different wall types.

19. Save the project.

Task 2: Add room tags.

1. Open the **Floor Plans: Floor 1 - Furniture Plan** view.
2. In the Status Bar, click (Select Elements by Face) to toggle it off. The icon should have a red X ( ) when it is off.

3. Hover the cursor over the open area inside the front entrance until you see the room element, as shown in Figure 16–25. The room elements do not display in this view but are available.

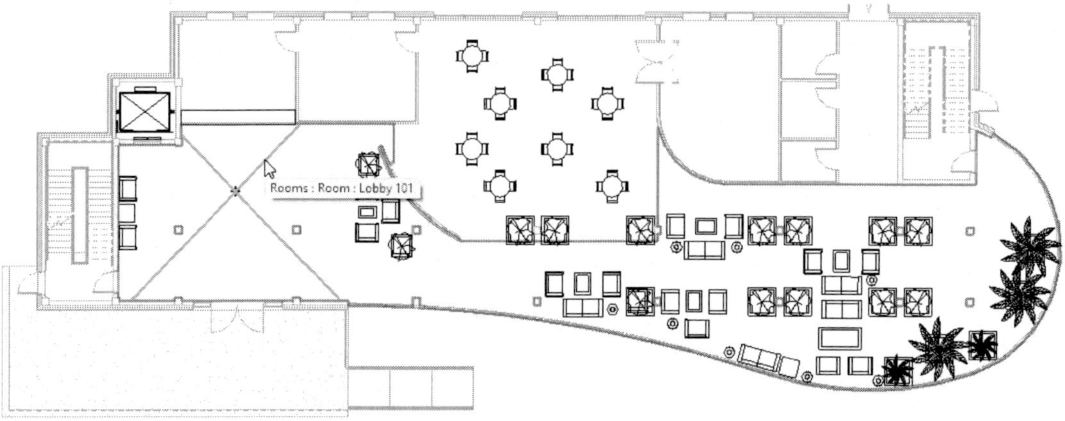

Figure 16–25

4. In the *Annotate* tab>*Tag* panel, click (Tag by Category). Note that you cannot tag rooms using **Tag by Category**.
5. Click (Modify).
6. In the *Annotate* tab>*Tag* panel, click (Room Tag). The room elements display. Place tags in the lobby, reception desk, and office, as shown in Figure 16–26.

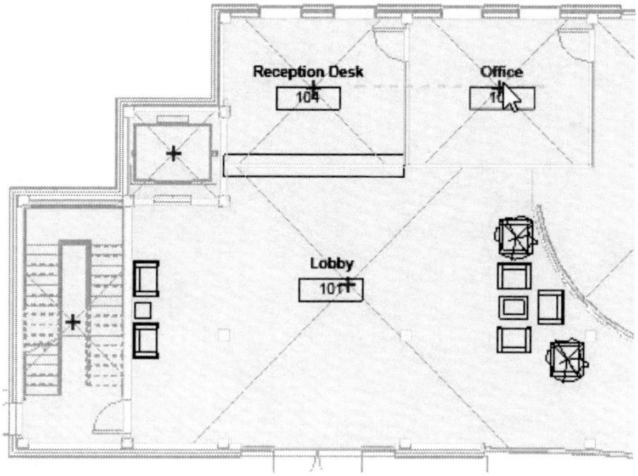

Figure 16–26

7. Click (Modify).
8. In the *Annotate* tab>*Tag* panel, click (Tag All).
9. In the *Tag All Not Tagged* dialog box, select the checkbox next to **Rooms** and click **OK**. Room tags are added to all of the rooms in the view that did not already have a tag.

10. Zoom in on the west stairs and move the tag outside the wall. A leader is automatically added to the room tag, as shown in Figure 16–27.

    Note: *Your room numbering may be different from the figure.*

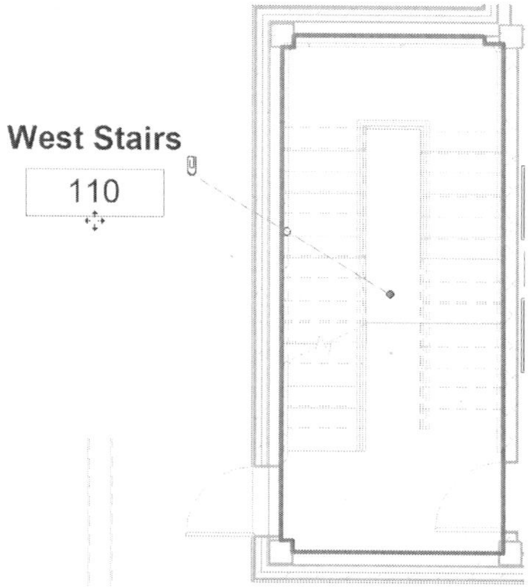

Figure 16–27

11. Click (Modify). Adjust the leader line as needed.
12. In the Status Bar, click (Select Elements by Face) to toggle it back on. The icon should not have a red X ( ) when it is on.
13. Save and close the project.

End of practice

16.2 Working with Schedules

Revit enables you to quickly create accurate schedules that can otherwise be time-consuming and difficult to maintain accurately throughout the lifecycle of a project. Schedules extract information from a project and display it in table form. Each schedule is stored as a separate view and can be placed on sheets, as shown in Figure 16–28. Any changes you make to the project elements that affect the schedules are automatically updated in both views and sheets.

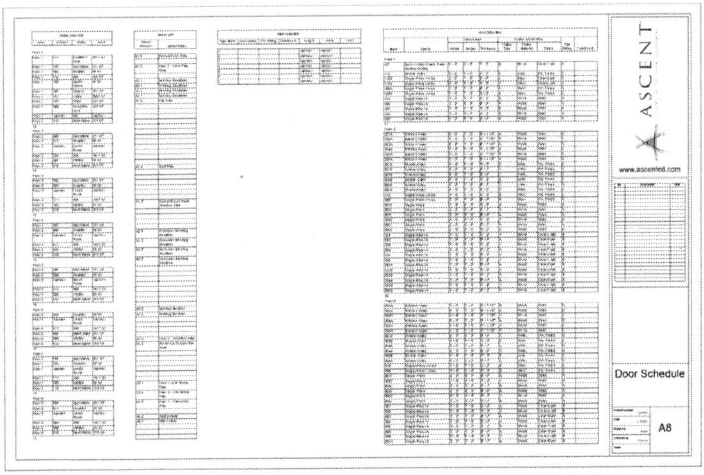

Figure 16–28

- Some of the default Revit templates have schedules included in them. For example the **Imperial Multi-discipline.rte** template file includes useful schedules. If there are no schedules in a project, you can create one of the following types of schedules:
  - (Schedule/Quantities) allows you to create building component schedules of elements in your project.
  - (Graphical Column Schedule) allows you to create a schedule for specific columns or all columns in the project including off-grid columns.
- Schedules can be created in templates so that they can be reused in multiple projects.
- You are not required to have actual elements in the model when you are creating schedules. You can schedule information that model elements contain.
- All properties that are stored in the model elements, as well as those specified by the user, can be added to schedules.

Building Component Schedules

A building component schedule is a table view of the type and instance parameters of a specific element. You can specify the parameters (fields) you want to include in the schedule. All of the parameters found in the type of element you are scheduling are available for use.

- Schedules are automatically filled out with the information stored in the instance and type parameters of related elements that are added to the model. Fill out additional information either in the schedule or in Properties.
- When selecting on a schedule's row, it will highlight in blue.
- You can drag and drop the schedule onto a sheet.
- You can zoom in to read small text in schedule views. Hold down <Ctrl> and scroll using the mouse wheel or press <Ctrl>+<+> to zoom in or <Ctrl>+<-> to zoom out.

How To: Create a Schedule

1. In the *View* tab>*Create* panel, expand (Schedules) and click (Schedule/Quantities), or in the Project Browser, right-click on *Schedules/Quantities (all)* and select **New Schedule/ Quantities...**.
2. In the *New Schedule* dialog box, select the type of schedule you want to create (e.g., Doors) from the *Category* list, as shown in Figure 16–29.

   Note: *In the Filter list drop-down list, you can specify the discipline(s) to show only the categories that you want to display.*

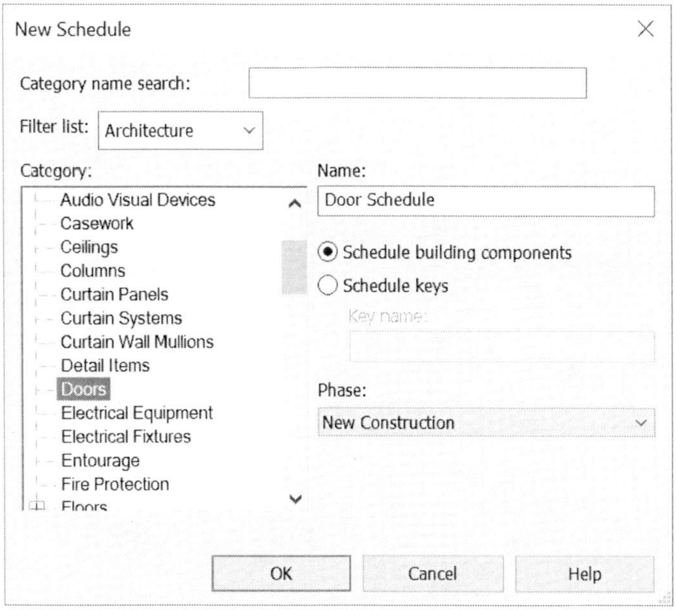

Figure 16–29

3. Revit assigns a name for the schedule. You can also type a new *Name* if the default does not suit.
4. If applicable, select *Schedule building components* and specify the *Phase*.
5. Click **OK**.

6. Fill out the information in the *Schedule Properties* dialog box. This includes the information in the *Fields*, *Filter*, *Sorting/Grouping*, *Formatting*, and *Appearance* tabs.
7. Once you have entered the schedule properties, click **OK**. A schedule view is created, displaying a report of the information configured in the schedule.

- Other elements that can be scheduled include model groups and Revit links.
- If a schedule is long, in the *Modify Schedule/Quantities* tab>*Appearance* panel, you can select  (Freeze Header) to keep the header row visible while you scroll through the schedule.

Schedule Properties – Fields Tab

In the *Fields* tab, you can select from a list of available fields and organize them in the order in which you want them to display in the schedule, as shown in Figure 16–30. You can also sort the available fields by *Parameter Type* (such as Project Parameters), *Discipline*, or *Value Type*.

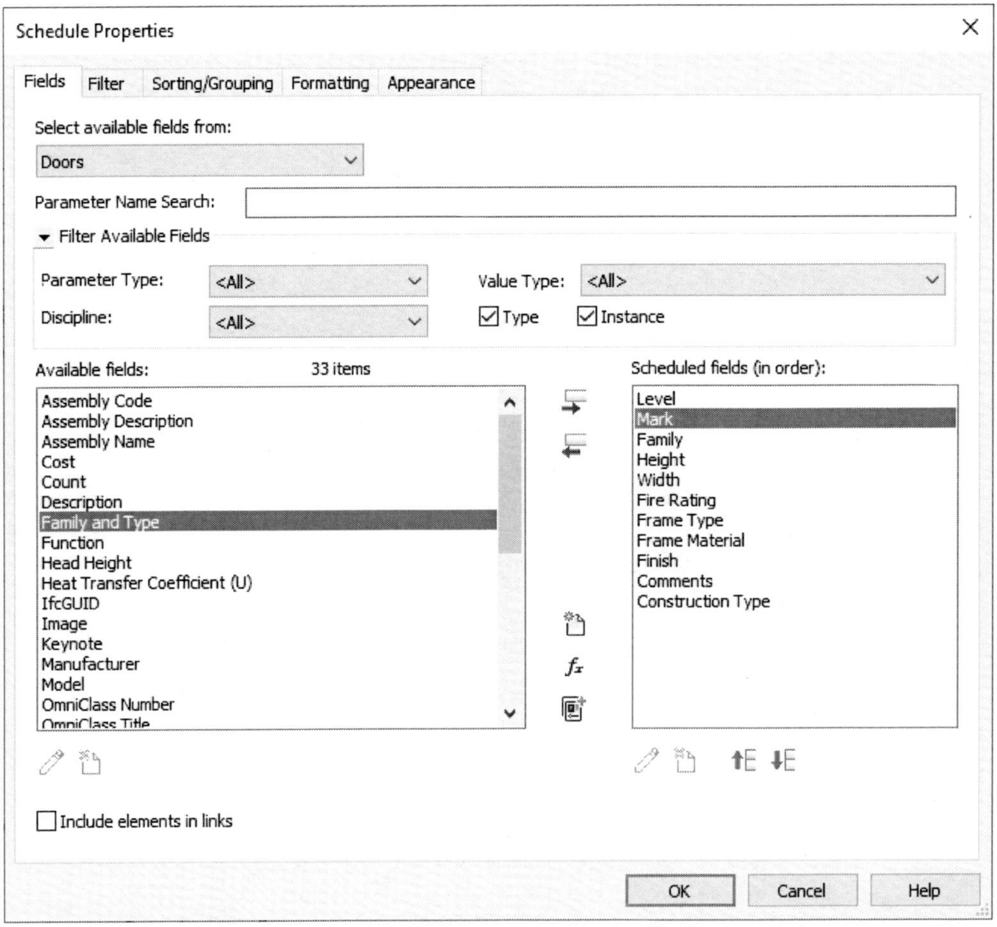

Figure 16–30

How To: Fill Out the Fields Tab

1. In the *Available fields* area, select one or more fields you want to add to the schedule and click (Add parameter(s)). The field(s) are placed in the *Scheduled fields (in order)* area.
2. Continue adding fields, as required.
   - Click (Remove parameter(s)) to move a field from the *Scheduled fields* area back to the *Available fields* area.

   Note: *You can also double-click on a field to move it from the Available fields area to the Scheduled fields area, and double-click on a field to remove it from the Scheduled fields area.*

   - Use (Move parameter up) and (Move parameter down) to change the order of the scheduled fields.

Other Fields Tab Options

Select available fields from	Enables you to select additional category fields for the specified schedule. The available list of fields depends on the original category of the schedule. Typically, they include room information.
Include elements in links	Includes elements that are in files linked to the current project, so that their elements can be included in the schedule.
(New parameter)	Adds a new field according to your specification. New fields can be placed by instance or by type.
(Add Parameter(s) from Service)	Import defined shared parameters from a project in Autodesk Forma.
(Add Calculated parameter)	Enables you to create a field that uses a formula based on other fields.
(Combine parameters)	Enables you to combine two or more parameters in one column.You can put any fields together even if they are used in another column.
(Edit parameter)	Enables you to edit custom fields. This is grayed out if you select a standard field.
(Delete parameter)	Deletes the selected custom fields. This is grayed out if you select a standard field.

Schedule Properties – Filter Tab

In the *Filter* tab, you can set up filters so that only elements meeting specific criteria are included in the schedule. For example, you might only want to show information for one level, as shown in Figure 16–31. You can create filters for up to eight values. All values must be satisfied for the elements to display.

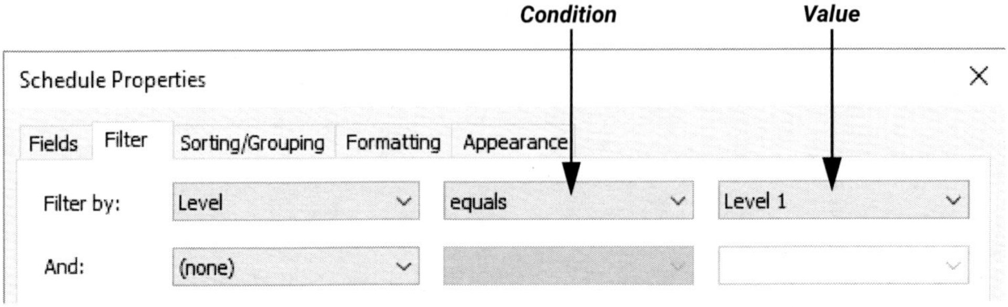

Figure 16–31

- The parameter you want to use as a filter must be included in the schedule on the *Fields* tab. You can hide the parameter once you have completed the schedule, if needed.

Filter by	
Field/Parameter	Specifies the field/parameter to filter. Not all fields/parameters are available to be used to filter.
Condition	Specifies the condition that must be met. This includes options such as **equal**, **not equal**, **greater than**, and **less than**.
Value	Specifies the value of the element to be filtered. You can select from a drop-down list of appropriate values. For example, if you set *Filter by* to **Level**, it displays the list of levels in the project.

Schedule Properties – Sorting/Grouping Tab

In the *Sorting/Grouping* tab, you can set how you want the information to be sorted, as shown in Figure 16–32. For example, you can sort by **Mark** (number) and then **Type**.

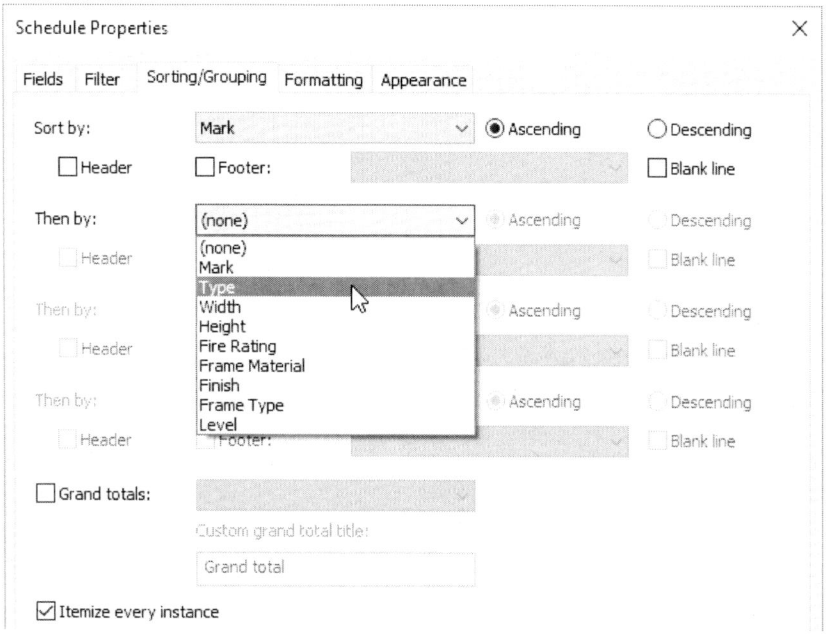

Figure 16–32

Sort by	Enables you to select the field(s) you want to sort by. You can select up to four levels of sorting.
Ascending/ Descending	Sorts fields in **Ascending** or **Descending** order based on an alphanumeric system.
Header/Footer	Enables you to group similar information and separate it by a **Header** with a title and/or a **Footer** with quantity information.
Blank line	Adds a blank line between groups.
Grand totals	Selects which totals to display for the entire schedule. You can specify a name to display in the schedule for the grand total.
Itemize every instance	If selected, displays each instance of the element in the schedule. If not selected, displays only one instance of each type based on the sorting/ grouping categories, as shown in Figure 16–33.

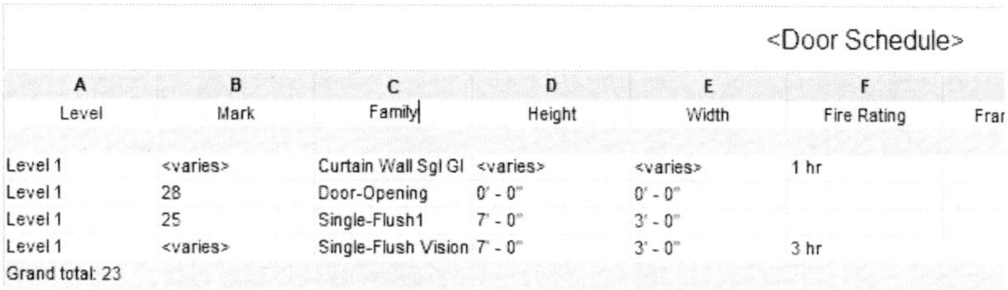

Figure 16–33

Schedule Properties – Formatting Tab

In the *Formatting* tab, you can control how the headers of each field display, as shown in Figure 16–34. The *Multiple values indication* options enable you to control how fields with multiple values display.

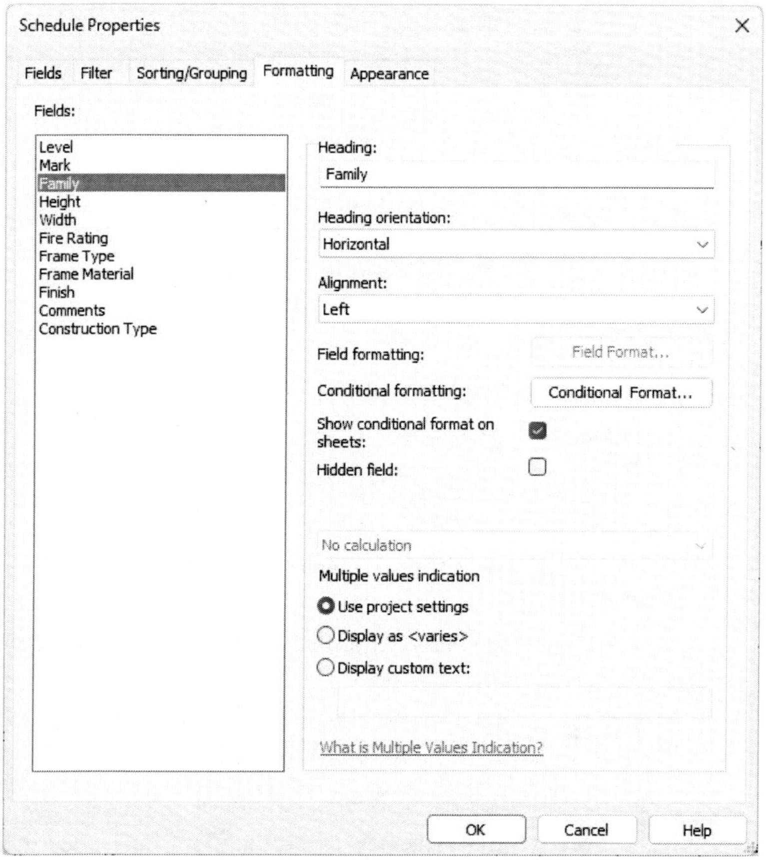

Figure 16–34

Fields	Enables you to select the field for which you want to modify the formatting.
Heading	Enables you to change the heading of the field if you want it to be different from the field name. For example, you might want to replace **Mark** (a generic name) with the more specific **Door Number** in a door schedule.
Heading orientation	Enables you to set the heading on sheets to **Horizontal** or **Vertical**. This does not impact the schedule view.
Alignment	Aligns the text in rows under the heading to be **Left**, **Right**, or **Center** justified.
Field Format...	Sets the units format for numerical fields, e.g., length, area, HVAC air flow, pipe flow, etc. By default, this is set to use the project settings.
Conditional Format...	Sets up the schedule to display visual feedback based on the conditions listed.
Hidden field	Enables you to hide a field. For example, you might want to use a field for sorting purposes, but not have it display in the schedule. You can also modify this option in the schedule view later.
Show conditional format on sheets	Select if you want the color code set up in the *Conditional Format* dialog box to display on sheets.
Calculation options	Select the type of calculation you want to use. • **No Calculation:** All values in a field are calculated separately. • **Calculate totals:** All values in a field are added together. This enables a field to calculate and display in the Grand Totals or Footers. • **Calculate minimum:** Only the smallest amount displays. • **Calculate maximum:** Only the largest amount displays. • **Calculate minimum and maximum:** Both the smallest and largest amounts display. Minimum and maximum calculations only show when **Itemize every instance** is unchecked in the *Sorting/Grouping* tab.
Multiple values indication	When a schedule is not set to itemize every instance, select how the value will display.

Hint: Hiding Columns

If you want to use the field to filter or sort, but do not want it to display in the schedule, select **Hidden field**. Alternatively, once the schedule is completed, select the column header, right-click on it, and select **Hide Columns**.

Schedule Properties – Appearance Tab

In the *Appearance* tab, you can set the text style and grid options for a schedule, as shown in Figure 16–35.

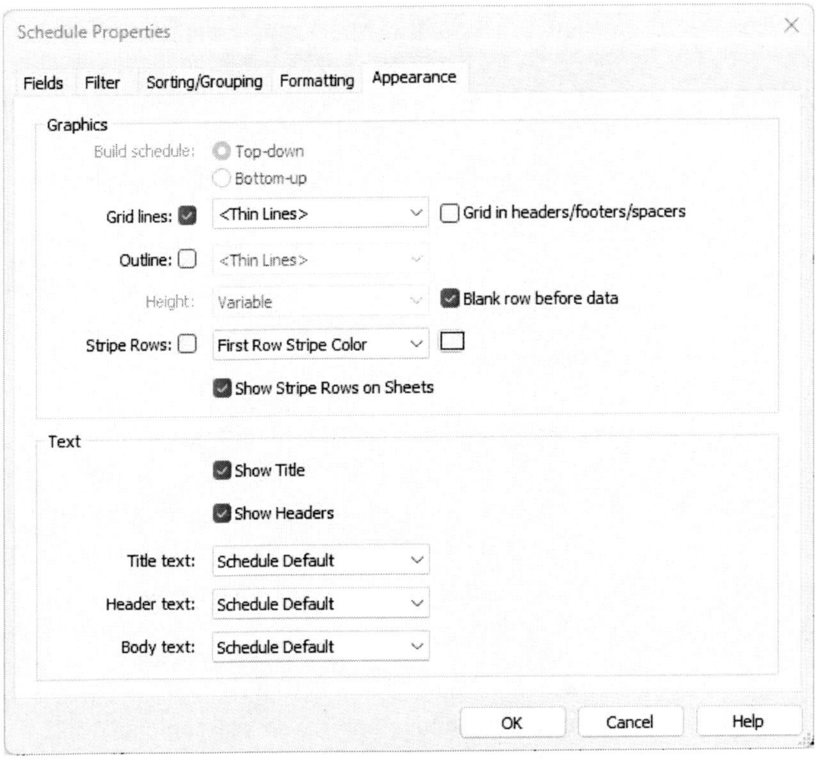

Figure 16–35

Grid lines	Displays lines between each instance listed and around the outside of the schedule. Select the style of lines from the drop-down list; this controls all lines for the schedule, unless modified.
Grid in headers/footers/ spacers	Extends the vertical grid lines between the columns.
Outline	Specify a different line type for the outline of the schedule.
Blank row before data	Select this option if you want a blank row to be displayed before the data begins in the schedule.
Stripe Rows	Select this option if you want to highlight alternating rows within the schedule to help differentiate the rows in large schedules.
Show Title/Show Headers	Select these options to include the text in the schedule.
Title text/Header text/ Body text	Select the text style for the title, header, and body text.

Schedule View Properties

Schedule views have properties, including the *View Template, View Name*, *Phases*, and methods of returning to the *Schedule Properties* dialog box (as shown in Figure 16–36). In the *Other* section, click the button next to the tab name that you want to open in the *Schedule Properties* dialog box. In the dialog box, you can switch from tab to tab and make any required changes to the overall schedule.

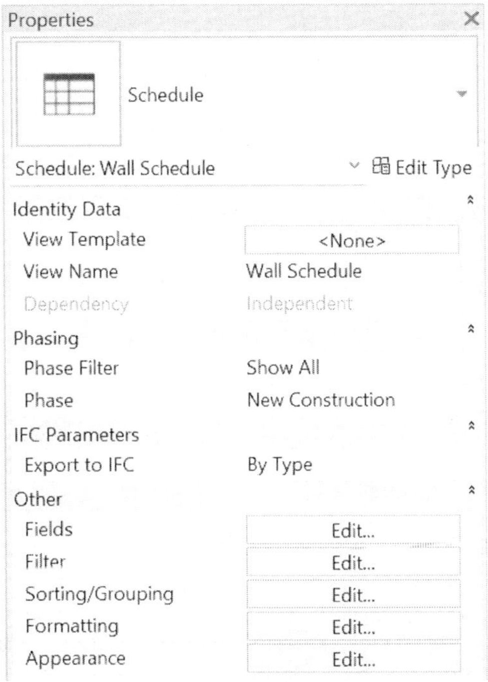

Figure 16–36

Just like other views, schedules can have view templates applied. When you specify a view template directly in the view, none of the schedule properties can be modified, as shown in Figure 16–37.

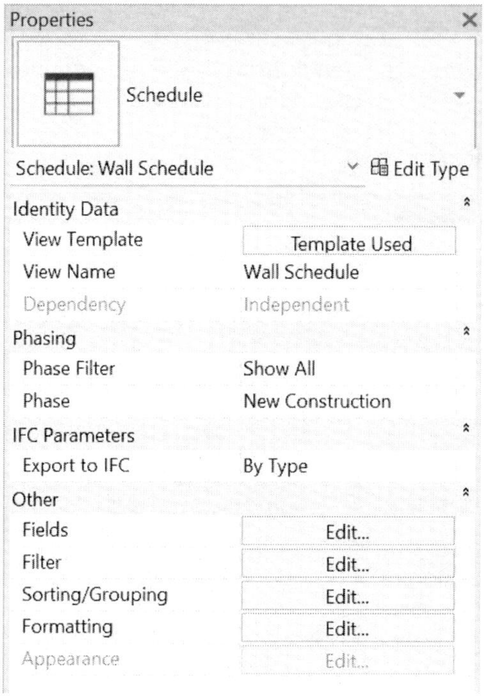

Figure 16–37

- Schedule view templates are type-specific. If you apply one to a different type of element, only the *Appearance* information is applied.
- If you apply a schedule view template to a schedule of the same type, it overrides everything in the existing schedule, including the fields.
- If you have a complicated schedule, you might want to create a view template for it to avoid losing that organization.
- To create schedule view templates, you need to create at least one from an existing view, then you can modify it and duplicate it in the *View Templates* dialog box.

Filtering Elements from Schedules

When you create schedules based on a category, you might need to filter out some of the element types in that category. For example, in Revit, doors (and windows) in curtain walls are automatically added to a door schedule, as shown at the top in Figure 16–38, but are typically estimated as part of the curtain wall rather than as a separate door. To remove them from the schedule, as shown at the bottom in Figure 16–38, assign a parameter that identifies them and then use that parameter to filter them out of the schedule.

Curtain wall doors displayed

Door Schedule- 1st

Door Type	Door Size			Frame		
	Width	Height	Thickness	Frame Type	Frame Material	Head Detail
	8' - 3 1/2"	9' - 4 1/4"				
	3' - 0"	7' - 0"	0' - 2"	A	Aluminum	
	3' - 0"	7' - 0"	0' - 2"	B	Aluminum	
	3' - 0"	6' - 8"	0' - 2"	C	Aluminum	

Curtain wall doors filtered out

Door Schedule- 1st

Door Type	Door Size			Frame		
	Width	Height	Thickness	Frame Type	Frame Material	Head Detail
	3' - 0"	7' - 0"	0' - 2"	A	Aluminum	
	3' - 0"	7' - 0"	0' - 2"	B	Aluminum	
	3' - 0"	6' - 8"	0' - 2"	C	Aluminum	
	3' - 0"	6' - 8"	0' - 2"	C	Aluminum	

Figure 16–38

- This type of filtering can be used for any schedule in any discipline.

How To: Filter Elements in a Schedule

1. Select an element (such as a door used in curtain walls) and modify the *Type Parameters*. Add a value to one of the parameters that you are not otherwise using in your schedule. For example, you could set *Construction Type* to **CW**, as shown Figure 16–39.

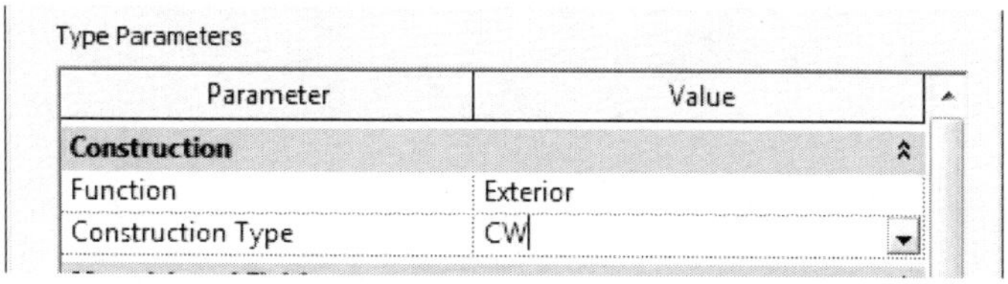

Figure 16–39

2. Create a schedule and include the field for the parameter you used (such as *Construction Type* in the above example).

3. Modify the *Filter* of the schedule so that the parameter does not equal the specified value. In the example shown in Figure 16–40, the filter is set so **Construction Type** > **does not equal** > **CW**. Any types that match this filter are excluded from the schedule.

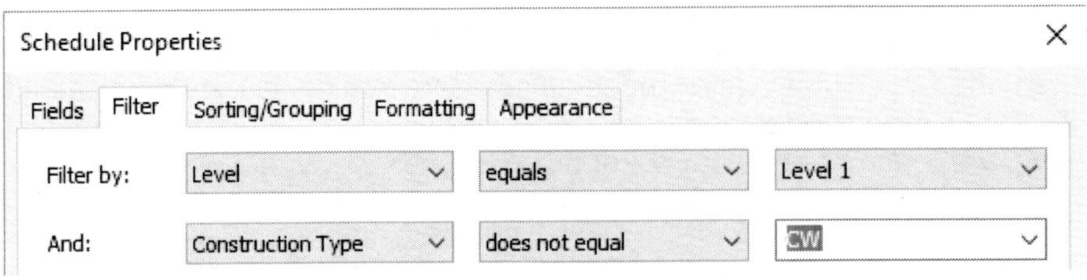

Figure 16–40

4. In the final schedule, the elements display with the specified value. Right-click on the column header for the parameter you used to filter the schedule and select **Hide Columns**. It is just used as a filter and does not need to be part of the final schedule.

Note: *Hiding a parameter/field in a schedule enables you to use it as a filter, but not have it visible in the schedule.*

Modifying Schedules

Information in schedules is bi-directional:

- Make changes to elements and the schedule automatically updates.
- Make changes to information in the schedule cells and the elements automatically update.

How To: Modify Schedule Cells

1. Open the schedule view.
2. Select the cell you want to change. Some cells have drop-down lists, as shown in Figure 16–41. Others have edit fields.

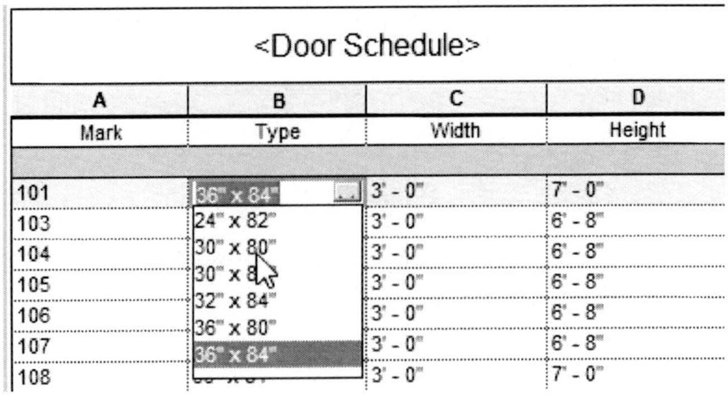

Figure 16–41

3. Add the new information. The change is reflected in the schedule, on the sheet, and in the elements of the project.

- If you change a type property, an alert box opens, as shown in Figure 16–42.

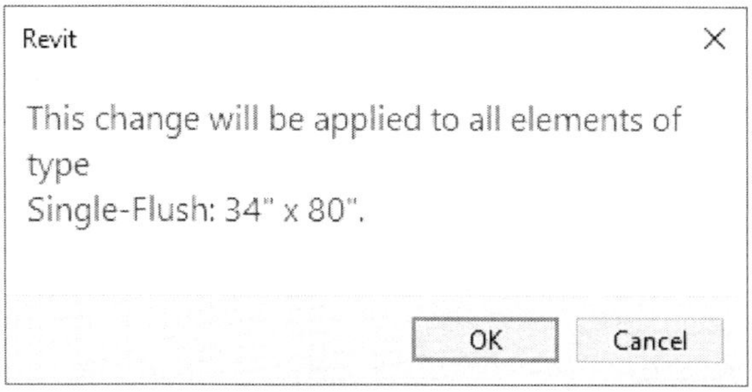

Figure 16–42

> ***Note:*** *If you change a type property in the schedule, it applies to all elements of that type. If you change an instance property, it only applies to that one element.*

- When you select an element in a schedule, in the *Modify Schedule/Quantities* tab>*Element* panel, you can click (Highlight in Model). This opens a close-up view of the element with the *Show Element(s) in View* dialog box, as shown in Figure 16–43. Click **Show** to display more views of the element. Click **Close** to finish the command.

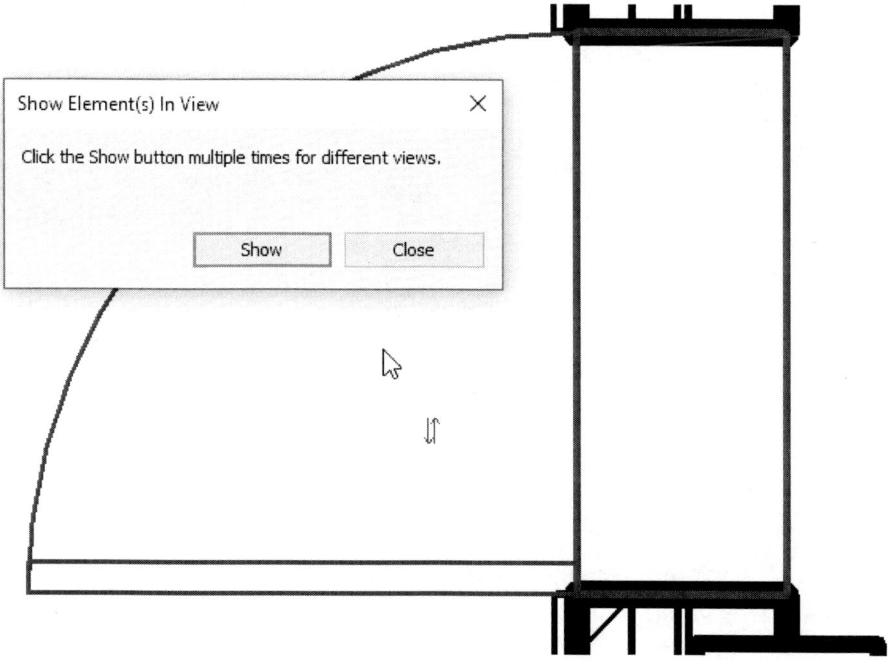

Figure 16–43

Hint: Customizing Schedules

Schedules are typically included in project templates, which are set up by the BIM manager or other advanced users. They can be complex to create as there are many options.

- For more information about creating schedules, refer to the ASCENT guide *Autodesk Revit BIM Management: Template and Family Creation*.

Modifying a Schedule on a Sheet

Once you have placed a schedule on a sheet, you can manipulate it to fit the information into the available space. Select the schedule to display the controls that enable you to modify it, as shown in Figure 16–44.

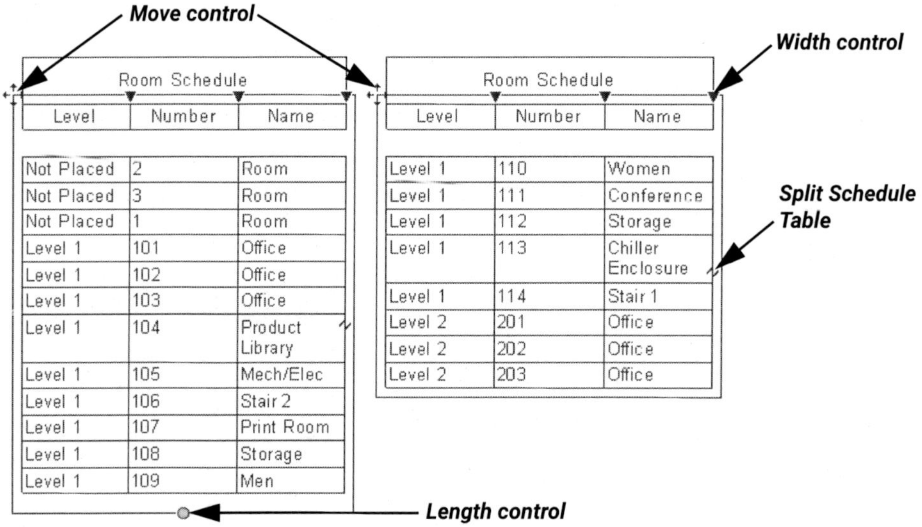

Figure 16–44

- The blue triangles modify the width of each column.
- The break mark splits the schedule into two parts.
- In a split schedule, you can use the arrows in the upper-left corner to move that portion of the schedule table. The control at the bottom of the first table changes the length of the table and impacts any connected splits.
- To unsplit a schedule, drag the Move control from the side of the schedule that you want to unsplit back to the original column.

Splitting a Schedule Across Multiple Sheets

When a schedule becomes too long, you need to be able to split it and place it on multiple sheets. You can split a schedule evenly or by setting a custom height. When a schedule has been split, you can expand **Schedules/Quantities (all)** in the Project Browser to see the segments of the schedule, as shown in Figure 16–45.

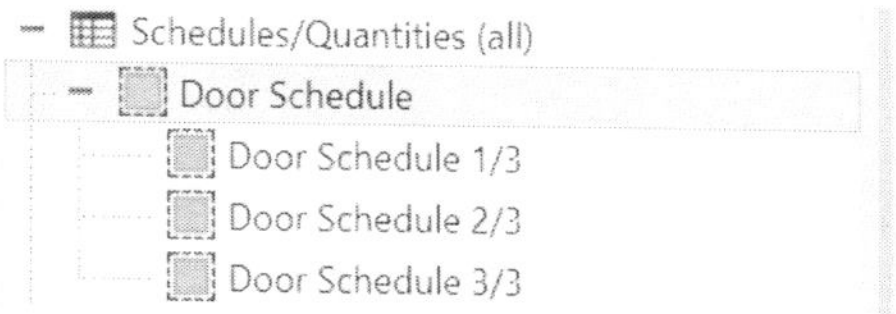

Figure 16–45

If the split is not what you wanted, you can delete the segmented schedules from the Project Browser. Do not delete the main schedule.

How To: Split a Schedule and Place It on Multiple Sheets

1. Make additional sheets, if needed. In a schedule view, in the *Modify Schedule/Quantities* tab>*Split* panel, click (Split & Place).
2. In the *Split Schedule and Place on Sheets* dialog box, select the sheets that you want to distribute the split schedule to, as shown in Figure 16–46.

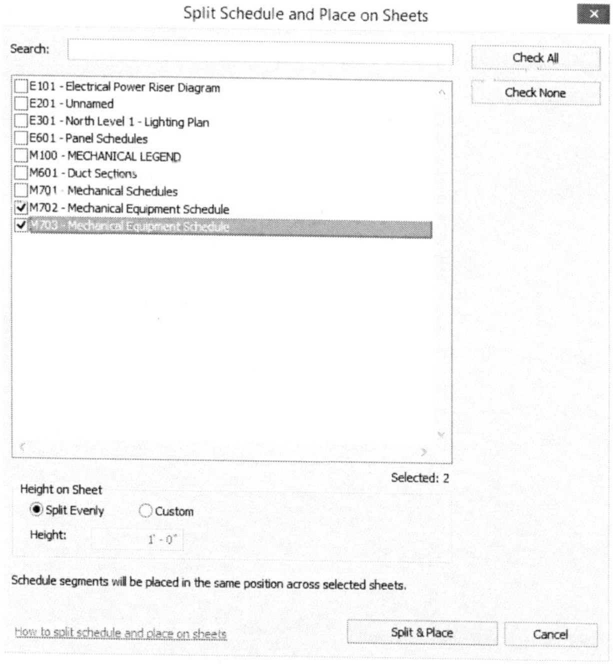

Figure 16–46

3. In the *Height on Sheet* section, select **Split Evenly** or **Custom**. If custom is selected, specify a *Height*.
4. Click **Split & Place**.
5. The first sheet selected in the list opens and the first segment of the split schedule is attached to your cursor. Place it on the sheet.
6. If you had selected multiple sheets in the *Split Schedule and Place on Sheets* dialog box, the rest of the segment schedule will automatically be placed exactly where you had initially placed the first segment of the schedule.
7. Open each sheet and use the control grips to adjust the columns and stretch the schedule to fit the sheet, as needed.

How To: Remove Split Schedules

1. In the Project Browser, expand the schedule.
2. Select the segmented schedules and press <Delete>, or right-click and select **Delete**.

Filtering by Sheet

If you place your schedule on a sheet that has a view on it, you can filter the schedule to only display the elements that are in that viewport. In Figure 16–47, the door schedule is only showing Floor 1 doors because the sheet contains the **Floor 1 - Plan** view and the **Filter by sheet** option has been selected.

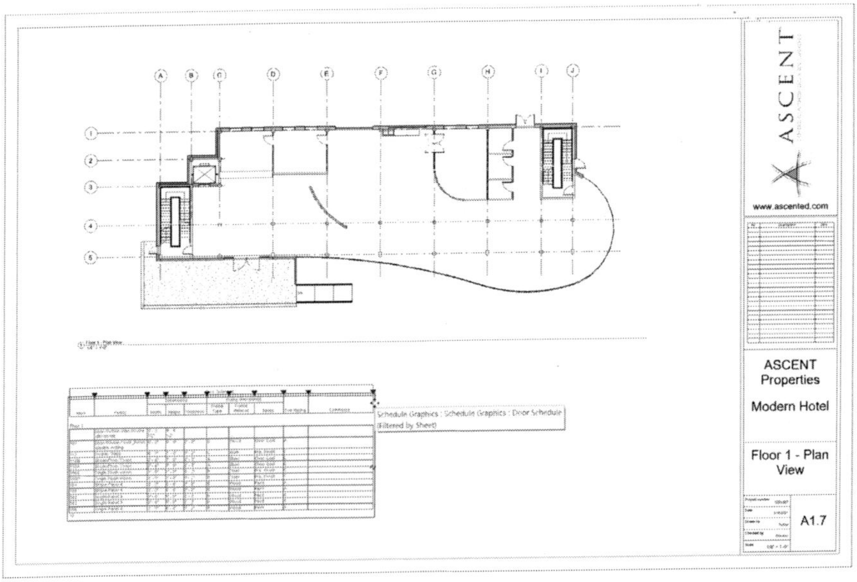

Figure 16–47

- If a view is changed or modified, the schedule and the same sheet will update accordingly.
- Schedules that are split across multiple sheets cannot use the **Filter by sheet** option.
- Panel and revision schedules cannot use the **Filter by sheet** option.

How To: Filter a Schedule by Sheets

1. Open a schedule view.
2. In Properties, click **Edit...** next to *Filter*.
3. In the *Schedule Properties* dialog box, check the checkbox for **Filter by sheet**, as shown in Figure 16–48.

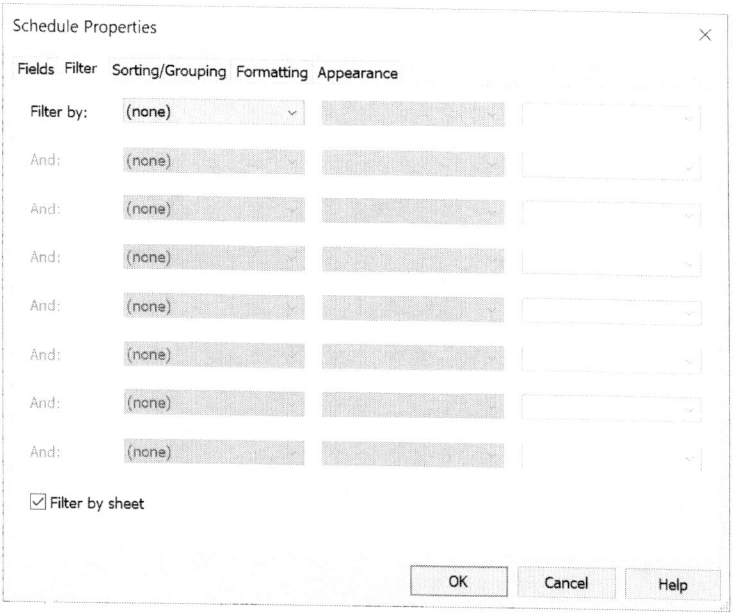

Figure 16–48

4. Click **OK**.
   - You cannot use this feature if you have split the schedule.

Practice 16b
Work with Schedules

Practice Objectives

- Update schedule information.
- Split a schedule and add it to multiple sheets.
- Add a schedule to a sheet.

In this practice, you will add information to a door schedule and to elements that are connected to the schedule. You will then place the schedule on a sheet, as shown in Figure 16–49.

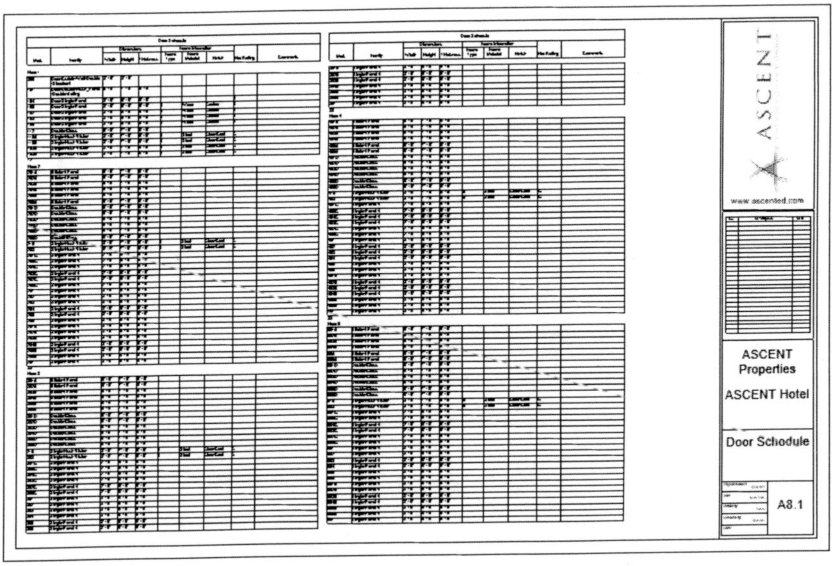

Figure 16–49

Task 1: Fill in schedules.

1. Open the project **Arch-Schedule.rvt** from the practice files folder.
2. Verify that you are in the **Floor Plans: Floor 1** view.
3. In the Project Browser, expand *Schedules/Quantities*. There are existing schedules in this project.

4. Double-click on **Door Schedule** to open it. The existing doors in the project are already populated with some of the basic information included with the door, as shown in Figure 16–50. Note that the doors are divided up into floors.

<Door Schedule>								
A	B	C	D	E	F	G	H	I
		Dimensions				Fram Information		
Mark	Door Type	Width	Height	Thickness	Frame Type	Frame Material	Finish	Fire Rating
Floor 1								
107	Door-Double-Flush_Panel-Double-Acting	6' - 0"	6' - 8"	0' - 2"				
104	Door-Single-Panel	3' - 0"	6' - 8"	0' - 2"				
105	Door-Single-Panel	3' - 0"	6' - 8"	0' - 2"				
102	Door-Single-Panel	3' - 0"	6' - 8"	0' - 2"				
103	Door-Single-Panel	3' - 0"	6' - 8"	0' - 2"				
106	Door-Single-Panel	3' - 0"	6' - 8"	0' - 2"				
112	Double-Glass	6' - 0"	7' - 0"	0' - 2"				
110B	Single-Flush Vision	3' - 0"	7' - 0"	0' - 2"				
110A	Single-Flush Vision	3' - 0"	7' - 0"	0' - 2"				
108A	Single-Flush Vision	3' - 0"	7' - 0"	0' - 2"				
108B	Single-Flush Vision	3' - 0"	7' - 0"	0' - 2"				

Figure 16–50

5. Close any other views that are open so the **Door Schedule** is the only view open.
6. In the *Mark* column, select **105**.
7. In the *Modify Schedule/Quantities* tab>*Element* panel, click (Highlight in Model).
8. Click **OK** to search in views to find the highlighted elements. In the *Show Element(s) In View* dialog box, click **Show** if you do not see a plan view of the door. If the view displays the door in a plan view, as shown in Figure 16–51, click **Close**.

Note: *The door that is found may or may not have a tag like the one shown in Figure 16–51.*

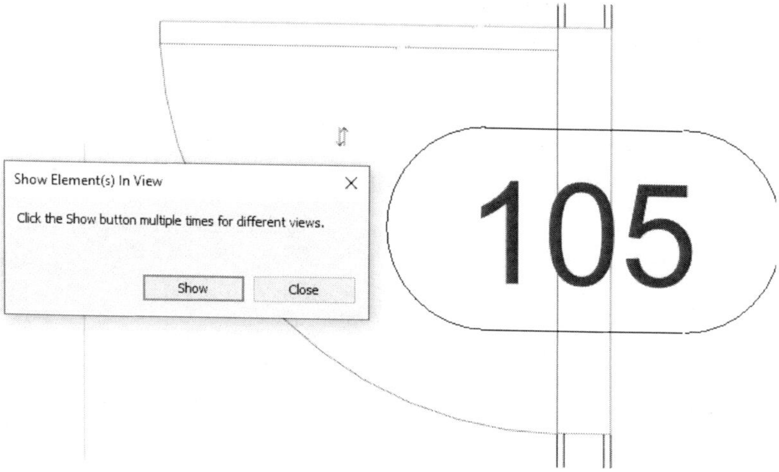

Figure 16–51

9. The door is still selected. In Properties, set the following:
   - *Frame Type:* **B**
   - *Frame Material:* **Wood**
   - *Finish:* **Coated**
10. Click (Edit Type).
11. In the *Type Properties* dialog box, in the *Identity Data* section, set the *Fire Rating* to **A**.
12. Click **OK** to finish.
13. Click (Modify).
14. Click the *Door Schedule* tab to switch to that view.
15. Note that the *Frame Type, Frame Material,* and *Finish* display for one door and the matching exterior doors have just the *Fire Rating*.

    Note: *The Frame Type and Frame Material did not populate on similar door types because the information you changed was in the element's instance property, whereas the Fire Rating change was the element's type property so it changes for all similar door types.*

16. In the **Door Schedule** view, for the *Frame Type, Frame Material*, and *Finish*, use the drop-down lists to change the options for the matching doors, as shown in Figure 16–52.

107	Door-Double-Flush_Panel-Double-Acting	6' - 0"	6' - 8"	0' - 2"				
104	Door-Single-Panel	3' - 0"	6' - 8"	0' - 2"	B	Wood	Coated	A
105	Door-Single-Panel	3' - 0"	6' - 8"	0' - 2"	B	Wood	Coated	A
102	Door-Single-Panel	3' - 0"	6' - 8"	0' - 2"	B	Wood	Coated	A
103	Door-Single-Panel	3' - 0"	6' - 8"	0' - 2"	B	Wood	Coated	A
106	Door-Single-Panel	3' - 0"	6' - 8"	0' - 2"	B	Wood	Coated	A
112	Double-Glass	6' - 0"	7' - 0"	0' - 2"				
110B	Single-Flush Vision	3' - 0"	7' - 0"	0' - 2"				
110A	Single-Flush Vision	3' - 0"	7' - 0"	0' - 2"				
108A	Single-Flush Vision	3' - 0"	7' - 0"	0' - 2"				
108B	Single-Flush Vision	3' - 0"	7' - 0"	0' - 2"				

Figure 16–52

17. In the **Door Schedule** view, specify the *Fire Rating* for some other doors in the schedule. When you change the fire rating, you are prompted to change all elements of that type. Click **OK**.
18. Open the **Floor Plans: Floor 1** view. Zoom and pan to the east stairs.
19. Select the interior door to the east stairs, then right-click and select **Select All Instances>In Entire Project**.
20. Look at the Status Bar beside (Filter) and note the number of doors, indicating that more doors have been selected than are in the current view.
21. In Properties, set the parameters in the *Construction* and *Materials and Finishes* sections as follows:
    - *Frame Type:* **A**
    - *Frame Material:* **Steel**
    - *Finish:* **Clear-coat**

22. Move the cursor into the view and click in an empty space in the view to clear the selection.

    Note: *No visual changes to the door display because these are just instance properties.*

23. Switch back to the **Door Schedule** view to see the additions. Note that more than the Floor 1 doors have been updated.
24. Set the *Fire Rating* for the **Single-Flush Vision** doors to **C**.
25. Click **OK** to apply the change to all elements, as shown in Figure 16–53.

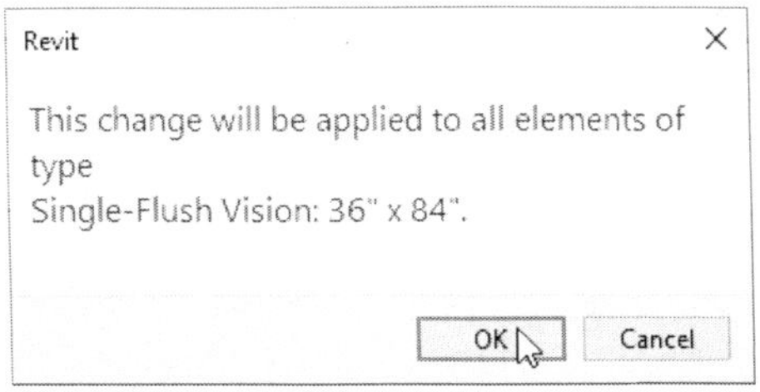

Figure 16–53

26. Save the project.

Task 2: Split and add a door schedule to sheets.

1. In the Project Browser, create three sheets using the title block **ASCENT_22X 34 Horizontal** with the name and sheet number of **A8.1 - Door Schedule**. Name the other two door schedules with a sequential sheet number.
2. Activate the **Door Schedule** view.
3. In the *Modify Schedule/Quantities* tab>*Split* panel, click (Split & Place).
4. In the *Split Schedule and Place on Sheets* dialog box, select the three door schedule sheets, as shown in Figure 16–54.

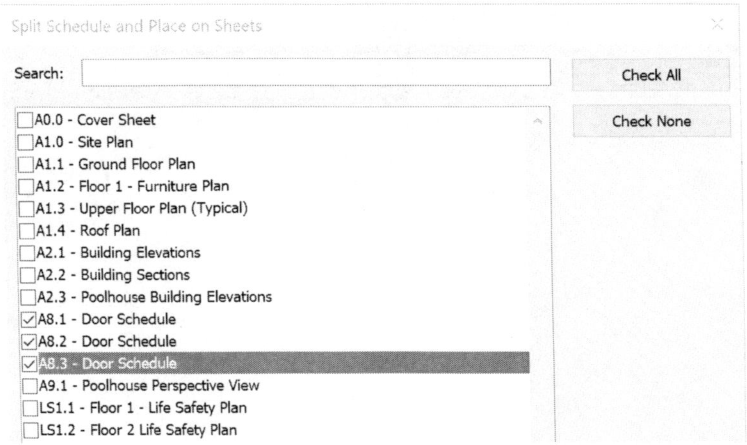

Figure 16–54

5. Click **Split & Place**.
6. The **Sheet A8.1 - Door Schedule** automatically opens and the first segment of the split schedule is attached to your cursor.
7. Place the door schedule in the upper-left corner of the sheet.
8. If not already opened, from the Project Browser, open sheet **A8.2** and **A8.3**. Note that the other segment of the split schedule has automatically been added to the sheets.
9. The schedule will be too long. Activate the **A8.1 - Door Schedule** view, select the schedule, and click (Split Schedule Table), as shown in Figure 16–55.

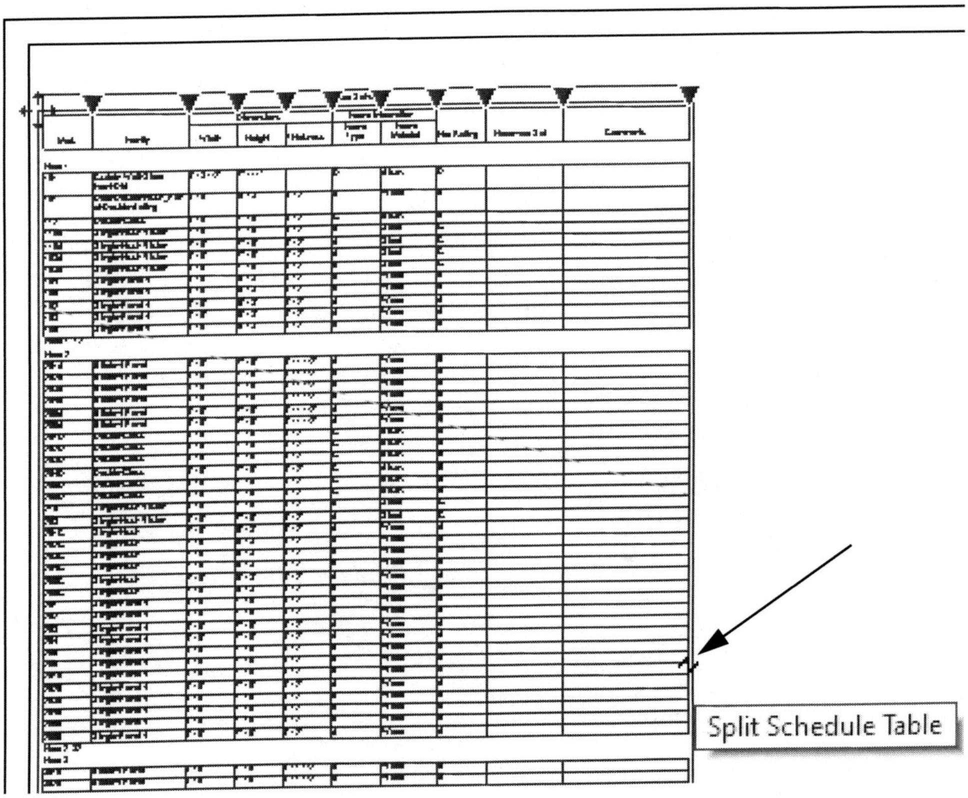

Figure 16–55

10. Select the individual schedules on the sheet and use the control grips at the bottom of the schedule to stretch it to fit the sheet, as shown in Figure 16–56.

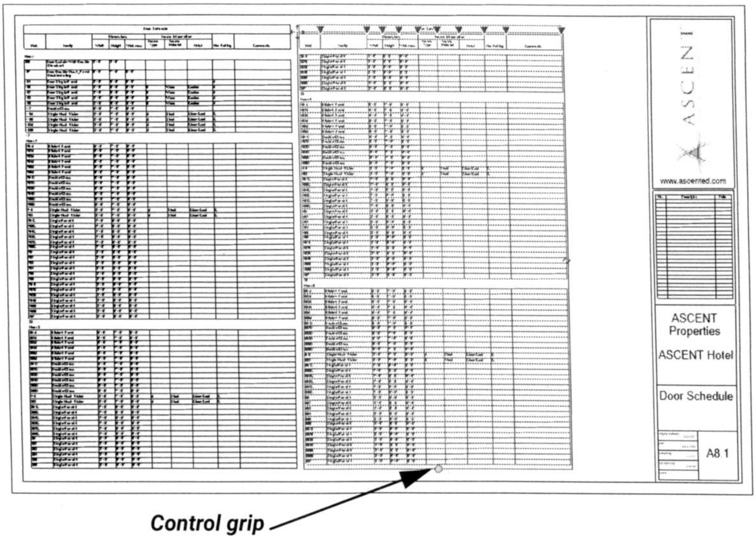

Figure 16–56

11. Zoom in and use the arrows at the top to modify the width of the columns so that the titles display correctly.
12. Click in an empty space in the view to clear the selection.
13. Open sheet **A8.2** and repeat the steps to resize and modify the door schedule.
    - You may find that you do not need the third sheet. You can right-click on the third sheet in the Project Browser and select **Delete** to remove it.
14. Switch back to the **Floor Plans: Floor 1** view and select the double-swing door at the kitchen.
15. In the Type Selector, change the type to **72" x 82"**. In Properties, add a *Frame Type*, *Frame Material*, and *Finish*.
16. Return to the sheet **A8.1 - Schedules**. The information is automatically populated.

Task 3: Modify and add a room schedule to a sheet.

1. From the Project Browser, open the **Room Schedule**. Close any other open views.
2. Note that for the RR name, both the room number and area show as **<varies>**. This means that on Floor 1, there are multiple restrooms with varying room numbers and square footage.
3. Open sheet **A1.2 Floor 1 - Furniture Plan**.

4. From the Project Browser, drag and drop the **Room Schedule** onto the sheet. Note that the schedule is showing all levels.
5. Activate the **Room Schedule** view. In Properties, click **Edit...** next to *Filter*.
6. In the *Schedule Properties* dialog box, check the **Filter by sheet** checkbox, as shown in Figure 16–57, and click **OK**.

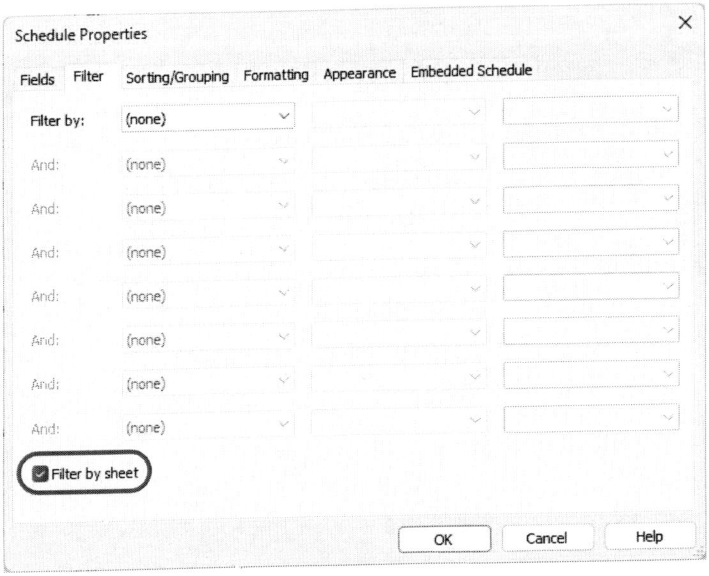

Figure 16–57

7. Activate the **A1.2 Floor 1 - Furniture Plan** sheet and note that the room schedule only shows the rooms that are in the viewport (e.g., Floor 1).
8. To see the schedule's ability to change depending on which viewports are placed on the sheet, drag and drop the **Floor 2** view onto the **A1.2 Floor 1 - Furniture Plan** sheet. (This view does not fit on the sheet.)
   - Note that the room schedule will automatically update with Floor 2's room information.
9. Delete the Floor 2 viewport, and note that the schedule updates to just show Floor 1's rooms.
10. Save and close the project.

End of practice

Chapter Review Questions

1. You can tag in a 3D view, but you first have to do what to the view?
    a. You cannot tag in a 3D view.
    b. Rename the view.
    c. Lock the view.
    d. Unlock the view.

2. Which of the following elements cannot be tagged using **Tag by Category**?
    a. Rooms
    b. Floors
    c. Walls
    d. Doors

3. If a view with walls has been placed on a sheet, what happens when you delete a wall in the view?
    a. You must delete the wall on the sheet.
    b. You must delete the wall from the schedule.
    c. The wall is removed from the model, but not from the schedule.
    d. The wall is removed from the model and any views, sheets, and schedules.

4. In a schedule, if you change type information (such as *Type Mark*), all instances of that type update with the new information.
    a. True
    b. False

5. You cannot remove split schedules once they have been created.
    a. True
    b. False

Command Summary

Button	Command	Location
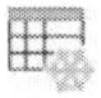	**Freeze Header**	• **Ribbon:** *Modify Schedule/Quantities* tab>*Titles & Header* panel
	**Highlight in Model**	• **Ribbon:** *Modify Schedule/Quantities* tab>*Element* panel
	**Material Tag**	• **Ribbon:** *Annotate* tab>*Tag* panel
	**Multi-Category**	• **Ribbon:** *Annotate* tab>*Tag* panel
	**Schedule/Quantities**	• **Ribbon:** *View* tab>*Create* panel, expand Schedules
	**Stair Tread/Riser Number**	• **Ribbon:** *Annotate* tab>*Tag* panel
	**Tag All Not Tagged**	• **Ribbon:** *Annotate* tab>*Tag* panel
	**Tag by Category**	• **Ribbon:** *Annotate* tab>*Tag* panel • **Shortcut: TG**
	**Tag Room (Room Tag)**	• **Ribbon:** *Architecture* tab>*Room & Area* panel • **Ribbon:** *Annotate* tab>*Tag* panel • **Shortcut: RT**

Chapter 17

Creating Details

Creating details is a critical part of the design process, as it is the step where you specify the exact information that is required to build a construction project. The elements that you can add to a model include detail components, detail lines, text, tags, symbols, and filled regions. Details can be created from views in the model, but you can also add 2D details in separate views.

Learning Objectives

- Create drafting views where you can add 2D details.
- Add detail components that show the typical elements in a detail.
- Annotate details using detail lines, text, tags, symbols, and patterns that define materials.

17.1 Setting Up Detail Views

Most of the work you do in Revit is exclusively with *smart* elements that interconnect and work together in the model. However, the software does not automatically display how elements should be built to fit together. For this, you need to create detail drawings, as shown in Figure 17–1.

> ***Note:*** *Details are created either in 2D drafting views or in callouts from plan, elevation, or section views.*

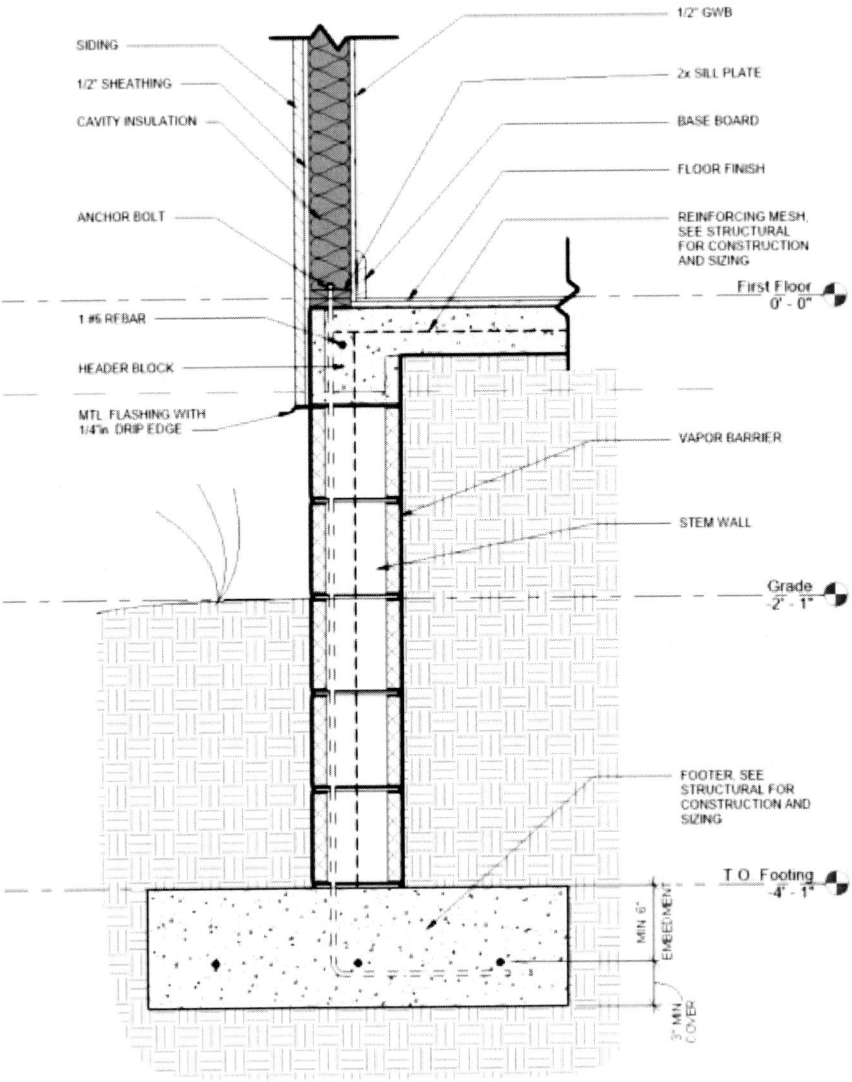

Figure 17–1

How To: Create a Drafting View

1. In the *View* tab>*Create* panel, click (Drafting View).
2. In the *New Drafting View* dialog box, enter a *Name* and set a *Scale*, as shown in Figure 17–2.

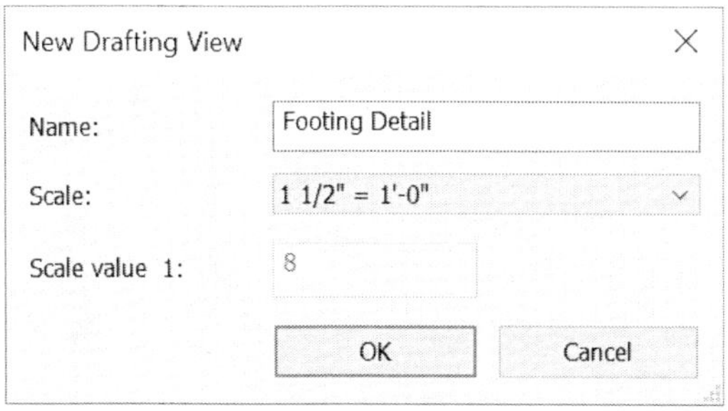

Figure 17–2

3. Click **OK**. A blank view is created with space in which you can sketch the detail.

   Note: *Drafting views are listed in their own section in the Project Browser.*

How To: Create a Detail View from Model Elements

1. Start the **Section** or **Callout** command.
2. In the Type Selector, select the **Detail View: Detail** type.
   - The marker indicates that it is a detail, as shown for a section in Figure 17–3.

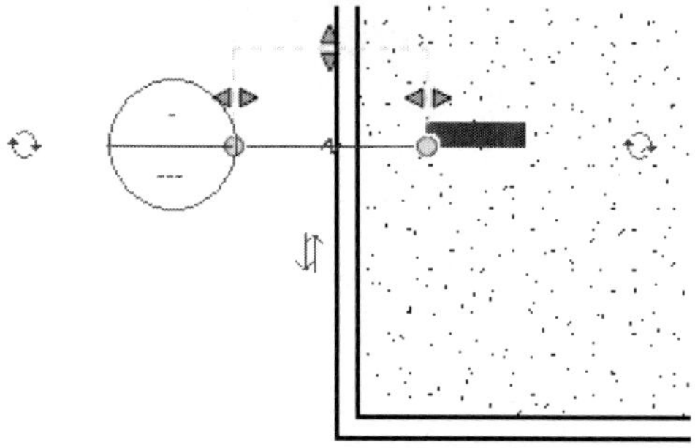

Figure 17–3

3. Place the section or a callout of the area you want to use for the detail.

   Note: *Callouts also have a Detail View type that can be used in the same way.*

4. Open the new detail.

- Change the detail level to see more or less of the element materials.
- Use the **Detail Line** tool to sketch on top of or add to the building elements.
- Because you are working with smart elements, a detail of the model is a true representation. When the building elements change, the detail changes as well, as shown in Figure 17–4.

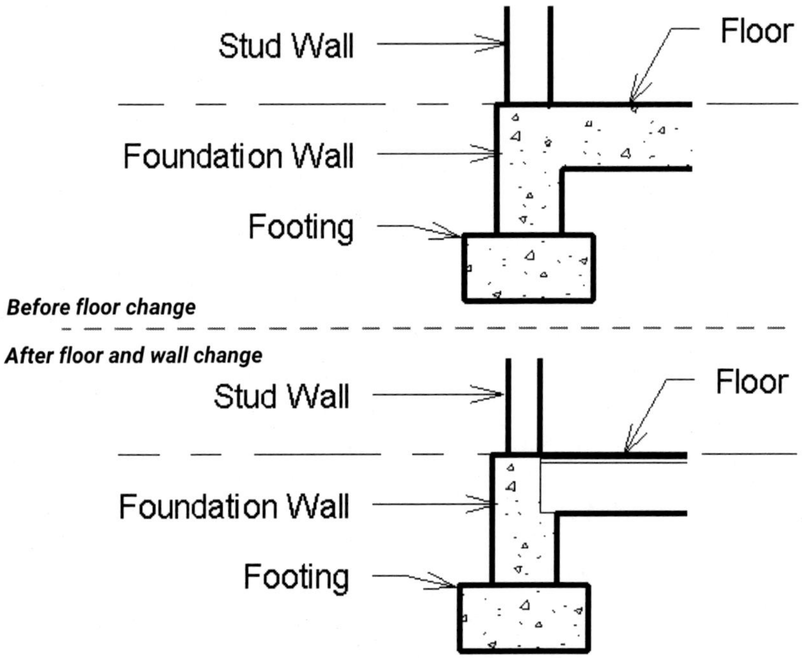

Figure 17–4

- You can create detail elements on top of the model and then toggle the model off so that it does not show in the detail view. In Properties, in the *Graphics* section, change *Display Model* to **Do not display**. You can also set the model to **Halftone**, as shown in Figure 17–5.

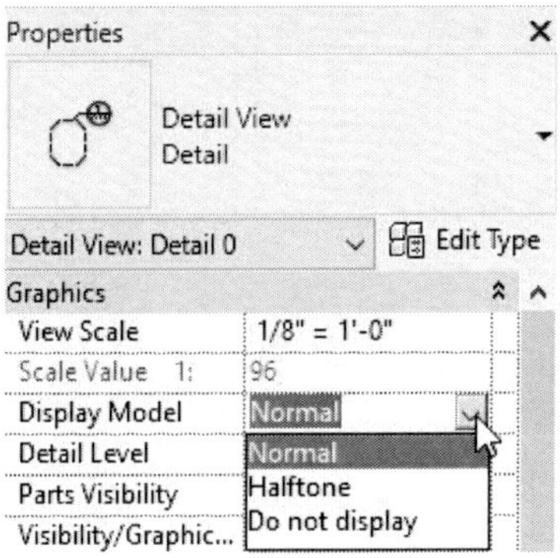

Figure 17–5

Referencing a Drafting View

Once you have created a drafting view, you can reference it in another view (such as a callout, elevation, or section view), as shown in Figure 17–6. For example, in a section view, you might want to reference an existing roof detail. You can reference drafting views, sections, elevations, and callouts.

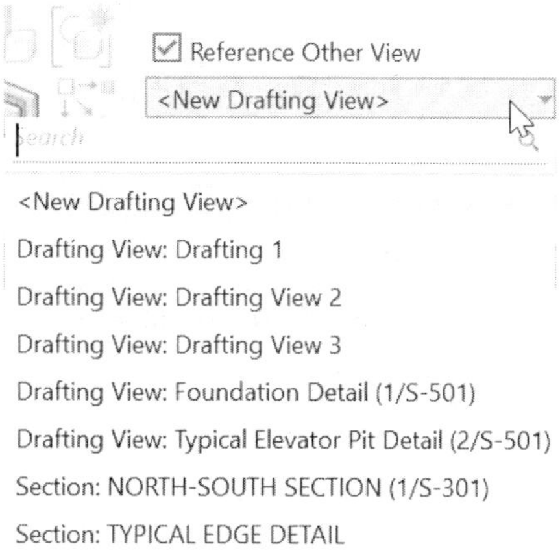

Figure 17–6

- You can use the search feature to limit the information displayed.

How To: Reference a Drafting View

1. Open the view in which you want to place the reference.
2. Start the **Section**, **Callout**, or **Elevation** command.
3. In the *Modify* contextual tab>*Reference* panel, select **Reference Other View**.
4. In the drop-down list, select a drafting view. If you do not have an existing drafting view, you can select **<New Drafting View>**.

   Note: *Depending on the command started, you will have different reference view options. For example, if you start the* ***Section*** *command and select* ***Reference Other View****, the view options that you can reference will be existing drafting views and section views.*

5. Place the view marker.
6. When you place the associated drafting view on a sheet, the marker in this view updates with the appropriate information.

- If you select **<New Drafting View>** from the drop-down list, a new view is created in the *Drafting Views (Detail)* area in the Project Browser. You can rename it as needed. The new view does not include any model elements.

- When you create a detail based on a section, elevation, or callout, you do not need to link it to a drafting view.
- You can change a referenced view to a different view. Select the view marker and in the ribbon, select the new view from the list.
- You can change the reference label that is on the marker by selecting the marker and changing the value for *Reference Label* in Properties.

Saving Drafting Views

To create a library of standard details, save the non-model specific drafting views to your server. They can then be imported into a project and modified to suit. They are saved as .RVT files.

Drafting views can be saved in two ways:

- Save an individual drafting view to a new file.
- Save all of the drafting views as a group in one new file.

How To: Save One Drafting View to a File

1. In the Project Browser, right-click on the drafting view you want to save and select **Save to New File...**.
2. In the *Save As* dialog box, specify a name and location for the file and click **Save**.

How To: Save a Group of Drafting Views to a File

Note: *You can save sheets, drafting views, model views (floor plans), schedules, and reports.*

1. In the *File* tab, expand (Save As), expand (Library), and then click (View).
2. In the *Save Views* dialog box, in the *Views* area, expand the drop-down list and select **Show drafting views only**.
3. Select the drafting views that you want to save, as shown in Figure 17–7.

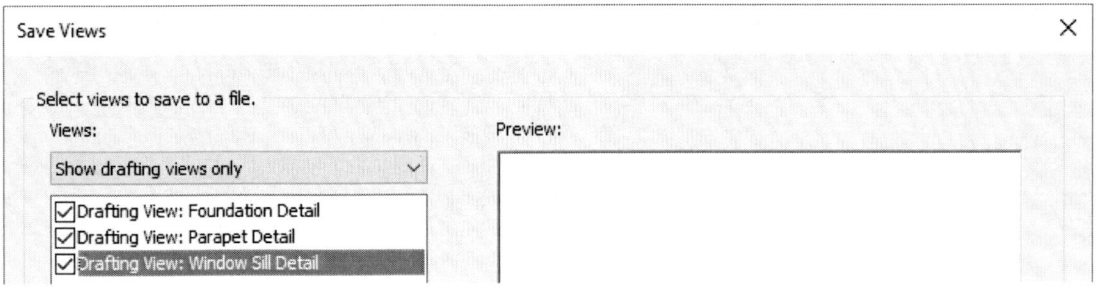

Figure 17–7

4. Click **OK**.
5. In the *Save As* dialog box, specify a name and location for the file and click **Save**.

How To: Use a Saved Drafting View in Another Project

1. Open the project to which you want to add the drafting view.
2. In the *Insert* tab>*Load from Library* panel, expand (Insert from File) and click (Insert Views from File).
3. In the *Open* dialog box, select the project in which you saved the detail and click **Open**.
4. In the *Insert Views* dialog box, limit the types of views to **Show drafting views only**, as shown in Figure 17–8.

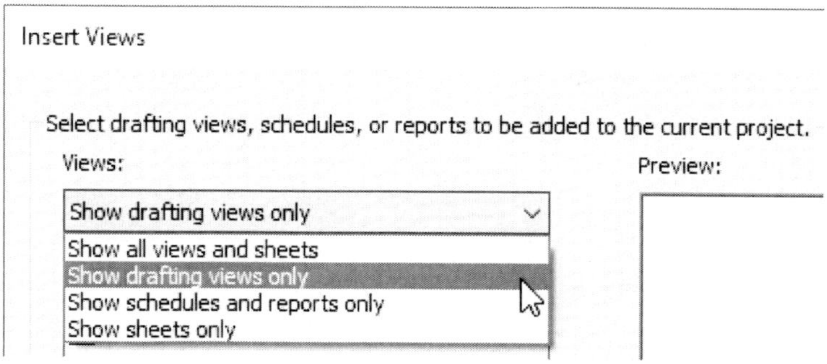

Figure 17–8

5. Select the view(s) that you want to insert and click **OK**.

Hint: Importing Details from Other CAD Software

You might already have a set of standard details created in a different CAD program, such as AutoCAD®. You can reuse the details in Revit by importing them into a temporary project. Once you have imported the detail, it helps to clean it up and save it as a view before bringing it into your active project.

1. In a new project, create a drafting view and make it active.
2. In the *Insert* tab>*Import* panel, click (Import CAD).
3. In the *Import CAD* dialog box, select the file to import. Most of the default values are what you need. You might want to change the *Layer/Level colors* to **Black and White**.
4. Click **Open**.
5. Use Revit detail lines and other tools to trace over the imported file.
6. Once finished, unpin the imported file, then select it and press <Delete>.

- If necessary, you can explode the imported file to modify it. This method is not recommended because it increases the file size and, depending on the importing objects, it could potentially take a long time to clean up and convert the objects to Revit-specific elements and styles.
  - Select the imported data. In the *Modify | [filename]* tab>*Import Instance* panel, expand (Explode) and click (Partial Explode) or (Full Explode). Click (Delete Layers) before you explode the detail. A full explode greatly increases the file size.
  - Modify the detail using tools in the *Modify* panel. Change all the text and line styles to Revit-specific elements.

17.2 Adding Detail Components

Revit elements, such as the casework section shown on the left in Figure 17–9, typically require additional information to ensure that they are constructed correctly. To create details such as the one shown on the right, you add detail components, detail lines, and various annotation elements

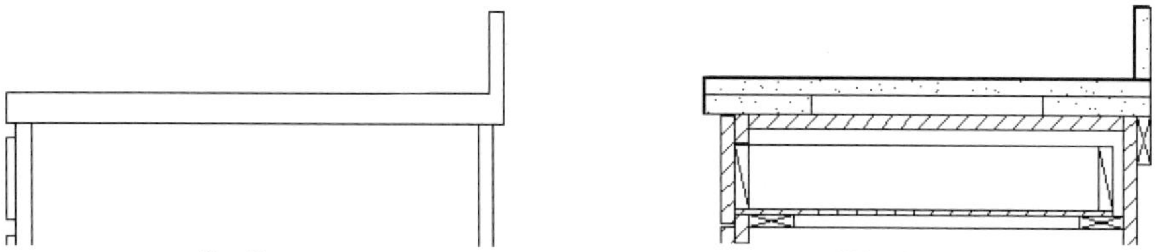

Section ***Detail built on section***

Figure 17–9

- Detail elements are not directly connected to the model, even if model elements display in the view.
- If you want to draw detail lines in 3D, use the **Model Line** tool. Detail Line is grayed out when you are in a 3D view or perspective view.

Detail Components

Detail components are families made of 2D and annotation elements. Over 500 detail components organized by CSI format are found in the *Detail Items* folder of the Revit Library.

How To: Add a Detail Component

1. In the *Annotate* tab>*Detail* panel, expand **Component** and click (Detail Component).
2. In the Type Selector, select the detail component type. You can load additional types from the Revit Library.
3. Many detail components can be rotated as you insert them by pressing <Spacebar>.

   Alternatively, select (Rotate After Placement) in the *Modify* contextual tab.
4. Place the component in the view.

Adding Break Lines

The break line is a detail component found in the Revit Library's *Detail Items\Div 01-General* folder. It consists of a rectangular area (shown highlighted in Figure 17–10) that is used to block out elements behind it. You can modify the size of the area that is covered and change the size of the cut line using the controls.

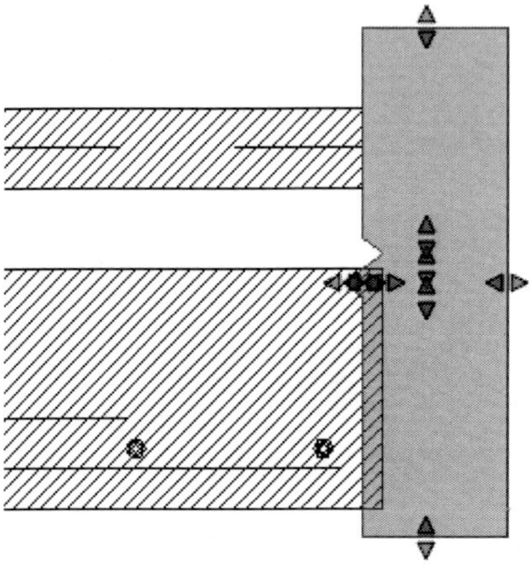

Figure 17–10

Hint: Working with the Draw Order of Details

When you select detail elements in a view, you can change the draw order of the elements in the *Modify | Detail Items* tab>*Arrange* panel. You can bring elements in front of other elements or place them behind elements, as shown in Figure 17–11.

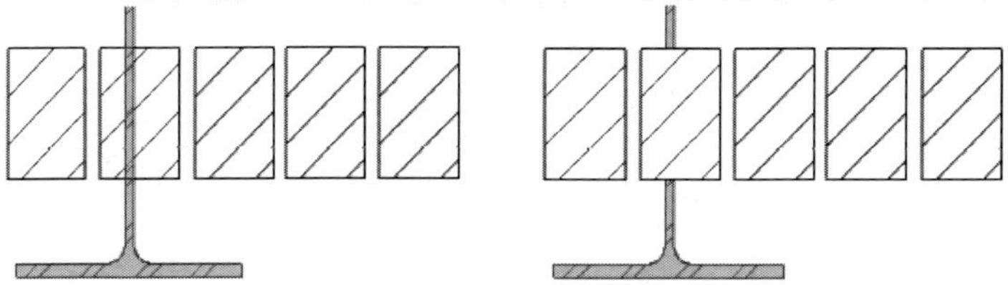

Draw order: front ***Draw order: back***

Figure 17–11

- (Bring to Front): Places element in front of all other elements.
- (Send to Back): Places element behind all other elements.
- (Bring Forward): Moves element one step to the front.
- (Send Backward): Moves element one step to the back.

You can select multiple detail elements and change the draw order of all of them in one step. They keep the relative order of the original selection.

Repeating Details

Instead of having to insert a component multiple times (such as brick or concrete block), you can use (Repeating Detail Component) and create a string of components, as shown in Figure 17–12.

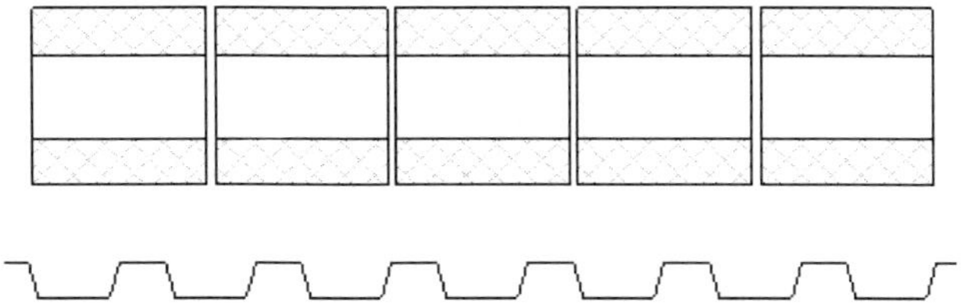

Figure 17–12

How To: Insert a Repeating Detail Component

1. In the *Annotate* tab>*Detail* panel, expand **Component** and click (Repeating Detail Component).
2. In the Type Selector, select the detail you want to use.
3. In the *Draw* panel, click (Line) or (Pick Lines) and type a value for the (Offset), if needed.
   - When using **Pick Lines**, you can click (Lock) in the *Draw* panel to lock the detail into place. To unlock it, select the detail in the view and click (Create or remove a length or alignment constraint).
4. The components repeat, as required, to fit the length of the sketched or selected line, as shown in Figure 17–13. You can lock the components to the line by clicking (Create or remove a length or alignment constraint).

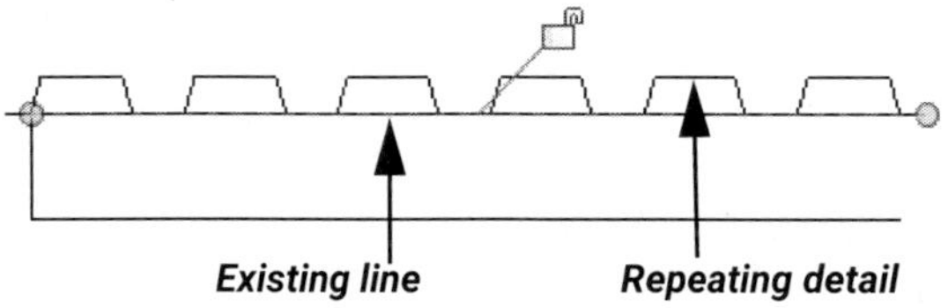

Figure 17–13

Hint: (Insulation)

Adding batt insulation is similar to adding a repeating detail component, but instead of a series of bricks or other elements, it creates the linear batting pattern shown in Figure 17–14.

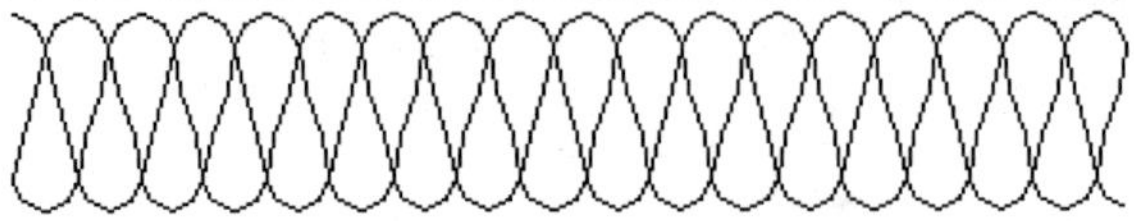

Figure 17–14

In the *Annotate* tab>*Detail* panel, click (Insulation). Before you place the insulation in the view, specify the (Offset) and other options in the *Modify | Place Insulation* tab>*Draw* panel (as shown in Figure 17–15), as well as the *Insulation Width* in Properties.

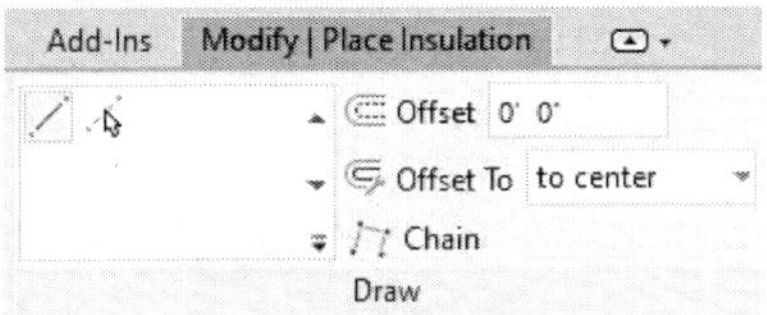

Figure 17–15

17.3 Annotating Details

After you have added components and sketched detail lines, you need to add annotations to the detail view. You can place text notes and dimensions, as shown in Figure 17–16, as well as symbols and tags. Filled regions are used to add hatching.

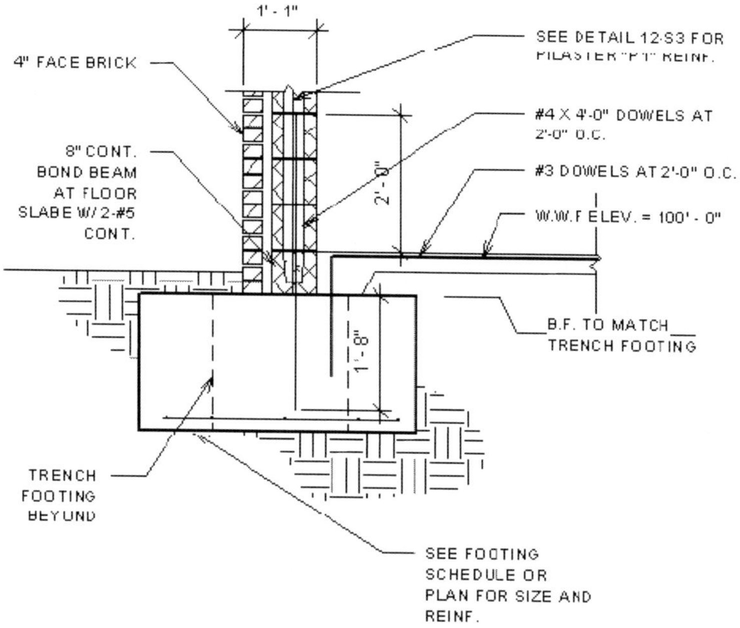

Figure 17–16

Filled Regions

Many elements include material information that displays in plan and section views, while other elements need more details to be added. For example, the concrete wall shown in Figure 17–17 includes material information, while the earth to the left of the wall needs to be added using the **Filled Region** command.

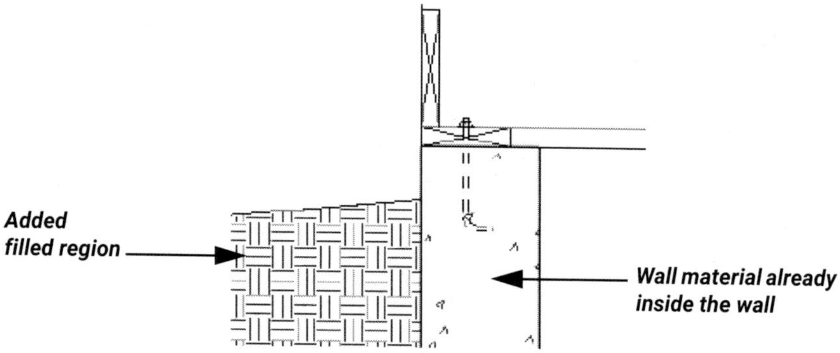

Figure 17–17

The patterns used in details are *drafting patterns*. They are scaled to the view scale and update if you modify it. You can also add full-size *model patterns*, such as a Flemish Bond brick pattern, to the surface of some elements.

How To: Add a Filled Region

1. In the *Annotate* tab>*Detail* panel, expand (Region) and click (Filled Region).
2. Create a closed boundary using the sketch tools.
3. In the *Line Style* panel, select the line style for the outside edge of the boundary. If you do not want the boundary to display, select the **<Invisible lines>** style.
4. In the Type Selector, select the fill type, as shown in Figure 17–18.

Figure 17–18

5. Click (Finish Edit Mode).

- You can modify a region by changing the fill type in the Type Selector or by editing the sketch.
- Double-click on the filled region or edge of the filled region to edit the sketch (if you have (Select elements by face) toggled on).

Hint: Creating a Filled Region Pattern Type

You can create a custom pattern by duplicating and editing an existing pattern type.

1. Select an existing region or boundary.
2. In Properties, click (Edit Type).
3. In the *Type Properties* dialog box, click **Duplicate** and name the new pattern.
4. Select the *Foreground/Background Fill Pattern* and *Pattern Color* and specify the *Line Weight* and *Masking*, as shown in Figure 17–19.

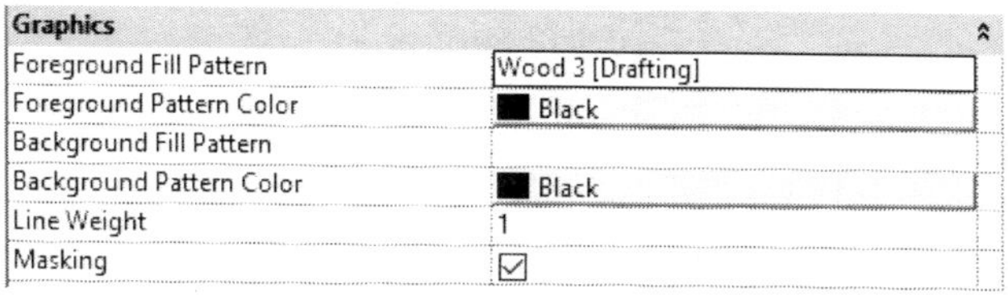

Figure 17–19

5. Click **OK**.

Alternatively, in the *Manage* tab>*Settings* panel, you can expand (Additional Settings) and select (Fill Patterns). You can select from two types of fill patterns: **Drafting** (as shown in Figure 17–20) and **Model**. Drafting fill patterns scale to the view scale factor. Model fill patterns display full scale on the model.

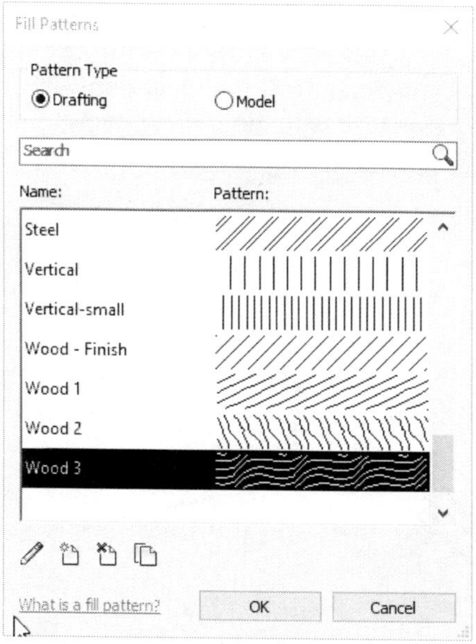

Figure 17–20

Adding Detail Tags

Besides adding text to a detail, you can tag detail components using (Tag By Category). The tag name is set in the *Type Parameters* for that component, as shown in Figure 17–21. This means that if you have more than one copy of the component in your project, you do not have to rename it each time you place its tag.

Note: *The* ***Detail Item Tag.rfa*** *tag is located in the Annotations folder in the Revit Library.*

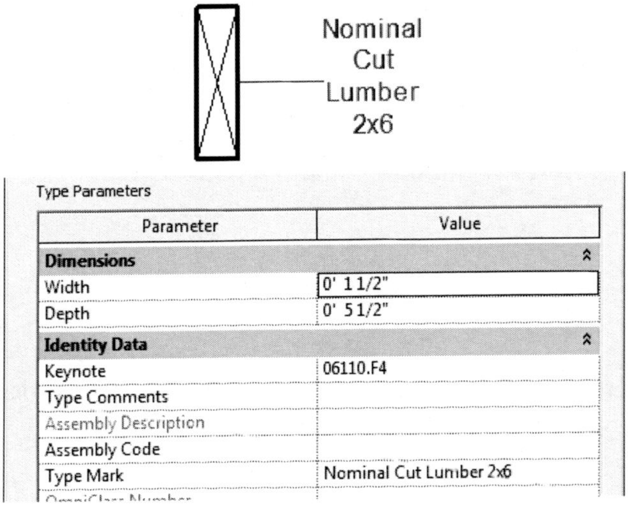

Figure 17–21

When you tag elements in a cropped view, the tag is placed at the default location of the element and might not display in the callout. In the View Control Bar, click (Do not Crop). Tag the elements, and then move the new tags in the crop window, as shown in Figure 17–22. Click (Crop View) to return to the area of the callout view.

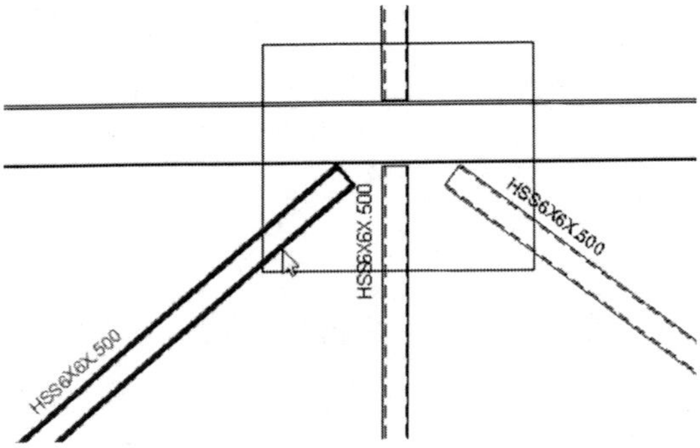

Figure 17–22

Linework

To emphasize a particular line or change the look of a line in elevations and other views, modify the lines with the **Linework** command. Changes made to lines with the **Linework** command are view-specific, applying only to the view in which you make them.

- The **Linework** command can be used on project edges of model elements, cut edges of model elements, edges in imported CAD files, and edges in linked Revit models.
- You cannot use the **Linework** command to change the line style of annotation lines like a dimension line or leader line.

How To: Adjust Linework

1. In the *Modify* tab>*View* panel, click (Linework), or type the shortcut **LW**.
2. In the *Modify | Linework* tab>*Line Style* panel, select the line style you want to use from the list.
3. Move the cursor and highlight the line you want to change. You can use <Tab> to toggle through the lines as needed.
4. Click on the line to change it to the new line style.
5. Click on other lines as needed or click (Modify) to end the command

- If the line is too long or short, you can modify the length using the controls at the end of the line.

Practice 17a
Create a Detail Based on a Section Callout

Practice Objectives

- Create a detail based on a section.
- Add filled regions, detail components, and annotations.

In this practice, you will create a detail based on a callout of a wall section. You will add repeating detail components, break lines, and detail lines, and add annotations to finish the detail. Figure 17–23 shows the completed detail.

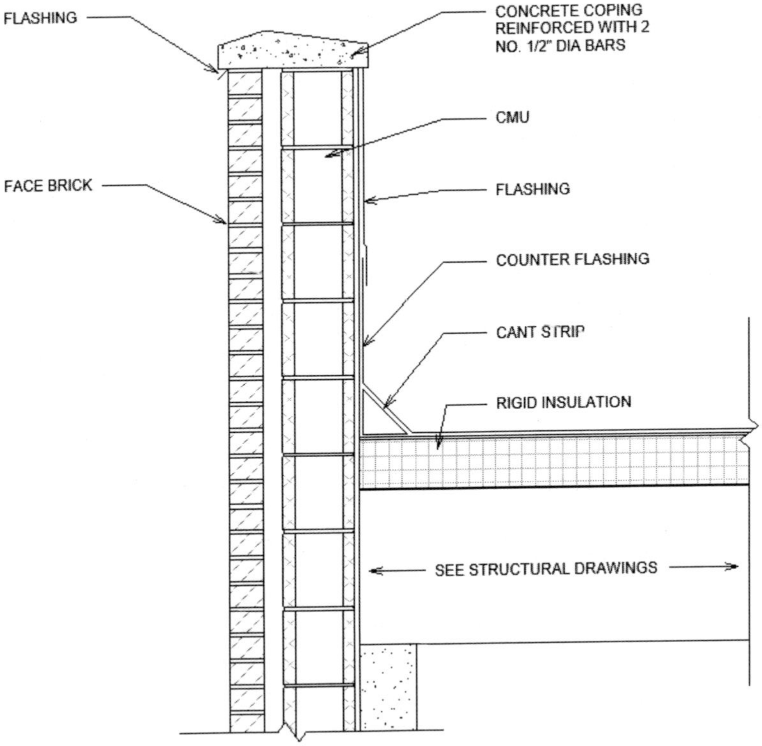

Figure 17–23

Task 1: Create a callout of a wall section.

1. Open the file **Arch-Detailing.rvt** from the practice files folder. If needed for reference, the completed detail is located in the practice files *Completed Details* folder.
2. Open the **Floor Plans: Floor 1** view.

3. Double-click on the wall section head shown in Figure 17–24. This guarantees that you open the correct section.

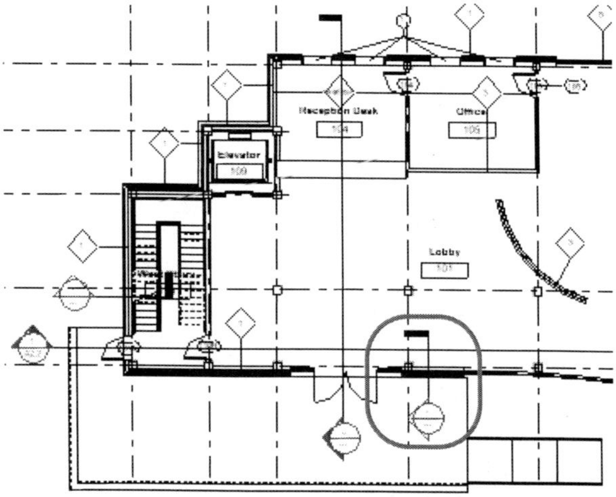

Figure 17–24

4. Zoom in to the top of the wall showing the parapet and the roof.
5. In the *View* tab>*Create* panel, click (Callout).
6. In the Type Selector, select **Detail View: Detail**, if not already selected.
7. Create a callout as shown in Figure 17–25. Use the grips to move the callout bubble location as needed.

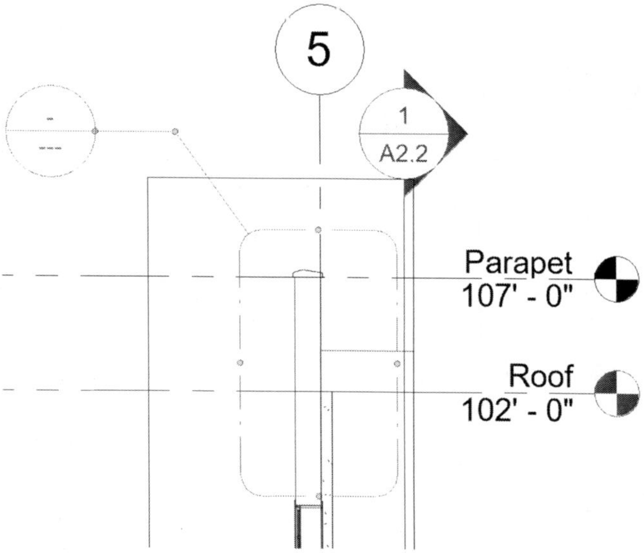

Figure 17–25

8. Click in an empty space in the view to clear the selection.
9. Double-click on the callout bubble to open the callout view.
10. In the View Control Bar, set the following:
    - *Scale:* **1"=1'-0"**
    - *Detail Level:* (Fine)
    - Click (Hide Crop Region) to turn the crop region off
11. Hide the levels, grids, and section markers (if displayed).
12. Select the wall, right-click, and select **Override Graphics in View>By Element**.
13. In the *View Specific Element Graphics* dialog box, in the *Cut Patterns* section, uncheck **Visible** for the *Foreground*, as shown in Figure 17–26. Click **OK**. The wall's layers still display but the layers' material detail does not.

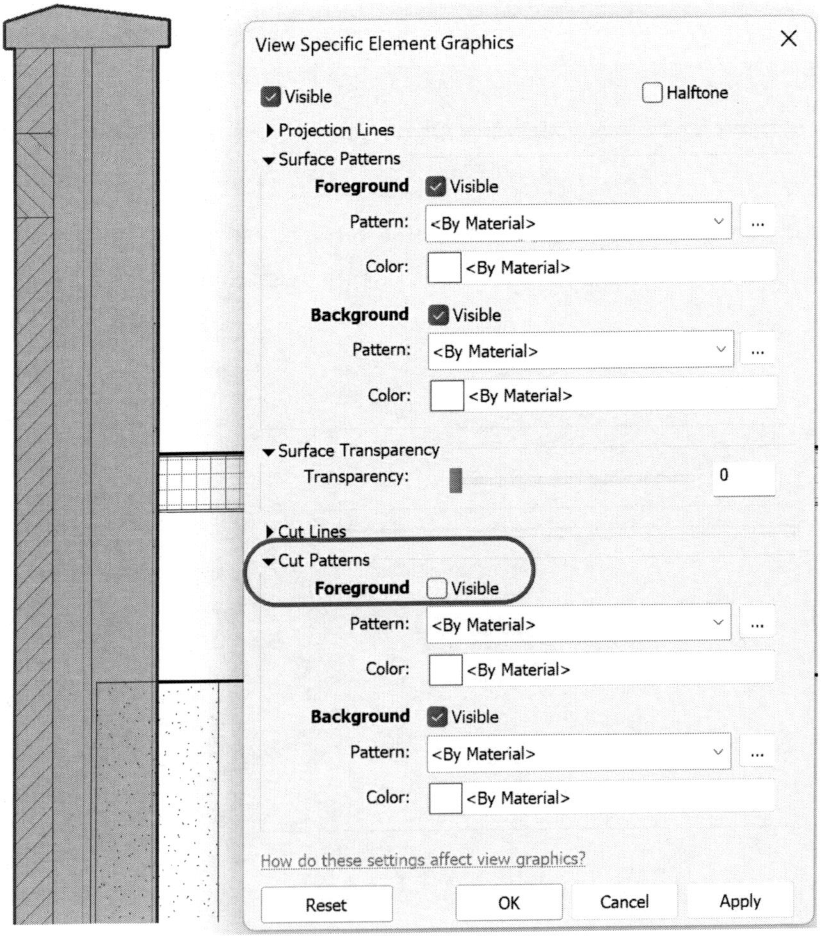

Figure 17–26

14. Click (Modify).
15. In the Project Browser, expand the *Detail Views (Detail)* section and rename the view to **Parapet Detail**.
16. Save the project.

Task 2: Add repeating detail components and break lines.

Note: *As you are working, toggle (Thin Lines) on and off to make it easier to draw.*

1. In the *Annotate* tab>*Detail* panel, expand **Component** and click (Repeating Detail Component).
2. In the Type Selector, set the type to **Repeating Detail: Brick**.
3. Draw the brick line from bottom to top, starting at the bottom of the wall up to the bottom of the parapet cap, as shown in Figure 17–27.

   Note: *Drawing from the bottom up ensures that "mortar" is between the cap and the brick. This is how the detail elements were created.*

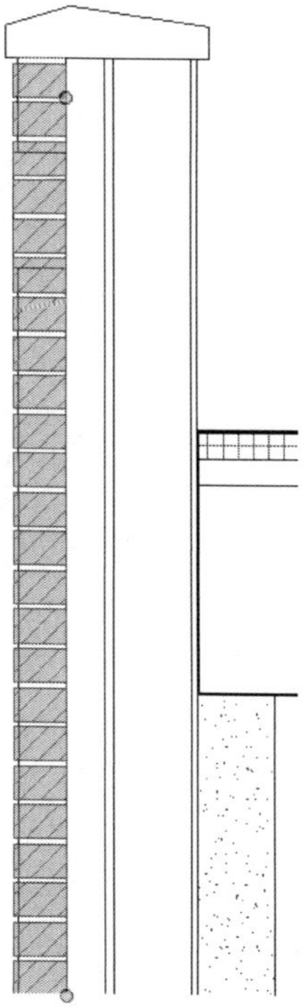

Figure 17–27

4. Click (Modify).
5. Zoom in to where the repeating brick meets the parapet cap and select the repeating brick.
6. Depending on where you ended the repeating brick, you may need to use the **Move** tool to move the repeating brick up to the parapet cap. Note that when you select it, you can see the gap for the mortar, as shown in Figure 17–28.

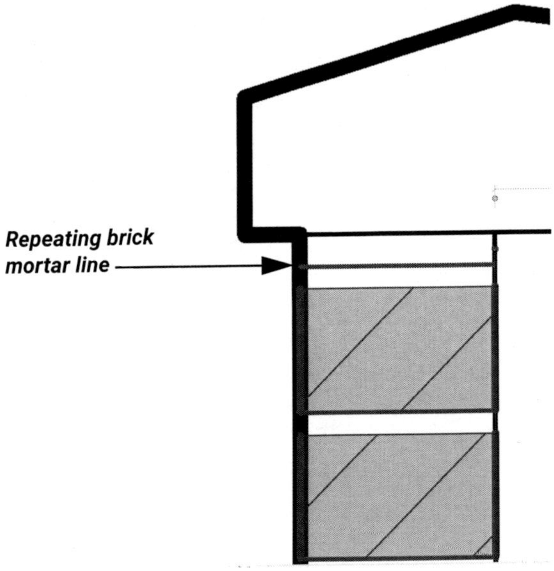

Figure 17–28

7. Start the **Repeating Detail Component** command again. In the Type Selector, select **Repeating Detail: CMU**. Draw top down on the other side of the wall, as shown in Figure 17–29.

   Note: *Revit lists the last tool you used at the top of the drop-down list.*

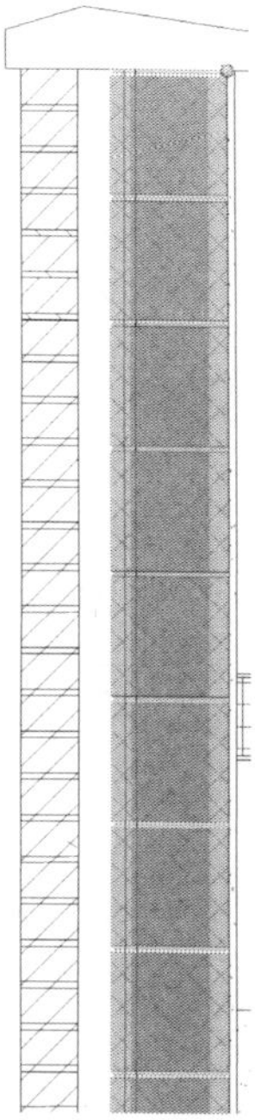

Figure 17–29

8. Click  (Modify).
9. In the *Annotate* tab>*Detail* panel, expand **Component** and click  (Detail Component).
10. In the *Modify | Place Detail Component* tab>*Mode* panel, click  (Load Family).
11. In the *Load Family* dialog box, navigate to the practice files *Families>Details* folder, select **Break Line.rfa**, and click **Open**.

12. Add break lines to the bottom and right side of the detail. Press <Spacebar> to rotate the break line as needed, and use the controls to modify the size and depth, as shown in Figure 17–30.
    - If you added the break line going in the wrong direction, select the break line in the view and press <Spacebar> until it is rotated correctly.

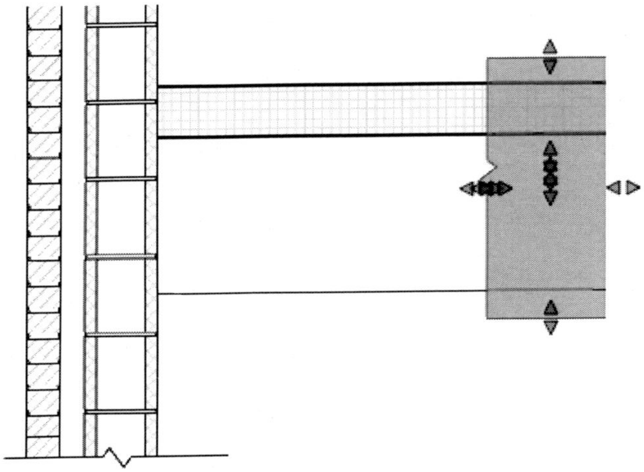

Figure 17–30

13. Click (Modify).
14. Save the project.

Task 3: Draw flashing using detail lines.

1. In the *Annotate* tab>*Detail* panel, click (Detail Line).
2. In the *Modify | Place Detail Lines* tab>*Line Style* panel, expand the *Line Style* drop-down list and select **Wide Lines**. In the *Draw* panel, select (Line) and toggle on (Chain).
3. Draw the flashing and the cant strip similarly to that shown in Figure 17–31. (The wall and details are set to halftone in the image for clarity.) Because **Chain** is toggled on, you will need to press <Esc> when you need to draw a new line.

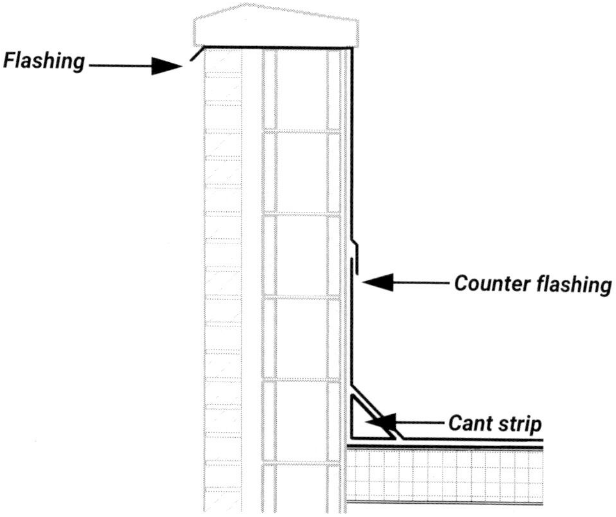

Figure 17–31

4. Click (Modify).
5. Save the project.

Task 4: Add a filled region.

1. Zoom in to the top of the parapet cap.
2. In the *Annotate* tab>*Detail* panel, expand (Region) and select (Filled Region).
3. In the *Draw* panel, select **Pick Lines**.
4. In the Type Selector, select **Concrete**, then select the lines that make up the parapet cap.
5. Click (Finish Edit Mode). The parapet cap now shows its concrete detail, as shown in Figure 17–32.

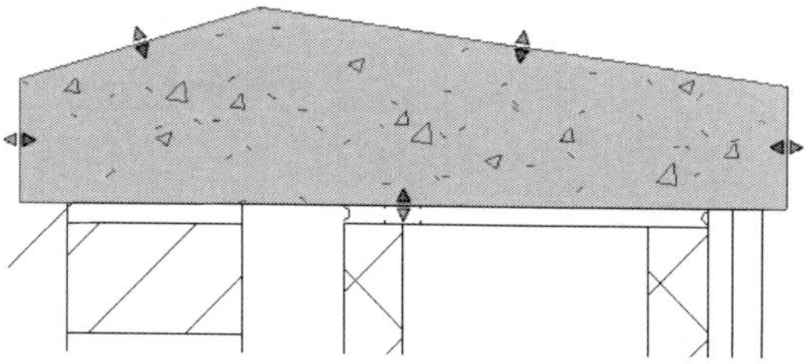

Figure 17–32

6. Click (Modify).
7. Save the project.

Task 5: Annotate the detail.

1. In the View Control Bar, toggle on **Show Crop Region**. Adjust the crop region to allow space for text.
2. In the Quick Access Toolbar or in the *Annotate* tab>*Text* panel, click A (Text).
3. In the Type Selector, select a text style (e.g., **1/8" Arial Narrow**).
4. In the *Modify | Place Text* tab>*Leader* panel, select A (Two-Segments).
   a. The first click will be the placement of the leader arrow.
   b. The second click will be the elbow of the leader line.
   c. The third click will be to place the text.
   d. Type the text and click away from the text to complete the annotation, as shown in Figure 17–33.

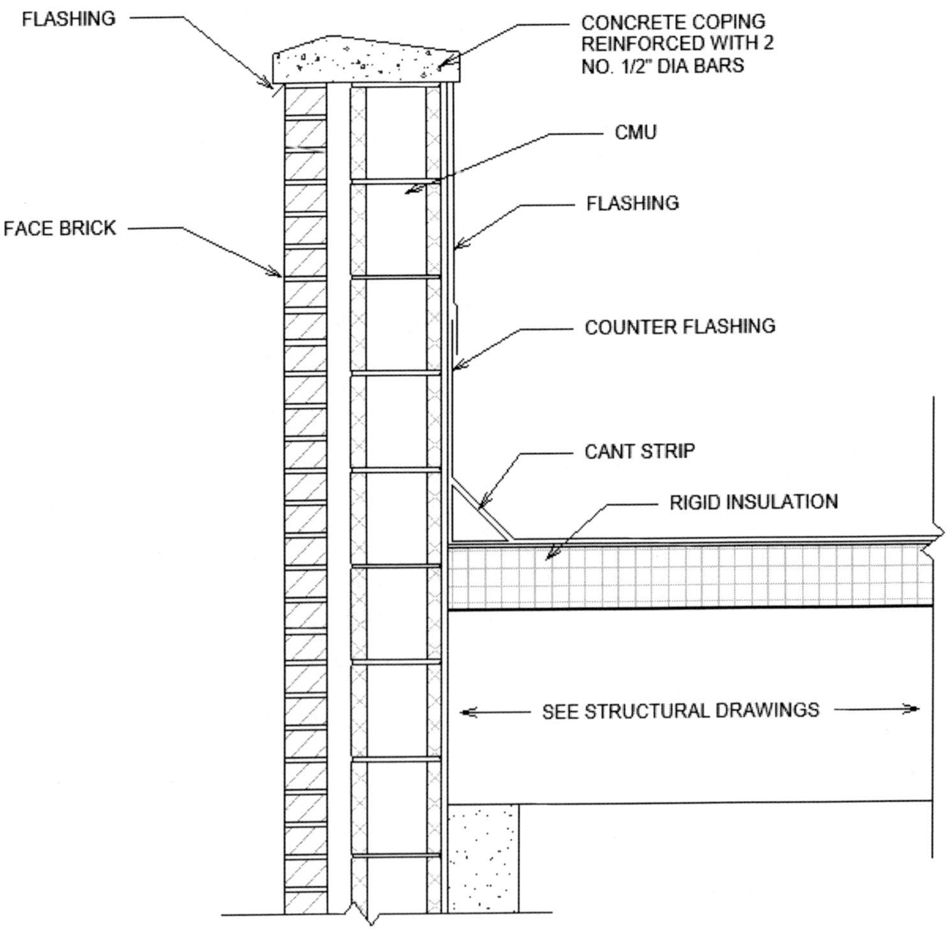

Figure 17–33

5. Select all the text notes on the right side of the wall.
6. In the *Modify | Text Notes* tab>*Multiple Align* panel, select (Distribute Vertically) to space the text out evenly based on the text box border.
7. With the text still selected, select (Align Elements Right). All the text will align to the rightmost text border.
8. Select (Align Elements Left) to align all the text to the leftmost text border.
9. Click (Modify).
10. Select the top-left flashing text and the top-right parapet cap. In the *Multiple Align* panel, click (Align Elements Top). The two text align vertically based on the topmost text border.
11. Modify the text on the left of the detail and adjust any of the leader lines as needed.
12. Save and keep the project opened.

At this point, you have a hybrid between detail items and model items. You can continue to add detail items to replace the roofing. You can also add structural elements if you have time.

End of practice

Practice 17b
Create a Detail in a Drafting View

Practice Objective

- Create and annotate details.

In this practice, you will create a footing detail in a drafting view. You will add detail components, lines, and annotations, as well as filled regions. You will place the view on a sheet and place a callout in another view that references this view. Figure 17–34 shows the completed detail.

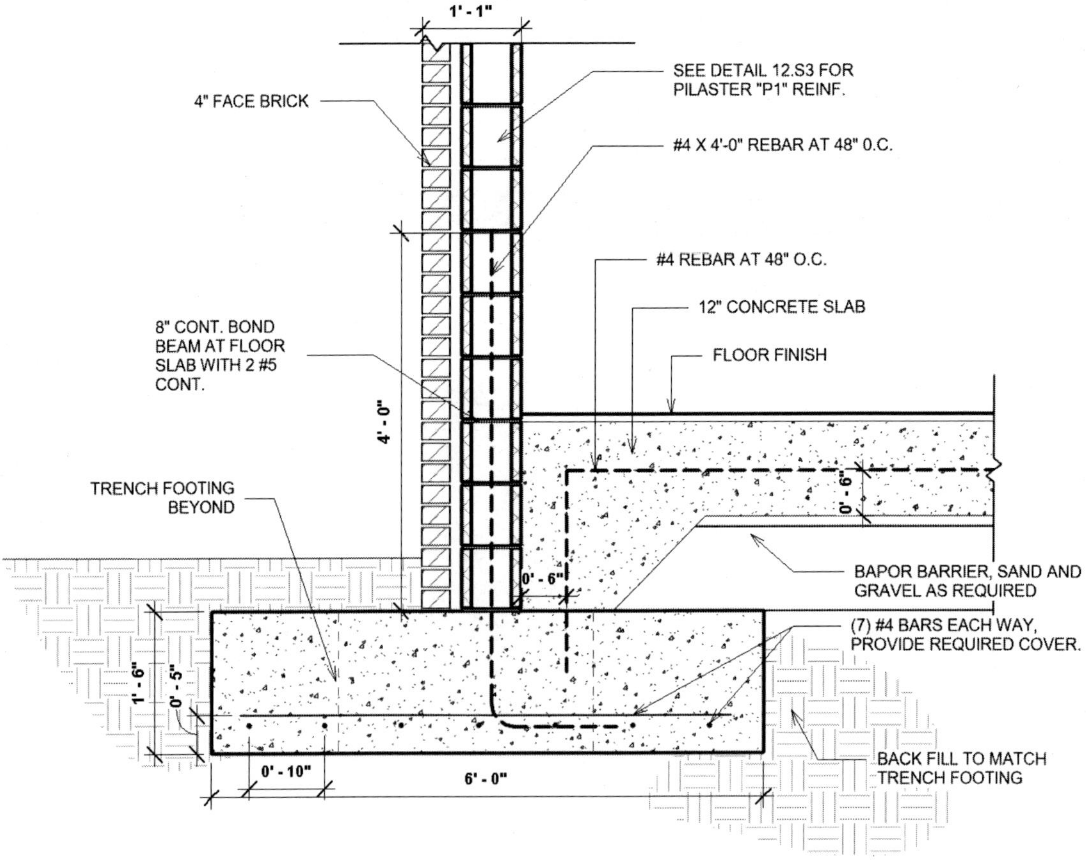

Figure 17–34

- This practice is designed with minimal direction so that you can apply what you have learned.

Task 1: Add filled regions.

1. Continue working in **Arch-Detailing.rvt**. If needed for reference, the completed detail is located in the practice files *Completed Details* folder.
2. In the *View* tab>*Create* panel, select (Drafting View). Create a drafting view named **Footing Detail** at a scale of **3/4"=1'-0"**.
3. In the *Annotate* tab>*Detail* panel, expand (Region) and click (Filled Region).
4. In the *Modify | Create Filled Region Boundary* tab>*Draw Style* panel, select (Line) and toggle on (Chain). In the *Line Style* panel, select **Medium Lines**.
5. Sketch the boundary of the floor slab, as shown in Figure 17–35.

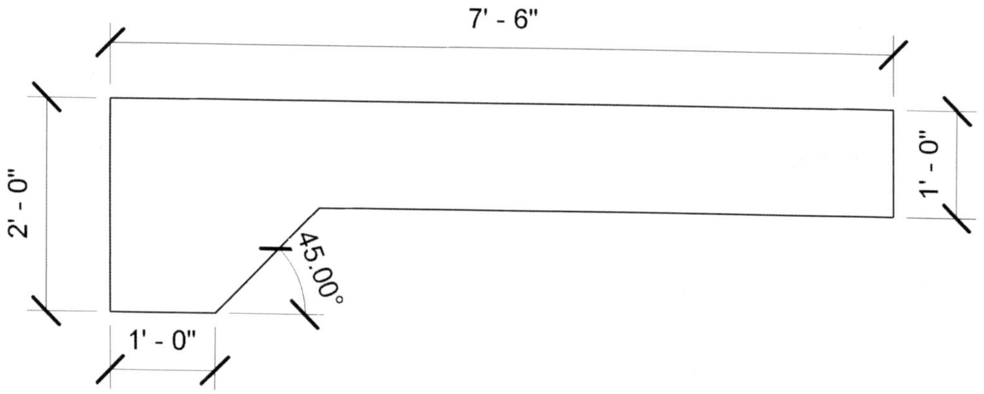

Figure 17–35

6. In the Type Selector, select **Filled region: Concrete**.
7. Click (Finish Edit Mode).
8. In the *Annotate* tab>*Detail* panel, expand **Component** and select (Detail Component). In the Type Selector, select **Concrete Footing-Rectangular-Section 72"x12"** and place it below the floor slab.

9. Create filled regions for the sections of earth around the footing using the **Earth** pattern, as shown in Figure 17–36. You can create the curved boundary lines by sketching splines and using the **<Invisible lines>** line style.

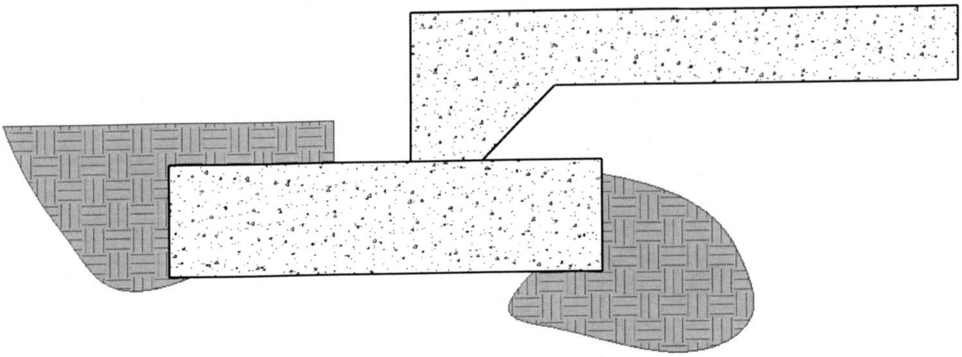

Figure 17–36

10. If the patterns cover over some elements, select the filled region and in the *Modify | Detail Items* tab>*Arrange* panel, click (Send to Back).

11. Create the wall by adding repeating detail CMU and Brick, as well as additional detail lines and rebar section details, as shown in Figure 17–37.

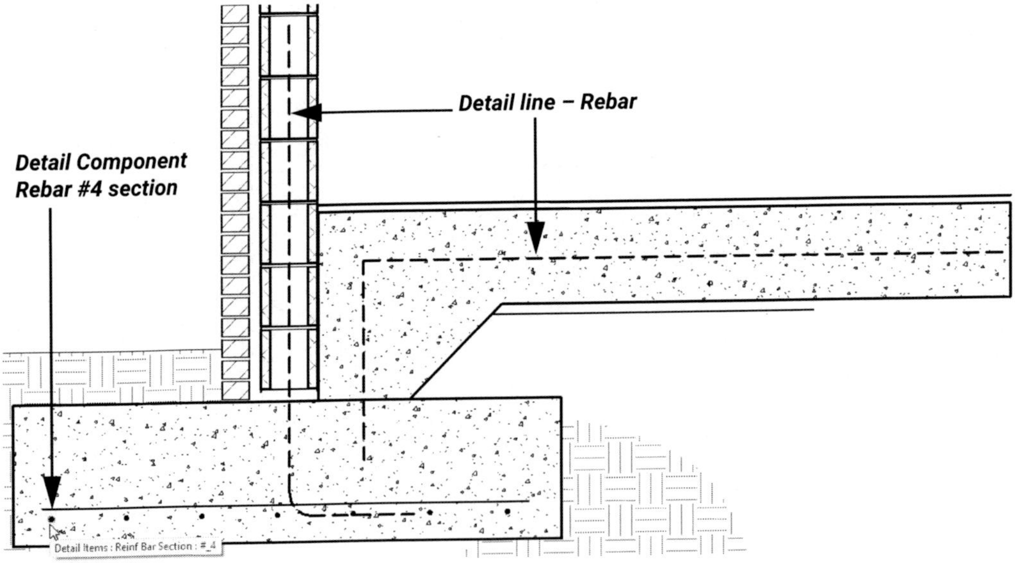

Figure 17–37

12. Add break lines, dimensions, and text with leaders, as shown in Figure 17–38.

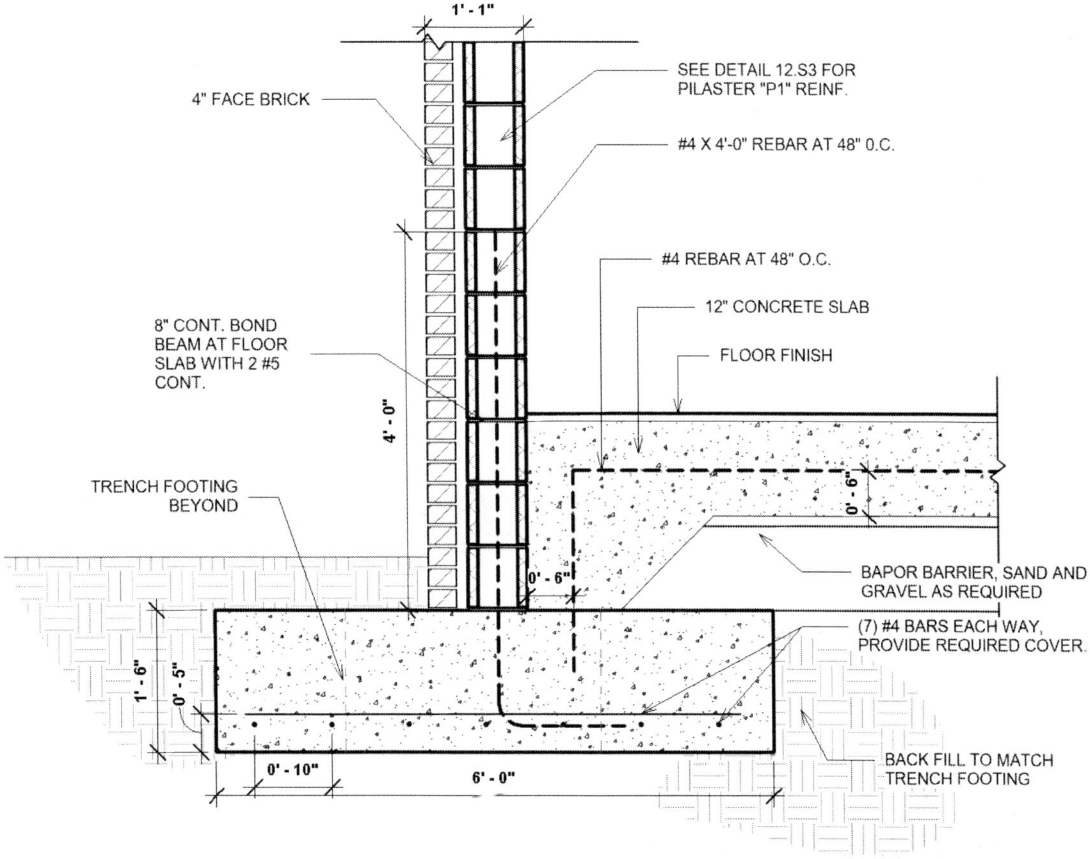

Figure 17–38

13. Save the project.

Task 2: Add the detail to a sheet and connect it to a detail callout.

1. Create a new sheet named **A5.1 - Wall Detail** and drag and drop the footing detail to this sheet.
2. Open the **Sections (Wall Section): Section 2** view.
3. Start the **Callout** command and select the **Detail View: Detail** type.
4. In the *Modify | Callout* tab>*Reference* panel, select **Reference Other View** and in the drop-down list, select **Drafting View: Footing Detail**.

5. Draw the callout around the footing area. The correct detail is referenced, as shown in Figure 17–39.

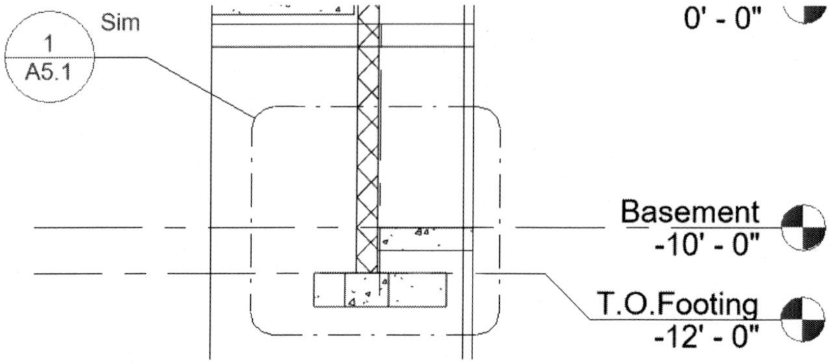

Figure 17–39

6. Save and close the project.

End of practice

Chapter Review Questions

1. Which of the following are ways in which you can create a detail? (Select all that apply.)
   a. Make a callout of a section and sketch over it.
   b. Draw all of the elements from scratch on the sheet.
   c. Import a CAD detail and modify or sketch over it.
   d. Insert an existing drafting view from another file.

2. How are detail components different from building components?
   a. There is no difference.
   b. Detail components are made of 2D lines and annotations only.
   c. Detail components are made of building elements, but only display in detail views.
   d. Detail components are made of 2D and 3D elements.

3. Which of the following statements is true when you sketch detail lines?
   a. Always the same width.
   b. Vary in width according to the view.
   c. Display in all views associated with the detail.
   d. Display only in the view in which they were created.

4. Which command do you use to add a pattern (such as concrete or earth, as shown in Figure 17–40) to part of a detail?

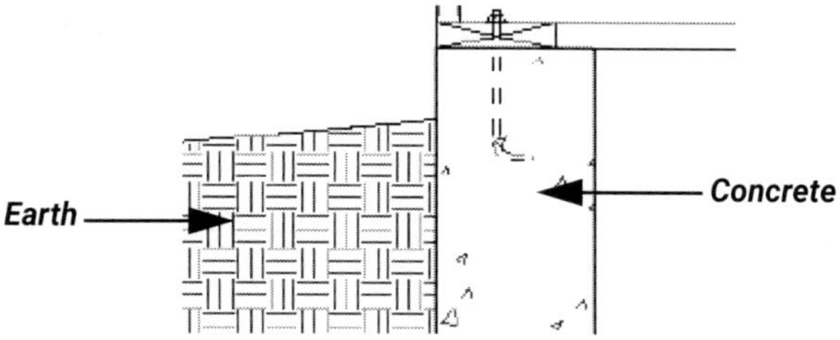

Figure 17–40

   a. Region
   b. Filled Region
   c. Masking Region
   d. Pattern Region

Command Summary

Button	Command	Location
CAD Import Tools		
	**Delete Layers**	• **Ribbon:** *Modify | <imported filename>* tab>*Import Instance* panel
	**Full Explode**	• **Ribbon:** *Modify | <imported filename>* tab>*Import Instance* panel, expand Explode
	**Import CAD**	• **Ribbon:** *Insert* tab>*Import* panel
	**Partial Explode**	• **Ribbon:** *Modify | <imported filename>* tab>*Import Instance* panel, expand Explode
Detail Tools		
	**Detail Component**	• **Ribbon:** *Annotate* tab>*Detail* panel, expand Component
	**Detail Line**	• **Ribbon:** *Annotate* tab>*Detail* panel
	**Insulation**	• **Ribbon:** *Annotate* tab>*Detail* panel
	**Filled Region**	• **Ribbon:** *Annotate* tab>*Detail* panel
	**Repeating Detail Component**	• **Ribbon:** *Annotate* tab>*Detail* panel, expand Component
View Tools		
	**Bring Forward**	• **Ribbon:** *Modify | Detail Items* tab>*Arrange* panel
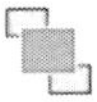	**Bring to Front**	• **Ribbon:** *Modify | Detail Items* tab>*Arrange* panel
	**Drafting View**	• **Ribbon:** *View* tab>*Create* panel
	**Insert from File: Insert Views from File**	• **Ribbon:** *Insert* tab>*Load from Library* panel, expand Insert from File
	**Send Backward**	• **Ribbon:** *Modify | Detail Items* tab>*Arrange* panel
	**Send to Back**	• **Ribbon:** *Modify | Detail Items* tab>*Arrange* panel

Index

W

Z

Made in United States
Cleveland, OH
23 October 2026

46780991R10420